terra australis 57

terra australis 57

Forty Years in the South Seas

Archaeological Perspectives on the
Human History of Papua New Guinea
and the Western Pacific Region

**Edited by Anne Ford, Ben Shaw
and Dylan Gaffney**

Australian
National
University

ANU PRESS

Australian
National
University

ANU PRESS

Published by ANU Press
The Australian National University
Canberra ACT 2600, Australia
Email: anupress@anu.edu.au

Available to download for free at press.anu.edu.au

ISBN (print): 9781760466435
ISBN (online): 9781760466442

WorldCat (print): 1426264665
WorldCat (online): 1426264597

DOI: 10.22459/TA57.2024

Cover design and layout by ANU Press. Cover photograph by Glenn R Summerhayes.

This book is published under the aegis of the Terra Australis Editorial Committee of the ANU Press.

Contents

List of figures   vii

List of tables   xiii

1. Introduction: Glenn Summerhayes' forty years in the south seas   1
   Ben Shaw, Anne Ford and Dylan Gaffney

Part 1: Glenn Summerhayes in Papua New Guinea

2. Recollection of Glenn Summerhayes' relationship with the Papua New Guinea National
   Museum and Art Gallery   21
   Kenneth Miamba, Loretta Hasu, Henry Arifeae, Betty Neanda, Jemina Haro, Joyce Taian and Dickson Kangi

3. Personal reflections on working with Professor Glenn Summerhayes in Papua New Guinea   29
   Roxanne Tsang and Jason Kariwiga

4. *Em i tisa blong mi*—On the value of community engagement in research   33
   Elizabeth Matisoo-Smith

Part 2: Lapita

5. The Lapita pottery of Tamuarawai (EQS), Emirau Island, Papua New Guinea: Studying the
   form and decoration of one of the earliest pottery assemblages in the western Pacific   51
   Nicholas W.S. Hogg and Glenn R. Summerhayes

6. Understanding social connections within the Bismarck Archipelago through petrographic
   and motif analyses of Mussau Lapita pottery assemblages   75
   Scarlett Chiu, Yuyin Su, David Killick, Patrick Kirch, Glenn R. Summerhayes, Jim Specht and Wallace Ambrose

7. Lapita pottery makers' marks: The memory of signs and wonders?   109
   Matthew Spriggs

8. An update on Late Lapita: Its manifestations and associated implications   127
   Stuart Bedford

Part 3: Interaction and exchange

9. Landscapes of exchange in the Willaumez Peninsula, West New Britain,
   Papua New Guinea   153
   Gustavo F. Bonnat, Robin Torrence and Peter White

10. The difficulty of sourcing prehistoric pottery from Bootless Bay, Central Province,
    Papua New Guinea   177
    Anne Ford, Jim Allen and Elaine Chen

11. Trading valuables to foreigners in south-east New Guinea in the nineteenth century:
    The case of *Conus* armshells   203
    Pamela Swadling, Robin Torrence and Jill Hasell

12. Raided and traded: Sourcing Marind-anim exotic stone objects, south-east Papua
    (Indonesia)   231
    Ian J. McNiven and Friedrich E. von Gnielinski

Part 4: Cultural landscapes

13. Mid–late Holocene diversification of cultural identities in the Massim islands and the formative development of *Kula*: Excavations at the Mumwa site, Panaeati Island   265

Ben Shaw, Simon Coxe, Jemina Haro, Vincent Kewibu, Kenneth Miamba and Lachlan Sharp

14. Echoes of distant pasts? New Britain, Vanuatu and Felix Speiser   297

Jim Specht

15. New 'mysterious mounds' in Southern Melanesia: An archaeological study of the Tivoli plateau (Lifou, Loyalty Islands, New Caledonia) and regional comparisons   319

Christophe Sand, Jacques Bolé and David Baret

16. The commons in prehistory: The case of Japan   339

Chris Gosden

Part 5: Cultural objects

17. Late Holocene potting traditions in the far western Pacific: Evidence from the Raja Ampat Islands, 3500–1000 BP   359

Dylan Gaffney and Daud Tanudirjo

18. Ancient starch and usewear analyses of an excavated pestle fragment from the Upper Kaironk Valley, Madang Province, Papua New Guinea   391

Judith H. Field, Adelle C. Coster, Ben Shaw, Elspeth Hayes, Richard Fullagar, Michael Lovave, Jemina Haro and Glenn R. Summerhayes

19. Heirlooming and shell money beads in the Solomon Islands   417

Katherine Szabó and Fiona Petchey

List of contributors   433

List of figures

Figure 1.1: Locations in Papua New Guinea where Glenn Summerhayes has undertaken archaeological fieldwork. — 2

Figure 1.2: Glenn in the Arawe Islands. — 3

Figure 1.3: Glenn sieving at the Boduna Island Lapita site, West New Britain, 1989. — 4

Figure 1.4: Glenn recording rock art on Feni Island, Bismarck Archipelago, 1998. — 5

Figure 1.5: Glenn with the research team on Feni Island, 1998. — 5

Figure 1.6: Glenn with the late Herman Mandui (white shirt) and local collaborators in the Ivane Valley, 2008. — 7

Figure 1.7: Professor Glenn Summerhayes receiving the Order of Logohu, 2014. — 8

Figure 1.8: Glenn wearing his trusty Swazi top, safety jandals and a woven beanie gifted to him by the Simbai community. Simbai, 2016. — 8

Figure 1.9: Glenn in his element, discussing archaeology with Kenneth Miamba (centre) and an interested public on Karkar Island, 2018. — 9

Figure 2.1: Glenn Summerhayes teaching Loretta Hasu field notebook recording techniques on Koil Island. — 26

Figure 3.1: Nidatha and Jason excavating at the Kosipe Mission Station, 2008. — 31

Figure 3.2: Some of the team excavating a site at the Kosipe Mission Station, 2008. — 31

Figure 4.1: (Left) Glenn talking to schoolchildren at Gomogom Cave. (Right) Glenn, Geoff and Lisa on day of departure from Koil. — 36

Figure 4.2: (Left) Jimmy Peter from Lihir Gold and the team. (Right) Glenn with Edward Salle (centre), Tatau, Tabar. — 37

Figure 4.3: (Left) Herman, Minol and Glenn on Manus. (Right) Glenn, Herman and Lisa at Lepong. — 39

Figure 4.4: (Left) Our arrival at Emirau in 2007. (Right) Glenn undertaking community consultation. — 39

Figure 4.5: (Left) Glenn arriving at Tamuarawai with Kelly and Lyn Amanga. (Right) School visit to the site. — 41

Figure 4.6: (Left) Glenn admiring a Lapita pot fragment. (Right) Fishhook recovered from Tamuarawai (2008). — 42

Figure 4.7: (Left) Dissecting rats 2007. (Right) Collecting genealogy and DNA in 2009, Emirau. — 43

Figure 4.8: (Left) 2010 Lunch on Emirau. (Right) Return of results, Emirau. — 44

Figure 5.1: The Bismarck Archipelago with locations discussed in text circled. — 53

Figure 5.2: (Top) Map of Emirau Island. (Bottom) Map of Tamuarawai (EQS) showing the site boundaries (outlined in grey) and the test pits (TP) and shovel pits (SP) excavated at the site. — 54

Figure 5.3: Vessel forms. — 57

Figure 5.4: Pottery from the site of Tamuarawai (EQS). — 58

Figure 5.5: Additional pottery from the site of Tamuarawai (EQS). — 58

Figure 6.1: Map of the Mussau Islands and nearby isles with locations of Lapita sites discussed in this paper. 76

Figure 6.2: Map showing the simplified geological zones within the Bismarck Archipelago region. — 78

Figure 6.3: Jaccard similarity measures of shared motifs between ECA, ECB and EHB and other Bismarck
Archipelago Lapita sites that have more than 20 different motifs recorded in the LPOD.   86

Figure 6.4: Distribution of undulated (a) and zigzag (b) motif themes among Bismarck Lapita sites.   88

Figure 7.1: Makers' marks identified by Donovan (1973:76) from sites RF-2 (here RL2) and SZ-8
in the Reefs–Santa Cruz Islands of the Southeast Solomons.   111

Figure 7.2: (A) RL2-265-85, an additional makers' mark missed by Donovan from the RF-2 site and
identified by Scarlett Chiu; (B) makers' mark on RL2 153/29 as identified by Donovan; (C) SZ8
116/1 as identified by Donovan.   112

Figure 7.3: Maker's marks on sherds from Talepakemalai site, Eloaua Island, Mussau Group.   113

Figure 7.4: Makers' marks from Teouma Lapita site, Efate Island, Vanuatu.   114

Figure 7.5: Makers' marks on Chinese Neolithic pottery and later Shang culture numerals
for comparison.   116

Figure 8.1: Summary of Late Lapita Tongan vessel forms. Not to scale.   131

Figure 8.2: Dentate and shell-impressed Lapita designs from Tonga.   132

Figure 8.3: Summary of Fijian Late Lapita vessel forms and decoration.   134

Figure 8.4: A selection of Vanuatu Late Lapita vessel forms and decoration.   136

Figure 8.5: Late Lapita zigzag dentate and flat tool stamped decoration from Vanuatu.   137

Figure 8.6: A range of Late Lapita New Caledonian vessel forms and decoration.   139

Figure 8.7: South Papuan coast Late Lapita vessel forms and decoration.   142

Figure 8.8: Shell-impressed sherds from Lapita sites across the distribution.   144

Figure 9.1: The Willaumez Peninsula showing the location of the Isthmus region, FRI site,
obsidian sources and the volcanic centres at Dakataua and Witori.   154

Figure 9.2: The tephrostratigraphy of the region defines the chronological phases used to monitor
cultural change.   156

Figure 9.3: The 25 test pits from the Isthmus region used in the study are spread around the edges
of the Kulu River floodplain, along the coastal divide and on the coastal plain.   157

Figure 9.4: Plot of the obsidian source reference samples (coloured symbols) versus artefacts (black dots).   160

Figure 9.5: Chronological changes in the percentage of obsidian artefacts from each source.   161

Figure 9.6: The percentage of obsidian artefacts from each source compared between test pits in coastal
and inland locations.   163

Figure 9.7: Changes in reduction stages through time at FRI and in the Isthmus region.   168

Figure 10.1: Bootless Bay with clay and sand sampling locations by Owen Rye.   180

Figure 10.2: PCA of Rye source pellets, using pXRF.   185

Figure 10.3: PCA of Rye source and Motupore pottery pellets, using pXRF.   186

Figure 10.4: Bivariate analysis of Rye source pellets, using pXRF.   186

Figure 10.5: Bivariate analysis of Rye source and Motupore pottery pellets, using pXRF.   187

Figure 10.6: PCA and HCA of Rye clays, using SEM. Triangles represented clays fired to 500 °C,
circles represent clays fired to 800 °C.   189

Figure 10.7: PCA of Motupore and Boera/Davage pottery, compared to Rye clays, using SEM.   191

Figure 10.8: Ternary plot diagram of clays and sands.   192

Figure 10.9: Ternary plot diagram of Motupore and Boera pottery: quartz, feldspar, pyroxene.   193

Figure 10.10: Ternary plot diagram of Motupore and Boera pottery: quartz, feldspar, shell.   194

Figure 10.11: SEM micrographs of Motupore pottery.   196

Figure 11.1: Papuan South Coast, showing places mentioned in the text.   204

Figure 11.2: The Massim, showing places mentioned in the text.   204

Figure 11.3: Ring armshells.   206

Figure 11.4: Brumer Islanders dancing on the deck of HMS *Rattlesnake* on 28 August 1849.
Conus armshells are worn above the elbows of some of the dancers.   207

Figure 11.5: Multiple segmented armshells.   208

Figure 11.6: The cultural valuation of armshells differed between the Massim and the Papuan
South Coast.   211

Figure 11.7: Bêche-de-mer fishing was the main economic activity in British New Guinea until
alluvial gold was discovered on Sudest in 1887.   213

Figure 12.1: Map of central-southern New Guinea showing Marind territory (brown line)
and igneous rock outcrops.   233

Figure 12.2: Marind stone axes and stone-headed clubs.   235

Figure 12.3: Marind men and stone-headed clubs.   237

Figure 12.4: Various hafted *imbassum*.   238

Figure 12.5: Marind *imbassum* stones collected by Paul Wirz between 1915 and 1922 and housed
in the Museum für Völkerkunde (now Museum of Cultures), Basel, Switzerland.   239

Figure 12.6: Marind *imbassum* and stone club heads, examined by IM and FvG.   241

Figure 13.1: (A) Map of Island New Guinea; (B) Massim island region; (C) Panaeati Island.   267

Figure 13.2: Calibrated radiocarbon dates from systematically excavated sites in the Massim region
with heuristic chronological divisions based on south coast and Massim datasets.   269

Figure 13.3: Aerial drone images of Mumwa and the surrounding landscape.   271

Figure 13.4: Stratigraphic profile of the Mumwa site, Squares A and C.   272

Figure 13.5: Lithic artefacts from Mumwa.   275

Figure 13.6: Tanged blade (A) and mortar rim (B) from Mumwa compared with other examples from
the Massim and island New Guinea.   276

Figure 13.7: Excavated pottery from Squares A–C and spade pits.   278

Figure 13.8: Surface pottery from Mumwa not well represented in excavation.   280

Figure 13.9: Box and whisker plot of decorated sherd thickness recovered from Square A, Mumwa,
attributed to SMCP or styles defined by Bickler (1998) for Woodlark Island.   281

Figure 13.S1: Early Period pottery (~1050–500 cal. BP) recorded on Woodlark Island.   291

Figure 13.S2: Late Period pottery (<500 cal. BP) recorded on Woodlark Island.   292

Figure 14.1: The western Pacific islands, showing the Near and Remote Oceania boundary, the major
island groups and the Bismarck (1), Solomon (2) and Coral (3) Seas.   298

Figure 14.2: New Guinea and the Bismarck Archipelago, showing the main places and language areas
cited in the text.   300

Figure 15.1: Location of Lifou Island in the western Pacific and positioning of site LWT085 of Tivoli.   320

Figure 15.2: GPS map of the location of the tumuli recorded in Tivoli. The group of low flat mounds
is highlighted.   321

Figure 15.3: Graph of the diameter/height of the tumuli recorded at Tivoli, differentiating the group
of low flat mounds.   322

Figure 15.4: Stratigraphic profile of the trench excavated in mound Tu.17.   325

Figure 15.5: Stratigraphic profile of Test pit 1 in mound Tu.20.   327

Figure 15.6: Map of mound Tu.42 and stratigraphic profile of Test Pit 1.   328

Figure 15.7: Profile of the fill of large coral blocks forming mound Tu.53.   330

Figure 15.8: Example of mound Tu.61, a large tumulus at the south-east edge of the site of Tivoli.   330

Figure 15.9: Tumulus KTU049 on the central plateau of the Isle of Pines, showing the double alignment of pebbles of the path leading to the top of the mound.   333

Figure 16.1: The major regions of Japan.   343

Figure 16.2: The Nishida site, Middle Jomon phase (Iwate prefecture).   344

Figure 16.3: Jomon pots excavated at the Komakino site.   344

Figure 16.4: The Komakino stone circles with a small central ring, two larger concentric circles with hints of a fourth ring outside of those and a series of stone alignments oriented on the movement of the sun or prominent features of the landscape.   346

Figure 16.5: The detailed chronology from the Late Jomon to Middle Yayoi showing the main pottery types and some important sites across Japan.   349

Figure 16.6: The Yayoi settlement at Etsuji village, Fukuoka prefecture, with a large rectangular building and granaries surrounded by a circle of round pit houses and two cemeteries to the south.   350

Figure 17.1: Map of circum-New Guinea islands showing key early pottery sites.   361

Figure 17.2: The northern Raja Ampat Islands.   363

Figure 17.3: Mololo Cave (WAI-1) site plan and excavation sequence showing Late Holocene radiocarbon determinations.   364

Figure 17.4: Manwen Bokor Cave (WAI-42) site plan and excavation sequence showing radiocarbon determinations.   367

Figure 17.5: Rims from Mololo Cave, Trench 1.   370

Figure 17.6: Harris matrix showing number of sherds per fabric group in each stratigraphic context at Mololo Cave.   371

Figure 17.7: Decorated sherds from Mololo Cave.   372

Figure 17.8: Harris matrix showing number of sherds with surface treatment in each stratigraphic context at Mololo Cave.   373

Figure 17.9: Provisional *chaînes opératoires* for four ceramic technical classes at Mololo Cave.   374

Figure 17.10: Rims from Manwen Bokor.   376

Figure 17.11: Number of sherds per techno-fabric group in each stratigraphic context at Manwen Bokor Cave.   377

Figure 17.12: Decorated potsherds from Manwen Bokor Cave, Unit 1, Layer 1 (001).   378

Figure 17.13: Rim form comparisons.   381

Figure 17.14: Circle stamp traditions from Island Southeast Asian late Neolithic and early Metal Age ceramics, alongside Lapita pottery.   383

Figure 18.1: The location of the Simbai–Kaironk Valleys.   395

Figure 18.2: Waisted chert artefacts as surface finds from the Upper Kaironk Valley.   396

Figure 18.3: Alvan spur excavation.   397

Figure 18.4: Microscopic wear documented on artefact KAI25-SP7-20cm-bs.   401

Figure 18.5: A sample of the starch grains recovered from the surface of KAI25-SP7-20cm-bs.   403

Figure 18.6: Representative examples of starch grains from the comparative reference set used in the analysis of the pestle fragment (KAI25-SP7-20cm-bs), Kaironk Valley, Madang Province, PNG.   404

Figure 18.7: Box plots of maximum diameter through the hilum, MaxD, starch grain area, starch grain perimeter and starch grain hilum position for the comparative reference set and the archaeological samples KAI25-SP7-20cm-bs (indicated in bold).   406

Figure 18.8: Histogram plots of size metrics.   407

Figure 18.9: Venn diagram indicating the number of grains of the KAI25-SP7-20cm-bs-2 artefact sample attributed to species in the reference set.   409

Figure 19.1: Community-held heirloom shell money being displayed by the priest of Outau Village, south of Lau Lagoon, eastern Malaita, May 2016.   419

Figure 19.2: Map of the Solomon Islands, showing key locations mentioned in the text.   420

Figure 19.3: Shell money string MAA Z10604/E1902.190 from the collections of the Museum of Archaeology and Anthropology, University of Cambridge.   421

Figure 19.4: Detail of *Chama* sp. red beads and white beads mainly manufactured from *Anadara antiquata* and *Tegillarca granosa* from Z10604/E1902.190 at 35× magnification.   422

Figure 19.5: Alternating white Arcidae and darker palm endocarp and plant stem beads from Z10604/E1902.190 at 35× magnification.   422

Figure 19.6: Shell money string Z10855 from the collection of the Museum of Archaeology and Anthropology, University of Cambridge.   423

Figure 19.7: White beads of various diameters and degrees of wear manufactured from a mix of *Anadara antiquata*, *Tegillarca granosa* and *Imbricariopsis punctata* from Z10855 at 30× magnification.   424

Figure 19.8: Bayesian modelling of calibrated radiocarbon determinations from beads from Z10604/E1902.190 and Z10855.   425

List of tables

Table 5.1: Radiocarbon determinations available for the site of Tamuarawai (EQS). 55

Table 5.2: Number of excavated sherds, number of excavated sherds following conjoining, sherds diagnostic of vessel form, decorated and plain sherds, and minimum number of vessels (MNV) for the site of Tamuarawai (EQS). 61

Table 5.3: Vessel forms identified at the site of Tamuarawai (EQS) Test Pits 1–2; Layers 1–4 and NP (no provenance). 62

Table 5.4: Vessel forms identified at the site of Tamuarawai (EQS) Test Pits 3–4 and Shovel Pit 15; Layers 1–4 and WF (wall fill). 62

Table 5.5: Frequency counts and proportion of decoration within Tamuarawai (EQS) Test Pits 1–2; Layers 1–4 and NP (no provenance) by sherd count (decorated sherds can be counted more than once). 64

Table 5.6: Frequency counts and proportion of decoration within Tamuarawai (EQS) Test Pits 3–4 and Shovel Pit 15; Layers 1–4 and WF (wall fill) by sherd count (decorated sherds can be counted more than once). 64

Table 5.7: Frequency counts and proportion of decoration within Tamuarawai (EQS) Test Pits 1–4 and Shovel Pit 15 by vessel form (vessels can be counted more than once). 65

Table 5.8: Counts and proportions of plainware vessels for the site of Tamuarawai (EQS), alongside the Early Lapita Arawe Islands sites of Adwe (FOH – Squares D, E, F) and Paligmete (FNY). 68

Table 6.1: Summary of temper groups and subgroups identified. 81

Table 6.2: Possible source(s) for samples excavated from ECA Area B and B-extension areas with well-controlled stratigraphic information. 85

Table 6.3: Jaccard similarity measures from EHB, ECA and ECB to other Bismarck Lapita pottery assemblages recorded in the LPOD. 86

Table 6.4: Distribution of different subcategories of both undulated and zigzag motif themes among Bismarck Lapita sites. 89

Table 6.S1: Summary of petrographic results. Dickinson's original grouping and inferred sources are included for comparison. 97

Table 9.1: Isthmus region test pits: Tephrostratigraphy and chronology. 158

Table 9.2: FRI Trench II, Walindi Plantation: Stratigraphy and chronology. 158

Table 9.3: Precision and accuracy of pXRF instrument. 159

Table 9.4: FRI II, Walindi Plantation: Chronological change in counts and weights of obsidian artefacts from each obsidian source. 162

Table 9.5: Isthmus region: Chronological change in counts and weights of obsidian artefacts from each obsidian source. 162

Table 9.6: Isthmus region: Assemblage composition by obsidian source. 165

Table 9.7: FRI II: Assemblage composition by obsidian source. 166

Table 9.8: Comparison of chronological change in the incidence of non-cortical artefacts in the Isthmus regions and FRI II (based on Tables 9.4 and 9.5). 166

Table 9.9: Discard rates for the Isthmus region based on data from 67 test pits. 170

Table 10.1: Results (weight %) of NIST 679 Brick Clay Standard shot using University of Otago. 185

Table 11.1: *Conus* collections made before 1900 and location.   215

Table 11.2: Provenanced nineteenth-century armshells.   216

Table 11.3: Ring armshells collected in the nineteenth century.   217

Table 11.4: Multi-segment armshells collected in the nineteenth century.   219

Table 11.5: The Mason Brothers collection acquired by the Australian Museum in 1883 (measurement external diameter).   221

Table 11.6: The armshell consignments made by Andrew Goldie to museums and to the organisers of the Sydney International Exhibition.   221

Table 11.7: List of armshells collected on Woodlark by the Italian missionaries.   222

Table 12.1: Descriptions of Marind stone objects.   243

Table 12.2: Outcropping igneous rock units across central New Guinea (Indonesia and Papua New Guinea) and Torres Strait (Australia). Rock types in bold match identified raw material types for sampled Marind stone objects (Table 12.1).   247

Table 13.1: Stratigraphic layers identified in Squares A–C at the Mumwa site.   272

Table 13.2: Radiocarbon accelerator mass spectrometer determinations from the Mumwa site.   273

Table 13.S1: Excavation data from Square A, Mumwa.   293

Table 13.S2: Excavation data from Square B, Mumwa.   294

Table 13.S3: Excavation data from Square C, Mumwa.   294

Table 13.S4: Excavated lithic artefacts from Mumwa.   295

Table 15.1: Morphological data of the tumuli recorded at Tivoli.   323

Table 15.2: Radiocarbon dates obtained from samples collected in tumuli from the plateau of the Isle of Pines (IoP) and from Païta (south-west Grande Terre).   331

Table 16.1: Chronology Jomon to Kofun.   343

Table 17.1: Late Holocene radiocarbon dates from Mololo (TR1 and TR2) and Manwen Bokor (Unit 1 and TP2).   365

Table 17.2: Number of ceramic fragments from excavated contexts at Mololo Cave.   368

Table 17.3: Formal and decorative description of pottery technical classes at Mololo Cave.   369

Table 17.4: Number of ceramic fragments from excavated contexts at Manwen Bokor Cave.   375

Table 17.5: Formal and decorative description of pottery technical classes at Manwen Bokor.   379

Table 18.1: A summary of the 13 tree taxa identified by Bulmer (1964) and updated by Gardner (2010), including local names and judged by Bulmer to likely be processed in mortars and pestles in the Kaironk Valley.   393

Table 18.2: Comparative reference starch and archaeological sample.   398

Table 19.1: Radiocarbon determinations from bead samples from Z10604/E1902.190 and Z10855.   424

1

Introduction: Glenn Summerhayes' forty years in the south seas

Ben Shaw, Anne Ford and Dylan Gaffney

This edited volume celebrates the career and achievements of Glenn Summerhayes, Foundation Chair and Professor of Anthropology at the University of Otago since 2005; and previously Head of Department at The Australian National University's (ANU) School of Archaeology and Natural History. In a career spanning more than four decades, Glenn has undertaken extensive research on the long-term human histories of the Asia-Pacific region, with a prominent focus on Papua New Guinea. For Glenn, Papua New Guinea is not just the geographic focus of his research. He has a passion for the communities he stays and works with, and the landscapes he works in. Throughout Glenn's career he has worked closely with the National Museum and Art Gallery of Papua New Guinea (NMAG) and the University of Papua New Guinea (UPNG). As a researcher he has made significant contributions to the archaeology of the region, and as an educator Glenn has mentored numerous students, many of whom now hold posts in academic faculties, museums and cultural heritage management organisations around the world. Figure 1.1 illustrates the geographical extent of fieldwork Glenn has undertaken across Papua New Guinea, culminating in an impressive 50 field seasons between 1986 and 2023.

The first two chapters of this volume present reflections by NMAG staff and former students of UPNG about working with Glenn. The many contributors of subsequent chapters have also worked with Glenn in some capacity throughout his career, and we, the editors of this volume, are former students of Glenn's who are fortunate to have him as a teacher, mentor, colleague and friend. This volume has been arranged into broad themes that reflect some of Glenn's many research interests and is a testament to Glenn's character as a person and his approach as an inclusive and collaborative researcher.

In the foreword of *Lapita Interaction* published in 2000, Matthew Spriggs stated that Glenn was 'a rare kind of archaeologist, being as much at home in front of a scanning electron microscope as in a Melanesian leaf-house discussing the day's excavation results' (p. vi). This statement is as true now as it was when the monograph was published 23 years ago.

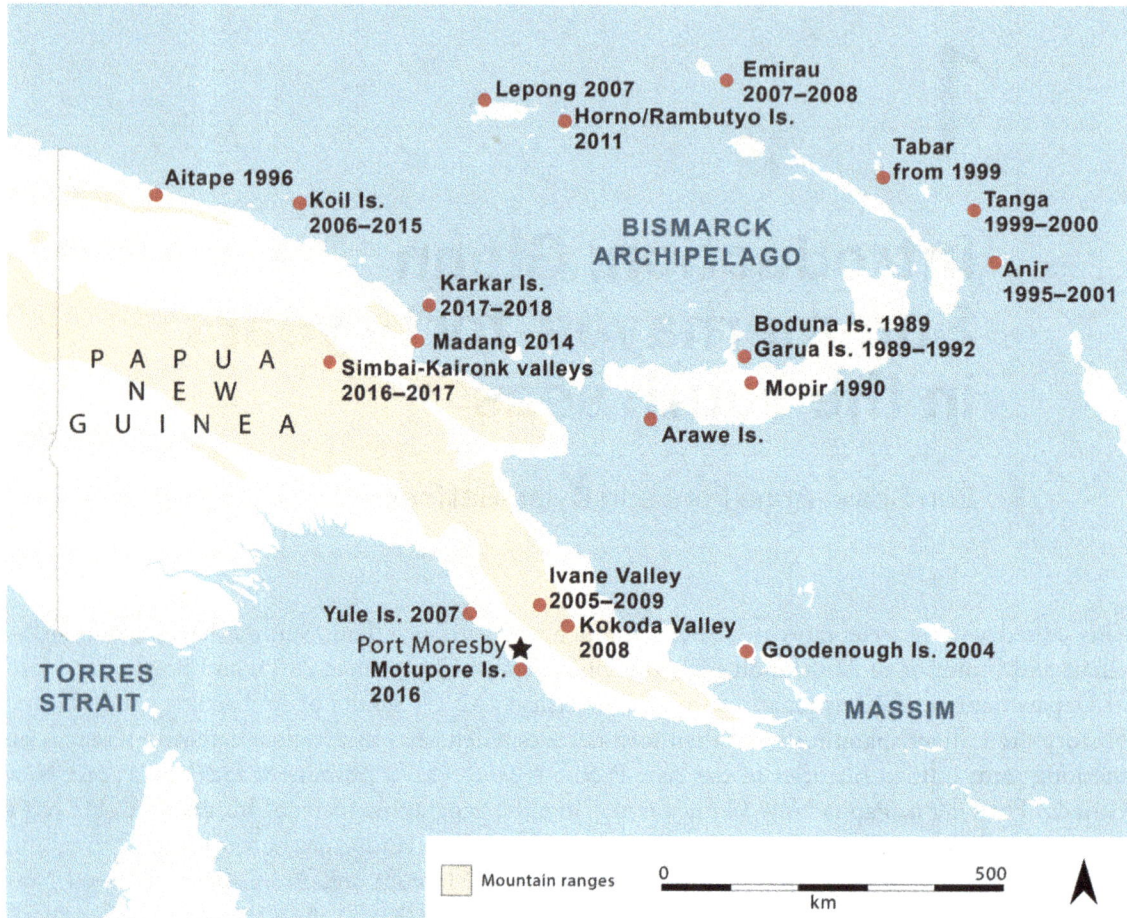

Figure 1.1: Locations in Papua New Guinea where Glenn Summerhayes has undertaken archaeological fieldwork.

Source: Dylan Gaffney.

Biography

Glenn Reginald Summerhayes was born in Redfern, Sydney, in 1954. He and his twin brother, Gregg, are two peas from the same pod and whenever Glenn makes a trip back to Sydney from his home in Dunedin, they share fond memories of their formative years growing up in Blacktown. Glenn's interest in archaeology was cultivated from the young age of eight when he was given C.W. Ceram's 1958 book *A Picture History of Archaeology*—jam-packed with images of discoveries from across the ancient world and with a whirlwind history of the discipline. Glenn was hooked. After finishing high school, Glenn went straight on to the University of Sydney where he completed a double major in history from 1973 to 1976, and was eager to delve into the archaeology courses on offer— there was just one problem. Glenn started university just prior to the 1974 abolishment of tertiary education fees, but was fortunate to have secured a teaching scholarship to cover the otherwise out of reach course costs. However, this limited his study options and bonded him into teaching four years of high school after graduation—a predicament of sorts. As it happened, and with uncanny timing, the bonded student scheme was abolished shortly after Glenn finished his undergraduate degree, and with only the requisite months of teaching placements under his belt Glenn was free to pursue archaeology as originally intended.

Glenn first cut his teeth on the chemical characterisation of pottery for his MA qualifying thesis in 1977–78, using the electron microprobe and X-ray fluorescence (XRF) spectrometry on a Javanese assemblage under the supervision of Michael Walker. During this time, Glenn joined the Public Service in the Department of Veterans Affairs, and what was to be a few short months of making a bit of money on the side to get him through his studies turned into 10 years of full-time employment. Time allowed, however, in early 1978 for Glenn to spend two months on his first excavation at Capertree rock shelter in New South Wales, led by then-PhD student Ian Johnson, where he also met long-time colleagues Sue O'Connor and Ken Aplin. By 1980 Glenn had started a master's on the Spanish Neolithic. Not making much progress without proficiency in the Spanish language, and with a desire to focus his attention on the Pacific, a fortuitous suggestion came from Richard Wright to talk with Jim Specht at the Australian Museum who had taught Glenn Pacific archaeology as an undergraduate. The meeting led to a swift change in project, to one investigating production patterns in Buka pottery industries of the northern Solomons, excavated by Jim as part of his PhD studies. Working part time on his thesis in between full-time work, Glenn completed his master's in 1986 (conferred 1987) under the supervision of Jim Specht and Peter White.

In 1989, Glenn sought to hone his archaeometry skillset when he began a PhD at La Trobe University in Melbourne under the supervision of Jim Allen and Chris Gosden. Here he was quickly introduced to another lifelong passion—fieldwork in Papua New Guinea. Over a whopping six field seasons in New Britain with the La Trobe–Australian Museum team, Glenn set to work combining the nuances of excavated cultural records with the highest resolution of pottery analyses (Figures 1.2 and 1.3). During this time, Glenn also took up a role as Curator of the Vanuatu collection at the Museum of Victoria, and later as a registrar for the Victorian Archaeological Survey. Completing his PhD in 1996, Glenn had identified that Lapita pottery was made from many different clay-temper recipes, mostly locally made. He developed the thesis that the movement of pottery from one place to another was epiphenomenal to the movement of ideas and people, providing a springboard for him and other archaeologists to investigate *why* objects were moved and what it meant for the people who moved them.

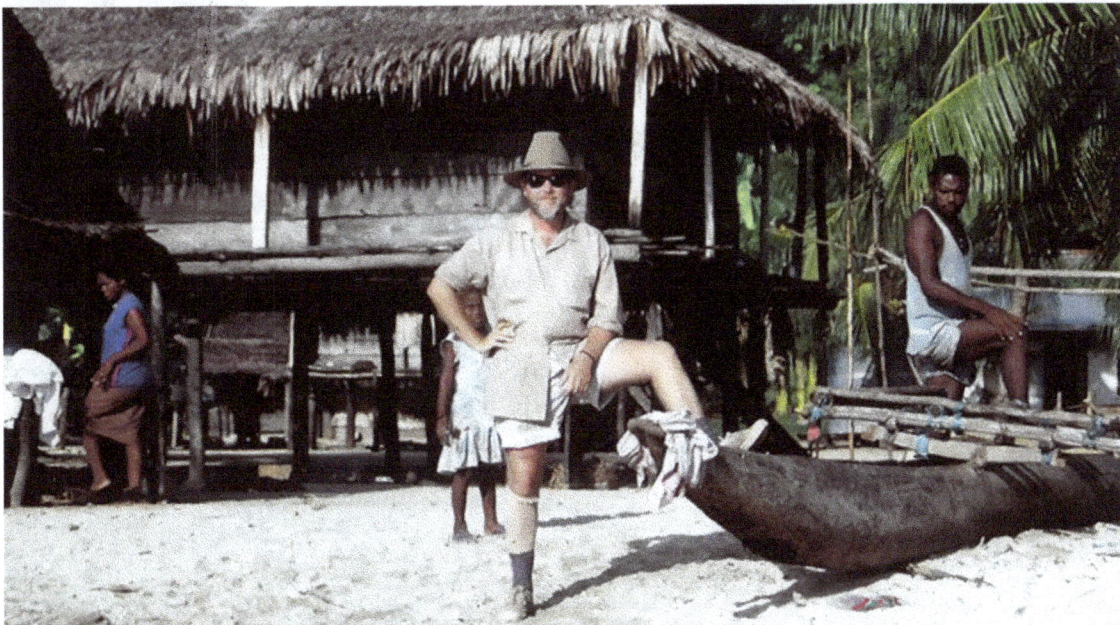

Figure 1.2: Glenn in the Arawe Islands.
Source: Photo by Chris Gosden.

Figure 1.3: Glenn sieving at the Boduna Island Lapita site, West New Britain, 1989.
Source: Photo by Jim Specht.

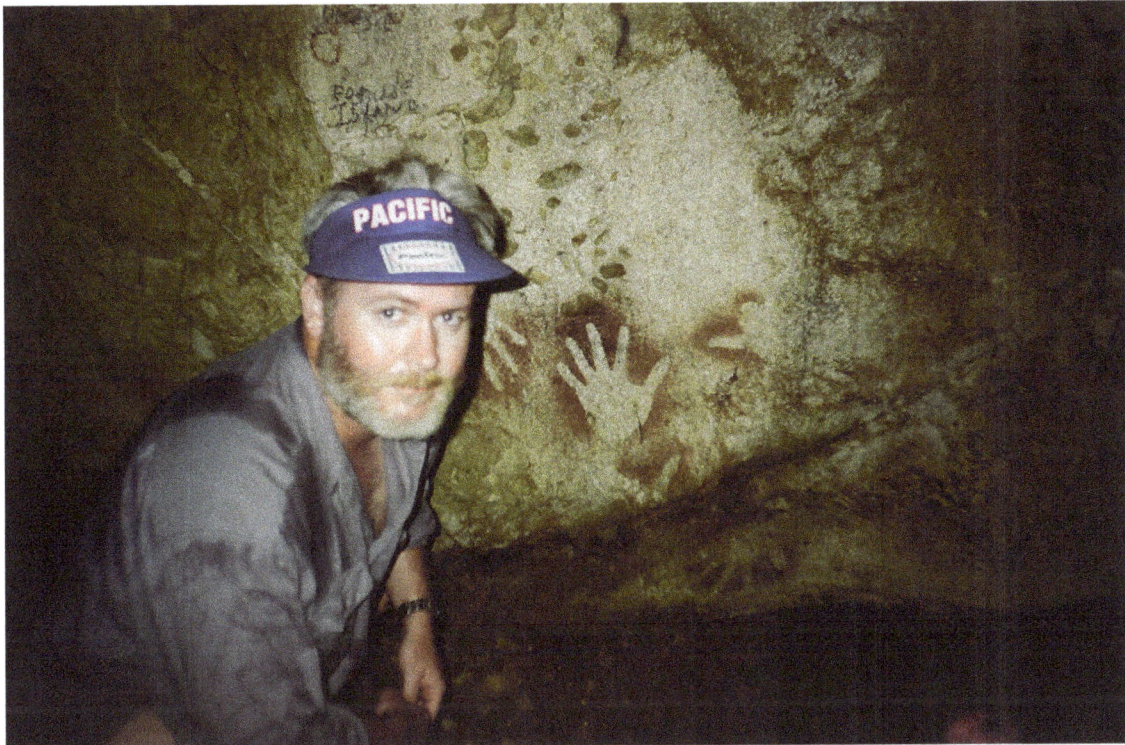

Figure 1.4: Glenn recording rock art on Feni Island, Bismarck Archipelago, 1998.
Source: Vicky Barnecutt.

Figure 1.5: Glenn with the research team on Feni Island, 1998.
Source: Vicky Barnecutt.

During his tenure as a PhD student, Glenn applied for a large three-year Australian Research Council (ARC) grant for a field-based project on the Anir Islands and in 1994 was awarded the grant in a competitive round against tenured academic researchers. It came as a pleasant surprise to Glenn, and took the ARC by surprise too it would seem, as shortly thereafter the rules were changed preventing students from applying for academic grants. While writing up his PhD thesis, Glenn was called back to the Public Service in Canberra in 1996, where he worked until 1998 when, having had his PhD conferred a couple of years prior, he was awarded an ARC Fellowship at ANU, equivalent to an ARC DECRA[1] nowadays.

The fellowship took him back to the Anir Islands for another three years where he got to work reconstructing past human settlement, including some of the earliest evidence for Lapita culture, and setting up several PhD students to work in the Bismarck Archipelago (see Figures 1.4 and 1.5).

Glenn was appointed as a tenured research fellow in the Department of Archaeology and Natural History in 2001 where he stayed until 2004, becoming head of department in the final year. With his young family, including wife Rieko and then two-year-old daughter Kyoka, Glenn moved to Dunedin in 2005 to take up a Professorship and the Chair of Anthropology at the University of Otago, having applied for the position on the advice of Atholl Anderson and Wal Ambrose. Glenn was Head of Department of Anthropology, Gender, and Sociology at Otago from 2005 to 2010, bringing with him his years of management experience in the Australian Public Service and formal qualifications in teaching.

Over a long career, Glenn has also worked in Southern Japan, Vanuatu and Micronesia. He has supervised 17 PhD students, 17 master's students and 28 honours students; holds honorary professorships at ANU and University of Queensland and is an honorary curator of the Archaeology and Pacific collections at the Otago Museum where he has contributed substantially to the H.D. Skinner Pacific Cultures gallery. His archaeological research has been presented in over 130 journal articles, book chapters, edited volumes and encyclopedia entries, and a seminal book titled *Lapita Interaction* based on a subset of his PhD thesis.

As a homage to the ongoing impact the research in that book has made since its publication in 2000, and as a nod to the positive influence Glenn made while at ANU, this Festschrift is published in the same *Terra Australis* series. While there is not space here to review all of his contributions to Papua New Guinea's past, we briefly list some highlights from his career below.

Research highlights

Of the many impacts Glenn has made on the archaeology of the Asia-Pacific region over the years, perhaps none has had more global reach than the 2010 publication in *Science* on the earliest evidence for a human presence in New Guinea. It took Glenn and his team five years of fieldwork with the Goilala people in the Ivane Valley, 2000 m above sea level, and then much longer in the lab with a large group of collaborators, to collate and interpret the cultural evidence from several sites (Figure 1.6). Demonstrating human occupation between 49,000 and 44,000 years ago, the montane sites in the Ivane Valley showcase how quickly people moved across the supercontinent of Sahul (Australia, New Guinea and Tasmania) and into new and unfamiliar environments. These sites have been important for understanding the deep time of human occupation in New Guinea, as well as for modelling the adaptability of modern humans during global migrations.

---

1   Discovery Early Career Researcher Award.

Figure 1.6: Glenn with the late Herman Mandui (white shirt) and local collaborators in the Ivane Valley, 2008.

Source: Photo by Ben Shaw.

Glenn's contribution to Lapita research has been unquestionably foundational to how archaeologists model the spread of Lapita peoples and the development of this cultural phenomenon. Glenn's heuristic definition of Early, Middle and Late Lapita phases was founded on detailed stylistic and chemical characterisation analyses presented in *Lapita Interaction* and numerous other articles, with these phases still widely used today. Some of the earliest Lapita sites have also been excavated by Glenn and his team in the Bismarck Archipelago that enabled the initial movements of Lapita people, objects and ideas, and interactions with indigenous peoples, to be modelled with increased nuance. The data generated has since formed the basis for many debates about the peopling of the Pacific region.

A major theme of Glenn's research has been the archaeology of trade and exchange. Glenn's innovative approaches to the stylistic and chemical characterisation of pottery is matched by his research on modelling the movement and use of obsidian in Papua New Guinea. Building on foundational work demonstrating that obsidian sources were chemically distinct, Glenn has had a major impact on modelling how Late Pleistocene and Holocene populations adapted to island life in the Bismarck Archipelago by tracing when, from where and how people sourced obsidian.

Investigations into the past 2000 years of cultural change led Glenn to connect his expertise on the Lapita period with his unrivalled knowledge of early ethnographic texts—whether that be in English, German, French or Dutch. This allowed him to reconstruct past population movements and changing exchange networks from the first footsteps through to the ethnographic present. Particularly relevant here are his excavations of Post-Lapita sites around New Ireland, along the south Papuan coast, in the Sepik and most recently in Madang. Drawing from his extensive personal library of early European accounts and spurred on by the unavailability of these texts in Papua New Guinea, Glenn has also championed the translation of several important ethnographic monographs, having donated copies of these volumes to libraries around the country.

For Glenn's contributions to the archaeology of Papua New Guinea Glenn was made an Officer of the Order of Logohu by the PNG Governor General in 2014—one of highest honours that can be bestowed upon a non-citizen (see Figure 1.7).

For his services to tertiary education and history in 2021 Glenn was awarded the prestigious Order of Australia medal. Glenn has also been made a Fellow of the Society of Antiquaries (FSA), a Fellow of the Linnean Society (FLS), Fellow of the Royal Anthropological Institute of Great Britain and Ireland (FRAI), and a Corresponding Fellow of the Australian Academy of the Humanities (FAHA). Officially retiring in 2024, Glenn has no plans on hanging up his boots or putting the brakes on pursuing his research interests, with recent fieldwork in June 2023 taking him and a team to Bogia on the north coast of Papua New Guinea.

Figure 1.7: Professor Glenn Summerhayes receiving the Order of Logohu, 2014.

Note: Professor Summerhayes (far right) receiving the Order of Logohu, with his wife Reiko (far left), and daughter Kyoka in front, with the Governor General of Papua New Guinea (mid right) and his wife Lady Esmie Ogio (mid left), at Government House in Port Moresby, 2014.

Source: Glenn Summerhayes.

Figure 1.8: Glenn wearing his trusty Swazi top, safety jandals and a woven beanie gifted to him by the Simbai community. Simbai, 2016.

Source: Photo by Ben Shaw.

Figure 1.9: Glenn in his element, discussing archaeology with Kenneth Miamba (centre) and an interested public on Karkar Island, 2018.

Source: Photo by Dylan Gaffney.

Reflections

On putting this volume together, the editors reflected on working with Glenn.

For Ben Shaw, there was a pivotal moment during his first trip to Papua New Guinea in 2008 as a master's student that solidified his passion for a career spent working in the country. Glenn, the late Herman Mandui and Ben had made the half-day walk from the airstrip at Woitape to Kosipe Mission in the Ivane Valley. There they met the rest of the team and in the days that followed, work slowly started on excavations and survey. However, word was soon sent that everyone was to return to the mission house as concerns were raised between different clan groups about accommodation arrangements and payments. At the meeting place Glenn sat patiently in the middle waiting for all those concerned to arrive. The meeting eventually started, the communities and Glenn spoke in turn, a fragile agreement was made but it seemed that grievances between clans ran deeper than the archaeological work, with the research a catalyst for bringing issues to the surface there and then. Glenn listened and was empathetic to the concerns but avoided being drawn into clan politics, a solution was reached and for the rest of the trip discussions continued. It was this event, involving real and reasonable community concerns and seeing Glenn's approach to what seemed like a very tricky diplomatic situation, one that from the sidelines was difficult to grasp at times, that convinced Ben that he wanted to keep working in Papua New Guinea with local communities.

For Anne Ford, it has been a privilege to have Glenn as a mentor and a friend. Anne first came to work with Glenn for her PhD because of his reputation in sourcing studies and for the chance to do research in Papua New Guinea. From the very first field trip to the beautiful island of Emirau where they excavated one of PNG's earliest Lapita sites, Anne was inspired by Glenn's passion for the people and the stories for this 'Land of the Unexpected'. From that first trip, Glenn showed her the importance of giving back the stories to the communities with which they worked, visiting schools, church gatherings and community events, as well as doing interviews on the radio which most people in PNG have access to. Glenn's ability to spread such knowledge is why they were even at Emirau in the first place—the villagers had uncovered Lapita pottery on the island and knew that it was important because of his work. Getting these stories back to the people they belong to should be a vital part of all archaeological research. Nothing quite compares to being on Fergusson Island in the D'Entrecasteaux Archipelago and having one of the high school students pull out their schoolbook and seeing the obsidian sources and trade networks that Glenn helped to map, and the student being so excited to discuss what they had learnt. Glenn's work with communities, his outreach and his passion for giving back to the people of PNG has inspired all the students who have worked with him, setting up an important role model for how we conduct our own fieldwork and research. Glenn—it's been an honour!

For Dylan Gaffney, what initially set Glenn apart was his ability to tell incredible stories about New Guinea. First, during undergraduate lectures full of vivid details about working in the Pacific. During BA Honours supervision meetings, these stories were told from his office—famously overflowing with all kinds of books, not just about PNG archaeology, but from all over the world (and many of them a few hundred years old), as well as numerous handcrafted objects like pottery, wooden bowls, woven mats, spears and carvings gifted to him by friends and dignitaries across the Pacific. It was in PNG itself, however, that Glenn really made sense—recounting the same stories over a cup of coffee in the mornings or scotch in the evenings. During Dylan's first trip to Madang as a 22-year-old MA student, it immediately became clear that it wasn't just Glenn's pioneering archaeometric work or theoretical modelling that made him such a successful archaeologist, but his ability to sincerely connect with people in PNG. His rapid-fire Tok Pisin, cutting wit and superb stories made him an instant favourite among people he worked with at Malmal and Bilbil. Even when discussions were delayed by a key clan leader's absence, potentially compromising the field season, Glenn never batted an eye, assuring Dylan that they had to move at the local pace and follow local etiquette. Every field season with Glenn—whether along the coast, in the highlands or in the islands—involved trips to local schools and community meetings to share the word about archaeology, whereby the giving back has been just as important as what was dug up.

Bibliography of Glenn R. Summerhayes

1. Clegg, J., D. Bell, H. Brayshaw, M. Coaldrake, E. Godden, P. Quay, G. **Summerhayes**, A. Urquhart and E. Wilson 1977. Science in the study of Australian Prehistoric Art. *Memoirs of the Victorian Archaeological Survey* 1:18–41.

2. **Summerhayes**, G.R. and M.J. Walker 1982. Elemental analysis and taxonomy of prehistoric pottery from Western Java. In W.R. Ambrose and P. Duerden (eds), *Archaeometry: An Australasian perspective*, pp. 60–67. Research School of Pacific Studies, The Australian National University, Canberra.

3. **Summerhayes**, G.R. 1987. Aspects of Melanesian ceramics. MA thesis, University of Sydney.

4. Fullagar, R., G.R. **Summerhayes**, B. Ivuyo and J. Specht 1991. Obsidian sources at Mopir, West New Britain Province, Papua New Guinea. *Archaeology in Oceania* 26:110–113. doi.org/10.1002/j.1834-4453.1991.tb00274.x.

5. **Summerhayes**, G.R. and M. Hotchkis 1992. Recent advances in Melanesian obsidian sourcing: Results of the 1990 and 1991 PIXE/PIGME analyses. In J.C. Galipaud (ed.), *Poterie Lapita et Peuplement*, pp. 127–134. ORSTOM, Nouméa.

6. **Summerhayes**, G.R. and J. Allen 1993. The transport of Mopir obsidian to Late Pleistocene New Ireland. *Archaeology in Oceania* 28:144–148. doi.org/10.1002/j.1834-4453.1993.tb00305.x.

7. **Summerhayes**, G.R., R. Bird, M. Hotchkiss, C. Gosden, J. Specht, R. Torrence and R. Fullagar 1993. Obsidian sourcing studies in Papua New Guinea using PIXE-PIGME analysis. In *Proceedings of the 8th Australian conference on nuclear techniques of analysis*, pp. 107–110. Australian Institute of Nuclear Science and Engineering, Lucas Heights.

8. **Summerhayes**, G.R., C. Gosden, R. Fullagar, J. Specht, R. Torrence, J.R. Bird, N. Shahgholi and A. Katsaros 1993. West New Britain obsidian. Production and consumption patterns. In B.L. Frankhauser and J.R. Bird (eds), *Archaeometry: Current Australasian research*, pp. 57–68. Research School of Pacific Studies, The Australian National University, Canberra.

9. Gosden, C., J. Webb, B. Marshall and G.R. **Summerhayes** 1994. Lolmo Cave: A mid-to-late Holocene site, the Arawe Islands, West New Britain Province, Papua New Guinea. *Asian Perspectives* 33:97–119.

10. Frankel, D. and G.R. **Summerhayes** 1995. Archaeological ceramics in Melanesia: A select bibliography. *La Tinja—Newsletter of Archaeological Ceramics* 8:12–19.

11. **Summerhayes**, G.R. 1996. Interaction in Pacific prehistory: An approach based on the production, distribution and use of pottery. Unpublished PhD thesis, La Trobe University, Melbourne.

12. **Summerhayes**, G.R., D. Frankel and J.M. Webb 1996. Electron microprobe analysis of pottery. In D. Frankel and J.M. Webb (eds), *Marki Aloni: An early and middle Bronze Age town in Cyprus*, pp. 175–180. Studies in Mediterranean Archaeology, vol 123. Paul Åströms Förlag, Sävedalen.

13. Torrence, R., J. Specht, R. Fullagar and G.R. **Summerhayes** 1996. Which obsidian is worth it? A view from the West New Britain sources. In J. Davidson, G. Irwin, F. Leach, A. Pawley and D. Brown (eds), *Oceanic culture history: Essays in honour of Roger Green*, pp. 211–224. New Zealand Journal of Archaeology, Dunedin.

14. **Summerhayes**, G.R. 1997. Losing your temper: The effect of mineral inclusions on pottery analyses. *Archaeology in Oceania* 32:108–117. doi.org/10.1002/j.1834-4453.1997.tb00376.x.

15. Bird, R., R. Torrence, G.R. **Summerhayes** and G. Bailey 1997. New Britain obsidian sources. *Archaeology in Oceania* 32:61–67. doi.org/10.1002/j.1834-4453.1997.tb00371.x.

16. Torrence, R. and G.R. **Summerhayes** 1997. Sociality and the short distance trader: Inter–regional obsidian exchange in the Willaumez region, Papua New Guinea. *Archaeology in Oceania* 32:74–84. doi.org/10.1002/j.1834-4453.1997.tb00373.x.

17. **Summerhayes**, G.R. 1998. The face of Lapita. *Archaeology in Oceania* 33:100.doi.org/10.1002/j.1834-4453.1998.tb00410.x.

18. **Summerhayes**, G.R., R. Bird, R. Fullagar, C. Gosden, J. Specht and R. Torrence 1998. Application of PIXE/PIGME to archaeological analysis of changing patterns of obsidian use in West New Britain, Papua New Guinea. In S. Shackley (ed.), *Archaeological obsidian studies: Method and theory*, pp. 129–158. Plenum Press, New York. doi.org/10.1007/978-1-4757-9276-8_6.

19. **Summerhayes**, G.R. 2000. The winds of change: Writing history before Europeans. *The Review of Archaeology* 21:6–10.

20. **Summerhayes**, G.R. 2000. *Lapita interaction*. The Australian National University, Canberra.

21. **Summerhayes**, G.R. 2000. What's in a pot? In A. Anderson and T. Murray (eds), *Australian archaeologist: Collected papers in honour of Jim Allen*. Coombs Academic Press, The Australian National University, Canberra.

22. **Summerhayes**, G.R. 2000. Recent archaeological investigations in the Bismarck Archipelago, Anir-New Ireland province, Papua New Guinea. *Bulletin of the Indo-Pacific Prehistory Association* 19:167–174.

23.   **Summerhayes**, G.R. 2000. Far Western, Western and Eastern Lapita: A re-evaluation. *Asian Perspectives* 39:109–138. doi.org/10.1353/asi.2000.0013.

24.   **Summerhayes**, G.R. 2001. Defining the chronology of Lapita in the Bismarck Archipelago. In G.R. Clark, A.J. Anderson and T. Vunidilo (eds), *The archaeology of Lapita dispersal in Oceania*, pp. 25–38. Pandanus Books, Canberra.

25.   **Summerhayes**, G.R. 2001. Lapita in the Far West: Recent developments. *Archaeology in Oceania* 36:53–63. doi.org/10.1002/j.1834-4453.2001.tb00478.x.

26.   **Summerhayes**, G.R. 2001. Trade and exchange, archaeology of. In N.J. Smelser and P.B. Baltes (eds), *International encyclopedia of the social and behavioral sciences*, pp. 15803–15807. Elsevier, Oxford. doi.org/10.1016/B0-08-043076-7/02079-9.

27.   **Summerhayes**, G.R. 2001. The history of Archaeometry. In T. Murray (ed.), *The encyclopaedia of archaeology: History and discoveries*, pp. 100–106. ABC Clio 4, Santa Barbara.

28.   Anderson, A., S. Bedford, I. Lilley, C. Sand, G.R. **Summerhayes** and R. Torrence 2001. An inventory of Lapita sites containing dentate-stamped pottery. In G.R. Clarke, A. Anderson and T. Vunidilo (eds), *The archaeology of Lapita dispersal in Oceania*, pp. 1–13. Pandanus Books, Canberra.

29.   Szabo, K. and G.R. **Summerhayes** 2002. Worked shell artefacts-new data from Early Lapita. In S. Bedford, C. Sand and D. Burley (eds), *Fifty years in the field: Essays in honour of Richard Shutler Jr's archaeological career*, pp. 91–100. New Zealand Archaeological Association, Auckland.

30.   **Summerhayes**, G.R. 2003. Modelling differences between Lapita obsidian and pottery distribution patterns in the Bismarck Archipelago, Papua New Guinea. In C. Sand (ed.), *Pacific archaeology: Assessments and prospects*, pp. 135–145. Nouvelle-Calédonie: Département Archéologie, Service des Musées et du Patrimoine, Nouméa.

31.   **Summerhayes**, G.R. 2003. The rocky road: The selection and transport of Admiralties obsidian to Lapita communities. *Australian Archaeology* 57:135–142. doi.org/10.1080/03122417.2003.11681772.

32.   Doelman, T., R. Torrence, N. Kononenko, B. Popov, G.R. **Summerhayes**, R. Bonetti, A. Guglielmetti, A. Manzoni and M. Oddone 2004. Acquisition and movement of volcanic glass in the Primoroye region of far eastern Russia. *Humane Problems of the Asian-Pacific Region Countries* 4:112–124.

33.   Kennett, D.J., A.J. Anderson, M.J. Cruz, G.R. Clark and G.R. **Summerhayes** 2004. Geochemical characterization of Lapita pottery via inductively coupled plasma – mass spectrometry (ICP – MS). *Archaeometry* 46:35–46. doi.org/10.1111/j.1475-4754.2004.00142.x.

34.   **Summerhayes**, G.R. 2004. The nature of prehistoric obsidian importation to Anir and the development of a 3,000 year old regional picture of obsidian exchange within the Bismarck Archipelago, Papua New Guinea. *Records of the Australian Museum* 29:145–156. doi.org/10.3853/j.0812-7387.29. 2004.1411.

35.   **Summerhayes**, G.R. and I. Scales 2005. New Lapita pottery finds from Kolombangara, western Solomon Islands. *Archaeology in Oceania* 40:14–20. doi.org/10.1002/j.1834-4453.2005.tb00575.x.

36.   **Summerhayes**, G.R. 2006. Lapita in the Pacific. *The Journal of New Zealand Studies in Japan* 13: 103–111.

37.   Fairbairn, A.S., G.S. Hope and G.R. **Summerhayes** 2006. Pleistocene occupation of New Guinea's highland and subalpine environments. *World Archaeology* 38:371–386. doi.org/10.1080/00438240 600813293.

38.   Specht, J. and G.R. **Summerhayes** 2007. The Boduna Island (FEA) Lapita site. *Technical Reports of the Australian Museum* 20:51–103. doi.org/10.3853/j.1835-4211.20.2007.1474.

39.   **Summerhayes**, G.R. 2007. New Zealand archaeology – Another 50 years. *The Review of Archaeology* 27:58–66.

40.   **Summerhayes**, G.R. 2007. Lapita colonisation of the Pacific. *South Pacific* 9: 69–82.

41. **Summerhayes**, G.R. 2007. The rise and transformation of Lapita in the Bismarck Archipelago. In S. Chui and C. Sand (eds), *From Southeast Asia to the Pacific: Archaeological perspectives on the Austronesian expansion and the Lapita Cultural Complex*, pp. 129–172. Academic Sinica, Taipei.

42. **Summerhayes**, G.R. 2007. Island Melanesian pasts: A view from archaeology. In J. Friedlaender (ed.), *Genes, language and culture history in the Southwest Pacific*, pp. 10–35. Oxford University Press, New York. doi.org/10.1093/acprof:oso/9780195300307.003.0002.

43. **Summerhayes**, G.R. 2007. Le Monde Oceanien. In G. Jehel (ed.), *Histoire Du Monde 500–1000–1500*, pp. 463–481. Le Temps Editions, Nante.

44. **Summerhayes**, G.R. and J. Allen 2007. Lapita writ small? Revisiting the Austronesian colonisation of the Papuan South Coast. In S. Bedford, C. Sand and S.P. Connaughton (eds), *Oceanic explorations: Lapita and Western Pacific Settlement*, pp. 97–122. Canberra: ANU E Press. doi.org/10.22459/TA26.2007.05.

45. Anderson, A. and G.R. **Summerhayes** 2008. Edge-ground and waisted axes in the Western Pacific Islands: Implications for an example from the Yaeyama Islands, southernmost Japan. *Asian Perspectives* 47:45–58. doi.org/10.1353/asi.2008.0001.

46. **Summerhayes**, G.R. 2008. Exchange systems. In D.M. Pearsall (ed.), *Encyclopedia of archaeology*, pp. 1339–1344. Elsevier, San Diego. doi.org/10.1016/B978-012373962-9.00106-0.

47. **Summerhayes**, G.R. 2008. Sourcing techniques in Landscape Archaeology. In B. David and J. Thomas (eds), *Handbook of landscape archaeology*. pp. 530–535. Left Coast Press, Walnut Creek CA.

48. **Summerhayes**, G.R. 2008. Becoming human. *The Review of Archaeology* 29:58–67.

49. Findlater, A.M., G.R. **Summerhayes**, W.R. Dickinson and I.A. Scales 2009. Assessing the anomalous role of ceramics in Late Lapita interaction: A view from Kolombangara, Western Solomon Islands. In P.J. Sheppard, T. Thomas and G.R. Summerhayes (eds), *Lapita: Ancestors and descendants*, pp. 101–117. New Zealand Archaeological Association, Auckland.

50. Matisoo-Smith, E., M. Hington, G.R. **Summerhayes**, J. Robins, H.A. Ross and M. Hendy 2009. On the rat trail in Near Oceania: Applying the commensal model to the question of Lapita colonisation. *Pacific Science* 63:465–475. doi.org/10.2984/049.063.0402.

51. Shaw, B., G.R. **Summerhayes**, H.R. Buckley and J.A. Baker 2009. The use of strontium isotopes as an indicator of migration in human and pig Lapita populations in the Bismarck Archipelago, Papua New Guinea. *Journal of Archaeological Science* 36:1079–1091. doi.org/10.1016/j.jas.2008.12.010.

52. Sheppard, P., T. Thomas and G.R. **Summerhayes** (eds) 2009. *Lapita: Ancestors and descendants*. New Zealand Archaeological Association, Auckland.

53. **Summerhayes**, G.R. 2009. Obsidian network patterns in Melanesia: Sources, characterisation and distribution. *IPPA Bulletin* 29:109–123.

54. **Summerhayes**, G.R. and A. Anderson 2009. An Austronesian presence in Southern Japan: Early occupation in the Yaeyama Islands. *Bulletin of the Indo-Pacific Prehistory Association* 29:76–91. doi.org/10.7152/bippa.v29i0.9481.

55. **Summerhayes**, G.R., M. Leavesley and A. Fairbairn 2009. Impact of human colonization on the landscape: A view from the Western Pacific. *Pacific Science* 63:725–745. doi.org/10.2984/049.063.0412.

56. Shaw, B., H.R. Buckley, G.R. **Summerhayes**, D. Anson, S. Garling, F. Valentin, H. Mandui, C. Stirling and M. Reid 2010. Migration and mobility at the Late Lapita site of Reber-Rakival (SAC), Watom Island using isotope and trace element analyses: A new insight into Lapita interaction in the Bismarck Archipelago. *Journal of Archaeological Science* 37:605–613. doi.org/10.1016/j.jas.2009.10.025.

57. **Summerhayes**, G.R. 2010. Lapita interaction: An update. In M.Z. Gadu and H. Lin (eds), *2009 International symposium on Austronesian studies*, pp. 11–40. National Museum of Prehistory, Taitung, Taiwan.

58. **Summerhayes**, G.R. 2010. Obsidian. In C. Sand, S. Bedford and S. Chambonniere (eds), *Lapita: Ancêtres Océaniens*, pp. 102–103. Musée du Quai Branly, Paris.

59. **Summerhayes**, G.R. 2010. The emergence of Lapita in the Bismarck Archipelago. In C. Sand, S. Bedford and S. Chambonniere (eds), *Lapita: Ancêtres Océaniens*, pp. 92–101. Musée du Quai Branly, Paris.

60. **Summerhayes**, G.R., M. Leavesley, A. Fairbairn, H. Mandui, J. Field, A. Ford and R. Fullagar 2010. Human adaptation and plant use in Highland New Guinea 49,000 to 44,000 years ago. *Science* 330:78–81. doi.org/10.1126/science.1193130.

61. **Summerhayes**, G.R., E. Matisoo-Smith, H. Mandui, J. Allen, J. Specht, N. Hogg and S. McPherson 2010. Tamuarawai (EQS): An early Lapita site on Emirau, New Ireland, PNG. *Journal of Pacific Archaeology* 1:62–75. pacificarchaeology.org/index.php/journal/article/view/10.

62. Dennison, J., G. **Summerhayes** and E. Matisoo-Smith (eds) 2010. *St Matthias Group*. Translation of Hans Nevermann, 1933 *St Mathias Gruppe*. University of Otago Studies in Prehistoric Anthropology 22. University of Otago, Dunedin.

63. Allen, J., G.R. **Summerhayes**, H. Mandui and M. Leavesley 2011. New data from Oposisi: Implications for the Early Papuan Pottery phase. *Journal of Pacific Archaeology* 2:69–81.

64. Reepmeyer, C., M. Spriggs, P. Lape, L. Neri, W.P. Ronquillo, T. Simanjuntak, G.R. **Summerhayes**, D. Tanudirjo and A. Tiauzon 2011. Obsidian sources and distribution systems in Island Southeast Asia: New results and implications from geochemical research using LA-ICPMS. *Journal of Archaeological Science* 38:2995–3005. doi.org/10.1016/j.jas.2011.06.023.

65. Spriggs, M., C. Reepmeyer, P. Lape, L. Neri, W.P. Ronquillo, T. Simanjuntak, G.R. **Summerhayes**, D. Tanudirjo and A. Tiauzon 2011. Obsidian sources and distribution systems in Island Southeast Asia: A review of previous research. *Journal of Archaeological Science* 38:2873–2881. doi.org/10.1016/j.jas.2011.06.015.

66. Shaw, B., H.R. Buckley, G.R. **Summerhayes**, C. Stirling and M. Reid 2011. Prehistoric migration at Nebira, south coast of Papua New Guinea: New insights into interaction using isotope and trace element concentration analyses. *Journal of Anthropological Archaeology* 30:344–358. doi.org/10.1016/j.jaa.2011.05.004.

67. Ambrose, W.R., F. Petchey, P. Swadling, H. Beran, L. Bonshek, K. Szabo, S. Bickler and G.R. **Summerhayes** 2012. Engraved prehistoric *Conus* shell valuables from southeastern Papua New Guinea: Their antiquity, motifs and distribution. *Archaeology in Oceania* 47:113–132. doi.org/10.1002/j.1834-4453.2012.tb00124.x.

68. Harlow, G.E., G.R. **Summerhayes**, H.L. Davies and E. Matisoo-Smith 2012. A jade gouge from Emirau Island, Papua New Guinea (Early Lapita context, 3300 BP): A unique jadeitite. *European Journal of Mineralogy* 24:391–399. doi.org/10.1127/0935-1221/2012/0024-2175.

69. Carson, M.T., H. Hung, G.R. **Summerhayes** and P. Bellwood 2013. The pottery trail from Southeast Asia to remote Oceania. *The Journal of Island and Coastal Archaeology* 8:17–36. doi.org/10.1080/1556 4894.2012.726941.

70. Dennison, J. and G.R. **Summerhayes** (eds) 2013. *Admiralty Islands*. Translation of Hans Nevermann, 1934 *Admiralties Inslen*. University of Otago Working Papers in Anthropology 1. University of Otago, Dunedin.

71. **Summerhayes**, G.R. and H. Buckley (eds) 2013. *Pacific archaeology: Documenting the past 50,000 years*. University of Otago, Dunedin.

72. **Summerhayes**, G.R. and M. Porr 2013. Die ersten Siedler Neuguineas. *Archäologie in Deutschland* 5:14–19.

73. **Summerhayes**, G.R. and A. Ford 2014. Late Pleistocene colonisation and adaptation in New Guinea: Implications for modelling modern human behaviour. In R. Dennell and M. Porr (eds), *Southern Asia, Australia, and the search for human origins*, pp. 213–228. Cambridge University Press, New York. doi.org/10.1017/CBO9781139084741.017.

74. **Summerhayes**, G.R., J. Kennedy, E. Matisoo-Smith, H. Mandui, W. Ambrose, C. Allen, C. Reepmeyer, R. Torrence and F. Wadra 2014. Lepong: A new obsidian source in the Admiralty Islands, Papua New Guinea. *Geoarchaeology* 29:238–248. doi.org/10.1002/gea.21475.

75. Dennison, J. and G.R. **Summerhayes** (eds) 2015. *The empress Augusta/Sepik River by Otto Reche.* Translated by John Dennison. Department of Anthropology & Archaeology, University of Otago, Dunedin.

76. Gaffney, D., A. Ford and G.R. **Summerhayes** 2015. Crossing the Pleistocene–Holocene transition in the New Guinea Highlands: Evidence from the lithic assemblage of Kiowa rockshelter. *Journal of Anthropological Archaeology* 39:223–246. doi.org/10.1016/j.jaa.2015.04.006.

77. Gaffney, D., G.R. **Summerhayes**, A. Ford, J.M. Scott, T. Denham, J. Field and W.R. Dickinson 2015. Earliest pottery on the New Guinea mainland reveals Austronesian influences in Highland environments 3000 years ago. *PLoS ONE* e0134497:1–15. doi.org/10.1371/journal.pone.0134497.

78. **Summerhayes**, G.R. 2015. Trade and exchange, Archaeology of. In J.D. Wright (ed.), *International encyclopedia of the social & behavioral sciences*, pp. 481–484. 2nd edition, Vol. 24. Elsevier, Oxford. doi.org/10.1016/B978-0-08-097086-8.13043-0.

79. Sutton, N., G.R. **Summerhayes** and A. Ford 2015. Regional interaction networks in southern Papua New Guinea during the Late Holocene: Evidence from the chemical characterisation of chert artefacts. *Proceedings of the Prehistoric Society* 81:343–359. doi.org/10.1017/ppr.2015.14.

80. Ford, A., M. Leavesley and G.R. **Summerhayes** 2016. Chief bilong PNG Akiologi: Papers in honour of Herman Mandui. *Journal of Pacific Archaeology* 7:1–3.

81. Gaffney, D., A. Ford and G.R. **Summerhayes** 2016. Sue Bulmer's legacy in highland New Guinea: A re-examination of the Bulmer Collection and future directions. *Archaeology in Oceania* 51:23–32. doi.org/10.1002/arco.5111.

82. Mialanes, J., B. David, A. Ford, T. Richards, I.J. McNiven, G.R. **Summerhayes** and M. Leavesley 2016. Imported obsidian at Caution Bay, south coast of Papua New Guinea: Cessation of long distance procurement c. 1900 cal BP. *Australian Archaeology* 82:248–262. doi.org/10.1080/03122417.2016.1252079.

83. Shaw, B., M. Leclerc, W.R. Dickinson, M. Spriggs and G.R. **Summerhayes** 2016. Identifying prehistoric trade networks in the Massim: Evidence from petrographic and chemical compositional pottery analyses from Rossel and Nimowa Islands in the Louisiade Archipelago, Massim region, Papua New Guinea. *Journal of Archaeological Science: Reports* 6:518–535. doi.org/10.1016/j.jasrep.2016.03.034.

84. Skelly, R., A. Ford, G.R. **Summerhayes**, J. Mialanes and B. David 2016. Chemical signatures & social interactions: Implications of west Fergusson Island obsidian at Hopo, east of the Vailala River (Gulf of Papua), Papua New Guinea. *Journal of Pacific Archaeology* 7:126–138.

85. Specht, J., C. Gosden, C. Pavlides, Z. Richards and G.R. **Summerhayes** 2016. Exploring Lapita diversity on New Britain's south coast, Papua New Guinea. *Journal of Pacific Archaeology* 7:20–29.

86. **Summerhayes**, G.R. 2016. Sourcing techniques in landscape archaeology. In B. David and J. Thomas (eds), *Handbook of landscape archaeology*, pp. 530–535. Routledge, New York.

87. Sutton, N., G. Vilgalys, G.R. **Summerhayes** and A. Ford 2016. Revisiting the late prehistoric sequence of the Port Moresby region of Papua New Guinea: The continuing contribution of Susan Bulmer. *Archaeology in Oceania* 51:41–49. doi.org/10.1002/arco.5110.

88. Vilgalys, G. and G.R. **Summerhayes** 2016. Do hiccups echo? Late Holocene interaction and ceramic production in southern Papua New Guinea. *Asian Perspectives* 55:62–88. doi.org/10.1353/asi.2016.0011.

89. Gaffney, D. and G.R. **Summerhayes** 2017. *An archaeology of Madang, Papua New Guinea.* University of Otago, Dunedin.

90. Heath, H., G.R. **Summerhayes** and H. Hung 2017. Enter the Ceramic Matrix: Identifying the nature of the early Austronesian settlement in the Cagayan Valley, Philippines. In P. Piper, H. Matsumura and D. Bulbeck (eds), *New perspectives in Southeast Asian and Pacific prehistory*, pp. 213–231. ANU Press, Canberra. doi.org/10.22459/TA45.03.2017.12.

91.   Roberts, P., D. Gaffney, J. Lee-Thorp and G.R. **Summerhayes** 2017. Persistent tropical foraging in the highlands of terminal Pleistocene/Holocene New Guinea. *Nature Ecology and Evolution* 1:1–6. doi.org/ 10.1038/s41559-016-0044.

92.   **Summerhayes**, G.R. 2017. Island Southeast Asia and Oceania interactions. In J. Habu, P.V. Lape and J.W. Olsen (eds), *Handbook of East and Southeast Asian archaeology*, pp. 659–673. Springer, New York. doi.org/10.1007/978-1-4939-6521-2_38.

93.   **Summerhayes**, G.R., J. Field, B. Shaw and D. Gaffney 2017. The archaeology of forest exploitation and change in the tropics during the Pleistocene: The case of Northern Sahul (Pleistocene New Guinea). *Quaternary International* 448:14–30. doi.org/10.1016/j.quaint.2016.04.023.

94.   Dennison, J. and G.R. **Summerhayes** (eds) 2017. *New Guinea*. Translation of M. Krieger, 1898 *Neu-Guinea*. University of Otago Working Papers in Anthropology No. 6. University of Otago, Dunedin.

95.   Gaffney, D., G.R. **Summerhayes** and K. Miamba 2018. An archaeological survey of inland Madang, Northeast Papua New Guinea. *Archaeology in New Zealand* 12:12–26.

96.   Gaffney, D., G.R. **Summerhayes**, M. Mennis, T. Beni, A. Cook, J. Field, G. Jacobsen, F. Allen, H. Buckley and H. Mandui 2018. Archaeological investigations into the origins of Bel trading groups around the Madang coast, northeast New Guinea. *The Journal of Island and Coastal Archaeology* 13:501–530. doi.org/10.1080/15564894.2017.1315349.

97.   **Summerhayes**, G.R. 2018. Coconuts on the move: Archaeology of Western Pacific. *The Journal of Pacific History* 53:375–396. doi.org/10.1080/00223344.2018.1520082.

98.   **Summerhayes**, G.R. 2018. An Austronesian presence in the Sakishima Islands: An archaeological update. In N. Guo and T. Shogimen (eds), *Proceedings of the Overseas Symposium in Otago: Japanese Studies Down Under: History, Politics, Literature and Art*, pp. 27–37. International Research Center for Japanese Studies, Kyoto.

99.   **Summerhayes**, G.R. 2018. Les premiers habitants de la Nouvelle-Guinée. In J.P. Demoule, D. Garcia and A. Schnapp (eds), *Une histoire des civilisations: Comment l'archéologie bouleverse nos connaissances*, pp. 138–143. La Découverte, Paris.

100.   Bedford, S., M. Spriggs, D. Burley, C. Sand, P. Sheppard and G.R. **Summerhayes** 2019. Debating Lapita: Distribution, chronology, society and subsistence. In S. Bedford and M. Spriggs (eds), *Debating Lapita: Distribution, chronology, society and subsistence*, pp. 5–33. ANU Press, Canberra. doi.org/ 10.22459/TA52.2019.01.

101.   Dennison, J. and G.R. **Summerhayes** (eds) 2019. *The Sepik and its catchment area*. Translation of W. Behrmann, 1917 *Der Sepik Neu-Guinea Der Sepik (Kaiserin Augusta-Flusz) und sein Stromgebiet*. University of Otago Working Papers in Anthropology No. 7. University of Otago, Dunedin.

102.   Gaffney, D., G.R. **Summerhayes**, K. Szabo and B. Koppel 2019. The emergence of shell valuable exchange in the New Guinea Highlands. *American Anthropologist* 121:30–47. doi.org/10.1111/aman.13154.

103.   Gaffney, D., G.R. **Summerhayes** and M. Mennis 2019. A Lapita presence on Arop/Long Island, Vitiaz Strait, Papua New Guinea? In S. Bedford and M. Spriggs (eds), *Debating Lapita: Distribution, chronology, society and subsistence*, pp. 115–134. ANU Press, Canberra. doi.org/10.22459/TA52.2019.06.

104.   Gaffney, D. and G.R. **Summerhayes** 2019. Coastal mobility and lithic supply lines in northeast New Guinea. *Archaeological and Anthropological Sciences* 11:2849–2878. doi.org/10.1007/s12520-018-0713-8.

105.   Radclyffe, C., G.R. **Summerhayes** and R. Walter 2019. Discovery of Talasea obsidian in a Post-Lapita deposit on the Arnavon Islands, Solomon Islands. *Journal of Pacific Archaeology* 10:73–79.

106.   **Summerhayes**, G.R. 2019. Austronesian expansions and the role of mainland New Guinea: A new perspective. *Asian Perspectives* 58:250–260. doi.org/10.1353/asi.2019.0015.

107.   **Summerhayes**, G.R. 2019. The archaeology of Melanesia. In E. Hirsch and W. Rollason (eds), *The Melanesian world*, pp. 43–62. Routledge, London. doi.org/10.4324/9781315529691-2.

108. **Summerhayes**, G.R., K. Szabó, M. Leavesley and D. Gaffney 2019. Kamgot at the lagoon's edge: Site position and resource use of an Early Lapita site in Near Oceania. In S. Bedfordand M. Spriggs (eds), *Debating Lapita: Distribution, chronology, society and subsistence*, pp. 89–103. ANU Press, Canberra. doi.org/10.22459/TA52.2019.04.

109. **Summerhayes**, G.R., K. Szabó, A. Fairbairn, M. Horrocks, S. McPherson and A. Crowther 2019. Early Lapita subsistence: The evidence from Kamgot, Anir Islands, New Ireland Province, Papua New Guinea. In S. Bedford and M. Spriggs (eds), *Debating Lapita: Distribution, chronology, society and subsistence*, pp. 379–402. ANU Press, Canberra. doi.org/10.22459/TA52.2019.18.

110. Sutton, N., G.R. **Summerhayes** and A. Ford 2019. Oposisi revisited: A fabric analysis of an early Papuan pottery assemblage from Yule Island, Papua New Guinea. *The Journal of Island and Coastal Archaeology* 14:411–425. doi.org/10.1080/15564894.2018.1531329.

111. Chynoweth, M., G.R. **Summerhayes**, A. Ford and Y. Negishi 2020. Lapita on Wari Island: What's the problem? *Asian Perspectives* 59:100–116. doi.org/10.1353/asi.2020.0009.

112. Field, J., G.R. **Summerhayes**, S. Luu, A.C.F. Coster, A. Ford, H. Mandui, R. Fullagar, E. Hayes, M. Leavesley, M. Lovave and L. Kealhofer 2020. Functional studies of flaked and ground stone artefacts reveal starchy tree nut and root exploitation in mid-Holocene highland New Guinea. *The Holocene* 30:1360–1374. doi.org/10.1177/0959683620919983.

113. Gaffney, D., K. Greig, D. Stoddart, M. Tromp, J. Field, S. Luu, A.C.F. Coster, T. Russell, H. Mandui and G.R. **Summerhayes** 2020. Tropical foodways and exchange along the Coastal Margin of Northeastern New Guinea. *Journal of Field Archaeology* 45:498–511. doi.org/10.1080/00934690.2020.1786285.

114. Shaw, B., J. Field, G.R. **Summerhayes**, S. Coxe, A.C.F. Coster, A. Ford, J. Haro, H. Arifeae, E. Hull, G. Jacobsen, R. Fullagar, E. Hayes and L. Kealhofer 2020. Emergence of a Neolithic in Highland New Guinea by 5000–4000 years ago. *Science Advances* eaay4573. doi.org/10.1126/sciadv.aay4573.

115. **Summerhayes**, G.R. 2020. Oceania. In E. Hermans (ed.), *A companion to the global early middle ages*, pp. 95–110. ARC Humanities Press, Leeds. doi.org/10.1017/9781942401766.005.

116. Douglass, K., D. Gaffney, T.J. Feo, P. Bulathsinhala, A.L. Mack, M. Spitzer and G.R. **Summerhayes** 2021. Late Pleistocene/Early Holocene sites in the montane forests of New Guinea yield early record of cassowary hunting and egg harvesting. *Proceedings of the National Academy of Sciences* 118:e2100117118. doi.org/10.1073/pnas.2100117118.

117. Gaffney, D., G.R. **Summerhayes**, S. Luu, J. Menzies, K. Douglass, M. Spitzer and S. Bulmer 2021. Small game hunting in montane rainforests: Specialised capture and broad spectrum foraging in the Late Pleistocene to Holocene New Guinea Highlands. *Quaternary Science Reviews* 253:106742. doi.org/10.1016/j.quascirev.2020.106742.

118. Grainger, A., G.R. **Summerhayes** and C. Gosden 2021. Investigating the nature of mobility patterns and interaction: Ceramic production at the Late Lapita site of Amalut, Papua New Guinea. *Australian Archaeology* 87:93–104. doi.org/10.1080/03122417.2020.1840489.

119. Hogg, N., G.R. **Summerhayes** and Y.E. Chen 2021. Moving on or settling down? Studying the nature of mobility through Lapita pottery from the Anir Islands, Papua New Guinea. *Technical Reports of the Australian Museum* 34:71–86. doi.org/10.3853/j.1835-4211.34.2021.1744.

120. Radclyffe, C., G.R. **Summerhayes**, J.M. Scott and R. Walter 2021. Pottery production and exchange in the last millennium in the Western Solomon Islands: A ceramic sequence for Choiseul. *Journal of Pacific Archaeology* 12:25–46.

121. **Summerhayes**, G.R. 2021. History of archaeology in Papua New Guinea: The early years up to 1960. In I.J. McNiven and B. David (eds), *The Oxford handbook of the archaeology of Indigenous Australia and New Guinea*, online edn. Oxford University Press, Oxford. doi.org/10.1093/oxfordhb/9780190095611.013.3.

122. **Summerhayes**, G.R. 2021. Kisim save long graun: Understanding the nature of landscape change in modelling Lapita in Papua New Guinea. In M.T. Carson (ed.), *Palaeolandscapes in archaeology: Lessons for the past and future*, pp. 291–312. Routledge, London. doi.org/10.4324/9781003139553-10.

123. Thomas, T., A. McStay, P. Sheppard and G.R. **Summerhayes** 2021. Interaction and isolation in New Georgia: Insights from the Nabo Point ceramic assemblage, Tetepare. *Archaeology in Oceania* 56:45–64. doi.org/10.1002/arco.5221.

124. Wang, N., S. Brown, P. Ditchfield, S. Hebestreit, M. Kozlikin, S. Luu, O. Wedage, S. Grimaldi, M. Chazan, K.L. Horwitz, M. Spriggs, G.R. **Summerhayes**, M. Shunkov, K.K. Richter and K. Douka 2021. Testing the efficacy and comparability of ZooMS protocols on archaeological bone. *Journal of Proteomics* 233:104078.

125. Field, J., B. Shaw and G.R. **Summerhayes** 2022. Pathways to the Interior: Human settlement in the Simbai-Kaironk Valleys of the Madang Province, PNG. *Australian Archaeology* 88:2–17. doi.org/10.1080/03122417.2021.2007600.

126. Hogg, N., Y.E. Chen, G.R. **Summerhayes**, G. Boswijk, S.W. Manning, A. Hogg and C. Gosden 2022. Building on the past: Refining our current understanding of Lapita stilt structures. *Australian Archaeology* 88:268–281. doi.org/10.1080/03122417.2022.2148184.

127. Mialanes, J., A. Ford, B. Goodall, M. Codlin, M. McCoy, G.R. **Summerhayes**, B. David, T. Richards and I.J. McNiven 2022. The stone artefacts of Tanamu 1. In B. David, K. Szabo, M. Leavesley, I.J. McNiven, J. Ash and T. Richards (eds), *The archaeology of Tanamu 1: A pre-Lapita to Post-Lapita site from Caution Bay, South Coast of Mainland Papua New Guinea*. Archaeopress, Oxford.

128. Roberts, P., K. Douka, M. Tromp, S. Bedford, S. Hawkins, L. Bouffandeau, J. Ilgner, M. Lucas, S. Marzo, R. Hamilton, W. Ambrose, D. Bulbeck, S. Luu, R. Shing, C. Gosden, G.R. **Summerhayes** and M. Spriggs 2022. Fossils, fish and tropical forests: prehistoric human adaptations on the island frontiers of Oceania. *Philosophical Transactions of the Royal Society B* 377:20200495. doi.org/10.1098/rstb.2020.0495.

129. **Summerhayes**, G.R. 2022. New Guinea's past: The last 50,000 years. In R.T. Jones and M.K. Martsuda (eds), *The Cambridge history of the Pacific Ocean*, pp. 406–433. Cambridge University Press, Cambridge. doi.org/10.1017/9781108539272.024.

130. **Summerhayes**, G.R. 2022. Sue Bulmer and New Guinea archaeology. In H. Howes, T. Jones and M. Spriggs (eds), *Uncovering Pacific pasts: Histories of archaeology in Oceania*, pp. 527–534. ANU Press, Canberra. doi.org/10.22459/UPP.2021.34.

131. Kerby, G., A. Ford, G.R. **Summerhayes**, M.G. Leavesley and J.M. Palin 2022. Fit for purpose: Investigating adaptations in late Pleistocene lithic technology to an island environment at Buang Merabak, New Ireland, Papua New Guinea. *World Archaeology* 54:317–337. doi.org/10.1080/00438243.2023.2172070.

132. **Summerhayes**, G.R. 2023. Reflections on populating the Western Pacific. In C. Nimura, R. O'Sullivan and R. Bradley (eds), *Sentient archaeologies: Global perspectives on places, objects, and practice. Essays in honour of Professor Chris Gosden*, pp. 9–18. Oxbrow Press, Oxford. doi.org/10.2307/jj.2373316.6.

133. Roberts, P., S. Hixon, R. Hamilton, M. Lucas, J. Ilgner, S. Marzo, S. Hawkins, S. Luu, C. Gosden, M. Spriggs and G.R. **Summerhayes** (in press). Assessing Pleistocene–Holocene climatic and environmental change in insular Near Oceania using stable isotope analysis of archaeological fauna. *Journal of Quaternary Science*.

Part 1:
Glenn Summerhayes in Papua New Guinea

2

Recollection of Glenn Summerhayes' relationship with the Papua New Guinea National Museum and Art Gallery

Kenneth Miamba, Loretta Hasu, Henry Arifeae, Betty Neanda, Jemina Haro, Joyce Taian and Dickson Kangi

Glenn's relationship with the National Museum and Art Gallery (NMAG)

Professor Glenn Summerhayes' interest in Papua New Guinea (PNG) archaeology began in 1986 when he worked on pottery from Jim Specht's fieldwork in North Solomons (Autonomous Region of Bougainville) for his MA dissertation at Sydney University (Summerhayes 1987). The Solomons research eventually paved the way for numerous archaeological projects in the Bismarck Archipelago, the north and south coasts of Papua New Guinea, the Central Highlands (Goilala) (Summerhayes et al. 2010), the northern fringes of the Papua New Guinea Highlands (Simbai-Kaironk) and the Sepik–Ramu trough.

During this time, the head of archaeology at PNG National Museum and Art Gallery (NMAG) in Port Moresby was Dr Pamela Swadling, until 1999 when the position became nationalised. National archaeologists such as Nick Araho, the late Herman Mandui, and Alois Kuaso worked in the prehistory branch and trained under Dr Swadling to be stewards of Papua New Guinea's archaeological and cultural heritage. Araho reported to Swadling as a principal curator. A few years later, Mandui joined as an impact archaeologist. He was followed by Kuaso in 1997 as a traditional sites curator—a junior role that Kenneth Miamba occupied in 2016 after Kuaso became the Deputy Director. Glenn has worked with four generations of PNG National Museum indigenous archaeologists.

Glenn's intimate connection with the prehistory staff from the museum began more than 36 years ago when he first set foot in Port Moresby. The late Herman Mandui was Glenn's closest colleague in PNG. Besides Mandui was the late Baiva Ivuyo, technical staff within the prehistory branch, and Kuaso, who was once a student of Glenn's at The Australian National University in Canberra. Henry Arifeae is another close colleague of Glenn's; they have worked together in PNG on many projects. Glenn is a great friend of NMAG and a stalwart of PNG archaeology. It will be a sad day when he finally hangs up his field boots and we no longer see him in our corridors.

PNG is everything to Glenn, a country where he devoted much of the energy and time of his career as a researcher, and a place he called a second home. A particular province in PNG he loves the most would be New Ireland, which he always calls 'Bilas peles' [beautiful place]. It was also during fieldwork in New Ireland that he met his wife.

On 2014 Queen's Birthday, Glenn was made an Officer of Logohu (OL) in Port Moresby, in recognition of his contribution to archaeological heritage and research in PNG.

His contribution to Papua New Guinea archaeology

Glenn's contribution to PNG archaeology is immeasurable. He is one of the few international archaeologists who has frequented the country despite its diverse cultural complexities, geographical constraints, remoteness and isolation, and sometimes negative stories in the media. He has contributed indispensable knowledge to the understanding of the prehistory of Papua New Guinea and the Pacific Islands.

In quest of the Lapita Cultural Complex, Glenn spent many years working in the Bismarck Archipelago and the north coast of Papua New Guinea. He has worked in Bougainville, New Ireland, New Britain, Central Province, Manus, Morobe, Madang and the Sepik. He also spent a few years on the south central Papuan coast, particularly Yule Island.

To further understand prehistoric exchange and interaction between the Austronesians and Papuan groups, he also undertook numerous projects on the mainland of New Guinea. His energetic pursuit of PNG archaeology has paid off with the two most significant discoveries up in the Ivane Valley of Goilala District, and the Simbai-Kairork Valley systems of Middle Ramu District.

In 2009 Glenn led a team of archaeologists and students into the Ivane Valley of Goilala. The discovery of the 50,000-year-old archaeological site in the Ivane Valley of Goilala District in the Central Highlands of Papua New Guinea is a significant achievement for the archaeology of Sahul and the country (Summerhayes et al. 2010). Not only did it set the earliest chronological age for the settlement history of the inhabitants of New Guinea and the Pacific. It was a discovery that also explained occupation and survival strategies in higher altitudes, and demonstrated that the colonisation of New Guinea and offshore islands was a rapid process. Today, we can hear bureaucrats and politicians in Papua New Guinea making profound statements, boasting about PNG's 50,000-year-old settlement history, 854 plus languages and diverse culture, in both the national and international arena.

In 2017 Glenn and a team of researchers from the University of New South Wales (UNSW) excavated a pottery site in Simbai, New Guinea Highlands. It was a very significant discovery that highlighted a possible route that may have facilitated the movement of people and ideas, domesticates and cultigens via the Sepik–Ramu corridors into the highlands, along the coast and across the Pacific.

His works have been highly influential in encouraging archaeologists and scientists around the world to focus their attention on Papua New Guinea. His inspiring undergraduate lectures in universities and schools during his visits have been the catalyst that attracts a growing number of young Papua New Guineans to take up studies in anthropology, archaeology and cultural heritage studies every year at PNG universities. We thank Glenn for his infectious enthusiasm and we hope that his school of thought will continue to inspire interest and research in PNG archaeology.

His support for NMAG

Had all the previous National Museum archaeologists still been around at this time, they would have recalled and mentioned in detail all that Glenn did to support NMAG. Below is what we have heard and observed during the last five years at the PNG Museum.

Good books on Papua New Guinea are hard to find in Port Moresby. Glenn would bring books to the National Museum or send a few copies with colleagues coming for fieldwork. We have gone through several books on the prehistory office shelves and found his signatures to be good as new. Some were translated versions on early German expeditions of the Sepik and the Admiralty Islands, a book project Glenn and others had been working on for some years.

Besides books, there was a donation of field equipment and gear for the branch and staff members. The prehistory staff members' personal field gear includes several gifts from Glenn. On the shelves are pieces of equipment that Glenn and colleagues donated and have been used by everyone who came to NMAG for research. We would not hesitate to exhibit these if we were asked to by any museums.

He also assisted former staff members on many occasions to attend international conferences and symposiums in many places in the Pacific, Australia, New Zealand and Asia. He ensured that the faces and voices of indigenous PNG archaeologists could be seen and heard in the international arena.

In preparation for the 2018 Asia-Pacific Economic Cooperation (APEC) Summit, the PNG National Museum refurbished its gallery spaces. A new exhibition was required but the time was insufficient. Glenn volunteered and wrote a didactic text and produced a map for the Lapita Cultural Complex and movement into the Pacific for the archaeology gallery.

In October 2019, Glenn successfully secured a Marsden Grant for major archaeological research in the lowland Middle Ramu area of Madang. He negotiated for two potential candidates from PNG to undertake postgraduate studies—a master's and a PhD—in archaeology at the University of Otago before he calls it a day.

A colleague and friend

Besides being an eminent scholar, Glenn has also proven to be a great friend of NMAG staff, students and many Papua New Guineans he met during his work.

Jemina Haro is a Technical Officer in the Prehistory Branch at NMAG (2015–2021):

I came to know Professor Glenn Summerhayes back in 2015. He came to NMAG to see the late Herman Mandui (Science Research and Consultancy Deputy Director). That time I got to introduce myself and meet him. I saw Glenn sitting at the Prehistory office chewing betel nut. I thought to myself, 'This white man is chewing betel nut?' He knew I was curious. He said he only chewed when he came to PNG to do work.

In 2016 we worked with his team on Motupore Island. I saw how great he worked and how the students looked up to him as a great mentor and talked well about how he has contributed to Papua New Guinea archaeology. Having read a few articles by Glenn he has done a lot for PNG archaeology.

I also worked with Professor Summerhayes on our Simbai–Kaironk trip in 2016. He led a team excavating one of the sites (Fundum), which was likely to be one of the oldest places where people lived in the Simbai–Kaironk valleys. He is a great man. I commend him for his research work in PNG.

Kenneth Miamba is a Traditional Sites Curator in the Prehistory Branch at NMAG (2016–2021):

In 2005, Glenn came to my high school (Brandi Secondary School) in Wewak and gave a talk on PNG archaeology that inspired me to study anthropology and sociology at the University of Papua New Guinea in 2007. I then met Glenn in June 2016, just after three months of employment with the National Museum and Art Gallery in Port Moresby. At the time Glenn (with Jim Allen, Anne Ford and Nick Sutton) was accompanying the staff and students from the University of Papua New Guinea on fieldwork to Motupore Island outside Port Moresby.

I was naïve and a bit shy to approach Glenn at the beginning without knowing that we would later be close friends and colleagues. I spent a few days on the island with the team and left for Aitape with other colleagues from the University of Papua New Guinea and the Notre Dame University, USA. A year later, Glenn and a team of academics, including students from the University of Otago, NZ, and UNSW, Australia, returned to Port Moresby for fieldwork in Simbai, Middle Ramu District of Madang Province. Jemina Haro (technical staff) and I from the museum accompanied the team on that trip.

There were a good number of us. We split into two teams, Fundum and Kaironk. Glenn picked all young fellows and had us in his team, the likes of Dylan Gaffney, Bennetine N'adrose and myself, a young local cook from Simbai Guest House and a few local youths, both males and females. We were excavating a 30,000-year-old site up on Fundum ridges, a saddle connecting the Bismarck and Schrader Range, overlooking Simbai Valley, eastward towards Ramu River and Kaironk Valley, westward down the Sepik River.

Glenn would check our progress at every 20-minute interval. He'd tell us about the book by Sir John Middleton on Karkar Island he read (in preparation for the Karkar project), retreated to the wind *haus* at a distance, smoke his cigarette, drink coffee and continue reading. At times some village elders would pop up and be invited by Glenn for a cigarette or coffee. We would hear an old version of New Guinea Tok Pisin coming from the thatched kunai roof, then followed by an outburst of laughter, as young Glenn lashed out his hilarious jokes.

During this time I got to know the persona of a great friend, colleague and mentor. One question he asked two other PNG colleagues and me on that trip, that is still fresh in my mind today, was: 'If I have to give you a small grant, where would you want to spend it?' I immediately responded that I would prefer to conduct archaeological research on the north coast of Papua New Guinea. He gave me an archaeology trowel and a tape measure and said: 'Keep this; I have been keeping it for 12 years. It's yours now, don't lose it'. I received it with a firm handshake, a gesture that I regarded as prophetic for something better to come.

From then on, I got to know Glenn better. We returned to Simbai in mid-2017 to excavate a 2,700-year-old pottery site, a significant discovery in the highlands of New Guinea. Then, later on, two trips to Karkar Island. Slow and careful we walked on the rugged mountain tracks and the slippery rocks across the cold rapids of the New Guinea Highlands, and sailed on the choppy waters of the Bismarck Sea.

Working with Glenn is fun. There is no hurry. He always ensures those with him are well and happy and the job executed very efficiently. His love for archaeology and places in PNG is so intense. He is a great archaeologist who has suburb public relations and field skills. The strength of his archaeology work lies in his character. He sees the positive side in every situation and every person. He has infectious humour. He is liked and admired by everyone who has met him.

One thing that gave Glenn the leverage to move around doing fieldwork is his mastery of pure Tok Pisin. He speaks an old version of Niugini Tok Pisin, something that he acquired while working in the Bismarck Archipelago and north coast of Papua New Guinea. In every community consultation in a village, he speaks in Tok Pisin and ends it with good humour. Here are popular lines from almost all of his talks in the villages that I have been with him: 'Mi wok moa long tripela ten krismas long planti hap bilong Papua Niu Guinea. Nau mi lapun nogut tru' [I have been working for more than 30 years at many places in Papua New Guinea. Now I am too old]. He used to stress the last sentence, which would make locals laugh. He is a friendly person. People get to approach him at ease. That enables him to get a great deal of information from locals very quickly.

Glenn knows well the social art of establishing a relationship and gaining respect from a New Guinean. As in every place in New Guinea and elsewhere in Melanesia, one must share to establish a relation, gain trust and make one another feel obligated. The two things that Glenn must have with him on fieldwork are coffee and British American Tobacco branded cigarettes, particularly Cambridge and Spear Rolls. Not that he loves smoking, but he shares a cup of coffee or a cigarette and cracks a joke to create friends. I have been around with Glenn in Madang for several field seasons. Elders would refer to him as *poroman* (friend), youngsters would call him papa, a few would humorously call him pater (father)—a word for a Catholic priest because of his grey hair and beard.

Glenn has a good sense of humour that also keeps those who work, and those around him, well at work and entertained. He would either say something or use facial expressions to express his sense of humour. During a busy day of work, one would hear a giggle or an outburst of laughter a few meters away from the dig site. Only to realise that people are chatting with him under the shades of trees or a temporary shelter.

Lukim yu! Gutpela poroman bilong mipela.

Loretta Hasu is the Manager, Access Education and Public Program at NMAG (2021):

Little did I know trowels would be a handy tool for archaeologists when I filled in my registration form at University of Papua New Guinea. Anthropology, sociology and archaeology was chosen as my major, fast forward to 6 months later and I read a notice outside the notice board of Kuri Dom building inviting students majoring in the strand and who have an interest in archaeology to submit their expression of interests for field research. Being the only female that year, I was fortunate enough to be selected to be part of Professor Glenn Summerhayes' team to Koil Island in the East Sepik Province.

Then, followed by archaeological projects on Yule Island along the coast, and to Kosipe in the hinterlands of the Central Province.

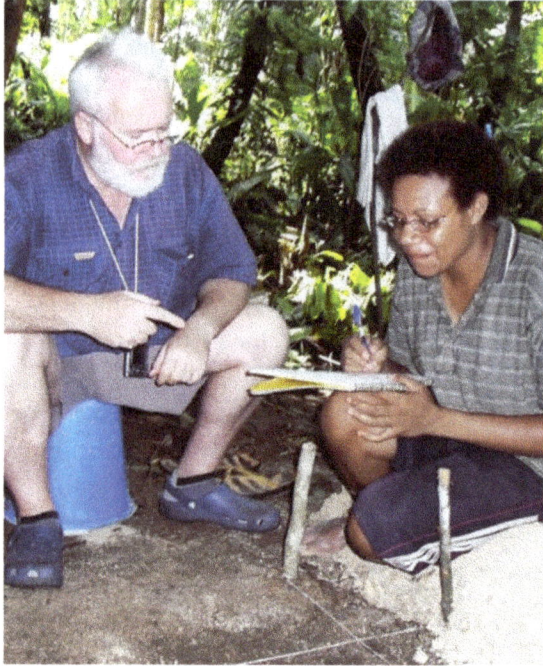

Figure 2.1: Glenn Summerhayes teaching Loretta Hasu field notebook recording techniques on Koil Island.

Source: Loretta Hasu.

Learning involved theories in class and practicals in the field, starting with community consultation first and foremost then to navigating through understanding techniques used in archaeology; from surface finds and landscape survey, soil stratigraphy, then to choosing an excavation site and coaching through the excavation processes using a trowel and the documentation processes simultaneously. This exposed me and others who were part of his team to other experts who accompanied him, from collecting samples of trees for dendrochronology to collecting swamp soil samples for the study of plant macrofossil remains, ethnobotanical studies and the use of field equipment such as dumpy levels, cameras and, of course, the trowel.

Being a student learning under his command was a motivation for me to pursue further studies in the field that I had developed an interest in. Glenn sees the future, which lies in training the upcoming generations. His legacy lives on in the knowledge he has imparted on the younger Papua New Guineans. May his legacy live on!

Betty Neanda is a Senior Technical Officer in the Prehistory Branch at NMAG (2016–2021):

I first met Glenn in 2016 on a visit to the Motupore Island archaeological salvage project by the University of Papua New Guinea (UPNG) and Otago University, NZ. The project involved young archaeologists from UPNG and Otago University, to help complete the thesis under their master's and PhD programs. A few staff members from the NMAG spent a week helping them in excavating the sites. During that time, I still remember Glenn, who was very welcoming and kind to everyone involved in the fieldwork. I was fascinated by his remarkable work. He makes sure everyone gets involved and understands the prehistory of the Papuan Region. I commend him for doing a lot of research about the prehistory of PNG.

Joyce Taian is Personal Assistant to the Deputy Director Corporate and Administration, NMAG (2003–2021):

I knew Professor Glenn Summerhayes way back in 2003 when I first started at the National Museum. He was the late Herman Mandui's best friend. The late Mandui used to call me his small sister. That's how I came to know Professor Summerhayes and often refer to him as a big brother.

During those days he chewed betel nut. He loved going out with his friends. Sometimes we went out together to have a few beers and smoke cigarettes at the late Mandui's residence. Sometimes we had fun out together during the fieldwork with the likes of the late Mandui, Nick Araho, Kari Heri, Baiva Ivuyo and Alois Kuaso. These are all Prehistory boys—sadly almost all have gone now. He is one of the great professors to work with. He has contributed a lot to PNG archaeology. There is a lot to say about him. I have tears in my eyes recalling fond memories of him and the late Herman Mandui. I'll end it here.

Dickson Kangi is a Community Representative and Guide from Kalam Guest House, Simbai, Middle Ramu District, Madang Province:

I was an infant at the time Ralph and Susan Bulmer did ethnobotany and archaeological research in the Kaironk Valley (Wañelek). Most of my peers only heard of the Bulmers and met their field assistant, the late Ian Saem Majnep. Little did we know about archaeology or what it was all about. We are well vested with legends of our mythical ancestors, migration history and trading routes. Professor Summerhayes and the team's presence and involvement with the surrounding communities and the result of their work helped us understand that ancient people passed through our territory thousands of years ago. The importance of community archaeology is that locals get firsthand information and learn from archaeologists. It motivates and encourages us to preserve our archaeological heritage.

On behalf of the People of Simbai, I thank Professor Summerhayes and the team for the three years of work in Simbai and Kaironk valleys. Your friendship with the locals, school visits and contribution to the Kalam Community and our Guest House during the years of fieldwork means a lot to us. It is a good start, and we are looking forward to hosting and supporting your colleagues with any research of this magnitude in the future.

The Kalam Tribe wishes you the best retirement.

Henry Arifeae is the Cultural Center Coordinator at the NMAG (2001–2021):

I met Glenn at a backyard party at the Arifeae Estate Residence in 2001, when this 'dashing handsome guy' walked in and 'pipped': 'G'day, I'm Glenn … mi wanpela archaeologist lo Australia National University, lon Canberra, Australia'. He was escorted in by the late Chief Archaeologist Herman Amaka Mandui (RIP). At first, I thought he was the local padre from the St Joseph's Catholic Church, around the corner from my house, in East Boroko. Herman laughed and said 'No! He is a colleague of mine … ' That was in 2001; fast forward, Glenn has been a personal friend/wantok for two decades. 20 years on and I must say 'I have learnt a lot from this maestro in the field of archaeology' and it is a very sad day for me to learn, he has finally called it quits from a vocation that has been his calling since leaving the Australian Public Service some time ago in the early years of his career!

Some of his famous quotes, in Tok Pisin: 'igo … igo … istap; na nau mi go simuk pastaim; you mas go lotu olgeta taim', and 'somewhere in New Guinea, husait i ken save, nobody knows!'

My family and I join in wishing Prof. Glenn Summerhayes all the best in his retirement from archaeology and acknowledge his immense contribution to this vocation in PNG!

All the best bro!

References

Summerhayes G.R. 1987. Aspects of Melanesian ceramics. Unpublished MA (Hons) thesis. Department of Anthropology, University of Sydney, Sydney.

Summerhayes G., M. Leavesley, A. Fairbairn, H. Mandui, J. Field, A. Ford and R. Fullagar 2010. Human adaptation and plant use in highland New Guinea 49,000 to 44,000 years ago. *Science* 330:78–81. doi.org/10.1126/science.1193130.

3

Personal reflections on working with Professor Glenn Summerhayes in Papua New Guinea

Roxanne Tsang and Jason Kariwiga

Roxanne Tsang

Professor Glenn Summerhayes is one of the most compelling New Guinea/Pacific archaeologists I have ever worked with. He was primarily involved in my archaeological career during my honours degree at the University of Papua New Guinea (UPNG) in Port Moresby, Papua New Guinea (PNG). As I recall from my archaeological field school seasons with him and other New Guinea archaeologists, namely: Professor Jim Allen, Dr Anne Ford and my UPNG lecturer and mentor Dr Matthew Leavesley at Motupore Island in PNG, and his lectures at UPNG, Glenn is one of those rare speakers that make listening to archaeology for hours a joy rather than a chore. I appreciated how he explained archaeology in its simplest terms; cutting down complex concepts to their barest essentials and inspiring his students in the process to do the same. For example, my fondest experience from working with him at Motupore was learning how to set up a dumpy level—I still remember how patient he was with me and other students. He is a true gentleman teacher!

In tandem with his practical mentorship, Glenn frequently circulates academic opportunities. To use another personal example, it was Glenn who shared the 17th International Speleology Congress Scholarship—an event which greatly interested me. Thanks to Glenn's support, I not only applied for but secured my first grant, which was used to attend and present at my first international conference in Sydney. There, I presented my first conference paper which also led to a publication, and coincided with my first caving excursions in New South Wales, culminating in my first consultant-archaeology job in Australia. This was just one of the many instances where Glenn was pivotal in paving the way for the future of archaeology. I remain indebted to him for constantly keeping our UPNG cohort in his thoughts and actions. Lastly, I want to sincerely thank him for his immense contribution to PNG's growing body of archaeological knowledge, and for his influence more broadly in the Pacific. His professionalism will continue to inspire me and many other students to carve out our path in a time of both uncertainty and opportunity. I wish him all the best for his retirement!

Jason Kariwiga

There is an old social science textbook once issued by the PNG Department of Education and used to teach primary school–aged students about the country's history. Published sometime in the late 1980/early 1990s, this book will have been the introduction to PNG's past for many generations of primary school students, including myself. Its title, author and most of its contents escape me—I'm not even sure if it's distributed across schools anymore. However, two short sections still stick out in my mind. The first of these outlines the magnificent Kuk and its ancient drainage ditches associated with early agriculture. The second describes the Pleistocene highland sites around Kosipe, complete with Peter White's initial occupation date of 26,000 years. I have since been fortunate enough to visit both places, but Kosipe stands out for me—it would, years later, the first place I ever did fieldwork and excavation. It was also at Kosipe that I first met Glenn Summerhayes.

Well, perhaps more accurately, I first met Glenn on a typically sweltering Port Moresby morning in early November 2008 at an Airlines PNG (now PNG Air) airport terminal. Terminal is too generous a word—it was more an open iron-roofed enclosure—but that's where I was introduced to Glenn by my UPNG lecturer Matt Leavesley. We were all there to catch the plane to Woitape station in the highlands of Goilala, and then make the arduous trek further north to the Ivane Valley and Kosipe Mission. My first impression of him was that unmissable white beard, but also that he spoke much better Tok Pisin than I did! Since then, I've had the pleasure of rubbing shoulders with him on many occasions during his various trips to the country.

Glenn's body of work and influence on Papua New Guinean archaeology is immense. His knowledge in this area is vast; I recall on one of his many trips to PNG, he stopped by the UPNG archaeology lab. At that time I was looking at Lapita pottery recovered from the mouth of the Liton River in Pomio, West New Britain. All week I had been searching the literature to find possible similarities in motif design from other Lapita sites. One look at the pottery and Glenn immediately fired off a couple of sites—saved me from more of the dreaded literature search! Glenn can also have a dry sense of humour. At Kosipe we used metal buckets during excavation and he used one in particular and its underside to sit on; on one of the first times out at the Vilaquav site, he remarked to all of us newbies (I was with my UPNG colleagues Nidatha Martin and Laura Naidi) that the first lesson of archaeology is to never sit on (Glenn's) bucket. It was only after a few days in I realised it was all tongue-in-cheek, but I still remember the lesson clearly! His ability to build genuine relationships with landowners and locals is very much the secret of his success in undertaking research in the country. There has been many a situation where his people skills have maintained good relations between researchers and locals.

Glenn's support of the archaeology program at UPNG also cannot be understated. Over the years he has freely given his time, from presenting public lectures on campus to meeting extensively with faculty. His photographs, words and slides are still used to teach students in the flagship 'Archaeology of Papua New Guinea', a course for second-year archaeology students. More profoundly, Glenn has been very generous with his funding and has had countless UPNG students accompany him into the field—I can certainly attest to the positive impact these excursions can have on young adults stepping into archaeology for the first time. His legacy will be his large body of work on PNG archaeology. Perhaps in time, the Kosipe section in primary school textbooks will be updated, complete with the new 50,000-year date, courtesy of Glenn's research.

Figure 3.1: Nidatha and Jason excavating at the Kosipe Mission Station, 2008.
Source: Jason Kariwiga.

Figure 3.2: Some of the team excavating a site at the Kosipe Mission Station, 2008.
Source: Jason Kariwiga.

Finally, and on a more personal level, for a 19-year-old just out of high school and with one year of university under his belt, Glenn left a huge impression on me at Kosipe. His knowledge, warmth and humour was (and is) infectious, and the overall experience left me wanting to do more archaeology. I have two favourite photographs from that fieldwork. The first (Figure 3.1) is a close-up of Nidatha and I smiling up at the camera as we excavate, while immediately behind us the late Herman Mandui is lifting a bucket of sediment. The second photograph (Figure 3.2) is a wide shot of a few of us; Glenn is excavating in the centre, side on to the camera in the foreground. Around him but close, Nidatha, Laura, Xavier (Carrah) and I are observing and working the sieves. I think both photographs highlight the most significant of Glenn's contributions: his role in inspiring and training future PNG archaeologists; support that has enabled Papua New Guineans and students all over the opportunity to participate fully in the archaeological process and discovery. That is a legacy worth emphasising.

4

Em i tisa blong mi— On the value of community engagement in research

Elizabeth Matisoo-Smith

Introduction

The need for community engagement and consultation is a topic that is receiving increasing attention in scientific research (Adams et al. 2014; Stilgoe et al. 2014; Tindana et al. 2017; Acabado 2020). In New Zealand, for example, major research funding agencies require discussion of consultation and community engagement in grant applications and are increasingly including scores for this in their assessments. Indigenous communities around the globe are calling for more and better consultation and engagement in research (Claw et al. 2018; Handsley-Davis et al. 2021). Archaeologists have perhaps been more aware of the need for such activities than other scientific researchers, due to the nature of fieldwork. Undertaking a field survey to even identify an archaeological site or environment generally requires discussions with the landowners and likely with the wider community who are traditionally linked to the region. The amount of time that an excavation requires also allows for engagement, and opportunities for discussion, as well as education for both the researchers and the communities. Other researchers who are interested in understanding and reconstructing human history can learn a lot from archaeologists when it comes to community engagement. I was lucky enough to learn about, and see the value of, community engagement firsthand from Glenn Summerhayes. What follows is a personal account of my fieldwork experiences which ultimately led to my working with Glenn in Papua New Guinea (PNG) for more than 10 years. I hope this story inspires others who have not had the opportunity to work with Glenn and see the impact he has had on the people of PNG and, as a result, on the field of Pacific archaeology.

I believe I first met Glenn in 1996 at the 3rd Lapita Conference held in Port Vila, Vanuatu, where I first presented my PhD research on mitochondrial DNA variation in Pacific rats (*Rattus exulans*). Our next meeting was four years later at the Easter Island Foundation's Pacific 2000 conference in Kamuela, on the Big Island of Hawai'i. The conference was held on the campus of a boarding school, which was fairly isolated and, much to the concern of many of the archaeologists in attendance, did not allow consumption of alcohol. Whether it was by design or just chance, a large contingent of archaeologists from The Australian National University (ANU) had been accommodated in a house off campus. What became known as ANU House, therefore, became the focus of post-session meals, drinks and discussions. Glenn was one of the archaeologists staying at ANU House and I remember that one night, for some reason probably related to the quality of food that was served on campus, we decided that we would cook dinner at the house for the crowd of archaeologists who had gathered there. Glenn and I ended up making a big pot of Japanese curry rice and we quickly became friends, sharing a love of food, wine and, of course, 'talking story'. Anyone who knows Glenn knows that he likes to talk and he certainly can tell a good story. It turns out that this is one of the things that makes him so successful in outreach and engagement.

Establishing a new model for tracking human mobility in the Pacific

My dissertation research involved the development and application of what is now generally referred to as the commensal approach for tracking prehistoric human migration. When I began my research, the field of molecular anthropology, while still in its infancy, was in crisis. It was in 1987 that Rebecca Cann, Mark Stoneking and Allan Wilson published their seminal article on human mitochondrial DNA (mtDNA) variation and how we could track human populations to a common maternal ancestor who lived in Africa some 200,000 years ago (Cann et al. 1987). Quickly researchers realised that mtDNA and other molecular markers could be valuable tools for reconstructing human migrations around the globe. While DNA proved to be a valuable scientific tool, indigenous communities were hesitant to engage with geneticists and other human biologists because of very legitimate concerns over unethical and unengaged research in the past (Lone Dog 1999). The Human Genome Diversity Project was generating significant debate and resistance (Cunningham 1998) and this was particularly strong in Australia and New Zealand. It became clear to me very quickly when I started my postgraduate research at the University of Auckland that it was highly unlikely that I would be able to use the new molecular tools to study human variation in the Pacific directly. But I was lucky enough to meet a colleague who helped me to identify another source of data and alternative approach to reconstructing population origins in Polynesia.

My PhD dissertation focused on studying mtDNA variation in Pacific rats (*Rattus exulans*) from throughout Polynesia in order to identify the origin of rats that were found in Aotearoa New Zealand. The commensal model for tracking human migration was based on the idea that if we could determine the origins and genetic relationships of the various plant and animal species that Polynesian and other Pacific peoples transported in their colonising canoes, we could use that information to reconstruct the population origins and identify interaction networks. For my dissertation research, I obtained fresh tissue samples from rats throughout Polynesia. Many of my samples were provided by biologists living or working in the islands who were able to trap rats for me and send me tissues. In the case of French Polynesia, however, I did my own fieldwork, travelling and trapping with my friend and colleague Dr Mere Roberts.

First fieldwork experiences in Polynesia — Informed but not engaged communities

Through colleagues in Papeete, I obtained contact details of local mayors or agricultural officers in many of the Society and Marquesas islands who allowed me access to gardens or other locations where I could set my traps. We generally stayed in small hotels or guest houses, and occasionally camped on site in the agricultural stations. We ventured out each evening to set traps in locations for which we had permission, and then cleared our traps first thing in the morning and undertook dissections in the field. This was a reasonably successful process that allowed me to collect enough samples to do my research, write my dissertation and to show that the commensal model did work (Matisoo-Smith et al. 1998). While I was fulfilling all of my official and legal obligations of having the correct research permits, working through national and local agencies in my fieldwork, I was relatively removed from, and not engaged with, the communities in which I was working. There certainly was gossip about these strange 'rat ladies' travelling around the islands of French Polynesia, and we found that people were expecting us but were rather sceptical about what we were really doing. As a result, we often had visitors to the field sites where we were working and sleeping so that people could try to see what we were up to in those pineapple fields. There seemed to be a bit of disappointment when they saw us working and doing exactly what we said we were: catching rats and collecting tissues from them. Other than these visits, and the wonderful Pacific hospitality we received from so many people we met, there was no real engagement in the research. As per my research permit agreements, I sent reports and publications back to the appropriate government agencies in Papeete, but this was the extent of communication of the results.

Given this success in applying the commensal model in Polynesia, the obvious next step was to extend the research on *R. exulans* further to the west to investigate the deeper origins of these Polynesian samples. This next phase of research involved samples provided mostly by the American Museum of Natural History, extending my sampling through Island Southeast Asia, New Guinea, the Solomon Islands and out into Remote Oceania. The results of this work indicated that there were three main haplogroups, or lineage clusters, of *R. exulans*. The rats from Remote Oceania belonged to what was labelled Group 3, and were quite distant from the rats from New Guinea and the Solomon Islands (Group 2) and from the *R. exulans* populations in the Philippines, Borneo and Sulawesi (Group 1). The Group 3 rats were linked to populations in Halmahera (Matisoo-Smith and Robins 2004). This result, or more specifically, the lack of Group 3 rats in New Guinea, was at odds with what we had expected to find based on the assumption that the rats were brought into the Pacific with Lapita colonists. Upon closer consideration, I realised that our result wasn't really testing the Lapita connection because all of the samples that I had from Near Oceania were from locations that had little or no evidence of Lapita occupation. This prompted another grant application to specifically target sampling of *R. exulans* from islands in the Bismarck Archipelago and determine if they might be ancestral to the rats found in Remote Oceania.

Lapita connections and an introduction to Papua New Guinea

There are few Pacific archaeologists who are more closely associated with the Bismarck Archipelago than Glenn Summerhayes, so I approached him to be a collaborator on a Marsden Fund application, which we submitted in early 2005. Later that year, I took my first trip to PNG and met Glenn in the field on Koil Island. I must admit that I was rather nervous about working in New Guinea, but Glenn arranged for me to meet his collaborators, Geoff Hope and Andy Fairbairn, at the airport in Brisbane so that we could all travel together from there. We immediately flew to Port Moresby and from there to Wewak, where we met with the local administrators and boarded the small boat for the two-hour trip to Koil.

As the boat approached the island, I heard the sound of drumming, which Geoff told me was letting the team know that we had arrived. Soon a small crowd appeared on the shore and there was Glenn and Herman Mandui, the archaeologist from the National Museum and Art Gallery and Glenn's close colleague and friend, waiting to meet us. Our gear was transported to Wanap village and I was introduced to the family with whom I would be living. I was sharing a room with Patricia, a young archaeology student from the University of Papua New Guinea (UPNG) who Glenn was co-supervising. I then started discussing with Glenn about how and where I might be able to set my rat traps. He quickly explained to me that my having free rein to set traps in the gardens was not possible as there were many locations where women were not allowed. He suggested that I explain my research to the community and give them my traps, asking for them to bring any rats that they trapped to me the next morning. I was a bit unsure about this approach, but trusted Glenn's advice.

That day I began showing people how to set the traps and explaining which rats I was interested in and that I expected that they would be found in houses and in gardens. With all of my traps handed out, I waited. Things started slowly. In the first few days, a few of the older children began bringing me dead rats, which I would take to the edge of the village, to record measurements and then dissect for the tissues I needed for DNA. Usually, the children would follow me, so I took the opportunity to show them how and why I measured the rats to make a tentative species identification. We would then have a short anatomy lesson as I measured and dissected each rat. There was much hilarity as I explained that we needed to count the nipples on each rat, because *R. exulans* only had eight nipples, while the other possible resident rat species had 10 or 12. After a few days, some of the women started bringing me dead rats, and they also began to observe the dissections and then take part in the data collection. Soon, rat trapping appeared to become a competition and everyone was bringing me rats. The community was engaged in the research and not only did they provide me with the samples I needed, we had numerous opportunities to talk about anatomy, taxonomy and, of course, anthropology. In addition to these informal educational opportunities, we also went around the island talking to schoolchildren about Lapita, archaeology, and, of course, my rat trapping. Interestingly, all 21 rats collected on Koil Island were identified as *Rattus tanezumi* (Matisoo-Smith et al. 2009). It appears that *exulans* were not introduced to Koil. While this result was initially disappointing, the lesson on the value of community engagement was priceless. As it turns out, however, finding which islands did <u>not</u> have *exulans* has been an important piece of information in trying to understand and interpret the results of this application of the commensal model.

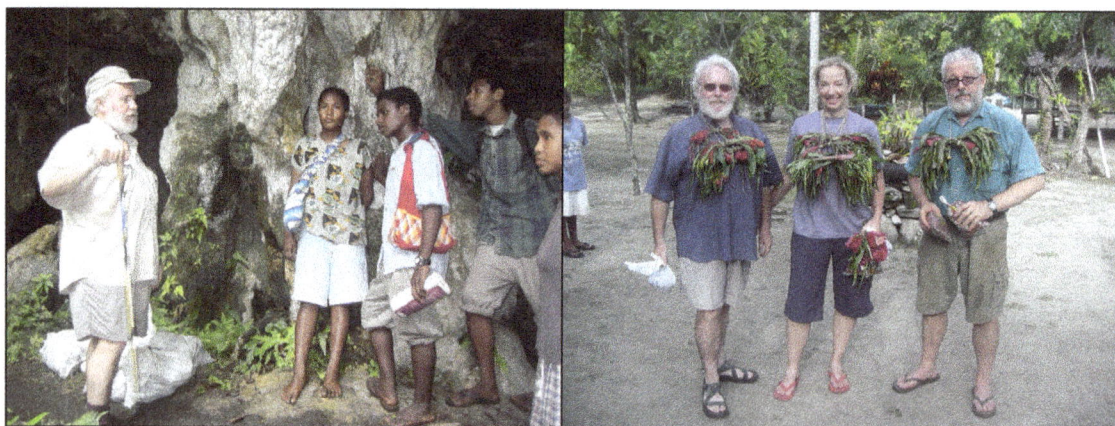

Figure 4.1: (Left) Glenn talking to schoolchildren at Gomogom Cave. (Right) Glenn, Geoff and Lisa on day of departure from Koil.

Source: Elizabeth Matisoo-Smith.

Rat catching in the Bismarck Archipelago

In 2006, we were granted funding from the Royal Society of New Zealand Marsden Fund to extend the commensal model in Near Oceania to address the Lapita connection, so Glenn and I planned a trip to the Bismarck Archipelago. Based on my experience in Koil, I came prepared with bags full of rat traps and the plan to engage in a similar approach for obtaining samples. After spending a few days in Port Moresby, where we organised permits, and met with officials at the National Research Institute and colleagues at UPNG and the National Museum and Art Gallery, we were ready to start our sampling trip. Again, we were accompanied by Herman Mandui, but we were also joined by two young Swedish students who were interested in Pacific archaeology and anthropology. Their supervisor had asked Glenn if they could travel to PNG with us. Of course Glenn said yes, as he is always willing to support the next generation of archaeologists. So, with rat traps packed and permits in hand, we flew from Port Moresby to Kavieng, New Ireland.

Within hours of our arrival in Kavieng, it was clear that Glenn was home. The number of people who called out from a passing vehicle or stopped us to chat was amazing. One of the first things Glenn had planned for Kavieng was a trip to the local radio station to set up an interview where we could talk about our research on air. Glenn talked about Lapita and I talked about mtDNA, rats and commensal models. With that done, we began arranging for visits to Lihir and Tabar. Again, Glenn and Herman had connections with people at the gold mine on Lihir, so we first flew from Kavieng to Lihir and were put up in accommodation at the mine. Over the next few days, we spoke to the local primary schoolchildren on Lihir, and one of the staff from Lihir Gold, Jimmy Peter, trapped rats for me around the compound.

We then arranged for a boat to take us to the nearby Tabar group, where we stayed for a few days. After giving a few community talks, I handed out traps and began collecting rats from the islands of Simberi and Tatau. Glenn and I gave several school talks on Tatau and Glenn put in a small test pit at a site where a local had found a waisted axe and shell adze. After five days in Tabar, with 27 rat samples in hand, we returned to Kavieng. From there we travelled by boat to nearby New Hanover, where, again, we gave talks about our research and the community became quite involved and excited about catching rats for my study.

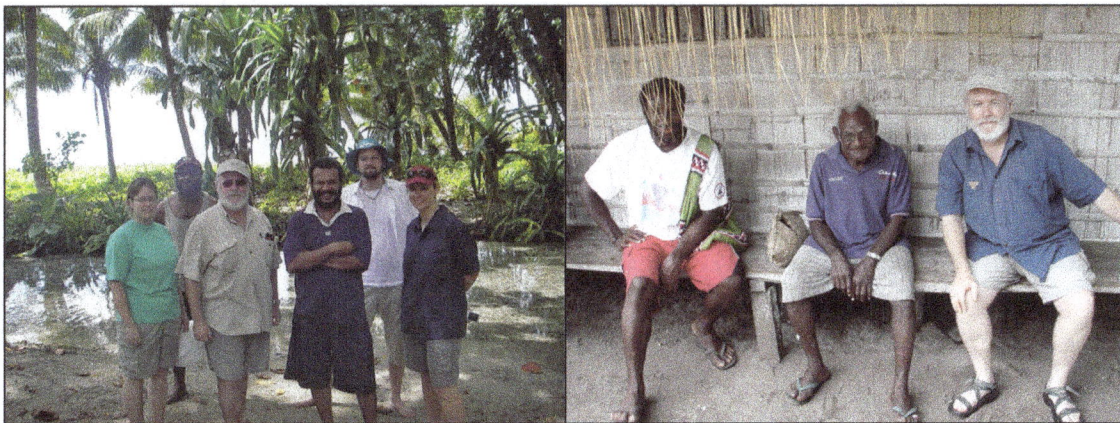

Figure 4.2: (Left) Jimmy Peter from Lihir Gold and the team. (Right) Glenn with Edward Salle (centre), Tatau, Tabar.
Source: Elizabeth Matisoo-Smith.

By the time we had returned to Kavieng again, the radio interview that we had recorded had aired. It turned out that a couple of school teachers from a small island called Emirau, in the St Matthias Group, were in Kavieng and heard the interview. Glenn, of course, had been explaining and describing Lapita pottery in his talk. The two teachers tracked us down via Jim Ridges, an English expat who lived in Kavieng, and explained that they had seen this pottery being dug up in their gardens on the island. We thanked them for the information and promised to keep in touch.

Manus, Minol and Mohe — Old friends and new obsidian sources

From Kavieng we flew to Manus Island, where we met up with Manus local and English professor at UPNG, Bernard Minol. We also met up with an old friend of Glenn's from his time in Anir, Father Paul Mohe, who was the Catholic Priest in Lorengau, the capital of Manus Province. It was decided that we would stay with Father Paul and that Glenn would speak to the congregation on Sunday and would explain our research. I will never forget the sight of Glenn in the pulpit giving a Lapita sermon! But several people met us afterwards and offered to collect rats, so traps and collection tubes of ethanol were handed out. We explained that just taking a bit of a tail snip would suffice since people would not be able to travel daily to drop off their rats and we did not expect for people to undertake a full dissection. The next day, Bernard travelled with us by boat up the north coast of the island, where we stopped off and met with communities and gave talks and left traps and tubes with friends and relatives of Bernard.

Earlier, Father Paul had told us about a possible new obsidian source that he had heard about, one that might turn out the be the mysterious Source-X that produced several obsidian flakes or the 'pitchstone' discoids, both of which had been recovered at the Pleistocene site of Pamwak (Fredericksen 1994, 1997). Again, Glenn's long-term engagement of communities in his research had hooked Father Paul. He became an archaeology enthusiast who spread the word and was always on the lookout for a Lapita site or a source of obsidian. He was also fascinated by biology, so I provided him with my first-year lecture slides and notes. We discussed human variation and how understanding population mobility and interaction in the past was essential for explaining human variation today. Father Paul was fascinated with the idea of Micronesian connections with Manus, particularly via the Western Islands. Those conversations led ultimately to ideas for a field project targeted at the Western Islands. While to date we have not been able to successfully fund such a trip, despite more than one grant application, it remains on my list of places I would love to visit and undertake research.

After meeting with communities and talking rats with Bernard's friends and family along the north coast of Manus, we decided that there might be enough time left in the day to travel further up the coast to see if we could find the new obsidian source. Father Paul had told us that it was discovered during forest clearance, as the logging company was cutting an access road. We arrived at the forestry base in the late afternoon, and after speaking with the manager, we jumped into the back of the truck to check out the location of interest. After approximately 10 kilometres we stopped at what appeared to be a large outcrop of exposed and weathered obsidian boulders, extending for almost 500 metres. We were told by the landowner that the name of the site was Lepong.

Figure 4.3: (Left) Herman, Minol and Glenn on Manus. (Right) Glenn, Herman and Lisa at Lepong.
Source: Elizabeth Matisoo-Smith.

Samples were collected from several of the boulders. These were subsequently analysed, with results indicating that the Lepong obsidian was the likely source of at least one of the 'pitchstone' flakes and one discoid from Pamwak, but that there was likely still another unidentified obsidian source providing raw material for the Late Pleistocene/Early Holocene sites on Manus (Summerhayes et al. 2014). Once again, Glenn's ability to educate and excite locals about archaeology, science and prehistory, and to maintain relationships that he established in the field, resulted in a valuable scientific discovery.

An invitation to Emirau

Manus was our last stop on the 2006 fieldwork tour of the Bismarck and Admiralty Archipelagos. We returned home and started making plans for the next year's work. After receiving photos of the pot sherds found by the teachers from Emirau Island, we decided to plan a visit to Emirau in 2007.

Figure 4.4: (Left) Our arrival at Emirau in 2007. (Right) Glenn undertaking community consultation.
Source: Elizabeth Matisoo-Smith.

The pottery that we saw in the photos was clearly Lapita pottery, and Emirau being so close to Mussau, the location of the early Lapita site of Talepakemalai, excavated by Pat Kirch and colleagues (Kirch 2001), meant that there were very possibly early Lapita sites on the island. So, in September 2007 we flew to Kavieng and started gathering our supplies for the six- to nine-hour, 140-kilometre boat trip to Emirau. We were joined on this trip, as always, by Herman Mandui, but also by Jim Specht from the Australian Museum, who had a long history of archaeological research in the Bismarcks, and Jim Ridges, the Kavieng resident who put us into contact with the teachers from Emirau, Kelly Amanga and Kenneth Vito Thomas.

After a relatively quick trip out to Emirau, we were met on the beach in Hamburg Bay by Kelly and Kenneth and we were taken for a walk through the bush towards the main village. About five minutes into the walk, a bunch of young men wielding spears jumped out and challenged us. Watching Kelly, I quickly realised that this was nothing to be concerned about and this was part of a ceremonial welcome, very much like a haka or challenge that I was used to seeing on marae in Aotearoa New Zealand. We were escorted into the village by this group of young warriors where we were officially welcomed by a very large gathering of the Emirau community. We were shown to our beautiful house and brought food and drink to recover from our trip. In the following days, we gave talks at the main school on the island and rode in the back of the big old truck, the only vehicle on the island, to speak to each of the villages, describing why we were there and talking about Lapita, commensal rats and DNA. Eventually, we were taken out to the gardens where Kelly had found the Lapita pottery and where we were told that he and Kenneth had undertaken an archaeological excavation with the schoolchildren.

It seems that the school and community had been preparing the site for our arrival. I will never forget the look on Glenn's face when we arrived—they had made a lovely gateway and decorated the walkway into the site.

I have since always teased Glenn about how easy it was to find a Lapita site! Kelly identified the various pits that they excavated and described the stratigraphy. The pottery recovered was kept back at the school, with all information about the location and depth of the finds. The next day, Herman and Soso, one of the local men, started excavating the first of two 1 × 1 m test pits next to the location identified by Kelly as having the most dense cultural material. Over the next few days we had most of the schoolchildren and a large number of adults out at the site, watching the 'experts' methodically excavate, sieve and map the two test pits and determine the extent of the site. In the meantime, several of the schoolchildren started trapping rats for me. They would deliver these to our house in the morning and we would then dissect them together and have our anatomy lessons and discussions about recording morphological data and species identifications. Once we were finished, we would head over to the excavations. Several traps were also given to one of the fishermen who was planning to head over to the small island of Tench, about five hours away by boat. Tench was, I was told, a small atoll where the women still used back-strapped looms for weaving and the men still undertook kite fishing—both evidence of cultural links with Micronesia. I was thrilled when the man returned with eight rat tails from Tench, as these might help us track Micronesian contacts.

Figure 4.5: (Left) Glenn arriving at Tamuarawai with Kelly and Lyn Amanga. (Right) School visit to the site.

Source: Elizabeth Matisoo-Smith.

After a week or so of excavating, Glenn advised the community that we had found exactly what they had described. This was indeed an Early Lapita site and they had done a surprisingly good job at excavating. They told us that the name of the location was Tamuarawai, which is now the recorded name of the site (EQS in the National Museum and Art Gallery site recording scheme) (Summerhayes et al. 2010). We took charcoal samples for dating along with several of the artefacts recovered, which included pottery, obsidian, shell hooks and remains of shell armbands. Sadly, we found no faunal remains other than fishbone. We decided that the site was clearly an important one and we promised that we would return the following year to undertake a further excavation and an archaeological survey of the rest of the island.

Return to Emirau (ours and Nevermann's) and the value of gifts

We did return to Emirau in 2008, along with several students of both Glenn and me. We were also joined that year by Jim and Jill Allen. Jim was one of the organisers of the Lapita Homeland Project in the early 1980s, but had never actually excavated a Lapita site, so was keen to be involved. Jill joined the team as our cook, working with the wonderful women in Kelly's family to provide us with beautiful curries and cakes. One of the students who joined us was Melanie Hingston. Melli was a PhD student from Germany who was taking over the rat mtDNA research as part of her PhD with me at the University of Auckland. In addition to trapping rats, she also found that she had a new job on the island. One of the things that Glenn has been committed to in his work in PNG is producing resources for local communities. He brought with him to Emirau on this trip several ethnographies, including a copy of Hans Nevermann's report on the St Matthias Group, which was written in the original German (Nevermann 1933). Nevermann was part of the German South Sea Expedition of 1908–1910 that visited Emirau. When Kelly and others realised that Melli was German, it became the nightly routine that she would sit down and read from Nevermann, providing the English translation of what he recorded.

There was much interest in Nevermann, and many very interesting discussions about the 'taim bifo' resulted from these public readings. One of the oldest men in the community, a lovely man named Naphtali Kapti, who spoke perfect English, was particularly interested—he remembered some of the people whose photographs were in the book, and spoke of them and his memories of the various cultural activities described with tears in his eyes. Many of the younger men were interested in the photographs and drawings of the designs and carvings of the spears, which they started reproducing, and the women were interested in the weaving. They found an older woman from Tench who remembered how to weave using the back-strapped loom and she started teaching other women. This lovely gift that Glenn brought to the island seemed to bring about a sort of cultural renaissance. Glenn later arranged for Nevermann, and several other ethnographies written by the Germans, to be formally translated into English by one of our colleagues, John Dennison (Nevermann et al. 2010), and copies have since been sent to UPNG, the New Ireland provincial archives and the descendant communities, in addition to being made available for purchase online.

Return of results

The archaeological fieldwork undertaken in 2007 and 2008 provided data and artefacts indicating that Tamuarawai was indeed an early Lapita site, with dates as early, if not earlier than Talepakemalai (Summerhayes et al. 2010).

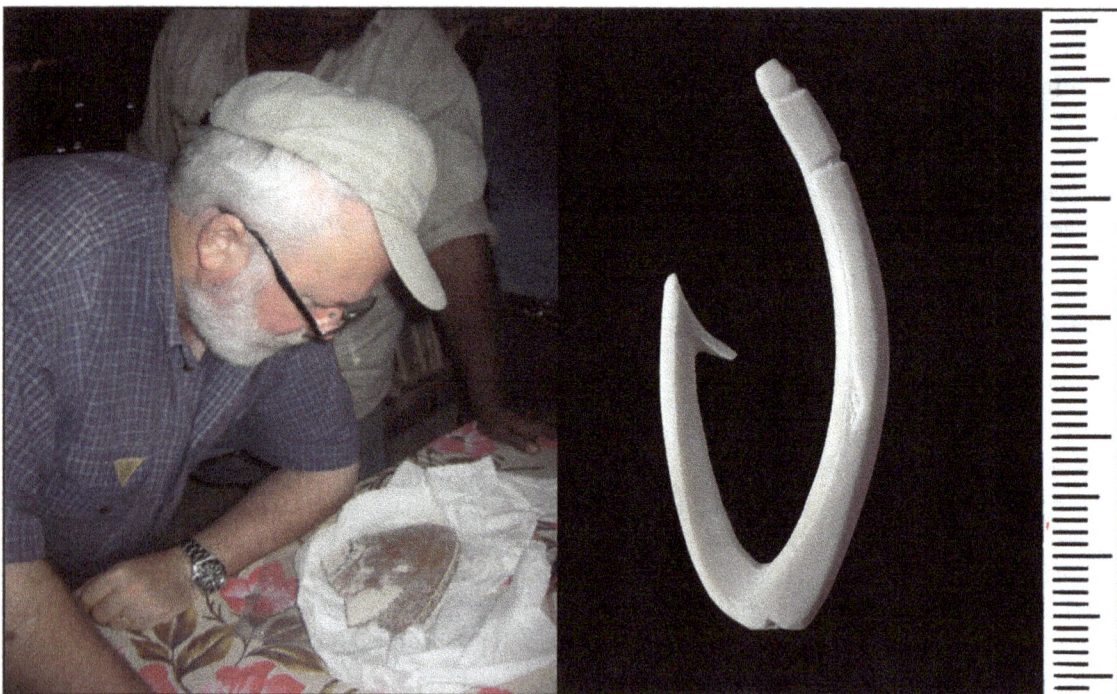

Figure 4.6: (Left) Glenn admiring a Lapita pot fragment. (Right) Fishhook recovered from Tamuarawai (2008).
Source: Elizabeth Matisoo-Smith.

We obtained mtDNA data from the Emirau and Tench rats, which were very interesting. The Emirau rats, like those from Lihir, Tabar and New Ireland, all belonged to the Group 2 haplogroup. But the *R. exulans* from Tench and Manus all belonged to the Group 3 lineages—like those we found in Remote Oceania (Matisoo-Smith et al. 2009). I was able to provide these results to the community during our field season in 2008, and I produced posters for the school and talked to them about what these results meant. As we were waiting on the beach, getting ready to board our boat back to Kavieng, I was approached by some of the women who had a question for me. They understood that I was using the DNA of the rats to track the movement of the people who settled the island. Why, they asked, didn't I just look at their mtDNA? I must admit that I was a bit taken aback. In the 15 years since I had started my research using mtDNA of commensals as a proxy for tracking human settlement, I never thought that the time would be right for undertaking human DNA sampling in the Pacific. The timing of the women's question was uncanny. I had recently been approached by National Geographic to see if I might be willing to join their Genographic project as the Principal Investigator responsible for collecting samples for mtDNA and Y-chromosome sequencing from Pacific Island communities. So, I told the women on Emirau that if that was something that they would be interested in, I might be able to do such a study.

The Genographic Project in PNG—From rat DNA to human DNA

When I returned to Aotearoa New Zealand, I began negotiations with National Geographic to investigate the possibility of working with Pacific communities and, if the communities were willing, to collect samples that could be part of the Genographic project. I returned to Emirau in 2009, with Glenn, Herman and several more archaeology students from the University of Otago. My 18-year-old daughter, Tessa, also joined us as my field assistant. While the archaeologists did some more surveying and excavation on the island, Tessa and I travelled around to the various villages on the island, talking about the Genographic project and collecting cheek swab samples from volunteers.

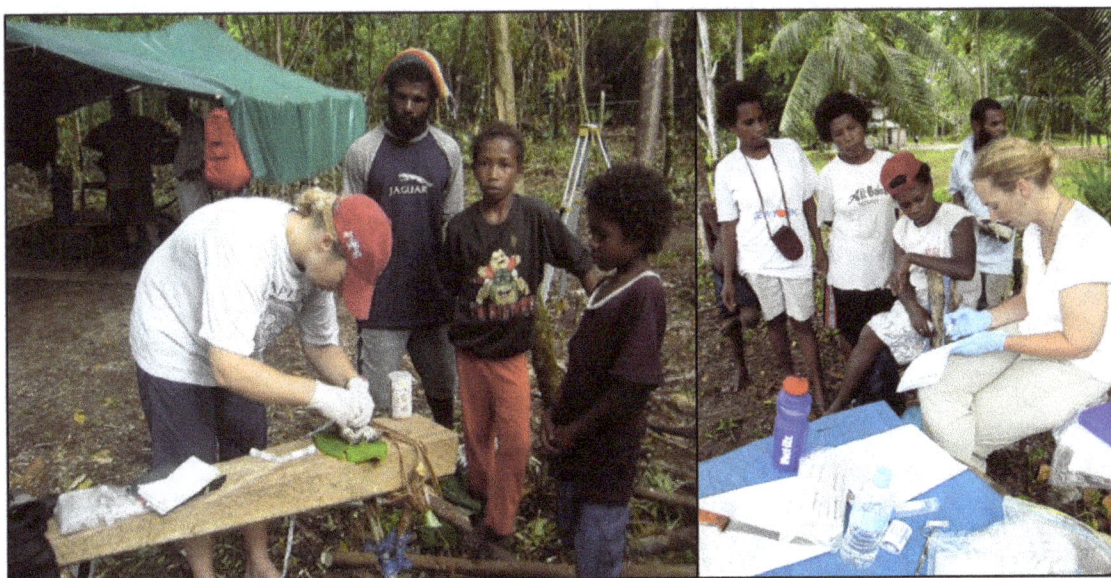

Figure 4.7: (Left) Dissecting rats 2007. (Right) Collecting genealogy and DNA in 2009, Emirau.
Source: Elizabeth Matisoo-Smith.

People already knew about mtDNA from the rat study that they had contributed to. They knew that mtDNA was maternally inherited and I explained that my sampling strategy was to try to sample the full mtDNA and Y-chromosome diversity on the island. In each village I visited, they pulled out a full genealogy that they had constructed over the last few years as part of a church program. They then identified the people that I should sample from each village to account for both mtDNA and Y-chromosome diversity. They also explained to me that their oral traditions were that the island was settled by four sisters and their descendants were represented by the four clans on the island. They asked me that in addition to the standard genealogical information that I collected from each participant that I also record which clan they belonged to. They wanted to know if the mtDNA results would be correlated to these clans. This was my first experience with community engaged and designed research—and approach that has proven to be invaluable.

Sadly, in December of 2008 there had been a king tide in PNG. It affected many coastal locations but it had totally swamped the low-lying atoll of Tench, ruining gardens and flooding the village. All 118 inhabitants of Tench were relocated to an emergency tent village on Emirau, and they were still there when we arrived. I approached the elders and explained the Genographic project to them and they agreed to take part in the study. When some of Kelly's family, who were travelling around the island with us, asked the people from Tench if they had their genealogies written down, they said no. In fact, they realised there was only one elderly gentleman who had any reliable knowledge of the genealogical history of the community. So they immediately sat down with him to start recording what he knew of the family relationships on Tench. We were thankful that this interaction meant that such valuable social information was not lost to the future generations from Tench.

A final return to Emirau and the value of engagement for interpretation of results

During the 2009 field season we collected over 150 DNA samples representing the 500 inhabitants of Emirau and Tench. Glenn, Herman and I returned to Emirau in 2010 to return the DNA results. Each participant got their individual results and we gave a public presentation about what we found generally. Posters were presented to the schools as well as a written report. We then explained that I would be staying at Kelly's place for the next few weeks and would be available to talk with people should they want further information or further explanation about their DNA results. Slowly, people began wandering over to Kelly's to hang out and talk.

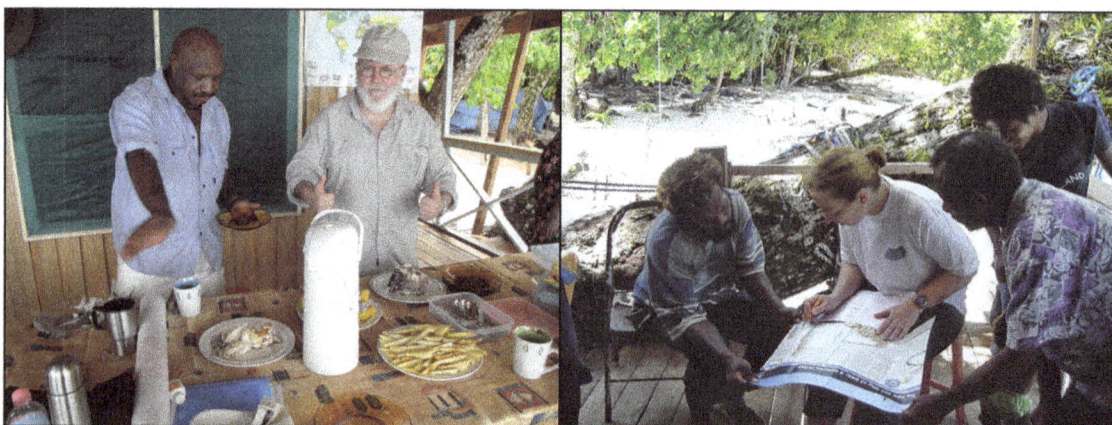

Figure 4.8: (Left) 2010 Lunch on Emirau. (Right) Return of results, Emirau.
Source: Elizabeth Matisoo-Smith.

They didn't always come forward immediately with a question, but in conversation they wanted to hear the explanation again, or they asked for clarification about what their results meant or, often more importantly, what they didn't mean. There was a small cohort of younger people, including Kelly's daughter, Jilda, who were really interested in DNA and human migrations and links to Pacific settlement. They became particularly good at explaining or clarifying results for people and we had several discussions about evolution, ethics and how local knowledge might improve interpretations of DNA results. These people became a valuable resource to me, as a researcher, and to the community as they could answer people's questions once we left.

We found that there were a handful of people who had an unusual mtDNA haplotype compared to the rest of the island and through conversations, we were able to determine that they all shared a distant common female ancestor who was from another island. This was information that was not registered in the genealogical data we collected because it was more than two generations in the past. This information is extremely valuable for interpreting genetic variation in the region, and it is information that we would never have had if we had not returned results in person and stayed around to discuss those results.

Epilogue

My last visit to PNG was in 2013, when Herman, Glenn and I visited Kavieng to consult over the development of a new project focusing on genome evolution and metabolic disease in the Pacific, a project now underway with colleagues from UPNG. Sadly, Herman passed away not long after that visit. In 2014, Glenn's dedication to the people and past of PNG was formally recognised when he was designated an Officer of the Order of the Logohu by the Governor General of Papua New Guinea. In addition to his research Glenn has left a legacy, having trained and mentored so many of the next generation of archaeologists from Australia, New Zealand, Japan, Taiwan and, of course, New Guinea. Through his research he has taught us all. The lessons that I have learned from Glenn about working with communities, establishing and maintaining long-term relationships in the field, and being inclusive of students and colleagues, have shaped the way I undertake research today. I thank him for this and am grateful that he is my friend, my colleague and *em i tisa blong mi*.

Acknowledgements

I thank the editors for inviting me to contribute to this volume. I dedicate this paper to four of our friends and colleagues who all contributed so much to our research in PNG, but are no longer with us—Father Paul Mohe, Mr Herman Mandui, Mr John Dennison and Prof Bernard Minol. We are privileged to have known and worked with you.

References

Acabado, S. 2020. Current archaeological practice in Southeast Asia: Collaboration, engagement, and community involvement in field research in Southeast Asia. *Journal of Community Archaeology & Heritage* 7(3):158–160. doi.org/10.1080/20518196.2020.1767370.

Adams, M.S., J. Carpenter, J.A. Housty, D. Neasloss, P.C. Paquet, C. Service, J. Walkus and C.T. Darimont 2014. Toward increased engagement between academic and indigenous community partners in ecological research. *Ecology and Society* 19(3):5. doi.org/10.5751/ES-06569-190305.

Cann, R.L., M. Stoneking and A.C. Wilson 1987. Mitochondrial DNA and human evolution. *Nature* 325: 31–36. doi.org/10.1038/325031a0.

Claw, K.G., M.Z. Anderson, R.L. Begay, K.S. Tsosie, K. Fox and N.A. Garrison 2018. A framework for enhancing ethical genomic research with Indigenous communities. *Nature Communications* 9(1):2957. doi.org/10.1038/s41467-018-05188-3.

Cunningham, H. 1998. Colonial encounters in postcolonial contexts—Patenting indigenous DNA and the Human Genome Diversity Project. *Critique of Anthropology* 18(2):205–233. doi.org/10.1177/0308275X 9801800205.

Fredericksen, C. 1994. Patterns in glass: Obsidian and economic specialisation in the Admiralty Islands. Unpublished PhD thesis, The Australian National University, Canberra.

Fredericksen, C. 1997. Changes in Admiralty Islands obsidian source use: The view from Pamwak. *Archaeology in Oceania* 32(1):68–73. doi.org/10.1002/j.1834-4453.1997.tb00372.x.

Handsley-Davis, M., E. Kowal, L. Russell and L.S. Weyrich 2021. Researchers using environmental DNA must engage ethically with Indigenous communities. *Nature Ecology & Evolution* 5(2):146–148. doi.org/ 10.1038/s41559-020-01351-6.

Kirch, P.V. 2001. *Lapita and its transformations in Near Oceania: Archaeological investigations in the Mussau Islands, Papua New Guinea, 1985–1988.* Berkeley Archaeological Research Facility Contribution 59. University of California Berkeley, Berkeley, CA.

Lone Dog, L. 1999. Whose genes are they? The Human Genome Diversity Project. *Journal of Health & Social Policy* 10(4):51–66. doi.org/10.1300/J045v10n04_04.

Matisoo-Smith, E. and J.H. Robins 2004. Origins and dispersals of Pacific peoples: Evidence from mtDNA phylogenies of the Pacific rat. *Proceedings of the National Academy of Sciences of the United States of America* 101(24):9167–9172. doi.org/10.1073/pnas.0403120101.

Matisoo-Smith, E., R.M. Roberts, G.J. Irwin, J.S. Allen, D. Penny and D.M. Lambert 1998. Patterns of prehistoric human mobility in Polynesia indicated by mtDNA from the Pacific rat. *Proceedings of the National Academy of Sciences of the United States of America* 95(25):15145–15150. doi.org/10.1073/ pnas.95.25.15145.

Matisoo-Smith, E., M. Hingston, G. Summerhayes, J. Robins, H.A. Ross and M. Hendy 2009. On the Rat Trail in Near Oceania: Applying the commensal model to the question of the Lapita colonization. *Pacific Science* 63(4):465–475. doi.org/10.2984/049.063.0402.

Nevermann, H. 1933. *St. Matthias-Gruppe.* Edited by G. Thilenius. Vol. 2. Ergebnisse der sudsee expedition, 1908- 1910. De Gruyter and Co., Hamburg.

Nevermann, H., J. Dennison, G. Summerhayes and L. Matisoo-Smith 2010. *St. Matthias group.* University of Otago Studies in Prehistoric Anthropology 22. Department of Anthropology, University of Otago, Dunedin.

Stilgoe, J., S.J. Lock and J. Wilsdon. 2014. Why should we promote public engagement with science? *Public Understanding of Science* 23(1):4–15. doi.org/10.1177/0963662513518154.

Summerhayes, G., E. Matisoo-Smith, H. Mandui, J. Allen, J. Specht, N. Hogg and S. McPherson 2010. Tamuarawai (EQS): An early Lapita site on Emirau, New Ireland, PNG. *Journal of Pacific Archaeology* 1:62–75.

Summerhayes, G.R., J. Kennedy, E. Matisoo-Smith, H. Mandui, W. Ambrose, C. Allen, C. Reepmeyer, R. Torrence and F. Wadra 2014. Lepong: A new obsidian source in the Admiralty Islands, Papua New Guinea. *Geoarchaeology* 29(3):238–248. doi.org/10.1002/gea.21475.

Tindana, P., M. Campbell, P. Marshall, K. Littler, R. Vincent, J. Seeley, J. de Vries and D. Kamuya 2017. Developing the science and methods of community engagement for genomic research and biobanking in Africa. *Global Health, Epidemiology and Genomics* 2:e13. doi.org/10.1017/gheg.2017.9.

Part 2: Lapita

5

The Lapita pottery of Tamuarawai (EQS), Emirau Island, Papua New Guinea: Studying the form and decoration of one of the earliest pottery assemblages in the western Pacific

Nicholas W.S. Hogg and Glenn R. Summerhayes

Abstract

Over a three-year period beginning in 2007, a new Lapita site called Tamuarawai was revealed. Tamuarawai, located on the island of Emirau in the northern Bismarck Archipelago of Papua New Guinea, belongs to a selected group of exceedingly rare Early Lapita sites that chronicle the arrival of Austronesian-speaking populations in the western Pacific. The primary archaeological signature of such populations is intricately decorated, complex pottery that is unique among all the sites of the Lapita range and represents an important source of information pertaining to the lives of the Early Lapita populations. The aim of this research is to document the full range of vessel forms and decoration of the pottery assemblages of this unique site, and to employ these data to further understand the lives of those that occupied it. Drawing upon both current understandings concerning the social functions of plain and decorated Lapita pottery and the distribution of vessel forms and their decoration, it looks to clarify the range of activities occurring across the site, and in so doing, to ascertain whether (1) it represented a specialised fishing camp or a hamlet when first settled in the Early Lapita Period, and (2) whether subsequent phases of occupation occurred after the Early Period, and if so, how this Lapita settlement changed over time. The study concludes that the ceramic and broader archaeological record indicates the site most likely represented a small hamlet occupied during the Early Lapita Period, with no subsequent phases of Lapita occupation. It further argues that separate activity areas, delineating between highly socially significant and more utilitarian activities, can be seen within the archaeological record.

Introduction

Early Lapita sites, concentrated in the Bismarck Archipelago of Papua New Guinea, represent the first steps by Austronesian-speaking populations into the Western Pacific (Pawley 2007; Summerhayes 2010a), a journey which would eventually see these peoples occupy some 293 known locations from Near Oceania through to Tonga and Samoa in Remote Oceania (Bedford et al. 2019:8). Lapita is an archaeologically reconstructed culture associated with the introduction of pottery into the Pacific region by groups of people from Island Southeast Asia, who interacted with indigenous populations and were the first inhabitants of the Remote Oceanic islands. Dating to ca 3300–3100 cal. BP (Specht and Gosden 2019:186; Summerhayes 2010b:Table 3; for an alternative view see Kirch 2021a:162–163, 2021b:512), the settlements of these colonising populations thus hold critical information concerning both the nature of the first Lapita populations, their material culture, lifeways and even ancestry, and the adaptations they underwent upon arrival into a new and foreign landscape. However, only 13 such sites have been discovered in the Bismarck Archipelago as of 2019 (Bedford et al. 2019:Table 1.1). Lapita pottery from the most recently discovered of these rare sites, Tamuarawai (Papua New Guinea National Museum and Art Gallery site code EQS), located on the island of Emirau in the northern Bismarck Archipelago of Papua New Guinea, is the focus of this research.

The aim of this study is to present the results of a formal and decorative analysis conducted upon pottery assemblages from EQS (Hogg 2022), and to employ this data to further understand the lives of those that lived at the site in the past. To achieve this, models concerning the social functions of Lapita pottery, typically divided into plainwares with an arguable utilitarian role and decorated wares that are seen as fulfilling a 'socially significant' role (Kirch 2017:95, 97; Summerhayes 2000b:303), alongside an understanding of the distribution of vessel forms and decoration across the site, are employed to investigate the possible range of activities being undertaken, and their spatial and chronological distribution. Ultimately, it looks to elucidate if Tamuarawai represented a specialised 'fishing camp' or a larger Lapita settlement when first occupied (Summerhayes et al. 2010:72), and to determine whether subsequent phases of occupation are evident in the archaeological record—and if so, how the settlement changed over time.

Tamuarawai, Emirau Island, St Matthias Group

The site of Tamuarawai (EQS) is located on the island of Emirau, lying in between the remaining islands of the St Matthias Group (see Figure 5.1), including the Mussau Islands, 25 km to the west, and the isolated island of Tench, which lies approximately 73 km to the east (Summerhayes et al. 2010:62). Located approximately 140 km to the north-west of the town of Kavieng, on the northern tip of New Ireland, the St Matthias Group represents the northernmost point of the Bismarck Archipelago (Kirch and Catterall 2001:28).

The site was excavated over three field seasons between 2007 and 2009 and covers some 22,500 m in extent (Bedford et al. 2019:Table 1.1). A total of four test pits (TP), including three 1 × 1 m test pits (TPs 1, 2 and 4) and one 2 × 2 m test pit (TP 3 A-D) were excavated, alongside a further 13 shovel pits (SP).

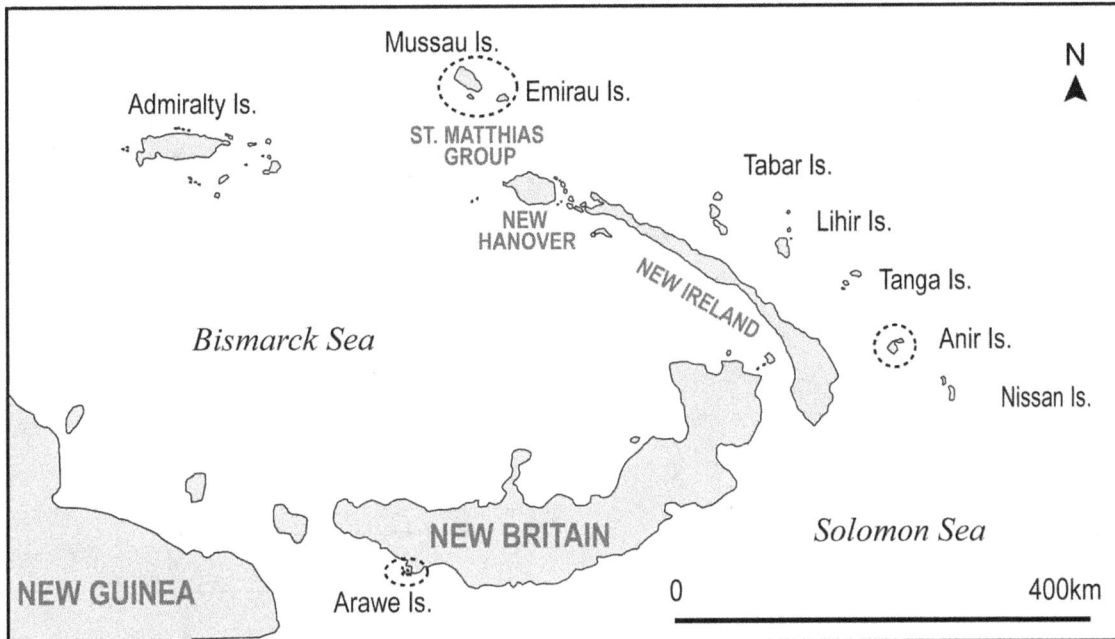

Figure 5.1: The Bismarck Archipelago with locations discussed in text circled.

Source: Illustration by authors.

SP 15, material from which is studied in this research, was 1 × 1 m in extent (Hogg 2022:100; Summerhayes et al. 2010:64). Stratigraphically, the same four layers were identified across the site: Layer 1 consists of a brown/black gardening soil which increases in thickness from 10 cm in the north to over 30 cm in the south; Layer 2 is a yellow/brown sand with variable thickness of between 8 and 30 cm; Layer 3 consists of an unconsolidated yellow/grey to white beach sand ranging in thickness between 15 and 40 cm; finally, Layer 4 is a coarse, gritty sand sitting on top of the underlying coral bedrock with a variable thickness of between 40 and 50 cm (Hogg 2022:Table 4.1; Summerhayes et al. 2010:64) (see Summerhayes et al. (2010) and Hogg (2022:98–102) for further details of the site's excavation and stratigraphy).

Initial occupation is represented by material in the basal layer of TP 1 and 3 A-D in the south-eastern corner of the site (Summerhayes et al. 2010:65, 67), and is dated by two determinations, Wk-21349 (charcoal), previously published by Summerhayes et al. (2010:Table 1) dating to 3350–3168 cal. BP, and a previously unpublished determination, Wk-49133 (marine shell) with a date of 3403–3111 cal. BP (see Table 5.1), indicating that the site was first occupied during the Early Lapita Period (3300–3100 cal. BP, hereafter referred to as Early Period) (Summerhayes 2010b:Table 3).

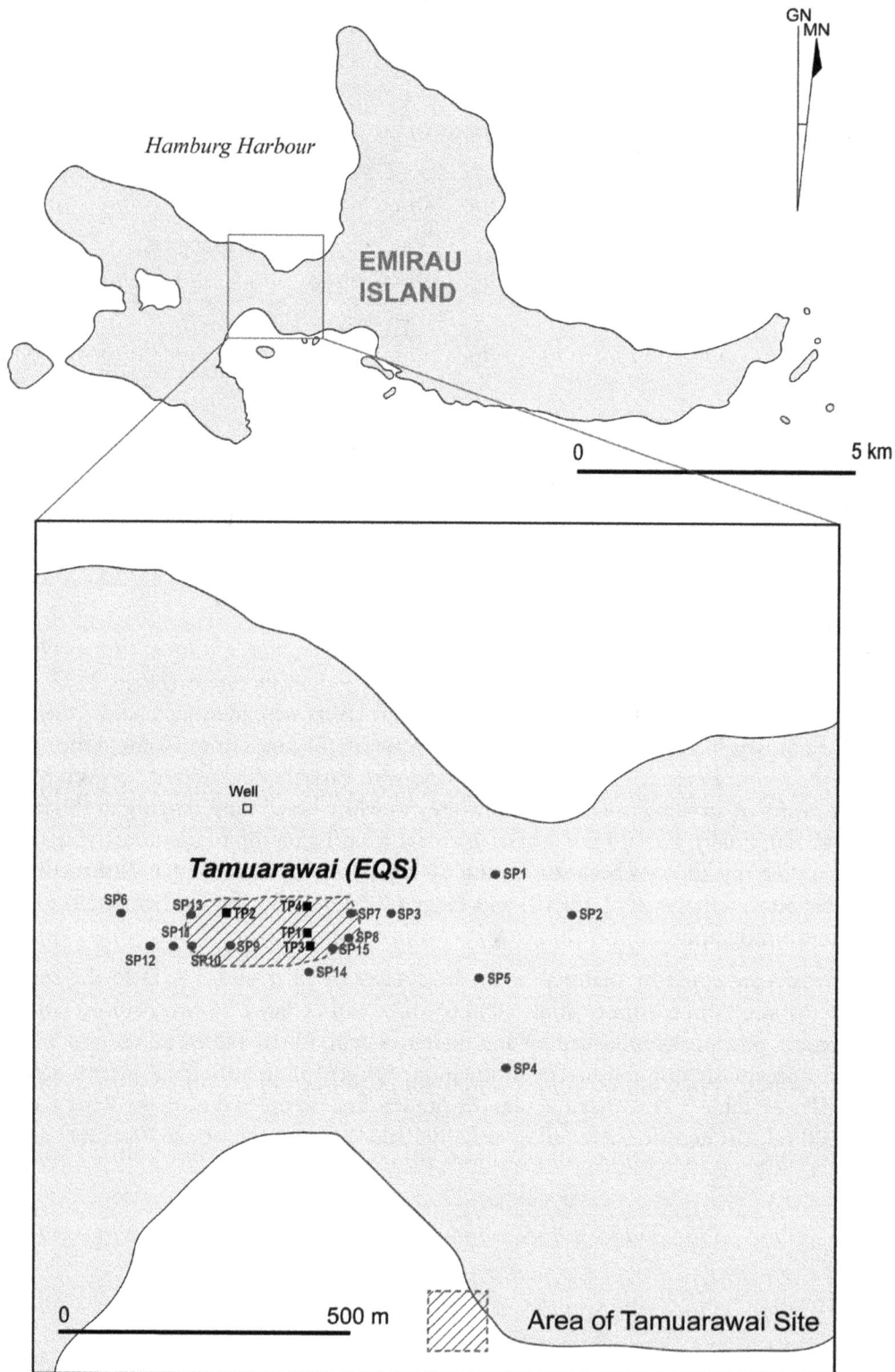

Figure 5.2: (Top) Map of Emirau Island. (Bottom) Map of Tamuarawai (EQS) showing the site boundaries (outlined in grey) and the test pits (TP) and shovel pits (SP) excavated at the site.

Source: Top map adapted from Summerhayes et al. (2010:Fig. 2). Bottom map adapted from Summerhayes et al. (2010:Fig. 6), readapted by Hogg (2011:Fig. 2.4).

Table 5.1: Radiocarbon determinations available for the site of Tamuarawai (EQS).

Lab reference	Sample type	Provenance	Uncalibrated range (BP)	Calibrated range cal. BP (1σ)	Calibrated range cal. BP (2σ)
Wk-21345	Charcoal	TP 2, Layer 4	2917 ± 31	3140–2999	3160–2965
Wk-21349	Charcoal	TP 1, Layer 4	3044 ± 31	3332–3185	3350–3168
Wk-49133	*Trachycardium* sp. Marine shell	TP 3 A, Layer 4 – Spit 17	3332 ± 21	3345–3200	3403–3111

Source: Hogg (2022), Table A1.1.

The site is believed to have represented several stilt structures built out over the water. A series of circular discolourations found in TP 3 B, approximately 10 cm in diameter with a depth of 2–3 cm and arranged in an apparent right-angle, are potentially related to these structures, although further work is required to confirm this for sure (Summerhayes et al. 2010:72). After initial occupation, geomorphological changes occurred, leading to the deposition of material onto a beach or sandbank (as represented by Layer 4 of TP 2 and 4) in the north of the site between 3160 and 2965 cal. BP (Wk-21345, charcoal), indicating deposition occurred either at the end of the Early Period or alternately during the Middle Period (3100–2900 cal. BP) (Summerhayes 2010b:Table 3). Finally, further undated depositional events occurred, as represented by Layers 3–1 across the site (Summerhayes et al. 2010:72).

A broad range of material culture was excavated from EQS besides the pottery assemblages at the heart of this study, including 563 pieces of obsidian (Muir 2017:Appendix 1), a range of shell valuables and other worked shell artefacts and an extremely rare jadeite stone chisel excavated in the vicinity of TP 1 (Summerhayes et al. 2010:65–72), which was transported some 1000 km from Northeast Papua (Indonesia) to the island (Harlow et al. 2012:395–396). From the shell artefacts, with the exception of a net sinker and a fishhook from TP 4 – Layer 4, and a drilled shell bead from Layer 3 of the same TP, all are concentrated in TP 1 and 3 A-D. TP 3 A-D contained the larger of the two assemblages, including four drilled shell beads, three fishhooks and blanks, two cowrie shell octopus lures and a net sinker, all of which came from Layer 4 with the exception of two shell beads from Layers 1–2. Alternatively, TP 1 is slightly smaller but includes both a *Conus* shell armband and a disk made of the same, from Layers 4 and 1, respectively, alongside a further three shell beads, two of which came from Layer 3 and one from Layer 1, and an additional fishhook blank from Layer 2 (Summerhayes et al. 2010:70).

Finally, from the faunal materials excavated (NISP = 1862) from TP 1, 3 A-D and 4, roughly 93 per cent were fishbones, with the remainder primarily composed of turtle bones (Summerhayes et al. 2010:70, Table 10). While the preponderance of fish is not surprising (for comparison, 58 per cent (*n* = 763) of the faunal remains of the Early Period deposits of Kamgot (ERA) in the Anir Group (*n* = 1311) were composed of fish) (Summerhayes et al. 2019:384), what is noteworthy is how few mammalian remains were identified (*n* = 24, 1.3 per cent) (Summerhayes et al. 2010:70, Table 10). ERA, for comparison, identified some 335 mammal bones, comprising 25.6 per cent of the assemblage (Summerhayes et al. 2019:380). Comparison of faunal remains by TP and layer shows very little difference in their distribution, with assemblages from all layers, irrespective of TP, dominated by fishbone, with turtle bone making most of the remainder. Finally, mammalian bones are primarily found in Layer 1 (Summerhayes et al. 2010:Table 10).

When viewed together, the archaeological record from Tamuarawai is something of a conundrum, with several outstanding questions. First, what did the site represent when it was first settled during the Early Period? As originally argued by Summerhayes et al. (2010:67–71, 72), the restricted range of fauna represented—composed primarily of fish and to a lesser extent turtle, with little to no mammalian remains—in addition to the small overall size of the site, suggests it may have represented a specialised 'fishing camp' (Summerhayes et al. 2010:72, Table 10). However, they also note that the broad range of material culture (including pottery, obsidian, worked shell artefacts and the green stone (jadeite) chisel) (see Harlow et al. 2012 for more details) and the possibility that a serious investment in time and labour may have been expended to build stilt structures out over the lagoon, are more akin to a village than a smaller specialised settlement (Summerhayes et al. 2010:67–71, 72, Tables 2–3). In the latter instance, the restricted nature of the faunal record was seen by Summerhayes et al. (2010:72) as a by-product of the process of colonisation, as populations were forced to rely on local food supplies while waiting for the establishment of their agricultural systems. While Summerhayes et al. (2010:72) specifically use the term 'village' when describing the possibility of the site being a larger settlement, we instead employ the term 'hamlet', representing a small settlement with fewer than 10 dwellings or structures (Kirch 2017:98), in order to better suit the small scale of the site in question.

Second, is there evidence in the archaeological record to suggest EQS is a multicomponent site with phases of occupation following the Early Period? The radiocarbon chronology is the basis for two possible scenarios: The first envisages all deposits within the TPs/SPs studied as relating to an Early Period occupation, with those in Layers 3 and 4 in TP 1 and 3 A-D and the nearby deposits in SP 15 associated with the initial occupation of the site, while those in Layers 3–4 of TP 1 and 2 relate to an expansion of the site's boundaries occurring around 3160 cal. BP. In this instance, Layer 2 is seen as relating to the continued use of the site during the Early Period, while Layer 1 consists of a mixture of a modern gardening soil and disturbed materials from the previous layer. The second posits that the cultural remains of EQS relate to multiple periods of occupation occurring at differing times in the past. This view acknowledges that the range of Wk-21345 overlaps with the theoretical range of the Middle Period (3100–2900 cal. BP) (Summerhayes 2010b:Table 3), and thus deposits in Layer 4 of TP 2 and 4 in the north and those within Layers 1–3 in this and other parts of the site, may derive from a later Middle Period occupation, while also considering that Layers 1–3 and SP 15 are undated and thus may derive from later depositional events.

These outstanding questions concerning the nature of the Lapita occupation at EQS are the central focus of this research. These questions are approached via an analysis of pottery assemblages excavated from TP 1–4 and SP 15, amounting to 3807 sherds, discussed in detail further below. The next section introduces the material culture at the heart of this study, Lapita pottery, and reviews previous research into the possible social functions it may have performed in the past.

Lapita pottery and its social functions

Early and Middle Period pottery from the Bismarck Archipelago has been the focus of a considerable amount of research (for example, see: Anson 1983, 1986; Hogg et al. 2021; Hunt 1989; Kirch 2001, 2021c; Sand 2015; Scahill 2020; and Summerhayes 2000b, 2001; among others), which has helped to delineate clear differences between the two sets of assemblages. The pottery of the Early Period, for example, is typified by the presence of high proportions of dentate-stamped vessels, predominantly open bowls/cups and pot stands (or bowls with such stands attached). Conversely, Middle Period assemblages have higher proportions of incised vessels, typically outcurving carinated jars (Hogg et al. 2021:81–82; Kirch and Chiu 2021:299–303; Specht and Summerhayes 2007:67–70; Summerhayes 2000b:163, 231–232, 2001:29–30). In addition, Early and Middle Period assemblages are associated with a unique inventory of decorative motifs that are only found on vessels of each period (Summerhayes 2000b:160–163), and were each produced with unique production strategies (see Summerhayes (2000b:167–229) for more detail on the production of vessels).

It is widely recognised within Lapita scholarship that this pottery can be divided into two main groups, plainwares and decorated wares, and that each set of assemblages performed a distinct role within Lapita society. Plainwares are widely accepted as performing utilitarian functions such as cooking or the storage of water (Summerhayes 2000a:303) or foodstuffs (Kirch 2017:97). Kirch and Chiu (2021:287), for example, recently argued that the general form of globular jars (equivalent to the Form VI—globular pots in Figure 5.3) identified within the Mussau Island assemblages, along with their restricted necks and lack of decoration beyond lip notching, in combination with the lack of evidence for their use in cooking, suggested these vessels were used to store either liquids or dry materials, such as sago flour.

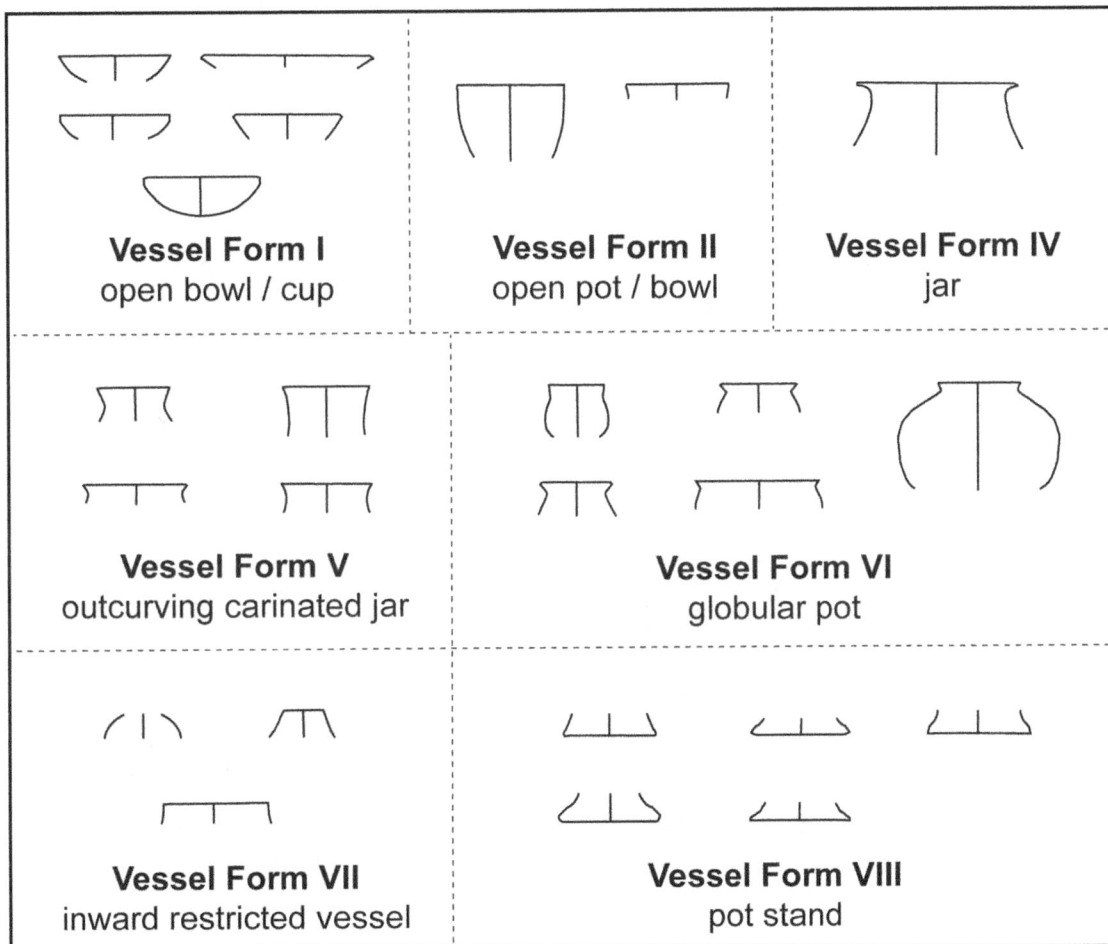

Figure 5.3: Vessel forms.
Source: Adapted from Summerhayes (2000b:Fig. 4.1–4.3).

Figure 5.4: Pottery from the site of Tamuarawai (EQS).

Note: (A) Form I (#EQS 110 & 126, TP 3 A-D); (B) Form VI (#EQS 1, TP 1).

Source: Illustration by authors.

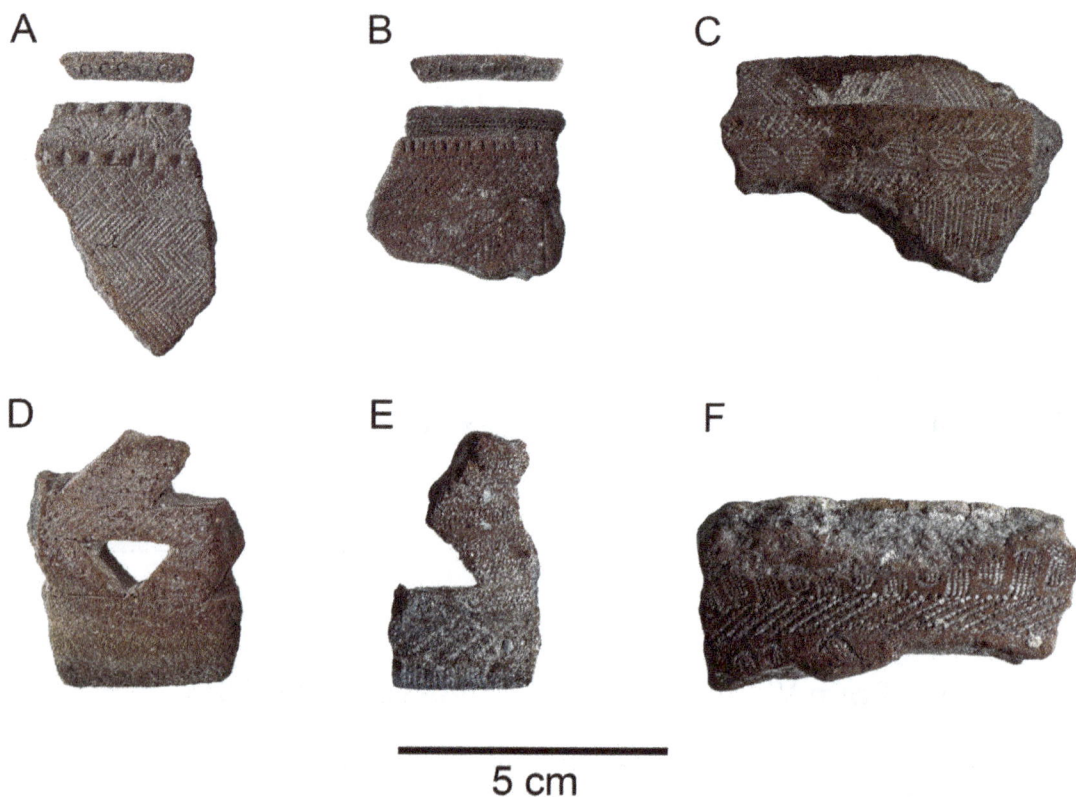

Figure 5.5: Additional pottery from the site of Tamuarawai (EQS).

Notes: (A) Form I (#EQS 127, TP 3 A-D); (B) Form I (#EQS 88, TP 3 A-D); (C) Form II (#EQS 89, TP 3 A-D); (D) Form VIII (#EQS 109, TP 3 A-D); (E) Form VIII (#EQS 129, TP 3 A-D); (F) Base with stand attachment (#EQS 296, TP 3 A-D).

Source: Illustration by authors.

Kirch (2017:97) further argues that such flour (produced from the pith of sago (*Metroxylon*) palm trees), which can last a long time when stored in a dry environment, may have provided an important staple food source for colonising populations prior to the establishment of their horticultural systems. However, the presence of external fire blackening, evidence of a vessel's use in cooking foodstuffs (Kirch and Chiu 2021:287), on a globular pot excavated from the Tamuarawai site (#EQS 1, Figure 5.4B), indicates the likelihood that some vessels of this form also performed this function in the past.

In opposition to plainwares, decorated wares (particularly dentate-stamped wares) are generally ascribed a function of high social significance; a number of models have been put forward to further understand the social function(s) performed by these vessels. Kirch (1997:145–146, 2017:96–97) for example, argued that dentate-stamped wares depicting anthropomorphic designs may have been employed as prestige items in marriage exchanges or other important social occasions. Later research by Chiu (2005:5, 2007:257–260, 2015:198–200, 2019:329–331) similarly argued for certain decorative motifs to have acted as highly prestigious 'crests' or symbols of houses or social groups within Lapita society, which acted as a means of differentiating between houses or groups of varying status, or to affect group cohesion depending upon the social situation. For their part, Summerhayes and Allen (2007:116–117) suggested, following the behavioural ecological approach of costly signalling, that decorated vessels acted as a means of establishing and maintaining social links between Lapita groups. They additionally argued, with specific reference to the Early Period when Lapita and non-Lapita populations first met, that such vessels were used as a means of signalling the strength of a Lapita population(s) to others (in the manner of a costly display), while simultaneously conferring values (whether prestigious or utilitarian in nature) onto said groups when engaged in exchange. Lastly, it is widely believed that the forms of decorated vessels directly related to the social occasions within which they were employed. This is particularly the case with dentate-stamped vessels that were elevated upon stands, which have been highlighted by a number of authors as being related to the preparation and presentation of food at important social events (Kirch 1997:122; Leclerc 2018:713; Marshall 2008:70; Summerhayes 2000a:303), or more specifically in the context of ceremonial feasts (Clark 2007:297; Jones 2015; Kirch 2021c:83) (for further discussion concerning the social function(s) of Lapita decorated wares see Best 2002:99–100; Noury 2019; Spriggs 1990, 1997:156–157, 2019; Terrell and Schechter 2009:53–54; and Terrell and Welsch 1997:568).

Significantly, excavations at the site of Talepakemalai (ECA), located in the Mussau Islands, and the discovery of a 'special-function' stilt structure within the Area B (Zone C) deposits, provide an arguable glimpse at how these decorated vessels may have been used in the Early Period (Kirch 2021c:79–83). The artefactual record of Area B is unique in the site due to the presence of a wide array of finely made shell objects, including *Spondylus*-shell beads and pendants, *Nautilus* shell discs, shell rings made of *Conus* and *Tridacna* shell, large 'rectangular units' made of *Conus* shell and more, alongside a small anthropomorphic bone sculpture, and significantly, highly decorated pedestalled bowls and dishes (equivalent to Forms I and VIII in this research, see Figure 5.3) (Kirch 2021c:79). Crucially, in addition to these artefacts the deposit also contains evidence of food waste (including shell and bone midden) and artefacts associated with food preparation (such as scrapers and peeling knives), which taken together are seen as possible evidence of feasting (Kirch 2021c:83).

Pottery analysis methodology

This section details the methodologies employed to analyse the form and decoration of the Tamuarawai pottery assemblages. Data generated from these analyses represents the primary foundation of this study and forms the basis for the interpretations offered in the discussion to follow.

The methodology employed to analyse the form of the EQS vessels was based around the principle that in the absence of complete vessels, the rim is the most diagnostic element of a vessel (Bedford 2006:76–77; Joukowsky 1980:351; Poulsen 1987:87; Summerhayes 2000b:33). The attributes of rim direction, rim profile, lip profile, extra rim features, thickness, orifice diameter (Summerhayes 2000b:35–36) and orientation and inclination angle (Irwin 1985:107) were analysed to assign sherds to vessel form. In addition, wherever possible rim sherds were combined with other types of sherds, including neck, body, base and pot stands, either by the physical conjoining of sherds or by comparison of pottery attributes where appropriate (see the attributes used to calculate MNV below), to ensure the correct identification of form. The vessel forms used were modelled after those defined by Summerhayes (2000b:33) and include: Form I—open bowl/cup; Form II—open pot/bowl; Form IV—jar; Form V—outcurving carinated jar; Form VI—globular pot; Form VII—inward restricted vessel; and Form VIII—pot stand (see Figure 5.3). No Form III vessels (possible open bowl with a horizontal rim) were identified in the assemblage.

Calculation of the minimum number of vessels (MNV) was primarily made with reference to rim sherds, but in a small number of cases was based upon other types of sherds (necks or carinations with parts of the body attached or bases), which could not have been associated with any rim sherds. Attributes used to calculate MNV include those listed above alongside those collected as part of the decorative analysis (including type of decoration (Tables 5.5, 5.6 and 5.7) and location of decoration) and fabric type (designed to broadly classify sherds based upon their predominant non-plastic inclusions; details of the fabrics identified in the assemblage can be found in Hogg (2022:Volume II—Appendix 5)). A more detailed discussion of the methodology employed to analyse the EQS assemblages can be found in Hogg (2022:127–165).

Results

Results from the formal and decorative analyses of the Tamuarawai assemblages are presented in the following section (representing the most up-to-date formal and decorative datasets available for EQS, thus superseding those in the earlier study of Hogg (2011:60–63, 89–96)). Discussion is first made of the vessel forms identified, followed by the types of decoration found and the association between said decoration and the vessels they adorned.

Distribution of vessel forms in the Tamuarawai Lapita site

TP 1–4 and SP 15 produced 3807 sherds, with the total dropping to 3754 sherds following conjoining; from these, 205 sherds were found to be diagnostic to vessel form (Table 5.2). It should be noted that the numbers of excavated sherds recorded in Summerhayes et al. (2010:Table 2) for TP 1 and 4 are equivalent to the 'Sherds excavated (conjoined)' in Table 5.2; however, the total numbers of sherds recorded differ slightly as a small number of sherds were added following the publication of the earlier paper.

Table 5.2: Number of excavated sherds, number of excavated sherds following conjoining, sherds diagnostic of vessel form, decorated and plain sherds, and minimum number of vessels (MNV) for the site of Tamuarawai (EQS).

Test pit/ Shovel pit	Sherds excavated	Sherds excavated (conjoined)	Diagnostic sherds	Decorated sherds	Plain sherds	MNV
TP 1	1167	1159	46	61	1098	16
TP 2	184	184	8	11	173	4
TP 3 A-D	1817	1776	120	119	1657	66
TP 4	411	411	15	23	388	7
SP 15	228	224	16	18	206	10
Total	3807	3754	205	232	3522	103

Source: Hogg (2022), Tables 6.1–6.6 and Table 6.10.

An MNV of 103 vessels was calculated for seven vessel forms present in the five assemblages studied from the site (Tables 5.3 and 5.4, Figures 5.4 and 5.5). From these, TP 3 A-D has by far the largest amount, with a total of 66 vessels identified to form, the majority of which are found in Layers 3 (14 per cent, $n = 9$) and 4 (80 per cent, $n = 53$). Form VI—globular pots are the most common (42 per cent, $n = 28$), followed by Form I—open bowls/cups (27 per cent, $n = 18$). The remaining vessels are primarily Form V—outcurving carinated jars and Form VIII—pot stands, alongside two Form II—open pots/bowls. Studying the distribution of vessels stratigraphically, Layer 4 is dominated by Forms VI (49 per cent, $n = 26$) and I (23 per cent, $n = 12$), with the remainder primarily made up of Forms V and VIII (13 per cent, $n = 7$ each). In Layer 3, the same range of forms are present, but the number of Form VI (22 per cent, $n = 2$) vessels has proportionally declined while those from Form I (44 per cent, $n = 4$) have increased. In Layers 1–2 only three vessels are present, including single examples of Forms I, II and V.

TP 1 has the second largest assemblage, with 16 vessels identified to form, with most coming from Layers 3 (25 per cent, $n = 4$) and 4 (38 per cent, $n = 6$). The most common by a considerable margin are Form VI—globular pots (50 per cent, $n = 8$), followed by vessels belonging to Forms I and VIII (13 per cent, $n = 2$ each). Vessels of these forms are predominantly found in Layers 3 and 4; the only exception is a Form VI—globular pot in Layer 1. Finally, three vessels are present in Layer 2, including a Form IV jar and two Form VII inward-restricted vessels (13 per cent, $n = 2$).

TP 4 and SP 15 are like those discussed above, in that they are both dominated by Form VI—globular pots (71 per cent for the former and 60 per cent for the latter), with the remainder being comprised of small numbers of Form I, V and VIII vessels. In TP 4, all vessels identified, excepting a single Form VI vessel, come from Layer 4.

Finally, TP 2, the smallest assemblage studied, is entirely comprised of vessels from two forms, Forms V and VII, with only one belonging to the latter. Form V vessels are found in all layers excepting Layer 4, while the single Form VII vessel comes from Layer 1.

Table 5.3: Vessel forms identified at the site of Tamuarawai (EQS) Test Pits 1–2; Layers 1–4 and NP (no provenance).

Vessel form	TP1												TP2									
	1	%	2	%	3	%	4	%	NP	%	Total	%	1	%	2	%	3	%	4	%	Total	%
I – open bowl/cup	0	0	0	0	0	0	1	17	1	50	2	13	0	0	0	0	0	0	0	0	0	0
II – open pot/bowl	0	0	0	0	0	0	0	0	0	0	0	0	0	0	0	0	0	0	0	0	0	0
IV – jar	0	0	1	33	0	0	0	0	0	0	1	6	0	0	0	0	0	0	0	0	0	0
V – outcurving carinated jar	0	0	0	0	1	25	0	0	0	0	1	6	1	50	1	50	1	100	0	0	3	75
VI – globular pot	1	100	0	0	2	50	4	67	1	50	8	50	0	0	0	0	0	0	0	0	0	0
VII – inward restricted vessel	0	0	2	67	0	0	0	0	0	0	2	13	1	50	0	0	0	0	0	0	1	25
VIII – pot stand	0	0	0	0	1	25	1	17	0	0	2	13	0	0	0	0	0	0	0	0	0	0
Totals	1	6	3	19	4	25	6	38	2	13	16	100	2	50	1	25	1	25	0	0	4	100

Source: Hogg (2022), Table A2.1 and Table A2.2.

Table 5.4: Vessel forms identified at the site of Tamuarawai (EQS) Test Pits 3–4 and Shovel Pit 15; Layers 1–4 and WF (wall fill).

Vessel form	TP 3 A-D										TP 4										SP 15	
	1-2	%	3	%	4	%	WF	%	Total	%	1	%	2	%	3	%	4	%	Total	%	Total	%
I – open bowl/cup	1	33	4	44	12	23	1	100	18	27	0	0	0	0	0	0	1	17	1	14	3	30
II – open pot/bowl	1	33	0	0	1	2	0	0	2	3	0	0	0	0	0	0	0	0	0	0	0	0
IV – jar	0	0	0	0	0	0	0	0	0	0	0	0	0	0	0	0	0	0	0	0	0	0
V – outcurving carinated jar	1	33	1	11	7	13	0	0	9	14	0	0	0	0	0	0	0	0	0	0	1	10
VI – globular pot	0	0	2	22	26	49	0	0	28	42	1	100	0	0	0	0	4	67	5	71	6	60
VII – inward restricted vessel	0	0	0	0	0	0	0	0	0	0	0	0	0	0	0	0	0	0	0	0	0	0
VIII – pot stand	0	0	2	22	7	13	0	0	9	14	0	0	0	0	0	0	1	17	1	14	0	0
Totals	3	5	9	14	53	80	1	2	66	100	1	14	0	0	0	0	6	86	7	100	10	100

Source: Hogg (2022), Tables A2.3–A2.5.

Distribution of decoration in the Tamuarawai Lapita site

From the 3754 sherds (following conjoining) identified in TP 1–4 and SP 15, 232 (6 per cent) were found to have evidence of decoration (see Table 5.2).

The most common decoration by far is dentate stamping, which comprises 36–61 per cent of decoration present, with the only exception being TP 1, where it is slightly less common (26 per cent, $n = 16$). Stratigraphically, it makes up 50–67 per cent of that identified in Layer 4 of all TPs studied and 33–60 per cent in Layer 3, except in TP 1 where it comprises 33 per cent ($n = 5$) in the former layer and only 11 per cent ($n = 1$) in the latter. In Layers 1 and 2, it declines further to comprise 46 per cent ($n = 5$) in the combined Layer 1–2 in TP 3 A-D, while being absent in Layer 2 of TP 2 and in both layers of TP 4. Alternatively, dentate stamping increases in the same layers of TP 1 from 15 per cent ($n = 3$) to 33 per cent ($n = 3$), and also reappears in Layer 1 of TP 2 (33 per cent, $n = 1$) (see Tables 5.5 and 5.6). Following the work of Kirch and Chiu (2021:281), the dentate stamping present at the site can for the most part be described as 'fine', with very small individual tine impressions arranged in a series of well-executed, orderly designs.

Notching is also very common and is found in all TPs/SPs studied, comprising between 17 and 41 per cent of decoration. The only exception is TP 2, where such decoration only makes up 9 per cent ($n = 1$). In Layer 4, this decoration makes up a substantial 24–42 per cent of that identified (aside from TP 2, where it is absent), while in Layer 3 it proportionally declines to comprise only 13–22 per cent of decoration. TP 1 is once again the exception, where it increases from 60 per cent ($n = 9$) in Layer 4 to 78 per cent ($n = 7$) in Layer 3. In Layer 2 notching comprises only 20 per cent ($n = 7$) of decoration in TP 1, while being entirely absent in the same layer of TP 2 and 4, prior to increasing to 22 per cent ($n = 2$) in TP 1–Layer 1 and reappearing in the same layer of TP 2 and 4. Finally, notching makes up 36 per cent ($n = 4$) of decoration in the combined Layers 1–2 in TP 3 A-D.

The decorative types of incision—cut-out, single tool impression, and perforation—are commonly employed in concert with dentate stamping and notching, with one or more comprising a large proportion of all identified decoration in each assemblage studied. In TP 1, for example, incision (13 per cent, $n = 8$) and perforation (12 per cent, $n = 7$) are the next most common types after dentate stamping and notching, while in TP 3 A-D and TP 2, it is cut-out (13 per cent, $n = 16$) and single tool impression (13 per cent, $n = 15$) for the former and incision (27 per cent, $n = 3$) for the latter. The only exception is SP 15, which has only single instances of cut-out and incision. From the four decoration types, incision appears for the first time in Layers 1 and 2 in TP 1 and 3 A-D to comprise 22 per cent ($n = 2$) and 30 per cent ($n = 6$) of decoration, respectively, in the former and 18 per cent ($n = 2$) in the combined Layer 1–2 of the latter, while also appearing in TP 2, Layers 2 (100 per cent, $n = 2$) and 3 (33 per cent, $n = 1$). Cut-out, single tool impression, and perforation are primarily concentrated in Layers 3 and 4.

The remainder of the decoration is spread over several decoration types, all comprising around 5 per cent or less of that identified in any given assemblage. The only exceptions are stick impression and carving, which comprise 27 per cent ($n = 3$) and 17 per cent ($n = 3$) of the small assemblages from TP 2 and SP 15, respectively. From these minor decorative types, the majority are restricted to a small number of assemblages and are primarily found in Layers 3–4; stamp impression, fingernail impression and plain bands are only found in TP 4, SP 15 and TP 3 A-D, respectively, while brushing is restricted to TP 3 A-D and SP 15. The only exceptions are cut, groove–channel and stick impression, which are widely distributed and are found in at least three of the assemblages studied.

Table 5.5: Frequency counts and proportion of decoration within Tamuarawai (EQS) Test Pits 1–2; Layers 1–4 and NP (no provenance) by sherd count (decorated sherds can be counted more than once).

Decoration type	TP 1												TP 2									
	1	%	2	%	3	%	4	%	NP	%	Total	%	1	%	2	%	3	%	4	%	Total	%
Dentate-stamped	3	33	3	15	1	11	5	33	4	50	16	26	1	33	0	0	1	33	2	67	4	36
Notched	2	22	4	20	7	78	9	60	3	38	25	41	1	33	0	0	0	0	0	0	1	9
Cut-out	1	11	0	0	0	0	4	27	0	0	5	8	0	0	0	0	0	0	0	0	0	0
Single tool imp.	0	0	1	5	0	0	1	7	1	13	3	5	0	0	0	0	0	0	0	0	0	0
Incised	2	22	6	30	0	0	0	0	0	0	8	13	0	0	2	100	1	33	0	0	3	27
Perforated	0	0	6	30	1	11	0	0	0	0	7	12	0	0	0	0	0	0	0	0	0	0
Cut	0	0	0	0	0	0	0	0	0	0	0	0	0	0	0	0	0	0	1	33	1	9
Grooved–channelled	0	0	0	0	0	0	0	0	1	13	1	2	0	0	0	0	0	0	0	0	0	0
Brushed	0	0	0	0	0	0	0	0	0	0	0	0	0	0	0	0	0	0	0	0	0	0
Stick imp.	1	11	0	0	0	0	0	0	0	0	1	2	1	33	1	50	1	33	0	0	3	27
Carved	0	0	0	0	0	0	0	0	0	0	0	0	0	0	0	0	0	0	0	0	0	0
Plain band	0	0	0	0	0	0	0	0	0	0	0	0	0	0	0	0	0	0	0	0	0	0
Fingernail imp.	0	0	0	0	0	0	0	0	0	0	0	0	0	0	0	0	0	0	0	0	0	0
Stamped imp.	0	0	0	0	0	0	0	0	0	0	0	0	0	0	0	0	0	0	0	0	0	0
Total decorated sherd count	9	–	20	–	9	–	15	–	8	–	61	–	3	–	2	–	3	–	3	–	11	–
Decoration frequency	9	–	20	–	9	–	19	–	9	–	66	–	3	–	3	–	3	–	3	–	12	–

Source: Hogg (2022), Table A4.2 and Table A4.3.

Table 5.6: Frequency counts and proportion of decoration within Tamuarawai (EQS) Test Pits 3–4 and Shovel Pit 15; Layers 1–4 and WF (wall fill) by sherd count (decorated sherds can be counted more than once).

Decoration type	TP 3 A–D										TP 4										SP 15	
	1–2	%	3	%	4	%	WF	%	Total	%	1	%	2	%	3	%	4	%	Total	%	Total	%
Dentate-stamped	5	46	9	60	56	61	1	100	71	60	0	0	0	0	4	44	6	50	10	44	11	61
Notched	4	36	2	13	22	24	0	0	28	24	1	100	0	0	2	22	5	42	8	35	3	17
Cut-out	0	0	2	13	14	15	0	0	16	13	0	0	1	11	0	0	0	0	1	4	1	6
Single tool imp.	1	9	0	0	13	14	1	100	15	13	0	0	0	0	1	8	1	8	2	9	0	0
Incised	2	18	0	0	0	0	0	0	2	2	0	0	0	0	0	0	0	0	0	0	1	6
Perforated	0	0	3	20	1	1	0	0	4	3	0	0	0	0	3	33	0	0	3	13	0	0
Cut	0	0	1	7	2	2	0	0	3	3	1	100	0	0	0	0	1	8	2	9	1	6

Decoration type	TP 3 A-D										TP 4										SP 15	
	1-2	%	3	%	4	%	WF	%	Total	%	1	%	2	%	3	%	4	%	Total	%	Total	%
Grooved–channelled	0	0	0	0	4	4	0	0	4	3	0	0	0	0	1	11	0	0	1	4	1	6
Brushed	0	0	0	0	6	7	0	0	6	5	0	0	0	0	0	0	0	0	0	0	1	6
Stick imp.	0	0	0	0	2	2	0	0	2	2	0	0	0	0	0	0	0	0	0	0	0	0
Carved	0	0	0	0	2	2	0	0	2	2	0	0	0	0	0	0	0	0	0	0	3	17
Plain band	0	0	1	7	1	1	0	0	2	2	0	0	0	0	0	0	0	0	0	0	0	0
Fingernail imp.	0	0	0	0	0	0	0	0	0	0	0	0	0	0	0	0	0	0	0	0	1	6
Stamped imp.	0	0	0	0	0	0	0	0	0	0	0	0	0	0	0	0	1	8	1	4	0	0
Total decorated sherd count	11	–	15	–	92	–	1	–	119	–	2	–	0	–	9	–	12	–	23	–	18	–
Decoration frequency	12	–	18	–	123	–	2	–	155	–	2	–	0	–	11	–	14	–	27	–	23	–

Source: Hogg (2022), Tables A4.4–A4.6.

Table 5.7: Frequency counts and proportion of decoration within Tamuarawai (EQS) Test Pits 1–4 and Shovel Pit 15 by vessel form (vessels can be counted more than once).

Decoration type	Vessel form															
	I	%	II	%	IV	%	V	%	VI	%	VII	%	VIII	%	Total	%
Dentate-stamped	18	75	2	100	0	0	1	7	0	0	0	0	10	83	31	30
Stick imp.	0	0	0	0	0	0	3	21	2	4	0	0	0	0	5	5
Single tool imp.	11	46	1	50	0	0	0	0	0	0	0	0	0	0	12	12
Fingernail imp.	1	4	0	0	0	0	0	0	0	0	0	0	0	0	1	1
Notched	2	8	0	0	0	0	6	43	17	36	2	67	0	0	27	26
Cut	2	8	0	0	0	0	0	0	1	2	0	0	2	17	5	5
Incised	0	0	0	0	1	100	1	7	0	0	0	0	0	0	2	2
Plain band	2	8	0	0	0	0	0	0	0	0	0	0	0	0	2	2
Cut-out	0	0	0	0	0	0	0	0	0	0	0	0	8	67	8	8
Grooved–channelled	0	0	1	50	0	0	0	0	0	0	0	0	0	0	1	1
Brushed	0	0	0	0	0	0	0	0	3	6	0	0	0	0	3	3
Plain	5	21	1	50	0	0	4	29	24	51	1	33	1	8	36	35
Total vessel count	24	–	2	–	1	–	14	–	47	–	3	–	12	–	103	–
Decoration frequency	41	–	5	–	1	–	15	–	47	–	3	–	21	–	133	–

Source: Authors' data.

Finally, studying vessel form alongside type of decoration (see Table 5.7) indicates that dentate stamping is restricted to Forms I (n = 18), II (n = 2) and VIII (n = 10), apart from a single Form V jar. Decorative types that typically occur alongside dentate stamping are similarly restricted. This includes single tool impression, only found on Form I (n = 11) and Form II vessels (n = 1), and cut-out, only present on Form VIII pot stands (n = 8). Similarly, incision is only found on Form IV and V jars (one vessel each). The last decoration type found on a significant number of vessels, notching, is most closely associated with Form VI (n = 17) vessels. The remainder of the decoration is only found on one vessel each, excepting stick impression, which is found on five vessels from Forms V (n = 3) and VI (n = 2), brushing, found on vessels of the latter form (n = 3), and cut, which is found on vessels from Forms I, VIII (n = 2 each) and VI (n = 1). Lastly, plainware vessels compose 35 per cent (n = 36) of the vessels identified and are dominated by Form VI vessels (67 per cent, n = 24).

Summary

Studying the form and decoration of the EQS assemblages, the following patterns were identified:

1. Excepting TP 2, all assemblages studied are dominated by Form VI vessels, while the remainder are generally comprised of vessels from Forms I and VIII and in some assemblages Form V.

2. Vessels in Layers 3 and 4 represent the majority of those identified in most assemblages, excepting TP 2, where vessels are found throughout Layers 1–3. Generally, vessels in Layers 1–2 represent forms already present in the underlying Layers 3–4, the exceptions being TP 1 and 2, which both have new forms in the former layers.

3. Decoration is dominated by fine dentate stamping in all assemblages studied, followed by notching. The only exception is TP 1, where this scenario is reversed. After notching, the most applied decoration types that typically occur alongside dentate stamping, are incision, cut-out, single tool impression, and perforation.

4. Dentate stamping is the dominant decoration in Layer 4 in most assemblages, followed by notching, excepting TP 1 where this scenario is reversed. In Layer 3, these decoration types decline, again apart from TP 1 where notching increases. Notching continues to decline in most assemblages through Layers 1–2, while dentate stamping declines in TP 3 A-D and 4, while alternately increasing in TP 1 and Layer 1 of TP 2. Incision appears in Layers 1–2 of TP 1 and 3 A-D and increases through Layers 3–2 in TP 2.

5. Dentate stamping is most commonly associated with Form I and VIII vessels, while the plainware assemblages are dominated by Form VI vessels.

The implications of the patterns seen in the form and decoration of the EQS pottery assemblages will be discussed in further detail in the following section. For further discussion of the vessel forms identified at EQS and their general characteristics, and for greater detail concerning the decoration types identified, see Hogg (2022:166–177).

Discussion

Multi or single-phase occupation?

Now that a clear picture has been outlined of the form and decoration of the EQS assemblages, the central questions of this research can be posed. First, what does the site of EQS represent, a single Early Period occupation or a multicomponent site with multiple phases of occupation over time?

Radiocarbon determinations securely date Layer 4 of TP 3 A-D and TP 1 to the Early Period. The high proportion of dentate-stamped decoration in combination with dentate-stamped Form I—open bowl/cups and Form VIII—pot stands comprising a large, or indeed all, of the decorated vessels within TP 1 and 3 A-D, further supports the dating of these deposits. Furthermore, the nearly identical pottery assemblages in Layers 3 and 4 of TP 3 A-D indicates that Layer 3 represents a continuation of this occupation. This suggests that SP 15, which has as high a proportion of dentate stamping as TP 3 A-D, as well as a number of Form I vessels, and Layer 3 of TP 1, which has a lower proportion of dentate stamping but with a Form VIII—pot stand, also date to this period.

In the north of the site, an additional radiocarbon determination dates Layer 4 of TP 2 and 4 to the tail end of the Early Period or to the Middle Period. Proportions of dentate stamping in TP 4, Layers 3–4, are similar to those of TP 3 A-D, which, alongside examples of dentate-stamped Form I and VIII vessels in the latter layer, suggest that these deposits also date to the Early Period. Finally, the basal layers of TP 2 are similar to the previously discussed assemblages in that they also have a high rate of dentate stamping, but differ in that they feature incised pottery, with only one vessel form represented, Form V. While the latter two aspects of the TP 2 pottery would seem to indicate a Middle Period assemblage, its comparative simplicity in terms of form and decoration when compared to others in the region (for example see: Hogg et al. 2021:Tables 4–5; Kirch and Chiu 2021:299–303; Specht and Summerhayes 2007:67–70; Summerhayes 2000b:91–123), in combination with the high rate of dentate stamping and the presence of ostensibly Early Period deposits in the same layers of TP 4 close by, strongly suggests the unique characteristics of this pottery relate to a specific social activity occurring within this part of the site, rather than being indicative of a later occupation.

Comparison of pottery in Layers 1–2 in TP 3 A-D and 4 with that in underlying layers shows unique proportions of decoration, particularly in relation to dentate stamping and notching, and vessel forms that differ from those in Layers 3–4 below, alongside the appearance of incision in TP 3 A-D. In TP 1 the difference between the upper and lower layers is more marked, with both incision and new vessel forms, Form IV and Form VII, the latter of which is also present in Layer 1 of TP 2, appearing within these layers. While the pottery in Layers 1–2 of these TPs provides perhaps the strongest evidence for later Lapita occupation at EQS, most of the forms and decoration present can be found in the underlying Early Period deposits, and thus could equally support continued deposition of material in this period as they could a later Lapita occupation. Significantly, even those forms and types of decoration that are absent from the Early Period deposits can be found in other contemporaneous assemblages in the Bismarck Archipelago (for example, see Hogg et al. 2021:Tables 4–5; Summerhayes 2000b:Tables 5.4, 5.7, 8.3, 8.6) and thus could represent internal changes within the existing Lapita settlement.

The results of the pottery analyses discussed above are further reinforced by reference to the faunal materials from TP 1, 3 A-D and 4, which are dominated by fishbones irrespective of TP or layer, while mammalian remains are incredibly rare and are primarily found in Layer 1. The fact that no substantial changes are seen in the faunal record through Layers 2–4, with mammalian bones being largely restricted to Layer 1, a modern gardening soil, indicates a continuance of the subsistence strategy practised from initial settlement. If the argument by Summerhayes et al. (2010:72) is correct and the dominance of fishbones reflects a lack of access to agricultural produce at initial settlement, this further suggests that the TPs/SP studied are representative of an Early Period occupation capped by modern deposits. Taken together, while later phases of occupation at EQS are possible, as it currently stands, the archaeological record is best interpreted as being derived from a single period of occupation during the Early Period.

Hamlet or fishing camp?

Following on from the above argument, the second primary question of this research can be posed: Does this pottery data support the site as being a fishing camp or a hamlet (Summerhayes et al. 2010:67–71, 72)? Looking at this debate from the perspective of the EQS pottery assemblages, it is apparent that a high proportion of vessels (by MNV) are plainware (35 per cent) (see Table 5.7). While this value is not aberrant for Early Period assemblages—50 per cent and 35 per cent of vessels from the Arawe Islands (western New Britain) sites of Paligmete (FNY) and Adwe (FOH – Squares D, E, F), respectively are plainwares, for example (Summerhayes 2000b:45, 126)—what is unusual is the restricted range of forms identified within this assemblage (Table 5.8).

Table 5.8: Counts and proportions of plainware vessels for the site of Tamuarawai (EQS), alongside the Early Lapita Arawe Islands sites of Adwe (FOH – Squares D, E, F) and Paligmete (FNY).

Vessel form	EQS		FOH		FNY	
	Plain vessels	%	Plain vessels	%	Plain vessels	%
I	5	14	14	13	2	8
II	1	3	17	16	6	24
III	N/A	N/A	11	10	3	12
IV	0	0	8	7	4	16
V	4	11	24	22	2	8
VI	24	67	25	23	4	16
VII	1	3	3	3	2	8
VIII	1	3	7	6	2	8
Total	36	100	109	100	25	100

Note: Percentages of plain vessels for EQS total 101% due to rounding.

Source: Authors' tabulation, and Summerhayes (2000b),Table 5.11 and Table 8.8.

In EQS the vast majority of the plain vessels are Form VI—globular pots (67 per cent), with vessels of Forms I (14 per cent) and V (11 per cent) making up the bulk of the remainder. In comparison, plainwares in FOH – Squares D, E, F and FNY (Summerhayes 2000b:Table 5.11, Table 8.8) are composed of vessels from four to five forms, each comprising a significant proportion of plainware vessels identified. Like globular pots in EQS, such vessels in FOH – Squares D, E, F and FNY are either plain or only have simple decoration applied to their lips (Summerhayes 2000b:Table 5.9, Table 8.8), which, based upon the arguments made above, suggests such vessels served a similar utilitarian function, such as cooking or food storage, within all of these settlements.

If globular pots were indeed used by the populations of Tamuarawai for utilitarian purposes, this suggests the activity associated with this pottery was being practised equally across the site, where such vessels comprise between 42 and 71 per cent of those identified, with the exception of TP 2 where they are absent. While the high proportion of globular pots lends credence to the possibility that the site had a utilitarian function, the presence of dentate-stamped vessels in every TP and SP studied, alongside a significant number of other decoration types (such as cut-outs, single tool impression, incision etc.; see Tables 5.5, 5.6 and 5.7), strongly suggests that a far more complex range of social activities were occurring. Accepting arguments for decorated wares to have played a differing socially significant role in society to plainwares, as discussed previously, their presence alongside utilitarian vessels gives considerable support to Tamuarawai representing a hamlet over that of a specialised fishing camp. In the earlier deposits in TP 1, 3 A-D and SP 15, the presence of a high proportion of plainware globular pots in almost every excavation unit and the dominance of fish within the faunal remains studied may well be related: upon arrival, colonising Lapita populations augmented their restricted diet of seafood by eating foodstuffs stored (perhaps sago flour), and possibly also cooked, in globular pots prior to the establishment of their agricultural systems. Whether this scenario also applies to the globular pots within the slightly later deposits in TP 4, or if perhaps another scenario applies (e.g. a drought impacting food supplies, or a change in vessel function) is uncertain.

Regarding the possible social activities involving decorated pottery within this hamlet, if the distribution of decoration and vessel forms is considered, one excavation area in particular stands out: TP 3 A-D. This assemblage is both one of the most heavily decorated of any of those studied, with 60 per cent of decorated pottery bearing dentate stamping alongside a further 11 decorative types (see Table 5.6), and has the highest proportions of the specialised dentate-stamped Form I—open bowls/cups and Form VIII—pot stands (see Table 5.4). The differences in the application of decoration and the high proportion of specialised vessels raises the possibility that a special-function structure, as discussed above for ECA Area B (Kirch 2021c:79–83), may have existed in this part of the site in the past. Furthermore, there is a possibility that this structure, if it indeed existed, may have extended further to the north to include the contemporaneous deposits of TP 1, as tentatively suggested by the presence of vessels from both Forms I and VIII in this assemblage. Furthermore, the presence of these same forms in the slightly later TP 4 deposits still further to the north, in conjunction with their complete absence, alongside vessels of Form VI, in the contemporaneous deposits in TP 2, may indicate that the locus of the social activities associated with TP 1 and 3 A-D may have shifted further to the north over time.

The possible presence of such a special-function structure in the vicinity of TP 1 and 3 A-D is further strengthened by the high concentration of shell valuables and other high-value items (including drilled shell beads, an armband and shell disk, and a jadeite stone chisel) in, or around, these TPs, mirroring the same in the deposits of ECA Area B discussed above. Finally, the abundance of faunal remains in the TP 1 and 3 A-D deposits and high proportion of utilitarian globular pots (one of which from TP 1 (#EQS 1, Figure 5.4B) has external fire blackening, indicative of its use in cooking), alongside specialised open bowls/cups and associated stands in the same deposits, suggests that the activity in this area potentially involved the cooking, presentation and consumption of foods, perhaps in the context of a 'feasting event' (Kirch 2021c:83). Finally, the possibility that the location of these feasts within the site shifted further to the north over time (to include TP 4), has additional tentative support in the presence of a small number of worked shell artefacts (representing the only other artefacts discovered after those in TP 1 and 3 A-D), and the presence of an abundance of fish remains in this deposit.

Conclusions

The data presented in this study allows the following conclusions.

First, radiocarbon determinations from Layer 4 of TP 1 and 3 A-D securely date the settlement of EQS to the Early Period, while that found in the same layer of TP 2 indicates a second later depositional event occurred during either the tail end of the former period or the Middle Period. The lack of determinations from Layers 1–3 across the site and SP 15 means they too could have been deposited later in time. However, while the pottery found in the upper layers of most TPs can be differentiated by the presence of either unique vessel forms and decoration types or proportions of such (or both), particularly TP 1 and TP 2, it is argued that these likely relate to either changes occurring over time within an Early Period settlement, or with regards to the latter TP, are interpreted as indicative of their use in a specific social activity. Thus, it is argued that the most likely scenario is the site represents a single phase of occupation during the Early Period.

Second, interpreting the differences in the proportions of vessel forms and types of decoration from the TP 1–4 and SP 15 assemblages, via an understanding of the theoretical social functions of plain and decorated pottery within Lapita society, it is argued that the presence of both plain and decorated ceramics within the same deposits suggests that the site represented a hamlet rather than a specialised fishing camp. It is further argued that the high proportions of largely plain globular pots within TP 1, 3 A-D and SP 15 may have resulted from colonising populations' need to augment their diets, composed predominantly of fish, with stored foods in anticipation of later agricultural produce.

Third, comparison of the decorated wares excavated from EQS highlighted the unique nature of the TP 3 A-D assemblages and to a lesser extent those from TP 1. The concentration of complex decorated pottery, particularly Form I and VIII vessels, a range of shell artefacts and other materials and an abundance of largely plain globular pots and faunal materials within the two deposits pointed to the possible presence of a special-function structure in this part of the site that may have been used for feasting events. The possibility that the location of such events may have shifted further to the north over time to include deposits in TP 4, was also raised.

Acknowledgements

Hogg recalls a story from his first trip to the island of Emirau in 2008 with Prof Glenn Summerhayes. When given the opportunity by Glenn to excavate a test pit in Tamuarawai alongside another junior colleague, the two were excited to find what they thought was an in situ feature. When seeing this feature himself, Glenn politely suggested all was not what it seemed, and told them to check again in the morning. After duly doing so, two somewhat embarrassed students realised their mistake—they had identified a modern rubbish pit dug into the topsoil. Taking this all in his stride Glenn, used this as a teaching opportunity, showing them where they had gone wrong, what to look out for next time and, equally importantly, through good-humoured jokes, why it's never a good idea to brag about something you have found—until you knew you actually found it! Hogg wishes to congratulate Glenn on his many years of fantastic research in Papua New Guinea, and to extend his personal gratitude for all of the help he has provided over three separate theses and more besides.

The authors would like to thank the communities of Emirau, in particular Kelly Amanga, Kenneth Vito Thomas and Pastor Wilson. In Kavieng we thank the New Ireland Provincial Administration, Leo and Rhondi Badcock, Kavieng Hotel, Peter McEwan and Shaun Yip; in Port Moresby, we thank the National Museum and Art Gallery of Papua New Guinea, Georgia Kaipu from the National Research Institute and Jim Robins of the University of Papua New Guinea (formerly of the National Research Institute). Many thanks to Anne Ford, Jim Specht, Elizabeth Matisoo-Smith, Matthew Hennessey, Matthew Leavesley, Jim Allen and Jill Allen for your hard work in the field. Thanks also to Adelie Filippi for the countless hours she put into photographing the EQS assemblages. Lastly, a special thanks to those that joined us in the field but are no longer with us: Herman Mandui of the National Museum and Art Gallery of Papua New Guinea and Jim Ridges of Kavieng. Funding for the fieldwork upon which this research is based was awarded to Elizabeth Matisoo-Smith and Glenn Summerhayes by the Royal Society Te Apārangi (Marsden Grant), while additional funds were provided by the University of Otago to Summerhayes, which allowed for the participation of Jim Allen, Jim Specht, Anne Ford, Matthew Hennessey and Nicholas Hogg. Hogg also wishes to acknowledge the support of the Taiwan Fellowship Program of the Ministry of Foreign Affairs, Republic of China (Taiwan), funding from which has facilitated the writing of this paper.

References

Anson, D. 1983. Lapita pottery of the Bismarck Archipelago and its affinities. Unpublished PhD thesis, University of Sydney, Sydney.

Anson, D. 1986. Lapita pottery of the Bismarck Archipelago and its affinities. *Archaeology in Oceania* 21:157–165. doi.org/10.1002/j.1834-4453.1986.tb00144.x.

Bedford, S. 2006. *Pieces of the Vanuatu puzzle: Archaeology of the north, south and centre.* Terra Australis 23. ANU E Press, Canberra. doi.org/10.22459/PVP.02.2007.

Bedford, S., M. Spriggs, D. Burley, C. Sand, P. Sheppard and G.R. Summerhayes 2019. Debating Lapita: Distribution, chronology, society and subsistence. In S. Bedford and M. Spriggs (eds), *Debating Lapita: Distribution, chronology, society and subsistence*, pp. 5–36. Terra Australis 52. ANU Press, Canberra. doi.org/10.22459/TA52.2019.01.

Best, S. 2002. *Lapita: A view from the East.* New Zealand Archaeological Association Monograph 24. New Zealand Archaeological Association, Auckland.

Chiu, S. 2005. Meanings of a Lapita face: Materialized social memory in ancient house societies. *Taiwan Journal of Anthropology* 3:1–47.

Chiu, S. 2007. Detailed analysis of Lapita face motifs: Case studies from Reef/Santa Cruz Lapita sites and New Caledonia Lapita Site 13A. In S. Bedford, C. Sand and S.P. Connaughton (eds), *Oceanic explorations: Lapita and western Pacific settlement*, pp. 241–264. Terra Australis 26. ANU E Press, Canberra. doi.org/10.22459/TA26.2007.15.

Chiu, S. 2015. Where do we go from here? Social relatedness reflected by motif analysis. In C. Sand, S. Chiu and N.W.S. Hogg (eds), *The Lapita Cultural Complex in time and space: Expansion routes, chronologies and typologies*, pp. 185–206. Archeologia Pasifika 4. Institute of Archaeology of New Caledonia and the Pacific, Nouméa.

Chiu, S. 2019. Measuring social distances with shared Lapita motifs: Current results and challenges. In S. Bedford and M. Spriggs (eds), *Debating Lapita: Distribution, chronology, society and subsistence*, pp. 307–334. Terra Australis 52. ANU Press, Canberra. doi.org/10.22459/TA52.2019.15.

Clark, G. 2007. Specialisation, standardisation and Lapita ceramics. In S. Bedford, C. Sand and S.P. Connaughton (eds), *Oceanic explorations: Lapita and western Pacific settlement*, pp. 289–299. Terra Australis 26. ANU E Press, Canberra. doi.org/10.22459/TA26.2007.17.

Harlow, G.E., G.R. Summerhayes, H.L. Davies and L. Matisoo-Smith 2012. A jade gouge from Emirau Island, Papua New Guinea (Early Lapita context, 3300 BP): A unique jadeitite. *European Journal of Mineralogy* 24:391–399. doi.org/10.1127/0935-1221/2012/0024-2175.

Hogg, N.W.S. 2011. Specialised production of Early-Lapita pottery: A skill analysis of pottery from the island of Emirau. Unpublished MA thesis, University of Otago, Dunedin.

Hogg, N.W.S. 2022. Fragments of a Lapita past: Investigating the emergence, transformations, and interactions of Lapita populations during the Early and Middle Periods of the Lapita Cultural Complex in the Bismarck Archipelago. Unpublished PhD thesis, University of Otago, Dunedin.

Hogg, N.W.S., G.R. Summerhayes and Y.-I.E. Chen 2021. Moving on or settling down? Studying the nature of mobility through Lapita pottery from the Anir Islands, Papua New Guinea. In J. Specht, V. Attenbrow and J. Allen (eds), *From field to museum—Studies from Melanesia in honour of Robin Torrence*, pp. 71–86. Technical Reports of the Australian Museum, Online 34. Australian Museum, Sydney. doi.org/10.3853/ j.1835-4211.34.2021.1744.

Hunt, T.L. 1989. Lapita ceramic exchange in the Mussau Islands, Papua New Guinea. Unpublished PhD thesis, University of Washington, Seattle.

Irwin, G. 1985. *The emergence of Mailu: As a central place in coastal Papuan prehistory.* Terra Australis 10. Department of Archaeology and Natural History and the Centre for Archaeological Research, The Australian National University, Canberra.

Jones, S. 2015. Eating identity: An exploration of Fijian foodways in the archaeological past. *Journal of Indo-Pacific Archaeology* 37:64–71. doi.org/10.7152/jipa.v37i0.15000.

Joukowsky, M. 1980. *A complete manual of field archaeology: Tools and techniques of field work for archaeologists.* Prentice-Hall International Inc, London.

Kirch, P.V. 1997. *The Lapita peoples: Ancestors of the Oceanic world.* Blackwell Publishers Inc., Cambridge MA.

Kirch, P.V. (ed.) 2001. *Lapita and its transformations in Near Oceania: Archaeological investigations in the Mussau Islands, Papua New Guinea, 1985–88, vol. 1. Introduction, excavations, chronology.* Contributions of the Archaeological Research Facility 59. University of California at Berkeley, Berkeley CA.

Kirch, P.V. 2017. *On the road of the winds: An archaeological history of the Pacific Islands before European contact.* University of California Press, Berkeley CA. doi.org/10.1525/9780520968899.

Kirch, P.V. 2021a. Radiocarbon dating and chronology of the Mussau sites. In P.V. Kirch (ed.), *Talepakemalai: Lapita and its transformations in the Mussau Islands of Near Oceania*, pp. 137–163. The Costin Institute of Archaeology Press, Los Angeles CA. doi.org/10.2307/j.ctv27tctrd.14.

Kirch, P.V. 2021b. Lapita and its transformations in the Mussau Islands. In P.V. Kirch (ed.), *Talepakemalai: Lapita and its transformations in the Mussau Islands of Near Oceania*, pp. 509–522. The Costin Institute of Archaeology Press, Los Angeles CA. doi.org/10.2307/j.ctv27tctrd.27.

Kirch, P.V. 2021c. Excavations at Talepakemalai (Site ECA). In P.V. Kirch (ed.), *Talepakemalai: Lapita and its transformations in the Mussau Islands of Near Oceania*, pp. 47–102. The Costin Institute of Archaeology Press, Los Angeles CA. doi.org/10.2307/j.ctv27tctrd.12.

Kirch, P.V. and C. Catterall 2001. The Mussau Islands: Natural and cultural environments. In P.V. Kirch (ed.), *Lapita and its transformations in Near Oceania: Archaeological investigations in the Mussau Islands, Papua New Guinea, 1985–88, vol. 1. Introduction, excavations, chronology*, pp. 28–56. Contributions of the Archaeological Research Facility 59. University of California at Berkeley, Berkeley CA.

Kirch, P.V. and S. Chiu 2021. Ceramic assemblages of the Mussau Islands. In P.V. Kirch (ed.), *Talepakemalai: Lapita and its transformations in the Mussau Islands of Near Oceania*, pp. 269–374. The Costin Institute of Archaeology Press, Los Angeles CA. doi.org/10.2307/j.ctv27tctrd.20.

Leclerc, M. 2018. The use of Lapita pottery: Results from the first analysis of lipid residues. *Journal of Archaeological Science: Reports* 17:712–722. doi.org/10.1016/j.jasrep.2017.12.019.

Marshall, Y. 2008. The social lives of lived and inscribed objects: A Lapita perspective. *The Journal of the Polynesian Society* 117:59–101.

Muir, A. 2017. Obsidian and interaction during the Early Lapita Period: An analysis of the lithic assemblage from Tamuarawai, Emirau Island. Unpublished BA (Hons) thesis, University of Otago, Dunedin.

Noury, A. 2019. Along the roads of the Lapita people: Designs, groups and travels. In S. Bedford and M. Spriggs (eds), *Debating Lapita: Distribution, chronology, society and subsistence*, pp. 335–348. Terra Australis 52. ANU Press, Canberra. doi.org/10.22459/TA52.2019.16.

Pawley, A. 2007. The origins of Early Lapita culture: The testimony of historical linguistics. In S. Bedford, C. Sand and S.P. Connaughton (eds), *Oceanic explorations: Lapita and western Pacific settlement*, pp. 17–49. Terra Australis 26. ANU E Press, Canberra. doi.org/10.22459/TA26.2007.02.

Poulsen, J. 1987. *Early Tongan prehistory: The Lapita period on Tongatapu and its relationships*. Terra Australis 12. ANH Publications and The Centre for Archaeological Research, The Australian National University, Canberra.

Sand, C. 2015. Comparing Lapita pottery forms in the southwestern Pacific: A case-study. In C. Sand, S. Chiu and N. Hogg (eds), *The Lapita cultural complex in time and space: Expansion routes, chronologies and typologies*, pp. 125–171. Archeologia Pasifika 4. Institute of Archaeology of New Caledonia and the Pacific, Nouméa.

Scahill, A. 2020. Early Lapita settlement in the colonisation process: The nature of an Early Lapita ceramic assemblage from Tamuarawai, Emirau Island, Papua New Guinea. Unpublished MA thesis, University of Otago, Dunedin.

Specht, J. and C. Gosden 2019. New dates for the Makekur (FOH) Lapita pottery site, Arawe Islands, New Britain, Papua New Guinea. In S. Bedford and M. Spriggs (eds), *Debating Lapita: Distribution, chronology, society and subsistence*, pp. 169–202. Terra Australis 52. ANU Press, Canberra. doi.org/10.22459/TA52. 2019.09.

Specht, J. and G.R. Summerhayes 2007. The Boduna Island (FEA) Lapita site. In J. Specht and V. Attenbrow (eds), *Archaeological studies of the middle and late Holocene, Papua New Guinea. Part IV*, pp. 51–103. Technical Reports of the Australian Museum Online 20. Australian Museum, Sydney. doi.org/10.3853/ j.1835-4211.20.2007.1474.

Spriggs, M. 1990. The changing face of Lapita: Transformation of a design. In M. Spriggs (ed.), *Lapita design, form and composition: Proceedings of the Lapita Design Workshop, Canberra, December 1988*, pp. 83–122. Occasional Papers in Prehistory 19. Department of Prehistory, Research School of Pacific studies, The Australian National University, Canberra.

Spriggs, M. 1997. *The Island Melanesians*. Blackwell Publishers Ltd., Oxford.

Spriggs, M. 2019. The hat makes the man: Masks, headdresses and skullcaps in Lapita iconography. In S. Bedford and M. Spriggs (eds), *Debating Lapita: Distribution, chronology, society and subsistence*, pp. 257–274. Terra Australis 52. ANU E Press, Canberra. doi.org/10.22459/TA52.2019.13.

Summerhayes, G.R. 2000a. What's in a pot? In A.J. Anderson and T. Murray (eds), *Australian Archaeologist: Collected papers in honour of Jim Allen*, pp. 291–307. Coombs Academic Publishing, Canberra.

Summerhayes, G.R. 2000b. *Lapita Interaction*. Terra Australis 15. ANH Publications and the Centre for Archaeological Research, The Australian National University, Canberra.

Summerhayes, G.R. 2001. Defining the chronology of Lapita in the Bismarck Archipelago. In G. Clark, A. Anderson and T. Vunidilo (eds), *The archaeology of Lapita dispersal in Oceania*, pp. 25–38. Terra Australis 17. Pandanus Books, Canberra.

Summerhayes, G.R. 2010a. The emergence of Lapita in the Bismarck Archipelago. In C. Sand and S. Bedford (eds), *Lapita: Ancêtres Océaniens*, pp. 93–101. Musée du quai Branly, Somogy Editions D'Art, Paris.

Summerhayes, G.R. 2010b. *Lapita interaction – An update*. 2009 International Symposium on Austronesian Studies. National Museum of Prehistory, Taitong.

Summerhayes, G.R. and J. Allen 2007. Lapita writ small? Revisiting the Austronesian colonisation of the Papuan south coast. In S. Bedford, C. Sand and S.P. Connaughton (eds), *Oceanic explorations: Lapita and western Pacific settlement*, pp. 97–122. Terra Australis 26. ANU E Press, Canberra. doi.org/10.22459/TA26. 2007.05.

Summerhayes, G.R., E. Matisoo-Smith, H. Mandui, J. Allen, J. Specht, N. Hogg and S. McPherson 2010. Tamuarawai (EQS): An Early Lapita site on Emirau, New Ireland, PNG. *Journal of Pacific Archaeology* 1(1):62–75.

Summerhayes, G.R., K. Szabó, A. Fairbairn, M. Horrocks, S. McPherson and A. Crowther 2019. Early Lapita subsistence: The evidence from Kamgot, Anir Islands, New Ireland Province, Papua New Guinea. In S. Bedford and M. Spriggs (eds), *Debating Lapita: Distribution, chronology, society and subsistence*, pp. 379–402. Terra Australis 52. ANU E Press, Canberra. doi.org/10.22459/TA52.2019.18.

Terrell, J.E. and E.M. Schechter 2009. The meaning and importance of the Lapita face motif. *Archaeology in Oceania* 44:45–55. doi.org/10.1002/j.1834-4453.2009.tb00046.x.

Terrell, J.E. and R.L. Welsch 1997. Lapita and the temporal geography of prehistory. *Antiquity* 71:548–572. doi.org/10.1017/S0003598X0008532X.

6

Understanding social connections within the Bismarck Archipelago through petrographic and motif analyses of Mussau Lapita pottery assemblages

Scarlett Chiu, Yuyin Su, David Killick, Patrick Kirch,
Glenn R. Summerhayes, Jim Specht and Wallace Ambrose

Abstract

Petrographic and motif analyses of Lapita pottery assemblages from the Talepakemalai (ECA), Etakosarai (ECB) and Etapakengaroasa (EHB) Lapita sites of the Mussau Islands help to illuminate the social lives of people living in the Bismarck Archipelago some 3000 years ago. Based on petrographic analysis, these early Mussau Lapita sites acquired pots from many parts of the Bismarck Archipelago, namely the Admiralty Islands, north-east and central north New Britain, northern and south-western New Ireland and the Tabar–Lihir–Tanga–Feni (TLTF) chain. None of our petrographic samples indicate sources from southern New Britain, even though ECA shares a high number of motifs with sites in the Kandrian region of south-western New Britain. There is also no evidence of imports from the northern coast of New Guinea. We suggest that the Mussau Lapita community was linked with at least two possible social networks based on pottery sources, motifs and obsidian distribution patterns.

Introduction

Located on the northern rim of the Bismarck Archipelago, the Lapita communities of the Mussau Islands have long been of particular interest to Pacific archaeologists. Egloff and others initially reported finds of fine dentate-stamped Lapita sherds on Eloaua island (ECA and ECB sites: see below) (Bafmatuk et al. 1980; Egloff 1975), while Allen and Specht, who also surveyed the area, found 16 possible archaeological sites (Allen et al. 1984:8–11, cited in Kirch 2001:58). During the 1985 Lapita Homeland Project and in subsequent field seasons in 1986 and 1988, Kirch and his team extended archaeological survey of this island group, and excavated at the Talepakemalai (ECA), Etakosarai (ECB) and Etapakengaroasa (EHB) Lapita sites (Figure 6.1) on Eloaua and Emananus islands, along with other sites of Lapita and Post-Lapita age (Kirch 1987, 2001, 2021c).

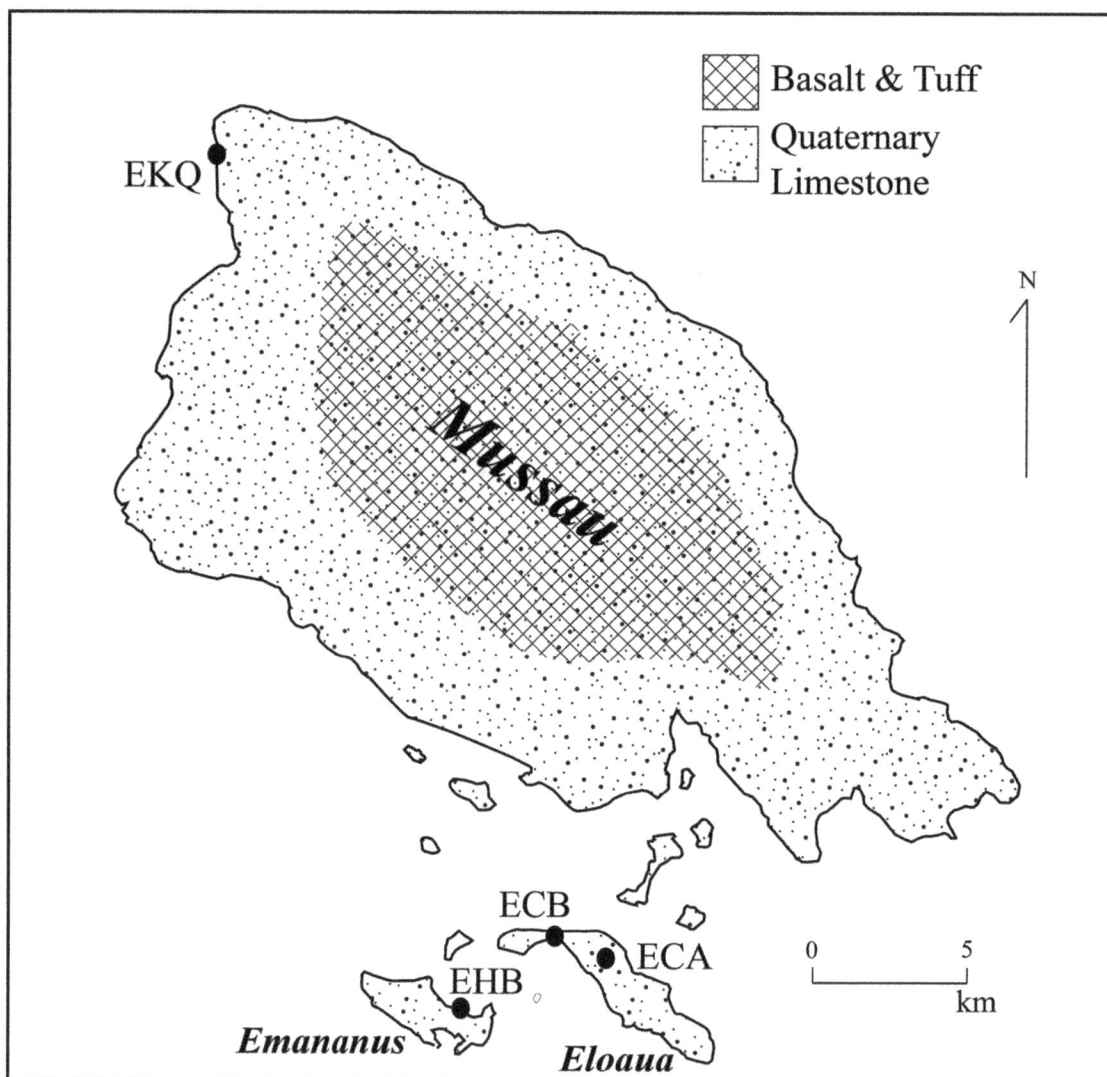

Figure 6.1: Map of the Mussau Islands and nearby isles with locations of Lapita sites discussed in this paper.

Source: Adapted from Kirch (2001:Fig. 3.1, 59), Warin and Jensen (1959:Plate 12).

The extensive Talepakemalai site (ECA) incorporated the remains of numerous stilt houses, including two sides of a stilt house and many posts belonging to other such structures. ECA is estimated to be up to 82,000 m² or more in size, thus representing the largest Lapita village site on record (Kirch 1997:167, 173; 2021b:155). In contrast, the smaller ECB (estimated at around 3000 m²) and EHB (about 1000 m²) sites are more likely to have been hamlets (Kirch 2021a:519). The Talepakemalai site has a waterlogged, subtidal deposit that preserved wooden stilt house posts, along with large quantities of pottery, obsidian flakes imported from both Lou and Talasea sources, adzes, scrapers, shell fishhooks, shell rings and ornaments. The range of materials associated with the Area B stilt house at Talepakemalai suggest that this was not an ordinary dwelling, but more likely a specialised structure such as a men's house, used for conducting ritual or community-related activities (Kirch et al. 2015:60). Potsherds from the undisturbed parts of the site are quite large, and around 260 vessels have been reconstructed (Kirch et al. 2015; Kirch and Chiu 2021).

Radiocarbon dating of the Mussau sites, previously reported by Kirch (2001), has recently been improved with the accelerator mass spectrometry (AMS) dating of short-lived organic materials such as *Canarium* nuts, coconut endocarp and similar samples, combined with Bayesian modelling and calibration (Kirch 2021c). The earliest Lapita site in Mussau is EHB on Emananus Island, which was estimated to have been established no later than 3350–3325 cal. BP (Kirch 2021a:512). The second earliest is the small ECB site, dated to around 3550–3475 cal. BP with unidentified wood samples, and 3500–3050 cal. BP based on calibrated shell dates. Both sets of dates suggest that ECB may be roughly contemporaneous with the main stilt house occupations at ECA Area B (Kirch 2021b:163). Cultural deposition at site ECA Area A, and the earliest deposits of the southern end of trenches W200 and W250, began at ca 3300–3200 cal. BP. The main stilt house occupation at Area B and B-extension dated to about 3200–2950 cal. BP (Kirch 2021a:512). Zones C_2-C_3 of this area started between 3234–3089 cal. BP and ended between 3155 and 3020 cal. BP, while Zone C_1 started between 3061-2836 cal. BP and ended between 2919-2724 cal. BP. The latest Lapita phase represented by the deposits at Area C and the northern ends of the W200 and W250 transects at ECA likely occurred between 3154 and 2970 cal. BP and ended between 2778 and 2492 cal. BP (Kirch 2021b: Table 5.5, 156).

Petrographic analysis of four sherds from ECA was conducted by Lohu, who reported that two samples (samples 1 and 2) contain high proportions of clinopyroxene having 'a relatively strong colouration (greenish yellow) … The andesite lithic grains also include the same, coloured pyroxenes' (Anson 1983:Appendix II, 290). These samples also contain plagioclase, opaques, volcanic lithics and hornblende, but lack quartz and calcareous sands (Anson 1983:Appendix II, 290). Based on his description, these two samples are likely to have been transported into ECA from the Tabar–Lihir–Tanga–Feni (TLTF) chain of islands, while samples 3 and 4 are from unknown volcanic islands.

Anson carried out X-ray fluorescence (XRF) and electron microprobe analysis on 16 ECA samples excavated by Egloff (1975). He concluded that they might have been transported from two or more distinctive clay sources. In a more extensive analysis of 172 sherds excavated by Kirch at ECA and other Mussau sites, Hunt compared the chemical compositions of one local Mussau clay and two clay samples from the Manus islands with the archaeological samples using a scanning electron microscope in conjunction with an X-ray analyser (Hunt 1989:121, 171; Kirch et al. 1991:158). Hunt identified 16 chemical composition groups in the archaeological samples, among which one is indistinguishable from a local Mussau clay, some are clustered with Hus (Ahus) and M'Buke clays of the Admiralty Islands, while others are from unknown sources exotic to Mussau (Hunt 1989:191). Pots made with clays from M'Buke Island off the south of Manus were found in ECA Area A, as well as in the ECB and EKQ (Epakapaka, a rockshelter Late Lapita site on the Mussau Island) samples, while Hus (off the north of Manus) clay was found at the much later post-Lapita Sinakasai (EKU) site (Figure 6.3) (Hunt 1989:121:195, Table 7.1, 203). Hunt concluded that ECB, ECA Area B and EHB had 12, 11 and 9 different compositional groups respectively (Hunt 1989:206). A small number of samples from ECB (12 per cent) and EKQ (9 per cent) with high amounts of calcareous sands clustered with local Mussau clay, while the rest of the samples were interpreted as exotic to the region (Kirch et al. 1991:159).

Dickinson (2000a) initially examined thin sections of 12 sherds excavated by Kirch at ECA, indicating that at least two sources exotic to Mussau were evidenced. Kirch subsequently invited Dickinson to sample a wider array of sherds from the ECA and EHB sites. Together, Dickinson and Kirch selected 49 sherds, basing their sampling on both macroscopic indications of temper variation and on stylistic traits of the pottery. Petrographic analysis of the combined sample of 61 sherds by Dickinson (2021b) resulted in the definition of 10 different calcareous, hybrid and volcanic temper groups, nearly all of which are exotic to the Mussau Islands. These samples had been sourced to the Admiralty Islands (Manus and nearby islands), Lavongai (and adjacent parts of New Ireland) and the TLTF alkalic chain (Dickinson 2021b:388); none of them resembles what Dickinson had examined from other archaeological assemblages within the Bismarcks (Dickinson 2021b:376). Our own petrographic analysis builds upon this pioneering research by the late professor Dickinson.

Simplified geology of the Bismarck Archipelago

Mussau Island, the largest island in the St Matthias Group located in the north of the Bismarck Archipelago, is comprised of basic volcanic and sub-volcanic rocks such as basalt and mafic andesite, surrounded by an apron of uplifted limestones of coral reef origin. At the central hilly part of the island, Mt Eunainaun rises c. 645 m above sea level, where basalts and tuffs (Warin and Jensen 1959:15) and epidotised porphyry have been reported (Thilenius 1927:440, cited from Kirch 2001:55). Evidence for metamorphism or faulting is not reported for this island. Rock samples collected by Kirch in 1985 near the Ekasi river on the eastern side of Mussau Island include both 'plutonic (intrusive) diorite-gabbro' and 'fine-grained igneous rocks of probably volcanic and hypabyssal origin' (Kirch 2001:33). The plutonic rocks were identified by Dickinson as 'highly porphyritic plutonics (gabbro)' (Kirch et al. 1991:146). The island's volcanic core is deeply weathered, with exposures of fine-grained workable clay (Hunt 1989:80–81, Fig. 5.1). Eloaua and Emananus islands to the south-west of Mussau Island are composed entirely of coral reefs surrounding upraised limestone (fossil reefs) (Dickinson 2006, 2021b), and thus lack clay sources or exposed volcaniclastic rocks.

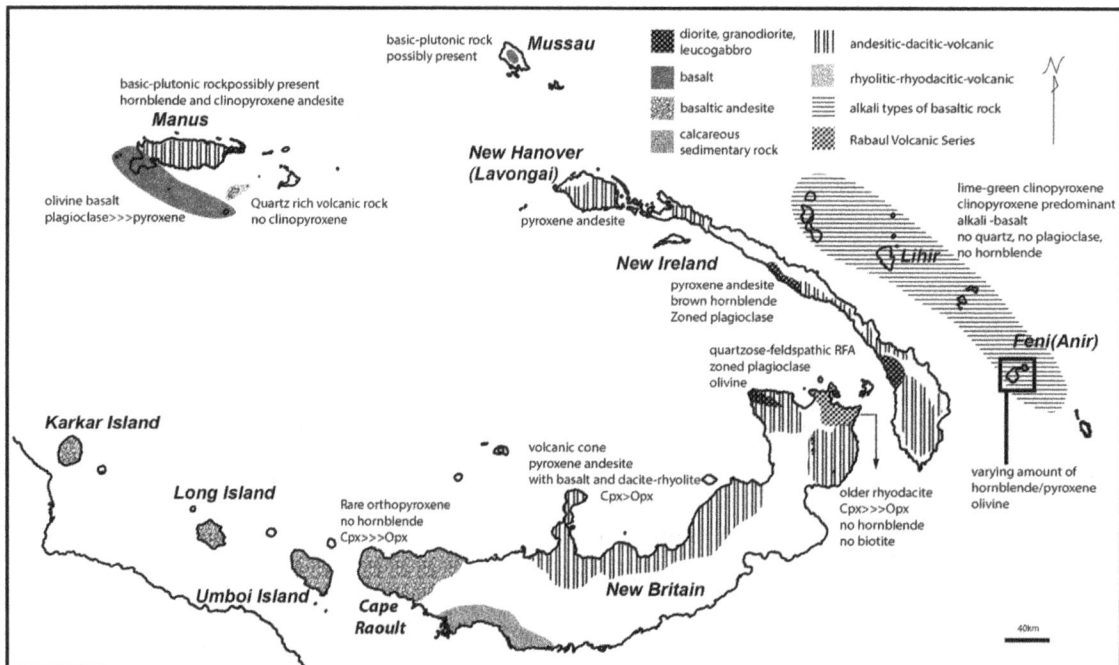

Figure 6.2: Map showing the simplified geological zones within the Bismarck Archipelago region.

Note: The map includes notes summarised from Dickinson's reports and geological references related to our own observations from available thin sections (after Blake and Miezitis 1967; Dickinson 2000a, 2021b; Jaques 1980; Page and Ryburn 1977; Rogerson 1989; Stewart and Sandy 1988).

Source: Authors' illustration; see also references cited.

The Bismarck Archipelago is a geologically complex region (Figure 6.2), with 'intersecting subduction zones, spreading centers, and transform faults' (Dickinson 2006:50) caused by various geological events that have transformed these island landscapes over the last four million years (Martinez and Taylor 1996:204).

In general, Paleogene volcanogenic assemblages of the ancestral Vitiaz Island arc 'contain both hornblende and clinopyroxene in widely varying proportions, but generally lack orthopyroxene or olivine in any appreciable amount'; these can be found in all the major islands (Dickinson 2006:52). During the Miocene, sequences of limestone accumulated across much of this region and beyond, forming thick layers of limestone on top of the Paleogene volcanic rock. New volcanoes then intruded into these limestone layers, forming volcanic landscapes mainly on New Britain and Bougainville during and after the Pliocene (Sheppard and Cranfield 2012:27). In addition, many islands are fringed by raised Pleistocene–Holocene coral reefs (Lindley 2006:404).

Dickinson (2021b) pointed out the difficulty in discriminating among different temper sources within the Bismarck Archipelago, given that most terrigenous sands are derived from similar volcanic parent rocks. Three out of five geotectonic temper classes defined by Dickinson (2006:11-14) are found within the Bismarck Archipelago: (1) andesitic arc tempers, (2) backarc/postarc tempers (lacking grains from plutonic or metamorphic rocks) and (3) dissected orogen tempers containing plutonic rocks (Dickinson 2006:Table 1, 13). Distinguishing one source from another largely depends on subtle variations in volcanic petrology and temper grain types, mostly based on the observation of archaeological ceramics and occasional sand and rock samples of this region (Dickinson 2021b).

Based on available geological reports, we have developed a simplified geological map of the region (Blake and Miezitis 1967; Dickinson 2000a, 2000b, 2021b; Hohnen 1978; Jaques 1980; Page and Ryburn 1977; Rogerson 1989; Stewart and Sandy 1988) (see Figure 6.2). We have also listed regional differences expected from local terrestrial sand tempers, data which we then use to differentiate temper sources. More detailed descriptions of these geological settings will be provided in another paper (Chiu et al. in prep.). It should be emphasised that the geology of the Bismarck Archipelago and eastern Papua New Guinea is still poorly known, and that detailed geological maps are not available for many parts of this region.

Petrographic analysis

In his effort to establish a generic classification system for all Oceanic temper types, Dickinson (2006) not only provided summary descriptions of what major sand grain types can be expected from each of the five geotectonic temper classes of the Pacific, he also employed various parameters to calculate ratios of certain rocks and minerals in order to further differentiate among various temper types within each geotectonic region (Dickinson 2006:Table 6, 29). Yet in doing so, he sometimes omitted the more geologically specific but rare index minerals or rocks in his temper summary tables, although these are usually described in the more general description of these regions. One such case is 'the greenish cast and faint yellowish pleochroism typical of aegirine-augite, a sodic variety of augite characteristic of alkalic volcanic suites' (Dickinson 2006:76) that only appears in ceramic samples made from the TLTF islands. This mineral had been described and was used by Dickinson to allocate samples to this particular island chain, however it was not listed in the point count tables when he reported analytical results of either the Kamgot (Dickinson 2000b) or Mussau (Dickinson 2021a) Lapita ceramic samples.

Therefore, we first reanalysed 59 of the samples from the ECA, ECB and EHB sites that Dickinson had previously analysed, in order to familiarise ourselves with the methods and classification principles that he used to identify possible sources (Dickinson 1996, 1997, 2021b). We started with a detailed description of the texture, size and weathering degree of tempers, types of minerals and rocks included. Based on our observations, we merged Dickinson's original temper Types A, B and H into two larger Groups 1 and 2; merged Types E and F into one (Group 5); and relocated one sample each from his Types C and G to our Group 8, while the rest of his original temper types remain the same (see Appendix, Table 6.S1).

Sampling strategy

According to Dickinson, the first group of 12 sherds were selected primarily to study the non-calcareous terrigenous tempers of the ECA assemblage, while the second group of 49 sherds were selected to represent the full range of variation in the Eloaua and Emananus temper types. All diagnostic sherds from Area B-extension and Area C were first examined macroscopically by Dickinson; nine calcareous dominate samples from Area B were selected to represent that particular temper type, and the other 40 were selected to represent the non-calcareous dominate temper types (Dickinson 2021b:375–376).

New samples

In 2017–19 Chiu thin-sectioned 182 additional samples from the Mussau assemblages curated in Kirch's laboratory. These new samples were selected from a subset of the entire assemblage due to constraints on time and funding. This subset includes many of the 266 reconstructed vessels, plus 95 sherds belonging to particular vessel or motif groups from the ECA, ECB and EHB sites, as well as sherds from 10 controlled excavation units of ECA Area B (units A14, A31, A32, A35, A36 (A14), A39, A40), and Area B-extension (units A66, A67, A68, A69). A total of 1216 sherds were first examined under a binocular microscope at 4-10×. Nine different mineral or rock fragments (based on colour and texture of the non-plastic inclusions) and their abundances were estimated and recorded in order to establish the range of variability in different temper groups present. Based on the observed ratio of minerals/rock fragments, we generated 260 preliminary temper groups.

Grouping was further refined based on the presence of different types of minerals or rock fragments, regardless of their relative ratios. This follows from Dickinson's warning that 'no reliable distinctions can be drawn between different temper types from megascopic estimates of relative proportions of light and heavy mineral grains and volcanic lithic fragments', due to the highly variable degree of placering in this region (Dickinson 2006:52). This led Chiu to condense the 260 preliminary groups to 30 temper groups. The next step was to measure sherd weight, as only 842 sherds heavier than 8 g (the minimum amount required for thin sectioning) were identified for further analysis. For each temper group, if the number of sherds was lower than 10, all were selected for further analysis. If the number of sherds was greater than 10, 20 per cent of the sherds were selected.

Analytical results

Combined with Dickinson's earlier analysis, a total of 241 thin sections from Mussau sherds were analysed at the Institute of History and Philology, Academia Sinica, Taipei, and at the School of Anthropology, University of Arizona. Based on observed inclusions, we clustered these samples into nine different temper groups, with two isolates (see Table 6.S1 in Appendix; two samples from the Post-Lapita EKQ site are omitted from the following discussion, thus the total number is 239 for this paper). Detailed petrographic descriptions will be published in a future paper (Chiu et al. in prep.); here we provide a summary of our results.

The ratio of various minerals and rocks, degree of weathering, appearance and the frequency of geologically specific index minerals that we observed in a given thin section sample all provide useful information for determining possible sources, by comparing them to the available geological maps and published and unpublished reports (Davies 2012; Dickinson 2000a, 2006, 2021b; Hohnen 1978; Summerhayes 2000; Warin and Jensen 1959) (Figure 6.2). As most samples contain large amounts of either reef detritus, opaque or only volcanic lithics, at this stage we can at best tentatively assign sherds to known volcanic regions within the Bismarck Archipelago, thus covering a rather large geological zone, or even to multiple possible sources. While the geology of this region is not yet mapped in sufficient detail to allow for more precise attributions—particularly on the north-east coast of New Guinea and in the Schouten Arc—it is nonetheless possible to suggest some source attributions (see Table 6.1).

Table 6.1: Summary of temper groups and subgroups identified.

Temper group and subgroups	The feature of geological area	Possible source	Number of samples
G1 Reef detritus-predominant fabric			**70**
1 Typical coral reef detritus, limeclast, with trace of volcanic lithics		unknown	28
2 Homogeneity reddish clay			11
3 Probable clay bulks			12
4 Weathered volcanic lithic			12
5 Yellowish-grey clay mineral			7
G2 Reef detritus-predominant hybrid fabric			**82**
1 Volcanic cone related	acid, intermediate and basic volcanic (no sub-volcanic, no dioritic, no plutonic)	volcanic zone along the north coast of New Britain	6
2 Heavy mineral	coral reef detritus and basic/intermediate volcanic	Mussau or basaltic Manus, Manus or Lavongai (or adjacent parts of New Ireland)	14
3 Quartz-feldspar	coral reef detritus and intermediate-acid/acid volcanic lithic	Lou island and the nearby rhyolitic islands	34
4 Slightly metamorphism	weathered intermediate plutonic/sub-volcanic area or sedimentary area	Manus or Lavongai (or adjacent parts of New Ireland), or Northern New Britain near Watom, or plutonic parts of New Ireland	28
G3 Coral reef detritus–opaque fabric			**23**
1 Coral reef detritus	coral reef detritus:placer sand (7:3). Basic volcanic area/pyroxene bearing intermediate volcanic	Mussau or basaltic Manus	7
2 Sub-volcanic & sediment	intermediate volcanic/sedimentary area with placer sand	Manus or Lavongai (or adjacent parts of New Ireland)	11

Temper group and subgroups	The feature of geological area	Possible source	Number of samples
3 Opaque	coral reef detritus:placer sand (3:7). Basic volcanic area/ pyroxene bearing intermediate volcanic	Mussau or basaltic Manus	5
G4 Opaque-dominant fabric	intermediate volcanic area with placer sand	Manus or Lavongai (or adjacent parts of New Ireland)	**8**
G5 Amphibole-feldspar fabric			**20**
1 Metavolcanics absent	basic or intermediate volcanic area	unknown basic or intermediate volcanic area	8
2 Epidote-bearing metavolcanics	weathered intermediate plutonic/sub-volcanic area or sedimentary area	Manus or Lavongai (or adjacent parts of New Ireland), or Northern New Britain near Watom, or plutonic parts of New Ireland	7
3 Prehnite-bearing metavolcanics	weathered intermediate plutonic/sub-volcanic area or sedimentary area	Manus or Lavongai (or adjacent parts of New Ireland), or Northern New Britain near Watom, or plutonic parts of New Ireland	5
G6 Pyroxene volcanic fabric			**15**
1 Basic volcanic with red iron oxide	basic volcanic area	unknown basic volcanic area	4
2 Alkali basalt, no lime-green clinopyroxene	alkali-rich basic volcanic area	TLTF alkalic chain(?)	1
3 Intermediate volcanic	intermediate volcanic	unknown intermediate volcanic	10
G7 Quartz-feldspar fabric			**9**
1 Quartz-feldspar fabric with silty clay	basic/intermediate/acid sub-volcanic/plutonic area	Northern New Britain near Watom, or plutonic parts of New Ireland	4
2 Quartz-feldspar fabric with dark matrix	basic/ intermediate/acid sub-volcanic/plutonic area	Northern New Britain near Watom, or plutonic parts of New Ireland	5
G8 Lime-green clinopyroxene	alkali-rich basic volcanic area	TLTF alkalic chain	**6**
G9 Two different pastes	mixed tempers	unknown	**4**
ECA69-05-004	no identifiable inclusion	unknown	**1**
ECA34-05-062	basic volcanic area	from unknown basic volcanic area	**1**
Total			**239**

Source: Authors' data.

Identified temper groups and subgroups, number of samples within each group, the feature of geological area they reflect and the possible source(s) are provided in Table 6.1. The reef detritus-predominant fabric group (G1) has 70 samples, all of which contain more than 30 per cent clay with more than 50 per cent reef detritus and limeclasts[1] and very few heavily weathered unidentifiable terrestrial fragments as tempers. Eighty-two samples that do contain a few identifiable rock fragments with roughly the same proportions of clay and reef detritus and limeclasts form the reef detritus-predominant hybrid fabric group (G2). Twenty-three samples that contain 30–50 per cent reef

---

1   Limeclasts are formed from terrestrial limestones, and have distinctive microstructures from those of coral.

detritus but without any limeclast, 25–70 per cent opaque minerals and very few other terrestrial grains, are classified as the coral reef detritus/opaque fabric group (G3). The opaque-dominant fabric group (G4) has eight samples, all of which contain more than 60 per cent opaque minerals (mostly iron and iron/titanium oxides) and roughly 15–20 per cent silicate minerals and rock fragments, indicating an intermediate volcanic origin with a high amount of placer sand sorting. Twenty samples in the amphibole-feldspar fabric group (G5) contain roughly more than 30–50 per cent feldspar, 10–20 per cent opaque minerals and less than 5 per cent pyroxenes. The 16 samples in the pyroxene volcanic fabric group (G6) are defined by roughly 15–25 per cent volcanic lithics, 10–20 per cent feldspar and more than 10 per cent pyroxene grains. Nine samples containing more than 50 per cent feldspar and quartz, and roughly 5–10 per cent heavy minerals with silty or dark clays are classified into the quartz-feldspar fabric group (G7). We have also classified eight samples that contain about 30 per cent clinopyroxene, especially the lime-green clinopyroxene (probably aegirine-augite (Dickinson 2004:1; Dickinson 2021b:382)), into the lime-green clinopyroxene fabric group (G8). Samples of this group likely derive from an alkali-rich basic volcanic region, as with the TLTF chain (Dickinson 2006).

Four samples with clays of contrasting colour but similar types of calcareous temper (two samples from ECB), or with similar clay but different suites of tempers (two ECA samples), are clustered under the two different pastes group (G9) (for more discussion about clay mixing, see Ho and Quinn 2021). Two samples cannot be classified with any other samples we examined. ECA69-05-004 consists of lumps of laterites with no identifiable temper, thus no origin can be identified. ECA34-05-062 contains extremely high amounts of heavily weathered, devitrified basic volcanic lithics in its matrix, unlike all other samples that also include basaltic or andesitic volcanic lithics that we have examined.

Ryburn reports that the coastal region of south-western New Britain starting from the Arawe Islands to the islands and hills east of Kandrian consists of raised coral reefs and terraces, backed by a raised marine platform that extends as much as 25 km inland (Ryburn 1976:6, Fig. 1, 5; Page and Ryburn 1977:Plate 1). Thus, any pottery made from this region is expected to contain large amount of limeclasts mixed with coral reef fragments, calcareous mudstone, siltstone, sandstone and conglomerate, except where terrestrial grains have been brought by rivers tapping into other geological zones located in interior highlands of western or central New Britain (namely the Pulie, Palicks and Andru Rivers) (Ryburn 1976:Fig. 1, 5). According to Ryburn (1976), there is probably a small inlier of volcanic breccia and tuff (indicative of the presence of basaltic and andesitic lavas) along the Anu River which runs close to the Kreslo site. Dickinson had also reported the local Kreslo tempers, which contain 'presence of appreciable hornblende, as well as pyroxene', that may be from such an intrusion (Dickinson 1998:2). Summerhayes has collected river sands (alluvial deposits) from four river mouths located on the south-western coast of New Britain (namely the Adi, Pulie, Anu and Alimbit Rivers) and analysed them with an electron microprobe (Summerhayes 2000:168; Fig. 11.1, 169). The same set of river sand samples plus 150 ceramic samples from six Arawe sites were later analysed by Wu with SEM-EDS (Wu 2016:Table 9.2, 302). The Arawe pottery samples were sourced to the above four river mouths according to the texture and composition of their inclusions (Summerhayes 2000:168; Wu 2016:303–306).[2] Yet none of these samples contains only calcareous sands.

---

2   Both authors reported what types of minerals can be found in the river sand and pottery samples, but no rock types specified. As they were using different methods to analyse their samples, we cannot compare our results directly to theirs.

Although samples of our Group 1 also contain only reef detritus and limeclasts that match the main characteristics of the above region, these calcareous grains alone are not diagnostic of any particular geological region (Dickinson 2006:4). At this stage we can only assign our G1 samples to unknown sources, since previous petrographic results of Kreslo and Arawe samples all contain volcanic and/or plutonic terrestrial grains with or without calcareous inclusions (Dickinson 1998, 2006:89).

Our results do not differ greatly from those previously obtained by Dickinson (2021b). After examining 180 new archaeological samples from well-controlled layers from Area B and Area B-extension of ECA, ECB and EHB, we have been able to add north-eastern and central northern New Britain and Mussau Island to the original list of possible sources identified by Dickinson (2021b:388) (Figure 6.2). The majority of samples contain mostly reef detritus with or without identifiable terrestrial grains. Only samples from the alkali-rich basaltic area with the distinctive lime-green clinopyroxene can be assigned to the TLTF chain, and those with excessive amounts of quartz and feldspar and rarely anything else can be assigned to rhyolitic volcanic islands such as Lou in the Admiralties. All other temper groups can be found in various parts of many islands in this region. The bottom line is that this is a challenging region for ceramic petrography. To pin things down more precisely would require a huge effort to sample many more localised potential clay and temper sources (for example, see Leclerc 2020).

Chronological changes in possible sources

Table 6.2 illustrates samples selected from ECA Area B and Area B-extension, where well-controlled stratigraphic layers and radiocarbon dates are available. Out of 190 samples selected from this excavation area, 63 contain almost entirely calcareous sands and therefore cannot be assigned to any known geological source. Another 11 are from unknown basic or intermediate volcanic areas. The remaining 116 samples could derive from five rather large geological zones within the Bismarcks. The first is Mussau itself, or the basaltic part of south-western Manus. The second is rhyolitic Lou and nearby islands in the Admiralties. The third is from the main island of Manus, New Hanover (Lavongai) Island, or adjacent parts of New Ireland with andesitic-dacitic volcanic temper.

Pots made on the Gazelle Peninsula in north-eastern New Britain or plutonic parts of central and south New Ireland, as well as pots made in Manus – New Ireland – New Britain arc all appear fairly early on in the Mussau sequence, quite consistently from the beginning of the chronological sequence at ECA Area B, Zone C_3. Pots made in the volcanic zone along the northern coast of New Britain and on the Willaumez Peninsula were imported into ECA at Zone C_2, only slightly later than those from other areas. However, pots imported from the alkali-rich volcanic TLTF chain seem to occur at Zone C_1 at ECA, which may be as much as 200 years later than Zones C_3 and C_2, although a shorter interval is not ruled out (Kirch 2021b:155–156).

Table 6.2: Possible source(s) for samples excavated from ECA Area B and B-extension areas with well-controlled stratigraphic information.

ECA Area B and B-extension	Possible source(s)										Total
	Mussau or basaltic Manus	Lou island and the nearby rhyolitic islands	Manus or Lavongai (or adjacent parts of New Ireland)	Northern New Britain near Watom, or plutonic parts of New Ireland	Manus or Lavongai (or adjacent parts of New Ireland), Northern New Britain near Watom, or plutonic parts of New Ireland	The volcanic zone along the north coast of New Britain	TLTF alkalic chain	Unknown basic volcanic area	Unknown intermediate volcanic	Unknown	
A	–	4	–	1	1	–	–	–	1	1	8
B1	–	4	7	1	7	2	1	2	1	14	39
B2	–	7	2	–	5	2	1	–	1	18	36
C1	–	7	3	1	3	1	3	1	1	14	34
C2	7	3	3	2	19	1	–	1	3	7	46
C3	1	6	2	2	7	–	–	–	–	9	27
Total	8	31	17	7	42	6	5	4	7	63	190

Source: Authors' data.

Motif analysis

Sampling strategy

Since 2011, Kirch and Chiu have reconstructed motifs and vessel forms occurring in the Mussau assemblages, and Chiu has studied other Lapita sites through collaborations with numerous scholars. Motifs included in the Lapita Pottery Online Database (LPOD, lapita.ihp.sinica.edu.tw) have been recorded in Excel tables, allowing specific motifs and their frequency in a given site to be extracted from the dataset. A total of 8502 decorated sherds that exhibit 1834 different motifs from 71 Lapita sites of the Bismarck Archipelago have been recorded in the LPOD. Fifty sites contain less than 20 different motifs and we have omitted them from the following analysis. Motifs that are too fragmented to recognise the original pattern, called TFGs, have been omitted as well. Therefore, 8313 decorated sherds with 1803 different motifs from 21 Bismarck Lapita sites are employed in this study.

The number of shared motifs among all sites is calculated with the Jaccard index of similarity (Real and Vargas 1996); QGIS 3.16 is used to plot the links representing weak to strong connections among these Early Lapita sites. Jaccard similarity indices between any two sites can be calculated by the number of motifs shared by these sites divided by the sum of the number of shared motifs plus the number of motifs that only appear at one site. We grouped those with a score higher than or equal to 0.2, less than 0.2 to 0.1, and less than 0.1 to form three clusters, in order to better illustrate their connections with other sites (Table 6.3 and Figure 6.3).

a. Links between Bismarck Lapita sites

b. Links between EHB to other Bismarck Lapita sites

c. Links betweem ECA to other Bismarck Lapita sites

d. Links between ECB to other Bismarck Lapita sites

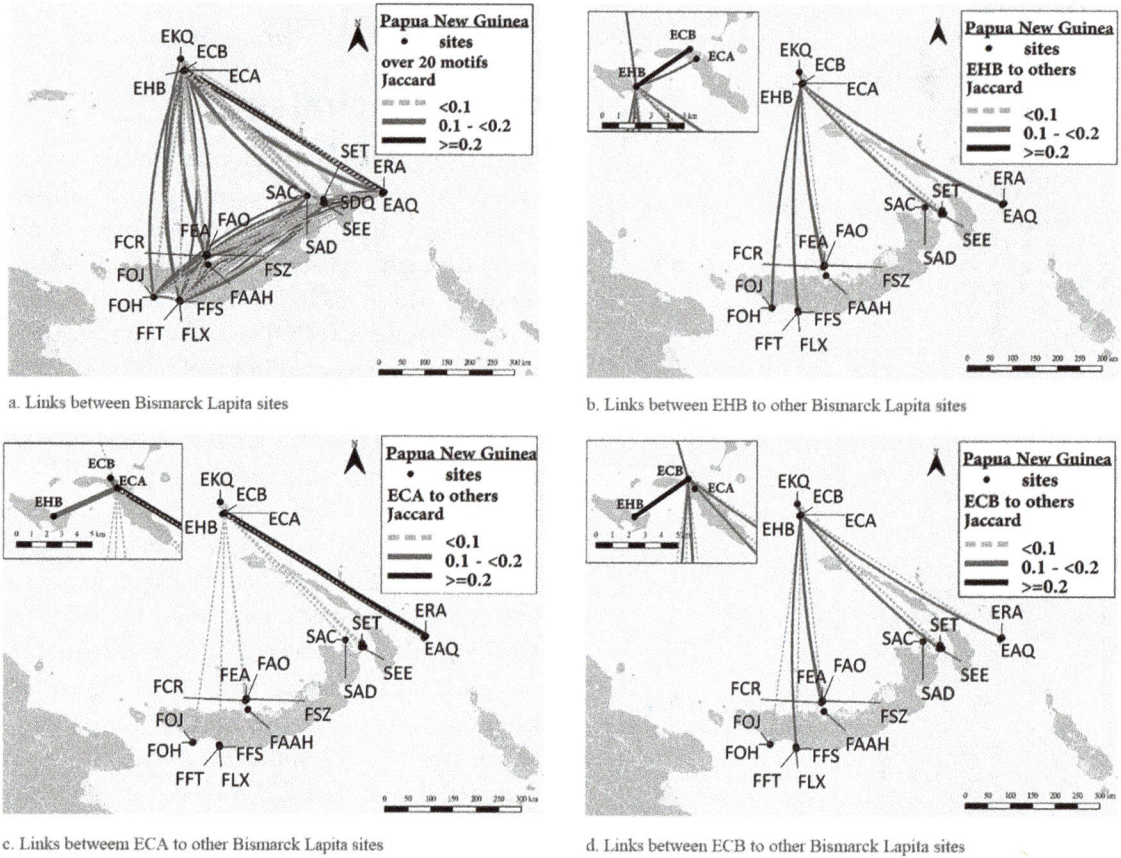

Figure 6.3: Jaccard similarity measures of shared motifs between ECA, ECB and EHB and other Bismarck Archipelago Lapita sites that have more than 20 different motifs recorded in the LPOD.

Source: Authors' illustration.

Table 6.3: Jaccard similarity measures from EHB, ECA and ECB to other Bismarck Lapita pottery assemblages recorded in the LPOD.

Jaccard site	Jaccard similarity score to EHB	Jaccard similarity score to ECB	Jaccard similarity score to ECA	Jaccard similarity score to ERA	Region
EHB	x	**0.214**	0.105	0.118	Mussau
ECB	**0.214**	x	0.143	0.154	Mussau
EKQ	0.191	0.137	0.051	0.065	Mussau
FFS	0.171	0.141	0.062	0.077	Kandrian
FEA	0.170	0.144	0.080	0.091	CN New Britain
SEE	0.160	0.144	0.080	0.105	Duke of Yorks
FSZ	0.137	0.082	0.036	0.039	CN New Britain
FFT	0.136	0.084	0.038	0.040	Kandrian
FCR	0.130	0.116	0.058	0.073	CN New Britain
EAQ	0.126	0.100	0.046	0.050	TLTF
FOH	0.124	0.097	0.039	0.049	Arawe
FLX	0.119	0.073	0.024	0.029	Kandrian
ERA	0.118	0.154	**0.219**	x	TLTF
FOJ	0.109	0.099	0.032	0.043	Arawe

Jaccard site	Jaccard similarity score to EHB	Jaccard similarity score to ECB	Jaccard similarity score to ECA	Jaccard similarity score to ERA	Region
ECA	0.105	0.143	x	**0.219**	Mussau
SAC	0.094	0.064	0.024	0.033	Watom
SAD	0.075	0.063	0.026	0.032	Watom
SET	0.071	0.050	0.017	0.019	Duke of Yorks
SDQ	0.064	0.050	0.013	0.019	Duke of Yorks
FAAH	0.057	0.046	0.015	0.015	CN New Britain
FAO	0.050	0.029	0.015	0.012	CN New Britain

Note: Jaccard similarity measures from EHB, ECA and ECB to other Bismarck Lapita pottery assemblages that have more than 20 different motifs recorded in the LPOD, sorted from highest to lowest based on the weight to EHB. The highest scores of each site are marked by bold font, those higher than 0.1 marked by italicised font. 'CN' should be read as 'Central North', and 'TLTF' as 'the Tabar–Lihir–Tanga–Feni chain'. Red highlight indicates first level of signficance

Source: Authors' data.

Because only a few assemblages in the Bismarck Archipelago have been fully recorded in the LPOD at this stage, we lack detailed information from sites located on Manus, New Ireland or the Arawe Islands. We also lack records from nearby Emirau Island where Lapita site Tamuarawai (EQS) has been reported (Summerhayes et al. 2010). This no doubt restricts our ability to fully understand the nature of exchange patterns among these islands with the Mussau sites. Future collaborations with archaeologists working on those assemblages are planned.

Analytical results

In contrast with what we observed from the petrographic analysis, in which only four ECA petrographic samples, from Zones C_1 (ECA-67-05-007 and ECA-67-05-011), B_2 (ECA69-01-004), and B_1 (ECA39-02-005) of ECA Area B and B-extension, have been provisionally sourced to the Feni (Anir) Islands, ECA shares the greatest number of motifs and degree of motif similarity with the contemporary Kamgot (ERA) Lapita site (Summerhayes 2007:146) (Table 6.3 and Figure 6.3). Anson had observed a similar pattern from his motif analysis, in which ECA was closely related to Ambitle (Site Malekolon (EAQ)). A second set of Ambitle samples was clustered with those from Talasea, indicating that communities in the TLTF chain shared motifs with Mussau and north New Britain communities (Anson 1986:Fig. 3, 16). ECA also has stronger links to both ECB and EHB, not surprisingly, as these sites were surely part of a single community that persisted over several centuries. However, unlike EHB and ECB, ECA shares a much lower degree of motif similarity with all other Lapita sites located in the Bismarck Archipelago (Table 6.3).

EHB shares the highest degree of motif similarity with ECB and EKQ in the Mussau islands, followed by sites located in the Kandrian region of southern New Britain, central north New Britain, the Duke of Yorks, the TLTF chain, the Arawe Islands and then ECA of Mussau (Table 6.3). It shares a lesser degree of motif similarity (less than 0.1) with SAC and SAD of Watom Island off eastern New Britain, SET and SDQ of the Duke of Yorks, and FAAH and FAO of central north New Britain. This indicates a wide and relatively strong connection between EHB and other Bismarck Lapita sites. ECB shows an almost identical pattern, sharing the strongest similarity with EHB and well connected to other sites, although not so much with ECA. ERA, on the other hand, shares an identical pattern to that of ECA, with the highest similarity with ECA, followed by ECB and EHB of the Mussau Islands, SEE of the Duke of Yorks, and not very much with all other Lapita sites in this region.

The motif similarity pattern analysis demonstrates a connection between Lapita sites located in the Mussau islands, northern coastal and north-eastern New Britain, the Duke of York islands, the southern TLTF chain, south-western New Britain and the Arawe Islands. The first four regions are also consistent with the results of our petrographic analysis. However, the relatively high degree of motif similarity shared between Mussau sites and south-western New Britain and the nearby Arawe Islands is unexpected, since petrographically no thin section samples of Mussau Lapita sites have been sourced to this region.

a. Undulated motif theme

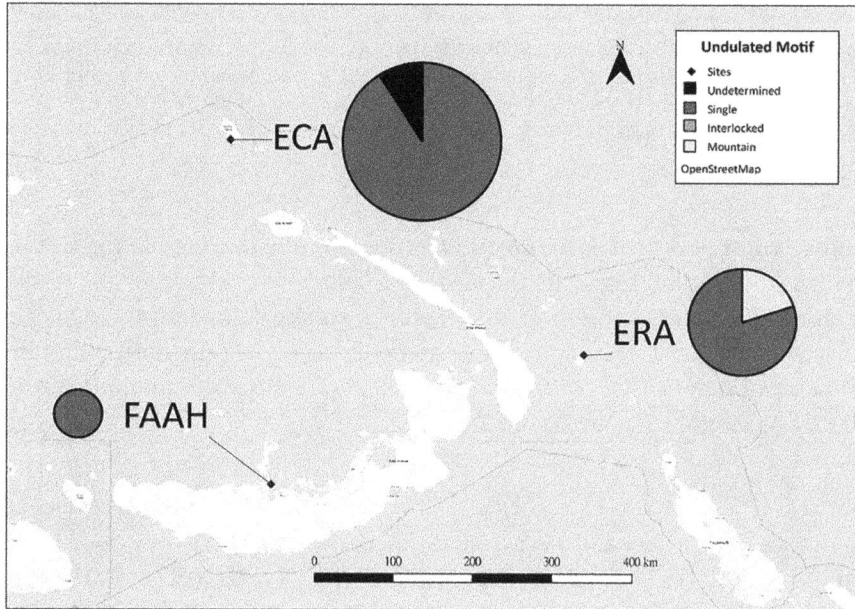

b. Zigzag motif theme

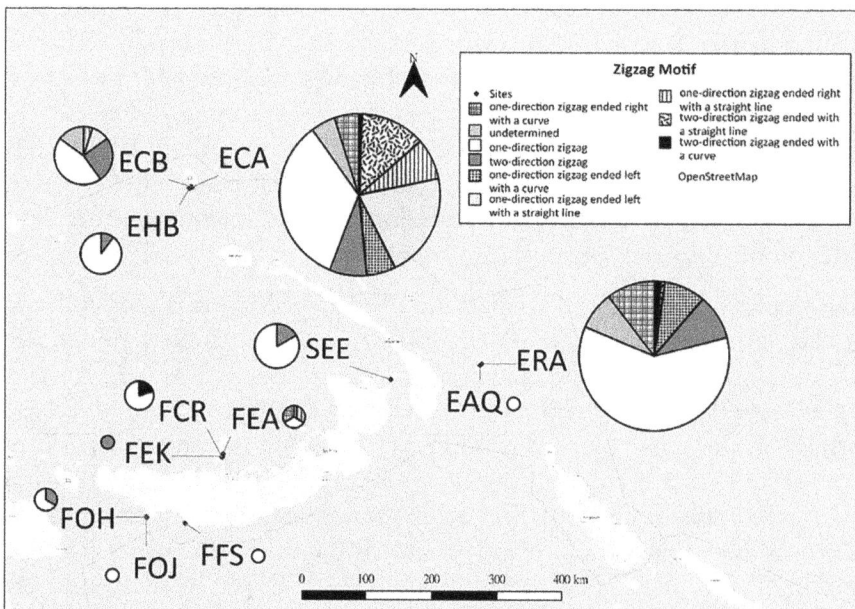

Figure 6.4: Distribution of undulated (a) and zigzag (b) motif themes among Bismarck Lapita sites.
Source: Authors' illustration.

Table 6.4: Distribution of different subcategories of both undulated and zigzag motif themes among Bismarck Lapita sites.

(A) Distribution of the undulated motif theme.			
undulated sub	**ECA**	**ERA**	**FAAH**
undetermined	1	–	–
single	10	4	1
interlocked	–	–	–
mountain	–	1	–
Total	11	5	1

(B) Distribution of the zigzag motif theme.												
zigzag sub	**EHB**	**ECA**	**ECB**	**ERA**	**EAQ**	**FEA**	**FFS**	**FEK**	**FOH**	**FOJ**	**FCR**	**SEE**
undetermined	–	8	3	11	–	–	–	–	–	–	–	–
one-direction zigzag ended right with a curve	–	8	–	14	–	1	–	–	–	–	–	–
one-direction zigzag	9	53	9	81	1	1	1	–	2	1	4	10
two-direction zigzag	1	12	5	13	–	–	–	1	1	–	–	2
one-direction zigzag ended left with a curve	–	9	–	12	–	–	–	–	–	–	–	–
one-direction zigzag ended left with a straight line	–	33	2	–	–	–	–	–	–	–	–	–
one-direction zigzag ended right with a straight line	–	13	1	–	–	1	–	–	–	–	–	–
two-direction zigzag ended with a straight line	–	20	–	1	–	–	–	–	–	–	–	–
two-direction zigzag ended with a curve	–	1	–	2	–	–	–	–	–	–	1	–
Total	10	157	20	134	1	3	1	1	3	1	5	12

Source: Authors' data.

In terms of major motif themes that are usually executed on the main surface of a vessel or ceramic object such as a pedestal stand, ECA and ERA have the highest number of undulated and zigzag motifs among all 70 Lapita sites in the Bismarck Archipelago recorded so far in the LPOD. This clearly sets both of them apart from other Bismarck Lapita sites (Table 6.4 and Figure 6.4). A previous motif distribution pattern analysis shows that only the single undulated category of the undulated motif theme is widely shared among Lapita sites in Papua New Guinea, the Solomon Islands, Vanuatu and New Caledonia. It does not appear in the Fiji–Tonga–Samoa region (Chiu 2019:324, Table 15.10). Single undulated motifs appear exclusively in ECA (Mussau), ERA (Anir) and FAAH (Talasea, New Britain) assemblages in the entire Bismarck Archipelago, while a subcategory of the undulated motif theme ('mountain') appears only at ERA (Anir) (Table 6.4A). Furthermore, ECA and ERA have the highest number and diversity of zigzag motifs among Bismarck Lapita sites (Table 6.4B), while only the simplest one-directional zigzag subtype occurs in most other Lapita assemblages throughout the whole Lapita realm (Chiu 2019:322, Table 15.8). What we see in the undulated and zigzag motif themes may be an indicator of a set of firmly controlled motif categories that were never widely shared beyond ECA and ERA.

Due to the high variation in the size of individual Lapita pottery assemblages recorded in the LPOD, sites with only a small number of motifs may get a much higher Jaccard similarity score as most of them share sets of the more geometric motifs, or the so-called zone markers that are commonly found on fragmented sherds. Finding the more complex 'index motifs' such as the zigzag and the undulated major motif themes may be a further way to investigate social relationships through motif analysis, as these motif themes are more likely to be used as group symbols with restricted usage among different social groups. Additional petrographic studies will surely enhance our current understanding of the Lapita exchange network.

Discussion

We have tried to assess the social connectedness of geographically dispersed communities during the Lapita period based on the assumption that people who produced and used pots decorated with the same motifs or their alloforms had a higher degree of social connectedness than those who do not share many motifs, and by assuming that people tend to acquire more pots and other materials from those with whom they have frequent exchanges or visits. As Lapita people also exchanged obsidian tools and raw materials rather extensively, comparing distributions of obsidian and pots may also help us better understand the dynamics of Lapita social networks.

As Summerhayes and others have previously noted, sites located in Mussau, New Britain, the Arawes, the Duke of Yorks, Anir and Nissan Islands during the early Lapita era all imported obsidian mainly from the Kutau/Bao source close to the Talasea region of West New Britain. In contrast, only Mussau and Kamgot in the Anir Islands acquired 20–50 per cent of their obsidian from the Lou source that was previously exclusively used by the Manus community in the pre-Lapita era (Allen 1996; Ambrose 2002; Fredericksen 1997a, b; Summerhayes 2009:116, Fig. 12; Summerhayes et al. 2014; Torrence et al. 2009:141). Lou obsidian was very rare in sites located on New Britain and the Duke of Yorks (Summerhayes 2003a:137) during this period. Over time, Mussau communities imported more obsidian from the nearby Lou source while importing less obsidian from New Britain. Kamgot went through a similar temporal shift in terms of obsidian exchange (Summerhayes 2009:116, Fig. 12-14), as did the Nissan Islands sites located further south of Anir (Spriggs 1991:241). On the south-west coast of New Britain, only a few pieces of Lou obsidian were found in Late or Post-Lapita times at the site of Apalo (FOH) on the Arawe Islands (Henderson 2017:62). Our petrographic results likewise suggest a large number of pots were likely imported into ECA from Lou Island and/or the nearby rhyolitic islands, beginning around 3234–3089 cal. BP and associated with the earliest Zone C_3 at ECA Area B and Area B-extension (Table 6.2). Pots imported from the northern part of New Britain where the Kutau/Bao obsidian source is located are found in slightly later stratigraphic contexts associated with Zone C_2 at ECA Area B and Area B-extension and are not as numerous as those acquired from Lou Island and/or the nearby rhyolitic islands. This pattern of ceramic exchange fits with the frequency patterns identified from the obsidian sources mentioned above.

Kirch has suggested that Lou obsidian might have reached the southern TLTF chain Lapita sites via Mussau (Kirch et al. 1991:158). Therefore, the high frequency of motifs shared by Mussau and Kamgot correlates with the fact that both acquired the majority of their obsidian from the Lou Island source in the Admiralties. As pots made from the TLTF chain only appear in Mussau assemblages in Zone C_1 of Area B and B-extension at ECA, these may represent stronger social networks between these two sites postdating 3000–2800 BP. Interestingly, this corresponds to an increased usage of Admiralty Islands obsidian at Kamgot (ERA) (Summerhayes 2009:116, Fig. 12-13). Therefore, at least in the Mussau and the TLTF chain regions, we find strong convergence in pottery and obsidian exchange patterns, suggesting that Lapita social networks, at certain times and places, involved multiple forms of material culture.

Motifs shared among Mussau assemblages that are similar to the ones located in central north New Britain—near Talasea and in the Arawe Islands—do not correlate with obsidian distribution patterns. Although pots made in central north New Britain did reach the Mussau islands, none from the Arawe and the Kandrian areas have been identified, despite the fact that the region's FOH and FOJ sites are said to be contemporary with ECB and ECA in Mussau (Summerhayes 2007:145) and the fact that sites located in this region also share motifs with Mussau sites (Figure 6.4). As Arawe and Kandrian consistently used Kutau/Bao obsidian without importing Admiralty obsidian before, during and after the entire Lapita sequence, the social and economic factors that led these two regions to network with Mussau communities are still unknown.

Petrographic analysis of 10 EHB and eight ECB samples provide little information on their possible sources. Only one ECB sample can be sourced to Mussau or basaltic Manus; one EHB sample to Lou and nearby rhyolitic islands. Another EHB sample can be sourced to basic and intermediate volcanic areas that include Mussau, basaltic Manus and Lavongai (or adjacent parts of New Ireland). Two sherds from each site can only be sourced to weathered intermediate plutonic/sub-volcanic areas or sedimentary areas, a vast region covering Manus, Lavongai (or adjacent parts of New Ireland), northern New Britain near Watom Island and plutonic parts of New Ireland. The rest of the samples cannot be sourced (see Appendix: Table 6.S1). Dickinson had reported that six Lapita sherds sent to him by Summerhayes from Kamgot were all locally made on the Anir Island of the TLTF chain (Dickinson 2000b). What we see here is that EHB and ECB share a higher degree of motif similarity with many sites located on New Britain, Duke of Yorks and the TLTF chain, yet there is little petrographic evidence that inhabitants of these two sites imported pots from all these areas. ECA has many exotic pots sourced to various regions, while ERA does not have any, yet these two sites are paired with one another in term of motifs, and do not share as many motifs with all other sites in the Bismarck Archipelago.

Summerhayes (2000) has proposed that Lapita communities shared not just pots, but more importantly, the concepts of how to make and decorate pots. He also demonstrated that Lapita pots were rarely transported between sites located on the north and south coasts of New Britain, and that early Lapita potters of south-western New Britain probably used locally available clays, tempered with grains collected from various river systems along the south coast of New Britain to Arawe region, to produce similarly shaped and decorated pots (Summerhayes 2003b:140). Samples from our two pastes group (G9), however rare, also show a similar pattern of a vessel using either different clays mixed with similar tempers, or similar clay with different tempers. Lapita potters used locally available raw materials to produce pots carrying similar motifs that were shared over extensive regions encompassing several island groups. Although direct material evidence through imported pottery for shared motifs is extremely rare, similar motifs with subtle differences can be traced throughout the Lapita realm (Chiu 2019). Further comparison among the Bismarck Lapita sites is needed before we can explore issues such as chronological or spatial patterns of preferred motifs or motif themes across this region. Yet, from data we have gathered so far, it is clear that inhabitants of the Mussau islands maintained close relationships with communities surrounding their island group for both obsidian and pottery, especially with Manus to the west and sites located on northern and north-eastern New Britain. Links to various parts of New Ireland were established quite early on as well, yet the connection to the TLTF chain was perhaps, based on our current data, a few decades later.

Conclusion

Comparing connection maps generated by the results of our petrographic and motif analysis of the Mussau sites, it is clear that the communities of the Bismarck Archipelago were highly connected. While the idea of how to make pots and of what motifs to be employed might be shared widely, even spreading beyond the Bismarck Archipelago and well into Remote Oceania, the physical sources of pots used at ECA were limited to Manus, New Ireland, the TLTF chain and north-eastern and central north of New Britain. Paired with the results from the obsidian sources and distribution ranges, we propose that there might have been at least two social networks existing in the Bismarck Archipelago. The first realm includes the Admiralties, the Mussau islands, the Duke of Yorks, the TLTF chain and possibly also parts of northern New Ireland and northern New Britain. Some sites (ECA and ERA in particular) of this first network share a high degree of motif similarity to many early Lapita sites outside of the Bismarcks. The second realm perhaps encompasses central north and southern New Britain including the Arawe Islands, although there is currently no evidence for the transport of pottery from the south coast of New Britain to the Mussau Islands.

Acknowledgements

We are delighted to offer this paper to Glenn Summerhayes as a sign of our respect and admiration for his contributions to Pacific archaeology, especially in the Bismarck Archipelago and New Guinea Highlands where he has helped to transform our understanding of the regional history. For each of us, in different ways, he has been a teacher, mentor, field companion and co-author on many projects, but most importantly we thank Glenn for his collegial friendship and ability to bring humour and common sense appropriate to every occasion. May our friendships continue for many more years.

We thank the Bishop Museum for lending us Papua New Guinean petrographic thin sections first worked on by the late William Dickinson. We also thank the School of Anthropology, University of Arizona, and the Archaeological Research Facility, University of California at Berkeley, for providing access to their laboratories. We want to thank Si-ru Chen and Jia-Zun Chang and the team members of Lapita Pottery Online Database for working on vessel and motif analyses over the years. We thank also Hsiung-Ming Liao for teaching Chiu and her assistants how to use QGIS, and Jennifer Kahn and Nick Hogg for commenting and proofreading drafts of this paper.

Finally, we would also like to thank the Ministry of Science and Technology (MOST-106-2410-H-001-023-MY2) and Academia Sinica (AS-TP-107-L18-2) for funding this project under Chiu's directorship. The Lapita Pottery Online Database has been funded by Academia Sinica through awards to Chiu since 2005.

References

Allen, J. 1996. The pre-Austronesian settlement of Island Melanesia: Implications for Lapita archaeology. *Transactions of the American Philosophical Society* 86(5), Prehistoric Settlement of the Pacific:11–27. doi.org/10.2307/1006618.

Allen, J., J. Specht, W. Ambrose and D.E. Yen 1984. *Lapita Homeland Project: Report of the 1984 field season.* ANU Press, Canberra.

Ambrose, W.R. 2002. From very old to new, obsidian artefacts in the Admiralty Islands. In C. Kaufmann, C.K. Schmid and S. Ohnemus (eds), *Admiralty Islands: Art from the south seas*, pp. 67–72. Museum Rietburg, Zurich.

Anson, D. 1983. Lapita pottery of the Bismarck Archipelago and its affinities. Unpublished PhD thesis, University of Sydney, Sydney.

Anson, D. 1986. Lapita pottery of the Bismarck Archipelago and its affinities. *Archaeology in Oceania* 21:157–165. doi.org/10.1002/j.1834-4453.1986.tb00144.x.

Bafmatuk, F., B. Egloff and R. Kaiku 1980. Islanders: Past and present. *Hemisphere* 25:77–81.

Blake, D.H. and Y. Miezitis 1967. *Geology of Bougainville and Buka Islands, New Guinea.* Vol. 93. Bureau of Mineral Resources, Geology and Geophysics, Canberra.

Chiu, S. 2019. Measuring social distances with shared Lapita motifs: Current results and challenges. In S. Bedford and M. Spriggs (eds), *Debating Lapita: Distribution, chronology, society and subsistence*, pp. 307–334. ANU Press, Canberra. doi.org/10.22459/ta52.2019.15.

Chiu, S., Y. Su, D. Killick and P. Kirch. In preparation. Petrographic results of Lapita pottery sampled from the Mussau assemblages.

Davies, H.L. 2012. The geology of New Guinea—the cordilleran margin of the Australian continent. *Episodes–Journal of International Geosciences* 35:87–102. doi.org/10.18814/epiiugs/2012/v35i1/008.

Dickinson, W.R. 1996. Sand tempers in Lapita sherds from the Mussau Islands. Petrographic Report WRD-123. Unpublished report on file with author, Academia Sinica, Taipei.

Dickinson, W.R. 1997. Inherent geologic ambiguity of potential sources for exotic Mussau Lapita temper on Manus, New Hanover (Lavongai), and New Ireland. Petrographic Report WRD-150. Unpublished report on file with author, Academia Sinica, Taipei.

Dickinson, W.R. 1998. Temper sands in Lapita sherds from the Kreslo site, New Britain. Petrographic Report WRD-175. Unpublished report on file with author, Academia Sinica, Taipei.

Dickinson, W.R. 2000a. Petrography of sand tempers in prehistoric Watom sherds and comparison with other temper suites of the Bismarck Archipelago. *New Zealand Journal of Archaeology* 20 (1998):161–182.

Dickinson, W.R. 2000b. Petrography of temper sands in Lapita sherds from the Kamgot site on Ambitle in the Feni Islands of the TLTF chain northeast of New Ireland. Petrographic Report WRD-200. Unpublished report on file with author, Academia Sinica, Taipei.

Dickinson, W.R. 2004. Petrography of sand tempers in Lapita sherds from the Balbalankin site on Anir (Ambitle) in the TLTF chain off New Ireland. Petrographic Report WRD-244. Unpublished report on file with author, Academia Sinica, Taipei.

Dickinson, W.R. 2006. *Temper sands in prehistoric Oceanian pottery: Geotectonics, sedimentology, petrography, provenance*. Geological Society of America Special Paper 406. The Geological Society of America, Boulder. doi.org/10.1130/2006.2406.

Dickinson, W.R. 2021a. Table S12.8. Frequency percentages of grain types in Types CD opaque-rich placer sands of Mussau tempers for Talepakemalai. In P.V. Kirch (ed.), *Talepakemalai: Lapita and its Transformations in the Mussau Islands of Near Oceania*. Cotsen Institute of Archaeology Press, Los Angeles. doi.org/10.25346/S6/GQBYJZ.

Dickinson, W.R. 2021b. Sand tempers in Mussau ceramics: Evidence for ceramic transfer from multiple unspecified localities with the Bismarck Archipelago. In P.V. Kirch (ed.), *Talepakemalai: Lapita and its Transformations in the Mussau Islands of Near Oceania*, pp. 375–390. Cotsen Institute of Archaeology Press, Los Angeles. doi.org/10.2307/j.ctv27tctrd.21.

Egloff, B.J. 1975. Archaeological investigations in the coastal Madang area and on Eloaue Island of the St Matthias Group. *Records of the Papua New Guinea Public Museum and Art Gallery* 5:15–43.

Fredericksen, C. 1997a. The maritime distribution of Bismarck Archipelago obsidian and Island Melanesian prehistory. *The Journal of the Polynesian Society* 106(4):375–393. www.jstor.org/stable/pdf/20706754.pdf.

Fredericksen, C. 1997b. Changes in Admiralty Islands obsidian source use: The view from Pamwak. *Archaeology in Oceania* 32:30–35. doi.org/10.1002/j.1834-4453.1997.tb00372.x.

Henderson, R. 2017. The changing nature of Lapita mobility and interaction: Insight from sourcing and technological analyses of obsidian from Apalo, West New Britain Province, Papua New Guinea. Unpublished Bachelor of Arts (Hons) thesis, University of Otago, Dunedin.

Ho, J.W.I. and P.S. Quinn 2021. Intentional clay-mixing in the production of traditional and ancient ceramics and its identification in thin section. *Journal of Archaeological Science: Reports* 37:102945. doi.org/10.1016/j.jasrep.2021.102945.

Hohnen, P.D. 1978. *Geology of New Ireland, Papua New Guinea*. Bulletin 194 (PNG 12), Australian Government Publishing Service, Northfield.

Hunt, T.L. 1989. Lapita ceramic exchange in the Mussau Islands, Papua New Guinea. Unpublished PhD thesis, University of Washington, Seattle.

Jaques, A.L. 1980. *Admiralty Islands, Papua New Guinea*. Papua New Guinea Geological Survey 1:250,000 Geological Series Explanatory Notes SN55-10, SA/55-11. Libra Press Limited, Hong Kong.

Kirch, P.V. 1987. Lapita and Oceanic cultural origins: Excavations in the Mussau Islands, Bismarck Archipelago, 1985. *Journal of Field Archaeology* 14:163–180. doi.org/10.1179/009346987792208493.

Kirch, P.V. 1997. *The Lapita peoples: Ancestors of the Oceanic world*. The peoples of South-East Asia and the Pacific. Blackwell Publishers, Cambridge.

Kirch, P.V. (ed.) 2001. *Lapita and its transformations in Near Oceania: Archaeological investigations in the Mussau Islands, Papua New Guinea, 1985–88*, vol. 1: *Introduction, excavations, chronology*. Archaeological Research Facility Contribution 59. University of California at Berkeley, Berkeley.

Kirch, P.V. 2021a. Lapita and its transformations in the Mussau Islands. In P.V. Kirch (ed.), *Talepakemalai: Lapita and its transformations in the Mussau Islands of Near Oceania*, pp. 509–522. Cotsen Institute of Archaeology Press, Los Angeles. doi.org/10.2307/j.ctv27tctrd.27.

Kirch, P.V. 2021b. Radiocarbon dating and chronology of the Mussau Sites. In P.V. Kirch (ed.), *Talepakemalai: Lapita and its transformations in the Mussau Islands of Near Oceania*, pp. 137–163. Cotsen Institute of Archaeology Press, Los Angeles. doi.org/10.2307/j.ctv27tctrd.14.

Kirch, P.V. (ed.) 2021c. *Talepakemalai: Lapita and its transformations in the Mussau Islands of Near Oceania.* Cotsen Institute of Archaeology Press, Los Angeles. doi.org/10.2307/j.ctv27tctrd.

Kirch, P.V. and S. Chiu 2021. Ceramic assemblages of the Mussau Islands. In P.V. Kirch (ed.), *Talepakemalai: Lapita and its transformations in the Mussau Islands of Near Oceania*, pp. 269–373. Cotsen Institute of Archaeology Press, Los Angeles. doi.org/10.2307/j.ctv27tctrd.20.

Kirch, P.V., T.L. Hunt, M.I. Weisler, V. Butler and M.S. Allen 1991. Mussau Islands prehistory: Results of the 1985–86 excavations. In J. Allen and C. Gosden (eds), *Report of the Lapita Homeland Project*, pp. 144–163. Department of Prehistory, The Australian National University, Canberra.

Kirch, P.V., S. Chiu and Y.-Y. Su 2015. Lapita ceramic vessel forms of the Talepakemalai site, Mussau Islands, Papua New Guinea. In C. Sand, S. Chiu and N. Hogg (eds), *The Lapita Cultural Complex in time and space: Expansion routes, chronologies and typologies*, pp. 49–62. Instiut d'archeologie de la Nouvelle-Calédonie et du Pacifique, Nouméa.

Leclerc, M. 2020. The natural variability of clay and its impact on provenance study of pottery in Vanuatu and further afield. *Geoarchaeology* 35(4):562–590. doi.org/10.1002/gea.21780.

Lindley, I.D. 2006. Extensional and vertical tectonics in the New Guinea islands: Implications for island arc evolution. In G. Lavecchia and G. Scalera (eds), *Frontiers in earth sciences: New ideas and interpretation*, pp. 403–426. Editrice Compositori, Roma.

Martinez, F. and B. Taylor 1996. Backarc spreading, rifting, and microplate rotation, between transform faults in the Manus Basin. *Marine Geophysical Researches* 18(2–4):203–224. doi.org/10.1007/bf00286078.

Page, R.W. and R.J. Ryburn 1977. K-Ar ages and geological relations of intrusive rocks in New Britain. *Pacific Geology* 12:99–105.

Real, R. and J.M. Vargas 1996. The probabilistic basis of Jaccard's index of similarity. *Systematic Biology* 45(3):380–385. doi.org/10.1093/sysbio/45.3.380.

Rogerson, R. 1989. *The geology and mineral resources of Bougainville and Buka islands, Papua New Guinea.* Vol. 16. Geological Survey of Papua New Guinea, Port Moresby.

Ryburn, R.J. 1976. *Cape Raoult–Arawe, Papua New Guinea.* Papua New Guinea Geological Survey 1:250,000 Geological Series Explanatory Notes SB/55-8, SB/55-12. Australian Government Publishing Service, Canberra.

Sheppard, S. and L.C. Cranfield 2012. *Geological framework and mineralization of Papua New Guinea-An update.* Vol. 65. Mineral Resources Authority, Papua New Guinea, Port Moresby.

Spriggs, M. 1991. Nissan, the island in the middle. Summary report on excavations at the north end of the Solomons and the south end of the Bismarcks. In J. Allen and C. Gosden (eds), *Report of the Lapita Homeland Project*, pp. 222–243. Department of Prehistory, Research School of Pacific Studies, Australian National University Press, Canberra.

Stewart, W.D. and M.J. Sandy 1988. Geology of New Ireland and Djaul Islands, Northeastern Papua New Guinea. In M.S. Marlow, S.V. Dadisman and N.F. Exon (eds), *Geology and offshore resources of Pacific Island Arcs—New Ireland and Manus region, Papua New Guinea*, pp. 13–30. Circum-Pacific Council for Energy and Mineral Resources, Houston, TX, USA.

Summerhayes, G.R. 2000. *Lapita interaction.* Terra Australis 15. Pandanus Books, Research School of Pacific and Asian Studies, The Australian National University, Canberra. openresearch-repository.anu.edu.au/handle/1885/127430.

Summerhayes, G.R. 2003a. The rocky road: The selection and transport of Admiralties obsidian to Lapita communities. *Australian Archaeology* 57:135–143. doi.org/10.1080/03122417.2003.11681772.

Summerhayes, G.R. 2003b. Modelling differences between Lapita obsidian and pottery distribution patterns in the Bismarck Archipelago, Papua New Guinea. In C. Sand (ed.), *Pacific archaeology: Assessments and prospects (Proceedings of the International Conference for the 50th Anniversary of the First Lapita Excavation, Koné-Nouméa 2002)*, pp. 135–145. Département Archéologie, Service des Musées et du Patrimoine de Nouvelle-Calédonie, Nouméa, New Caledonia.

Summerhayes, G.R. 2007. The rise and transformations of Lapita in the Bismarck Archipelago. In S. Chiu and C. Sand (eds), *From Southeast Asia to the Pacific: Archaeological perspectives on the Austronesian expansion and the Lapita Cultural Complex*, pp. 141–184. Center for Archaeological Studies, Research Center for Humanities and Social Sciences, Academia Sinica, Taipei.

Summerhayes, G.R. 2009. Obsidian network patterns in Melanesia: Sources, characterisation and distribution. *Indo-Pacific Prehistory Association Bulletin* 29(2009):109–123.

Summerhayes, G.R., E. Matisoo-Smith, H. Mandui, J. Allen, J. Specht, N. Hogg and S. McPherson 2010. Tamuarawai (EQS): An Early Lapita Site on Emirau, New Ireland, PNG. *Journal of Pacific Archaeology* 1(1):62–75.

Summerhayes, G.R., J. Kennedy, E. Matisoo-Smith, H. Mandui, W. Ambrose, C. Allen, C. Reepmeyer, R. Torrence. and F. Wadra 2014. Lepong: A new obsidian source in the Admiralty Islands, Papua New Guinea. *Geoarchaeology* 29(3):238–248. doi.org/10.1002/gea.21475.

Thilenius, G. 1927. *Ergebnisse der Südsee-Expedition 1908–1910*. Vol. I Allgemeines. L. Friederichsen & Co., Hamburg.

Torrence, R., P. Swadling, N. Kononenko, W. Ambrose, P.I.P. Rath and M.D. Glascock 2009. Mid-Holocene social interaction in Melanesia: New evidence from hammer-dressed obsidian stemmed tools. *Asian Perspectives* 48(1):119–148. doi.org/10.1353/asi.0.0014.

Warin, O.N. and A.R. Jensen 1959. *Report of investigation of islands in the Territory of Papua and New Guinea, phosphate survey, 1958*. Bureau of Mineral Resources, Geology and Geophysics, Canberra.

Wu, P. 2016. What happened at the end of Lapita: Lapita to Post-Lapita pottery transition in West New Britain, Papua New Guinea. Unpublished PhD thesis, University of Otago, Dunedin. ourarchive.otago.ac.nz/handle/10523/6817.

Appendix: Supplementary table

Table 6.S1: Summary of petrographic results. Dickinson's original grouping and inferred sources are included for comparison.

Thin section ID	New group	Subgroup	Dickinson's group	Sources inferred by Dickinson	Probable resource		sample ID
					Sources inferred by us	The feature of geological area	
ECA002	G1 Reef detritus-predominant fabric	Sub1 Typical modern reef debris			unknown	modern reef debris & limeclast & volcanic lithic	ECA31-04-004
ECA008							ECA31-07-037
ECA023							ECA32-07-037
ECA035							ECA36-15-008
ECA067							ECA50-05-053+50-06-005
ECA070							ECA52-02-018
ECA073							ECA53-03-038
ECA097							ECA68-01-029
ECA104							ECA68-09-007
ECA105							ECA68-09-008
ECA113							ECA93-04-006-Pot
EHB001							EHB08-07-003
ECA121							ECA-V-030
ECA124							ECA-V-049
ECA128							ECA-V-062
ECA137							ECA-V-130
ECA140							ECA-V-143
ECA148							ECA-V-235
ECA151							ECA-V-239
ECA155							ECA-V-243
ECA161							ECA47-07-026
ECA164							ECA42-09-030
ECB008							ECB07-07-020

Thin section ID	New group	Subgroup	Dickinson's group	Sources inferred by Dickinson	Probable resource Sources inferred by us	The feature of geological area	sample ID
EHB02-03-008			A	unknown			EHB02-03-008
ECA88-04-012			A				ECA88-04-012
ECA87-05-006			B	Admiralty bimodal zone—rhyolitic to rhyodacitic			ECA87-05-006
ECA69-05-007			B				ECA69-05-007
ECA66-08-024			B				ECA66-08-024
ECA007		Sub2 Homogenous reddish clay			unknown	modern reef debris & limeclast	ECA31-07-033
ECA045							ECA39-08-005+39-09-004
ECA069							ECA52-02-013
ECA106							ECA69-02-003
ECA130							ECA-V-089
ECA141							ECA-V-173
ECA149							ECA-V-237
ECA160							ECA40-10-007
ECB007							ECB07-03-008
EHB01-09-006			B	Admiralty bimodal zone—rhyolitic to rhyodacitic			EHB01-09-006
ECA66-03-007			B				ECA66-03-007
ECA006		Sub3 Probable clay bulks			unknown	modern reef debris, less grains	ECA31-07-028
ECA011							ECA31-08-016
ECA077							ECA54-02-051
ECA078							ECA54-02-055
ECA091							ECA67-03-017
ECA093							ECA67-04-011
ECA107							ECA69-02-007
ECA110							ECA69-05-001+002+009
ECA115							ECA-V-031
ECA143							ECA-V-196
ECA69-06-001			A	Admiralty bimodal zone—rhyolitic to rhyodacitic			ECA69-06-001
ECA88-04-007			A	unknown			ECA88-04-007

Thin section ID	New group	Subgroup	Dickinson's group	Sources inferred by Dickinson	Probable resource: Sources inferred by us	The feature of geological area	sample ID
ECA005		Sub4 Weathered volcanic lithic			unknown	modern reef debris & heavily weathered volcanic lithic	ECA31-07-021
ECA013							ECA31-10-020
ECA020							ECA32-05-004
ECA031							ECA35-12-024
ECA063							ECA50-03-024
ECA064							ECA50-04-020_046
ECA068							ECA52-02-011
ECA071							ECA52-03-026+53-02-032
ECA079							ECA54-02-056
ECA147							ECA-V-234
ECA154							ECA-V-242
ECA88-07-004			A	unknown			ECA88-07-004
ECA018		Sub5 Yellowish-grey clay mineral			unknown	modern reef debris with pale yellow matrix	ECA32-04-003
ECA081							ECA54-06-014
ECA134							ECA-V-105
EHB01-05-012			A	unknown			EHB01-05-012
ECA88-04-004			B	Admiralty bimodal zone—rhyolitic to rhyodacitic			ECA88-04-004
ECA66-08-015			A				ECA66-08-015
EHB01-04-019			B				EHB01-04-019
ECA072	G2 Reef detritus—predominant hybrid fabric	Sub1 Volcanic cone related			Volcanic zone along the north coast of New Britain	acid, intermediate and basic volcanic	ECA53-03-009-Pot
ECA085							ECA66-03-019
ECA090							ECA67-02-023
ECA100							ECA68-06-009
ECA116							ECA-V-001
ECA019							ECA32-05-003

Thin section ID	New group	Subgroup	Dickinson's group	Sources inferred by Dickinson	Probable resource — Sources inferred by us	Probable resource — The feature of geological area	sample ID
ECA022		Sub2 Heavy mineral			Mussau or basaltic Manus, Manus or Lavongai (or adjacent parts of New Ireland)	modern reef debris & basic volcanic & intermediate volcanic area	ECA32-07-022
ECA034							ECA36-14-024+029
ECA051							ECA40-06-008
ECA092							ECA67-04-010
ECA098							ECA68-03-011
ECA132							ECA-V-095
ECA133							ECA-V-107
ECA138							ECA-V-132
ECA159							ECA38-08-033
ECA166							ECA53-02-035
EHB003							EHB-V-003
ECA90-02-001			H	Manus, and Lavongai (and adjacent parts of New Ireland), andesitic-dacitic volcanic rocks, associated in some instances with cogenetic subvolcanic hypabyssal intrusions			ECA90-02-001
ECA66-03-016A			H				ECA66-03-016A
ECA004		Sub3 Quartz-feldspar			Lou island and the nearby rhyolitic islands	modern reef debris & intermediate-acid/acid volcanic lithic	ECA31-07-009+016+026+0xx
ECA009							ECA31-07-041
ECA010							ECA31-08-015+017
ECA014							ECA32-01-005
ECA016							ECA32-03-009
ECA017							ECA32-04-002
ECA021							ECA32-06-003
ECA024							ECA32-07-051+053
ECA026							ECA32-09-056

Thin section ID	New group	Subgroup	Dickinson's group	Sources inferred by Dickinson	Probable resource		sample ID
					Sources inferred by us	The feature of geological area	
ECA028							ECA33-05-053+058_51-03-029+034
ECA030							ECA34-01-012+34-02-013
ECA032							ECA36-14-004
ECA036							ECA36-18-016+37-07-022
ECA041							ECA37-06-016
ECA042							ECA37-06-033+058
ECA043							ECA37-06-040
ECA050							ECA40-06-005
ECA056							ECA40-11-023
ECA082							ECA54-06-024
ECA083							ECA54-06-027
ECA117							ECA-V-002
ECA118							ECA-V-003
ECA120							ECA-V-026
ECA125							ECA-V-051
ECA152							ECA-V-240
ECA156							ECA14-03-002
ECA162							ECA47-07-027
EHB004							EHB01-04-008
ECA68-03-005			B	Admiralty bimodal zone—rhyolitic to rhyodacitic			ECA68-03-005
ECA67-05-005			B				ECA67-05-005
ECA68-01-024			B				ECA68-01-024
ECA67-06-023			B				ECA67-06-023
ECA66-03-16B			B				ECA66-03-16B
ECA66-07-003			B				ECA66-07-003

Thin section ID	New group	Subgroup	Dickinson's group	Sources inferred by Dickinson	Probable resource		sample ID
					The feature of geological area	Sources inferred by us	
ECA029		Sub4 Slight metamorphism			weathered intermediate plutonic/ sub-volcanic area or sedimentary area	Manus or Lavongai (or adjacent parts of New Ireland), Northern New Britain near Watom, or plutonic parts of New Ireland, near coastline	ECA33-08-100
ECA037							ECA36-19-004
ECA046							ECA39-12-012
ECA049							ECA40-06-004
ECA052							ECA40-07-012+015
ECA053							ECA40-11-012
ECA058							ECA40-11-031
ECA062							ECA50-02-019_020_021
ECA075							ECA53-06-067+082
ECA076							ECA53-06-073
ECA086							ECA66-04-001
ECA087							ECA66-07-026
ECA089							ECA66-08-025
ECA099							ECA68-03-014
ECA103							ECA68-08-008
ECA108							ECA69-03-003
ECA109							ECA69-04-003
ECA112							ECA69-06-015
ECA123							ECA-V-045
ECA126							ECA-V-060
ECA129							ECA-V-082
ECA131							ECA-V-094
ECA142							ECA-V-179
ECA150							ECA-V-238
ECA153							ECA-V-241
ECA163							ECA53-02-029
ECA167							ECA54-01-020
ECA168							ECA17-06-037
EHB002							EHB-V-002

Thin section ID	New group	Subgroup	Dickinson's group	Sources inferred by Dickinson	Probable resource		sample ID
					Sources inferred by us	The feature of geological area	
ECA057	G3 Coral reef detritus–opaque fabric	Sub1 Coral reef detritus			Mussau or basaltic Manus	modern reef debris & placer sand (70%:30%) & basic volcanic area/pyroxene bearing intermediate volcanic	ECA40-11-030
ECA095							ECA67-06-014
ECB001							ECB10-02-015_021
ECA16-08-017			C	Quartz-bearing felsitic tempers derived from Lou			ECA16-08-017
ECA67-06-012			C				ECA67-06-012
ECA66-08-009			C				ECA66-08-009
ECA66-07-016			C				ECA66-07-016
ECA025		Sub2 Sub-volcanic & sediment			Manus or Lavongai (or adjacent parts of New Ireland), Northern New Britain near Watom, or plutonic parts of New Ireland, near coastline	intermediate volcanic/sedimentary area with placer sand	ECA32-08-008
ECA038							ECA36-19-005
ECA047							ECA39-13-007
ECA048							ECA39-13-012
ECA065							ECA50-05-011
ECA080							ECA54-05-004
ECA088							ECA66-08-010
ECA096							ECA67-07-011
ECB002							ECB11-02-013
ECA122							ECA-V-037
ECB009							ECB14-02-014
ECA17-06-020		Sub3 Opaque	C	Quartz-bearing felsitic tempers derived from Lou	Mussau or basaltic Manus	modern reef debris & placer sand (30%:70%) & basic volcanic area/pyroxene bearing intermediate volcanic	ECA17-06-020
ECA66-07-019			C				ECA66-07-019
ECA68-07-006			C				ECA68-07-006
ECA17-06-030			C				ECA17-06-030
ECA68-07-027			C				ECA68-07-027
ECA054	G4 Opaque-dominant fabric				Manus or Lavongai (or adjacent parts of New Ireland)	placer sand & intermediate volcanic area with placer sand	ECA40-11-016
ECA139							ECA-V-015
ECA144							ECA-V-138
ECA145							ECA-V-228
ECA119							ECA67-02-010
ECA19-01-029			D	Quartz-bearing felsitic tempers derived from Lou			ECA19-01-029
ECA67-02-014			D				ECA67-02-014
ECA67-02-010			D				ECA67-02-010

Thin section ID	New group	Subgroup	Dickinson's group	Sources inferred by Dickinson	Probable resource		sample ID
					Sources inferred by us	The feature of geological area	
ECA012	G5 Amphibole-feldspar fabric	Sub1 Metavolcanics absent			unknown basic or intermediate volcanic area	unknown basic or intermediate volcanic area	ECA31-09-040
ECA084							ECA66-02-016+018
ECA127							ECA-V-061
ECA135							ECA-V-125
ECA146							ECA67-02-017
ECA157							ECA33-03-004
ECB004							ECB-V-011
ECA13-01-003			F	Manus, and Lavongai (and adjacent parts of New Ireland), andesitic-dacitic volcanic rocks, associated in some instances with cogenetic subvolcanic hypabyssal intrusions			ECA13-01-003
ECA015		Sub2 Epidote-bearing metavolcanics			Manus or Lavongai (or adjacent parts of New Ireland), Northern New Britain near Watom, or plutonic parts of New Ireland	weathered intermediate plutonic/sub-volcanic area or sedimentary area	ECA32-03-005
ECA074							ECA53-06-027-Pot
ECA027							ECA32-10-008+009
ECA66-07-021			F				ECA66-07-021
ECA67-02-017			F				ECA67-02-017
ECA68-07-010			F				ECA68-07-010
EHB1-03-015			F				EHB1-03-015
ECA16-07-015		Sub3 Prehnite-bearing metavolcanics	F	Manus, and Lavongai (and adjacent parts of New Ireland), andesitic-dacitic volcanic rocks, associated in some instances with cogenetic subvolcanic hypabyssal intrusions	Manus or Lavongai (or adjacent parts of New Ireland), Northern New Britain near Watom, or plutonic parts of New Ireland	weathered intermediate plutonic/sub-volcanic area or sedimentary area	ECA16-07-015
ECA13-02-001			E				ECA13-02-001
ECA18-01-008			E				ECA18-01-008
ECA16-05-003			E				ECA16-05-003
ECA68-03-003			E				ECA68-03-003

Thin section ID	New group	Subgroup	Dickinson's group	Sources inferred by Dickinson	Probable resource		sample ID
					Sources inferred by us	The feature of geological area	
ECA039	G6 Pyroxene volcanic fabric	Sub1 Basic volcanic with red iron oxide			unknown basic volcanic area	unknown basic volcanic area	ECA37-02-006+007
ECA066							ECA50-05-020+023
ECB003							ECB13-02-004
ECA69-02-006			G	Manus, and Lavongai (and adjacent parts of New Ireland), andesitic–dacitic volcanic rocks, associated in some instances with cogenetic subvolcanic hypabyssal intrusions			ECA69-02-006
ECA033		Sub2 Alkali basalt, no lime-green clinopyroxene			TLTF alkalic chain(?)	alkali-rich basic volcanic area	ECA36-14-018
ECA003		Sub3 Intermediate volcanic			unknown intermediate volcanic	unknown intermediate volcanic	ECA31-06-009
ECA114							ECA-V-016
ECA136							ECA-V-127
ECA69-07-027			G	Manus, and Lavongai (and adjacent parts of New Ireland), andesitic–dacitic volcanic rocks, associated in some instances with cogenetic subvolcanic hypabyssal intrusions			ECA69-07-027
ECA69-07-019			G				ECA69-07-019
ECA16-06-017			G				ECA16-06-017
EHB01-06-005			G				EHB01-06-005
ECA87-06-001			G				ECA87-06-001
ECA68-01-042			G				ECA68-01-042
ECA67-06-029			G				ECA67-06-029

Thin section ID	New group	Subgroup	Dickinson's group	Sources inferred by Dickinson	Probable resource		sample ID
					Sources inferred by us	The feature of geological area	
ECA060	G7 Quartz-feldspar fabric	Sub1 Quartz-feldspar fabric with silty clay			Northern New Britain near Watom, or plutonic parts of New Ireland	basic/intermediate/acid sub-volcanic/plutonic area	ECA42-09-050+051
ECA061							ECA47-07-031
ECA90-04-009			J1	Manus, and Lavongai (and adjacent parts of New Ireland), andesitic-dacitic volcanic rocks, associated in some instances with cogenetic subvolcanic hypabyssal intrusions			ECA90-04-009
ECA92-03-003			J2				ECA92-03-003
ECA001		Sub2 Quartz-feldspar fabric with dark matrix			Northern New Britain near Watom, or plutonic parts of New Ireland	basic/intermediate/acid sub-volcanic/plutonic area	ECA14-01-004
ECA040							ECA37-02-009
ECA101							ECA68-07-016
ECA102							ECA68-07-026
ECA165							ECA47-05-010
ECA044	G8 Lime-green clinopyroxene fabric				TLTF alkalic chain	alkali-rich basic volcanic area	ECA39-02-005
ECA17-07-043			K	TLTF alkalic chain			ECA17-07-043
ECA17-05-006			K				ECA17-05-006
ECA67-05-011			K				ECA67-05-011
ECA69-01-004			C	Quartz-bearing felsitic tempers derived from Lou			ECA69-01-004
ECA67-05-007			G	Manus, and Lavongai (and adjacent parts of New Ireland), andesitic-dacitic volcanic rocks, associated in some instances with cogenetic subvolcanic hypabyssal intrusions			ECA67-05-007

Thin section ID	New group	Subgroup	Dickinson's group	Sources inferred by Dickinson	Probable resource		sample ID
					Sources inferred by us	The feature of geological area	
ECA059	G9 Two different pastes				unknown	mixed tempers	ECA40-11-045
ECA094							ECA67-05-020
ECB005							ECB-V-017
ECB006							ECB-V-018
ECA111	Loner A				unknown	no identifiable inclusion	ECA69-05-004
ECA158	Loner B				unknown basic volcanic area	unknown basic volcanic area	ECA34-05-062

Note: Dickinson samples marked in blue.

Source: Authors' data and Dickinson (2021b).

7

Lapita pottery makers' marks: The memory of signs and wonders?

Matthew Spriggs

Abstract

What have been described as makers' marks on Lapita pottery were first reported by Donovan in 1973 and have been noted sporadically ever since. As Donovan herself noted, the placement and complexity of at least some of them refute the idea that they are merely 'the result of trials with tools'. So what are they? Ancient DNA analysis links the early Lapita people of Vanuatu and Tonga (and thereby by extension everywhere else in the Lapita distribution) directly back to Taiwan and on the latest evidence beyond, to the southern coastal regions of the Chinese mainland. These new data open up the geographic range of legitimate comparison for aspects of Lapita design and material culture. In particular, suggested links between the iconography of the Lapita 'double head' motifs and those on Liangzhu culture (5200–4200 BP) jade objects from the area around modern Shanghai, noted by Spriggs (2019), allow further comparisons with that culture in regard to incised signs on Liangzhu pottery. These have been proposed by some to be part of a widespread Chinese Neolithic phenomenon seen as the precursor to full writing systems by the time of the Shang culture. Are the Lapita makers' marks a distant memory of these Chinese developments?

you may not make use of strange arts or go in search of signs and wonders – Leviticus 19:26.[1]

Introduction

The art of writing for *Festschriften* has become an increasingly dying one, as papers become ever more rigorously reviewed to international journal standards and their very constrained formats. For me, the ideal Festschrift paper should be a somewhat whimsical and 'out-there' take on an interesting academic problem related to the work of the honouree. This chapter is offered in that spirit. I know that Glenn views the death of the art with the same shake of the weary old head as I do. So, I am happy to attempt a revolt against the current trend of too-perfect, too-serious and frequently all-too-tedious Festschrift papers.

---

1   This is taken from *The Bible in Basic English*, published by Cambridge University Press, 1965 (translation by S.H. Hooke).

The problem to be addressed here is a real one; what are the marks on Lapita pots that are dentate stamped, which are separate from and clearly not part of the decorative designs found on them, often occurring on the underside or the inside of pots and so not immediately visible unless looked for? These have been variously labelled as pot-marks, trademarks and decorator's marks, and were first noted for Lapita pots by Lorna Donovan in the second volume of her master's thesis (Donovan 1973). I use the more neutral term makers' marks, simply meaning deliberate, non-decorative marks made on the pot by the potter or potters prior to firing, using the same technique as used in the decoration of the pot—in this case, dentate stamping.

The 'out-there' take is to consider whether there is a link between such makers' marks and those on Chinese Neolithic pottery, taken by some scholars to be the precursors of writing. The link may be seen as somewhat of a chimaera given the distances involved between the Lapita realm and China. One might invoke convergent evolution, such marks appearing independently in distant societies because they served similar purposes. But I argue that just such a direct link is now possible to conceive of, because of advances in ancient DNA studies in China, Southeast Asia and Near and Remote Oceania pertinent to the origins of the initial stream of Lapita migrants into Remote Oceania (Lipson, Cheronet et al. 2018; Lipson, Skoglund et al. 2018; Lipson, Spriggs et al. 2020; McColl et al. 2018; Posth et al. 2018; Skoglund et al. 2016; Wang et al. 2021; Yang et al. 2020; Yu and Li 2021): a southern East Asian origin for the early Lapita people and a southern East Asian origin for their makers' marks.

I have elsewhere suggested that some distinctive elements of the Lapita design system, particularly the 'double head' motifs, can be traced back to representations on jade objects found in, among other places, the Liangzhu culture (5200–4200 BP) of the Yangtze region (Spriggs 2019) and I would like to extend that assertion here. If such a connection is allowed, then it permits us to look at other potential parallels in that and other preceding and neighbouring Chinese Neolithic cultures. These include makers' marks that have been plausibly identified as precursors to the development of writing in China during the Bronze Age. The perhaps whimsical suggestion is that the marks on Lapita pots could have had a similar function to those on Neolithic Chinese vessels. They are not, of course, actual writing but they could be what would, under different circumstances, lead towards the development of writing. Clearly this path was not taken in the Pacific in Lapita and later times—to assert otherwise leads to madness rather than whimsy and is surely not what the endangered art of Festschrift writing should encourage.

The corpus of Lapita Makers' marks

So, what are these marks and how common are they? The starting point must be Donovan (1973:II:75–76). Table 4 in her thesis, labelled 'Suggested Decorator's Marks' within a section titled 'Trade Marks', includes images of 11 marks from site SE-RF-2 (there RL2) and one from site SE-SZ-8 in the Reef Islands and Santa Cruz in the Southeast Solomons (Figure 7.1), excavated by Roger Green (Green and Cresswell 1976). Part of the short text reads:

> Of course, the suggestion that marks could be the result of trials with tools, in preparation for the design further up the vessel wall, cannot be ruled out. Though some do fit easily into this category, others show more purpose and placed as they are, on plain sherds, away from the decoration, seem to indicate a means of recognition.

/	RL2 78/9	↲	RL2 125/23	)|(	RL2 108/4
/	RL2 29/26	▮▮/▮//▮⦅	RL2 161/81	/	RL2 29/2
⦅⦅	RL2 59/43	⌒	SZ8 116/1	☰	RL2 60/63
ι/	RL2 31/2	⊥⊥⊥	RL2 61/72	🪶	RL2 153/29

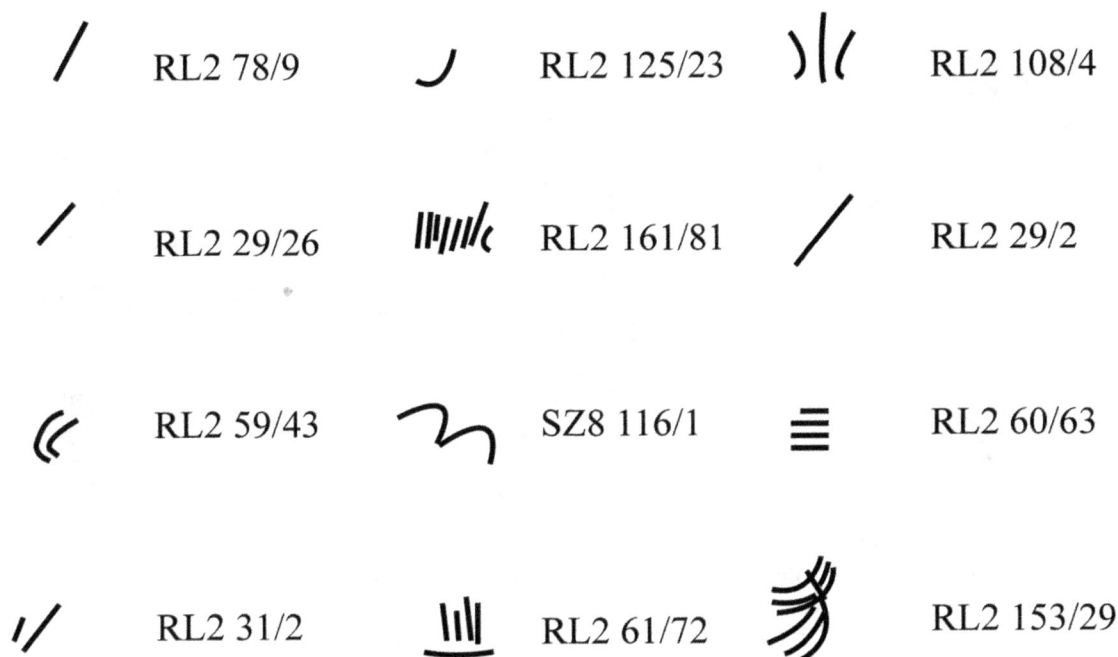

Figure 7.1: Makers' marks identified by Donovan (1973:76) from sites RF-2 (here RL2) and SZ-8 in the Reefs–Santa Cruz Islands of the Southeast Solomons.

Source: Redrawn by Stuart Bedford.

These collections have subsequently been studied by Scarlett Chiu as part of the Lapita Pottery Online Database (LPOD),[2] although only 5 of the 12 sherds were included in that restudy.[3] Of these five sherds, reanalysis suggests that the two with the simplest of marks of the whole series (RL2 125/23 and 29/26), a straight line and a curved line, are just incidental scratches (or not able to be differentiated from such), while a third small body sherd (RL2 29/2) does not bear any mark such as attributed by Donovan to it, its external surface bearing a standard dentate-stamped complex design. If it did possess a longer straight-line mark beyond merely a scratch, it would have been noticed by the LPOD recording team; possibly the sherd was mislabelled by Donovan or renumbered at some later stage.

The two remaining sherds (Figure 7.2B–C: RL2 153/29 and SZ8 116/1) indeed bear what appear to be makers' marks: two adjacent curved stamps of about 12 tines each arranged parallel to each other and touching in the case of the SZ8 sherd, and five curved stamps of about 12 tines each with the three below overlapping the two above in the RL2 sherd, so the sequence starts with the top two and then the bottom three.[4] The SZ8 marks appear on the plain exterior of the lower part of a large vessel and those of the RL2 sherd on the exterior of a plain body sherd, vessel form unknown.

---

2   The LPOD database (last accessed 27 May 2022) is accessible at: lapita.rchss.sinica.edu.tw/web/?cat=4.

3   I thank Scarlett Chiu for looking through the database for me in search of these and other makers' marks. It may be that the other seven sherds were undecorated body sherds and so not studied for the LPOD, or that they have lost or changed their labels, or were perhaps destroyed as part of other studies to produce thin sections or in related provenance studies. Further examination of the collection, currently impossible because of COVID entry restrictions to New Zealand at time of writing, is warranted.

4   Donovan's drawing (here Figure 7.1) suggests three below and three above, but the photo kindly supplied by Scarlett Chiu from LPOD clearly shows only five stamps.

Figure 7.2: (A) RL2-265-85, an additional makers' mark missed by Donovan from the RF-2 site and identified by Scarlett Chiu; (B) makers' mark on RL2 153/29 as identified by Donovan; (C) SZ8 116/1 as identified by Donovan.

Source: Photographs A and B by Scarlett Chiu. Photograph C by Stuart Bedford.

It is notable (see Figure 7.1) that the 'missing' seven sherds, with the exception of RL2 78/9, are what one might call 'complex' marks consisting of more than a single stamp: two in the case of RL2 59/43 (curved) and RL2 31/2 (straight), three in the case of RL2 108/4 (two curved and one straight), four for RL2 60/63 (straight), five for RL2 61/72 (straight) and eight in the case of RL2 161/81 (seven straight and one curved stamp). This strongly suggests that when relocated six of them at least will indeed turn out to qualify as makers' marks.

In addition, Chiu located a further sherd from the collection with a makers' mark, RL2-265-85, which has two parallel straight or slightly curved stamp impressions on the inside of the flat base of a pot, of at least five tines each (Figure 7.2A).

Heading back into Near Oceania,[5] in the Bismarck Archipelago there are examples only from Eloaua (site ECA) in the Mussau Group (Figure 7.3A–B), excavated by Kirch (2021). They consist of one simple (single line) possible makers' mark (ECA 42-09-18 & 19 and 20) and one complex (three stamps) mark (ECA 66-07-014). A third sherd (ECA-V-234) displays some deeply incised lines on the inside rim of an otherwise dentate-stamped pot. These are clearly deliberate but are arguably a form of decoration. As these lines were not created using the decorative technique of dentate stamping found elsewhere on the pot, they are excluded from further consideration here.

The single-line makers' mark is found on the base of a flat-bottomed dish and is made using a stamp of about 16 tines. The straightness of the line suggests it was not two stamps of 8 tines end to end. It is hardly visible at all, which casts doubt on whether it was done to be seen, but post-depositional weathering could possibly account for that. Similar single lines were postulated as makers' marks in the Reefs–Santa Cruz pottery but two of them appear to be merely scratches, another claimed by Donovan was not noticed on the sherd indicated and the fourth and final example is one of the 'missing' sherds.

---

5   I am greatly indebted to Scarlett Chiu for bringing these two Near Oceanic examples to my attention, derived from her analysis of the LPOD.

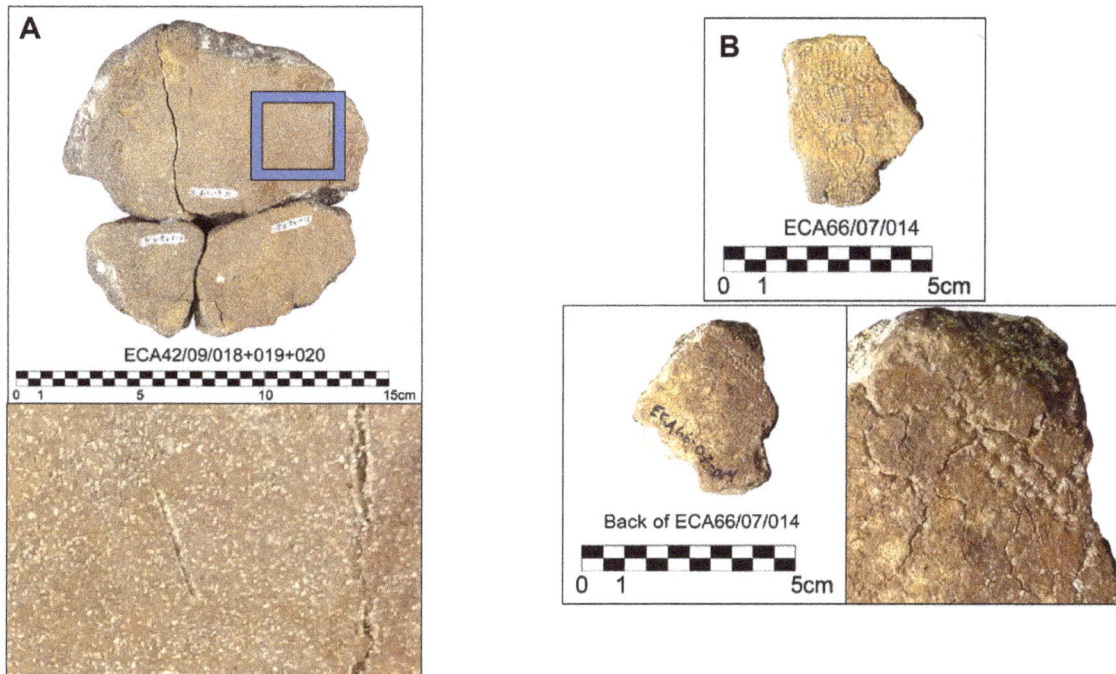

Figure 7.3: Maker's marks on sherds from Talepakemalai site, Eloaua Island, Mussau Group.

Notes: (A) ECA42-09-18 & 19 & 20 with maker's mark indicated; (B) ECA-66-07-014 showing design, interior surface and close-up of interior makers' mark.

Source: Photographs by Scarlett Chiu, used with the permission of Patrick Kirch.

The ECA 66-07-014 sherd has three parallel straight dentate lines of different lengths consisting of at least seven tines in one, whose true extent is obscured by a crack and the sherd edge, more than nine in the middle line and only about four in the third line. The marks appear on the interior of a dentate-decorated sherd.

The final examples come from the Teouma Lapita cemetery site on Efate, Vanuatu, and were excavated as part of a joint Vanuatu Cultural Centre/Kaljoral Senta (VKS) and The Australian National University salvage and research project between 2004 and 2010, directed by the VKS Directors of the time, and Stuart Bedford and the author (Bedford et al. 2006, 2010). One sherd in particular (Figure 7.4A) is what first prompted my interest in such makers' marks. It comes from Teouma Dish 2 (TD2) with joining sherds coming from Layer 3 burial deposits in Area 2, Squares A3 and B4 excavated in 2005; several further sherds from the same vessel were more widely scattered. The marks occur on the exterior of the curving base of a dish on an attached stand and begin 6 mm below the wall-base join. They consist of what may be four impressions of curved dentate stamps with about 16 tines running right to left and four further slightly curved stamps with 7 or 8 tines running left to right, to produce the most complex of the makers' marks encountered so far in Lapita assemblages.

The other makers' mark occurs on an otherwise plain exterior just below the carination of a presumably dentate-decorated vessel from Layer 2 of Square I1, bag 3240, also excavated in 2005 (Figure 7.4B). It consists of two diverging and partially overlapping straight stamps of 17 or 18 tines each.

Figure 7.4: Makers' marks from Teouma Lapita site, Efate Island, Vanuatu.

(A) Maker's mark on Teouma Dish 2 (TD2) showing placement on the vessel, with the start of the attached ring foot to the bottom of the upper photograph; (B) makers' mark on sherd 3720.

Source: Photographs by Stuart Bedford.

What do the makers' marks represent?

The first point to be made is how rare such marks are among the Lapita corpus. In Scarlett Chiu's interrogation of the LPOD she found five cases out of 35,494 sherds examined from 94 different sites.[6] In addition, Teouma, which represents one of the largest Lapita pottery assemblages found to date, produced only two examples out of many thousands of sherds. There are seven 'missing' sherds from SE-RF-2 reported by Donovan, of which six could plausibly be considered makers' marks. This gives a maximum total of 14 sherds from four sites across the Early Western and Western Lapita provinces. No makers' marks have been reported from Eastern Lapita contexts,[7] nor from the many thousands of Lapita sherds excavated in New Caledonia or in the Arawe Islands off New Britain in the Bismarck Archipelago.

---

6   Chiu found one such mark among 3760 sherds from SZ-8, two out of 7289 sherds she examined from site RF-2 and two out of 4580 sherds from ECA (pers. comm. 12 and 13 January 2022).

7   I do not include here identical possible makers' marks found on otherwise completely plain vessels from the Late Lapita/ Transitional 2600 BP Level 1 at the Sigatoka site, Viti Levu, Fiji, reported by Lawrence Birks (1973:35, 101, 166) from 1965–1966 excavations and by Dave Burley and Bill Dickinson (2004:19) from 1998 excavations. Birks (1973:35) describes the best-preserved example as being 'three pellets (or possibly one) of clay have been placed against the pot wall about 4.0 cms below the lip and squeezed out by pressure from three fingertips held close together'. Given the lack of any decoration on these vessels the marks may have been executed to identify the work of a single potter but equally could merely represent a very minimalist form of decoration.

There is no doubt that a few have been missed, part of the point of this paper being to encourage researchers to look more closely at their assemblages with makers' marks in mind. With some small sherds, what have until now been considered parts of Lapita designs may in fact be makers' marks or fragments of them. But one doubts if further examination would greatly increase the numbers. Nearly 300 Lapita sites are known (Bedford et al. 2019) and yet currently not even 2 per cent of them have produced such marks, and those only covering part of the full geographic range of Lapita.

This precludes them from being considered as trademarks, such as are known on Motu pottery from near Port Moresby, Papua New Guinea. Jim Allen (2017:302, 305) illustrates several from his excavation on Motupore Island in that region, where they were common. He quotes James Chalmers (1887:122): 'every woman has her private mark and marks everything she makes'; also Murray Groves (1960:11, 13): 'each woman in a household makes her own pots with her own trade mark on them … traditionally they used simple geometric figures as trade marks'. Allen (2017:303) notes that these trademarks are incised designs 'isolated by undecorated space (and thus not part of a continuous band of decoration) and occurring almost exclusively on the interior rims of globular pots', which were very largely undecorated and so less distinctive. He also notes that for pots that do not bear such trademarks, 'more extensive decoration on the bowls may have provided sufficient identification of the maker'. While this could be a factor in the rarity of makers' marks on Lapita pottery there is little evidence that those so marked were any less decorated or distinctive than other pots without makers' marks.

The special situation of Motu pottery is that it was trade ware, with pots moving beyond the household and the village as part of the traditional *hiri* exchange system to the Gulf of Papua, with the trade 'done by an agent acting for more than one potter and thus needing to distinguish between the pots in his care' (Allen 2017:305). This could never be the explanation for such marks on Lapita pots because the overwhelming evidence is that they were rarely exchanged between islands, and indeed that the rare movement of pots between islands may have been incidental to other practices such as marriage exchanges (Spriggs 2020:185, 194).

The simplest explanation would be that the Lapita makers' marks are just 'trials with tools' but one wonders why such trials with dentate stamps would be necessary in the first place? Another suggestion might be doodles, done by a bored potter. This cannot be excluded but even doodles generally represent *something* and so are pictographs of some kind. Their regular placement also needs to be considered.

A Chinese connection?

Very comparable marks appear on Chinese Neolithic pottery from the seventh to the fifth millennium BP, some seemingly exact parallels for Lapita examples (Figure 7.5). These are interpreted in very contrasting ways by different Chinese specialists. One school sees them as potential precursors to writing, or even as marking a transition towards writing in the case of examples from the Liangzhu culture (5200–4200 BP) and other related cultures (Dematté 1999, 2010; Li et al. 2003; Postgate et al. 1995). Others, most consistently William Boltz (1986, 2000; also Bagley 2004; Keightley 2006), take the stance that writing developed in a very short period of time during the later Shang culture as state formation required a recording system, either for economic transactions, as in the usually postulated sequence for the origin of writing across the world, or for divinatory purposes.

Figure 7.5: Makers' marks on Chinese Neolithic pottery and later Shang culture numerals for comparison.

Notes: (A) From Panpo site, Shaanxi Province, Yangshao culture, c. 7000–6000 BP (selected and redrawn from Lu and Aiken 2004:41); (B) from Liangzhu, Zhejiang Province, Liangzhu culture, 5200–4200 BP (from Boltz 1986:Fig. 3); (C) from Banshan and Machang sites, Gansu Province, Majiayao culture 5300–4000 BP (from Boltz 1986:Fig. 3); (D) from Liuwan, Qinghai Province, later Majiayao culture, 4300–4000 BP (selected and redrawn from Boltz 1986:Fig. 3 and Kaogu 1976:Fig. 1); (E) Shang numerals 1–10 (from Postgate et al. 1995:Fig 1b).

Source: Redrawn by Stuart Bedford.

In a now-classic paper, Nicholas Postgate, Tao Wang and Toby Wilkinson (1995:459) noted the need to establish criteria for 'differentiating between genuine writing, on the one hand, and symbols or systems of symbols which resemble it, on the other', noting that no simple criterion was likely to be decisive. They continue:

> Symbols may well perform a similar function to writing, such as making a statement of ownership; the difference is that writing needs always to correspond to a segment of language. Moreover, a writing system is only valid if it communicates: there has to be a reader as well as a writer, and for the system to function it must therefore be a finite system, with each side sharing the same repertoire. While it is reasonable to deny that a single sign on a potsherd proves the existence of writing, it may be difficult to decide whether a combination of such symbols represents a writing system if their meaning is unknown (Postgate et al. 1995:459–460).

They also note the difficulty that the earliest independent writing systems originated with 'symbols that could well have conveyed a message independently of their role within the system', given that such scripts are mostly logographic, with 'each symbol corresponding to a word' (1995:460–461).

Trigger (1998:54–55) notes that using graphic recording systems to represent ideas ('semasiography') is common in small-scale societies and includes using signs to record names. Such potential 'logographs' where a graph stands for a whole word may evolve into writing after developing as a more systematic system to record additional categories of information such as numerical data.

In their section on Chinese writing, Postgate, Wang and Wilkinson reject as precursors to writing the early Yangshao culture pottery with incised signs usually placed, pre-firing, on the black band running round the outer rim of select vessel types, although occasionally on the base of the pot. Such pots, dating to 7–6000 BP in the Yellow River valley at sites such as Banpo and Jiangzhai (Figure 7.5A), were often used in child burials, and so had a ritual association. At these sites more than 200 sherds with usually single marks consisting of one to seven incised strokes have been found and similar signs are found on more than one vessel and in more than one site (Dematté 2010:2124–2215). Postgate et al. (1995:467, cf. Boltz 1986) consider all such earlier Neolithic marks as 'numerical or potters' marks' and therefore not writing.

Ping-ti Ho (1975:233) claims the marks on Banpo pots include the earliest representation of numerals in the world, but as David Keightley points out in a review, this assertion is based on a very selective comparison with later Shang and Chou period numerals. Keightley (1977:391) notes that until such marks are found in a Neolithic context,

> which requires a definite meaning (such as, to take an ideal case, ten vessels a mark for 1 to 10 scratched on each one) the conclusions are bound to be speculative.

Postgate et al. (1995) seem less sure about the pre-Yangshao culture Jiahu site, Wuyang, Henan Province just south of the Yellow River, a Neolithic site dating to 8600–7500 BP, where turtle plastron and carapaces and bones are engraved with signs, some of them identical to later Chinese characters. They conclude that 'one cannot *a priori* rule out the possibility that these were short texts with a symbolic meaning of some kind' relating to divination (ibid.:467). There is further discussion of this site by Xueqin Li and colleagues (2003), who note incised marks on nine tortoise shells and two on bone associated with graves dating to 8600–8200 BP. They associate them with divination, illustrating four of them and comparing them to later Shang culture characters. Up to eight out of 11 signs are considered comparable to Shang numerals 1, 2, 8, 10 and 20, while three are comparable to characters for eye, window and possibly a human figure. All but the eye and human figure signs are comparable to examples illustrated in Figure 7.5 (and also in Lapita pottery). There are, however, specialists such as Dematté (2010:213) who suggest that the signs may in fact be recent forgeries on old bones!

Signs on pottery jars of the Dawenkou culture (c. 6000–4500 BP), which developed from Yangshao, get an honourable mention by Postgate et al. (1995), some of them combining more than one incised element, but these authors follow Boltz (1986) in considering them 'clan name' representations. They occur as both incised and painted signs, generally associated with adult burials but with child burials at one site (Dematté 2010:215–218). They seem unlike the makers' marks we have been discussing until now and were on occasion filled with red colour to be prominently displayed on the pot. Such prominence is the opposite of what we see with Lapita makers' marks examples.

Postgate et al. (1995) definitively date the emergence of writing in China to 4500–4000 BP, associated with both the Liangzhu culture (5200–4200 BP) in the Yangzi Valley, immediately south of the Dawenkou culture and in close contact with it (cf. Dematté 1999:252), and the contemporary

Late Longshan culture (4500–4000 BP) of the Middle and Lower Yellow River Valley to the north (Postgate et al. 1995:468), deriving from the Dawenkou culture in Shandong and also in contact with the Liangzhu culture. But the 'inscriptions' on pottery of these cultures, with five and eight signs incised (Liangzhu), and 11 signs in five vertical rows (Longshan), as well as an even more elaborate 'inscription' in a similar cursive script from Longqiu, Gaoyou, Jiangsu Province (illustrated by Postgate et al. (1995)), seem far more elaborate than the Neolithic makers' marks illustrated in Figure 7.5, which includes examples from the Liangzhu culture itself (Figure 7.5B). It is often not clear, particularly in secondary sources, where on the pots these simpler Liangzhu marks occur but illustrations suggest on the base of some flat-bottomed vessels, so 'hidden', but also prominently on the middle body of others.

The Majiayao culture (5300–4000 BP) developed from Yangshao and its final phase, Machang culture (4300–4000 BP), partly overlapped in time with Liangzhu and the earliest Bronze Age cultures. On Machang culture painted pots associated with burial use (Figure 7.5C, D),[8] we find painted signs on the lower otherwise unpainted body of the pot or on the base of flat-bottomed vessels (*Kaogu* 1976)—that is, in less easily visible positions. One interpretation given by the excavators of the Liuwan site was that they may have related to specific clan pottery workshops.

There is no definitive relation between the more elaborate Longshan and Liangzhu 'inscriptions' and the earliest identifiable writing in Chinese. If they are in fact writing, they could well represent a quite different language or, as Dematté (2010:214) suggests for some of the cursive script examples, could be recent forgeries or in one case represent a child's doodles. Dematté (1999) traces the lineage between these various cultures, mediated through Longshan to Early Bronze Age Erlitou cultures and on to Shang, to make a convincing case for their influence on at least the form of writing that developed in the later Shang, a Yellow River culture heavily influenced by eastern coastal cultures such as Liangzhu. Both Liangzhu and Longshan cultures had certainly reached a threshold in terms of social complexity and state formation where one might envisage true writing as being necessary or at least extremely useful for administrative purposes—Renfrew and Liu (2018) suggest the Liangzhu culture as the earliest state society in East Asia.

The earliest recognisably Chinese logographic script is found on turtle plastrons and bovid scapulae used for divinatory purposes at Anyang, Henan Province, and on bronze ritual vessels dating from Late Shang culture contexts c. 3400–3200 BP (Postgate et al. (1995) provide illustrations and references). Scholars argue whether there was also a larger corpus of writing on perishable materials, such as wooden or bamboo strips or silk, that related to more solely economic transactions. Boltz (2000) rejected the idea, but Bagley (2004) is among those who make this claim; for similar debates elsewhere in the world see Postgate et al. (1995:463–464).

Returning to the more obvious makers' marks on Neolithic pottery, Li et al. (2003) examine and provide references for a range of sources, but do not include the more detailed treatment of this issue by Dematté (1999; see also Dematté 2010 for an update). They conclude that:

> The present state of the archaeological record in China … does not permit us to say exactly in which period of the Neolithic the Chinese invented their writing. What did persist through these long periods was *the idea of sign use*. Although it is impossible at this point to trace any direct connection from the Jiahu signs to the Yinxu [Anyang] characters, we do propose that

---

8   One notes that in Boltz's illustrations of Machang culture signs from Liuwan, he omits those that seem to resemble later Shang graphs more closely (Compare *Kaogu* 1976:Fig. 17 with Boltz 1986:Fig. 3c and 2000:Fig. 1, number iii). He does the same with those of Yangshao age as well: compare Lu and Aiken (2004:Fig. 4) with Boltz (1986:Fig. 3a and 2000:Fig. 1, number i). Fig. 7.5, here, restores the more complex signs so omitted.

slow, culture-linked evolutionary processes adopting the *idea* of sign use, took place in diverse settings around the Yellow River. We should not assume that there was a single path or pace for the development of a script. (Li et al. 2003:41; italics in original)

That said, as has been shown earlier, the societies under consideration had interconnections with each other, either in terms of direct ancestry or in having clear direct cultural connections allowing diffusion of sign systems or at least 'the idea of sign use' as Li et al. put it in the quotation above.

Dematté (2010:213) sees these marks as 'early signaries and counting systems that served basic recording needs in non-complex societies' and suggests they were 'mnemonic marks for simple recording functions (pot-marks or tallies such as lines, crosses, combs etc.)'. Later, he opines that they 'were used to keep track of quantities, types and probably names' (Dematté 2010:224). Lu and Aiken (2004) try to assess how many of the Neolithic pot-marks could represent numbers, using early Shang numerals as their comparator (see Figure 7.5E for the latter). They concluded that many signs could indeed be so interpreted. But we should remember the strictures of sinologist John De Francis (1991:118–119) on 'claiming a genetic relationship between symbols simply on the basis of the resemblance between the two'. In that paper he demonstrates the exact match between 19 such Neolithic signs and those used currently in proofreading by American writers and publishers!

A common theme is the association of such marks with ritual activities (as well as Dematté 1999, 2010, see Keightley 1996). The pots on which these marks occur are frequently found in burials and so such a link is indeed not unlikely. The highly decorated Lapita pots with a display rather than cooking function would fit such a link too, and indeed at the Teouma Lapita cemetery in Vanuatu such pots also accompany burials, including having skeletal remains placed inside some of them (Kirch 2021:93–97; Leclerc et al. 2018; Summerhayes 2000).

Of the other Lapita sites with such marks, the spatial layout of RL-2 has been extensively studied by Green and colleagues (Green and Pawley 1999; cf. Sheppard and Green 1991). Sherd density was greatest in association with a rectangular structure interpreted as the main house of the settlement, and particularly in its south-eastern quadrant. Based on ethnographic analogy with 'house societies' (cf. Chiu 2005) and the lack of evidence for separate ritual structures, Green and Pawley (1999:81) suggest 'Ritual activity may well have been focused within the main dwelling house', where the greatest quantity of decorated pottery was in fact recovered. SZ-8 was a large Lapita settlement site but when excavated was found to be heavily disturbed and no details of its internal layout were revealed in excavation (Green et al. 2008). The main stilt house structure at Talepakemalai, site ECA, Area B, is interpreted as a ritual structure 'focused around some form of ancestor cult' (Kirch 2021:520–521). Kirch notes the presence of particularly high concentrations of fine decorated pottery, shell valuables and imported obsidian, curated human remains, a unique anthropomorphic bone figurine and a ceramic drum, and evidence of feasting.

In the three Lapita sites with makers' marks for which we can interpret details of site layout and function, a ritual emphasis has been suggested, either as a cemetery, or a house-like structure with evidence for ritual activity. Scholars such as Scarlett Chiu and Arnaud Noury attempt to 'read' the meaning of particular Lapita designs as clan or 'house' symbols or otherwise denoting social connectedness, or as representative of ancestral or cosmogonic figures (Chiu 2005, 2015, 2019; Noury 2005, 2019; Noury and Galipaud 2011).

The Lapita makers' marks are not part of the designs as such and are often hidden inside the vessel itself, or below the carination or on the base of flat-bottomed vessels, as are some of the Chinese examples. Do these hidden locations also convey social information? Although not writing as such, could they too be 'read' by those initiated into their meaning?

Liangzhu to Lapita?

The Liangzhu culture developed out of the Hemudu and Songze cultures, the former seen by Peter Bellwood and others as the *Urkultur* or original culture that leads to the Neolithic cultures of Taiwan (for instance Bellwood 1997, 2005, 2013). Liangzhu cultural traits occur in the mainland Chinese coastal provinces opposite Taiwan (Zhi and Hung 2010:20), Liangzhu culture influences into northern Taiwan Neolithic Dabenkeng cultures are attested in stone artefacts, pottery types and jade cutting techniques (Kuo 2019:83–86, 88) and genetic connections posited between Liangzhu and Austronesian populations of Taiwan (Li et al. 2007). More speculatively, recent genetic studies of mainland China and Taiwan draw a link between genetic patterns and an ancestral form of Austronesian language on the Chinese mainland in the coastal region south of the mouth of the Yangzi River (Huang et al. 2022; Wang et al. 2021; Yang et al. 2020; Yu and Li 2021). Cultural connections continued between Liangzhu and successor cultures, and later phases of the Taiwan Neolithic (after the initial Dabenkeng cultures and prior to the Neolithic spread south from Taiwan into Southeast Asia c. 4000 BP) and its manifestation in the western Pacific as Lapita less than a millennium later (Kuo 2019:125–135).

I am ever more convinced of a direct link between the double head or head and mask motifs of both Liangzhu and Lapita cultures and hope to pursue that link in a future paper. If Liangzhu design can be linked to Lapita, just as ancient DNA now links Lapita back to mainland China and Austronesian languages link Lapita at least back to Taiwan, and by extension the mainland, then can we perhaps also link the Chinese Neolithic tradition of signs on pots to later Lapita examples? While one branch of the Chinese Neolithic tradition of signs plausibly leads on to the earliest recognisable Chinese writing of the Shang dynasty, could another branch lead through Taiwan ultimately to Lapita makers' marks on pottery?

Arguably, this too was linked to elite communication and understood by only a few. The Lapita design system itself was doubtless full of symbolic meaning that could be 'read' to varying extents by participants in that culture. With the collapse of elites at the end of Lapita (Earle and Spriggs 2015:522–525), the design system and associated signs or makers' marks became irrelevant and forgotten and that lineage of signs died out. It certainly didn't develop into any later Pacific script, there being none prior to European contact—the only possible exception, Rapa Nui's *rongorongo* script, is generally believed to be a post-European contact phenomenon (Fischer 1997).

There is, however, a major gap between China and the Lapita realm where no early Neolithic makers' marks are known, Island Southeast Asia itself so far drawing a blank.[9] Beyond northern Luzon there is a dearth of early pottery sites, other than cave sites, and what sites there are consist of small assemblages of generally plain or red-slipped pottery. Where open sites are known, as on Sulawesi, decorated pottery assemblages of any size tend to occur only in late Neolithic assemblages, generally after 3100 BP, and thus are not relevant to the origins of Lapita (Spriggs 2011:517–521, cf. Azis et al. 2018). In what are sometimes decorated pottery samples of thousands of sherds in Lapita sites, we have seen that makers' marks are rare. Island Southeast Asian ceramic assemblages tend to be much smaller and therefore the chance of finding such marks is similarly reduced. Makers' marks have never been a focus of any study in Island Southeast Asia and researchers may have mistaken them as parts of decorative motifs; again, hopefully this paper will encourage a more systematic look.

---

9   I am grateful to Peter Bellwood, Philip Beaumont, Dylan Gaffney and Sue O'Connor for responding to my email queries seeking examples of early Island Southeast Asian makers' marks.

Conclusion

In what I hope is in the best 'old-school' tradition of Festschrift writing, being a somewhat whimsical and 'out-there' take on an interesting academic problem, I have pursued the question of Lapita makers' marks as far as one can sanely go (some may think considerably beyond!). Lapita derives in part, and for its earliest phases perhaps in very large part, from the Neolithic traditions of Eastern China, particularly that region around the Lower Yangzi River and further south. Concerning those Neolithic traditions, plausible arguments have been made, particularly by Chinese scholars, for a system of signs that developed into what became the Chinese script of the Late Shang period, itself contemporary with the earliest possible dates for Lapita in the Bismarck Archipelago 3400–3200 BP.

It does not seem beyond possibility that this system of signs, in its pre-writing stage of course, was also useful to elites as the Island Southeast Asian Neolithic spread into the Pacific as Lapita, just as the Lapita design system on the pots was. The echo of these 'signs and wonders' might thus be found as far distant from their origins as the Bismarck Archipelago, the Reef–Santa Cruz Islands and central Vanuatu. The Island Southeast Asian distribution gap needs to be looked at further: at present there are very few substantial assemblages of decorated pottery prior to 3100 BP outside of Taiwan and very little synthesis of surface treatments on pottery from anywhere in the region of interest.

Let me at least hope that having suggested this with suitable caveats, I might yet escape the trials and afflictions of Job and will not have to repent in dust and ashes and answer thus to all concerned:

> [He said] Who is this who makes dark the purpose of God by words without knowledge?
> For I have been talking without knowledge about wonders not to be searched out. Job 42:3.[10]

And may I fervently hope that they will be able to say of Glenn, again like Job, that after reading his Festschrift he lived 'a hundred and forty years after this, long enough to see his grandchildren and great-grandchildren. And then he died at a very great age' (Job 42:16, 17).[11]

Acknowledgements

First, I would like to acknowledge Glenn Summerhayes for his clear-eyed scholarship and for his fellowship and good conversation over many decades. Scarlett Chiu has been extremely helpful in providing Lapita examples of makers' marks but is in no way implicated in the interpretive liberties I have taken with them. I invited her to become a co-author, but she probably very wisely declined once she had read the draft text. Stuart Bedford displayed his usual technological acumen in producing Figures 7.1 and 7.5 and assisting with the other figures as well as providing additional photographs and information on Teouma and SZ-8 examples of makers' marks. Patrick Kirch and Patrick McCoy are thanked for information and permissions, and Peter Bellwood, Phillip Beaumont, Dylan Gaffney and Sue O'Connor are thanked for discussion of the lack of makers' marks in Island Southeast Asia. Rosemary Leona and William Hazell are thanked for enduring long and rambling discourses about Chinese writing and Lapita during preparation of this paper in Port Vila, Vanuatu. Two anonymous reviewers helped me hone the arguments to the best of my ability.

---

10   This is taken from *The Bible in Basic English*, published by Cambridge University Press, 1965 (translation by S.H. Hooke).

11   This is the version from the *Good News for South Pacific Students Bible*, published by the Bible Society in the South Pacific, Suva, Fiji, 1992 edition.

References

Allen, J. 2017. *Excavations on Motupore Island, Central District, Papua New Guinea, Vol. 1*. University of Otago, Working Papers in Anthropology 4. University of Otago, Dunedin.

Azis, N., C. Reepmeyer, G. Clark, Sriwigati and D.A. Tanudirjo 2018. Mansiri in North Sulawesi: A new dentate-stamped pottery site in Island Southeast Asia. In S. O'Connor, D. Bulbeck and J. Meyer (eds), *The archaeology of Sulawesi: Current research on the Pleistocene to the Historic Period*, pp. 191–205. Terra Australis 48. ANU Press, Canberra. doi.org/10.22459/TA48.11.2018.12.

Bagley, R.W. 2004. Anyang writing and the origin of the Chinese writing system. In S.D. Houston (ed.), *The first writing: Script invention as history and process*, pp. 190–249. Cambridge University Press, Cambridge.

Bedford, S., M. Spriggs and R. Regenvanu 2006. The Teouma Lapita site and the early human settlement of the Pacific Islands. *Antiquity* 80(310):812–828. doi.org/10.1017/S0003598X00094448.

Bedford, S., M. Spriggs, H. Buckley, F. Valentin, R. Regenvanu and M. Abong 2010. A cemetery of first settlement: Teouma, South Efate, Vanuatu/Un cimetière de premier peuplement: le site de Teouma, sud d'Efate, Vanuatu. In C. Sand and S. Bedford (eds), *Lapita: Oceanic ancestors/Lapita: Ancêtres Océaniens*, pp. 140–161. Musée de Quai Branly/Somogy, Paris.

Bedford, S., M. Spriggs, D.V. Burley, C. Sand, P. Sheppard and G.R. Summerhayes 2019. Debating Lapita: Distribution, chronology, society and subsistence. In S. Bedford and M. Spriggs (eds), *Debating Lapita: Distribution, chronology, society and subsistence*, pp. 5–33. Terra Australis 52. ANU Press, Canberra. doi.org/10.22459/TA52.2019.01.

Bellwood, P. 1997. *Prehistory of the Indo-Malaysian Archipelago*. Revised Edition. University of Hawai'i Press, Honolulu. doi.org/10.1515/9780824874681.

Bellwood, P. 2005. *First farmers: The origins of agricultural societies*. Blackwell Publishing, Oxford.

Bellwood, P. 2013. *First migrants: Ancient migration in global perspective*. Wiley-Blackwell, Chichester.

Birks, L. 1973. *Archaeological excavations at the Sigatoka Dune site, Fiji*. Bulletin of the Fiji Museum 1. Fiji Museum, Suva.

Boltz, W.G. 1986. Early Chinese writing. *World Archaeology* 17(3):420–436. doi.org/10.1080/00438243.1986.9979980.

Boltz, W.G. 2000. The invention of writing in China. *Oriens Extremus* 42:1–17.

Burley, D.V. and W.R. Dickinson. 2004. Late Lapita occupation and its ceramic assemblage at the Sigatoka Dune site, Fiji and their place in Oceanic prehistory. *Archaeology in Oceania* 39:12–25. doi.org/10.1002/j.1834-4453.2004.tb00553.x.

Chalmers, J. 1887. History and description of pottery trade. A Papuan Enoch Arden. In J.W. Lindt (ed.), *Picturesque New Guinea*, pp. 118–125. Longmans, Green and Co, London.

Chiu, S. 2005. Meanings of a Lapita face: Materialised social memory in ancient house societies. *Taiwan Journal of Anthropology* 3(1):1–47.

Chiu, S. 2015. Where do we go from here? Social relatedness reflected by motif analysis. In C. Sand, S. Chiu and N. Hogg (eds), *The Lapita cultural complex in time and space: Expansion routes, chronologies and typologies*, pp. 185–206. Archeologia Pasifika 4. Institut d'archéologie de la Nouvelle-Calédonie et du Pacifique (IANCP), Nouméa.

Chiu, S. 2019. Measuring social distances with shared Lapita motifs: Current results and challenges. In S. Bedford and M. Spriggs (eds), *Debating Lapita: Distribution, chronology, society and subsistence*, pp. 307–334. Terra Australis 52. ANU Press, Canberra. doi.org/10.22459/TA52.2019.15.

Dematté, P. 1999. The role of writing in the process of state formation in Late Neolithic China. *East and West* 49(1–4):241–272.

Dematté, P. 2010. The origins of Chinese writing: The Neolithic evidence. *Cambridge Archaeological Journal* 20(2):211–228. doi.org/10.1017/S0959774310000247.

Donovan, L.J. 1973. A study of the decorative system of the Lapita potters in Reefs and Santa Cruz Islands, Vol. 2 (Appendices). Unpublished MA thesis, University of Auckland, Auckland.

Earle, T.K. and M. Spriggs 2015. Political economy and prehistory: A Marxist approach to Pacific sequences. *Current Anthropology* 56(4):515–544. doi.org/10.1086/682284.

Fischer, S.R. 1997. *Rongorongo: The Easter Island script*. Clarendon Press, Oxford.

Green, R.C. and M.M. Cresswell (eds) 1976. *Southeast Solomon Islands cultural history: A preliminary survey*. Royal Society of New Zealand Bulletin 11. Royal Society of New Zealand, Wellington.

Green, R.C. and A. Pawley 1999. Early Oceanic architectural forms and settlement patterns: Linguistic, archaeological and ethnological perspectives. In R. Blench and M. Spriggs (eds), *Archaeology and language III: Artefacts, languages and texts*, pp. 31–89. Routledge, London and New York.

Green, R.C., M. Jones and P. Sheppard 2008. The reconstructed environment and absolute dating of SE-SZ-8 Lapita site on Nendö, Santa Cruz, Solomon Islands. *Archaeology in Oceania* 41(2):49–61. doi.org/10.1002/j.1834-4453.2008.tb00030.x.

Groves, M. 1960. Motu pottery. *Journal of the Polynesian Society* 69:3–22.

Ho, P. 1975. *The cradle of the east: An enquiry into the indigenous origins of technologies and ideas of Neolithic and Early Historic China, 5000–1000 B.C.* University of Chicago Press, Chicago and Chinese University of Hongkong, Hongkong.

Huang, X., Z.-Y. Xia, X. Bin, G. He, J. Guo, A. Adnan, L. Yin, Y. Huang, J. Zhao, Y. Yang, F. Ma, Y. Li, R. Hu, T. Yang, L.-H. Wei and C.-C. Wang 2022. Genomic insights into the demographic history of the Southern Chinese. *Frontiers in Ecology and Evolution* 10:853391. doi.org/10.3389/fevo.2022.853391.

Kaogu 1976. Qinghai Ledou Liuwan yuanshi shihui mudi fanyang de zhuyao wenti. *Kaogu* 1976(6):365–377.

Keightley, D.N. 1977. Ping-Ti Ho and the origins of Chinese civilization. *Harvard Journal of Asiatic Studies* 37(2):381–411. doi.org/10.2307/2718679.

Keightley, D.N. 1996. Art, ancestors and the origins of writing in China. *Representations* 56:68–95. doi.org/10.2307/2928708.

Keightley, D.N. 2006. Marks and labels: Early writing in Neolithic and Shang China. In M.T. Stark (ed.), *Archaeology of Asia*, pp. 177–201. Blackwell, Oxford. doi.org/10.1002/9780470774670.ch9.

Kirch, P.V. (ed.) 2021. *Talepakemalai: Lapita and its transformations in the Mussau Islands of Near Oceania*. Monumenta Archaeologica 47. Cotsen Institute of Archaeology Press, Los Angeles CA. doi.org/10.2307/j.ctv27tctrd.12.

Kuo, S-C. 2019. *New frontiers in the Neolithic archaeology of Taiwan (5600–1800BP): A perspective of maritime cultural interaction*. Springer Nature, Singapore. doi.org/10.1007/978-981-32-9263-5.

Leclerc, M., K. Taché, S. Bedford, M. Spriggs, A. Luquin and O.E. Craig 2018. The use of Lapita pottery: Results from the first analysis of lipid residues. *Journal of Archaeological Science: Reports* 17:712–722. doi.org/10.1016/j.jasrep.2017.12.019.

Li, H., Y. Huang, L.F. Mustavich, F. Zhang, J.-Z. Tan, L.-E. Wang, J. Qian, M.-H. Gao and L. Jin 2007. Y chromosomes of prehistoric people along the Yangtze River. *Human Genetics* 122:383–388. doi.org/10.1007/s00439-007-0407-2.

Li, X., G. Harbottle, J. Zhang and C. Wang 2003. The earliest writing? Sign use in the seventh millennium BC at Jiahu, Henan Province, China. *Antiquity* 77 (295):31–44. doi.org/10.1017/s0003598x00061329.

Lipson, M., O. Cheronet, S. Mallick, N. Rohland, M. Oxenham, M. Pietrusewsky, T.O. Pryce, A. Willis, H. Matsumura, H. Buckley, K. Domett, G.H. Nguyen, H.H. Trinh, A.A. Kyaw, T.T. Win, B. Pradier, N. Broomandkhoshbacht, F. Candilio, P. Changmai, D. Fernandes, M. Ferry, B. Gamarra, E. Harney, J. Kampuansai, W. Kutanan, M. Michel, M. Novak, J. Oppenheimer, K. Sirak, K. Stewardson, Z. Zhang, P. Flegontov, R. Pinhasi and D. Reich 2018. Ancient genomes document multiple waves of migration in Southeast Asian prehistory. *Science* 361:92–95. doi.org/10.1126/science.aat3188.

Lipson, M., P. Skoglund, M. Spriggs, F. Valentin, S. Bedford, R. Shing, H. Buckley, I. Phillip, G.K. Ward, S. Mallick, N. Rohland, N. Broomandkhoshbacht, O. Cheronet, M. Ferry, T.K. Harper, M. Michel, J. Oppenheimer, K. Sirak, K. Stewardson, K. Auckland, A.V.S. Hill, K. Maitland, S.J. Oppenheimer, T. Parks, K. Robson, T.N. Williams, D.J. Kennett, A.J. Mentzer, R. Pinhasi and D. Reich 2018. Population turnover in Remote Oceania shortly after initial settlement. *Current Biology* 28(7):1157–1165. doi.org/10.1016/j.cub.2018.02.051.

Lipson, M., M. Spriggs, F. Valentin, S. Bedford, R. Shing, W. Zinger, H. Buckley, F. Petchey, R. Matanik, O. Cheronet, N. Rohland, R. Pinhasi and D. Reich 2020. Three phases of ancient migration shaped the ancestry of human populations in Vanuatu. *Current Biology* 30(24):4846–4856. doi.org/10.1016/j.cub.2020.09.035.

Lu, W. and M. Aiken 2004. Origins and evolution of Chinese writing systems and preliminary counting relationships. *Accounting History* 9(3):25–51. doi.org/10.1177/103237320400900303.

McColl, H., F. Racimo, L. Vinner, F. Demeter, T. Gakuhari, J.V. Moreno-Mayar, G. Van Driem, U. Gram Wilken, A. Seguin-Orlando, C. De la Fuente Castro, S. Wasef, R. Shoocongdej, V. Souksavatdy, T. Sayavongkhamdy, M. Mokhtar Saidin, M.E. Allentoft, T. Sato, A.-S. Malaspinas, F.A. Aghakhanian, T. Korneliussen, A. Prohaska, A. Margaryan, P. De Barros Damgaard, S. Kaewsutthi, P. Lertrit, T.M. Huong Nguyen, H.-C. Hung, T. Minh Tran, H. Nghia Truong, G. Hai Nguyen, S. Shahidan, K. Wiradnyana, H. Matsumae, N. Shigehara, M. Yoneda, H. Ishida, T. Masuyama, Y. Yamada, A. Tajima, H. Shibata, A. Toyoda, T. Hanihara, S. Nakagome, T. Deviese, A.-M. Bacon, P. Duringer, J.-L. Ponche, L. Shackelford, E. Patole-Edoumba, A. Tuan Nguyen, B. Bellina-Pryce, J.-C. Galipaud, R. Kinaston, H. Buckley, C. Pottier, S. Rasmussen, T. Higham, R.A. Foley, M. Mirazón Lahr, L. Orlando, M. Sikora, M.E. Phipps, H. Oota, C. Higham, D.M. Lambert and E. Willerslev 2018. The prehistoric peopling of Southeast Asia. *Science* 361:88–92. doi.org/10.1126/science.aat3628.

Noury, A. 2005. *Le Reflet de L'Âme Lapita*, Tome I. Noury Éditions, Versailles.

Noury, A. 2019. Along the roads of the Lapita people: Designs, groups and travels. In S. Bedford and M. Spriggs (eds) *Debating Lapita: Distribution, chronology, society and subsistence,* pp. 335–348. Terra Australis 52. ANU Press, Canberra. doi.org/10.22459/TA52.2019.16.

Noury, A. and J.-C. Galipaud 2011. *Les Lapita: Nomades du Pacifique*. IRD Éditions, Marseille. doi.org/10.4000/books.irdeditions.653.

Postgate, N., T. Wang and T. Wilkinson 1995. The evidence for early writing: Utilitarian or ceremonial. *Antiquity* 69(264):459–480. doi.org/10.1017/s0003598x00081874.

Posth, C., K. Nägele, H. Colleran, F. Valentin, S. Bedford, K.W. Kami, R. Shing, H. Buckley, R. Kinaston, M. Walworth, G.R. Clark, C. Reepmeyer, J. Flexner, T. Maric, J. Moser, J. Gresky, L. Kiko, K.J. Robson, K. Auckland, S.J. Oppenheimer, A.V.S. Hill, A.J. Mentzer, J. Zech, F. Petchey, P. Roberts, C. Jeong, R.D. Gray, J. Krause and A. Powell 2018. Language continuity despite population replacement in Remote Oceania. *Nature Ecology and Evolution* 2:731–740. doi.org/10.1038/s41559-018-0498-2.

Renfrew, C. and B. Liu 2018. The emergence of complex society in China: The case of Liangzhu. *Antiquity* 92(364):975–990. doi.org/10.15184/aqy.2018.60.

Sheppard, P.J. and R.C. Green 1991. Spatial analysis of the Nenumbo (SE-RF-2) Lapita site, Solomon Islands. *Archaeology in Oceania* 26(3):89–101. doi.org/10.1002/j.1834-4453.1991.tb00272.x.

Skoglund, P., C. Posth, K. Sirak, M. Spriggs, F. Valentin, S. Bedford, G.R. Clark, C. Reepmeyer, F. Petchey, D. Fernandes, Q. Fu, E. Harney, M. Lipson, S. Mallick, M. Novak, N. Rohland, K. Stewardson, S. Abdullah, M.P. Cox, F.R. Friedlaender, J.S. Friedlaender, T. Kivisild, G. Koki, P. Kusuma, D.A. Merriwether, F.-X. Ricaut, J.T.S. Wee, N. Patterson, J. Krause, R. Pinhasi and D. Reich 2016. Genomic insights into the peopling of the Southwest Pacific. *Nature* 538:510–513. doi.org/10.1038/nature19844.

Spriggs, M. 2011. Archaeology and the Austronesian expansion: Where are we now? *Antiquity* 85(328): 510–528. doi.org/10.1017/s0003598x00067910.

Spriggs, M. 2019. The hat makes the man: Masks, headdresses and skullcaps in Lapita iconography. In S. Bedford and M. Spriggs (eds), *Debating Lapita: Distribution, chronology, society and subsistence*, pp. 255–275. Terra Australis 52. ANU Press, Canberra. doi.org/10.22459/TA52.2019.13.

Spriggs, M. 2020. The political economy of prestige practices in the Pacific: Understanding Lapita and after. In T. Thomas (ed.), *Theory in the Pacific, the Pacific in Theory: Archaeological perspectives*, pp. 180–199. Routledge, London. doi.org/10.4324/9780203730973-8.

Summerhayes, G. 2000. What's in a pot? In A.J. Anderson and T. Murray (eds), *Australian Archaeologist: Collected papers in honour of Jim Allen*, pp. 291–307. Coombs Academic Publishing, Canberra.

Trigger, B. 1998. Writing systems: A case study in cultural evolution. *Norwegian Archaeological Review* 31(1):39–62. doi.org/10.1080/00293652.1998.9965618.

Wang, C.C., H.-Y. Yeh, A.N. Popov, H.-Q. Zhang, H. Matsumura, K. Sirak, O. Cheronet, A. Kovalev, N. Rohland, A.M. Kim, S. Mallick, R. Bernardos, D. Tumen, J. Zhao, Y.-C. Liu, J.-Y. Liu, M. Mah, K. Wang, Z. Zhang, N. Adamski, N. Broomandkhoshbacht, K. Callan, F. Candilio, K.S. Duffett Carlson, B.J. Culleton, L. Eccles, S. Freilich, D. Keating, A.M. Lawson, K. Mandl, M. Michel, J. Oppenheimer, K.T. Özdoğan, K. Stewardson, S. Wen, S. Yan, F. Zalzala, R. Chuang, C.-J. Huang, H. Looh, C.-C. Shiung, Y.G. Nikitin, A.V. Tabarev, A.A. Tishkin, S. Lin, Z.-Y. Sun, X.-M. Wu, T.-L. Yang, X. Hu, L. Chen, H. Du, J. Bayarsaikhan, E. Mijiddorj, D. Erdenebaatar, T.-O. Iderkhangai, E. Myagmar, H. Kanzawa-Kiriyama, M. Nishino, K.-I. Shinoda, O.A. Shubina, J. Guo, W. Cai, Q. Deng, L. Kang, D. Li, D. Li, R. Lin, Nini, R. Shrestha, L.-X. Wang, L. Wei, G. Xie, H. Yao, M. Zhang, G. He, X. Yang, R. Hu, M. Robbeets, S. Schiffels, D.J. Kennett, L. Jin, H. Li, J. Krause, R. Pinhasi and D. Reich 2021. Genomic insights into the formation of human populations in East Asia. *Nature* 591:413–419. doi.org/10.1038/s41586-021-03336-2.

Yang, M.A., X. Fan, B. Sun, C. Chen, J. Lang, Y.C. Ko, C.H. Tsang, H. Chiu, T. Wang, Q. Bao, X. Wu, M. Hajdinjak, A.M.-S. Ko, M. Ding, P. Cao, R. Yang, F. Liu, B. Nickel, Q. Dai, X. Feng, L. Zhang, C. Sun, C. Ning, W. Zeng, Y. Zhao, M. Zhang, X. Gao, Y. Cui, D. Reich, M. Stoneking and Q. Fu 2020. Ancient DNA indicates population shifts and admixture in northern and southern China. *Science* 369: 282–288. doi.org/10.1126/science.aba0909.

Yu, X. and H. Li 2021. Origin of ethnic groups, linguistic families, and civilizations in China viewed from the Y chromosome. *Molecular Genetics and Genomics* 296:783–797. doi.org/10.1007/s00438-021-01794-x.

Zhi, Z. and H.-C. Hung 2010. The emergence of agriculture in southern China. *Antiquity* 84:11–25. doi.org/10.1017/s0003598x00099737.

8

An update on Late Lapita: Its manifestations and associated implications

Stuart Bedford

Abstract

It is now more than 20 years since Summerhayes introduced the concept and framework of Early, Middle and Late Lapita in an attempt to more accurately define and categorise the distinctive pottery found across an extensive zone in the south-west Pacific. Since that time, the terminology has been universally accepted and many more sites containing Late Lapita have been uncovered. This paper summarises current knowledge in relation to Late Lapita pottery across the distribution and what it implies in terms of Late Lapita societies. It suggests that while there are a series of motifs and decorative techniques that show similarity across the distribution, as argued by Summerhayes, the current evidence is overwhelmingly indicative of increasing regional diversification in Late Lapita pottery styles. Communities who had been established for several generations began to build an increasingly local identity, comprising both elements of their heritage and regionally specific social and physical environments.

Introduction

Lapita pottery first appeared on the global stage, or at least to a select educated elite, more than 100 years ago with the publication of Father Otto Meyer's finds of very distinctive highly decorated pottery from Watom Island in the Bismarck Archipelago (Meyer 1909). Since that time, generations of interested and informed individuals, through the implementation of formalised small and major archaeological research projects, have contributed to the current understanding of what Lapita pottery represented and its position in the history of Pacific colonisation and settlement (Kirch 2017:74–106; Sand 2010a). It was from the 1970s that regional and chronological variation in Lapita pottery was first identified. Green carried out detailed summaries of Lapita pottery, based on vessel shape and the style and frequency of decoration, ultimately identifying regionally distinct styles, namely Western and Eastern, which he suggested were influenced by both temporal and spatial aspects (Green 1979). A distinctive Far Western style, thought only to be found in the Bismarck Archipelago, was soon added (Anson 1986). The idea that Lapita provinces (Far Western, Western, Eastern and Southern) was perhaps a better way of conceptualising Lapita was also subsequently proposed (Kirch 1997; Sand 2000). Finally, the later characterisation and relabelling of Lapita pottery across its distribution as Early, Middle and Late by Summerhayes largely replaced the long-standing geographically specific terms and provinces (Summerhayes 2000, 2001). This both moved away from geographic-specific terms but also argued for connections across the distribution from New Guinea to Tonga during the Middle Period (former Western) and although diluted, even into the Late Lapita Period.

While the distinctive pottery has always been a focus of Lapita culture studies, the poor preservation and mixing of most Lapita sites and the generally small nature of the sherds from the now 293 sites (Bedford et al. 2019), has always been a challenge in terms of defining vessel form and full designs, and therefore in determining levels of similarity or difference. Another related challenging aspect of Lapita pottery studies is determining the definitive chronology of particular sherds from sites that might represent mixed deposits encompassing Lapita occupation over several generations. The end of Lapita is also generally associated with sites that date within a flat section of the radiocarbon calibration curve so dates often have a standard deviation that covers hundreds of years, which makes them of limited use in determining in any fine detail the period that Late Lapita encompasses.

It was this situation, of primarily dealing with small mixed sherds, that originally stimulated a focus on motif comparisons (Anson 1986; Green 1979) and perpetuated it as a major area of research (Chiu 2019; Chiu and Sand 2005; Noury 2019; Summerhayes 2000). However, there are inherent pitfalls in placing too much emphasis on the quantitative comparison of motif suites as attributes, as the complexity of dentate-stamped application or the position on a vessel can be equally suggestive of different periods, regional connections or divergence (Burley and Leblanc 2015:181; Sand 2015). Equally problematic is whether motifs are in fact being shared or are simply derived from earlier more complex designs, friezes or bands (Burley et al. 2002; Sand 2015).

While there is variation across the Lapita distribution and there are many challenges related to mixed deposits, chronological accuracy and gaps in sampling, for the purposes of this discussion a broad definition of Early, Middle and Late Lapita is outlined. There is of course an arbitrary element to aspects of any chronological and stylistic division of Lapita as it was a pottery tradition that represents continuous production over more than 400 years, at least in some regions. There are no abrupt breaks in the pottery style. Early Lapita appears in the Bismarck Archipelago at around 3200 to 3000 BP across a number of sites and is largely restricted to that region (Kirch 2021:162–163; Specht and Gosden 2019).[1] Distinctive vessel forms that dominate the earliest assemblages and are not found in sites further east include: open bowls that are sometimes on stands and in some cases have stepped rims and legs; flat dishes with cut-outs on the rim; and base and pedestal stands with excising and or full cut-outs through the vessel wall. Other forms that are common and found in later assemblages include jars, some of which were carinated. Fine dentate stamping where the decoration is tightly spaced is dominant, sometimes in association with applied relief, but coarser dentate, incised and plain vessels are also present (e.g. Kirch 2021:318–319; Summerhayes 2000:231). Middle Lapita develops from around 3000 BP and is associated with the rapid movement and initial colonisation of previously uninhabited islands from the Reefs–Santa Cruz across to Tonga. Carinated jars and flat dishes, some of which are connected to stands or pedestals,[2] dominate the assemblages. Carinated jars with incurving rims also feature. The dentate stamping is less fine and the designs less concentrated (Sand 2015:145–160). Incised and plainware vessels remain a component of the assemblages. From around 2800 BP Late Lapita develops and is described by most researchers,

---

1   In the earliest sites in the Reefs–Santa Cruz (SZ8) and Vanuatu (Makué), there are a very limited number of sherds/vessel forms that suggest some elements of Early Lapita. These are primarily excised stands and dishes with collared and cut-out rims (see Bedford 2015:37; Sand 2015:147–149).

2   The majority of which are not excised and none have cut-outs through the vessel walls.

in contrast to Early and Middle, comprising fewer vessel forms (i.e. stands and dishes have dropped out) of smaller dimensions, carinated vessels became less common and unique new vessel forms appear. The dentate decoration comprises more simplified patterns executed in an open and sparse style, often in the form of single lines (curved or linear) with stamps whose teeth were rectangular in form and were around 1–2 mm in size, as opposed to the earlier needle-point dentate. A new distinctive decorative technique, namely shell impression, is also present. Zone markers, a defining feature of Middle Lapita designs, particularly on carinated vessels, become rare. Overall, Late Lapita is thought to have undergone a simplification in both form and decoration that involved diminished input of labour and a shift away from stricter social rules relating to vessel form and design use in association with pottery function (Bedford 2015, 2019; Bedford and Galipaud 2010; Burley et al. 2002; Burley and Dickinson 2004; Clark 2007; Clark and Anderson 2009; David et al. 2011; Sand 2015; Specht 1968:131–132; Summerhayes 2000; Wu 2016). It is difficult to be definitive regarding the timing of the end of Lapita due to the flat section of the calibration curve at this crucial period, but most archaeologists would agree that dentate stamping continuing anywhere much beyond 2700 BP seems highly unlikely (Burley et al. 2018; Kirch 2021:163; Sand 2010b:233).

The focus of this paper is to profile Late Lapita pottery, that phase of production that demonstrates some connection with the final use of dentate stamping across the distribution, and discuss what it implies in terms of Late Lapita societies. Current data suggests that while there are a series of motifs and decorative techniques that show similarity across the distribution, as argued by Summerhayes, the overall trend is indicative of regional diversification, with some near neighbour connections developing in Late Lapita pottery styles. Communities who had been established for several generations began to build an increasingly local identity, comprising both elements of their shared heritage, and regionally specific social and physical environments.

Late Lapita

This review of Late Lapita is necessarily selective and restricted, largely due to logistical considerations, but also to enhance accuracy. It focuses on *stylistic attributes*, primarily on vessel form and decoration where dentate stamping has been recorded and securely provenanced. Other associated vessel forms are discussed and an exception is made for shell-impressed decoration that is generally recognised as a distinctive and unique decorative technique that appeared in association with the demise of dentate stamping. Incised decoration is another significant component of the Lapita story generally, including the Late period, but is not focused on here. Pottery production and compositional aspects are also not included, although most researchers have demonstrated that Late Lapita pottery overwhelmingly tends to be produced with locally available clays and tempers.

After undertaking a census of available data in theses, published material and online databases that include Late Lapita across the distribution, it is quickly apparent that there are major gaps in the data available. In some regions in Remote Oceania, it is well defined and represented in both vessel form and full design motifs. These include particularly Fiji and Tonga and to a lesser extent New Caledonia and Vanuatu. Others, where a distinctive Late Lapita pottery style is more difficult to determine, include Samoa, where there is only one known Lapita site to date, the submerged site of Mulifanua (Green 1974:172; Petchey 1995). However, the sherds from that site in combination with the limited number of Lapita sherds from Futuna and 'Uvea Islands (Sand 1990, 1998) all provide some detail on Late Lapita and can be connected with the much more robust Tongan pottery sequence. Perhaps surprisingly, the Reefs–Santa Cruz Lapita pottery collections, which number in the thousands of sherds, provide limited detail on Late Lapita. Most of the sites were heavily mixed and the sherds are generally small. In Near Oceania, the situation is varied, with the Solomon Islands having a very limited number of sites, mostly in the intertidal zone, where the dentate-stamped sherds are again generally small. In the Bismarck Archipelago, where the largest number of Lapita sites are known, the sherds from Late Lapita sites tend to be small and often come from mixed deposits. While there is abundant evidence of expanded or more open designs, the use of less refined tools, and sherds with shell impression, establishing full design structures and vessel forms is difficult (Wu 2016). On mainland New Guinea, the sites located at Caution Bay provide important data relating to this period, as they are all essentially date to the Late Lapita Period and there are a number of reconstructable vessels (David et al. 2011).

Regional profiles

Tonga

The Tongan archipelago is almost the ideal situation archaeologically for defining Late Lapita in the far east of the distribution. Over many decades, focused research has recorded 34 Lapita sites across 12 islands, almost all of which are described as Late (Bedford et al. 2019). There is only a single major site, that of Nukuleka on Tongatapu, which has been identified as a founding settlement, where Middle Lapita–style pottery is well represented (Burley et al. 2012). The later transition from Late Lapita to plainware is argued to be generally easily identifiable, with Lapita occupations largely located on beach sands, while plainware sites tend to be associated with stratigraphy that indicates a build-up of sediments and rapid midden accumulations (Burley et al. 2001:101). However, even in such potentially ideal conditions there are limitations on precise definitions for Late Lapita, particularly due to sherd size.

In a summary of vessel typology, Burley et al. (2002:217) cautioned that as different types were established primarily through rims only, it could only be considered as a general approximation and that it was likely that an extremely high degree of variation in vessel form existed in the Tongan decorated pottery assemblage overall.[3] Connaughton (2014), who specifically focused on trying to define and delineate Late Lapita and Polynesian Plainwares in Tonga, further refined this. The broad summary of vessel forms is outlined as follows: small cups/bowls of less than 12 cm in diameter, everted to straight-rimmed bowls, inverted rimmed bowls, short-necked jars, everted rim jars and a distinctive collared rim jar (see Figures 8.1 and 8.2). All assemblages are dominated by everted rim jars (both carinated and globular), while bowls with everted/straight rims and inverted rims are the second and third most dominant forms. These two forms dominate all collections and account for between 25 and 54 percent of all vessel forms. Vessels with handles also appear in Tonga during Late Lapita, although this is poorly defined (Burley et al. 2002:216–217, Table 3; Connaughton 2014:96–101, Fig. 4-2, 5-2; Kirch 1988:158, Fig. 95).

---

3   This is particularly emphasised in the category 'strongly everted jars', where carinated vessels are grouped together with flat-bottomed dishes (although are not considered associated with Late Lapita) and carinated and globular jar forms are combined (Burley et al. 2002:Fig. 2). This broad grouping is acknowledged (Burley et al. 2002:217, 223) but it has also demonstrated that carinated sherds are a dominant feature of many sites and often associated with decoration (Burley et al. 2002:Table 4; Connaughton 2014; Kirch 1988:158).

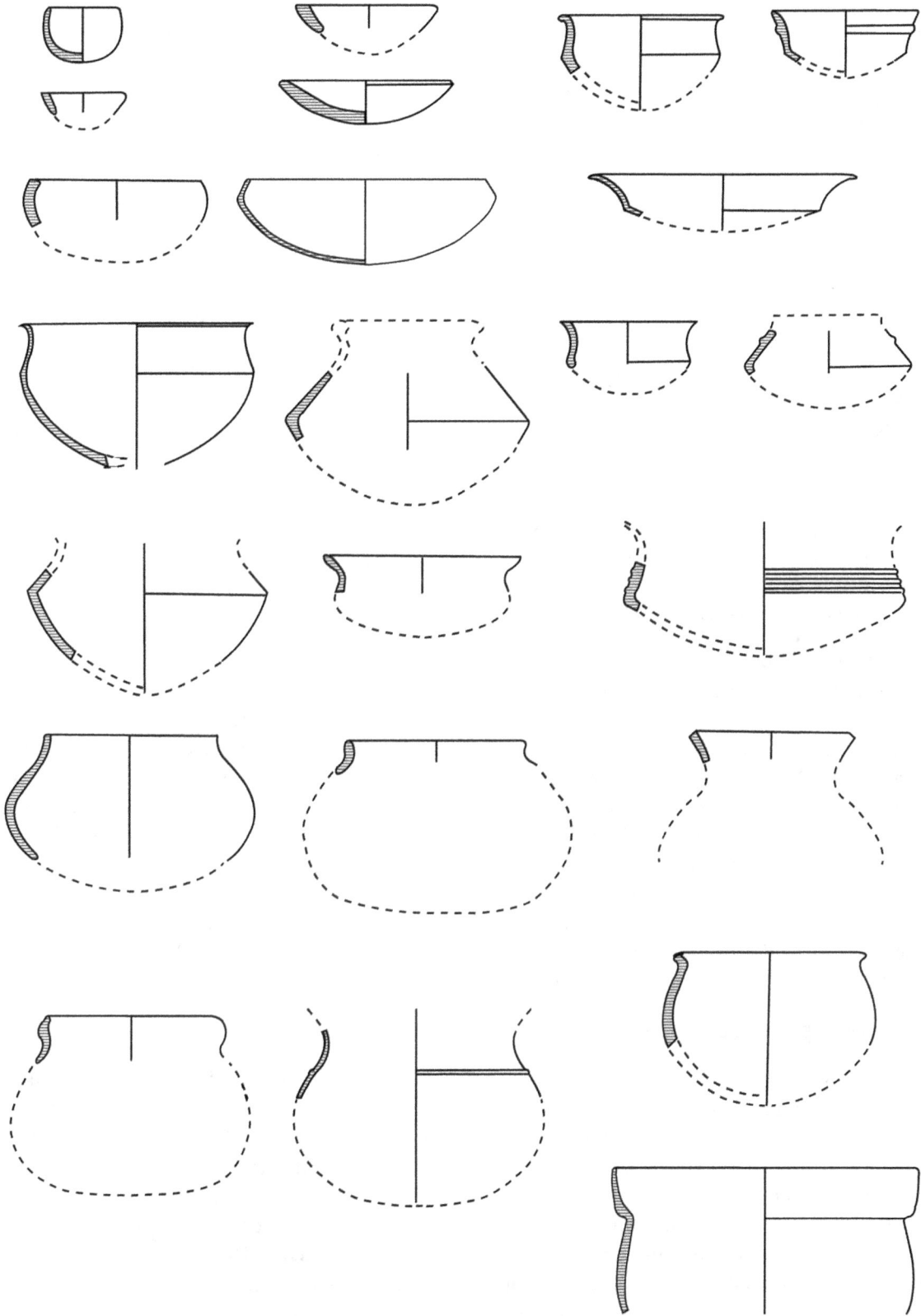

Figure 8.1: Summary of Late Lapita Tongan vessel forms. Not to scale.

Source: Derived from Burley et al. (2002); Connaughton (2014); Kirch (1988) and Poulsen (1987).

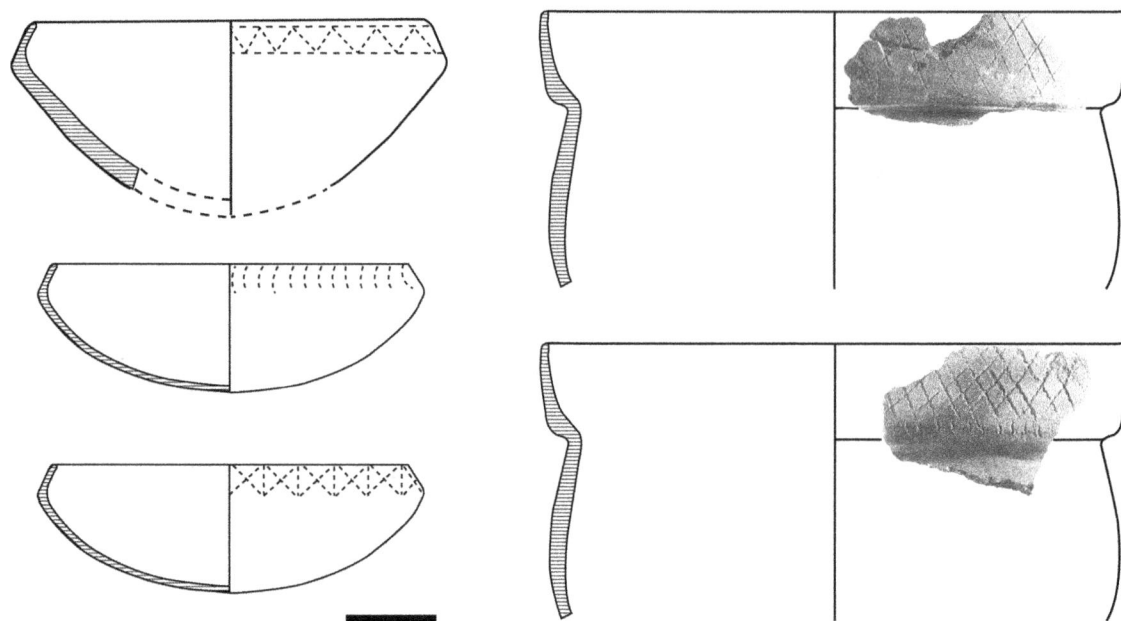

Figure 8.2: Dentate and shell-impressed Lapita designs from Tonga.

Note: The crosshatched motif on the collared vessels are in dentate stamping and shell impression. Black scale is 5 cm.

Source: Adapted from Poulsen (1987).

Late Lapita decoration in Tonga is characterised by expanded and simplified dentate-stamped designs that are consistently applied across the range of vessel forms (Burley et al. 2002:220, 223; Connaughton 2014:166). Over 230 design motifs, categorised into 25 themes, have been identified across Tonga. This includes the Nukuleka site, so the data may be skewed in terms of what characterises Late Lapita,[4] but it is significant to note that across all the recorded sites only a very small number of design motifs dominate. Six categories account for over 70 per cent of motif applications in the assemblage as a whole (Burley et al. 2002:Table 7, Fig. 3). The dentate-stamped designs overwhelmingly comprise single lines (see Figure 8.2). Other decorative features that are common include applied relief, occurring as raised horizontal bands (sometimes multiple and often notched), vertical bars and as nubbins. Incision and shell impression is present and used frequently to apply the same suite of motifs as dentate stamping (e.g. Figure 8.2) and can be found in combination on the same vessel in several cases (Burley et al. 2002:218, Table 5).

Samoa, Futuna, 'Uvea

The number of Lapita sites and recovered pottery from Samoa, Futuna and 'Uvea is very limited, compared to other regions. They comprise the single submerged site of Mulifanua for Samoa (Green 1974; Petchey 1995), one site on Futuna and three on 'Uvea (Frimigacci 2000; Sand 1990, 1998). Despite the limited assemblages, they do provide some detail as to the nature of Lapita in the region and the connections with near neighbours. The focus here is pottery from Mulifanua where, over a number of years, a significant number of diagnostic sherds (558), albeit small and worn, have been collected and studied in some detail (Green 1974:170–175; Petchey 1995:55–89). The dentate decoration illustrated from this site is striking for the domination of single-line dentate with notable gaps between stamping—that is, the designs are expanded and simple (Green 1974:172; Petchey

---

4   Although the site is heavily mixed, Burley et al. (2002:222) argue that the same design percentages are valid for Nukuleka.

1995:Fig. 3.5–9, Table 3.5). Notched applied relief is also present. These features and the motifs have clear parallels with Late Lapita decoration in Tonga. Vessel form is more difficult to establish and is more speculative due to sherd size. Petchey (1995:Table 3.8) proposed seven suggested vessel forms, most of which have parallels in the Tongan and Fijian Late Lapita, including collar-rimmed vessels, shallow bowls and cups.

Fiji

The well-preserved archaeological deposits identified in the Sigatoka dunes of Viti Levu Island in Fiji provide an almost unique and ideal situation in regard to defining Late Lapita pottery. A series of three discrete cultural horizons were long ago identified at the dunes (Birks 1973), each separated by layers of sterile sand, which incorporated different phases of the Fijian ceramic sequence. The tight chronological window represented in each of the phases and the limited disturbance of the large collections of pottery,[5] enabled the reconstruction of a whole series of vessels that date to the Late Lapita phase, found in the Level 1 deposits (Birks 1973; Burley and Connaughton 2010; Burley and Dickinson 2004; Petchey 1995). The collections from the different phases at Sigatoka have been crucial to the establishment of the Fijian pottery sequence and have allowed the identification, from much more fragmented collections, of the same vessel forms and decoration across much of Fiji.

A whole series of archaeological investigations have been undertaken at Sigatoka over more than 60 years. Major excavations associated with Level 1 deposits include the pioneering excavations of the Birks in 1965 and 66 (994 m² associated with Level 1 deposits) (Birks 1973); salvage excavations in 1993 following exposure of materials due to cyclone damage (Hudson 1994; Petchey 1995); and in 1998 and 2000, 85 m² was excavated when Level 1 deposits were exposed through natural erosion (Burley and Dickinson 2004). The Birks' identified a total assemblage of 87 diagnostically complete pottery vessels, along with partial vessels, pot lids, pot rests and pottery disks (Birks 1973:51–53). The main vessel forms comprised: open-necked jars (Type 1, five subtypes), bowls (Type 2, five subtypes), narrow-neck water jars (Type 3, four subtypes) and covers/lids (Type 4), then pot rests and discs (Figure 8.3). Pottery recovered from the 1993 excavations was more fragmentary. For example, 338 Lapita sherds were assigned to only four vessels. The four vessels were all carinated jars with outcurving rims (Type 1D), decorated predominately with single-line dentate stamping producing expanded motifs (Petchey 1995:106, Table 4.3). The later (1998, 2000) excavations identified 22 whole vessels, which largely aligned with the same earlier Birks typology, with the addition of a Type 2 variant (Figure 8.3e) (see Burley and Dickinson 2004:18, Table 2 and Appendix A for a summary). Another later find, following erosion from the same Level 1 zone, were large pieces of a carinated (Type 1D) vessel. The decoration was simple single-line dentate producing an expanded motif (Figure 8.3q) (Burley and Connaughton 2010:145). It both confirmed Lapita connections and a variation on vessel form and design that had earlier been identified in 1993 (Petchey 1995:112–116).

If the pottery recovered from these three periods of excavation is accepted as representing Late Lapita in Fiji, then it is characterised by a range of vessel forms with limited decoration, apart from notching on the rim of Type 1 vessels (Figure 8.3). It is overwhelmingly a plainware collection but there are a number of decorative techniques used, including dentate stamping on specific vessel forms (Birks 1973:51, Table 2; Petchey 1995:112–116). These are single-line dentates on the rim and body of Type 1 vessels (Figure 8.3d–f, n, p, q) and inverted rim, Type 2E bowls (Figure 8.3o). Other decorative techniques include shell impression (Birks 1973:162, Plate 25), incision, and rare applied relief (one example of nubbins and two of continuous notched applied horizontal relief (Birks 1973:154, Plate 8)).

---

5   Described as in good condition and 'undisturbed since deposition' (Birks 1973:17).

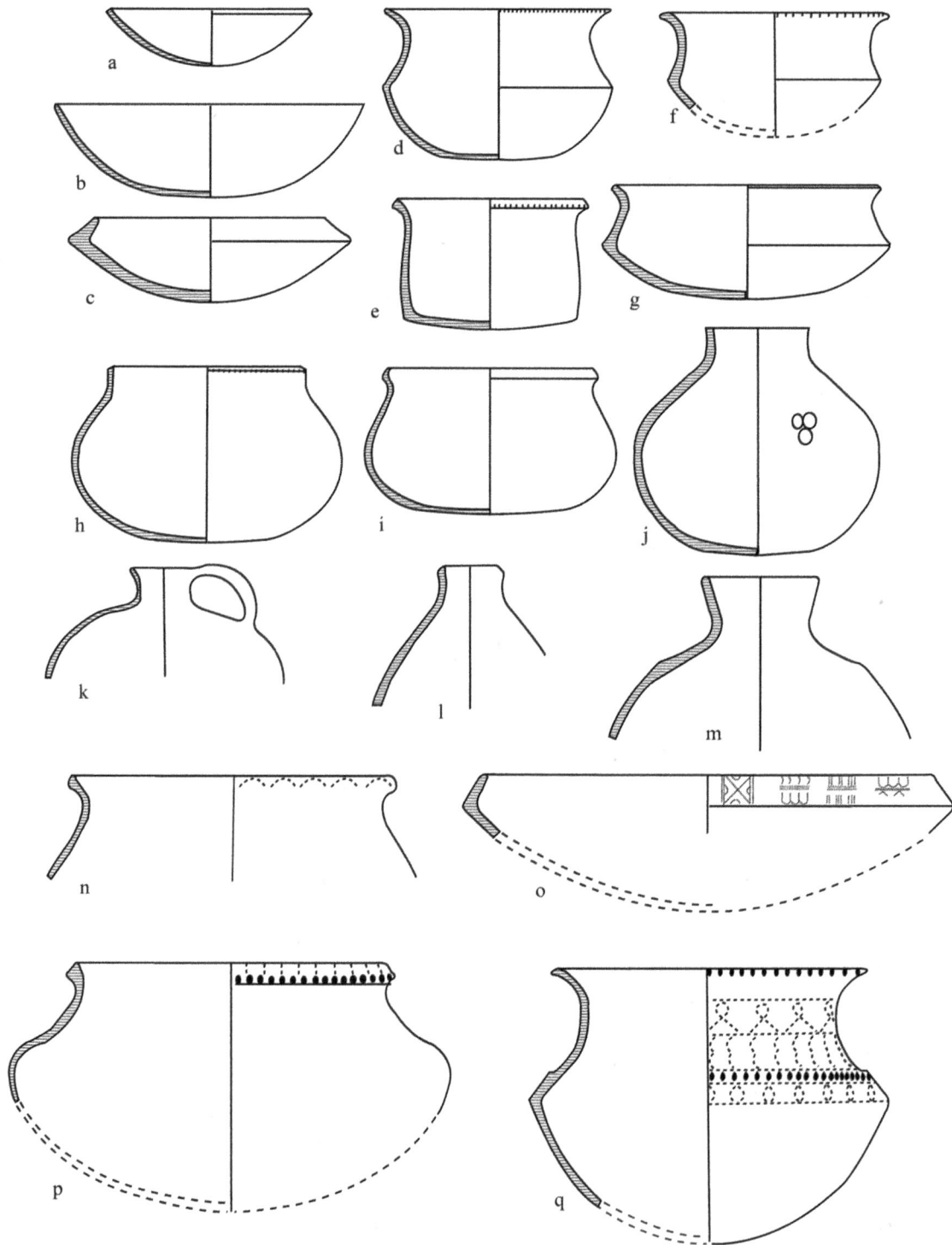

Figure 8.3: Summary of Fijian Late Lapita vessel forms and decoration.

Notes: Stands are not illustrated. Not to scale. (a–b) Type 2A; (c) Type 2E; (d), (f), (g) Type 1D; (e) Type 2 other; (h–i) Type 1C; (j) Type 3A; (k) Type 3B; (l) Type 3C; (m) Type 3A, (n, p) Type 1A, (o) Type 2E, (q) Type 1D.

Source: Derived from Birks (1973); Burley and Dickinson (2004) and Burley and Connaughton (2010).

Vanuatu

Across the Vanuatu archipelago, 30 Lapita sites have been identified (Bedford et al. 2019). However, many have collections of a limited number of small decorated or diagnostic sherds that provide limited information beyond dentate motifs. Those that are most useful in establishing Late Lapita in Vanuatu are those located on the islands of north-east Malakula, namely Vao and Uripiv, the Teouma site on Efate in central Vanuatu, and on Aneityum, the southernmost inhabited island of the archipelago. Lapita pottery from Malakula has been outlined and summarised (Bedford 2019) but even at these well-preserved sites, it is difficult to definitively tease out what might be Middle and/or Late Lapita. Rather, chronological and regional change in pottery form and decoration appears likely to have been very rapid in all periods, but this aspect is often obscured by both broad categorisations of Lapita pottery and radiocarbon dates (Bedford 2019:236). Even Middle Lapita on Vao clearly shows the development of new vessel forms and dentate-stamped designs when compared to other regions. Despite these challenges, a number of distinctive pottery features from these islands gives some indication of the last phase of Lapita in the north. A number of these features can also be identified among the very mixed collections retrieved from nearby Malo Island (Hedrick n.d.). There are the standard features, expanded motifs, larger dentate teeth, appearance of shell impression and a more limited range of vessel forms along with the development of other distinctive forms (Figures 8.4 and 8.5). The latter includes a carinated vessel that has an inverted rim and a ledge on the lower section of the carination (Figure 8.4j). Late Lapita vessel forms in the north as identified thus far are primarily restricted to carinated and globular jars with varying rim forms. Open bowls, so commonly seen in sites further east, are absent. Unrestricted zigzag decoration, both dentate and incised, is a signature feature (Figure 8.5). Shell-impressed decoration, in association with the Late Lapita decorative suite, has been recorded at Teouma and at sites on Malo and Santo Islands.

The Teouma Lapita site on Efate encompasses an occupation period of potentially several hundred years that starts with first arrival and Middle Lapita through to the Post-Lapita Erueti Phase (Bedford et al. 2010). More than 400 vessels have been identified associated with the Lapita period, which includes vessels primarily decorated with dentate stamping, but also incision and applied relief, and much rarer, shell impression. Like many other Lapita sites of prolonged occupation, it is not always easy to differentiate chronological phases in the pottery sequence and identify what might be definitively Late Lapita. A further complicating factor at the site was the identification of both fine and expanded dentate decoration (the latter usually assumed to be a feature of Late Lapita) in the earliest occupation phase of the site. A distinct zone of the site associated with the Lapita phase of occupation also had a high percentage of incised and plain carinated jars (Spriggs and Bedford 2013). There are, however, a number of distinct vessel forms and motifs that can be identified as Late Lapita at the site and others that might be categorised as such more tentatively, namely carinated and globular jars (Figure 8.4e, f). Again, open bowls are not present. An example of the very distinctive carinated vessel found in Malakula is also present at Teouma. A step or ledge is present on the underside of the carination and it is decorated with its own distinct face motif (Figure 8.4l). Other very simple dentate-stamped motifs occur on outcurving jars and globular incurving jars. Shell impression occurs on two vessels and a single sherd is decorated with a curved flat stamp (Figure 8.5g).

Figure 8.4: A selection of Vanuatu Late Lapita vessel forms and decoration.

Notes: (a) Impressed circles and single-line dentate, Vao Island; (b) single-line crosshatch on rim, Teouma, Efate Island; (c) globular jar with incurving rim, dentate stamping on rim (Vao); (d) globular jar with incurving rim, note step on rim (Vao); (e) globular jar with incurving rim and soft carination, single-line dentate (Teouma); (f) globular jar with incurving rim, (Teouma); (g–h) globular jars with incurving rim and step, dentate on rim (Vao); (i) globular jar with incurving rim, simple dentate, Uripiv Island; (j) carinated jar with inverted rim and step below carination (Uripiv); (k) carinated jar with expanded dentate motif (Uripiv); (l) carinated jar with inverted rim and step below carination, expanded dentate-stamped face motif (Teouma).

Source: Author's archive.

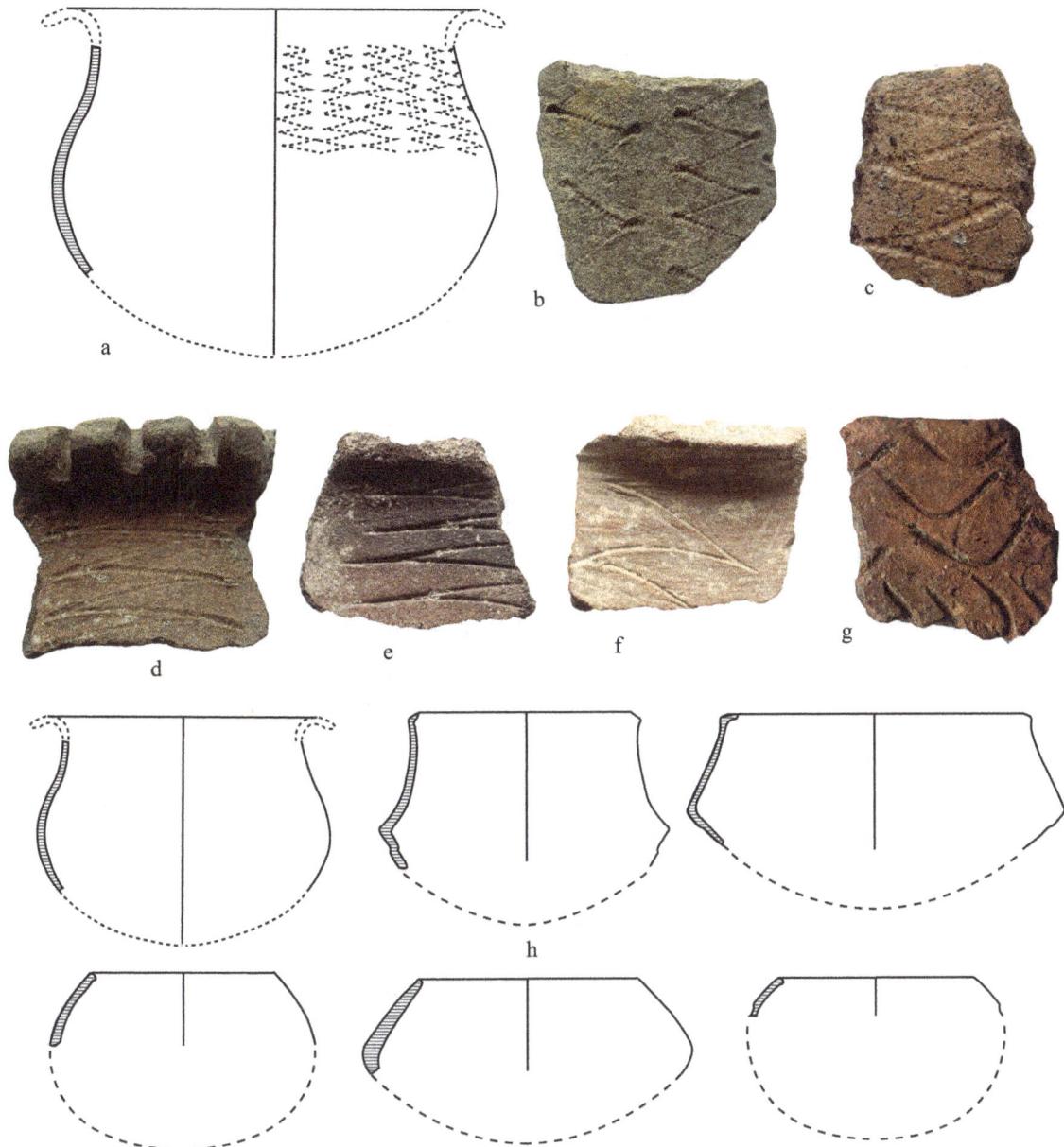

Figure 8.5: Late Lapita zigzag dentate and flat tool stamped decoration from Vanuatu.

Notes: (a–b) Dentate-stamped, Vao Island; (c) dentate-stamped, Aneityum Island; (d) flat tool zigzag (Vao); (e–f) flat tool and or incised zigzag motif (Aneityum); (g) flat tool, crescent-shaped impressed motif, rim sherd, Teouma, Efate Island; (h) a selection of Late Lapita vessel forms found in Vanuatu.

Source: Author's archive.

On Aneityum, the only Lapita site thus far discovered is located at Anelcauhat Harbour on the south-east of the island (Bedford et al. 2016). All sherds are generally small and the only vessel form associated with Late Lapita at the site is a globular jar with outcurving rim. Decoration is dominated by unrestricted dentate-stamped, incised and/or impressed zigzag motifs (Figure 8.5c, e, f). Impressed zigzag and other motifs, which appear to have been made using a flat stamp, have also been identified in Late Lapita deposits in the Loyalty Islands (Sand 2010b:132, Photo 51; Sand et al. 2002:139, Fig. 10). In summary, Late Lapita across Vanuatu itself shows both variation and some level of similarity, but is very different, particularly in vessel form and dentate decoration, to what is identified as Late Lapita found in sites further east. Perhaps not surprisingly, closer affiliation, at least in some aspects, is found with sites in New Caledonia.

New Caledonia

New Caledonia has long been endowed with a multitude of Lapita sites (current total 38) identified across the Grand Terre and the adjacent Loyalty Islands (Bedford et al. 2019). The discovery over generations of large sherds from various sites and particularly the 15 largely reconstructable vessels from the burial pit at Koné have greatly enriched the definition of Lapita in New Caledonia. However, mixing of deposits at most sites is again a challenge in determining chronological phases of the pottery sequence, but a broad summary is outlined here, gleaning information primarily from Sand (2010b:97–167).[6] The colonising phase in New Caledonia is characterised by Middle Lapita, identified at a whole series of sites across the islands. It is also a phase that goes through rapid transformation with a tendency towards a diminished suite of vessel forms of decreasing size and the development of a suite of distinctive dentate motifs. This has led researchers there to position and label Lapita from New Caledonia as a Southern Lapita variant or province (Sand 2010b:167). Late Lapita pottery displays further transformation and local variation, particularly between the Grand Terre and the Loyalties. There is an increase in the number and range of incised motifs, simplified, often single-line dentate-stamped motifs (Sand 2010b:Photo 56, Fig. 77) and the appearance of shell impression as a decorative technique (Sand 2010b:Photo 36). Vessel forms become more restricted, with carinated (generally less angular) and globular jars dominating, but also distinctive, unique vessels appearing (Figure 8.6). Unrestricted dentate-stamped zigzag motifs are common, and as noted above, the same motifs are produced in the Loyalties with a flat-edged tool. Paddle-impression also first appears in association with simple dentate stamping. Open bowls are absent.

---

6   Of the 38 identified sites in New Caledonia, 15 are classified as encompassing the period from Early to Late within the local ceramic series (Bedford et al. 2019).

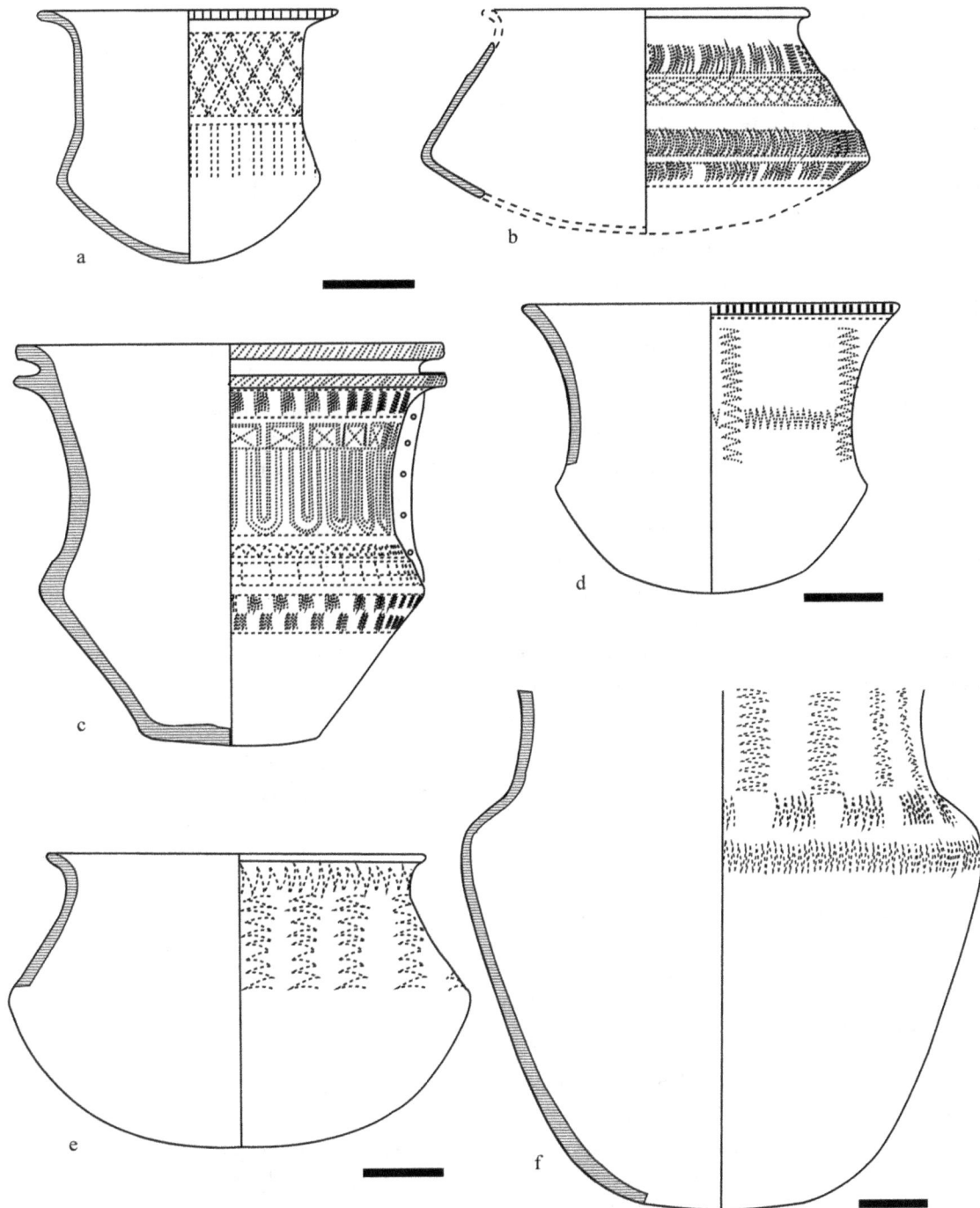

Figure 8.6: A range of Late Lapita New Caledonian vessel forms and decoration.

Notes: Zigzag dentate is prominent. (a) Patho site, Maré Island; (b) St-Maurice, Vatcha, Iles des Pines; (c–e) vessels from the Kurin site, Maré Island; (f) Lapita site, Koné. Black scales are 5 cm.

Source: All derived from Sand (2010b).

Reefs–Santa Cruz

The Lapita sites from the Reefs–Santa Cruz Islands have been central to much of the Lapita debate since their identification and excavation in the early 1970s. Due to their key location, as the first islands beyond Near Oceania, along with the abundant evidence for Lapita settlement, they were identified as both a key gateway into Remote Oceania and a central node of connection back to the homeland in the Bismarcks (Green 1979). The extensive excavations and recovery of thousands of decorated sherds were instrumental in the pioneering classification systems of Lapita pottery that were primarily based on motifs, and ultimately led to the identification and labelling of a distinctive Western and Eastern Lapita style (Green 1979). However, what has always been recognised was the shallow nature of all of the sites, the heavy mixing of the deposits and the small size of the vast majority of the sherds. Of the 9748 sherds (dentate, incised, other and plain) analysed by Donovan (1973) from the three major sites (RL2 [4545], RL6 [1549] and SZ8 [3654]), the majority came from the uppermost layer of all sites (described as garden soil) and surface collections (Donovan 1973:12–13, Tables 5a, 7a, 9a).[7] Donovan identified and compiled a list of 99 motifs and associated alloforms from all of the pottery collections (1973:Appendix III, 1–64), which provided a foundational dataset for comparison that has been used for decades (i.e. Chiu 2019). Identification of vessel form was not attempted by Donovan due to small sherd size, but following a vast increase in the number of sites discovered elsewhere since, including a whole series of almost complete vessels, a reliable definition of vessel forms and associated designs has been recently completed by Sand (2015:146–159). However, almost all of the forms and designs illustrated are associated with complex vessel forms and/or designs that are most compatible with the Middle Lapita Phase. Only a single jar with outcurving rim, which displays a motif comprising very simple single-line dentate and incision, stands out as being potentially Late Lapita (Sand 2015:156, Fig. 34).

In summary, the Reefs–Santa Cruz collections overall provide limited information in terms of defining Late Lapita, both due to the mixed nature of the deposits but also because most of the sites may indeed not date to that period (Bedford et al. 2019:Table 1.1, 14–15). Donovan's assessment of levels of skill in relation to the decoration of the sherds, where a 5-point scale was established, is instructive. It is significant to note that of the 5742 sherds that were assessed, only 177 (3%) were classified as fitting into the two lowest levels of skill (4 and 5) (1973: Appendix III, 77, Table 3). Shell impression was present although rare (10 examples) (Donovan 1973:Appendix III Table 5), as were unrestricted zigzag motifs and single-line dentate stamping.

Solomon Islands

The main Solomons chain has presented major challenges—much to do with geomorphological complexities—in terms of identifying Lapita sites, and some have even argued that the region was largely leap-frogged during much of the Lapita period (Sheppard 2011).[8] Sites where dentate-stamped sherds have been recovered are extremely rare. Three sites have been identified in the intertidal zone in New Georgia Province that provide some insights into the Late Lapita Period, although the small number of dentate-stamped sherds[9] and questions over chronology make determining full vessel form, design and possible associations with much of the collections difficult. Simple, single and parallel dentate stamping appears on carinated jars from Honiavasa and it is also found in

---

7   Dentate-stamped sherds from the surface (S) and uppermost Layer A (LA), from the various sites were as follows: RL2, S 40 (1.6%), LA:1647 (66%) 67% of total (2494); RL6, LA:586, 62% of total (949); SZ 8, S:416 (18%), LA: 789 (35%), 53% of total (2261).

8   Ten sites in total, seven in the North Solomons, and three in New Georgia (Bedford et al. 2019).

9   Seven from Nusa Roviana and Honiavasa (Felgate 2003:240, Table 16) and 5 from Poitete, Kolombangara Island (Summerhayes and Scales 2005).

association with horizontal notched applied relief and incision on one outcurving rim vessel from Nusa Roviana (Felgate 2001:Fig. 3). Shell-impressed decoration is also present at Honiavasa (Felgate 2003:228, Fig. 49). At Poitete, Kolombangara Island, dentate stamping is again simple and designs expanded; and vessel forms identified were restricted to carinated and globular jars with outcurving rims (Summerhayes and Scales 2005:15). Open bowls were not identified at any of the sites. Much greater numbers of dentate-stamped sherds have been found in the northern Solomons, including four sites on Buka (DJQ) and Sohano islands (DAF, DAA, DKC) and three on Nissan (DFF, DGD/2, DES) but all have been classified as Middle Lapita (Bedford et al. 2019; Spriggs 1991). Although there are hints of features that might indicate Late Lapita it is difficult to assess as the vast majority of the sherds come from intertidal deposits and only a limited number are illustrated.

Bismarck Archipelago

The Bismarck Archipelago is where Lapita was first identified and where by far the largest number of Lapita sites (88) have been identified to date (Bedford et al. 2019). The sites range from major settlements covering several 1000 m² to find spots where several sherds were found on the surface. The early sites in the Bismarck Archipelago were long ago identified as the earliest and most complex phase of the ceramic tradition, the Early Lapita style (Anson 1986; Green 1979). Summerhayes, in a series of publications where motifs, vessel form and production strategies were compared, has argued that the pottery from a number of these early sites is largely the same in almost all aspects indicating its arrival as a package (Summerhayes 2000, 2010). Early Lapita is largely restricted to this region although there are hints of certain decorative features, somewhat diluted, that are present in the earliest sites as far east as New Caledonia and Vanuatu (Bedford 2015). However, like most other regions in the Pacific, mixing of the Lapita deposits, at the vast majority of the identified sites, along with small sherd size has hindered defining a fully comprehensive Lapita pottery sequence. Designation of what might be described as Middle and/or Late Lapita often tends to be assigned through the radiocarbon dating of a site, rather than through pottery seriation or recognisably distinctive features. However, there are decorative features across many sites that can be associated with Late Lapita, including simpler often single-line dentate-stamped motifs, expanded designs, a more restricted range and some unique vessel forms, along with the appearance of shell- and flat tool-impressed (both curved and straight) decoration. For the purposes of this summary, the research of Wu (2016), who specifically focused on defining Late Lapita in West New Britain, is particularly informative. Her research built on that of Summerhayes (2000) and it highlights a whole series of distinctive dentate designs, vessel forms and decorative techniques that are likely to be associated with Late Lapita. However, it also demonstrates the mixed nature of many of the sites where designations as to period are assigned primarily through radiocarbon dates that at the end of Lapita fall into a flat section of the calibration curve.[10]

Wu (2016:374–376) and Summerhayes (2000:232–234) summarise and define Late Lapita from the Arawes and Garua as follows. There is a dramatic reduction in the range of vessel forms with flat dishes, stands and bowls dropping out. Vessel form became dominated by outcurving rim jars, and a new form, an outcurving rolled rim jar, appeared. Some of the latter were carinated. Dentate decoration continued but was coarser and less elaborately executed. Motifs often comprised well-spaced single lines and are found in combination or association with other decorative techniques including fingernail impression, wide incision, channelling, stick-impressed appliqué layers, scalloped appliqué layers and shell impression. Distinctive expanded motifs are seen particularly with a style

---

10   Wu noted that at some sites the Late Lapita samples were small and that the layers tended to be heavily mixed often with Post-Lapita contexts (2016:249).

of 'face' motif (sometimes a combination of dentate stamping and other techniques) that seems distinctive to the region and period (Specht 1991:Fig. 7a, b; Summerhayes 2000:121, Fig. 7.11; Wu 2016:240, Fig. 6.34a). Plain arc and straight-line stamping was also abundant. Also noted was some variation between sites.

Mainland Papua New Guinea

The discovery of Lapita pottery on the southern coast of mainland Papua New Guinea was a major advance, breaking through what appeared to be a Lapita boundary of long standing (McNiven et al. 2011). The recovered pottery is also very valuable in terms of discussions of Late Lapita, as almost all of the pottery discovered thus far dates to that period. The sites comprise primarily of those found in the Caution Bay area and a single site, named Hopo, on the east of the Vailala River in the Gulf of Papua (Skelly et al. 2014). Several decorated and plain vessel forms can be identified (Figure 8.7). Plain vessels include carinated jars with outcurving rims and globular jars with restricted rims (David et al. 2011:Fig. 6), while decorated vessels can be definitively identified on carinated jars and shallow bowls with straight or everted rims (David et al. 2011:Fig. 2; McNiven et al. 2012:Fig. 6). Overall, the dentate decorations are simple, expanded and applied with tools with coarse teeth. Shell impression is present (David et al. 2019:Fig. 3.12; McNiven et al. 2012:Fig. 7, c and e), as are impressed curved lines made with a flat tool (David et al. 2011:Fig. 2, b, e and h), a similar decorative technique noted in the Bismarcks, Vanuatu and New Caledonia during this period.

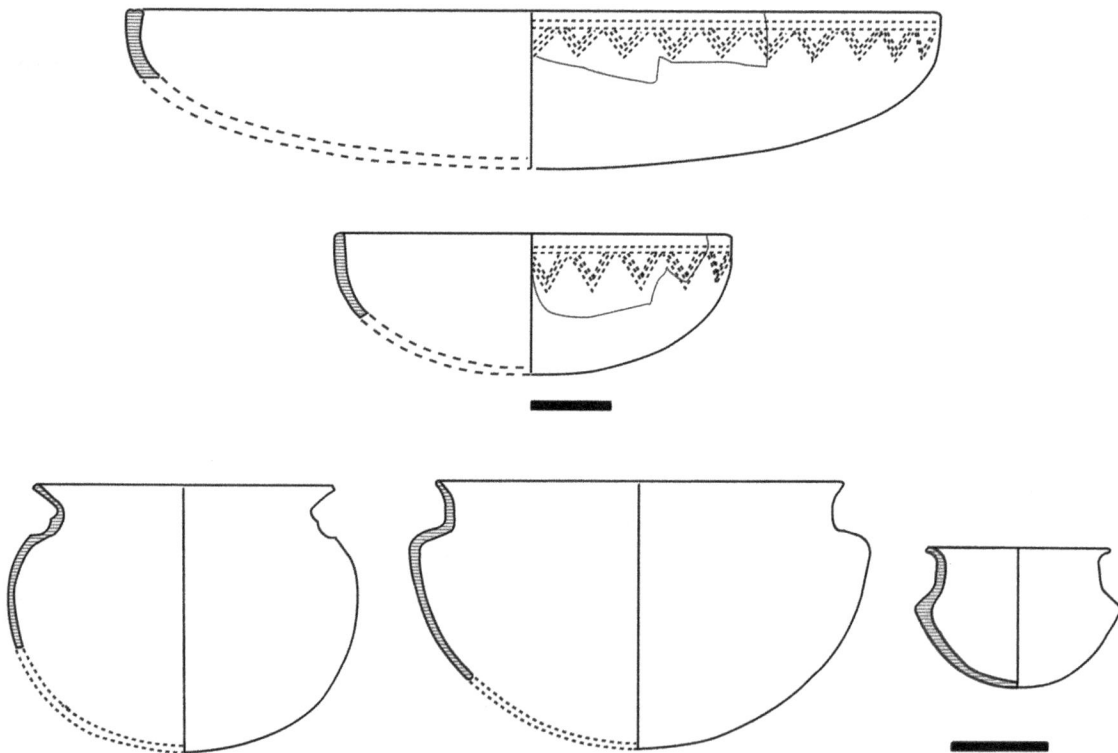

Figure 8.7: South Papuan coast Late Lapita vessel forms and decoration.
Note: Black scales are 5 cm (upper) and 10 cm (lower).
Source: Derived from McNiven et al. (2012:Fig. 6) and David et al. (2011:Fig. 6).

Discussion

This census of Late Lapita across the south-west Pacific is cursory at best, but it has highlighted a number of key aspects and challenges in profiling and classifying this phase of pottery production. Some might question the validity of dividing Lapita pottery sequences into rigid phases at all when in reality, there is no abrupt break and the divisions are simply a heuristic device to aid in the description and the clarification of chronological change. There is the question as to how accurate and well-defined the various phases of Lapita are, particularly given the often-mixed nature of most sites, the limited accuracy of radiocarbon dating and the potential that the pottery is changing within a generation and not over hundreds of years. Other factors such as taphonomic bias, sampling strategies, varied site functionality and the quantification of motifs also play a role in further complicating accurate profiling of Lapita pottery and discussions of similarities and differences. This seems particularly pertinent for defining Late Lapita in many places.

Despite these hurdles, the data we have at hand does provide us with a basic, general summary of Late Lapita, much of which was identified decades ago. There is a reduction in the range of vessel forms and the appearance of new vessel forms. Dentate stamping becomes very simple, motifs are expanded, and often single-lined and new decorative techniques appear, including shell (Figure 8.8) and flat tool impression. Late Lapita from Fiji and Western Polynesia is the best defined and most detailed due to the dominance of Late Lapita in that region and some unique preservation situations. Late Lapita is overwhelmingly plain, with a range of distinctive jars, open bowls and vessels with handles. Carinated jars, both plain and decorated, are well represented. Many of the vessel forms are restricted to this area and are not found further west. Dentate stamping is simple and expanded. Shell impression and unrestricted zigzag dentate and or incised motifs also appear. In Vanuatu and New Caledonia, Late Lapita vessel form seems even more restricted, with carinated and globular outcurving and incurving rim jars dominating. Open bowls are not present and a number of unique vessel forms appear. Dentate stamping is simple, and both shell impression and flat tool impression appear. In the Bismarcks, vessels become restricted, primarily to outcurving rim jars, some of which are carinated. A range of new decorative techniques appear, including shell and flat tool impression. Dentate stamping is simple and motifs are expanded and less structured. Open bowls have not been identified. Finally, on the mainland of New Guinea, a similar pattern emerges: restricted vessel forms but including some regional variants, expanded dentate decoration and shell and flat tool impressed motifs. Distinctive shallow bowls are present there.

Looking across the entire Lapita distribution, the evidence during the Late Lapita Period overwhelmingly indicates increasing divergence in the pottery between and across archipelagos. However, there are key indicators that suggest some level of continued interconnectedness remained across much of the Lapita region. The appearance of new and distinctive decorative techniques during this period, such as shell and flat tool impression, along with simple motifs such as unrestricted simple zigzag designs, are strong evidence of such connections. Moreover, as Summerhayes noted, 'these similarities were not the product of pottery exchange. They were the product of information exchange that necessitates the movement of people. Communication was ongoing indicating a more socially interactive network' (2000:233).

Figure 8.8: Shell-impressed sherds from Lapita sites across the distribution.

Notes: (a) Moiapu 3, Caution Bay; (b) FSZ, Garua Island, Bismarcks; (c) carinated vessel, RF2, Southeast Solomons; (d–e) New Caledonia (Sand 2010b:Photo 36); (f) carination with vertical nubbin, Teouma, Efate Island; (g) Port Olry, Santo Island; (h–i) Tonga. Of the nine sherds illustrated with shell decoration here, four are carinated vessels.

Source: (a) David et al. (2019); (b) Wu (2016:Fig. 8.5a); (c) DigitalNZ: digitalnz.org/records/32425050/lapita-sherd; (d–e) Sand (2010b:Photo 36); (f–g) Author's archive; (h–i) Poulsen (1987).

Conclusion

During the late phase of Lapita across its distribution, from New Guinea to Samoa, we would expect and assume that Late Lapita pottery shows considerable variation. Regional and local variation in vessel form and dentate design is seen during the Middle Lapita period and the processes involved are further amplified as time and distance are extended and varied population movement is registered across the region (Posth et al. 2018). These drivers of diversity shaped all aspects of society, including pottery production, during the Lapita period and were likely to be increasingly influential with the passing of each generation. Lapita groups managed to find and colonise whole archipelagos across vast areas of the Southwest Pacific, including previously uninhabited, increasingly isolated islands as they moved east. High levels of interconnectivity during this period were essential for the long-term viability of these small colonising communities. As populations grew and became self-sustaining, contacts beyond the local region were diluted but they did continue. Late Lapita pottery indicates clear connections with near neighbours (i.e. southern Vanuatu with the Loyalty Islands) but the appearance of certain distinctive decorative features across the entire distribution also confirms some wider level of interconnectivity, the further elucidation of which has yet to be fully determined.

Acknowledgments

Since I embarked on a PhD at The Australian National University in 1995, focusing on the archaeology of Vanuatu, Lapita has always loomed large. Equally prominent has been the figure of Glenn Summerhayes, dating from initial encounters with him during my studies and subsequent career. He also pointed me in the right direction for this paper regarding Late Lapita in the Bismarcks. He has always been a font of knowledge and lots of fun, especially when behind the Weber barbeque. In all that time, we have only managed fieldwork once together, on Wala Island in Vanuatu, but hopefully in the near future a planned expedition can be undertaken and an advance in Lapita knowledge may be the result. Christophe Sand provided key information and images associated with Lapita from New Caledonia. Financial support for my research, and that associated with the Vanuatu data generated here, has come from the Australian Research Council, The Australian National University, the Australia-Pacific Science Foundation, National Geographic, the Sasakawa Foundation and the Max Planck Institute. Two reviewers provided productive comments and key references.

References

Anson, D. 1986. Lapita pottery of the Bismarck Archipelago and its affinities. *Archaeology in Oceania* 21(3): 157–165. doi.org/10.1002/j.1834-4453.1986.tb00144.x.

Bedford, S. 2015. Going beyond the known world 3000 years ago: Lapita exploration and colonization of Remote Oceania. In C. Sand, S. Chiu and N. Hogg (eds), *The Lapita Cultural Complex in time and space: Expansion routes, chronologies and typologies*, pp. 25–48. Archeologia Pasifika 4. Institut d'archéologie de la Nouvelle-Calédonie et du Pacifique, Nouvelle-Calédonie.

Bedford, S. 2019. Lapita pottery from the small islands of northeast Malakula, Vanuatu: A brief overview and implications. In S. Bedford and M. Spriggs (eds), *Debating Lapita: Distribution, chronology, society and subsistence*, pp. 225–241. Terra Australis 52. ANU Press, Canberra. doi.org/10.22459/TA52.2019.11.

Bedford, S. and J.-C. Galipaud 2010. Chain of islands: Lapita occupation of Northern Vanuatu. In C. Sand and S. Bedford (eds), *Lapita: Ancêtres océaniens/Oceanic Ancestors*, pp. 122–137. Musée du quai Branly/Somogy, Paris.

Bedford, S., M. Spriggs, H. Buckley, F. Valentin, R. Regenvanu and M. Abong 2010. A cemetery of first settlement: Teouma, South Efate, Vanuatu. In C. Sand and S. Bedford (eds), *Lapita: Ancêtres océaniens/Oceanic Ancestors*, pp. 140–161. Musée du quai Branly/Somogy, Paris.

Bedford, S., M. Spriggs and R. Shing 2016. 'By all means let us complete the exercise': The 50-year search for Lapita on Aneityum, southern Vanuatu and implications for other 'gaps' in the Lapita distribution. *Archaeology in Oceania* 51:122–130. doi.org/10.1002/arco.5100.

Bedford, S., M. Spriggs, D. Burley, C. Sand, P. Sheppard and G. Summerhayes 2019. Debating Lapita: Distribution, chronology, society, and subsistence. In S. Bedford and M. Spriggs (eds), *Debating Lapita: Distribution, chronology, society and subsistence*, pp. 5–38. Terra Australis 52. ANU Press, Canberra. doi.org/10.22459/TA52.2019.01.

Birks, L. 1973. *Archaeological excavations at Sigatoka Dune site, Fiji*. Bulletin of the Fiji Museum No. 1. Fiji Museum, Suva.

Burley, D. and J. Connaughton 2010. Completing the story: A Late Lapita dentate stamped pot from Sigatoka, Fiji. *Archaeology in Oceania* 45(3):144–146. doi.org/10.1002/j.1834-4453.2010.tb00090.x.

Burley, D. and W.R. Dickinson 2004. Late Lapita occupation and its ceramic assemblage at the Sigatoka Sand Dune site, Fiji, and their place in Oceanic prehistory. *Archaeology in Oceania* 39:12–25. doi.org/10.1002/j.1834-4453.2004.tb00553.x.

Burley, D. and K. LeBlanc 2015. Obfuscating migration and exchange: The misconceptions of an Eastern Lapita Province. In C. Sand, S. Chiu and N. Hogg (eds), *The Lapita Cultural Complex in time and space: Expansion routes, chronologies and typologies*, pp. 173–184. Archeologia Pasifika 4. Institut d'archéologie de la Nouvelle-Calédonie et du Pacifique, Nouvelle-Calédonie.

Burley, D., W.R. Dickinson, A. Barton and R. Shutler Jr 2001. Lapita on the periphery: New data on old problems in the kingdom of Tonga. *Archaeology in Oceania* 36(2):89–104. doi.org/10.1002/j.1834-4453.2001.tb00481.x.

Burley, D., A. Storey and J. Witt 2002. On the definition and implications of Eastern Lapita ceramics in Tonga. In S. Bedford, C. Sand and D. Burley (eds), *Fifty years in the field: Essays in honour and celebration of Richard Shutler Jr's archaeological career*, pp. 213–226. New Zealand Archaeological Association Monograph 25. New Zealand Archaeological Association, Auckland.

Burley D., M. Weisler and J.-x. Zhao 2012. High precision U/Th dating of first Polynesian settlement. *PLoS ONE* 7(11):e48769. doi.org/10.1371/journal.pone.0048769.

Burley D., S.P. Connaughton and G. Clark 2018. Early cessation of ceramic production for ancestral Polynesian society in Tonga. *PLoS ONE* 13(2):e0193166. doi.org/10.1371/journal.pone.0193166.

Chiu, S. 2019. Measuring social distances with shared Lapita motifs: Current results and challenges. In S. Bedford and M. Spriggs (eds), *Debating Lapita: Distribution, chronology, society and subsistence*, pp. 309–336. Terra Australis 52. ANU Press, Canberra. doi.org/10.22459/ta52.2019.15.

Chiu, S. and C. Sand 2005. Recording of the Lapita motifs: Proposal for a complete recording method. *Archaeology in New Zealand* 48(2):133–150.

Clark, G. 2007. Specialisation, standardisation, and Lapita ceramics. In S. Bedford, C. Sand and S.P. Connaughton (eds), *Oceanic explorations: Lapita and Western Pacific settlement*, pp. 289–299. Terra Australis 26. ANU E Press, Canberra. doi.org/10.22459/TA26.2007.17.

Clark, G. and A. Anderson 2009. Colonisation and culture change in the early prehistory of Fiji. In G. Clark and A. Anderson (eds), *The early prehistory of Fiji*, pp. 407–437. Terra Australis 31. ANU E Press, Canberra. doi.org/10.22459/ta31.12.2009.16.

Connaughton, S.P. 2014. Emergence and development of Ancestral Polynesian Society in Tonga. Unpublished PhD thesis, Simon Fraser University, Vancouver. summit.sfu.ca/item/14822.

David, B., I.J. McNiven, T. Richards, S.P. Connaughton, M. Leavesley, B. Barker and C. Rowe 2011. Lapita sites in the Central Province of mainland Papua New Guinea. *World Archaeology* 43(4):576–593. doi.org/10.1080/00438243.2011.624720.

David, B., K. Aplin, H. Peck, R. Skelly, M. Leavesley, J. Mialanes, K. Szabó, B. Koppel, F. Petchey, T. Richards, S. Ulm, I. McNiven, C. Rowe, S.J. Aird, P. Faulkner and A. Ford 2019. Moiapu 3: Settlement on Moiapu Hill at the very end of Lapita, Caution Bay hinterland. In S. Bedford and M. Spriggs (eds), *Debating Lapita: Distribution, chronology, society and subsistence*, pp. 61–88. Terra Australis 52. ANU Press, Canberra. doi.org/10.22459/ta52.2019.03.

Donovan, L. 1973. A study of the decorative system of the Lapita potters in Reefs and Santa Cruz Islands, Vol. 2 (Appendices). Unpublished MA thesis, University of Auckland, Auckland.

Felgate, M. 2001. A Roviana ceramic sequence and the prehistory of Near Oceania: Work in progress. In G.R. Clark, A.J. Anderson and T. Sorovi-Vunidilo (eds), *The archaeology of Lapita dispersal in Oceania*, pp. 39–60. Terra Australis 17. Pandanus Books, The Australian National University, Canberra. hdl.handle.net/1885/210368.

Felgate, M. 2003. Reading Lapita in Near Oceania: Intertidal and shallow-water pottery scatters, Roviana Lagoon, New Georgia, Solomon Islands. Unpublished PhD thesis, University of Auckland, Auckland. researchspace.auckland.ac.nz/handle/2292/997.

Frimigacci, D. 2000. La préhistoire d'Uvea (Wallis). Chronologie et périodisation. *Journal de la Société des Océanistes* 111:135–163. doi.org/10.3406/jso.2000.2131.

Green, R.C. 1974. Pottery from the lagoon at Mulifanua, Upolo. In R.C. Green and J.M. Davidson (eds), *Archaeology in Western Samoa*, pp. 170–175, Volume 2. Bulletin of the Auckland Institute and Museum 7. Auckland Institute and Museum, Auckland.

Green, R.C. 1979. Lapita. In J.D. Jennings (ed.), *The prehistory of Polynesia*, pp. 27–60. Harvard University Press, Cambridge. doi.org/10.4159/harvard.9780674181267.c3.

Hedrick, J. n.d. Archaeological investigation of Malo prehistory: Lapita settlement strategy in the northern New Hebrides. Unpublished Manuscript draft of PhD thesis, University of Pennsylvania, Philadelphia.

Hudson, E. 1994. Sigatoka Dune site archaeological rescue project 1993. Report. Auckland Uniservices, Auckland.

Kirch, P.V. 1988. *Nuiatoputapu. The Prehistory of a Polynesian Chiefdom*. Thomas Burke Memorial Washington State Museum Monograph No. 5. Burke Museum, Seattle.

Kirch, P.V. 1997. *The Lapita peoples: Ancestors of the Oceanic world*. Blackwell, Cambridge.

Kirch, P.V. 2017. *On the road of the winds. An archaeological history of the Pacific Islands before European contact*. University of California Press, California. doi.org/10.1525/9780520968899.

Kirch, P.V. (ed.) 2021. *Talepakemalai: Lapita and its transformations in the Mussau Islands of Near Oceania*. Monumenta Archaeologica 47. Cotsen Institute of Archaeology Press, Los Angeles. doi.org/10.2307/j.ctv27tctrd.12.

McNiven, I., B. David, T. Richards, K. Aplin, B. Asmussen, J. Mialanes, M. Leavesley, P. Faulkner and S. Ulm 2011. New direction in human colonisation of the Pacific: Lapita settlement of south coast New Guinea. *Australian Archaeology* 72:1–6. doi.org/10.1080/03122417.2011.11690525.

McNiven, I., B. David, K. Aplin, J. Mialanes, B. Asmussen, S. Ulm, P. Faulkner, C. Rowe and T. Richards 2012. Terrestrial engagements by terminal Lapita maritime specialists on the southern Papuan coast. In S. Haberle and B. David (eds), *Peopled landscapes: Archaeological and biogeographic approaches to landscapes*, pp. 119–154. Terra Australis 34. ANU E Press, Canberra. doi.org/10.22459/ta34.01.2012.05.

Meyer, O. 1909. Funde prähistorischer Töpferei und Steinmesser auf Vuatom, Bismarck-Archipel, *Anthropos* 4(1):251–252.

Noury. A. 2019. Along the roads of the Lapita people: Designs, groups and travels. In S. Bedford and M. Spriggs (eds), *Debating Lapita: Distribution, chronology, society and subsistence*, pp. 337–350. Terra Australis 52. ANU Press, Canberra. doi.org/10.22459/ta52.2019.16.

Petchey, F. 1995. The archaeology of Kudon: Archaeological analysis of Lapita ceramics from Mulifanua, Samoa and Sigatoka, Fiji. Unpublished MA thesis, University of Auckland, Auckland.

Posth, C., K. Nägele, H. Colleran, F. Valentin, S. Bedford, K. Kami, R. Shing, H. Buckley, R. Kinaston, M. Walworth, G.R. Clark, C. Reepmeyer, J. Flexner, T. Maric, J. Moser, J. Gresky, L. Kiko, K.J. Robson, K. Auckland, S.J. Oppenheimer, A.V.S. Hill, A.J. Mentzer, J. Zech, F. Petchey, P. Roberts, C. Jeong, R.D. Gray, J. Krause and A. Powell 2018. Language continuity despite population replacement in Remote Oceania. *Nature Ecology & Evolution* 2:731–740. doi.org/10.1038/s41559-018-0498-2.

Poulsen, J. 1987. *Early Tongan prehistory: The Lapita period on Tongatapu and its relationships*. Terra Australis 12. Department of Prehistory, Research School of Pacific Studies, The Australian National University, Canberra. openresearch-repository.anu.edu.au/handle/1885/127427.

Sand, C. 1990. The ceramic chronology of Futuna and Alofi: An overview. In M. Spriggs (ed.), *Lapita design, form and composition*, pp. 123–133. Occasional Papers in Prehistory No. 19. Department of Prehistory, Research School of Pacific Studies, The Australian National University, Canberra.

Sand, C. 1998. Archaeological research on 'Uvea Island, Western Polynesia. *New Zealand Journal of Archaeology* 18:91–123.

Sand, C. 2000. The specificities of the 'Southern Lapita Province': The New Caledonian case. *Archaeology in Oceania* 35:20–33. doi.org/10.1002/j.1834-4453.2000.tb00448.x.

Sand, C. 2010a. Oceanic origins: The history of research on the Lapita traditions. In C. Sand and S. Bedford (eds), *Lapita: Ancêtres océaniens/Oceanic Ancestors*, pp. 30–39. Musée du Quai Branly/Somogy, Paris.

Sand, C. 2010b. *Lapita Calédonien. Archéologie d'un premier peuplement insulaire océanien*. Travaux et documents océanistes. Société des Océanistes, Paris. doi.org/10.4000/books.sdo.1128.

Sand, C. 2015. Comparing Lapita pottery forms in the Southwestern Pacific: A case study. In C. Sand, S. Chiu and N. Hogg (eds), *The Lapita Cultural Complex in time and space: Expansion routes, chronologies and typologies*, pp. 125–171. Archeologia Pasifika 4. Institut d'archéologie de la Nouvelle-Calédonie et du Pacifique, Nouvelle-Calédonie.

Sand, C., J. Bolé and A. Ouetcho. 2002. Site LP0023 of Kurin: Characteristics of a Lapita Settlement in the Loyalty Islands (New Caledonia). *Asian Perspectives* 41(1):129–147. doi.org/10.1353/asi.2002.0010.

Sheppard, P.J. 2011. Lapita colonization across the Near/Remote Oceania boundary. *Current Anthropology* 52(6):799–840. doi.org/10.1086/662201.

Skelly, R., B. David, F. Petchey and M. Leavesley 2014. Tracking ancient beach-lines inland: 2600-year-old dentate-stamped ceramics at Hopo, Vailala River Region, Papua New Guinea. *Antiquity* 88:470–487. doi.org/10.1017/s0003598x00101127.

Specht, J. 1968. Preliminary report of excavations on Watom Island. *Journal of the Polynesian Society* 77(2): 117–134. www.jstor.org/stable/20704542.

Specht, J. 1991. Kreslo: A Lapita pottery site in southwest New Britain, Papua New Guinea. In J. Allen and C. Gosden (eds), *Report of the Lapita Homeland Project*, pp. 189–204. Occasional Papers in Prehistory 20. Department of Prehistory, The Australian National University, Canberra.

Specht, J. and C. Gosden 2019. New dates for the Makekur (FOH) Lapita pottery site, Arawe Islands, New Britain, Papua New Guinea. In S. Bedford and M. Spriggs (eds), *Debating Lapita: Distribution, chronology, society and subsistence*, pp. 169–202. ANU Press, Canberra. doi.org/10.22459/ta52.2019.09.

Spriggs, M. 1991. Nissan: The island in the middle. In J. Allen and C. Gosden (eds), *Report of the Lapita Homeland Project*, pp. 222–243. Occasional Papers in Prehistory No. 20. Department of Prehistory, Research School of Pacific Studies, The Australian National University, Canberra.

Spriggs, M. and S. Bedford 2013. Is there an incised Lapita phase after dentate-stamped pottery ends? Data from Teouma, Efate Island, Vanuatu. In G. Summerhayes and H. Buckley (eds), *Pacific archaeology: Documenting the past 50,000 years*, pp. 148–156. Otago University Publications in Archaeology, No. 25. Otago University, Dunedin.

Summerhayes, G.R. 2000. *Lapita interaction*. Terra Australis 15. Pandanus Books, The Australian National University, Canberra. hdl.handle.net/1885/127430.

Summerhayes, G.R. 2001. Far Western, Western, and Eastern Lapita: A re-evaluation. *Asian Perspectives* 39(1–2):109–138. doi.org/10.1353/asi.2000.0013.

Summerhayes, G.R. 2010. Lapita interaction—an update. In M.Z. Gadu and H. Lin (eds), *2009 International symposium on Austronesian studies*, pp. 11–40. National Museum of Prehistory, Taitung, Taiwan.

Summerhayes, G. and I. Scales 2005. New Lapita pottery finds from Kolombangara, western Solomon Islands. *Archaeology in Oceania* 40:14–20. doi.org/10.1002/j.1834-4453.2005.tb00575.x.

Wu, P.-h. 2016. What happened at the end of Lapita: Lapita to Post-Lapita pottery transition in West New Britain, Papua New Guinea. Unpublished PhD thesis, University of Otago, Dunedin. ourarchive.otago.ac.nz/handle/10523/6817.

Part 3: Interaction and exchange

9

Landscapes of exchange in the Willaumez Peninsula, West New Britain, Papua New Guinea

Gustavo F. Bonnat, Robin Torrence and Peter White

Abstract

The well-preserved tephrostratigraphy stretching across the Willaumez Peninsula in West New Britain, Papua New Guinea, provides a unique opportunity to monitor landscapes of cultural exchange over a considerable period of human history, extending from the Pleistocene to the recent past. An approach integrating pXRF geochemical characterisation and measurements of reduction intensity is used to analyse a substantial sample of obsidian artefacts from the FRI site and 25 test pits in the Isthmus region, located at the base of the Willaumez Peninsula. Obsidian exchange is shown to have been a persistent feature of social life, but variations in the mix of sources used and the kinds of objects transferred may also indicate changes in how social networks were constructed. As the frequency and severity of volcanic events decreased through time and population rose in response, the role of obsidian in creating links may have been partially replaced by other objects, such as stone axe blades.

Social role of exchange

In many areas of coastal Papua New Guinea, relatively large quantities of flaked obsidian artefacts are ubiquitous within archaeological contexts (e.g. Fredericksen 1997; Gaffney et al. 2018; Golitko et al. 2012; Irwin and Holdaway 1996; Mialanes et al. 2016; Shaw et al. 2021; Summerhayes 2009; Summerhayes et al. 1998; White et al. 2006). Obsidian was also distributed widely by people colonising other parts of Melanesia (e.g. Reepmeyer 2021; Summerhayes 2009). Since obsidian can only be acquired from a few sources but was often transported over long distances, it seems reasonable to assume that this raw material was highly prized. Evidence from a growing number of studies, however, shows that consumption patterns do not fit those expected for a raw material that is valued. Except for the highly worked stemmed tools (e.g. Torrence et al. 2013), throughout history in Melanesia obsidian was treated in a very unsystematic, casual and wasteful manner (e.g. Allen and Bell 1988; Hanslip 2001; Sheppard 1992, 1993; Torrence 2011) and neither the size nor quantity of artefacts decreases in a consistent linear fashion with distance from the raw material sources (Galipaud et al. 2014; Reepmeyer 2021; Specht 2002), as might be expected in a down-the-line exchange system (e.g. Renfrew 1977; Torrence 1986:115–138). The stone tool technology used to process obsidian primarily yielded irregular and highly varying flake forms struck from nodules in an unsystematic manner. Retouched tools are rare. These patterns conform well to the definition of what Binford (1979, cf. Parry and Kelly 1987; Nelson 1991) originally termed an 'expedient technology': that is, made with little effort, used briefly and discarded quickly. The largely unretouched tools were employed in a wide variety of tasks, mainly associated with cutting relatively soft materials (e.g. Kononenko 2011, 2012), functions that could easily have been carried out with other materials close at hand and more easily procured, such as bamboo, shells, thorns, rat's teeth, etc.

The expedient nature of obsidian assemblages in Melanesia raises an important question. Why was this raw material procured from outcrops, transported over a considerable distance, and then treated in such a wasteful manner? Peter Sheppard (1993) first addressed this issue with respect to obsidian assemblages at Lapita sites on the Reef–Santa Cruz Islands. He proposed that for people who had moved into uninhabited lands away from social safety nets, the role of obsidian was not primarily as a raw material for useful tools, but as an exchange good that would create and strengthen social bonds. Once the exchange had been made, the obsidian itself had lost its value and, consequently, it was consumed in a seemingly careless fashion. Subsequently, in their hypothetical reconstruction of changes in exchange patterns in the Willaumez Peninsula (WP) of West New Britain, Papua New Guinea (Figure 9.1), Torrence and Summerhayes (1997) and Torrence (2004a) also argued that the exchange of obsidian was mainly directed at social rather than economic ends.

Figure 9.1: The Willaumez Peninsula showing the location of the Isthmus region, FRI site, obsidian sources and the volcanic centres at Dakataua and Witori.

Source: Illustration by authors.

Building on these ideas, Torrence (2005, 2011) proposed that obsidian was often selected as an object for exchange because its physical properties (i.e. discrete sources, black colour, lustrous surface, conchoidal fracture) made it ideal for cementing social relations. Most recently, Reepmeyer (2021) has suggested another social role for this distinctive raw material. He argues that obsidian was used in Remote Oceania as a marker of ethnic identity so that the early colonists coping with the risks associated with moving into an unfamiliar environment could easily recognise people they could trust.

Obsidian has also played an important role in creating and strengthening social connections among communities across time and in other parts of the world (e.g. Kristensen et al. 2019; Freund 2018; Lazzari and Sprovieri 2020; Peterson et al. 1997; Torrence 2005). All small groups depend on external links for their survival, because regular access to marriage partners is necessary for social and biological reproduction. Exchange systems of various forms are therefore extremely widespread throughout the recent and deep past. The benefits of social ties are especially high in environments with extreme levels of selection, such as those that experience 'frequent, very severe environmental perturbations' serious enough to cause local extinctions (Torrence and Doelman 2007:43). As discussed by Torrence (2016, 2019), the adoption of systems of exchange can reduce the impacts of environmental disasters by increasing a society's 'resilience', defined as the ability to maintain continuity by avoiding or withstanding failure (Conolly and Lane 2018; Lorenz 2013), and therefore reducing its vulnerability to future environmental forcing agents (Riede 2019).

Stimulated by the pioneering studies of Wiessner (1982) and Cashdan (1985, 1990), who described how exchange systems among the Kalahari Bushmen helped ensure that widely dispersed, small groups had access to necessary resources despite demographic and environmental challenges, this paper proposes that obsidian exchange helped build resilience to the effects of infrequent but catastrophic volcanic eruptions in the WP region of West New Britain, Papua New Guinea (Figure 9.1). When viewed over very long time periods, changes in the character of social networks created by obsidian exchange can be linked to the character of the volcanic forcing agents. The study expands on previous obsidian characterisation studies in the WP region by using a substantially enlarged dataset acquired with portable X-ray fluorescence (pXRF) technology, combined with a study of lithic technology focusing on reduction intensity. The results confirm the general patterns previously reported, but also contribute further information about the variety of social strategies adopted by small social groups subject to regularly occurring environmental disasters.

Study area and sample selection

The Willaumez Peninsula on New Britain Island in Papua New Guinea (Figure 9.1) is an excellent setting for investigating the relationships between the risks inherent in highly active volcanic environments and the ways in which populations developed a measure of resilience through using exchange to amplify social networks. During the period of human occupation, beginning at least by c. 40,000 BP, the region has been impacted by seven large volcanic events (volcanic explosivity index (VEI) 5 or greater) that would have necessitated abandonment for at least four to five generations, if not longer, as well as several smaller events that would have created hardships, although on a lesser scale (Neall et al. 2008; Torrence 2016:Table 1; Torrence et al. 2004; Torrence et al. 2009). We predict that as a consequence of repeated experience of environmental catastrophes in the WP, societies developed mechanisms that enabled them to sustain or improve their resilience. Torrence (2016) has proposed that formalised systems of exchange would have helped establish safety nets, facilitate safe evacuation, secure refuges until return was possible and provide essential backup during recolonisation.

Between 1999 and 2002, archaeological research took advantage of the extensively studied tephra stratigraphy (Machida et al. 1996; McKee et al. 2011; Neall et al. 2008) (Figure 9.2a) to conduct an archaeological study of buried contexts (Specht and Torrence 2007a; Torrence 2000, 2001, 2002a, 2008; Torrence and Doelman 2007; Torrence et al. 1999), using the landscape approach developed on Garua Island (Torrence 2002b; Torrence and Stevenson 2000). To monitor changes in the way exchange operated, obsidian assemblages from two areas situated between the two major obsidian sources at Kutau-Bao and Mopir were selected for analysis: the Isthmus region, located at the intersection of the WP and mainland New Britain, and the site of FRI (Figure 9.1). A key feature of both settings is the well-studied and dated regional tephrostratigraphy (Figure 9.2a), reconstructed through collaborative archaeological and geological research (Machida et al. 1996; McKee et al. 2011; Neall et al. 2008). The sequence is comprised of a series of layers derived from eruptions of the Witori and Dakataua volcanoes (Figure 9.1). Dates for the components of the stratigraphy have been obtained from Bayesian analyses of radiocarbon dates recovered from soils formed on the volcanic deposits (McKee et al. 2011; Petrie and Torrence 2008). A summary of the key stratigraphic layers, associated dates, and periods used in the study is presented in Tables 9.1 and 9.2.

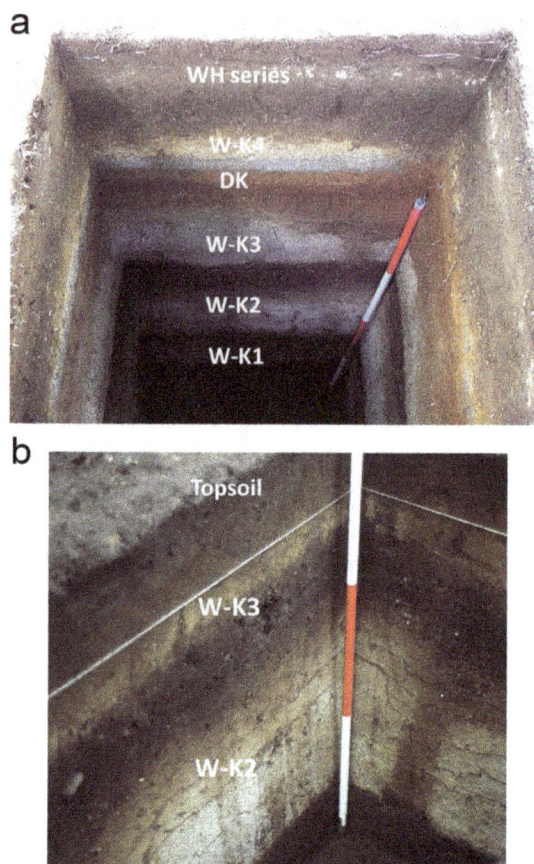

Figure 9.2: The tephrostratigraphy of the region defines the chronological phases used to monitor cultural change.

Notes: (a) Isthmus region; (b) FRI II.

Source: (a) Illustration by authors; (b) illustration by authors based on photograph by Jim Specht.

Given changes in the depth of tephras with increasing distance from the volcanic centres, not all layers are well preserved across the study area (see Torrence et al. 2009 for isopachs of tephras). Possibly due to heavy rains and subsequent erosion during the event, the W-K1 tephra which marks the boundary between Periods 2 and 3 is frequently absent in stratigraphic profiles. Where W-K1 is missing, the deposits underlying W-K2 have been treated as a separate time slice, called Period 3.2 because they may contain a mixture of Periods 2 and 3. Periods 7 and 8 are grouped together because it was difficult to discriminate among the thin W-H tephras in the field. Period 1, which is equivalent to the earliest settlement of the region during the late Pleistocene and early Holocene, is not represented in this sample as it has only been reliably documented at the Kupona Na Dari site (FABM) (Torrence et al. 2004).

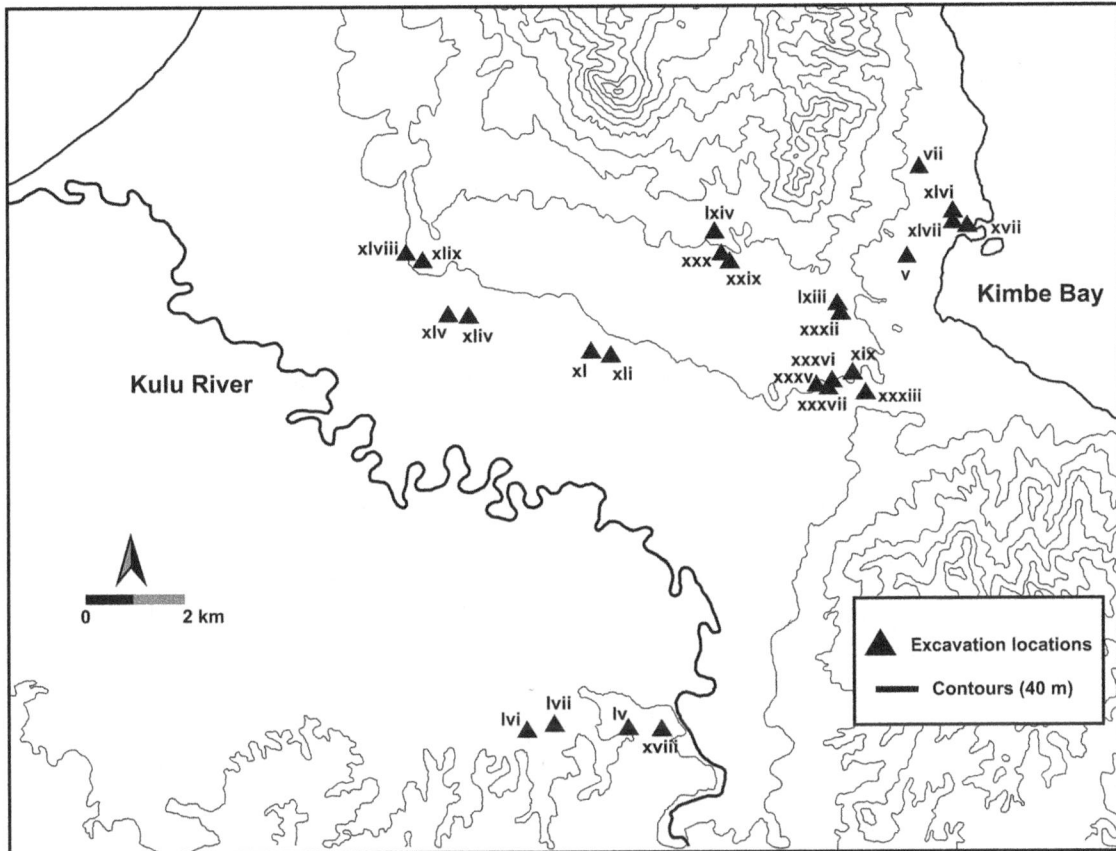

Figure 9.3: The 25 test pits from the Isthmus region used in the study are spread around the edges of the Kulu River floodplain, along the coastal divide and on the coastal plain.

Source: Illustration by authors based on a draft by Trudy Doelman.

To trace changes in the procurement, exchange and production of obsidian artefacts through time in the Isthmus region, a sample of 1614 artefacts was selected from 25 one-metre-square test pits (Figure 9.3). Excellent preservation of the volcanic stratigraphy was the most important criterion for sample selection, ensuring that the finds could be confidently assigned to chronological phases. The second aim in choosing samples was to reflect environmental variation across the region in terms of proximity to the coast and variation in elevation. Some of the local settings were radically altered after the W-K2 event, when areas in what are now the inland, upland regions that were originally situated near the sea became completely landlocked after volcanic sediment flooding down from hills to the south filled in the tidal basin (Torrence et al. 2009). Finally, since the sample sizes in some of the layers of the selected test pits were quite small, it was necessary to augment these with artefacts from the same stratigraphic context in a nearby test pit. This explains why the number of test pits in Table 9.1 differs among the periods.

Table 9.1: Isthmus region test pits: Tephrostratigraphy and chronology.

Period	Stratigraphic position	Approximate date	Test pits (N)
7/8	WH series up to present	post 500 cal. BP	9
6	Between Dk/W-K4 & WH series	c. 1300–500 cal. BP	16
5	Between W-K3 & DK/W-K4	c. 1600–1300 cal. BP	12
4	Between W-K2 & W-K3	c. 3200–1600 cal. BP	14
3.2	Below W-K2 where W-K1 is not preserved	pre 6000–3200 cal. BP	12
3	Between W-K1 & W-K2	6000–3200 cal. BP	9
2	Pre W-K1	pre 6000 cal. BP	8

Notes: Dk = the Dakataua eruption, known as the Dk event; W-K = Witori eruptions, numbered as W-K1 through WK-4.
Source: Authors' data.

As the difference in distance between the sources and the test pits in our sample is negligible, we included an additional assemblage of 613 obsidian artefacts from the FRI site at Walindi Plantation (Figure 9.1). Located at about 1 km inland from the present coastline, FRI is spread over several ridges situated at c. 95 m above sea level, with a commanding view of the ocean (Specht et al. 1991; Specht and Torrence 2007b; Torrence et al. 1990). Several trenches and test pits were excavated at the site in 1989 by Jim Specht, assisted by Glenn Summerhayes and a team of volunteers from the Australian Museum. The sample of obsidian artefacts used here is derived from Trench II, where the volcanic stratigraphy was well preserved (Table 9.2; Figure 9.2b). Phase 4 at the top of the site (c. post 500 BP) 'contains items of European date' (Specht et al. 1991:284). The W-K4/Dk horizon that marks the boundary between Periods 5 and 6 in the Isthmus was not preserved at this location, so the chronological divisions are slightly different from those identified in the Isthmus region.

Table 9.2: FRI Trench II, Walindi Plantation: Stratigraphy and chronology.

FRI phase	Isthmus period	Stratigraphic position	Approximate date
4	7/8	Topsoil	c. post 500 BP
3	5, 6	Post W-K3	1600–500 cal. BP
2	4	Between W-K2 and W-K3	3200–1600 cal. BP
1	2, 3	Pre W-K2	pre 3200 cal. BP

Source: Authors' data and Specht (pers. comm. 2021).

Detecting exchange

Inferences about the history of obsidian exchange in the study area stem from two methods: (1) geochemical characterisation of the artefacts and (2) position of the artefacts within the reduction sequence in which a nodule was converted into fragments, some presumably used as tools.[1] Our characterisation study of obsidian artefacts in the WP benefits from a long history of field research at the West New Britain obsidian outcrops (e.g. Fullagar et al. 1991; Specht 1981; Specht et al. 1988; Torrence et al. 1992) coupled with geochemical studies mainly employing the PIXE-PIGME technique pioneered by Roger Bird (Bird et al. 1981, 1997; Summerhayes 2009; Summerhayes et al. 1993, 1998), together with subsequent studies of source variation using LA-ICP-MS (e.g. Ambrose

---

1   The complete geochemical and lithic technology datasets used in this study can be freely accessed at zenodo.org/record/8274857.

et al. 2009; Reepmeyer et al. 2016).[2] Following key developments in instrumentation, portable X-ray fluorescence analysis (pXRF) of obsidian source material and artefacts has greatly enlarged the number of samples that can be measured at relatively low cost. In addition, constraints on the selection of samples due to artefact size have been lessoned considerably, thereby greatly reducing potential sampling biases (e.g. Torrence et al. 2013; Mialanes et al. 2016; Mulrooney et al. 2014, 2016). It is now feasible to analyse large numbers or even entire archaeological assemblages (e.g. Sheppard et al. 2010). Building on these significant developments, we used a Bruker Tracer 5i pXRF spectrometer equipped with an 8-μm Be detector window to analyse 613 samples from Trench II at site FRI (Figures 9.1 and 9.2b) and 1614 artefacts from 25 one-metre-square excavations in the Isthmus region (Figures 9.2a and 9.3).

The Tracer 5i instrument has an X-ray tube with a Rh target and a 20 mm^2 silicon drift detector with a typical resolution of less than 140 eV at 250,000 cps. Nine elements were measured: Mn, Fe, Zn, Ga, Rb, Sr, Y, Zr and Nb. The in-built obsidian calibration program, based on many years of development by Bruker, was used to convert XRF measurements to elemental values. Precision and accuracy of the calibrated results were evaluated as satisfactory by comparison between measurements of the well-characterised obsidian standards WNB4198 (Wekwok AD2000) and WNB4209 (Kutau-Bao source) taken before, during and after runs with results from Bird et al. (1997) analyses using PIXE-PIGME (Table 9.3).

Table 9.3: Precision and accuracy of pXRF instrument.

Elements	Wekwok AD2000					Kutau-Bao				
	pXRF WNB4198 (N = 27)			PIXE-PIGME (Bird et al. 1997) (N = 12)		pXRF WNB4209 (N = 27)			PIXE-PIGME (Bird et al. 1997) (N = 12)	
	Mean	SD	RSD (%)	Mean	SD	Mean	SD	RSD (%)	Mean	SD
Mn	465	20	4	520	17	459	20	4	523	22
Fe	13,968	309	2	17,000	500	8343	219	3	10,500	55
Zn	66	4	5	n/a	n/a	59	3	5	n/a	n/a
Ga	14	2	14	n/a	n/a	9	1	11	n/a	n/a
Th	11	1	10	n/a	n/a	1	1	75	n/a	n/a
Rb	145	4	3	161	5	50	2	4	55	4
Sr	63	2	3	72	3	182	4	2	206	9
Y	38	2	5	36	2	21	1	5	20	2
Zr	287	7	2	366	5	142	4	3	151	7
Nb	38	2	5	47	3	2	1	57	1	2

Source: Authors' data and Bird et al. (1997).

The obsidian artefacts were grouped into obsidian chemical groups with discriminant analysis using JMP 14.0 software. The confusion matrix, based on multiple runs of 143 well-characterised samples from the four major obsidian sources in the WP (53 Baki; 32 Kulu; 33 Gulu and 25 Mopir), yielded a 100 per cent successful classification of the samples to their known source. The artefacts were then successfully matched to this source group training set (cf. Pengilley et al. 2019). No outliers were detected. The high level of discrimination of WNB obsidians that is obtained with pXRF is demonstrated in Figure 9.4, which compares the principal components scores for the first two components of both the sources and the artefacts in the study based on the nine elements measured.

---

2   PIXE-PIGME: proton-induced X-ray emission and proton-induced gamma ray emission, respectively; LA-ICP-MS: laser ablation inductively coupled plasma mass spectrometry.

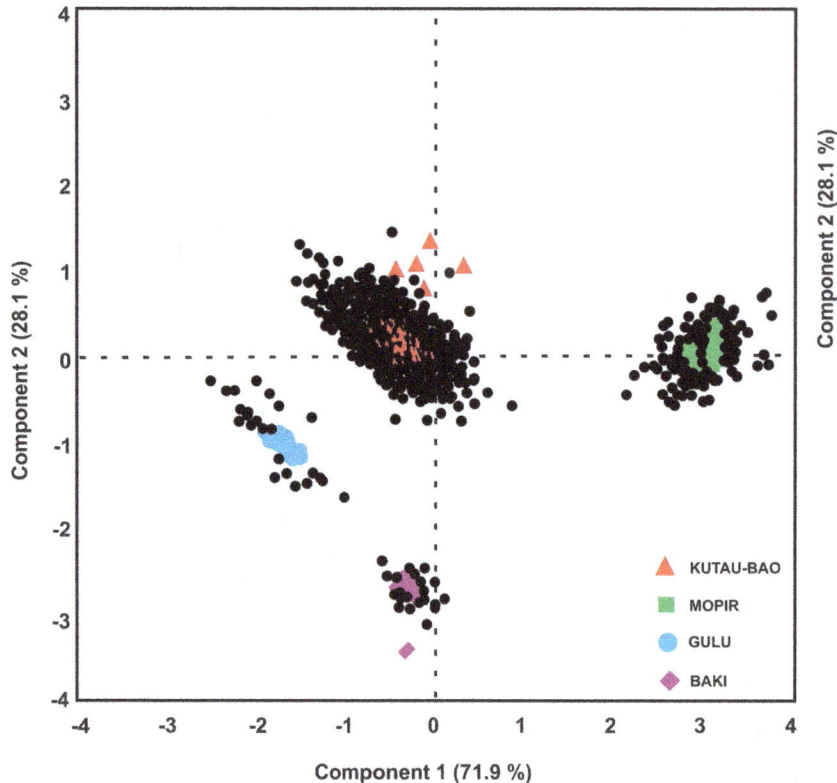

Figure 9.4: Plot of the obsidian source reference samples (coloured symbols) versus artefacts (black dots).

Notes: Using the results of a principal components analysis (JMP) of the calibrated data from the pXRF analysis, the artefacts can be unambiguously assigned to their source.

Source: Illustration by authors.

After considering the movement of obsidian from the different sources based on the geochemical analysis, in the second component of the study we examine patterns of consumption measured by the nature and degree of reduction of nodules in relation to distance from the sources using well-established techniques (e.g. Ditchfield 2016; Eerkens et al. 2008; James et al. 2022; Lin and Premo 2021; Shott, J. 2015; Shott, M. 1994; Sullivan and Rozen 1985). Once a piece of obsidian had been exchanged and the social connection between giver and receiver initiated or consolidated, what was its subsequent role and how was it consumed? Before addressing this question directly, it is useful to consider several potential scenarios (cf. Franco 2014). Beginning at the outcrops, the first key factor is how the raw material was treated. Unfortunately, we lack enough data from the quarries to answer this question and so we consider trajectories based on three potential outputs: (1) unmodified nodules; (2) partially reduced cores or preforms of tools which were finished off and used in other locations; or (3) final artefact form made at the quarries and transported to another location where it was exchanged and then used. A second factor to consider is whether the procured raw material, preform or artefact was consumed directly by the maker or was exchanged and then modified and/or used. Finally, since material acquired from the quarries might be partially consumed before it was exchanged, the number of transactions made in the movement from the source to the final point of discard will affect the character of the archaeological record. Since some artefact life histories could end up with similar outcomes in terms of the composition of the lithic assemblage and distribution across the landscape, it may not be possible to discriminate among all possibilities, but as we try to show, the potential options can be constrained.

a

FRI II N= 613

b

Isthmus region N= 1614

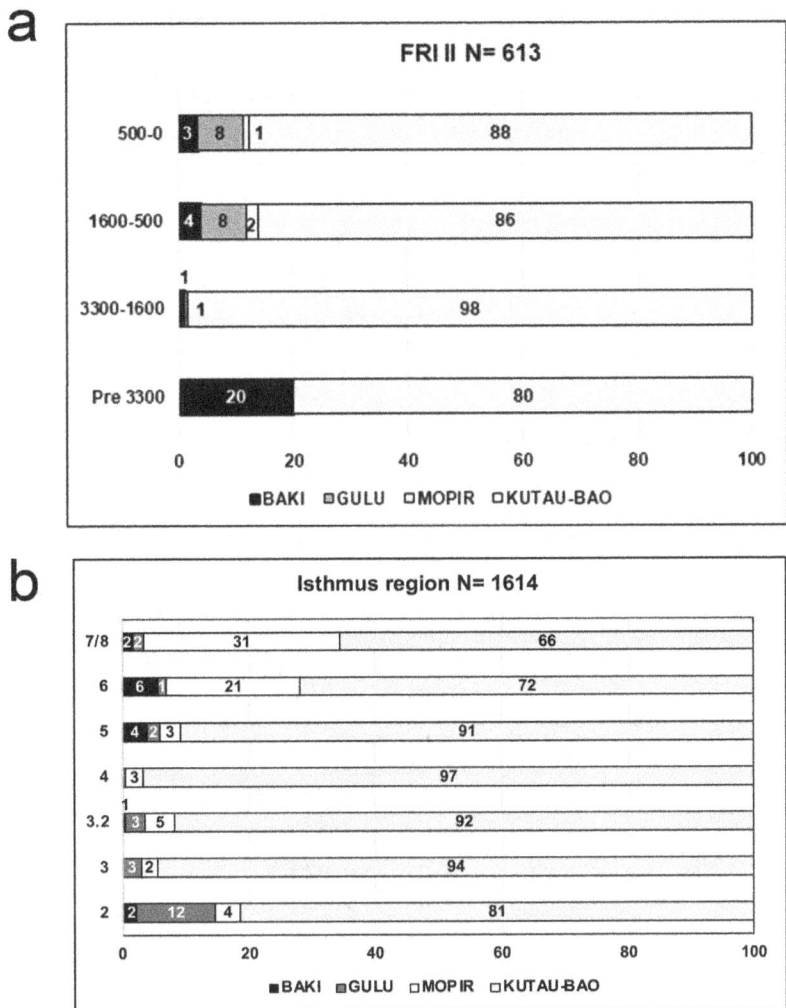

Figure 9.5: Chronological changes in the percentage of obsidian artefacts from each source.

Notes: (a) FRI II; (b) Isthmus region.

Source: Illustration by authors.

Geochemistry and social exchange

The results of the pXRF characterisation analysis are presented in Tables 9.4 and 9.5 and Figures 9.4 and 9.5. In both the Isthmus region and at FRI II, stone acquired from the Kutau-Bao obsidian source was by far the dominant raw material, although its abundance varied through time, with notable changes following major volcanic events. This result is perhaps not surprising since the Kutau-Bao outcrops contain ample quantities of excellent quality raw material and cover a much larger area than the Baki and Gulu outcrops (Figure 9.1) (Torrence et al. 1992). Fission track dates for the formation of the obsidian sources show that Kutau-Bao is probably the only source which has emerged since human occupation of the region, probably not until 12,000 years BP (Torrence et al. 2004:Table 5). The impact on communities of observing the eruption in which Kutau-Bao appeared might also have been a factor in its popularity (Torrence in press). Variations in the consumption patterns of the primary source of obsidian imply changes in the social mechanisms responsible for its distribution.

Table 9.4: FRI II, Walindi Plantation: Chronological change in counts and weights of obsidian artefacts from each obsidian source.

Phase	Counts					Weights (g)				
	Baki	Gulu	Kutau-Bao	Mopir	Total	Baki	Gulu	Kutau-Bao	Mopir	Total
4	6	14	156	2	178	7.7	44.3	322.6	2.7	377.3
3	2	4	44	1	51	5	9.4	108.3	0.5	123.2
2	4	2	363	0	369	7.5	0.4	724.4	0	732.3
1	3	0	12	0	15	14.1	0	21.6	0	35.7
Total	15	20	575	3	613	34.4	54.2	1177	3.1	1268.7
%	2	3	94	1<	100	3	4	92	<1	100

Note: The percentages of each source based on counts are reported in Figure 9.5a.
Source: Authors' data.

Table 9.5: Isthmus region: Chronological change in counts and weights of obsidian artefacts from each obsidian source.

Period	Counts					Weights (g)				
	Baki	Gulu	Kutau-Bao	Mopir	Total	Baki	Gulu	Kutau-Bao	Mopir	Total
7/8	3	3	115	55	176	4.2	0.9	179.0	110.8	294.9
6	21	5	266	78	370	20.9	0.6	466.6	135.6	623.7
5	6	3	137	5	151	7.1	0.5	351.9	9.2	368.7
4	0	1	177	5	183	0	0.1	284.4	10.5	295.0
3.2	1	6	177	9	193	0.2	6.8	211.5	9.5	228.0
3	0	11	343	9	363	0	25.7	546.6	9.3	581.6
2	4	22	145	7	178	1	26.6	180.6	5.3	213.5
Total	35	51	1360	168	1614	33.3	62.3	2220.7	290.2	2605.5
%	2	3	84	10	100	1	2	85	11	100

Note: The percentages of each source based on counts are reported in Figure 9.5b.
Source: Authors' data.

Turning to the minor sources, obsidian from the Baki and Gulu outcrops are reasonably well represented in the Pleistocene levels of Kupona Na Dari (Torrence 2004a), but since they are only present in very small amounts throughout the Holocene chronological sequences in both our study areas, it is not surprising that there are no consistent trends in their abundance in the sample pits. In FRI, the quantity of Gulu obsidian is consistently small, although it increased after the W-K3 eruption c. 1700 cal. BP (Table 9.4). In contrast, Baki was c. 40 per cent by weight prior to 3300 cal. BP (i.e. Periods 2 and 3), nearly disappeared during 3300–1600 cal. BP, and then only made a minor contribution in the most recent deposits (Table 9.4; Figure 9.5a). The opposite chronological pattern is witnessed in the Isthmus, where Gulu obsidian was most plentiful in Period 2, but subsequently decreased and only contributed very minor amounts later in time (Table 9.5; Figure 9.5b), whereas the Baki source made a brief appearance at the beginning of the sequence, but then immediately disappeared until Period 5 when it reappeared, although it never exceeded 5 per cent of the assemblage (Table 9.5; Figure 9.5b).

Coastal vs Inland Distribution

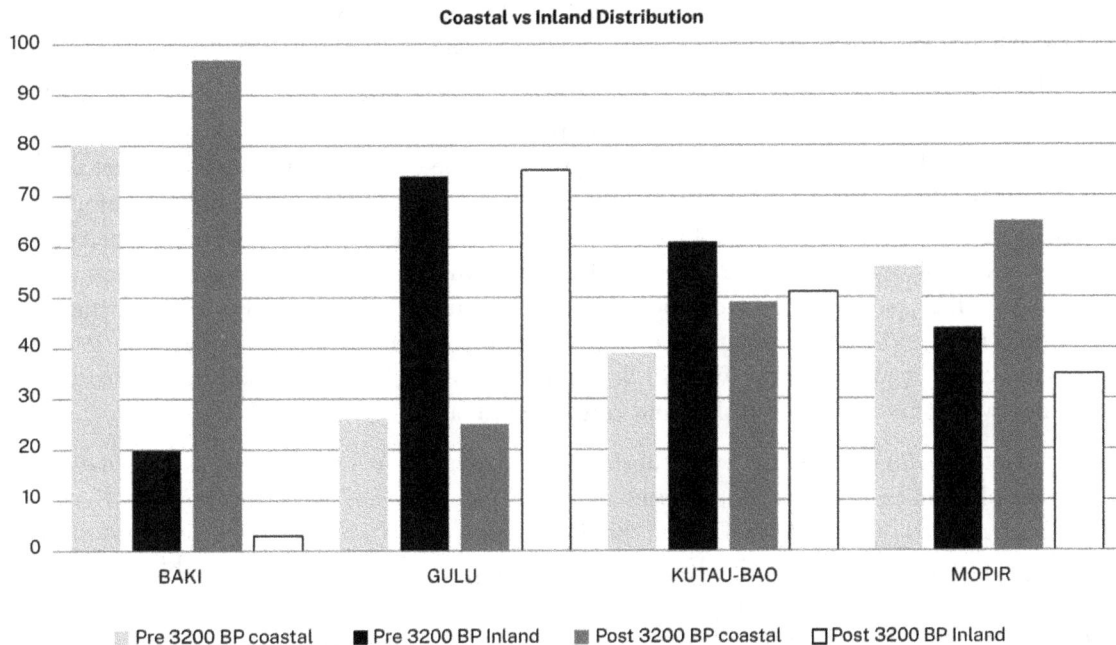

Figure 9.6: The percentage of obsidian artefacts from each source compared between test pits in coastal and inland locations.

Source: Illustration by authors.

It seems likely that the uses of the two minor sources reflect social ties involving only a small sector of the population that chose to interact outside the wider network dominated by people who used Kutau-Bao obsidian. Through time, obsidian from Gulu is most common among the Isthmus test pits situated in the inland regions (Table 9.5; Figure 9.6). Possibly it was primarily transported directly south from the major outcrops on the western side of the WP and then was carried inland, rather than moving east along the north coast as in the case of the bulk of the other obsidians. This route would have been especially convenient before the W-K2 eruption, because there was a large bay located in what is now the flood plain of the Kulu River (Figure 9.1; Torrence et al. 2009). In contrast, Baki obsidian is most common in coastal locations, which makes sense given its location on Garua Island (Figures 9.1 and 9.6).

In both the Isthmus and at FRI the most striking pattern in obsidian consumption is the largest peak of Kutau-Bao obsidian in the period immediately following the W-K2 eruption (c. 3300–1600 cal. BP or Period 4), representing 97 and 99 per cent of the samples respectively (Tables 9.4 and 9.5; Figure 9.5). The loss of Baki obsidian at FRI II is contemporary with its drastic decline at sites situated near the outcrops on Garua Island (Torrence 2004a; Torrence and Summerhayes 1997). Torrence and Summerhayes (1997) and Torrence (2004a) argued that the monopoly of Kutau-Bao obsidian at this time implied the existence of a specialised exchange system, perhaps along the lines described by Mead (1930) for coastal villages in the southern part of the Admiralty Islands. In this model, each community specialises in a raw material or product (e.g. obsidian, pottery, baskets, fish, taro, etc.), even if residents can easily produce the material locally, and they acquire other products through trade. This kind of exchange system is an effective way to integrate small, isolated groups by promoting the regular social interchange necessary for facilitating marriage ties and access to assistance when needed. The adoption of an exchange system that ensures frequent intercourse also makes sense for a population recolonising a region following the large-scale W-K2 volcanic eruption, at a time when small, isolated groups would have been susceptible to fluctuations in population size that could lead to failure.

Given the mix of obsidian sources in both regions, the formal trading system may have begun to break down after 1600 cal. BP. After the W-K3 eruption, the pXRF results show a gradual decline in the percentage of Kutau-Bao obsidian in favour of more heterogeneous assemblages comprising the minor sources Gulu and Baki (Tables 9.4 and 9.5; Figure 9.5). Possibly through time, a well-integrated exchange system focusing on Kutau-Bao obsidian was gradually replaced by a more fluid situation in which people negotiated their social connections independently. In the Isthmus, a change to a more individualised pattern of social interaction was further accentuated in Period 6 (1300–500 cal. BP) following the W-K4/Dk event (McKee et al. 2011), when the dominance of Kutau-Bao was significantly diminished and continued to fall in Period 7/8.

Another key element in the history of obsidian procurement in the Isthmus is the pattern of occurrence of obsidian from the Mopir obsidian source, located to the east in the Hoskins Peninsula (Fullagar et al. 1991) (Figure 9.1). During the Pleistocene, Mopir was the most common obsidian source represented at the Kupona Na Dari site, comprising 36 per cent of the assemblage (Torrence et al. 2004), but by the early Holocene (Periods 2–3) its incidence had declined markedly in the wider Isthmus region, where it comprised only c. 4 per cent (Table 9.5). The actual quantities of Mopir obsidian before and after W-K2 are admittedly small, but there is no significant change in the proportions they make up of the total assemblage (Figure 9.5b). Contrary to previous suggestions that Mopir disappeared from assemblages in the region because the W-K2 volcanic event increased the difficulty of reaching the outcrops (e.g. Summerhayes et al. 1998; Torrence 2004a; Torrence et al. 1996), in the WP it is present in roughly the same very small proportion before and after the eruption. It is worth noting that Mopir is also present, again in small quantities, in assemblages elsewhere in New Britain during Period 4, contemporary with Lapita pottery (White and Harris 1997).

Mopir continued as a minority source up until the W-K4/DK event, marking the boundary of Period 6. At this point, however, the proportion of Mopir obsidian increased markedly and continued to grow in Period 7/8. Similarly, all three artefacts from FRI II assigned to the Mopir source were recovered from post 1600 cal. BP contexts in Phase 3 (Table 9.4; Figure 9.5a). The rise in the contribution of Mopir obsidian after the Dk and W-K4 volcanic events (which McKee et al. (2011) show occurred very close together in time) may represent a significant change in the structure of regional social networks in the WP. It seems likely that the volcanic disasters played a role in the shift from the dominance of Kutau-Bao to a marked rise in the amount of Mopir obsidian in the Isthmus, but had less impact further north at FRI. Based on a Bayesian analysis of radiocarbon dates that bracket the eruptions, the Isthmus region was abandoned for c. 100 years following the W-K4 eruption. In contrast, since W-K4 tephra has not been identified near the Kutau-Bao sources, the immediate local consequences of that event were probably minimal. However, dates from Garua Island indicate the northern part of the WP was abandoned for c. 235 years after the Dk event, which occurred just slightly earlier (Petrie and Torrence 2008:Table 7), indicating that the northern WP was much more seriously impacted by the larger magnitude Dakataua eruption (Machida et al. 1996). The decline in Kutau-Bao obsidian in the Isthmus, and to a lesser extent at FRI, may be the consequence of reduced population sizes near the sources. When the Isthmus community returned after W-K4, opportunities for social networks to the north-west were probably still scarce and so people may have looked to the east for alternative lifelines. Through the process of initiating and reinforcing ties through exchange and marriage ties, they acquired obsidian from the Mopir source.

Evidence for a reorientation of social networks to the east in the most recent periods is also indicated by the novel importation of ground stone axes produced from raw material in the Hoskins Peninsula where Mopir is also situated (Pengilley et al. 2019).

Tracing exports from the quarries

Building on the characterisation study, the reduction analysis explored the nature of social relations through the material that was exchanged. A limitation of the study is the lack of excavated data that could provide information about how raw material was treated at the obsidian outcrops before it was distributed. An examination of the five general classes of artefacts—cores, flakes, microflakes (less than 1 cm^2), nonflake debris (often termed 'shatter') and tools—shows that in the Isthmus region the assemblage is dominated by flakes (85–92 per cent) (Table 9.6). The scarce cores (1 per cent) all preserve multidirectional flake scars, indicating that they had been heavily reduced in an unsystematic manner, possibly in the context of use rather than primarily as a source of flakes. Not surprisingly, given their rarity in other assemblages in West New Britain, there are no formal tools (Kononenko 2011; Torrence 2011). A very few small stemmed tools, all made on casual flakes (cf. Kononenko et al. 2010), have been recovered from the Isthmus test pits, but none occurred in our sample. The tools identified in the assemblage (4 per cent) are comprised of flakes with irregular, light, marginal retouch or edge damage. It is probable that some unmodified flakes had been selected for use because of the specific shape of the cutting edge, although Kononenko (pers. comm. 2020) has found that edge characteristics are not a reliable predictor of wear patterns in obsidian assemblages in this region. Given the results of Kononenko's (2011) usewear analyses of assemblages from Garua Island, it is likely that many of the flakes in our sample had also been used in a casual manner for a short period (cf. Torrence 1992, 2011). The expedient consumption of obsidian supports Sheppard's (1993) proposition that it was social relations that stimulated its movement rather than its value as a utilitarian good.

Since sample sizes from the Gulu, Baki and Mopir sources are small, interpretations of past behaviour based on assemblage composition alone are tentative (Tables 9.6, 9.7). The make-up of the assemblage sourced to Gulu is distinctive from the other sources, possibly reflecting change through time, since most of it dates to Period 2 (pre 6000 cal. BP). The relatively high proportion of Gulu microflakes and nonflake debris, together with a single core, is possibly indicative of waste from tool manufacture rather than assemblages comprised of discarded tools. Another major difference among the assemblages is the absence of cores sourced to Mopir despite the relatively large sample of artefacts recovered.

Table 9.6: Isthmus region: Assemblage composition by obsidian source.

Category	Baki		Gulu		Kutau-Bao		Mopir		Total	
	N	%	*N*	%	*N*	%	*N*	%	*N*	%
Cores	0	0	1	2	21	2	0	0	22	1
Flakes	31	88	35	68	1150	84	154	92	1370	85
Microflakes	1	3	6	12	50	4	5	3	62	4
Nonflake debris	2	6	5	10	81	6	5	3	93	6
Tools	1	3	4	8	58	4	4	2	67	4
Total/%	35	2	51	3	1360	84	168	10	1614	100

Source: Authors' data.

Table 9.7: FRI II: Assemblage composition by obsidian source.

Category	Baki		Gulu		Kutau-Bao		Mopir		Total	
	N	**%**	**N**	**%**	**N**	**%**	**N**	**%**	**N**	**%**
Cores	1	7	1	5	7	1	0	0	9	1
Flakes	13	86	18	90	528	92	3	100	562	92
Nonflake debris	0	0	1	5	26	5	0	0	27	4
Tools	1	7	0	0	14	2	0	0	15	3
Total/%	15	3	20	3	575	94	3	1<	613	100

Source: Authors' data.

The incidence of cortex, defined as the unmodified surface of an obsidian block extracted from the outcrops, is a useful indicator of how intensely raw material has been worked. The degree of reduction at the sites is a consequence of the form in which the material left the quarry together with the number of exchange episodes through which it passed. Given that FRI and the Isthmus region are within 10 or 22–33 km, respectively, of the Kutau-Bao obsidian outcrops, one would expect the preservation of cortex on some artefacts if raw nodules had been the main quarry output, because the number of exchanges among different communities over this short distance is unlikely to have been very high.

In contrast, the distance from the Mopir outcrops (45–55 km) should be large enough that cortex would have been removed from the initial quarried nodules moving 'down-the-line' among multiple recipients. As expected, the very small number of Mopir artefacts at FRI probably arrived as flakes and do not retain cortex. In contrast, during Periods 6–7/8 in the Isthmus, when there are reasonable sample sizes for Mopir obsidian, only 86–89 per cent are non-cortical, compared to 95–97 per cent for Kutau-Bao (Table 9.8), indicating differences in the exchange patterns from the two obsidian sources, either in terms of the form in which obsidian was transported and/or a smaller number of links between Mopir and the places where the obsidian was discarded.

Table 9.8: Comparison of chronological change in the incidence of non-cortical artefacts in the Isthmus regions and FRI II (based on Tables 9.4 and 9.5).

	ISTHMUS					FRI II			
Period	Kutau-Bao		Mopir		Phase	Kutau-Bao		Mopir	
	N	**%**	**N**	**%**		**N**	**%**	**N**	**%**
7/8	112	97	49	89	4	149	84	2	100
6	252	95	67	86	–	–	–	–	–
5	120	88	0	0	3	42	71	1	100
4	174	98	0	0	2	334	75	0	0
3.2	174	98	0	0	1	14	100	0	0
3	339	99	0	0	–	–	–	–	–
2	142	98	0	0	–	–	–	–	–

Source: Authors' data.

At FRI, cortex is absent in the Kutau-Bao assemblage dating pre 3300 cal. BP, suggesting that either quarried raw nodules passed through several hands, each of which consumed some of the nodule before exchanging it onward, or more likely, decorticated, preformed or finished artefacts were exchanged . In later periods at FRI, when cortical flakes range between 25 and 29 per cent of the total, unworked nodules or only partially worked preforms were imported. In contrast, by the time obsidian reached Isthmus consumers, there was practically no original surface of the nodule remaining on the imports, although the larger incidence of cortex in Period 5, after the W-K3 event, might be significant as this is also the time when the dominance of Kutau-Bao obsidian decreased. To track changes in the imports further, we consider additional indices for measuring changes in the degree to which obsidian nodules were reduced.

Reduction intensity and exchange

Since by far the largest proportion of the artefacts in the Isthmus region are noncortical flakes (Table 9.8), obsidian must have been imported as either preforms or finished objects. To refine the description of the assemblage, we used a method for characterising reduction intensity that focuses on dorsal scars. Following previous approaches (e.g. Andrefsky 1998; Callahan 1979; Shott 1994; Symons 2003), the obsidian archaeological assemblages were grouped into three stages.

1. Initial stage reduction: flakes with cortex covering more than 50 per cent of the dorsal surface. They have little or no platform preparation and tended to be the larger artefacts.
2. Mid-stage reduction: flakes with one or two dorsal scars. The majority of these preserved no cortex.
3. Late-stage reduction: flakes with three or more dorsal scars and including all the microflakes. No cortex was preserved on these flakes.

Sample sizes for Baki and Gulu obsidian artefacts were considered too small for this analysis, but the proportion of the various reduction stages for Kutau-Bao and Mopir obsidian (Periods 6–8) in the Isthmus region is depicted in Figures 9.7b and 9.7c.

Beginning with the consumption patterns for Kutau-Bao, the major change through time occurred between Periods 3 and 4, when there is a marked decrease in late-stage reduction. This pattern reflects the simultaneous change at FRI from 100 per cent noncortical artefacts to a quarter retaining some cortex (Table 9.8; Figure 9.7a). The absence of cortex and the large numbers of flakes with multiple dorsal scars (late-stage reduction) in Periods 2 and 3 in the Isthmus suggest that a preform or finished artefact was produced at the obsidian quarries and then exchanged. It is notable that at this time large, highly retouched stemmed blades and flakes were made at all the obsidian quarries, although the focus of production was at the Kutau-Bao outcrops (Araho et al. 2002; Torrence et al. 2013). Several stemmed tools have been recovered from a disturbed context in the Isthmus region at site FABN, located near test pits xlviii and xlix (Figure 9.3). Torrence (2004b; Torrence et al. 2013) and Specht (2005) have argued that stemmed tools were valuable objects that established or enhanced social status, but this does not preclude their being recycled following the transaction or ceremony in which they played a role. It is even possible that stemmed tools were deliberately destroyed as part of a ritual and the resulting flakes were recycled.

Moving through time into Period 4, contemporary with the near monopoly of Kutau-Bao obsidian in both areas there is a marked increase in mid-stage reduction. This indicates that the material leaving the quarries had not been converted into a final product but was only partially worked or reduced. If the dominance of a single obsidian source does signify a specialised exchange system, as proposed above, it is interesting that the people residing at the obsidian quarries were not controlling the exports to the same degree as they had previously. Obsidian was clearly circulating in a partially preformed state, since initial reduction is absent, but not in the final form, as previously. From Period 5, when the dominance of Kutau-Bao obsidian began to decline, the material imported into the Isthmus region was less worked prior to discard, as indicated by the appearance of flakes from initial stage reduction, and this trend continued. It seems likely that in Periods 5–8 access to the quarries was less regulated. People could more freely obtain unworked nodules and/or these passed through fewer exchange partners before reaching the Isthmus in a less reduced stage than during the exchange of stemmed tools in Periods 2–3.

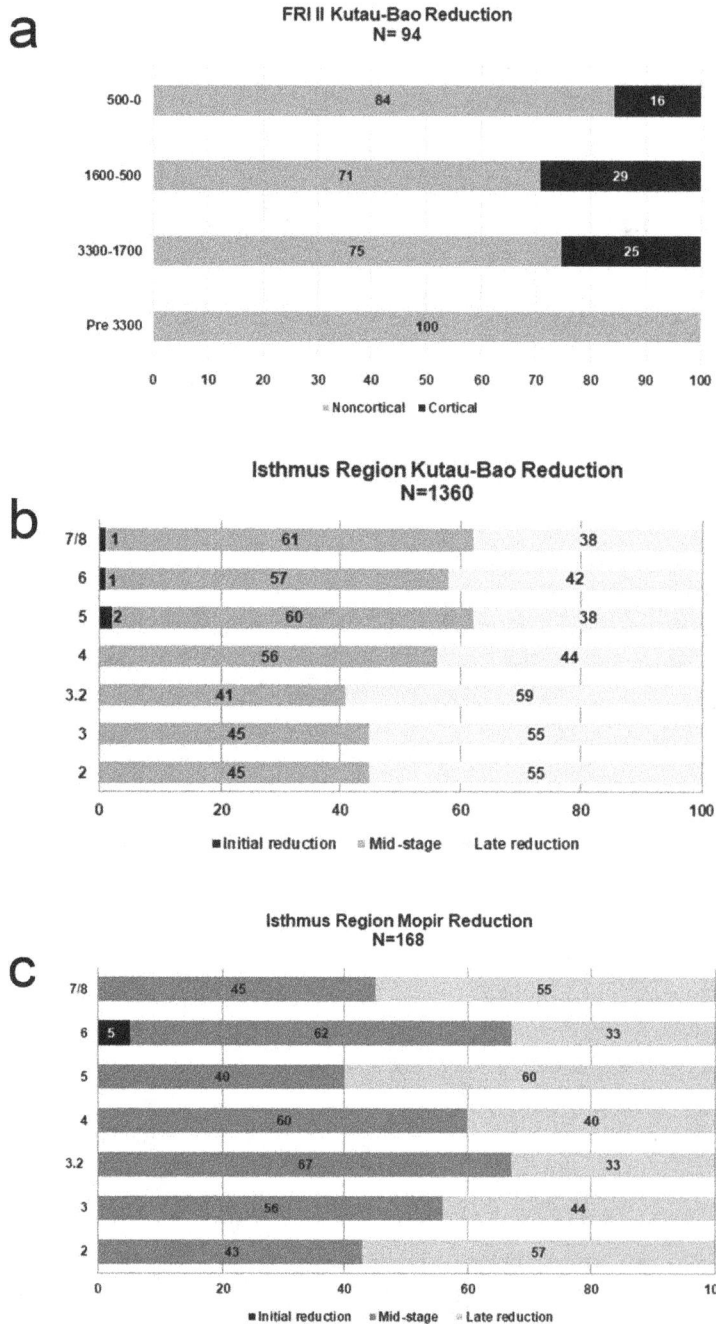

Figure 9.7: Changes in reduction stages through time at FRI and in the Isthmus region.

Notes: (a) FRI II Kutau-Bao reduction based on the percentage of cortical versus noncortical artefacts; (b) Isthmus region: changes in the degree of reduction for Kutau-Bao obsidian based on the percentage of artefacts at different stages; (c) Isthmus region: changes in the degree of reduction for Mopir obsidian based on the percentage of artefacts at different stages.

Source: Illustration by authors.

The exchange networks incorporating Mopir obsidian can also be inferred based on the mix of reduction stages for the most recent two periods with adequate sample sizes (Table 9.4; Figure 9.7c). As noted above, after the combined disaster of W-K4/Dk, larger amounts of Mopir obsidian were imported into the Isthmus area, indicating a significant shift in social connections. Given the incidence of initial and mid-stage reduction in the samples together with the amounts of cortex (Table 9.8), it also seems likely that partially or unworked nodules were exchanged through the reoriented social networks, much the same as with Kutau-Bao at this time.

Building resilience through social networks

Reconstructed using a combination of geochemical source characterisation and stone tool technology, the history of obsidian exchange within the Isthmus region of the WP in West New Britain in the period from the late Pleistocene up to the recent past is an excellent illustration of how populations have coped with the challenges of living in an active volcanic environment. In Periods 2 and 3 (pre 6000–3200 cal. BP), formalised valuables in the form of stemmed tools were made at all the sources, but only those comprised of Kutau-Bao obsidian arrived at FRI or the Isthmus region, where they were subsequently expended and converted into flakes and debris. The additional presence of very small quantities of Baki or Gulu obsidian at this time suggests that a few groups also established networks outside the ceremonial exchange in which Kutau-Bao circulated. Following the W-K2 event, in Period 4 (3200–1600 cal. BP) a much more tightly integrated exchange system was adopted in which only nodules or preforms from the Kutau-Bao source were used, possibly in exchange for other local specialities. This Kutau-Bao–dominated network began to break down after the W-K3 event. In Period 5 (1600–1300 cal. BP) and subsequently, there was a gradual shift from a well-coordinated pattern to one in which individuals forged their own exchange links, thereby reducing the length of the chain connecting the sources with the consumers. Finally, since the Dk disaster had a major impact on groups who controlled the Kutau-Bao obsidian sources in the northern WP (Periods 6–8, 1300 cal. BP onward), residents in the Isthmus region broadened their social networks to the east, resulting in an increase in Mopir obsidian and the introduction of stone axes produced in the same region.

The long history of obsidian consumption in the WP illustrates the importance of exchange for groups with low and unstable population levels as a result of volcanic activity. Although obsidian was not essential for utilitarian tasks, we argue it played a crucial role in creating and solidifying the social networks that sustained the small populations following a disaster as well as supporting colonising groups when they returned. When the scale of the volcanic eruptions diminished and smaller areas were subject to very serious impacts, however, there was more scope for people to diversify in terms of how and with whom they made connections. For example, in line with a reduction in the severity and spatial scale of the volcanic disasters experienced in the WP (Machida et al. 1996), there was a decrease in the length of time during which the area was abandoned (Petrie and Torrence 2008). Consequently, population levels in the Isthmus region probably rose over time, as reflected by the steadily increasing rate of discard for obsidian artefacts per year as illustrated in Table 9.9 (cf. Torrence 2016:10, Table 2). With decreased environmental challenges and a growing population, groups were able to solve their needs locally and the requirement for strong nonlocal connections was reduced. Consequently, the exchange systems that distributed obsidian were gradually loosened up and possibly played a lesser role in social life. The change in the role of obsidian probably created opportunities for alterative social and ceremonial practices.

Table 9.9: Discard rates for the Isthmus region based on data from 67 test pits.

Period	Number of artefacts discarded per year
3	0.3
4	0.9
5	1
6	1.4
7/8	1.8

Source: Torrence (2016:Table 2).

To test our proposal for the role of exchange in creating and strengthening social networks that ensured adequate resilience among groups inhabiting places prone to severe environmental perturbations, future studies could compare and contrast the distribution and use of obsidian in other areas of Papua New Guinea (e.g. Admiralty Islands or the south coast of the mainland and adjacent archipelagos) or indeed in other regions of the world with different environmental histories and challenges. It is interesting to note, for example, that Fergusson Island obsidian does not have the same persistence through time as the New Britain sources (e.g. Golitko et al. 2012; Irwin and Holdaway 1996; Mialanes et al. 2016; Shaw et al. 2021). Can changes in the mix of obsidian sources at sites in the Admiralty Islands (e.g. Fredericksen 1997) be connected with the volcanic history of Manus Island? With the advantages of portable technology, there are now many exciting possible avenues for examining relationships between obsidian exchange, social strategies and risks caused by environmental variation.

Acknowledgements

Archaeological fieldwork in New Britain was funded by the Australian Research Council, Australian Museum and New Britain Palm Oil Ltd and supported by the PNG National Museum and Art Gallery, West New Britain Cultural Centre, Walindi Plantation and Resort, and Mahonia Na Dari Research Institute. Bonnat's research visit to Sydney was supported by Consejo Nacional de Promoción Científica y Tecnológica (Estadías en el Exterior CONICET 2017). We are especially grateful to the people of West New Britain for permission to work on their lands, for sharing knowledge and assisting with the fieldwork, and for their welcoming hospitality over the years. We are very appreciative of assistance from the following: Jim Specht for permission to include the FRI study and for his very perceptive comments on this paper; Max Benjamin, who brought the FRI site to Specht's attention—he and Cecilie Benjamin were keen supporters of our archaeological research; Bob Wilson, Mike Hoare, Jaimie Graham and Kefu Boromana and their teams, who welcomed us into the plantations they managed and provided much logistical support; the many volunteers from Australia, Great Britain and Papua New Guinea who helped with the fieldwork; Trudy Doelman, who organised key databases and maps; and Nina Kononenko for help with Figure 9.1. The PXRF study was assisted by advice from Bruce Kaiser, Val Attenbrow and Christabel Brand. We thank the reviewers for pointing out where the paper needed to be strengthened. A very special thanks to Glenn Summerhayes for introducing Torrence to PIXE-PIGME, for many good times shared during fieldwork, but especially for his leadership in showcasing the importance and potential of obsidian characterisation studies in Pacific archaeology.

References

Allen, M.S. and G. Bell 1988. Lapita flaked stone assemblages: Sourcing, technological, and functional studies. In P.V. Kirch and T.L. Hunt (eds), *Archaeology of the Lapita Cultural Complex: A critical review*, pp. 83–98. Thomas Burke Memorial Washington State Museum Research Report 5. Thomas Burke Memorial Museum, Seattle.

Ambrose, W., C. Allen, S. O'Connor, M. Spriggs, N. Oliveira and C. Reepmeyer 2009. Possible obsidian sources for artefacts from Timor: Narrowing the options using chemical data. *Journal of Archaeological Science* 36:607–615. doi.org/10.1016/j.jas.2008.09.022.

Andrefsky, W. 1998. *Lithics: Macroscopic approaches to analysis.* Cambridge University Press, Cambridge.

Araho, N., R. Torrence and J.P. White. 2002. Valuable and useful: Mid-Holocene stemmed obsidian artifacts from West New Britain, Papua New Guinea. *Proceedings of the Prehistoric Society* 68:61–81. doi.org/10.1017/S0079497X00001444.

Binford, L. 1979. Organization and formation processes: Looking at curated technologies. *Journal of Anthropological Research* 35:255–273. doi.org/10.1086/jar.35.3.3629902.

Bird, J.R., P. Duerden, W.R. Ambrose and B.F. Leach 1981. Pacific obsidian catalogue. In F. Leach and J. Davidson (eds), *Archaeological studies of Pacific stone resources*, pp. 31–43. BAR International Series 104. British Archaeological Reports, Oxford.

Bird, J.R., R. Torrence, G.R. Summerhayes and G. Bailey 1997. New Britain obsidian sources. *Archaeology in Oceania* 32:61–67. doi.org/10.1002/j.1834-4453.1997.tb00371.x.

Callahan, E. 1979. The basics of biface knapping in the Eastern Fluted Point Tradition: A manual for flintknappers and lithic analysts. *Archaeology of Eastern North America* 7:1–180.

Cashdan, E. 1985. Coping with risk: reciprocity among the Basarwa of Northern Botswana. *Man* 20:454–474. doi.org/10.2307/2802441.

Cashdan, E. 1990. Risk and uncertainty in tribal and peasant economies: An introduction. In E. Cashdan (ed.), *Risk and uncertainty in tribal and peasant economies*, pp. 1–16. Westview Press, Boulder.

Conolly, J. and P. Lane 2018. Vulnerability, risk, resilience: An introduction. *World Archaeology* 50:547–553. doi.org/10.1080/00438243.2019.1591025.

Ditchfield, K. 2016. An experimental approach to distinguishing different stone artefact transport patterns from debitage assemblages. *Journal of Archaeological Science* 65:44–56. doi.org/10.1016/j.jas.2015.10.012.

Eerkens, J., A. Spurling and M. Gras 2008. Measuring prehistoric mobility strategies based on obsidian geochemical and technological signatures in the Owens Valley, California. *Journal of Archaeological Science* 35:668–680. doi.org/10.1016/j.jas.2007.05.016.

Franco, N. 2014. Lithic artifacts and the information about human utilization of large areas. In P. Escola and S. Hocsman (eds), *Lithic artefacts, mobility and site functionality problems and perspectives*, pp. 116–127. BAR International Series S2628. British Archaeological Reports, Oxford.

Fredericksen, C. 1997. The maritime distribution of Bismarck Archipelago obsidian and Island Melanesian prehistory. *Journal of the Polynesian Society* 106:375–393.

Freund, K. 2018. A long-term perspective on the exploitation of Lipari obsidian in central Mediterranean prehistory. *Quaternary International* 468:109–120. doi.org/10.1016/j.quaint.2017.10.014.

Fullagar, R., G.R. Summerhayes, B. Ivuyo and J. Specht 1991. Obsidian sources at Mopir, West New Britain Province, Papua New Guinea. *Archaeology in Oceania* 26:110–114. doi.org/10.1002/j.1834-4453.1991. tb00274.x.

Gaffney, D. G.R. Summerhayes, M. Mennis, T. Beni, A. Cook, J. Field, H. Buckley and H. Mandui 2018. Archaeological investigations into the origins of Bel trading groups around the Madang coast, northeast New Guinea. *Journal of Island and Coastal Archaeology* 13:501–530. doi.org/10.1080/15564894.2017. 1315349.

Galipaud, J-C., C. Reepmeyer, R. Torrence, S. Kelloway and J.P. White 2014. Long distance connections in Vanuatu: New obsidian characterisations for the Makué site, Aore Island. *Archaeology in Oceania* 49:110–116. doi.org/10.1002/arco.5030.

Golitko, M., M.M. Schauer and J.E. Terrell 2012. Identification of Fergusson Island obsidian on the Sepik coast of northern Papua New Guinea. *Archaeology in Oceania* 47:151–156. doi.org/10.1002/j.1834-4453. 2012.tb00127.x.

Hanslip, M.D. 2001. Expedient technologies? Obsidian artefacts in Island Melanesia. Unpublished PhD thesis, The Australian National University, Canberra.

Irwin, G. and S. Holdaway 1996. Colonisation, trade and exchange: From Papua to Lapita. In J. Davidson, G. Irwin, B. Leach, A. Pawley and D. Brown (eds), *Oceanic culture history: Essays in honour of Roger Green*, pp. 225–235. New Zealand Journal of Archaeology Special Publication. New Zealand Archaeological Association, Dunedin.

James, L., K. Joyce, K. Magargal and B. Codding 2022. A stone in the hand is worth how many in the bush? Applying the marginal value theorem to understand optimal toolstone transportation, processing and discard decisions. *Journal of Archaeological Science* 137:105518. doi.org/10.1016/j.jas.2021.105518.

Kononenko, N. 2011. Experimental and archaeological studies of use-wear and residues on obsidian artefacts from Papua New Guinea. *Technical Reports of the Australian Museum* 21:1–244. doi.org/10.3853/j.1835-4211.21.2011.1559.

Kononenko, N. 2012. Middle and late Holocene skin-working tools in Melanesia: Tattooing and scarification? *Archaeology in Oceania* 47:14–28. doi.org/10.1002/j.1834-4453.2012.tb00111.x.

Kononenko, N., J. Specht and R. Torrence 2010. Persistent traditions in the face of natural disasters: Stemmed and waisted stone tools in late Holocene New Britain, Papua New Guinea. *Australian Archaeology* 70: 17–28. doi.org/10.1080/03122417.2010.11681908.

Kristensen, T., P. Hare, R. Gotthardt, N. Eastern, J. Ives, R. Speakman and J. Rasic 2019. The movement of obsidian in Subarctic Canada: Holocene social relationships and human responses to a large-scale volcanic eruption. *Journal of Anthropological Archaeology* 56:101114. doi.org/10.1016/j.jaa.2019.101114.

Lazzari, M. and M. Sprovieri 2020. Weaving people and places: Landscapes of obsidian circulation in NW Argentina. A long term view (ca. CE100–1436). *Journal of Anthropological Archaeology* 59:101172. doi.org/ 10.1016/j.jaa.2020.101172.

Lin, S. and L. Premo 2021. Forager mobility and lithic discard probability similarly affect the distance of raw material discard from source. *American Antiquity* 86:845–863. doi.org/10.1017/aaq.2021.66.

Lorenz, D. 2013. The diversity of resilience: Contributions from a social science perspective. *Natural Hazards* 67:7–24. doi.org/10.1007/s11069-010-9654-y.

Machida, H., R. Blong, J. Specht, R. Torrence, H. Moriwaki, Y. Hayakawa, B. Talai, D. Lolok and C. Pain 1996. Holocene explosive eruptions of Witori and Dakataua caldera volcanoes in West New Britain, Papua New Guinea. *Quaternary International* 34–36:65–78. doi.org/10.1016/1040-6182(95)00070-4.

McKee, C., V. Neall and R. Torrence 2011. A remarkable pulse of large-scale volcanism on New Britain Island, Papua New Guinea. *Bulletin of Volcanology* 73:27–37. doi.org/10.1007/s00445-010-0401-8.

Mead, M. 1930. Melanesian middlemen. *Natural History* 30:115–130.

Mialanes, J., B. David, A. Ford, T. Richards, I. McNiven, G.R. Summerhayes and M. Leavesley 2016. Imported obsidian at Caution Bay, south coast of Papua New Guinea: Cessation of long distance procurement c. 1,900 cal. BP. *Australian Archaeology* 82:248–262. doi.org/10.1080/03122417.2016.1252079.

Mulrooney, M., A. McAlister, C.M. Stevenson, A.E. Morrison and L. Gendreau 2014. Sourcing Rapa Nui mata'a from the collections of Bishop Museum using non-destructive pXRF. *Journal of the Polynesian Society* 123:301–338. doi.org/10.15286/jps.123.3.301-338.

Mulrooney, M., R. Torrence and A. McAlister 2016. The demise of a monopoly: Implications of geochemical characterization of a stemmed obsidian tool from the Bishop Museum collection. *Archaeology in Oceania* 51:62–69. doi.org/10.1002/arco.5069.

Neall, V., R. Wallace and R. Torrence 2008. The volcanic environment for 40,000 years of human occupation on the Willaumez Isthmus, West New Britain, Papua New Guinea. *Journal of Volcanology and Geothermal Research* 176:330–343. doi.org/10.1016/j.jvolgeores.2008.01.037.

Nelson, M. 1991. The study of technological organisation. *Archaeological Method and Theory* 3:57–100.

Parry, W. and R. Kelly 1987. Expedient core technology and sedentism. In J.K. Johnson and C.A. Morrow (eds), *The organisation of core technology*, pp. 285–304. Westview Press, Boulder.

Pengilley, A., C. Brand, J. Flexner, J. Specht and R. Torrence 2019. Detecting exchange networks in New Britain, Papua New Guinea: Geochemical comparisons between axe-adze blades and in situ volcanic rock sources. *Archaeology in Oceania* 54:200–213. doi.org/10.1002/arco.5188.

Peterson, J., D.R. Mitchell and M.S. Shackley 1997. The social and economic contexts of lithic procurement: Obsidian from Classic period Hohokam sites. *American Antiquity* 62(2): 231–259. doi.org/10.2307/282508.

Petrie, C. and R. Torrence 2008. Assessing the effects of volcanic disasters on human settlement in the Willaumez Peninsula, Papua New Guinea: A Bayesian approach. *The Holocene* 18(5):729–744. doi.org/10.1177/0959683608091793.

Reepmeyer, C. 2021. Modelling prehistoric social interaction in the South-western Pacific: A view from the obsidian sources in northern Vanuatu. In J. Specht, V. Attenbrow and J. Allen (eds), *From field to museum: Studies from Melanesia in honour of Robin Torrence*, pp. 137–148. Technical Reports of the Australian Museum Online 34. Australian Museum, Sydney. doi.org/10.3853/j.1835-4211.34.2021.1748.

Reepmeyer, C., W.R. Ambrose and G.R. Clark 2016. Contributions of LA-ICP-MS to obsidian sourcing in the Pacific. In L. Dussubieux, M. Golitko and B. Gratuze (eds), *Recent advances in laser ablation ICP-MS for archaeology*, pp. 141–162. Springer, Berlin. doi.org/10.1007/978-3-662-49894-1_10.

Renfrew, C. 1977. Alternative models for exchange and spatial distribution. In J.A. Sabloff and C.C. Lamberg-Karlovsky (eds), *Ancient civilisation and trade*, pp. 3–60. University of New Mexico Press, Albuquerque.

Riede, F. 2019. Doing palaeo-social volcanology: Developing a framework for systematically investigating the impacts of past volcanic eruptions on human societies using archaeological datasets. *Quaternary International* 499:266–277. doi.org/10.1016/j.quaint.2018.01.027.

Shaw, B., G. Irwin, A. Pengilley and S. Kelloway 2021. Village-specific Kula partnerships revealed by obsidian sourcing on Tubetube Island, Papua New Guinea. *Archaeology in Oceania* 56:32–44. doi.org/10.1002/arco.5224.

Sheppard, P.J. 1992. A report on the flaked lithic assemblages from three Southeast Solomons Lapita sites (SE-SZ-8, SE-RF-2, SERF-6). In J.-C. Galipaud (ed.), *Poterie Lapita et peuplement. Actes du colloque Lapita Nouméa Janvier 1992*, pp. 145–153. ORSTOM, Nouméa.

Sheppard, P.J. 1993. Lapita lithics: Trade/exchange and technology. A view from the Reefs/Santa Cruz. *Archaeology in Oceania* 28:121–137. doi.org/10.1002/j.1834-4453.1993.tb00303.x.

Sheppard, P.J., B. Trichereau and C. Milicich 2010. Pacific obsidian sourcing by portable XRF. *Archaeology in Oceania* 45:21–30. doi.org/10.1002/j.1834-4453.2010.tb00074.x.

Shott, J. 2015. Glass is heavy, too: testing the field-processing model at the Modena obsidian quarry, Lincoln County, southeastern Nevada. *American Antiquity* 54:179–184. doi.org/10.7183/0002-7316.80.3.548.

Shott, M. 1994. Size and form in the analysis of flake debris: Review and recent approaches. *Journal of Archaeological Method and Theory* 1:69–110. doi.org/10.1007/BF02229424.

Specht, J. 1981. Obsidian sources at Talasea, West New Britain, Papua New Guinea. *Journal of the Polynesian Society* 90:337–356.

Specht, J. 2002. Obsidian, colonising and exchange. In S. Bedford, C. Sand and D. Burley (eds), *Fifty years in the field: Essays in honour and celebration of Richard Shutler Jr's archaeological career*, pp. 37–49. New Zealand Archaeological Association Monograph 25. New Zealand Archaeological Association, Auckland.

Specht, J. 2005. Stone axe blades and valuables in New Britain, Papua New Guinea. In C. Gross, H. Lyons and D. Counts (eds), *A polymath anthropologist: Essays in honour of Ann Chowning*, pp. 15–22. Research in Anthropology and Linguistics Monograph 8. University of Auckland, Auckland.

Specht, J. and R. Torrence 2007a. Lapita all over: Land-use on the Willaumez Peninsula, Papua New Guinea. In S. Bedford, C. Sand and S. Connaughton (eds), *Oceanic explorations: Lapita and western Pacific settlement*, pp. 71–96. Terra Australis 26. ANU E Press, Canberra. doi.org/10.22459/TA26.2007.04.

Specht, J. and R. Torrence 2007b. Pottery of the Talasea area, West New Britain Province. In J. Specht and V. Attenbrow (eds), *Archaeological studies of the middle and late Holocene, Papua New Guinea, Part IV*, pp. 131–196. Technical Reports of the Australian Museum 20 (online). Australian Museum, Sydney. doi.org/10.3853/j.1835-4211.20.2007.1476.

Specht, J., R. Fullagar, R. Torrence and N. Baker 1988. Prehistoric obsidian exchange in Melanesia: A perspective from the Talasea sources. *Australian Archaeology* 27:3–16. doi.org/10.1080/03122417.1988.12093158.

Specht, J., R. Fullagar and R. Torrence 1991. What was the significance of Lapita pottery at Talasea? *Bulletin of the Indo-Pacific Prehistory Association* 11:281–294.

Sullivan, A. and K. Rozen 1985. Debitage analysis and archaeological interpretation. *American Antiquity* 50:755–779. doi.org/10.2307/280165.

Summerhayes, G.R. 2009. Obsidian network patterns in Melanesia. Sources, characterization and distribution. *Bulletin of the Indo-Pacific Prehistory Association* 29:110–124.

Summerhayes, G.R., C. Gosden, R. Fullagar, J. Specht, R. Torrence, J.R. Bird, N. Shagholi and A. Katsaros 1993. West New Britain obsidian: Production and consumption patterns. In B.L. Fankhauser and J.R. Bird (eds), *Archaeometry: Current Australasian research*, pp. 57–68. Occasional Papers in Prehistory 22. Department of Prehistory, Research School of Pacific Studies, The Australian National University, Canberra.

Summerhayes, G.R., J.R. Bird, R. Fullagar, C. Gosden, J. Specht and R. Torrence 1998. Application of PIGME-PIXE to archaeological analysis of changing patterns of obsidian use in West New Britain, Papua New Guinea. In S. Shackley (ed.), *Archaeological obsidian studies: Method and theory*, pp. 129–158. Plenum Press, New York. doi.org/10.1007/978-1-4757-9276-8_6.

Symons, J. 2003. Obsidian artefacts and land-use in the mid-Holocene of the Willaumez Peninsula, Papua New Guinea. *Australian Archaeology* 57:128–134. doi.org/10.1080/03122417.2003.11681771.

Torrence, R. 1986. *Production and exchange of stone tools.* Cambridge University Press, Cambridge.

Torrence, R. 1992. What is Lapita about obsidian? A view from the Talasea sources. In J.-C. Galipaud (ed.), *Poterie Lapita et peuplement. Actes du colloque Lapita Nouméa Janvier 1992*, pp. 111–126. ORSTOM, Nouméa.

Torrence, R. 2000. Archaeological fieldwork in West New Britain, PNG. May–June 2000. Unpublished report to the National Museum and Art Gallery, Papua New Guinea, Port Moresby.

Torrence, R. 2001. Archaeological fieldwork in West New Britain, PNG. June–July 2001. Unpublished report to the National Museum and Art Gallery, Papua New Guinea, Port Moresby.

Torrence, R. 2002a. Archaeological fieldwork in West New Britain, PNG June–August 2002. Unpublished report to the National Museum and Art Gallery, Papua New Guinea, Port Moresby.

Torrence, R. 2002b. The archaeology of cultural landscapes on Garua Island, Papua New Guinea. *Antiquity* 76:766–776. doi.org/10.1017/S0003598X00091213.

Torrence, R. 2004a. Now you see it, now you don't: Changing obsidian source use in the Willaumez Peninsula, Papua New Guinea. In J. Cherry, C. Scarre and S. Shennan (eds), *Explaining social change: Studies in honour of Colin Renfrew*, pp. 115–125. McDonald Institute for Archaeological Research, Cambridge.

Torrence, R. 2004b. Pre-Lapita valuables in island Melanesia. In V. Attenbrow and R. Fullagar (eds), *A Pacific odyssey: Archaeology and anthropology in the western Pacific. papers in honour of Jim Specht*, pp. 163–172. Records of the Australian Museum, Supplement 29. Australian Museum, Sydney. doi.org/10.3853/j.0812-7387.29.2004.1413.

Torrence, R. 2005. Valued stone: How so? In. I. Macfarlane, R. Paton and M. Mountain (eds), *Many exchanges: Archaeology, history, community and the work of Isabel McBryde*, pp. 357–372. Aboriginal History Monograph 11. The Australian National University, Canberra.

Torrence, R. 2008. Punctuated landscapes: Creating cultural places in volcanically active environments. In B. David and J. Thomas (eds), *Handbook of landscape archaeology*, pp. 333–343. Left Coast Press, Walnut Creek CA.

Torrence, R. 2011. Finding the right question: Learning from stone tools on the Willaumez Peninsula, Papua New Guinea. *Archaeology in Oceania* 46:29–41. doi.org/10.1002/j.1834-4453.2011.tb00097.x.

Torrence, R. 2016. Social resilience and long-term adaptation to volcanic disasters: The archaeology of continuity and innovation in the Willaumez Peninsula, Papua New Guinea. *Quaternary International* 396:6–16. doi.org/10.1016/j.quaint.2014.04.029.

Torrence, R. 2019. Social responses to volcanic eruptions: A review of key concepts. *Quaternary International* 499:258–265. doi.org/10.1016/j.quaint.2018.02.033.

Torrence, R. in press. Something about Kutau: obsidian source selection in Papua New Guinea. In F.-X. le Bourdonnec, M. Shackley and M. Orange (eds), *Sourcing obsidian*. Springer, New York NY.

Torrence, R. and T. Doelman 2007. Problems of scale: Evaluating the effects of volcanic disasters on cultural change in the Willaumez Peninsula, Papua New Guinea. In J. Grattan and R. Torrence (eds), *Living under the shadow: The cultural impacts of volcanic eruptions*, pp. 42–66. Left Coast Press, Walnut Creek CA.

Torrence, R. and C.M. Stevenson 2000. Beyond the beach: Changing Lapita landscapes on Garua Island, PNG. In A. Anderson and T. Murray (eds), *Australian archaeologist: Collected papers in honour of Jim Allen*, pp. 324–345. Coombs Press, Canberra.

Torrence, R. and G.R. Summerhayes 1997. Sociality and the short distance trader: Intra-regional obsidian exchange in the Willaumez region. *Archaeology in Oceania* 32:74–84. doi.org/10.1002/j.1834-4453.1997. tb00373.x.

Torrence, R., J. Specht and R. Fullagar 1990. Pompeiis in the Pacific. *Australian Natural History* 23(6):456–463.

Torrence, R., J. Specht, R. Fullagar and J.R. Bird 1992. From Pleistocene to present: Obsidian sources in West New Britain Province, Papua New Guinea. *Records of the Australian Museum* 42:83–98. doi.org/10.3853/j.0812-7387.15.1992.86.

Torrence, R., J. Specht, R. Fullagar and G.R. Summerhayes 1996. Which obsidian is worth it? In J. Davidson, G. Irwin, F. Leach, A. Pawley and D. Brown (eds), *Oceanic culture history: Essays in honour of Roger Green*, pp. 211–224. New Zealand Journal of Archaeology Special Publication, Dunedin.

Torrence, R., J. Specht and B. Boyd 1999. Archaeological fieldwork on Numundo and Garu Plantations, West New Britain, Papua New Guinea. Unpublished report to the National Museum and Art Gallery, Papua New Guinea, Port Moresby.

Torrence, R., V. Neall, T. Doelman, E. Rhodes, C. McKee, H. Davies, R. Bonetti, A. Guglielmetti, A. Manzoni, M. Oddone, J. Parr and R. Wallace 2004. Pleistocene colonisation of the Bismarck Archipelago: New evidence from West New Britain. *Archaeology in Oceania* 39:101–130. doi.org/10.1002/j.1834-4453.2004. tb00568.x.

Torrence, R., V. Neall and B. Boyd 2009. Volcanism and historical ecology on the Willaumez Peninsula, Papua New Guinea. *Pacific Science* 63:507–535. doi.org/10.2984/049.063.0404.

Torrence, R., S. Kelloway and J.P. White 2013. Stemmed tools, social interaction, and voyaging in early-mid Holocene Papua New Guinea. *Journal of Island and Coastal Archaeology* 8:278–310. doi.org/10.1080/15 564894.2012.761300.

White, J.P. and M.N. Harris 1997. Changing sources: Early Lapita period obsidian in the Bismarck Archipelago. *Archaeology in Oceania* 32:97–107. doi.org/10.1002/j.1834-4453.1997.tb00375.x.

White, J.P., H. Jacobsen, V. Kewibu and T. Doelman 2006. Obsidian traffic in Southeast Papuan Islands. *Journal of Island and Coastal Archaeology* 1:101–108. doi.org/10.1080/15564890600583579.

Wiessner, P. 1982. Risk, reciprocity, and social influences on !Kung San economics. In E. Leacock (ed.), *Politics and history in band societies*, pp. 61–84. Cambridge University Press, Cambridge.

10

The difficulty of sourcing prehistoric pottery from Bootless Bay, Central Province, Papua New Guinea

Anne Ford, Jim Allen and Elaine Chen

Abstract

Various attempts have been made to characterise and source prehistoric pottery assemblages from the south Papuan coast. Foremost among these is the assemblage from the late prehistoric site on Motupore Island near Port Moresby. Here, a specialised pottery industry produced wares that were traded both locally and over long distances. The earliest attempts to source this pottery were experimental and imprecise but offered important insights into the offshore distribution of Motupore pottery. The problematic nature of this early work is most evident in the inability of subsequent studies to reproduce the earlier results. Overcoming this problem was compounded by the loss of early data samples and results in the Canberra fires of 2003. This paper recounts the history of sourcing studies of Motupore pottery. As part of this history, we began an attempt to reconstruct the lost data, as well as using newer techniques to reinvestigate Motupore pottery production and exchange. Expectations that these newer techniques would succeed in matching the early results were not fulfilled. We consider various explanations for this and think that chemical alterations to the sherd fabrics through time and during burial are a likely cause.

Introduction

Glenn Summerhayes provided the genesis of this paper. His long association with sourcing obsidian and pottery is a central aspect of his wide contribution to Pacific archaeology, beginning 40 years ago (e.g. Summerhayes and Walker 1982; Summerhayes 1987). In particular, Glenn popularised the use of the electron microprobe to analyse pottery (Summerhayes 1996, 2000). This technology enabled the clay component of sherds to be analysed separately from their mineral inclusions, an important advance on the then dominant PIXE analysis that could not separate these components (Summerhayes 1997). Prehistoric pottery sourcing on the Papuan south coast in the last quarter of the twentieth century mirrored these changes. The novel methods developed by Owen Rye, a professional potter and, in the 1970s, a Research Fellow in the Prehistory Department of The Australian National University (ANU), relied on proton-induced X-ray emission (PIXE) for chemical analyses of pottery from the Motupore site in Bootless Bay near Port Moresby, with analyses carried out at the Australian Atomic Energy Commission Research Establishment at Lucas Heights (AAEC) in Sydney. The PIXE technology is now replaced by more precise and less laborious approaches. Using PIXE to determine the geochemistry of sherds required that the sherd fabric be crushed and formed into pelletised targets. Rye's target pellets were retained as a data source, but, disastrously, most of his pellets and all of his associated data notebooks were lost in the Canberra bushfire of 2003. As described elsewhere (Allen 2017:369–370), a chance conversation with Glenn in 2012 in Dunedin led to him producing a bag of Rye's pellets he had rescued from the AAEC 30 years earlier. Glenn had kept and moved these samples with him, for no apparent reason or use, other than that they were historical data. Only Glenn would have done this.

The existence of the samples led to a fanciful plan to recreate Rye's data and techniques as a basis for further sourcing, a project of false starts and other problems that modified greatly over the following years. The serendipity continued in 2016 when two of us (AF and JA) were working in the National Museum and Art Gallery of Papua New Guinea. Our colleague there, Alu Guise, heard us discussing Rye's work, left the laboratory and returned with the remainder of Rye's original Bootless Bay clay and sand samples. We had assumed that these had been lost in the Canberra fire. With these raw material samples, we could immediately implement new analyses and ask a different range of questions. These included using more modern technology to compare the Bootless Bay clays with each other to see how similar or different they might be and to determine which useful elements they contained. The same could be done for the filler (temper) sands. Overall, these samples provided us with an independent path to analyse and compare sherds made with Bootless Bay raw materials and those made with foreign materials, rather than relying on the crushed pelleted produced by Rye.

This paper reports the work from 2016 onwards. It is appropriate that this research be reported here. If not for Glenn, it would never have happened.

Scope of this paper

Various attempts to source prehistoric pottery from Papuan south coast sites have occurred in the last 50 years, but the most concerted effort involved pottery from the island site of Motupore in Bootless Bay, some 15 km east of Port Moresby CBD. Excavation of this site in the 1970s allowed Owen Rye to undertake a full technological assessment of Motupore pottery (Rye 1976, 1977, 1981; Rye and Allen 1980, 2017; Rye and Duerden 1982; see also Allen and Duerden 1982; Allen and Rye 1982). Rye's specific aims included determining whether pottery recovered from Motupore and other Bootless Bay sites had in fact been manufactured with local materials, and to set up chemical and other technological signatures for Bootless Bay ceramics to allow their identification at other local and distant sites.

Here we offer a brief history of Rye's innovative approach to what was in the 1970s a perplexing question—how to characterise the chemical signature(s) of a pottery assemblage where the ingredients, clay and filler/temper were derived from different geological zones and potentially mixed in differing proportions. We then summarise his principal results. Secondly, we report new geochemical analyses of Motupore pottery using contemporary techniques that offer a firmer scientific characterisation of that assemblage.

Historically there have been difficulties noted with Rye's work. In particular, Frankel et al. (1994) attempted to source pottery from the Gulf sites in the Kerema region by replicating the sourcing study of Allen and Rye (1982), again using PIXE. This study employed reference samples used in the original Bootless Bay analysis and included 40 sherds from Motupore. Essentially it failed to source any of the sample sherds to the Bootless Bay reference samples, with one of the major difficulties being that multiple analyses of the same samples produced variable results. It was considered that this might reflect analysis of the data using cluster analysis rather than Rye's less precise allocations, although John Chappell (pers. comm. to JA 2015) believed that the AAEC PIXE technology was also unreliable. Thus, fundamental to our new analyses was the question of whether Rye's PIXE results could be duplicated using more modern techniques. Before this we begin by putting Motupore into its historical context.

Motupore Island and the *hiri*

Motupore Island, also known as Motu Hanua, is recognised as an ancestral village of the Western Motu, the coastal population encountered in Port Moresby Harbour in the nineteenth century (Murray 1912). The first systematic excavations occurred there from 1970 until 1975 and were finally reported in Allen (2017). Work began as a field school for students from the University of Papua New Guinea, but the aims of the excavation expanded as the extent and significance of the site was revealed from a total of more than 200 m² of excavation. The site's importance concerned both its relatively undisturbed nature and the richness of its artefactual remains; for example, excavations recovered more than half a million medium (>1 cm²) to large pottery sherds, more than 28,000 of which were diagnostic rim and decorated pieces. The following summary of Motupore history is drawn from Allen's conclusions, based on extensive artefactual analysis and a wide range of other evidence (see Allen 2017 and associated references for details).

Motupore was settled around 1200 AD by ancestral Motu, who, based on earlier pottery studies, likely came from the Boera area, 35 km to the west, a village with whom they maintained social ties. Motupore was abandoned around 1700 AD, probably as a result of local warfare reflecting population pressure on local resources. While its inhabitants likely practised some horticulture, economically they were primarily fishermen and traders. They arrived with pottery-making skills, demonstrated not only by the vast sherdage on the site, but also by pot firing locations and the frequency of firing-damaged sherds. During the site's lifetime, 11 or more satellite hamlets were established in Bootless Bay, together with a further contemporary village-size settlement at Taurama on the Bay's western edge (Figure 10.1). It is assumed that many or most of the women in these other communities were also potters and that the pottery was traded, along with shell artefacts such as strings of small shell beads (*ageva*), both locally and at a distance for food and raw materials.

Historically the Western Motu traded pottery, fish and shell artefacts throughout the year, but annually men from multiple Motu villages mounted a seaborne expedition called the *hiri* that transported thousands of Motu pots to villages in the Papuan Gulf, some 300 km to the west, to be exchanged for sago and canoe logs, and to gain prestige. Much is known about the historical *hiri* (e.g. see papers in Dutton 1982), but archaeology demonstrates that the late prehistoric villages in Bootless Bay, especially Motupore, were part of this history. Motupore pottery shows evolutionary time trajectories from complex to simple in both pottery forms and decoration that by the early twentieth century had evolved to the point where undecorated ovoid cooking pots with restricted necks and everted rims had become the dominant trade ware of the *hiri* (Groves 1960). A century ago, the *hiri* was explained by European observers as a response to wet season starvation in the Port Moresby villages (see Oram 1982 for summary). It is now better understood as part of a complex socio-economic strategy deliberately adopted and developed by the Western Motu and now glossed as subsistence trading (Allen 2017:616–621).

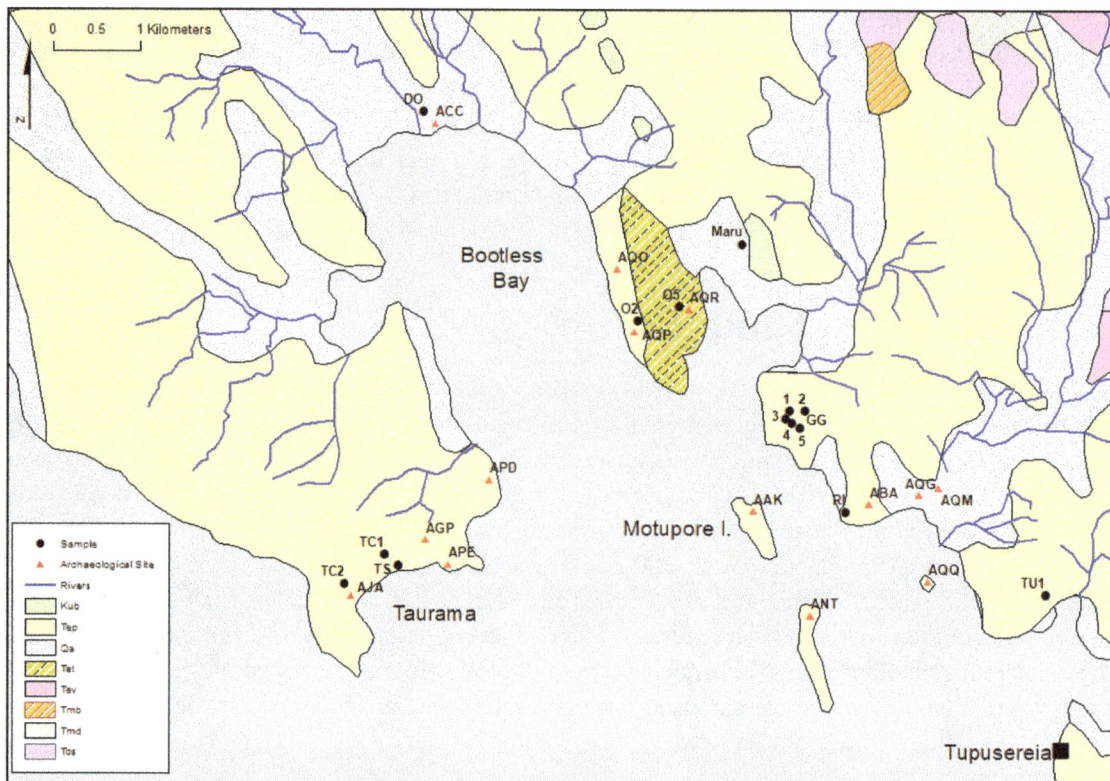

Figure 10.1: Bootless Bay with clay and sand sampling locations by Owen Rye.
Source: From Allen (2017:Fig. 9.1).

Sourcing pottery on the Papuan south coast

Archaeological studies of Papuan (and New Guinean) pottery production and trade grew out of a long tradition of ethnographic observation (e.g. Chalmers 1887; Seligman 1910; Stone 1876), culminating in the remarkable book by May and Tuckson (1982). Because of this connection between pottery and trade, there have been a number of pottery sourcing or characterisation studies completed on the south coast of Papua New Guinea (e.g. Bickler 1997; Frankel et al. 1994; Marsaglia et al. 2016; Rye and Duerden 1982; Summerhayes and Allen 2007; Sutton et al. 2019; Vigalys and Summerhayes 2016; Worthing 1980a, 1980b, 1982; Worthing and Swadling 1980). In particular, multiple sourcing studies have aimed at establishing a link between the Port Moresby region as a pottery-producing area and Gulf Province sites known historically or assumed to have been pottery consumers within the *hiri* trade network, although these studies have varied in terms of both methodology and results.

The sourcing techniques utilised have included petrography (Frankel et al. 1994; Marsaglia et al. 2016; Worthing 1980a, 1980b, 1982; Worthing and Swadling 1980), X-ray fluorescence or XRF (Bickler 1997) and PIXE (Rye and Duerden 1982; see also Allen and Duerden 1982). Different techniques mean that different information has been retrieved from the pottery. For the XRF/PIXE analyses for example, crushed pottery samples were used, which combined both clay and temper materials together into an overall 'signature'. In contrast, petrography involved thin-section analysis of microscope slides that largely removed the clay contribution from the analysis and instead focused on mineral inclusions to source sherds to geological locations.

Previous studies have also varied in terms of their scales of analysis when suggesting source locations for pottery. For example, Bickler's (1997) focus was regional, identifying Papuan Gulf pottery as deriving from either the Port Moresby or Yule Island regions. In contrast, Worthing (1982) suggested more focused source localities, identifying five close to Port Moresby: Eastern Bootless Bay, Motupore/Western Bootless Bay, Port Moresby/Fairfax Harbour, Lea Lea and Boera. Even more localised, Rye distinguished three prehistoric clay-temper combinations that were sourced within Western Bootless Bay itself. The problem with these previous studies is that different approaches have meant that it is difficult to integrate them, even where the same source and recipient site assemblages have been used, such as in the study by Frankel et al. (1994) noted above.

Previous pottery sourcing studies from Bootless Bay

The Rye PIXE study

The earliest pottery sourcing in Bootless Bay by Owen Rye asked simple questions. Were there local materials suitable for making pots and if so which, if any, were used by Motupore potters? Did sources change over time in the Motupore assemblage? Could Motupore pottery be distinguished from pots made in Port Moresby/Fairfax Harbour (Rye and Allen 2017)? And leading from this, might we be able to identify Motupore pottery in Gulf sites thought to reflect an early version of the *hiri* trade?

Rye (1981) surveyed the Bootless Bay inlet and obtained three sand samples and 12 clays from different locations (see Figure 10.1; see Allen (2017:331–335)). Sands from Taurama (labelled TS) and Motupore (MS) beaches were largely identical, but a distinctive mineralised black sand was recorded at two mainland locations. The nearest, c. 1 km from Motupore, was labelled R1. Of the clays, two from near the Taurama site (T1 and T2) and one on the mainland nearest Motupore (GG3) became important in the Rye analysis, but other sources also produced viable clays for making pottery.

Rye used different combinations of these sands and clays to determine the workability of these particular materials. The experiment involved making more than 850 small clay briquettes of known clay/sand compositions, firing them in the laboratory at various controlled temperatures and monitoring their post-firing viability (for example, some disintegrated because of CaO hydration of the calcite present in the shell component of the TS and MS sands). The 'successful' briquettes not only demonstrated the viability of each combination, they also provided proxy sources against which to compare the archaeological sherds.

At that time ANU archaeologists were closely associated with the AAEC at Lucas Heights, carrying out elemental sourcing of obsidian using PIXE. Rye set up experiments with AAEC physicist Peter Duerden to create PIXE characterisations of Motupore ceramics. The results were not perfect, with individual ceramic samples showing variability when measurements were repeated at different positions on the sample. Despite this, it was possible to determine 'an overall pattern of minor and trace element composition which differs from that of another clay' (Duerden et al. 1980:451).

Because of the uneven surfaces on pottery, the procedure required the sample to be crushed into a homogenous powder and compressed into a metal cap approximately 1 cm in diameter, with one smooth, exposed clay surface. These caps, the target pellets, were slow to make but had the advantage that around 150 could be processed in a day when measured in the Lucas Heights 3 MeV Van Der Graaff accelerator. Experimentation suggested that the most useful elements for the project were the major elements Si, Al, K, Ca, Ti and Fe, and the minor elements V, Sr and Rb and together these were the ones used in the archaeological sourcing project (Rye and Duerden 1982), although Allen and Rye (1982:111) noted the use of the major elements Mg, Al, Si, K, Ca and Ti, with the trace elements of V, Ni, Ga and Sr.

Each measurement of the pottery pellets produced a spectrum that was assessed for similarity with the source pellet spectra. Initially, peak area counts were obtained for the elements; however these could not be normalised to cater for counting conditions between runs (Allen and Rye 1982:110), so peak area ratios were used instead. Sherds were then allocated to source based on how they 'intersected' with a source plot. In the first run, allocations were made at two standard deviations, but for following runs one standard deviation marked the boundary for inclusion (Allen and Duerden 1982:50). This increased the percentage of 'unknowns' fourfold, from 2.5 per cent to 10.8 per cent between runs 1 and 2. While it was possible and probably likely that some unknowns were foreign sherds made from materials different to the target sources in use, it was equally likely that unknowns might be reflecting the variability within individual sherds made from local materials.

The Worthing sherd mineralogy study

In the mid-1970s a small project was set up by Dr Mike Worthing, then of the Geology Department, University of Papua New Guinea, to identify the mineralogy of pottery sherds from the Port Moresby region using standard thin sections and then to identify groupings within the wider set. Rye and Allen supplied Worthing with samples of Bootless Bay clays and sands and 42 sherds excavated from Motupore.

Worthing (1980a, 1980b, 1982) and Worthing and Swadling (1980) report the full project which also included samples from Boera and nearby Lea Lea. For Bootless Bay and Motupore, Worthing determined that the Bootless clays were too similar to relate the Motupore sherds to particular Bootless Bay sources and therefore he chose to focus upon the mineral inclusions in the filler sand. His initial results, however, noted that the Motupore and Taurama sands were likewise mineralogically indistinguishable, but the R1 sand was identifiable because of the presence of pyroxenes and gabbro fragments.

Worthing initially identified three mineralogical groups for the 42 Motupore sherds. The most numerous (~55 per cent) comprised Bootless Bay clays mixed with beach sands, consistent with the Motupore and Taurama sands. A smaller group (~15 per cent) was separated by the presence of R1 sand; Worthing assumed, but could not demonstrate, that this sand had also been mixed with Bootless clays. Unexpectedly, Worthing allocated four of the Motupore sherds to a Boera source suggesting a connection that would grow in importance in Rye's later studies. Worthing considered that a further nine sherds (which he labelled Group F) might reflect sources originating between Boera and Bootless Bay, and for no better reason nominated the intermediate Fairfax Harbour area as a possible location. Further details and implications of this study are reported in Rye and Allen (2017:345–349).

Rye's PIXE results

Three runs were undertaken at Lucas Heights, involving 816 sherds. Some 605 derived from Motupore while the remainder included other Bootless Bay sites, coastal and inland sites nearer to Port Moresby Harbour, sites near Boera, one site named Poukama on the mainland near Yule Island and one Papuan Gulf site called Popo excavated by Jim Rhoads (1980, 1994). The sherds external to Motupore were largely included on the basis of similarities in vessel decoration with Motupore sherds; the exceptions here were the five sherds from Poukama. These carried no stylistic similarities to Motupore sherds and were included as a negative sample. All five sourced as 'unknown'. Because of the results of the petrographic studies by Worthing, proxy source briquettes now also included representatives from Boera, Fairfax Harbour (Hanuabada village) and Galley Reach to the west (from the Western Motu pottery-making village of Manumanu).

The detailed results of this sourcing program appear in references already cited and are also summarised at length by Rye and Allen (2017:358–367).

Here we merely list the main results achieved, noting differences between these results and those of Worthing.

1. PIXE could not separate some Bootless clay sources. However, although the two sources close to Taurama (T1, T2) and the mainland source (GG3) were 'almost identical' (Allen and Duerden 1982:48), Rye was satisfied that he could distinguish them, with perhaps a 5 per cent error. These three sources provided the clays for the vast majority of Motupore pottery; however Worthing could not differentiate these Bootless clays using petrography. Rye also recognised the presence of R1 sand in some sherds but did not differentiate these. In his study they grouped within the GG3 clay category.

2. While the GG3 source occurred frequently among the Motupore sherd assemblage, the combined Taurama sources were consistently more frequent.

3. The Boera sourced sherds noted for Motupore by Worthing also occurred regularly throughout the site sequence in Rye's analysis.

4. Only a single sherd from Motupore was sourced to Fairfax Harbour. This suggested that Fairfax Harbour was not the source of Worthing's Group F.

5. For Motupore, no significant associations could be made between particular clay sources and ceramic changes through time, or with ceramic decorations or ceramic morphologies.

6. Analysis of 211 sherds from beyond Motupore showed a frequent presence of the T1, T2 and GG3 clays. In other Bootless Bay sites, these clays comprised ~77 per cent of that sample; at six sites near Boera ~70 per cent; at seven sites on the Port Moresby coast and in the hinterland ~69 per cent and at the Popo site in the Gulf ~65 per cent. (It should be recalled that these ex-Motupore samples were not random but were included because their decorations were similar to Motupore sherd decorations.) Notably the numerical precedence the Taurama clays over GG3 clays continued in these samples.

These results formed the basis for reconstructing spheres of socio-economic influence for the Motupore traders. They helped develop the ideas that:

1. Motupore and Taurama were related and closely interacting sites where the two-way flow of pots and/or pot-making raw materials was a likely proxy for other close social ties, invisible in the archaeological record;

2. That the two-way flow of pottery between Boera and Motupore (and Taurama) from Motupore's first settlement to abandonment was a strong indicator of social connectedness that implied the Boera area was the likely ancestral homeland of the Motupore/Taurama settlers;

3. That a lack of connection with Fairfax Harbour, located between Motupore and Boera, made the connection with Boera more pronounced;

4. That the presence of sherds of Bootless Bay clay in Gulf sites demonstrated that trading pottery from the Western Motu region to the Gulf of Papua was a practice much older than the ethnographic *hiri*.

Also, sherds with GG3 clay and R1 sand posed the question of whether these pots were made on Motupore or a different Bootless Bay site. The distributional data (Rye and Allen 2017:347–348) remains equivocal on this point.

The new project

In 2016, with the Summerhayes' target pellet collection and the Rye clays and sand from Bootless Bay, we undertook three analyses to compare with Rye's conclusions. We report each in turn.

Reanalysing Rye's pellets using pXRF

Among the pellets retained by Summerhayes the only useful ones were those for which we could establish some identification from the remnant documentation. This resulted in a sample of 146 items, including 27 pellets from Rye's original briquettes that represented known clay sources, 97 pellets from archaeological sherds that Rye had attributed to particular sources, and 22 pellets from archaeological sherds that were unidentified by source.

The aims of this analysis were (1) to determine, using portable X-ray fluorescence (pXRF) rather than PIXE, if the sources could be distinguished from each other, as per the original PIXE project; and (2) if the first proved possible, to determine if the archaeological pellets could be attributed to these sources.

We recognised that the latter objective was severely limited because the source sherds only represented three of Rye's original seven Bootless Bay sources: U1 (Tupesereia clay and Motupore sand); U2 (Tupesereia clay and R1 sand); and T2 (Taurama 2 clay and Taurama sand). (Note that Rye variously used U1 or TU1 or U2 or TU2 to refer to the Tupesereia clay. Here we use U1 and U2 to indicate the pellet combinations, and TU1 for the clay source and any clay samples obtained from here.) Two out of Rye's three important sources, T1 and GG3, were missing, with only T2 represented. Rye had eventually eliminated the Tupesereia clay from his analysis (Allen and Duerden 1982:48), deciding that he could not distinguish between Tupesereia clay and GG3 clay. He thus subsumed both clays under the GG3 rubric.

Methods

The pellets were analysed using a Bruker Tracer III-SD pXRF, using two settings (15 kv 23µA with a vacuum; and 40 kv 10.7µA with a 0.001" Ti, 0.012 Al filter (Bruker's yellow filter)), for a 300-second run time on each setting. These settings were chosen to reflect the original elements used in the Motupore pottery sourcing study (Allen and Duerden 1982). Elements were tested to identify which setting provided more accurate results and the following were selected: vacuum (Si, Al, K, Ti) and yellow filter (Ca, Fe, Sr, Rb). A pelletised international standard (NIST679—Brick Clay) was also analysed to understand the accuracy of the instrument before each run and after 15 samples during a run. The results of this analysis are presented in Table 10.1.

Calibration to parts per million for the pellets was completed in S1CalProcess using Bruker's Mudrock Major calibration for the vacuum setting and Bruker's Mudrock Trace calibration for the yellow filter setting.

Table 10.1: Results (weight %) of NIST 679 Brick Clay Standard shot using University of Otago.

	Al	Si	K	Ca	Ti	Fe	Rb	Sr
Univ. of Otago average (n = 15)	10.15	22.94	2.29	0.97	0.62	8.53	0.016	0.005
SD	0.23	0.54	0.02	0.06	0.01	0.15	0.0005	0.0001
RSD (%)	2.31	2.36	0.98	5.87	2.37	1.27	2.99	3.03
NIST values	11.01	24.34	2.43	0.16	0.58	9.05	–	0.007

Notes: SD = standard deviation; RSD = relative standard deviation.

Source: Authors' summary of results.

To determine if there were any groupings within the pXRF data, Principal Component Analysis (PCA) and Hierarchical Cluster Analysis (HCA) were performed, using SPSS Version 25. Prior to statistical analysis, all elemental values were logarithm base-10 transformed. As part of the PCA, the Kaiser-Meyer-Olkin measure of sampling adequacy (value >0.5) and Bartlett's test of sphericity ($\alpha = \leq 0.05$) were also applied to determine if the data was suitable for PCA. No rotation of the data was applied. For the HCA, Ward's method was used.

Results

As noted, Rye found that the U1, U2 and GG3 clays were largely indistinguishable from each other, but in our first PCA (Figure 10.2) U1 and U2 quite clearly separate out from each other, as does T2. Elements that are important to creating separation, as can be seen from the loadings in Figure 10.2, include Si versus Ca/Sr. Ca and Sr are usually linked elements and likely relate to the amounts of shell in the pelletised sample, whereas Si relates to the amount of quartz or chert in the beach sand temper.

A second PCA was run incorporating 119 pellets made from Motupore pottery that were mostly attributed to sources during the original PIXE project. Not all of the pellets included source information. Of the pellets sourced by the original PIXE project, 15 were attributed to T1, 29 to T2, 30 to GG3, and 23 to Boera. Figure 10.3 includes these original sourcing locations, and compares these to Rye's source pellets, which shows little correlation, particularly with U1 and U2 sources.

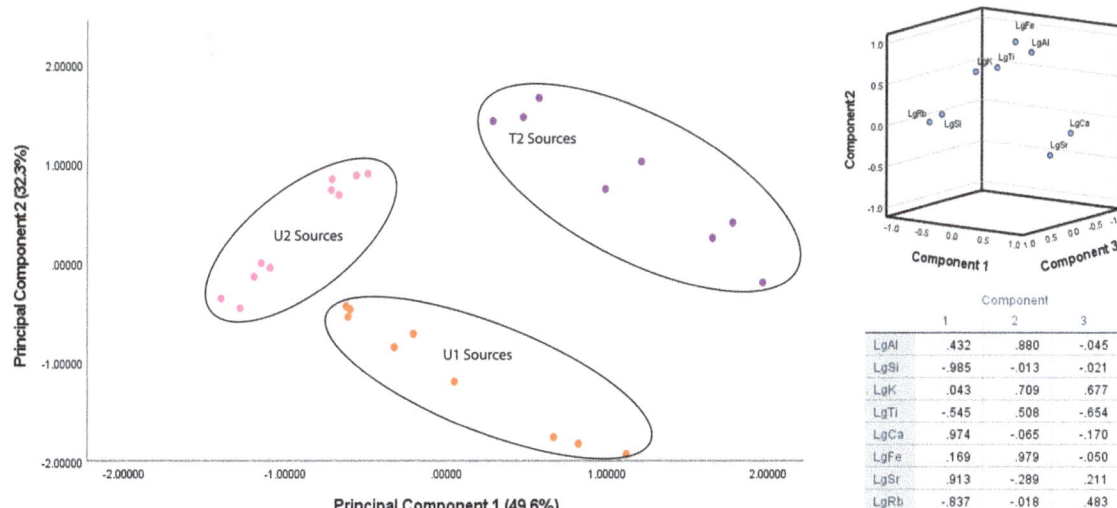

	Component		
	1	2	3
LgAl	.432	.880	-.045
LgSi	-.985	-.013	-.021
LgK	.043	.709	.677
LgTi	-.545	.508	-.654
LgCa	.974	-.065	-.170
LgFe	.169	.979	-.050
LgSr	.913	-.289	.211
LgRb	-.837	-.018	.483

Figure 10.2: PCA of Rye source pellets, using pXRF.

Source: Authors.

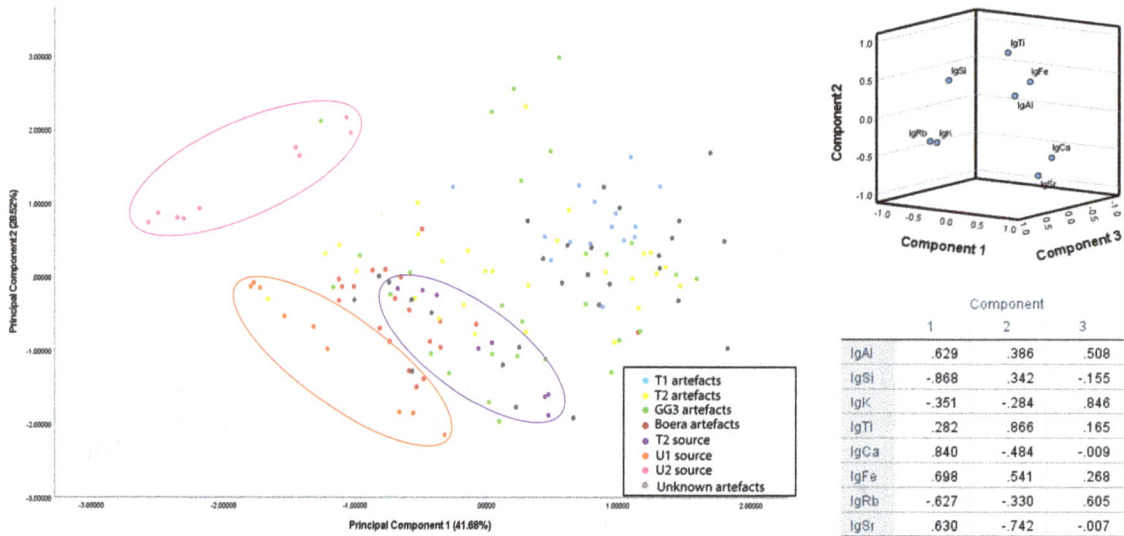

Figure 10.3: PCA of Rye source and Motupore pottery pellets, using pXRF.
Source: Authors.

For the T2 source, there is overlap with the archaeological pottery, some of which was originally attributed to this source, but which also includes numbers of sherds previously attributed to Boera and GG3 sources. Removing the sources, there is some clustering of the pottery into two larger groups: one which includes predominantly Boera and T2-attributed artefacts, and the second which consists of T1 and T2-attributed artefacts. GG3-attributed artefacts are spread across the PCA.

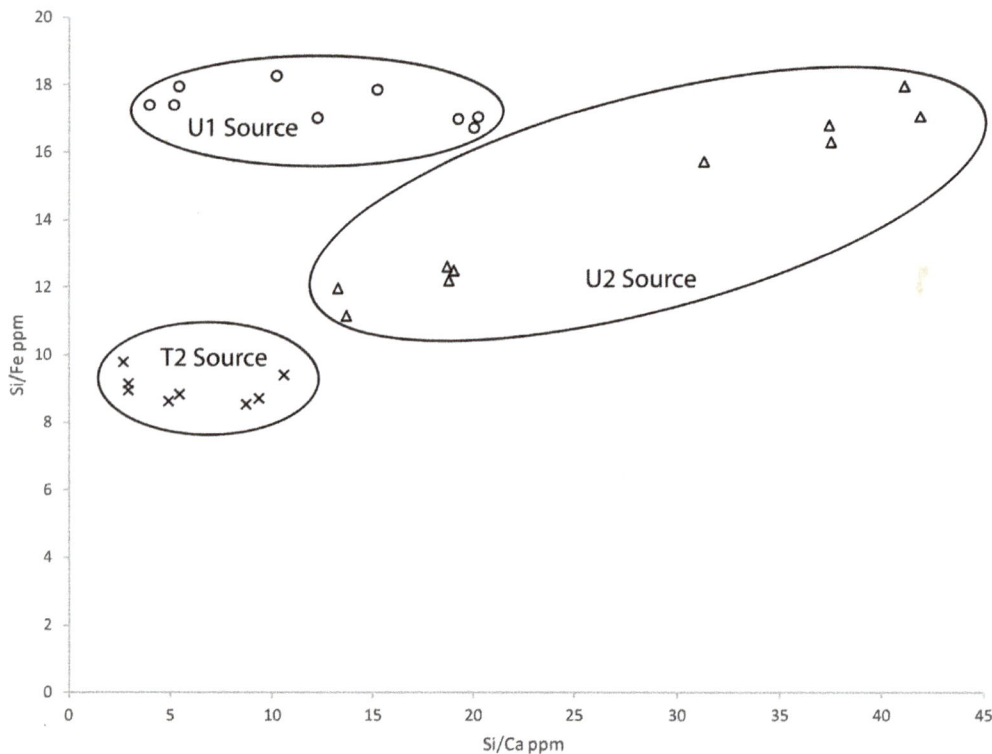

Figure 10.4: Bivariate analysis of Rye source pellets, using pXRF.
Source: Authors.

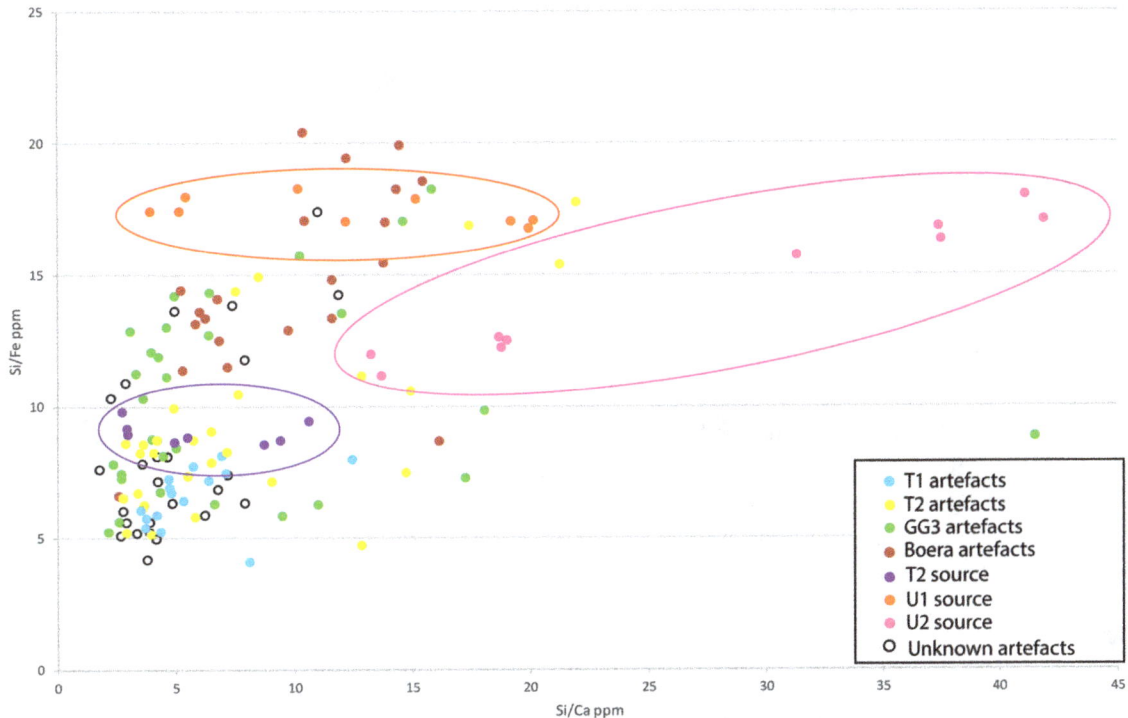

Figure 10.5: Bivariate analysis of Rye source and Motupore pottery pellets, using pXRF.
Source: Authors.

To test whether the lack of clarity of the archaeological pottery reflected minor fluctuations in pXRF counts caused by the level of precision and accuracy of the machine, a second analysis was completed where ratios of elements were used, rather than parts per million for each element. A similar analysis was undertaken in the original PIXE studies, although which specific peak ratios were used was not reported (Allen and Duerden 1982). Figure 10.4 demonstrates that this type of analysis, where ratios of the major elements are involved in the loadings of the PCA, successfully distinguishes between Rye's sources. Similar to the PCA results, the bivariate analysis shows that the source pellets are spread across a range of values, largely driven by the proportions of clay/temper used in making them. For example, the U1 and T2 sources decrease in Ca levels as the amount of temper is decreased, which likely reflects decrease in shell in the temper.

While some studies (e.g. Buhring et al. 2015) have suggested that different temper proportions do not prevent the identification of different clay sources in bulk sample analysis, other studies have noted that there can be a considerable effect on overall geochemical composition (Bentley 2000; Chiu 2003:222; Chiu et al. 2020). This appears to be particularly exacerbated for shell/coral tempers because of the degradation of Ca and Sr (Ambrose 1982; Cogswell et al. 1998), to the point where studies using crushed bulk samples with these types of tempers have used statistical methods to try and cater for this 'dilution' effect (Chiu et al. 2020; Cogswell et al. 1998) or have removed Ca/Sr from their geochemical compositions altogether (Shaw et al. 2016).

Once the archaeological pottery is added, a clear link between the pottery and a source is difficult to discern (Figure 10.5; compare Figure 10.2). This result indicates that while there appears to be some grouping of the pottery into 'sources' attributed by the original PIXE work, particularly with the Boera and T1-attributed artefacts, T2 and GG3-attributed artefacts are spread across a range of values. Another difference from the PCA results is that some of the Boera-attributed sherds align with the U1 source, however, examination of other elements, particularly Al, indicate that this is unlikely to be a true match. The importance of this result, where Boera trends into the T2 source in the PCA but to U1 in the bivariate, is that it indicates that the choice of elements used to attribute sherds to a 'source' may directly impact which 'source' is assigned, making this potentially a result of the statistical analysis employed, rather than a real difference in the archaeological pottery itself.

A geochemical analysis of Bootless Bay clays using the scanning electron microscope (SEM)

Here we reanalysed the Museum clay samples obtained by Rye from Bootless Bay. The purpose of this analysis was to determine if we could distinguish the clay samples geochemically using a scanning electron microscope (SEM). The clay samples were Taurama 1 (TC1), Taurama 2 (TC2), O5, Guma's Garden 3 (GG3), Guma's Garden 5 (GG5), Maru and Tupesereia 1 (U1) (see Figure 10.1).

Geologically, all of these clays derive from a similar geological zone (Figure 10.1): the Eocene-aged Paga chert (Tep) which is described as 'partly calcareous, siliceous argillite and shale, calcilutite, chert, and minor calcarenite and dolomite' (Pieters 1978:39). The exception is O5, which originates in a similar aged geological zone known as Tatana calcarenite (Tet), which is calcarenite, minor calcirudite and glauconite.

Methods

The raw clay samples were made into small briquettes suitable for analysis. They were first ground with a mortar and pestle to create a homogenous powdered material. Distilled water was then added to the clay and balls were formed with the wet material averaging 2 cm in diameter. The balls were then left in a drying room for three days at a temperature of 20 °C. Two batches of the seven clay samples were then fired at different temperatures: 500 °C and 800 °C. These temperatures were chosen to reflect possible open firing conditions that were likely utilised at Motupore (Rye and Allen 2017:342–343) and to identify what effects firing might have on the geochemical signature of the clays, as previous studies have noted some effects above 700 °C (Rye and Duerden 1982). To fire the clay samples, the balls were placed in a furnace which was set to the required temperature for an hour, then the heat source was turned off and the samples were left in the furnace until they were cool enough to be removed. These clay samples were then turned into plugs, using HillQuist epoxy, and polished to one micron. Prior to SEM analysis, the plugs were carbon-coated.

Quantitative geochemical analysis of the clay matrix was then completed on a Hitachi Tabletop Scanning Electron Microscope (SEM), using a Bruker QUANTAX energy dispersive X-ray spectrometer (EDS) and ESPRIT Compact acquisition and processing software. Before each analysis session, the EDS was calibrated with a pure copper standard. Additionally, a spot point analysis on a NMNH 115900 Plagioclase standard was recorded to track the stability of machine conditions. For clay analysis, five areas of each sample were examined. The clay matrix areas were carefully chosen after observation at 100×, 1000× and 2000× magnification. After capturing a 1024 × 960 pixel electron micrograph at 50,000× magnification, a spot analysis was then undertaken to collect elemental data. Each spot point measurement was acquired for 60 seconds.

For the statistical analysis, methods were the same as described for the pXRF data.

Results

Of the seven Rye clays shot for analysis, all of these included samples fired to 800 °C, with two additional samples of TC1 and GG5 fired to 500 °C. Elements included in the PCA analysis included Na, Mg, Al, Si, K, Ca, Ti and Fe. As noted above, each clay sample was analysed five times and all shots were then plotted individually within the PCA (Figure 10.6).

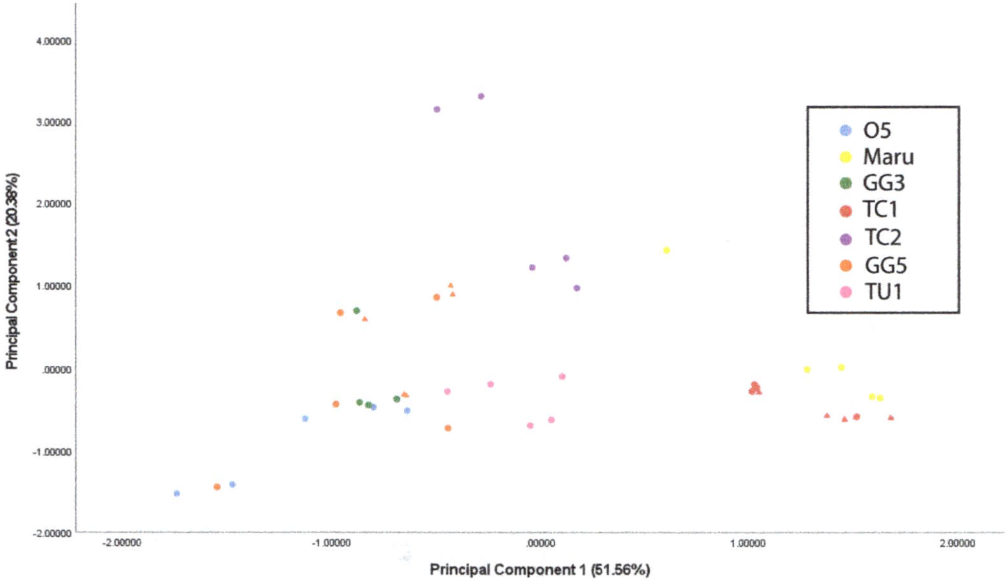

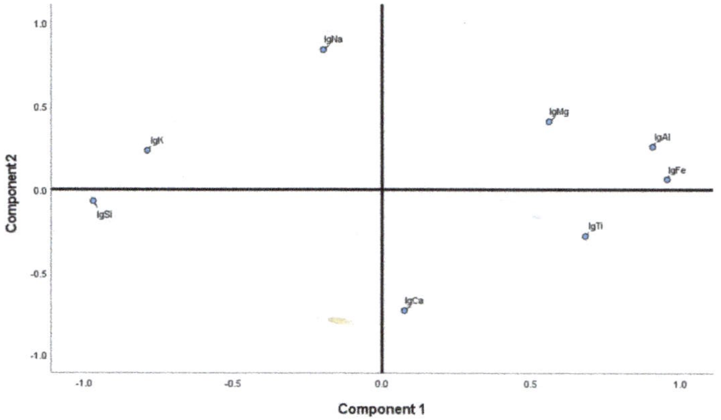

	Component 1	Component 2
lgNa	-.198	.842
lgMg	.560	.411
lgAl	.908	.263
lgSi	-.969	-.070
lgK	-.789	.240
lgCa	.074	-.736
lgTi	.681	-.273
lgFe	.957	.063

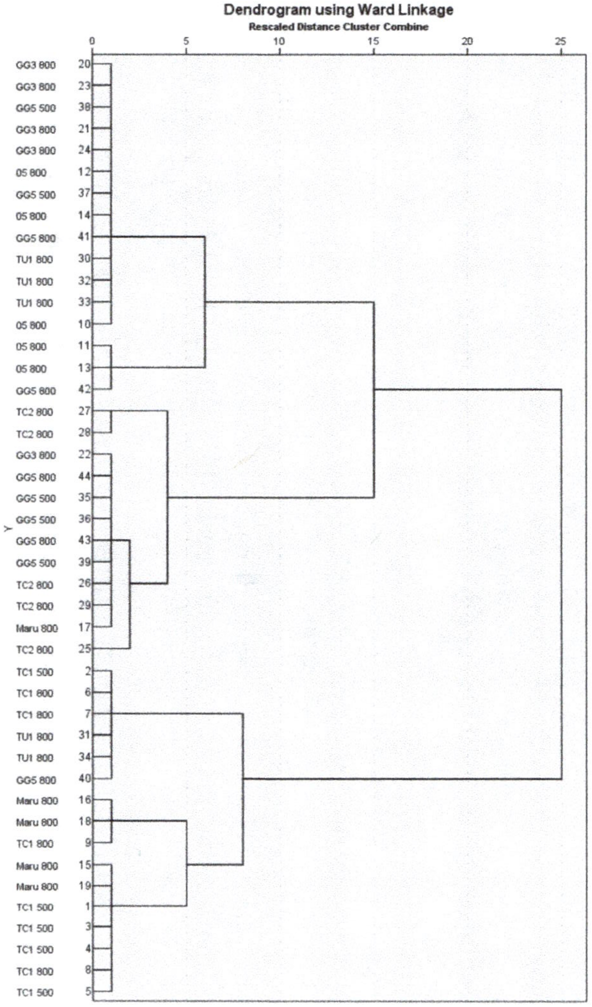

Figure 10.6: PCA and HCA of Rye clays, using SEM. Triangles represented clays fired to 500 °C, circles represent clays fired to 800 °C.

Source: Authors.

The PCA indicates fairly good source separation; in particular, there appears to be little change in signature according to firing temperature utilised (see GG5 and TC1). There is some overlap between sources, for example GG3, GG5 and O5, which likely reflects the geographic proximity of these sources (Figure 10.1). TC1 tends to cluster well, associated with Maru. TC2 and TU1 also tend to exist by themselves, although TU1 is closer to O5 and GG3/GG5. Distinction between the clay sources is largely driven by Al, Si and Fe in Principal Component 1 and Na and Ca in Principal Component 2.

The groupings of the clays were further tested using the HCA. Again, it is noted here that the TC1 and GG5 clays cluster together regardless of firing temperature. Similar results to the PCA are also demonstrated, with TC1 and Maru clustering at one end, with the GG3/GG5, plus O5 at the other. TC2 is largely with the GG cluster, although there is one outlier, and TU1 splits across both clusters. The results of both the PCA and HCA would therefore indicate real differences between at least the GG3/GG5/O5 cluster and the TC1/Maru cluster, with TU1 and TC2 being intermediary between the two. The close relationship between all these clays likely reflects their common geological origin.

Comparing Bootless Bay clays and Motupore sherds using the SEM

Given that some geochemical separation could be made between the Bootless Bay clays, we then tried to match archaeological sherds from Motupore with these clay sources. This comparison used 120 sherds from Motupore and 10 sherds from the Boera/Davage site complex. From Motupore, sherds were selected to provide 20 sherds from each of the six stratigraphic/analytical phases (1–6) (Allen 2017:129–131). Each of the six groups contained a mixture of forms (ovoid pots and restricted/unrestricted bowls) and decorated/undecorated items. In particular, a deliberate inclusion in each unit (where possible) was both painted and unpainted pottery since Rye and Allen (2017:356) suggest that painting is associated with a lighter coloured fabric that in turn is associated with lower amounts of shell temper than the unpainted sherds. The 10 sherds from Boera/Davage were part of a surface sample selected at random but which included both painted and unpainted pottery. While undated, this sample was 'prehistoric' on the basis of forms and decorations and considered to be a representative sample of Boera fabric sufficient for comparison.

Methods

The sherds were cut, cleaned and turned into plugs, following the same methodology as outlined above for Rye's clays. The benefit of using a cut sample of pottery versus a crushed sample is that the clay matrix and the mineral inclusions can be distinguished. Two different types of analysis were therefore conducted: the first was a clay matrix analysis, following the same procedures for the Rye clay analysis already described. However, for this analysis Na was excluded because it is likely that seawater was used to produce the archaeological pottery samples, whereas distilled water was used for the clay briquettes. The second analysis was a temper analysis: for this, micrograph images were captured at a high resolution, 2000 × 1875 pixels. One or two temper abundant areas per sample were selected at 100× magnification to examine the mineral inclusions, following the procedure below:

1. Map-scanning analysis was firstly conducted to obtain data from the entire view, in order to identify the main mineral groups. With the assistance of phase maps and mixed maps of the nominated elements: Na, Mg, Al, Si, K, Ca, Ti and Fe, it is possible to distinguish different minerals or inclusions visually. While a 32µs dwell time per pixel was set for map imaging, all the qualitative data were captured with a 128µs dwell time per pixel, which makes an acquisition time of approximately 8 minutes.

2. After each type of mineral or inclusion was grouped using the map scan, a follow-up spot point analysis was then completed to further define the chemical composition of each mineral group. Minerals or inclusions were then identified based on their geochemical signature. Finally, minerals/inclusions were quantified as to their abundance, borrowing the idea of point counting from sedimentary petrology, that is to count the grain types/clay matrix falling beneath the intersection points of a rectilinear grid on the printed out 2000 × 1875 pixels SEM maps, resulting in a 100-point count for each SEM map. While frequency counting has been used most commonly in the Pacific (Dickinson 2006), the two other studies to have employed petrographic analysis of temper on the south coast of Papua New Guinea (Marsaglia et al. 2016; Worthing 1980a, 1980b, 1982) both employed point counting.

Results 1. Clay matrix

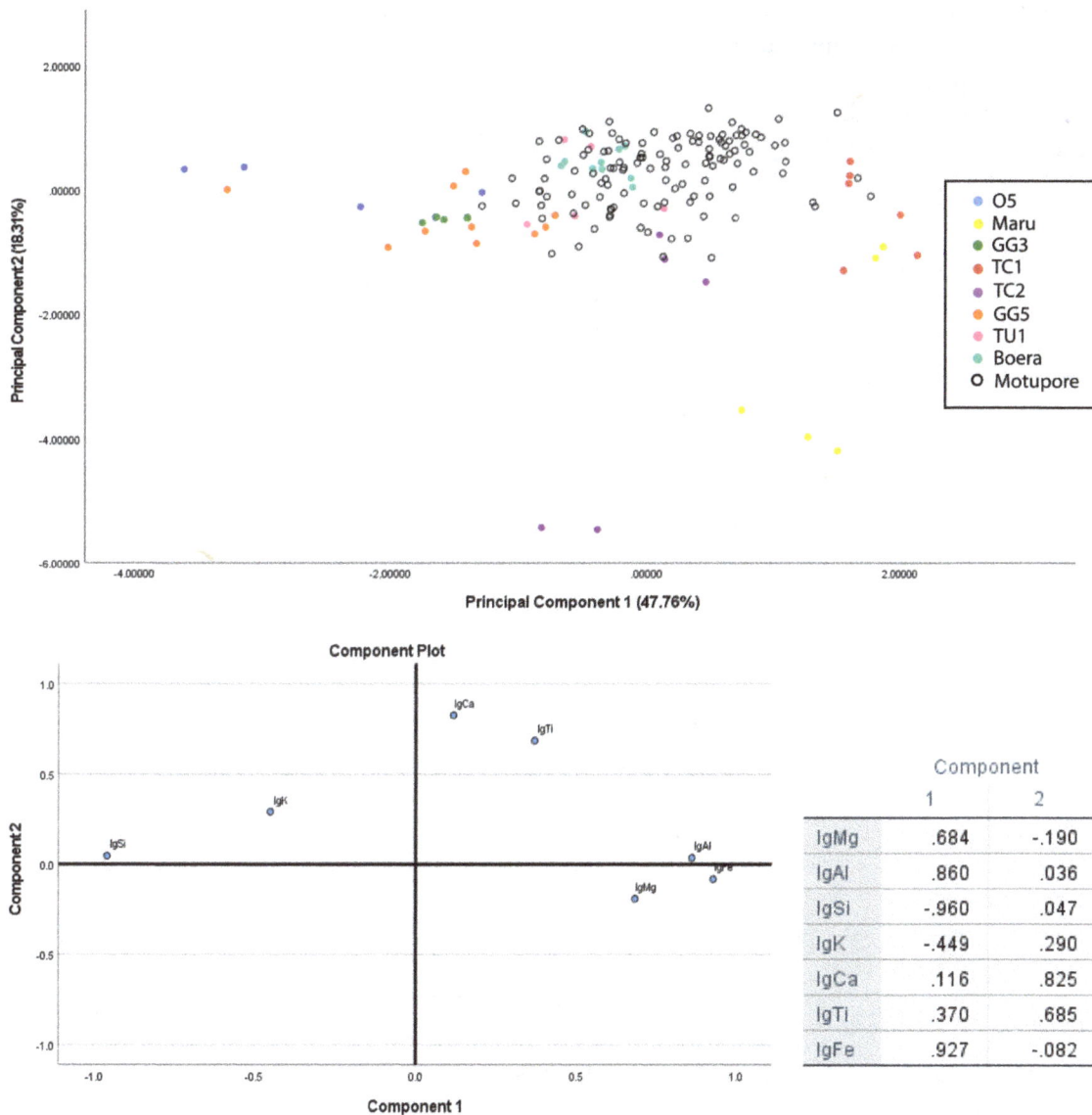

Figure 10.7: PCA of Motupore and Boera/Davage pottery, compared to Rye clays, using SEM.
Source: Authors.

Figure 10.7 represents the PCA which compares the Motupore pottery to pottery from Boera/Davage and to the Bootless Bay clays. Following the previous analysis, the clays largely fall out into the same clusters. However, there is little overlap with the archaeological pottery from either Motupore or Boera/Davage, with most of the archaeological pottery forming its own group independent of the clays. Boera/Davage appears to cluster quite tightly, but this cluster overlaps with the Motupore pottery; if the source of this pottery was not known it would be lost within the Motupore pottery. Since it is unlikely that the Boera/Davage sherds originated in Bootless Bay, it is probable that the source clays of Boera/Davage and Motupore are too similar to distinguish through geochemistry. As analysis using the SEM mainly identifies major elements, incorporating trace or rare earth elements might assist with providing distinctions between the two localities.

Results 2. Temper

The vast majority of the sherds from Motupore and Boera share a very similar suite of mineral inclusions that reflects the local geology. These include shell fragments, indicating the use of beach sands as temper, as well as minerals dominated by quartz and plagioclase feldspar. Accessory minerals in these sherds include K-feldspar, hornblende, pyroxenes, epidote and mica. Some rocks and opaques are also present but these are in smaller amounts.

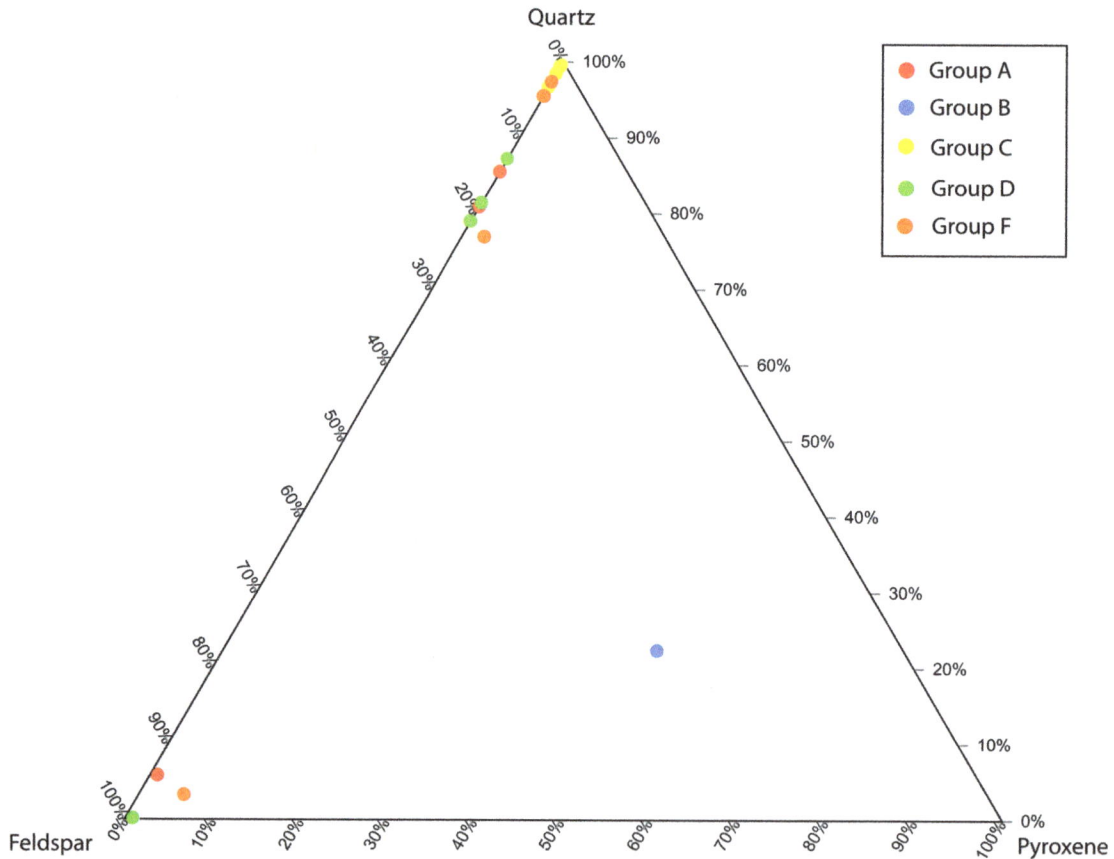

Figure 10.8: Ternary plot diagram of clays and sands.
Source: Authors' interpretation of data from Worthing (1982).

For the current study, the chert versus quartz/feldspar ratios used by Worthing (1982) to distinguish between source areas could not be measured as the geochemistry of quartz and chert is too similar under the SEM to be able to distinguish between them. However, ternary plots of Worthing's geological samples of clay and temper (drawn from Worthing 1982:Table 1), show distinctions between Group A (Boera) and Group C (Western Bootless Bay/Motupore) based on quartz/feldspar ratios, with a second distinction able to be made with Group B (Eastern Bootless Bay—R1 Sand) based on pyroxene levels (Figure 10.8). Using these ratios, Group D (Lea Lea) overlaps with Boera and Group F (putatively 'Port Moresby Harbour') overlaps with Western Bootless Bay, reflecting their respective locations.

Temper comparisons between Boera and Motupore are more interesting. Figure 10.9 shows that pottery from Boera is likely to have a higher feldspar content than a large proportion of pottery from Motupore. The second point is that pottery sherds from Motupore with mica present are also more likely to have a higher feldspar content, and tend to overlap with Boera pottery. Worthing (1982) noted that mica is a distinguishing mineral of pottery from Boera/Lea Lea, and suggests that Motupore sherds with mica inclusions were originally manufactured in Boera.

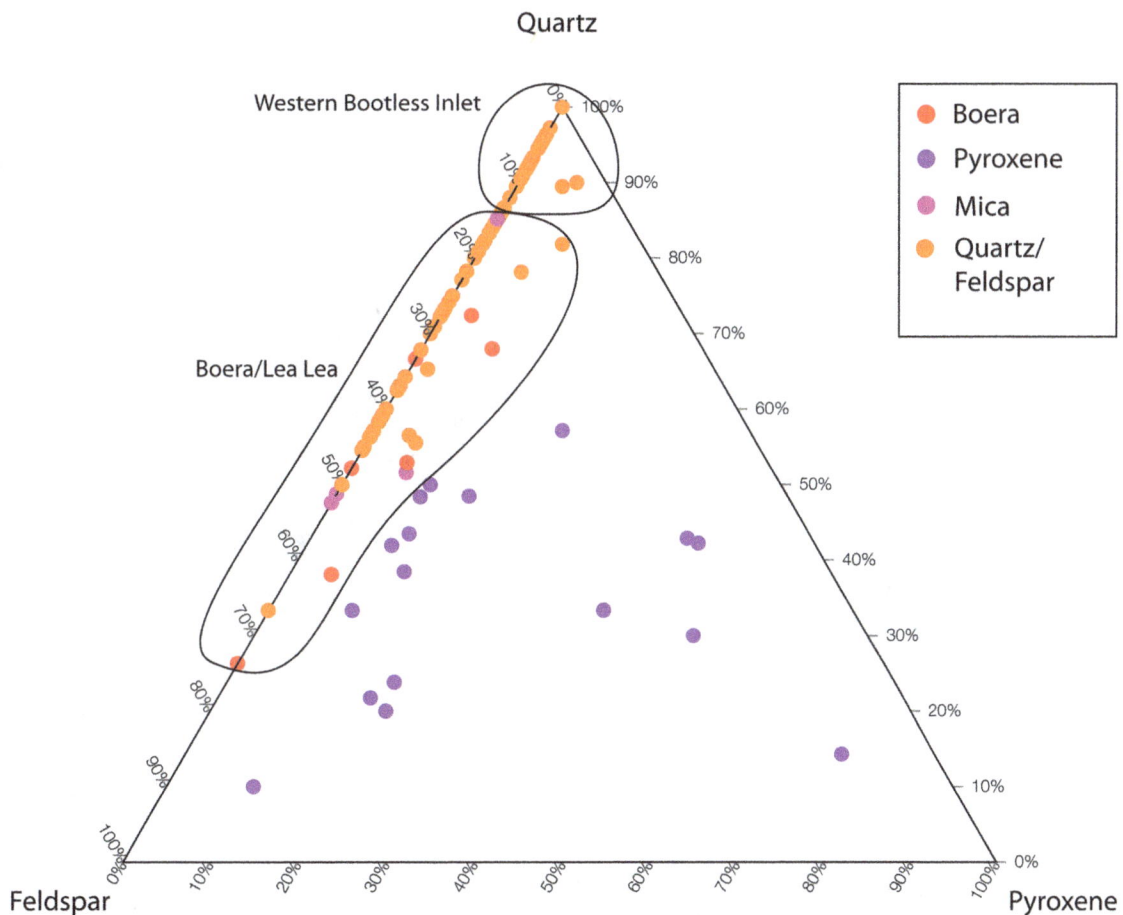

Figure 10.9: Ternary plot diagram of Motupore and Boera pottery: quartz, feldspar, pyroxene.
Source: Authors.

A third point is that some pottery from Motupore contains high levels of pyroxenes, which also tend to have a higher feldspar content than other Motupore pottery. While these sherds may overlap with the feldspar content of Boera sherds, they are distinguishable from Boera sherds on higher pyroxene counts that match Worthing's Group B (R1 sand) pottery, attributed by Rye to the GG3 clay source.

The distinctions noted between Worthing's Groups A, B and C were difficult to apply to the archaeological pottery as the quartz/feldspar ratios show an array of values. In Figure 10.9 a distinction has been made between these groups, largely based on the presence of mica and the values of the Boera pottery, as well as reference to Figure 10.8 which shows the Worthing results. A second ternary diagram (Figure 10.10) was plotted to test the 'realness' of these groups but this time replacing pyroxene with shell, and again, this shows that the pyroxene (or Group B) related pottery largely clumps together with no shell present (although there are some outliers here), and the Boera/mica pottery also clusters together within the centre of the plot, indicating middle ranges of shell, and consistent quartz/feldspar values.

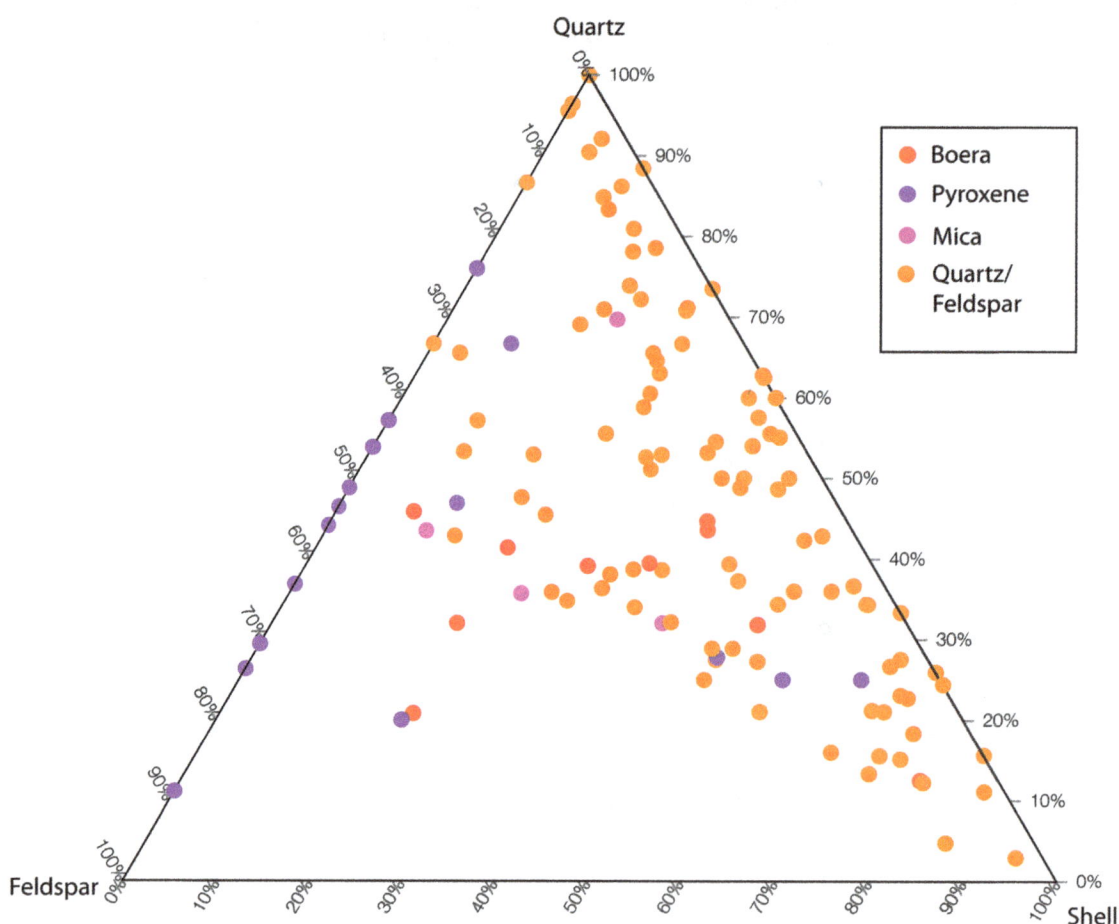

Figure 10.10: Ternary plot diagram of Motupore and Boera pottery: quartz, feldspar, shell.
Source: Authors.

Summary

The present project has reviewed a number of geochemical techniques to assess the ability to distinguish between geological sources of clay and temper sands and to associate these raw materials with archaeological pottery. Particularly significant in this study is the proximity of the raw material sources to each other, with effectively all of the clay and temper sands deriving from the same geological unit of the Paga chert. While using crushed samples or clay matrix alone did not allow for connection to specific geological locales, unlike that originally specified by the original PIXE work (see Rye and Allen 2017), mineralogical analysis of the temper sands using SEM did provide some important distinctions between specific sources. Because of the relatedness of the geology, these distinctions are largely identified as proportions of the same minerals or components (shell) which makes them particularly sensitive to issues such as the percentage of the sherd assemblage actually analysed. Improvements to this methodology may allow for further distinctions to be made.

Discussion

Given the accumulated physical, chemical, and archaeological evidence previously amassed for Bootless Bay, we do not doubt that prehistoric potters there made pots using Bootless Bay raw materials. Indeed, a case might be made that it was the availability of these materials that underwrote the settlement and expansion of the Taurama and Motupore sites and wider settlement in Bootless Bay over five centuries. That we cannot provide a coherent demonstration of such usage in this study or those that preceded us emphasises the complexities of sourcing a composite material such as pottery, especially when compared, for example, to the precise and separate chemical compositions of different obsidians.

Given that we began this study with the original Rye clays from Bootless Bay we expected that our new approach might confirm Rye's central conclusions. This expectation rose when we were able to chemically separate the Bootless Bay clays from each other, but this merely exacerbated our disappointment when we failed to relate the Motupore sherd sample in any meaningful way to these clay 'sources'. At the same time, we were able to take instructive lessons from these experiments. Here we summarise the more important of these.

pXRF analysis of the Rye pellets

Both PCA and HCA indicated our methodology could distinguish between Rye's three sets of available source pellets but pXRF analysis was unable to match the archaeological pellets to these sources, apart for a partial, perhaps coincidental, overlap with the T2 source. Beyond this, this test was of little value because two sets of source pellets employed clay from eastern Bootless Bay excluded by Rye as unlikely to have been preferred to nearer sources. Our results, with virtually no overlap between the archaeological pellets and the eastern sources, appeared to support this. But while lack of overlap might be explained by the physical distance between the eastern sources and the archaeological sample, lack of overlap with the nearer T2 source suggested a different explanation. While Rye's source briquettes were subjected to manufacturing and firing conditions that mimicked the archaeological pottery, these samples could not recreate the effects that use or burial of the pottery might have in creating functional or post-depositional effects on the pottery constituents. This was most clearly seen during SEM analysis in the amount of shell present in the archaeological pottery, which was visibly eroded in some, but not all, archaeological samples (Figure 10.11). The erosion of shell affected Ca/Sr values that are a clear driver in grouping the archaeological samples. We carried this idea forward into the SEM analyses.

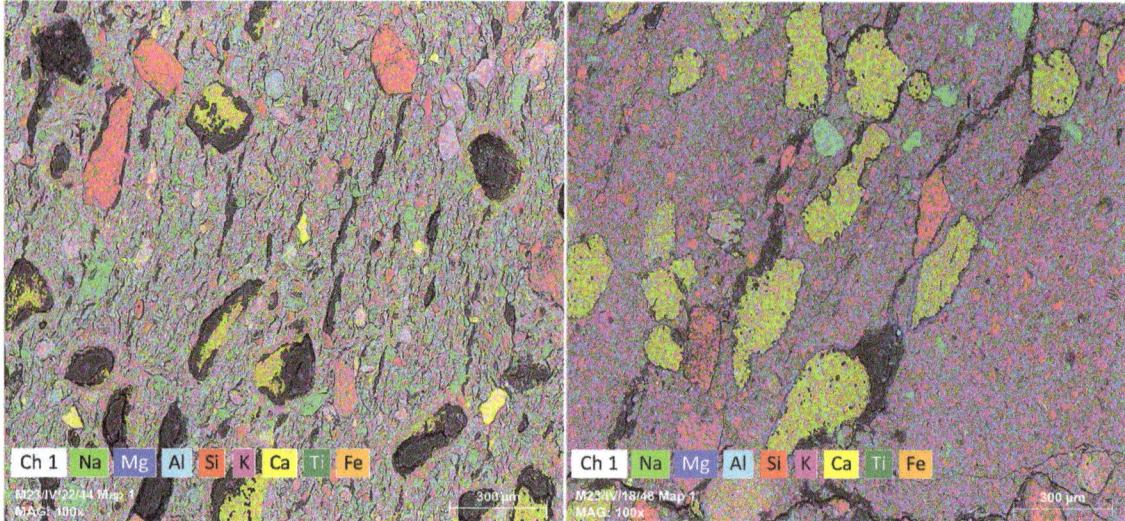

Figure 10.11: SEM micrographs of Motupore pottery.

Notes: (Left) pottery with erosion of shell creating voids; (Right) pottery with more intact shell.

Source: Authors.

SEM analyses of Bootless Bay clays and archaeological sherds

The SEM analyses to some extent mirrored the pXRF analyses in that while we could differentiate between the Bootless Bay clays, especially distinguishing between the T1, T2 and GG3 sources that formed Rye's three major groups, it was difficult to relate the Motupore sherds to any of the clays (see Figure 10.7).

In searching for reasons to explain this difficulty, the noted erosion of shell in the archaeological samples opened up the question of whether the addition or leaching of other elements might explain the differences between the archaeological pottery and the clays (see Schneider 2016 for a comprehensive overview of these types of issues). For the current study, we note three possible areas that might provide explanations: (1) that our source briquettes differed in some significant chemical way from the archaeological samples; (2) that the uses the pottery was put to may have occasioned chemical changes; or (3) that post-depositional burial might have altered the clay geochemistry. The loss of shell temper in the fabric of buried sherds is an example of the latter. Figure 10.11 indicates that this occurred at different rates for Motupore sherds. A study by Golitko et al. (2012) noted the post-depositional leaching of barium that affected pottery geochemical composition sufficiently to make samples appear to derive from different 'sources', while Ambrose (1982) and Bearat et al. (1992) also record change in particular elements due to the nature of the burial contexts of the pottery.

In terms of briquette differences, while our briquettes were made using distilled water, Motu potters used seawater (Groves 1960:15) and Motupore potters likely did as well, as its use in preference to fresh water increased the range of successful firings (Rye and Allen 2017:337–338); and additionally, Motupore has no surface fresh water source. Using salt water may be chemically significant in enriching the pottery samples in Na and Cl (Ambrose 1982). Ethnographically, some newly fired Motu pots were coated with mangrove dye and water pots vigorously rubbed with leaves to make them watertight (Groves 1960:17). The difficulty here is understanding what exact affect each stage of a pot's life can have on its geochemistry and being able to separate these effects to create an 'unbiased' source identity. While many studies simply exclude possibly affected elements, this may be a different way of introducing bias into the results as some excluded elements may reflect genuine differences in source location. Pottery from more distinct geologies might withstand these exclusions but this research suggests that for pottery from closely related geologies this could become an insurmountable obstacle.

Characterisation of Motupore sherds

As Figure 10.7 demonstrates, while the intersection of the archaeological sherds with the clay sources is poor, the sherds themselves cluster quite well, with relatively few outliers. This suggests that their characterisation, either chemically or mineralogically, might provide groups that stand as the equivalent of a Motupore or Bootless Bay source for external comparisons, even though these groups do not align closely with the clay sources. However, it is also worth noting here that the Boera sherds fit within this cluster as well, therefore perhaps this should be considered to reflect a more general coastal Port Moresby regional signature, similar to that identified by Bickler (1997), rather than solely Bootless Bay.

The types of inclusions in the archaeological pottery are also similar, making it difficult to distinguish between them qualitatively, but as Worthing (1982) showed, the proportions of these can reflect different temper suites. Five of Worthing's six groups were largely based on chert versus quartz/feldspar ratios, with Group B, the R1 sand, recognised as having little shell and the presence of pyroxenes and gabbro fragments.

A limitation of our study was our inability to distinguish chert, a clear marker of Worthing's results. However, the SEM analysis improved upon other parts of Worthing's analysis, as the geochemical approach provides the ability to distinguish more easily between quartz and feldspar, as well as between pyroxenes and amphiboles (see Marsaglia et al. 2016 who note difficulty with this). Petrography of thin sections, in addition to SEM analysis, would therefore be a way forward for improving this type of analysis. A second improvement would be additional map scanning using the SEM. Since our analysis included a large number of sherds, only one map scan was completed for each sherd. However, for a small sample, an additional map scan was completed to compare the results. While this analysis showed that there was not a large difference in quartz/feldspar ratios, it did become important for the identification of important accessory minerals such as mica. Therefore, it is possible that mica is under-represented in the current analysis.

Going forward

While our current analyses indicate the difficulties of relating Bootless Bay archaeological sherd fabrics to local geological sources, they have opened up a different approach to characterising these assemblages for comparison with other local and distant assemblages. Common archaeological practice at present is to point to comparisons between decoration techniques and motifs and vessel morphology, to which we envisage the addition of associated defining chemical tests.

It is assumed that continued research will expand and refine defining characteristics, but for the moment we can begin by identifying that archaeological pottery from Bootless Bay may be differentiated into 'source' groups based on a number of factors, including:

1.   Chert versus quartz/feldspar ratios, similar to that proposed by Worthing (1982).

2.   Distinctions between quartz and feldspar abundance, which may distinguish between Motupore, Boera and R1 (see Figure 10.9), in conjunction with the identification of associated minerals such as mica and pyroxene (see next two points).

3.   The presence of mica that, in turn, indicates a Boera source.

4.   The presence of pyroxenes that indicate use of the R1 sand.

This work continues.

Acknowledgements

This research was funded by a University of Otago Humanities Research Grant. We thank Alu Guise from the National Museum and Art Gallery of Papua New Guinea for finding the original Rye clay/sand samples. At the University of Otago, we would like to thank Helen Heath for processing the clay samples into briquettes for analysis, and Les O'Neill and Heather Sadler for their assistance in figure production.

References

Allen, J. 2017. *Excavations on Motupore Island, Central District, Papua New Guinea*. 2 Volumes. University of Otago Working Papers in Anthropology, No. 4. Department of Anthropology & Archaeology, University of Otago, Dunedin.

Allen, J. and P. Duerden 1982. Progressive results from the PIXE program for sourcing prehistoric Papuan pottery. In W. Ambrose and P. Duerden (eds), *Archaeometry: An Australian perspective*, pp. 45–59. Research School of Pacific Studies, The Australian National University, Canberra.

Allen, J. and O.S. Rye 1982. The importance of being earnest in archaeological investigations of prehistoric trade in Papua. In T. Dutton (ed.), *The* hiri *in history. Further aspects of long distance Motu trade in Papua*, pp. 99–115. Pacific Research Monograph 8. The Australian National University, Canberra.

Ambrose, W. 1982. Clays and sands in Melanesian pottery analysis. In J.C. Galipaud (ed.), *Poterie Lapita et Peuplement*, pp. 169–176. ORSTOM, Nouméa.

Bearat, H., D. Dufournier and Y. Nouet 1992. Alterations of ceramics due to contact with seawater. *Archaeologia Polona* 30:151–162.

Bentley, R.A. 2000. Provenience analysis of pottery from Fijian hillforts: Preliminary implications for exchange within the archipelago. *Archaeology in Oceania* 35:82–91. doi.org/10.1002/j.1834-4453.2000.tb00458.x.

Bickler, S.H. 1997. Early pottery exchange along the south coast of Papua New Guinea. *Archaeology in Oceania* 32(2):151–162. doi.org/10.1002/j.1834-4453.1997.tb00381.x.

Buhring, K.L., C.S. Azémard and P.J. Sheppard 2015. Geochemical characterization of Lapita ceramics from the Western Solomon Islands by means of portable X-Ray Fluorescence and Scanning Electron Microscopy. *The Journal of Island and Coastal Archaeology* 10(1):111–132. doi.org/10.1080/15564894.2014.880759.

Chalmers, J. 1887. History and description of pottery trade. A Papuan Enoch Arden. In J. Lindt *Picturesque New Guinea*, pp. 118–125. Longmans, Green and Co, London.

Chiu, S. 2003. The socio-economic functions of Lapita ceramic production and exchange: A case study from Site WKO013A, Koné, New Caledonia. Unpublished PhD thesis, University of Berkeley, California. www.proquest.com/docview/305336522?pq-origsite=gscholar&fromopenview=true.

Chiu. S., D. Killick, C. Sand, Y. Su, J.R. Fergusson and J-H. Chao 2020. Petrographic and chemical analyses of sherds from the Kurin Lapita site (Loyalty Islands, New Caledonia), ca. 3000–2700 BP. *Journal of Archaeological Science: Reports* 33:102542. doi.org/10.1016/j.jasrep.2020.102542.

Cogswell, J.W., H. Neff and M.D. Glascock 1998. Analysis of shell-tempered pottery replicates: Implications for provenance studies. *American Antiquity* 63(1):63–72. doi.org/10.2307/2694776.

Dickinson, W.R. 2006. *Temper sands in prehistoric Oceanian pottery: Geotectonics, sedimentology, petrography, province.* Geological Society of America Special Paper 406. The Geological Society of America, Boulder. doi.org/10.1130/2006.2406.

Duerden, P., J.R. Bird, M.D. Scott. E. Clayton, L.H. Russell and D.D. Cohen 1980. PIXE-PIGME Studies of Artefacts. *Nuclear Instruments and Methods* 168:447–452. doi.org/10.1016/0029-554x(80)91292-6.

Dutton, T. (ed.) 1982. *The* hiri *in history. Further aspects of long distance Motu trade in Papua.* Pacific Research Monograph 8. The Australian National University, Canberra.

Frankel, D., K. Thompson and R. Vanderwal 1994. Kerema and kinomere. In *Archaeology of a Coastal Exchange System: Sites and Ceramics of the Papuan Gulf.* Research Papers in Archaeology and Natural History, No. 25. pp. 1–52. Division of Archaeology and Natural History, Research School of Pacific and Asian Studies, The Australian National University, Canberra.

Golitko, M., J.V. Dudgeon, H. Neff and J.E. Terrell 2012. Identification of post-depositional chemical alteration of ceramics from the north coast of Papua New Guinea (Sandaun Province) by time-of-flight-laser ablation-inductively coupled plasma-mass spectrometry (TOF-LA-ICP-MS). *Archaeometry* 54(1): 80–100. doi.org/10.1111/j.1475-4754.2011.00612.x.

Groves, M. 1960. Motu pottery. *The Journal of the Polynesian Society* 69(1):3–22.

Marsaglia, K.M., K.G. Kramer, B. David and R.J. Skelly 2016. Petrographic analyses of sand/temper inclusions in ceramics of Kikinui, Kikori River and modern sand samples from the Gulf Province (Papua New Guinea). *Archaeology in Oceania* 51:131–140. doi.org/10.1002/arco.5097.

May, P. and M. Tuckson 1982. *The Traditional Pottery of Papua New Guinea.* Bay Books, Sydney.

Murray, J.H.P. 1912. *Papua or British New Guinea.* T. Fisher Unwin, London.

Oram, N. 1982. Pots for sago: The *hiri* trading network. In T. Dutton (ed.), *The* hiri *in history: Further aspects of long distance Motu trade in Papua,* pp. 1–34. Pacific Research Monograph 8. The Australian National University, Canberra.

Pieters, P.E. 1978. *1:250,000 Geological Series—Explanatory Notes—Port Moresby–Kalo–Aroa, Papua New Guinea.* Australian Government Publishing Service, Canberra.

Rhoads, J. 1980. Through a glass darkly: Present and past land-use systems of Papuan sagopalm users. Unpublished PhD thesis, The Australian National University, Canberra. openresearch-repository.anu.edu.au/handle/1885/96947.

Rhoads, J.W. 1994. The Popo site. In D. Frankel and J. Rhoads (eds), *Archaeology of a coastal exchange system: Sites and ceramics of the Papuan Gulf.* Research Papers in Archaeology and Natural History, No. 25. pp. 53–69. Division of Archaeology and Natural History, Research School of Pacific and Asian Studies, The Australian National University, Canberra.

Rye, O.S. 1976. Keeping your temper under control: Materials and the manufacture of Papuan pottery. *Archaeology and Physical Anthropology in Oceania* 11(2):106–137. www.jstor.org/stable/40386262.

Rye, O.S. 1977. Pottery manufacturing techniques: X-ray studies. *Archaeometry* 19(2):205–211. doi.org/10.1111/j.1475-4754.1977.tb00200.x.

Rye, O.S. 1981. *Pottery technology: Principles and reconstruction.* Manuals on Archaeology 4. Taraxacum Inc, Washington.

Rye, O.S. and J. Allen 1980. New approaches to Papuan pottery analysis. *Journal de la Société des Océanistes* 69(36):305–314. www.persee.fr/doc/jso_0300-953x_1980_num_36_69_3045.

Rye, O.S. and J. Allen 2017. Technological studies of Motupore pottery. In J. Allen (ed.), *Excavations on Motupore Island, Central District, Papua New Guinea,* pp. 331–370. University of Otago Working Papers in Anthropology, No. 4. Department of Anthropology & Archaeology, University of Otago, Dunedin.

Rye, O.S. and P. Duerden 1982. Papuan pottery sourcing by PIXE: Preliminary studies. *Archaeometry* 24: 59–64. doi.org/10.1111/j.1475-4754.1982.tb00648.x.

Schneider, G. 2016. Mineralogical and chemical alteration. In A.M.W. Hunt (ed.), *The Oxford handbook of archaeological ceramic analysis,* pp. 162–180. Oxford University Press, Oxford. academic.oup.com/edited-volume/34668/chapter/295390288.

Seligman, C.G. 1910. *The Melanesians of Papua New Guinea.* Cambridge University Press, Cambridge.

Shaw, B., M. Leclerc, W. Dickinson, M. Spriggs and G.R. Summerhayes 2016. Identifying prehistoric trade networks in the Massim region, Papua New Guinea: Evidence from petrographic and chemical compositional pottery analyses from Rossel and Nimowa Islands in the Louisiade Archipelago. *Journal of Archaeological Science: Reports* 6:518–535. doi.org/10.1016/j.jasrep.2016.03.034.

Stone, O.C. 1876. Description of the country and the natives of Port Moresby and neighbourhood, New Guinea. *Journal of the Royal Geographical Society* 46:34–62. doi.org/10.2307/1798668.

Summerhayes, G.R. 1987. Aspects of Melanesian ceramics. Unpublished MA thesis, University of Sydney, Sydney.

Summerhayes, G.R. 1996. Interaction in Pacific prehistory: An approach based on the production, distribution and use of pottery. Unpublished PhD thesis, La Trobe University, Melbourne.

Summerhayes, G.R. 1997. Losing your temper: The effect of mineral inclusions on pottery analyses. *Archaeology in Oceania* 32:108–117. doi.org/10.1002/j.1834-4453.1997.tb00376.x.

Summerhayes, G.R. 2000. *Lapita interaction.* Terra Australis 15. The Australian National University, Canberra. openresearch-repository.anu.edu.au/bitstream/1885/127430/1/TA_15.pdf.

Summerhayes, G.R. and J. Allen 2007. Lapita writ small: Revisiting the Austronesian colonisation of the Papuan coast. In S. Bedford, C. Sand and S. Connaughton (eds), *Oceanic explorations: Lapita and Western Pacific settlement,* pp. 97–122. Terra Australis 26. ANU Press, Canberra. doi.org/10.22459/ta26.2007.05.

Summerhayes, G.R. and M.J. Walker 1982. Elemental analysis and taxonomy of prehistoric pottery from Western Java. In W. Ambrose and P. Duerden (eds), *Archaeometry: An Australasian perspective,* pp. 60–67. Department of Prehistory, Research School of Pacific Studies, The Australian National University, Canberra.

Sutton, N., G.R. Summerhayes and A. Ford 2019. Oposisi revisited: A fabric analysis of an Early Papuan Pottery assemblage from Yule Island, Papua New Guinea. *Journal of Island and Coastal Archaeology* 14(3): 411–425. doi.org/10.1080/15564894.2018.1531329.

Vigalys, G. and G. Summerhayes 2016. Do hiccups echo? Late Holocene interaction and ceramic production in southern Papua New Guinea. *Asian Perspectives* 55(1):61–88. doi.org/10.1353/asi.2016.0011.

Worthing, M. 1980a. South Papuan coastal sources of potsherds from the Gulf area of PNG. *Oral History* 8:87–100.

Worthing, M.A. 1980b. The mineralogy and sources of Port Moresby potsherds from the Gulf area of Papua New Guinea. *Science in New Guinea* 7(3):157–162.

Worthing, M.A. 1982. A petrographic method of sourcing potsherds from the Port Moresby area of Papua New Guinea. *Archaeology in Oceania* 17(2):79–82. doi.org/10.1002/j.1834-4453.1982.tb00041.x.

Worthing, M.A. and P. Swadling 1980. South Papuan coastal sources of potsherds from the Gulf area of Papua New Guinea. Unpublished report on file with author. University of Otago, Dunedin.

11

Trading valuables to foreigners in south-east New Guinea in the nineteenth century: The case of *Conus* armshells

Pamela Swadling, Robin Torrence and Jill Hasell

Abstract

This chapter examines why and how 170 valuable *Conus* armshells collected from two areas of Papua New Guinea during the nineteenth century were traded to foreigners. The different histories of European contact on the eastern Papuan South Coast and the Massim region, particularly with respect to the introduction of iron in the former area and services in the latter, had a major impact on the acquisition of these artefacts into museum collections. Armshells remain important valuables for the people of south-east New Guinea. To recognise this continued significance, Papua New Guinea gave a regional armshell name to one of its currency denominations.

Introduction

Rings made from *Conus* shell and worn on the arm, commonly called armshells, are important valuables for the villagers living on the Papuan South Coast as well as in the islands to the south-east of the New Guinea mainland, known as the Massim region, and especially communities involved in the *Kula* network (see Figures 11.1 and 11.2).

The modern state of Papua New Guinea recognises their significance by using *Toea*, a regional name for a *Conus* armshell, for a modern currency denomination (Mira 1986:29). Currently, information about these artefacts is not readily available. For instance, the Bank of Papua New Guinea's currency website (Anon. 2020) has no information about how most *Toea* were made on Mailu Island or in the Massim and then traded to the Port Moresby area. The first inaugural Mailu Island *Toea* armshell festival was held in 2016. Deveni Temu (pers. comm. 2021) reported that the festival's organisers are interested in obtaining more information about the history of armshell production. Helping to provide this information is the prime aim of this chapter.

This study is based on 170 armshells, most of which are currently held in 12 institutions, although some were lost during World War II. Around 40 of these armshells have information about where they were collected. This general lack of provenance is overcome by examining when the armshells were acquired, foreign activities at the time and what is known about the activities of the collectors.

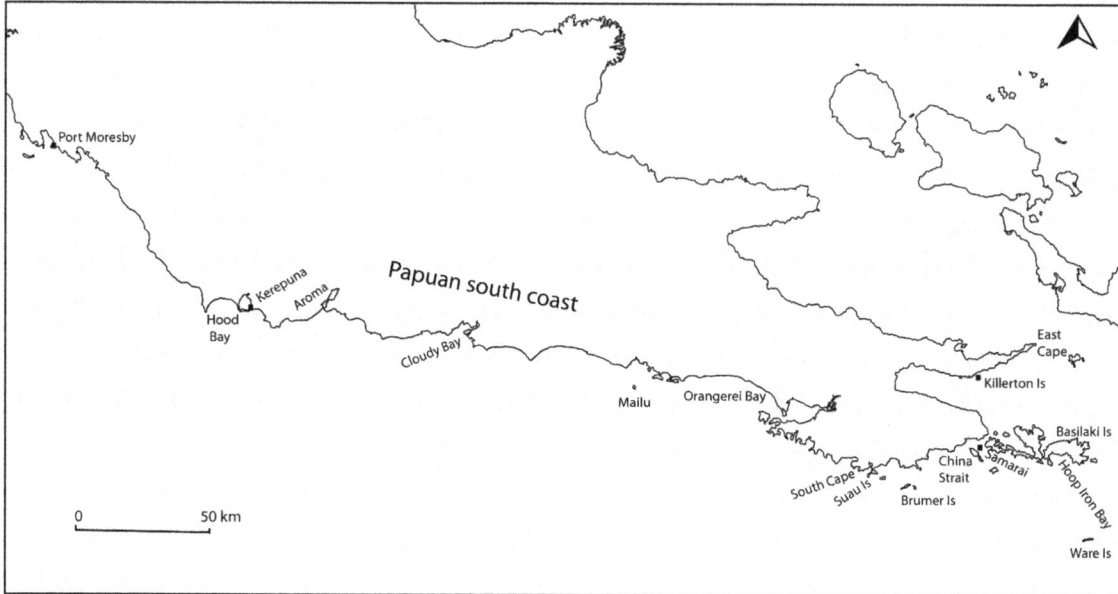

Figure 11.1: Papuan South Coast, showing places mentioned in the text.
Source: Drawn by author.

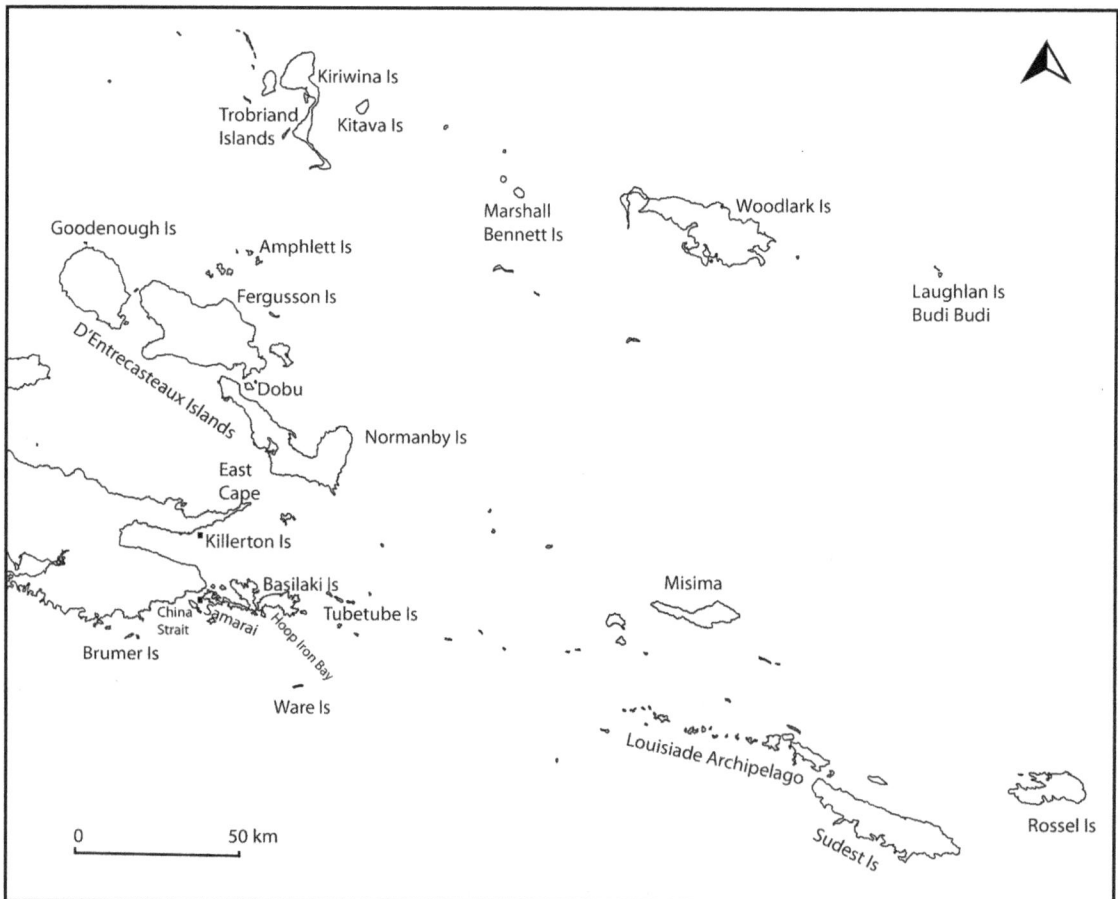

Figure 11.2: The Massim, showing places mentioned in the text.
Source: Drawn by author.

Most armshells from the eastern Papuan South Coast were collected between 1876 and 1884. By contrast, most of the armshells from the Massim were acquired during the 1890s. Although regular foreign visits to the Massim by Europeans and Americans began in the 1820s, interaction with local communities on the Papuan South Coast did not take place until the 1870s. Most of the early visitors to the Massim were searching for natural resources, such as whale oil or bêche-de-mer. They did not specifically seek artefacts but did bring iron to trade for provisions. By contrast, when foreigners began visiting the eastern Papuan South Coast in the 1870s, collectors and museums had become interested in acquiring curios. Again, as in the Massim, iron was the product most eagerly sought during the initial trade exchanges with foreigners on the Papuan South Coast.

Before discussing the trade in armshells to foreigners, some background information needs to be presented about the morphology, sources, variation in decoration, size and value of the armshells themselves. This information is presented in Part 1 of this chapter. Part 2 covers differences in the different contact histories experienced by villagers in the Massim compared to those on the eastern Papuan South Coast, with an emphasis on the importance of iron in these exchanges. Part 3 examines the collectors who procured the armshells that are now in museum collections. Part 4 considers the different acquisition agencies, including ships' crews, traders, scientists, missionaries and government officers. Part 5 then looks at the geographical variation in armshell decoration in south-east New Guinea. The conclusion considers what can be learned from armshell collections about Papuan social connections and their interactions with foreigners.

Part 1: Morphology, sources, variation in decoration, sizes and value

Conus armshells are made from the wider upper body of the shell of *Conus leopardus* and *C. litteratus* shells. The World Register of Marine Species gives a maximum length of 220 mm for *C. leopardus* and 170 mm for *C. litteratus*, though some *C. leopardus* shells have been reported up to 250 mm in length (Cernohorsky 1978:129). There are two types of armshells: most are made from a complete ring of *Conus* shell, whereas some are made by joined segments of *Conus* shell.

Ring armshells

Armshells made from the outer whorl of large cone shells are illustrated in Figure 11.3. In the Port Moresby region on the Papuan South Coast, these armshells are known as *Toea* and are a required component in Motuan brideprice payments. In 1876 such a payment was 10 armshells, but by the early 1900s the number required was up to 40 (Seligman 1910:77; Turner 1878:479). In their annual trading expedition to the Papuan Gulf, armshells were also one of the products the Motu took with them to pay for sago and canoe hulls. In 1885, one trading canoe (*Lakatoi*) is recorded as taking 57 *Toea* (Barton 1910:114). If Barton's number of 57 is representative of those taken on one *Lakatoi*, the four *Lakatoi* that went to the Papuan Gulf in 1885 could have been carrying some 230 *Toea* altogether. Clearly armshells were a very important cultural asset. In 1902, Barton (1904) reports, Motuans were willing to pay two pounds sterling for a large armshell. This was a lot of money, as the annual salary at that time for a village constable was only one pound. Some 15 years later, armshells in Port Moresby were attaining prices of up to 30 pounds, far more than what was paid for the same artefact amongst the Massim (Malinowski 1922:86).

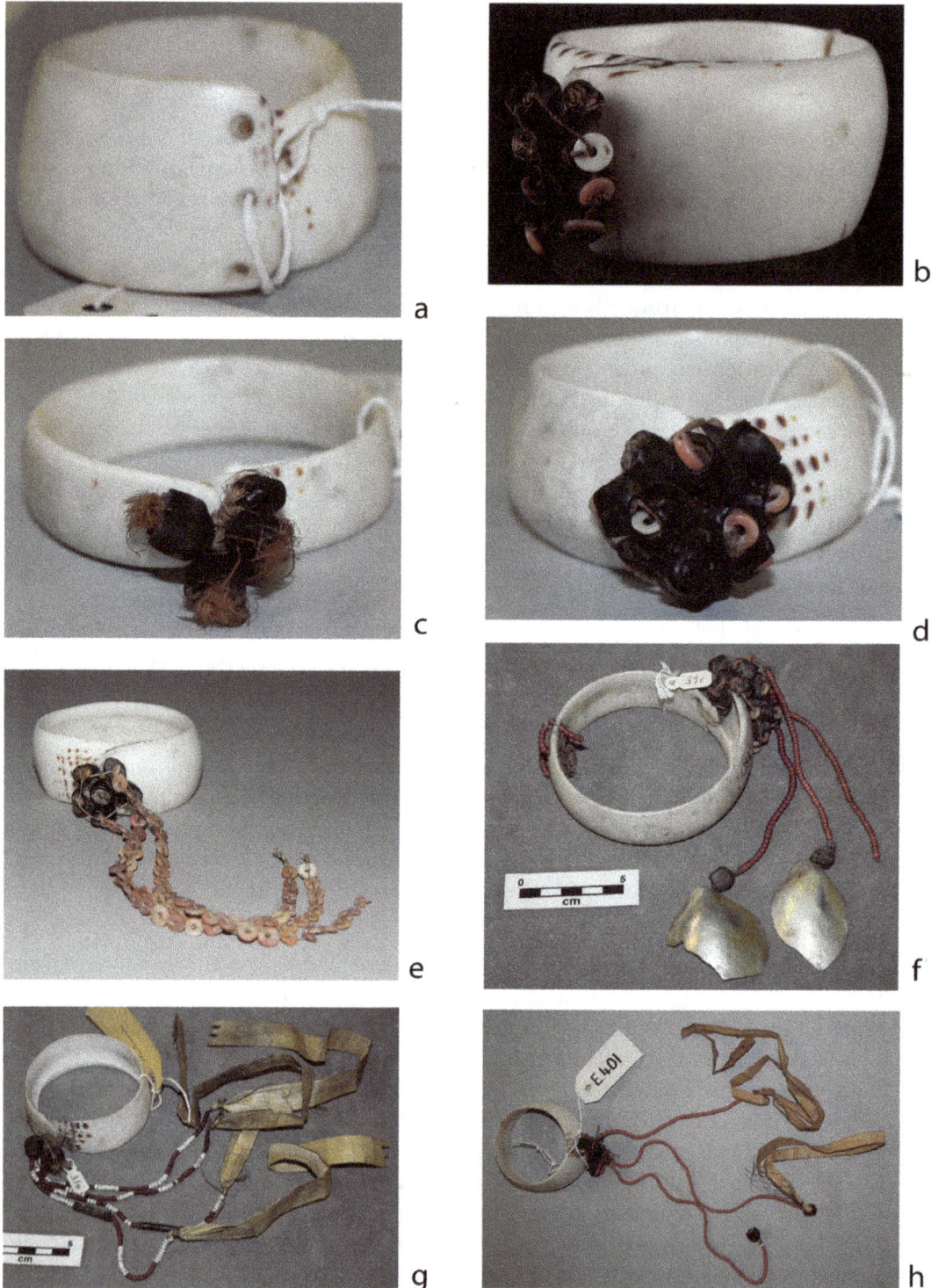

Figure 11.3: Ring armshells.

Notes: (a) A15906-2, Australian Museum, 1883, Mason Brothers artefact dealers in Sydney, max. diameter 81 mm, internal diameter 65 mm, decoration 3 holes; (b) 11421, Auckland War Memorial Museum, 1879, collected by Andrew Goldie at Pure (?Pari) in Port Moresby, Toea, max. external diameter 80 mm, decoration rosette of banana seeds, some with inserted shell beads; (c) A15913, Australian Museum, 1883, Mason Brothers artefact dealers in Sydney, max. external diameter 85 mm, internal diameter 66 mm, decoration 4 banana seeds with red fibre inserts; (d) A15903, Australian Museum, 1883, Mason Brothers artefact dealers in Sydney, max. external diameter 85 mm, internal diameter 65 mm, decoration rosette of banana seeds with inserted shell beads; (e) Oc1980, Q.226, British Museum, 1876, Rev. S. MacFarlane, max. external diameter 80 mm, decoration rosette of banana seeds with inserted shell beads, 3 strings of shell beads; (f) ABDUA 390, University of Aberdeen Museums, 1898, Sir William MacGregor collection, max. external diameter 99 mm, internal diameter 85 mm, 2 joins one at lip, the other on circumference, decoration rosette of banana seeds with inserted shell beads, 3 strings of glass trade beads, pendants: 2 banana seeds and 2 pearl shells; (g) ABDUA 394, University of Aberdeen Museums, 1898, Sir William MacGregor collection, max. external diameter 74 mm, internal diameter 67 mm, decoration rosette of 3 banana seeds, no inserts, 4 strings of glass trade beads, including 2 black organic tubular beads and pandanus streamers; (h) E401, Australian Museum, 1887, Rev. W. Wyatt Gill, max. external diameter 87 mm, internal diameter 68 mm, rosette of banana seeds with some shell bead inserts, 3 strings of glass trade beads, pendants: 2 banana seeds, 2 pandanus streamers.

Sources: (a) Copyright: The Australian Museum, photo Robin Torrence; (b) Copyright: The Auckland War Memorial Museum; (c–d) Copyright: The Australian Museum, photo Robin Torrence; (e) Copyright: The Trustees of the British Museum; (f–g) Copyright: University of Aberdeen Museums, photo Robin Torrence; (h) Copyright: The Australian Museum, photo Robin Torrence. These photographs are shared under a Creative Commons Attribution-NonCommercial-ShareAlike 4.0 International (CC BY-NC-SA 4.0) licence.

Figure 11.4: Brumer Islanders dancing on the deck of HMS *Rattlesnake* on 28 August 1849. *Conus* armshells are worn above the elbows of some of the dancers.
Source: Scene by marine artist Oswald Brierly, held by the Mitchell Library, State Library of New South Wales.

In the Massim, ring armshells were among the valuables used in peacemaking, marriage, mortuary and other payments (Macintyre 1983a; Weiner 1988). In some areas they were often worn as an arm ornament (see Figure 11.4). In the *Kula* exchange network, armshells (*Mwali*) were once secondary in value to *Doga* (circular boar's tusk pendants). In the late nineteenth and early twentieth centuries armshells came to replace circular boar's tusks as the primary valuable, being exchanged for necklaces *(Soulava)* in the *Kula* (Malinowski 1922; Swadling and Bence 2016). Malinowski used the Kiriwina names for these valuables in his book *Argonauts of the Western Pacific*, but other terms are used elsewhere in the *Kula* ring. For ease of discussion, the term *Mwali* is also used here to refer to a *Kula* armshell valuable.

Multi-segmented armshells

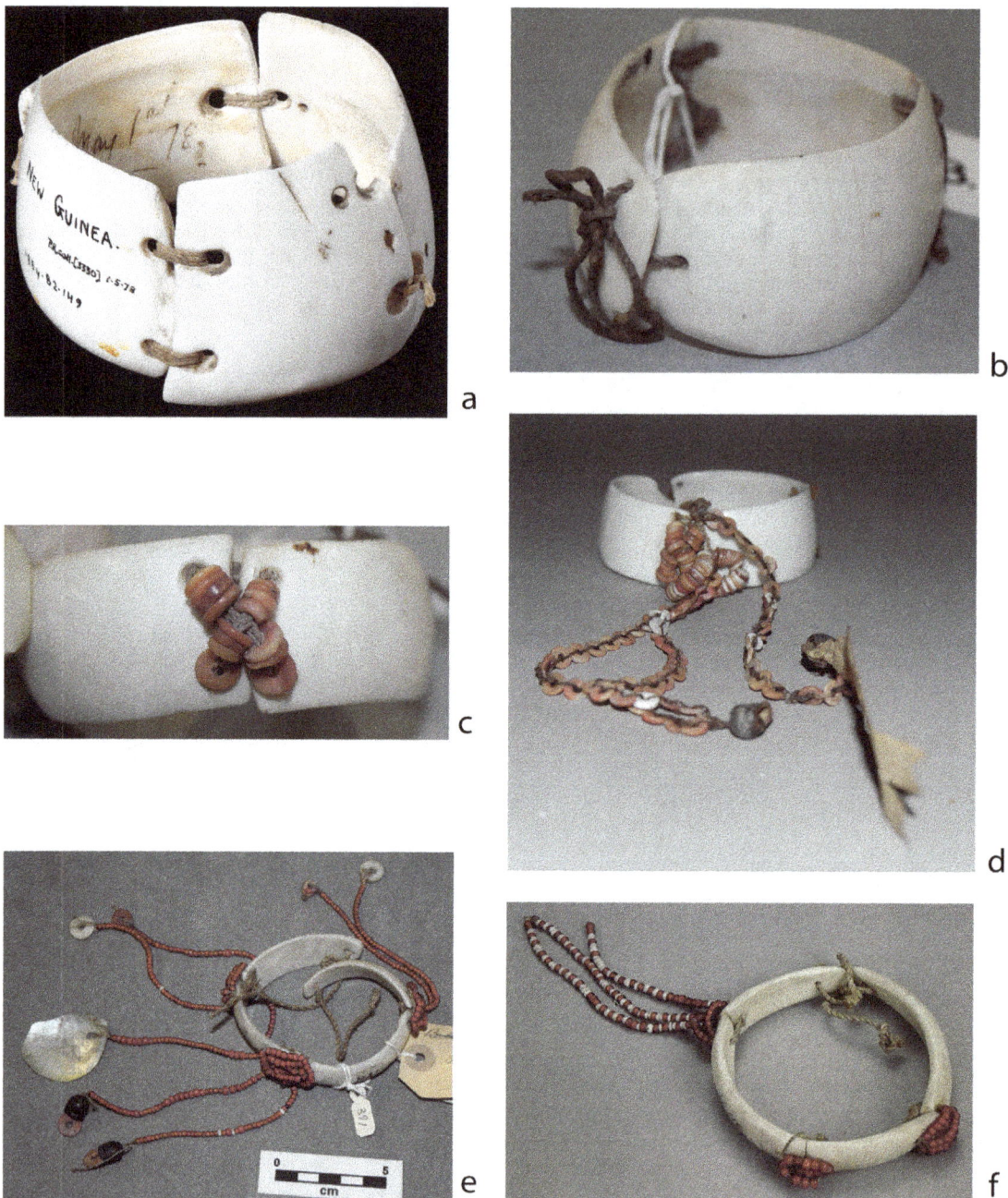

Figure 11.5: Multiple segmented armshells.

Notes: (a) 1884.82.149, Pitt Rivers Museum, prior to 1878, max. external diameter 70 mm, 4 segments; (b) B1907, Australian Museum, 1884, H.I. Renwick, max external diameter 73 mm, internal diameter 60 mm, 3 segments; (c) B1910, Australian Museum, 1884, H.I. Renwick, max. external diameter 67 mm, internal diameter 64 mm, 3 segments, decoration cross of red shell beads on one join, banana seed off a cord on another; (d) Oc1886, 1016.13, British Museum, 1886, Captain W.H. Henderson, max. external diameter 80 mm, decoration rosette of shell beads, 3 strings of shell beads, pendants: 2 banana seeds, one pandanus streamer; (e) ABDUA 391, University of Aberdeen Museums, 1898, Sir William MacGregor collection, max. external diameter 82 mm, 4 segments, rosettes of glass trade beads at joins, 7 glass trade bead strings, pendants: 2 banana seeds, 6 shell beads, 1 pearl shell; (f) H0136442, National Museum of Ethnology, Osaka, Rev. George Brown, from Budi Budi, Laughlan Islands, max. external diameter 79 mm, 4 segments, rosettes of glass trade beads at 3 joins, 3 strings of glass trade beads from 1 rosette.

These are less common and are usually made of three to four, or occasionally more, segments (see Figure 11.5). Almost all examples have been collected in the Massim. Broad multi-segmented arm ornaments seem to be restricted to the southern Massim, and to early collections. The large examples include those deposited at Pitt Rivers Museum by an unknown collector, by H.J. Renwick at the Australian Museum and by an ethnographic example on Rossel Island (Armstrong 1928). Other examples are narrower. Malinowski collected multi-segmented armshells in the Trobriands, and his collection notes record that the local name is *Nuripuapua* (Norick 1976). Some are configured as *Mwali*, but Malinowski makes no mention of them in his 1922 ethnography *Argonauts of the Western Pacific*. In terms of numbers, most examples of multi-segmented armshells in museum collections come from Budi Budi (Laughlan Islands) and the Trobriand Islands.

Despite being more difficult and time-consuming to make, multi-segmented armshells are not as valuable as ring armshells. C. Salerio, an Italian missionary on Woodlark Island from 1852 to 1855, found those made from segments were of less value and on this island were used by women (Affleck 1981). It is currently not known whether there is a link between the multi-segmented armshells of the Massim and those that are considered markers for Lapita (Langley et al. 2019). It is possible that there may be some continuity as Late Lapita sites have been found in the Massim (Shaw et al. 2020).

Source areas for *Conus* shells in south-east New Guinea and the location of manufacturing communities

In the northern Massim, *Conus* shells are obtained from the reefs off western Kiriwina in the Trobriand Islands and off south-east Woodlark Island. To the south they are obtained from reefs in the Louisiade Archipelago, as well as from the barrier reef system that extends from near Sudest eastwards along the Papuan South Coast as far as Aroma. There was limited *Conus* fishing in the Port Moresby region.

In the Massim, ring armshells are produced in the Trobriand and Woodlark islands, on Ware and elsewhere in the Louisiades. In the Trobriands some villages specialise in the fishing and making of armshells. Both the Kavataria and Kaileuna (Kayleula) communities in the Trobriands fished for cone shells to make armshells prior to the commencement of the pearling industry in 1892. By 1915 the Kavataria community was completely absorbed by the pearling industry and had ceased to produce armshells. On Woodlark, armshells are made from *Conus* specimens found when carrying out other activities. Armshells from the Louisiade Archipelago were traded via Ware islanders to Tubetube and Misima, thence onto Woodlark (Belshaw 1955:25; Damon 1980:284; Lepowsky 1983:474–475; Malinowski 1922:502–504; Malinowski 1988; Seligman 1910; Shaw and Langley 2017; Swadling and Bence 2016).

On the Papuan South Coast, ring armshells are made by the Mailu, who trade them to the Aroma to their west, as well as other armshells that originate from the *Kula* network. The armshells then move through exchange relationships down the line, by which means they reach Port Moresby and subsequently the Papuan Gulf (Malinowski 1988; Saville 1926; Seligman 1910). The supply from Mailu and the *Kula* region was supplemented by limited manufacture at Boera, a Motu village west of Port Moresby (Oram 1982:13). Malinowski (1922:481) observed that multi-segmented armshells are imported into the Trobriands via Kitava from the smaller islands.

Armshell decoration in the late nineteenth and early twentieth centuries

Armshells are not always decorated. Museum collections made in the late nineteenth century, from both the Massim and the Papuan South Coast, indicate that many armshells were traded without being decorated.

The decorating of armshells with rosettes of banana seeds with inserted shell beads was formerly done both in the Massim and at Mailu. An armshell decorated in this way is illustrated on the two-kina banknote. The armshell shown came from Milne Bay Province (Mira 1986:145).

In 1914 when the Mailu produced an armshell, they also bored holes and attached a banana seed rosette with shell bead inserts (Malinowski 1988:165). In the Trobriands, *Conus* were fished and made into armshells, but not decorated. Decoration was applied when the armshells reached Dobu. The Dobuans received new *Conus* armshells as *Kula* gifts, either directly from the Trobriands or through the Amphletts. Once received, the Dobuans bored holes in the armshell's lip. This allowed wild, black banana seeds with inserted shell beads to be attached (Malinowski 1922:503).

In the late nineteenth and early twentieth centuries, *Kula* exchange valuables (*Mwali*) not only had rosettes of banana seeds with inserted beads but also other decorations to make them more enticing. These additions included strings of beads, shell pendants and pandanus streamers. Other less common configurations included rosettes made solely with shell beads or strings of beads.

Both the nature of artefact assemblages as well as comments by observers from the 1870s indicate that Port Moresby's shell bead industry was in decline. Octavius Stone, who arrived there in 1875 and stayed for some months, reports that some men and women wore short strings of shell beads as ear decoration, but double and treble string red shell bead (*Ageva*) necklaces were very rare. The brideprice paid for the daughter on one of the principal chiefs at (Tanapata) Hanuabada did not include such a necklace (Stone 1879:8–10).

Stone, Otto Finsch and members of the Cooke Daniels Expedition were only able to acquire a few beads when they visited Tatana, the renowned shell bead–making village, between 1875 and 1903 (Swadling and Bence 2016). The diminished shell bead supply impacted on the decoration applied to shell armshells in the Port Moresby region (see Tables 11.2 and 11.3, later in the chapter). The two armshells that Andrew Goldie collected from 'Pure' (perhaps Pari?) in Port Moresby in 1879, are decorated with eight banana seeds, with four red and one white inserted shell beads (see Figure 11.3b). Other unprovenanced armshells collected in the 1870s and early 1880s from the South Coast, probably from the Port Moresby region, have rosettes of banana seeds, but the seeds lack shell bead inserts. One provenanced example is the armshell that Otto Finsch acquired at Ihli, Hood Bay in the Port Moresby region in 1882 (Finsch 1887). It has an external diameter of 80 mm, eight banana seeds, but no shell bead inserts. Another armshell now in the Australian Museum collection has red fibre inserted in the banana seeds presumably as a replacement for shell beads (see Figure 11.3c).

Armshell sizes and value

An armshell's size can be assessed by using either its maximum external diameter, or preferably, the internal diameter that fits over the arm. The Mailu increased the internal diameter by further grinding away the inside of armshells (Malinowski 1988:264–265, Plate 28; Saville 1926:154–155). Both diameters have been used by museum catalogues and reported in the literature. A useful way to compare these measurements is to plot them as shown in Figure 11.6.

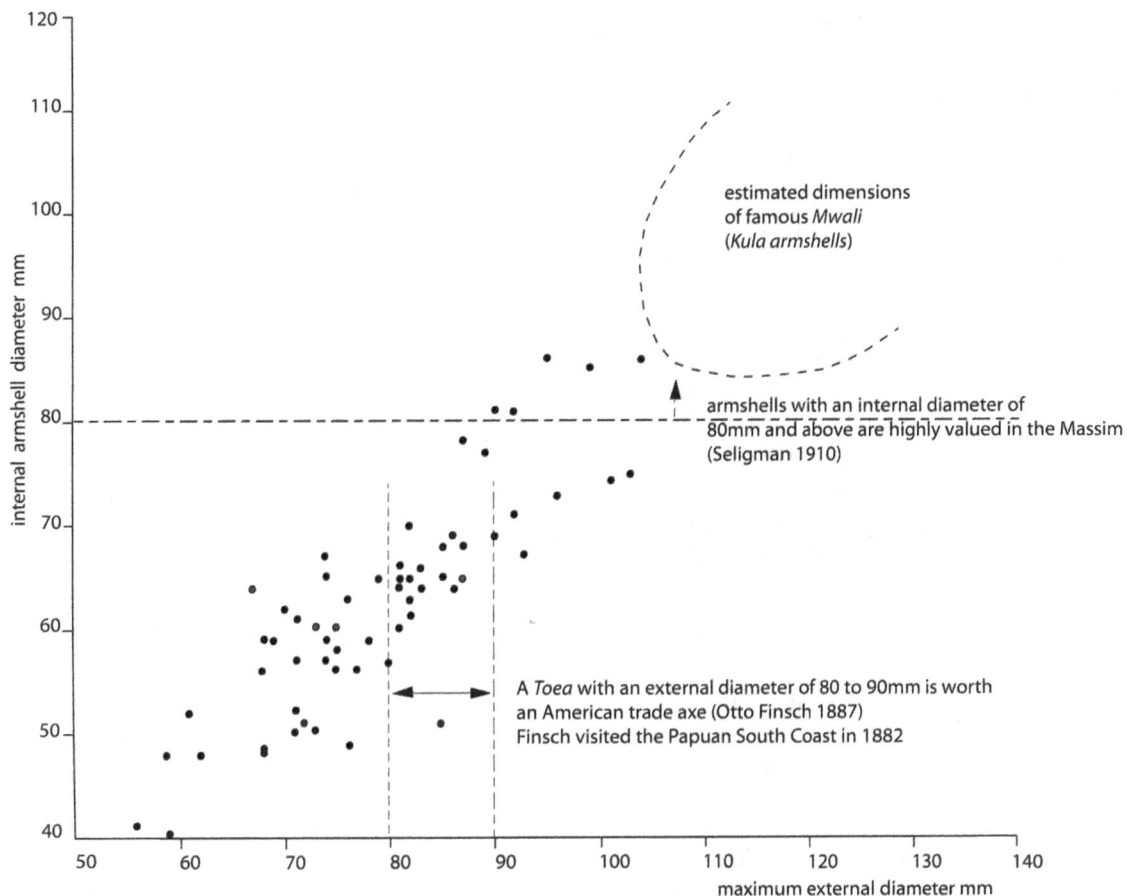

Figure 11.6: The cultural valuation of armshells differed between the Massim and the Papuan South Coast.

Notes: This reflects the predominant use of the larger *Conus leopardus* in the northern Massim and the smaller *C. litteratus* in the southern Massim and on the Papuan South Coast.

Source: Drawn by author.

Naturally larger *Conus leopardus* have the potential to produce wider diameters than those of the smaller species, *C. litteratus*. In the Massim, armshells with an internal diameter of 80 mm are highly valued (Seligman 1910:513–514), whereas smaller armshells are found in the Louisiades and on the Papuan South Coast. In 1882 Otto Finsch found that highly valued armshells on the South Coast had an external diameter of 80 to 90 mm (Finsch 1887:154–155). The difference between the external and internal diameters is evident in Figure 11.6.

In the *Kula* region of the Massim, armshells large enough to fit over the upper arm are considered the most valuable. Famous *Mwali* have a personal name and history. Documented examples include *Nimoa*, which has an external diameter of 140 mm, seen at Tubetube (Macintyre 1983a:112) and *Nimov* with an external diameter of 113 mm, recorded at Woodlark (Bickler 1998:355). At the other end of the *Mwali* size range are very small arm shells which are used by young men entering *Kula* relationships. They provide something to *Kula* especially when larger armshells are scarce (Campbell 1983:237–240). Museum collections indicate that the internal diameters of these smaller armshells range from 45 to 65 mm (see Figure 11.6).

Part 2: The impact of iron on contact histories

The Massim

Iron was introduced to the northern Massim by whalers from the late 1820s. During their voyages of six months or more, whalers required enough firewood to boil whale blubber down into oil. They also needed water and fresh provisions. An account of a shore visit by whalers to an island in the Bismarck Archipelago mentions that the boats had to return to their ship when all the iron supplies ran out (Gray 1989:54). Supplying tomahawks would have sped up the provision of firewood, and in the case of Kiriwina and Woodlark Island iron would also have been traded for yams.

The *Woodlark*, captained by George Grimes, is the first whaler recorded in the northern Massim. Grimes named Woodlark Island during his ca 1826 to 11 June 1827 voyage out of Sydney. The *Woodlark*, as well as other whalers such as the *Marshall Bennett*, made subsequent visits to the northern Massim. *The Shipping Gazette* and *Sydney General Trade List of 1851* note that the deep water off the north coast of Woodlark Island gave whalers a safe anchorage for acquiring wood and fresh provisions. Another favoured location was Cape Dennis at the northern tip of Kiriwina. It was known in London and the United States that whalers could trade hoop iron for plenty of yams at Cape Dennis. In October 1836, Captain R.L. Hunter of the *Marshall Bennett* reported that Trobrianders there waded out to their whaleboats with baskets of yams to exchange for hoop iron. Clearly, the islanders were confident and familiar with these kinds of interactions (Hunter 1939). Visits by whalers started to decline in the 1860s and only a few, such as the *Avola*, came in the 1870s (Anon. 1839, 1851:231, 1966; Gray 1989; Laracy 2010; Moore 2003:118).

The Catholic Mission on Woodlark Island (1847–56), passing ships, including those on Admiralty surveys, and wrecked ships provided other sources of iron. *Mnoumnou* (iron) was the first Muruan word missionaries heard on their arrival at Woodlark (Moore 2003:119, 123). The missionaries on Woodlark found that villagers were more interested in acquiring material goods than spiritual teaching (Laracy 2010:143; Salerio et al. 1983).

Iron was salvaged from wrecked ships including the Sydney whaler *Mary*, wrecked in 1841 in the Laughlan group (Budi Budi); the island trader *Gazelle* at the entrance to Guasopa Harbour at Woodlark Island in 1855 and the *Saint Paul* on the north coast of Rossel Island in 1858. Iron from these wrecked ships, as well as the trade iron from whalers, missionaries and other foreign visitors resulted in traditional stone tools being replaced by iron ones. By 1870 the production of stone blades at Suloga on Woodlark Island had ceased (Affleck 1971:25; Bickler and Turner 2002:40; Damon 1983:55; Laracy 2010:142; Liep 2009:85; Liep and Affleck 1983:121; Seligman 1910:33).

In 1849 the crew of the British Admiralty survey ship HMS *Rattlesnake* found that the villagers of the Louisiade Archipelago were familiar with iron. Macgillivray mentions that villagers from Sudest, and nearby Piron and Brierly Islands, sought hoop iron to haft their axe shafts. They were also keen to acquire iron axes. The people of Brumer (Brummer) Island, on the South Coast near the eastern tip of New Guinea, were also observed to be familiar with hoop iron. As in the Louisiades, hoop iron was the article the villagers most prized (Macgillivray 1852).

By 1873 Captain Moresby found that the islanders at East Cape were receiving iron from the Louisiade Archipelago, whereas by this date those living at the eastern tip of New Guinea had little apart from some sharpened bolts and spike nails. Moresby found the demand for hoop iron so keen near the tip of New Guinea that he gave the name Hoop Island Bay to a favoured anchorage on Basilaki (Moresby) Island (Moresby 1875:29, 1876:187).

In the 1870s the new foreign industry of bêche-de-mer fishing bought iron to south-eastern New Guinea. Its commencement occurred after Captain John Moresby had undertaken his three maritime surveys in 1873–4. Moresby's first voyage was from Torres Strait to Fairfax Harbour (later Port Moresby) and back to Cape York. The second was from Cape York to the China Strait, Louisiade Archipelago and Milne Bay to Sydney. In January 1874 he returned to England via Port Moresby, China Strait, East Cape, the D'Entrecasteaux Islands and up the north coast of New Guinea (Moresby 1876). No bêche-de-mer traders were observed by Moresby, but it is likely that his voyages made potential traders aware of the extensive reefs off the eastern tip of New Guinea.

These traders brought iron to the Massim during the 1870s and 1880s, but their small boats and focus on obtaining bêche-de-mer meant they had no interest in collecting curios such as armshells. The Australian traders seeking bêche-de-mer mostly lived on their boats and paid locals with tobacco pipes, knives and tobacco. For example, one of the first boats seeking bêche-de-mer was a brig, the *Rita* from Sydney. It was observed by the missionary Samuel MacFarlane in 1876 at anchor on the north side of Mekinley Island in the China Strait. The crew were on shore cutting wood, where a tent was erected. The captain said they were fishing for bêche-de-mer and had been out 10 months, and had been stationed at Mekinley Island for 10 days and were about to leave (MacFarlane 1877:360).

In 1877 the *Torres Strait Fisheries Act* was passed, regulating bêche-de-mer fishing in Torres Strait (Moore 1991:422). To avoid the restrictions imposed by this Act traders began to focus their activity on the uncontrolled reefs of the Louisiade Archipelago. It quickly became the main industry in British New Guinea protectorate until gold was discovered on Sudest Island in 1887. Gold then became the primary export (Figure 11.7).

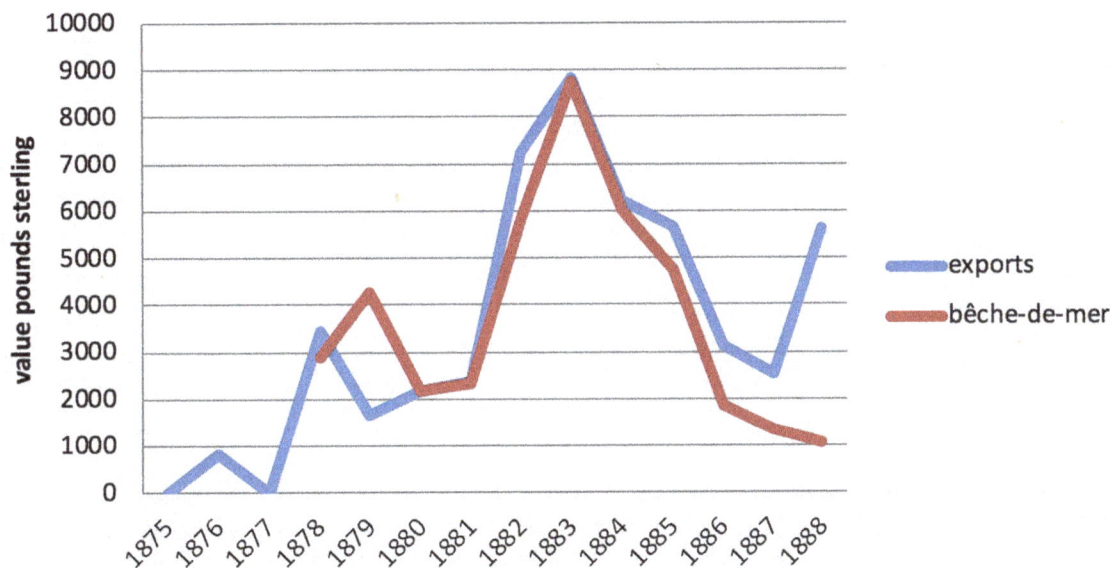

Figure 11.7: Bêche-de-mer fishing was the main economic activity in British New Guinea until alluvial gold was discovered on Sudest in 1887.
Source: Musgrave (1889:22, 36).

Many bêche-de-mer traders had violent deaths at the hands of the local people. In 1878 William Ingham and six of his crew were killed on Brooker (Utian) Island in the Calvados chain of the Louisiade Archipelago (Moore 1991:414). Bêche-de-mer trading also brought Nikolai Miklouho-Maclay, the Russian anthropologist, to the Trobriands in late November 1879. He was travelling on the *Sadie F. Caller*, an American schooner that traded for this product (Webster 1984:234). In 1885 Lindt (1887:84) observed a trader called Kissack living on Teste (Ware Island), who made a living by entrusting trade items, including knives, tobacco pipes and tobacco, to Ware men, who bartered them in the Louisiade Archipelago for bêche-de-mer and coconuts. Lindt thought that this trading activity, which they undertook for bêche-de-mer traders, was how the Ware became the central link and source of influence within the Louisiade Archipelago, but they were only doing what they had long done as the principal agents in the southern *Kula* (Lepowsky 1983:476).

The eastern Papuan South Coast

Unlike its early introduction in the Massim, iron was not obtained by villagers on the eastern Papuan South Coast until the 1870s when ships began visiting. Both Captain Moresby and D'Albertis visited in 1873. When the corvette D'Albertis was travelling on was anchored off Orangerie Bay in 1873, he was able to acquire some bird of paradise plumes there (D'Albertis 1877:38–39). Some iron had been introduced to villagers at Redscar Bay, some 60 km west of Port Moresby, by London Missionary Society missionaries. In 1873 Moresby found the mission was staffed by South Sea Islanders and was poorly provisioned. In November 1874, the missionary G.W. Lawes settled in what became Port Moresby township (Beale 1974; Lacey 1972; Gibbney 1974a). Consequently, there was an increasing availability of foreign trade goods in the region.

In the 1870s iron quickly became the most desired foreign trade item on the Papuan South Coast to the east of Port Moresby. In April 1876 two missionaries, Lawes and MacFarlane, left Port Moresby to visit the Papuan South Coast as far as China Strait. They had previously travelled as far as Hood Bay. In 1876 MacFarlane, when at Kerepuna, was impressed by the adjustability and durability of stone axes, but what the villagers wanted to acquire from the missionaries was hoop iron. MacFarlane (1877) mentions that hoop iron was sought at Dedele (Cloudy Bay), Toulon Island (Mailu Island), past Dufaure Island (Mugula Island in Orangerie Bay–Mullins Harbour), a bay between Eagle Point and Roux Islands, Leocardie Island (to the east of South Cape), Mekinley Island (a small island in the northern part of China Strait) and Heath Island (Rogeia, an island in the China Straits).

At Leocardie Island for example, some 45 canoes came out to the mission ship, with their occupants clamouring for hoop iron. By then the missionaries' supply of hoop iron was running out and to meet their demands some old metal plates on the *Ellangowan* were cut up. MacFarlane and Lawes concluded that hoop iron was the article in demand and they realised there was no point extending their voyage without it. They recommended anyone wishing to visit these parts should bring a good supply of hoop iron with them as it would allow them to obtain vegetables and also valuable curiosities. They returned to Port Moresby on 22 April 1876 (MacFarlane 1877).

In the 1870s and early 1880s missionaries on the Papuan South Coast soon realised that the only practical way of gaining a foothold was to buy their way in via hoop iron, tomahawks, glass beads and tobacco (Jones 1974:90). As the missionary James Chalmers stated in 1886, 'The gospel of the New Guineans is red beads, tobacco, tomahawks and hoop iron' (Anon. 1886:1). This was the time when villagers were willing to part with prized valuables if they could acquire tomahawks and hoop iron. In the early 1880s a tomahawk/American axe was a prize worth a *Conus* armshell (Finsch 1887:154–155).

Part 3: Who collected the armshells now in museum collections?

Many individuals, including ships' crews, traders, missionaries, visitors, a scientist and government officers made armshells collections in the late nineteenth century, as shown in Table 11.1. This selection includes most of the large collections and covers the period from 1849 to 1900. Information about the places where armshells were collected is known for only a small number of armshells. To find out more about where in Papua New Guinea the objects could have been acquired, it is essential to examine data about collectors, their museum acquisition dates and, if available, when they were collected, together with information about geographic changes in the extent of government control, as well as missionary, commercial and scientific visits to south-east New Guinea. The armshells with known collection locations are listed in Table 11.2.

Table 11.1: *Conus* **collections made before 1900 and location.**

Collector/dealer/year	*Collected*/deposited	Location	Number
1840s			
Captain Owen Stanley	*1849/1851*	British Museum	2
1850s			
Father C. Salerio	*1852–1855*	Civic Museum, Milan	7
1870s			
Captain John Moresby	1875	British Museum	2
Anon.	*1878*	Pitt Rivers Museum	6
Rev. Samuel MacFarlane	1876–1886	British Museum	3
Rev. James Chalmers	*1876–1886*	British Museum	4
Andrew Goldie	1879	Auckland War Memorial Museum	2
1880s			
Rev. William Wyatt Gill	*1882*	British Museum	2
Otto Finsch	*1882*	American Museum of Natural History	2
Mason Brothers	1883	Australian Museum	22
H.J. Renwick	1884	Australian Museum	4
Otto Finsch	*1885*	American Museum of Natural History	2
Captain Hillel F. Liljeblad	1885	Australian Museum	2
Hugh Romilly	1886	British Museum	17
Captain William H. Henderson	1886	British Museum	1
Rev. William Wyatt Gill	1887	Australian Museum	7
Lord and Lady Brassey	*<1889*	Hastings Museum	3
1890s			
Andrew Goldie	*<1890*	Cumbrae Museum, Scotland	1
Sir William MacGregor	1892–1897	Queensland Museum	6
Sir William MacGregor	1892–1897	PNG National Museum and Art Gallery (repatriation from Queensland Museum)	1
Rev. George Brown	*1891–1905*	National Museum of Ethnology (Minpaku), Japan	39
Sir William MacGregor	*<1898*	University of Aberdeen Museum	27
Rev. Samuel B. Fellows	*<1900*	National Gallery of Australia	8
Total armshells			**170**

Source: Authors' summary.

Table 11.2: Provenanced nineteenth-century armshells.

Collector	Location	Armshell	Decoration
	MASSIM		
Captain O. Stanley	Louisiade Archipelago	2 segments	One with shell beads
Father C. Salerio	Woodlark Is	Ring	Holes, shell beads
Father C. Salerio	Woodlark Is	4 rings	None
Father C. Salerio	Woodlark Is	2 segments	None
Otto Finsch	Dinner Is., Samarai	Ring	Holes, banana seed rosette, shell bead inserts, red glass trade beads
Otto Finsch	Duau, Normanby Is.	Ring	Holes, 4 banana seeds, shell bead inserts
Otto Finsch	Teste (Ware) Is.	Ring	Hole
Sir W. MacGregor	Goodenough Is.	2 rings	None
Sir W. MacGregor	Goodenough Is.	Ring	Holes, banana seed rosette, shell bead inserts
George Brown	Dobu Is.	Ring	3 holes
George Brown	Dobu Is.	Ring	Holes, banana seed rosette, shell bead inserts
George Brown	Dobu Is.	Ring	Holes, banana seed rosette, shell bead inserts, 2 strings glass trade beads
George Brown	Dobu Is.	Ring	Holes, banana seed rosette, shell bead inserts, 3 strings glass trade beads, shell pendant
George Brown	Dobu Is.	Ring	Holes, banana seed rosette, shell bead inserts, 7 strings glass trade beads, 2 shell pendants, pandanus streamers
George Brown	Laughlin Is. (Budi Budi)	Segment	Glass trade bead rosette, 3 strings glass trade beads
George Brown	Laughlin Is. (Budi Budi)	Segment	2 glass trade bead rosettes
	PAPUAN SOUTH COAST		
Andrew Goldie	Pure (?Pari), Pt. Moresby	2 rings	Holes, rosette of 8 banana seeds with some shell bead inserts
Otto Finsch	Ihli, Hood Bay	Ring	Holes, rosette of 8 banana seeds
Otto Finsch	Maupa, Aroma	Ring	2 holes
Lord and Lady Brassey	Toulon (Mailu) Is.	Ring	Holes, rosette of banana seeds, shell bead inserts
Sir W. MacGregor	Milport Harbour	Segment	Cross rosette of glass trade beads
Sir W. MacGregor	Milport Harbour	Segment	None
	ORO		
Sir W. MacGregor	Holnicote Bay	2 segments	None

Source: Authors' summary.

Although whalers were active in the Massim from the 1820s to 1870s and are known to have frequently visited Kiriwina and Woodlark Islands (Gray 1989, 1999), we were unable to locate any *Conus* armshells that they collected. The same is true of the later bêche-de-mer traders. Some armshells originally held at the Norwich Castle Museum but transferred to Liverpool in 1965 to replace artefacts destroyed by bombing in 1941 were once thought to predate 1851. Although this date is given in the Norwich object list, it is not correct as Captain T.H. Foster did not deposit his collection at Norwich until 1919 (Macintyre 1983b:82; Marion Servat-Fredericq pers. comm. 2019). Tables 11.3 and 11.4 list the ring and multi-segmented armshells within five time periods, where possible: the 1840s, 1850s, 1870s to 1884, 1885–89 and the 1890s.

Table 11.3: Ring armshells collected in the nineteenth century.

Object	1850s	1870s–84									1885–9					1890s			
	Salerio	Moresby	Anon. Pitt Rivers	MacFarlane	Chalmers	Goldie	Gill	Finsch	Mason Brothers	Renwick	Finsch	Liljeblad	Romilly	Gill	Brassey	MacGregor O	MacGregor A	Brown	Fellows
no holes	4	–	1	–	–	–	–	–	3	–	–	–	6	–	–	–	8	16	2
1 hole	–	–	–	–	–	–	–	–	3	–	1	–	1	–	–	–	–	4	–
2 holes	–	–	–	–	–	–	–	–	2	–	–	–	1	–	–	–	3	–	1
3 holes	–	–	–	–	–	–	1	–	3	–	–	–	–	–	–	–	–	2	1
5 holes	–	–	–	–	–	–	–	–	–	1	–	–	–	–	–	–	–	–	–
broken lateral lip	–	1	–	–	1	–	–	1	1	–	–	–	6	–	–	–	2	8	4
1 short string shell beads	1	–	–	–	–	–	–	–	–	–	–	–	–	–	–	–	–	–	1
rosette 3–8 banana seeds	–	–	–	–	1	–	1	1	1	–	–	–	–	–	–	–	–	–	–
rosette 4 banana seeds fibre inserts	–	–	–	–	–	–	–	–	1	–	–	–	–	–	–	–	–	–	–
rosette 3–4 banana seeds shell bead inserts	–	–	–	–	–	–	–	–	3	–	1	–	–	–	–	–	1	1	–
rosette banana seeds shell bead inserts	–	1	1	–	2	2	–	–	3	–	1	1	2	1	1	1	2	2	3
rosette banana seeds shell bead inserts,1 string shell beads	–	–	–	–	–	–	–	–	2	–	–	–	–	–	–	–	–	–	–
rosette banana seeds shell bead inserts,2 strings shell beads, pendants pearl shell cowrie or *Tridacna* ring	–	–	–	2	–	–	–	–	–	–	–	–	2	–	–	–	–	–	–
rosette banana seeds shell bead inserts, 3 shell bead strings	–	–	–	1	–	–	–	–	–	–	–	–	–	–	–	–	–	–	–
rosette banana seeds shell bead inserts, 3 shell bead strings, pendants banana seed pearl shell	–	–	–	–	–	–	–	–	–	–	–	–	–	–	–	1	–	–	–
rosette shell beads, 3 shell bead strings, pendant banana seeds	–	–	1	–	–	–	–	–	–	–	–	–	–	–	–	–	–	–	–
BELOW: GLASS TRADE BEADS PRESENT																			
rosette banana seeds, shell beads and glass red trade beads	–	–	–	–	–	–	–	–	–	–	1	–	–	–	–	–	–	–	–
rosette banana seeds, 1 string red glass trade beads, pendant banana seeds	–	–	–	–	–	–	–	–	–	–	–	–	–	1	–	–	–	–	–
rosette banana seeds, 1 string glass trade beads	–	–	–	–	–	–	–	–	–	–	–	–	–	1	–	–	–	–	–
rosette banana seeds shell bead inserts, 1 string glass trade beads	–	–	–	–	–	–	–	–	–	–	–	–	–	–	–	–	1	–	–

Object	Date range: 1850s	1870s–84									1885–9				1890s				
	Salerio	Moresby	Anon. Pitt Rivers	MacFarlane	Chalmers	Goldie	Gill	Finsch	Mason Brothers	Renwick	Finsch	Liljeblad	Romilly	Gill	Brassey	MacGregor O	MacGregor A	Brown	Fellows
rosette banana seeds, shell bead inserts, 1 string shell beads, 1 string red glass trade beads, pendants cowrie or *Tridacna* ring	–	–	–	–	–	–	–	–	–	–	–	–	–	1	–	–	–	–	–
rosette banana seeds, 2 strings glass trade beads, pandanus streamer	–	–	–	–	–	–	–	–	–	–	–	–	–	–	–	–	2	–	–
rosette banana seed shell bead inserts, 2 strings glass trade beads	–	–	–	–	–	–	–	–	–	–	–	–	–	–	–	–	–	1	1
rosette banana seed shell inserts, 3 strings glass trade beads, pendants pearl shell	–	–	–	–	–	–	–	–	–	–	–	–	–	–	–	–	1	–	–
rosette banana seeds, shell bead inserts, red trade beads, 3 strings red glass trade beads, pendants banana seeds, pandanus streamer	–	–	–	–	–	–	–	–	–	–	–	–	–	1	–	–	1	–	–
rosette banana seeds, 4 strings glass trade beads, pendant banana seeds and/or pandanus streamer	–	–	–	–	–	–	–	–	–	–	–	–	–	–	–	–	2	–	–
rosette banana seeds shell bead inserts, 4 strings glass trade beads, pendants 3 shells	–	–	–	–	–	–	–	–	–	–	–	–	–	–	–	–	1	–	–
rosette banana seeds shell bead inserts, 5 strings glass trade beads, pendants 3 shells	–	–	–	–	–	–	–	–	–	–	–	–	–	–	–	–	1	–	–
rosette banana seeds shell bead inserts, 7 strings glass trade beads, pendants 2 shells, pandanus streamer	–	–	–	–	–	–	–	–	–	–	–	–	–	–	–	–	1	–	–
rosette banana seeds and trade beads, 8 strings glass trade beads, pendants pearl shell, pandanus steamers	–	–	–	–	–	–	–	–	–	–	–	–	–	–	–	–	–	1	–
1 string red glass trade beads, pendants banana seeds, pandanus streamer	–	–	–	–	–	–	–	–	–	–	–	–	–	1	–	–	–	–	–

Source: Authors' summary.

Table 11.4: Multi-segment armshells collected in the nineteenth century.

Object	1840s Stanley	1850s Salerio	1870-84 Anon. (Pitt Rivers)	1870-84 Renwick	1885-90 Henderson	1885-90 Romilly	1890s MacGregor O	1890s MacGregor P	Brown
3–4 segments	2	2	3	1	–	–	3		–
3 segments, cross rosette, shell beads, banana seed	–	–	–	2		–	–	–	–
3 segments, rosette shell bead, 3 shell bead strings, pendants, banana seeds, pandanus	–	–	–	–	1	–	–	–	–
BELOW: GLASS TRADE BEADS PRESENT	–	–	–	–	–	–	–	–	–
3 segments, rosettes red glass trade beads, 4 strings trade beads	–	–	–	–	–	–	–	–	2
4 segments, rosettes red glass trade beads, 3 strings glass trade beads	–	–	–	–	–	–	–	–	1
4 segments, 7 strings glass trade beads, pendants, shell, banana seeds with inserted shell beads	–	–	–	–	–	–	–	1	–
2 segments, 1 string red and blue glass trade beads	–	–	–	–	–	1	–	–	–
2 segments, cross rosette blue glass trade beads	–	–	–	–	–	–	1	–	–

Source: Authors' summary.

Part 4: Acquisition agencies

Conus armbands were mainly acquired on the Papuan South Coast in exchange for highly desirable iron objects prior to 1884; whereas in the Massim iron was initially important, but most large armshell collections were obtained there after 1891 in return for some service (Swadling et al. 2022). It is now useful to look more carefully at the people who obtained the artefacts and deposited them in museums.

Ships' crews

In 1849, on 28 August, men and women from Brumer Island came onboard HMS *Rattlesnake* wearing *Conus* armshells. Brumer Island is located just east of Suau Island near the eastern tip of New Guinea (Macgillivray 1852). The villagers danced for the crew. Oswald Brierly, the marine artist on board, recorded the scene (Figure 11.4). On this voyage, two small three-segment armshells were collected in the Louisiade Archipelago, one of which is decorated with some shell beads. They were donated to the British Museum by Captain Owen Stanley in 1851.

Two armshells were collected by Captain Moresby during his Admiralty surveys in south-east New Guinea in 1873–4. During his 1873 voyage, Moresby sought to find a safe passage to China via the eastern tip. Finding a safe passage would mean that ships would no longer have to sail to the east of Rossel Island to avoid the Barrier Reef (Beale 1974). Moresby did not record where he collected the two armshells, but one likely place is at the anchorage he called Hoop Iron Bay on Basilaki, or Moresby Island, one of the islands off the eastern tip of New Guinea. Armshells in the Pitt Rivers Museum collection deposited before 1885 were probably collected by crew during early Admiralty voyages to eastern New Guinea.

Theodore Bevan, who was a bêche-de-mer trader on the south-east coast from 1884 to 1888, observed that naval officers bought curios and also allowed their crews to barter for curios (Bevan 1890:95, 132). Captains W.H. Henderson, H.F. Liljeblad and J.T. Bebrouth deposited armshells in museums. Henderson RN was the Commander of HMS *Nelson* and was in New Guinea for about five weeks during the proclamation of the British New Guinea protectorate in 1884 (Chalmers 1887:81). The *Nelson* was the flagship carrying Commodore Erskine who was responsible for the proclamation. In this task he was assisted by the missionary James Chalmers. The proclamation in the Massim was declared at the London Missionary Society Stations, located at Diner Island (Samarai), Teste (Ware Island) and the Killerton Islands near East Cape (Lyne 1885).

It is likely that Henderson collected the *Mwali* he deposited at the British Museum at the Killerton Islands as the people at East Cape participated in such exchanges. Although Malinowski (1922:82) considered Samarai (one of the East End Islands) and Ware to be within the *Kula* ring, we have been unable to find any *Conus* armshells from these localities configured as *Mwali*. Their characteristic decoration consists of rosettes made of banana seeds with shell bead inserts. Captain Liljeblad is reported as having been familiar with the Papuan coast (Edelfeld 1887:127). He deposited two *Conus* armshells in the Australian Museum in 1885. Both armshells are decorated with banana seeds with shell bead inserts and have maximum external diameters of 81 and 83 mm respectively. Captain J.T. Bebrouth worked for Burns Philp and deposited a Massim-style armshell at the Queensland Museum in ca 1887. It has not been located in the collection (Susan Davies pers. comm. 2019) and is therefore not listed in Table 11.1.

Ships' crews probably acquired curios to earn extra income, once sold to artefact dealers in ports such as Sydney and Brisbane. The oldest material from New Guinea at the Queensland Museum consists of a Papuan tomahawk, as well as an axe, bow and paddle donated by Edmund Connor, a naval officer, in April 1874 (Susan Davies pers. comm. 2019). H.J. Renwick, who may have been a naval officer, deposited four armshells at the Australian Museum in 1884. In 1881 A. and H.J. Renwick donated other artefacts from the Papuan South Coast and other South Sea Islands to the Australian Museum. In 1885, when Lindt visited KapaKapa village, east of Port Moresby, he observed that villagers wanted a good tomahawk in exchange for their stone axe or club. The value of curios on the Papuan South Coast had been enhanced by the high demand resulting from the large number of Admiralty vessels visiting during the 1884 proclamation of British New Guinea. When ships were in sight prices inflated, and declined once they had departed (Lindt 1887:60, 68).

Traders

Lyne (1885:198) observed in his account of the 1884 proclamation of British New Guinea that there was currently little interaction between the people of the Massim and Europeans. His observation suggests that the armshells collected by traders prior to 1885 probably came from the Papuan South Coast and no further into the Massim than East Cape and Ware Island. Andrew Goldie, a major trader based in Port Moresby, had not extended his activities to East Cape until 1879 (Davies 2012:136). In 1886 the shipping company Burns Philp began running a monthly steamer service from Thursday Island to Port Moresby and would go along the Papuan South Coast, and if required went as far as East Cape (Douglas and Burns 1887:12).

Mason Brothers were artefact dealers in Sydney, and in 1883 the Australian Museum purchased a collection of 22 armshells from them. These artefacts would have been purchased from ships' crews, travellers and missionaries, as well as traders, including Andrew Goldie. The Mason Brothers collection of 22 armshells has seven armshells with rosettes of banana seeds and shell bead inserts.

The large armshell with the broken lip and those with single strings of red beads are likely to have been obtained or to have originated from the Massim, whether this was by traditional trade or through foreign collectors is not known. Table 11.5 has the maximum external diameters for this collection.

Table 11.5: The Mason Brothers collection acquired by the Australian Museum in 1883 (measurement external diameter).

mm	70–74	75–79	80–84	85–89	90–94	95–99	100+
no holes	2	–	1	–	–	–	–
1 hole	2	1	–	–	–	–	–
2 holes	–	–	1	–	1	–	–
3 holes	–	1	2	–	–	–	–
broken lateral lip	–	–	–	–	–	–	1
4 banana seeds with fibre inserts	–	–	1	1	–	–	–
5 banana seeds	1	–	–	–	–	–	–
3 banana seeds shell bead inserts	–	1	1	–	–	–	–
rosette banana seeds shell bead inserts	–	–	2	1	–	–	–
rosette banana seeds shell bead inserts, 1 string shell beads	–	–	–	–	–	2	–

Source: Authors' summary.

The trader Andrew Goldie arrived in Port Moresby in 1876, and it is likely that six of the eight armshells he acquired in 1878–79 were *Toea* as he notes that these were used by locals for purchasing their wives. Goldie's museum and exhibition consignments were all made by 1880, apart from one armshell in his personal collection that he took to Scotland (Table 11.6). While Mason Brothers were Goldie's agents, there is no evidence that the collection purchased by the Australian Museum was Goldie's 1880 offer to the museum (Davies 2012:148). Four wrist ornaments from Aroma were initially thought to be armshells but are likely to be coix-seed armlets and are not included in Table 11.6 (Davies 2012:157–161; Susan Davies pers. com. 2020). The Auckland War Memorial Museum has two armshells from Port Moresby. They feature in the museum's online catalogue, Nos. 11420 and 11421; see Figure 11.3b for 11421. This armshell was acquired by Andrew Goldie at Pure (possibly 'Pari'), Port Moresby in 1879. It is decorated with eight banana seeds, with one white and four red shell bead inserts, and has an external diameter of 80 mm.

Table 11.6: The armshell consignments made by Andrew Goldie to museums and to the organisers of the Sydney International Exhibition.

Museum	date	number	offered	acquired	shown
Australian	1878	2	–	x	–
Auckland War Memorial	1879	2	–	x	–
Sydney International Exhibition	1879	4	–	–	x
Australian (January)	1880	36	x	–	–
Australian (August)	1880	6*	x	–	–
Australian (August)	1880	9*	x	–	–
Australian (August)	1880	9*	x	–	–
Queensland	1880	1	–	x	–
Cumbraes, Millport, Scotland (pers. coll.)	before 1890	1	–	x	–

* may be from different areas as listed separately in the same consignment.

Source: Authors' summary.

When Goldie returned to Scotland in 1890, he took back a collection of artefacts which his descendants later deposited at the Cumbraes Museum in Millport. These were all good examples with one exception, an armshell with a broken lip (Davies 2012:163). His consignment records and inability to acquire a better example to take to Scotland suggests that these artefacts ceased to be easily acquired after 1880 in the Port Moresby region. The two armshells (*Toea*) held in the Auckland War Memorial Museum are the only nineteenth-century armshells clearly provenanced to Port Moresby. Otto Finsch's example was acquired in Hood Bay in 1882. The Hood Bay armshell with its rosette of eight banana seeds was considered by Finsch to be an exceptionally good *Toea*. Similar examples with rosettes of three to five banana seeds were collected by the missionaries Chalmers and Gill and there is also an example in the Mason Brothers collection (see Table 11.3). The inserting of red fibre into an armshell, which is decorated with four banana seeds, may have substituted for the shortage in shell beads (Figure 11.3c).

Lord and Lady Brassey made a round-the-world trip in their yacht and were in the Cape York–Torres Strait area in August 1887, but did not sail along the Papuan South Coast. It is not known where they acquired the two armshells labelled from Toulon Island (Mailu) and a *Mwali*-configured armshell, now held in the Hastings Museum (Sarah French pers. comm. 2019). One of the armshells from Mailu is damaged, in that there is a lot of fine cord extending from the rosette of banana seeds. This may indicate that the shell beads that had once been inserted have been removed. This armshell has not been included in Table 11.5.

Scientists

Otto Finsch was interested in ethnology and ornithology. When travelling along the Papuan South Coast in 1882 he collected two armshells in what is now Central Province. One was obtained in Hood Bay and the other at Maupa in Aroma. Both are held at the American Museum of Natural History. In 1884 Finsch was involved in reconnaissance voyages on the steamer *Samoa*. These led to the declaration of northeast New Guinea and the Bismarck Archipelago as a German protectorate in November 1884 (Howes 2018). On a voyage on the *Samoa* in 1885, Finsch visited parts of British New Guinea. These included the Trobriands, Normanby, Fergusson and Killerton (East Cape) islands, Milne Bay, Diner (Samarai) and Teste (Ware) islands, as well as East Cape to the German border. Finsch collected two armshells from the Massim, which are now in the American Museum of Natural History. One is from Dinner Island (Samarai) and the other is from Duau (Normanby Island) (Finsch 1888). Another armshell from Teste/Tschas (Ware Island) is mentioned in his collection notes, held by the American Museum of Natural History.

Missionaries

The Italian missionaries, who replaced the French Marists on Woodlark Island in 1852, made a small collection of armshells (Table 11.7). After the mission was abandoned in 1855 these armshells and other artefacts were deposited at the Civic Museum in Milan. They were displayed in 1863, but unfortunately were destroyed in 1943 during World War II (Affleck 1981; Salerio et al. 1983).

Table 11.7: List of armshells collected on Woodlark by the Italian missionaries.

Cat. No.	Description
198	Bracelet of white shell, highly valued for its size and for being adorned with red rings made from shell. Used in trade exchange, Woodlark, etc.
199	2 small armshells of less value on account of being composed of various pieces. Used by women of Woodlark. (One sent to Pigorini in exchange for reptiles 5/1880.)
209	2 white bracelets used in Woodlark and on the islands to the west.
210	2 others, similar but smaller.

Source: Authors' summary.

MacFarlane and James Chalmers, both members of the London Missionary Society, visited south-eastern New Guinea in 1876. McFarlane landed two Loyalty Islands teachers at Teste (Ware) Island and others at East Cape. Chalmers arrived on the south-east mainland near Suau Island with two Rarotongan teachers (Wetherell 1988). These visits and subsequent follow-up visits would have provided both men with opportunities to acquire armshells. Those acquired by MacFarlane are decorated with banana seeds with inserted shell beads and strings of shell beads, with some of the strings having pendants, whereas those collected by Chalmers are not elaborate *Kula* artefacts but consist of two armshells with banana seeds that have inserted shell beads, an armshell with just banana seeds and another with the notches of drill holes on its broken front edge. MacFarlane's sale of his armshells in London in 1886 is explained by his retiring from mission work in New Guinea that year (Gibbney 1974b). The collection made by Chalmers is also likely to predate 1886 as by this time he had shifted his missionary activities to areas west of Port Moresby (Lacey 1972:151).

Another missionary, W. Wyatt Gill, who travelled with Chalmers to Suau in 1882, had acquired similar armshells. One has banana seeds with inserted shell beads and the other has drilled holes but no decoration. The difference in decoration between the armshells collected by MacFarlane compared to those of Chalmers and Gill is because East Cape is within the *Kula* exchange network, whereas Suau on the Papuan South Coast lies outside it. In the 1880s missionary activity expanded on the Papuan South Coast, but it was not until 1891, through the auspices of Sir William MacGregor, that George Brown, as the General Secretary of the Methodist Australasian Missions, was able to establish Dobu and the other Methodist missions in the Massim. Based in Sydney, Brown made five visits to the Massim. The first was a reconnaissance trip in 1890 to select the first mission site, the second in 1891 to establish the founding mission station at Dobu under W.E. Bromilow. Brown's third visit was in 1897; two others followed, the last in 1905 (Brown 1908; MacGregor 1893).

The only provenanced armshells in Brown's large collection come from Dobu and the Laughlan Islands (Budi Budi). The only time he visited the Laughlan Islands was on his first reconnaissance trip. It is likely that most of the armshells in his collection were acquired by mission staff on his behalf and were given by villagers in payment for some service. Brown's collection is now held at the National Museum of Ethnography in Osaka. Fellows established the first mission in the Trobriands at Kiriwina in 1894. The large collection he made demonstrates both an interest in artefacts, as well as the strong personal ties that he had with his parishioners. It is recorded that Fellows was gifted armshells as a service payment for his role in peacemaking. A comprehensive part of his collection was gifted to his friend Sir William MacGregor, who deposited it at the University of Aberdeen Museum in 1899 (see Swadling et al. 2022). When he retired, Fellows took the remainder of his collection to Australia where it was later deposited at the National Gallery of Australia.

Government officers

Hugh Hastings Romilly came to the western Pacific as a British roving Deputy Commissioner and made his first cruise to New Guinea in 1881. At various times between 1884 and 1886 he held the post of Administrator of British New Guinea. In 1886 when on sick leave he supervised the New Guinea exhibits for the Colonial and Indian Exhibition in London (Langdon 1976). Sir William MacGregor was in British New Guinea from 1888 to 1898, initially as Administrator and later as Lieutenant-Governor. During his tenure, MacGregor formed strong relationships with other Europeans in British New Guinea. The largest armshell in MacGregor's official collection was obtained through a government officer, C.A.W. Monckton, who had established a friendship with a prestigious leader (*bigman*) on Goodenough Island (Monckton 1921:36–37). MacGregor acquired some lower-grade armshells during his official travel. As noted above, the comprehensive collection of armshells he deposited at Aberdeen was a gift to MacGregor from Fellows, the first missionary in the Trobriand Islands (Swadling et al. 2022).

Part 5: Geographic variation in armshell decoration

The demise of shell bead production in the Port Moresby region impacted armshell decoration (Swadling and Bence 2016). In 1879 Goldie collected two armshells that are decorated with banana seed rosettes, but only some of the seeds have shell bead inserts. The armshell Finsch collected in 1882 only has a banana seed rosette but lacks shell bead inserts. Other unprovenanced armshells collected in the 1870s and early 1880s also have banana seeds rosettes which lack shell bead inserts.

The armshell from Toulon (Mailu) Island in the Brassey collection shows that armshells made there in the nineteenth century were decorated with rosettes of banana seeds with shell bead inserts. The same decoration was documented in the 1920s by Malinowski (1988) and Saville (1926). The same decoration of a rosette of banana seeds with shell bead inserts is also found in the *Kula* region, and is also part of a *Mwali*, see Table 11.3. Although Ware and the islands of Samarai to Basilaki, off the eastern tip of New Guinea, were recognised by Malinowski (1922) to be in the *Kula* network, these islands have not yielded armshells configured as *Mwali*, either in publications or museum collections. Instead, they are comparable to those at Mailu.

The oldest *Mwali* in museum collections are likely to have been acquired from East Cape where they would have been exchanged with villagers from Duau (southern and Eastern Normanby) and Tubetube (Figure 11.5d). These ring and multi-segment armshells lack banana seeds and instead are decorated with shell bead rosettes. Many of the shell bead rosettes are arranged in a cross formation. Shell beads would have been plentiful in the East Cape, Duau and Tubetube area as Ware islanders brought *Bagi* (shell beads) from the Louisiades to this region (Lepowsky 1983:474–475). Banana seeds are imports in some parts of the Massim. In the early twentieth century, Amphlett Islanders obtained them on Fergusson Island and traded them to the Trobriands (Malinowski 1922:287).

Conus shells were fished by people in the Kayleula (Keileuna) and Kavataria districts in the Trobriands and made into finished armshells elsewhere. Those from Kavataria were polished before they were taken to Dobu, whereas the Kayleula gave two shaped but unpolished shells as a *Kula* gift to the Amphlett Islanders. There they were polished and taken as *Kula* gifts to Dobu. The Dobuan recipients of armshells from the Trobriands and Amphletts then bored the holes for attaching banana seeds and shell beads, and thus the *Kula* valuables were configured as *Mwali*. (Malinowski 1922:502–503). When the pearl boom began in the Trobriand Islands in 1892, large quantities of glass trade beads became available to decorate *Mwali* (Swadling et al. 2022). Tables 11.3 and 11.4 indicate that it was not until the mid-1880s that glass trade beads were first used to decorate armshells, and by the 1890s they were widely used. The earliest use of glass trade beads is the armshell Finsch collected at Samarai in 1885, which has a rosette of banana seeds with inserted shell beads, with red glass trade beads strung across the rosette.

Conclusion: Trading armshells to foreigners and Papuan social connections

Foreign economic activity began in the Massim in the 1820s but large armshell collections were not made until Methodist missionaries did so in the 1890s. These armshells were not acquired in return for iron implements, but as payment for providing some service. Prior to that period, only small numbers had been collected by a Catholic missionary on Woodlark Island in the 1850s, the crew of British Admiralty ships in 1849 and by 1875, by London Missionary Society missionaries at East Cape and Ware Island in the 1870s, and a scientist in the 1880s.

By contrast, on the Papuan South Coast trading armshells to foreigners began with the arrival of missionaries and traders in the 1870s. In due course these agencies expanded their activities along the coast. By 1884 London Missionary society missionaries had established a bridgehead in the Massim as far as East Cape and Ware Island. They brought iron, which was keenly sought by villagers who were initially willing to trade their armshell valuables for this new commodity. Within a decade the cultural value of armshells increased, especially for those Papuans who lived far from where most *Conus literatus* and *C. leopardus* are fished and produced into armshells. When increasing numbers of armshells were required for economic and social activities in the early 1880s, the Motu ceased to trade armshells for foreign commodities. For them the cultural value of armshells had become higher than any foreign trade good.

The people living in the Massim and on the Papuan South Coast share a related cultural heritage. This is evident not only from the pottery styles they share, such as between Mailu on the Papuan South Coast and Tubetube Island in the Massim (Shaw et al. 2021), but also by the comparable armshell decoration that was used in the late nineteenth and early twentieth centuries along much of the eastern Papuan South Coast and in the Massim. This shared heritage was recognised by the government of Papua New Guinea when a currency denomination was named after a Papuan South Coast *Conus* armshell (the *Toea*) and the drawing of a Massim armshell was placed on the two-kina banknote.

Acknowledgements

We wish to thank Jim Allen, Chris Ballard, Faye Belsey; Harry Beran; Lissant Bolton, Hannah Clarke; Susan Davies; Sarah French; Emma Gray; Robin Hide; Crispen Howarth; Peter Matthews; Christopher Morton; Fuli Pereira; Zoë Richardson, Marion Servat-Fredericq; Ben Shaw, Jim Specht; Glenn Summerhayes, Deveni Temu and Peter White for useful comments and information. We also thank Martha Macintyre and Ian McNiven for their constructive review comments.

References

Affleck, D. 1971. Murua or Woodlark Island: A study of European–Muruan contact to 1942. Unpublished BA (Hons) thesis. The Australian National University, Canberra.

Affleck, D. 1981. Catalogue of the Civic Museum collection Milan, Italy (Displayed in 1863 … destroyed in 1943). A translation of the descriptions given to those items which originate from within or close to the Kula area. Paper presented at the 1981 Kula Conference, Charlottesville, Virginia.

Anon. 1839. *The nautical magazine* (London):37–39 (cited by Wisse 2018:57).

Anon. 1851. *The shipping gazette and Sydney general trade list* (NSW), Saturday 9 August 1851:231.

Anon. 1886. Report of an interview with the Rev. James Chalmers. *Pall Mall Gazette*, 30 September 1886:1.

Anon. 1966. Article in *The Daily Mercury*, New Bedford, Mass., March 10. In R. Gerard Ward (ed.), *American activities in the central Pacific, 1790–1870: A history, geography, and ethnography pertaining to American involvement and Americans in the Pacific taken from contemporary newspapers etc*. Vol. 7, pp. 507–509. Gregg Press, Ridgewood, NJ (cited by Wisse 2018:55).

Anon. 2020. Currency. Bank of Papua New Guinea. www.bankpng.gov.pg/payment-system/currency.

Armstrong, W.E. 1928. *Rossel Island: An ethnological study*. Cambridge University Press, Cambridge.

Barton, F.R. 1904. Report on Central Division British New Guinea, and the addendum to the report. *Annual Report of British New Guinea for 1902–03*:16–20.

Barton, F.R. 1910. The annual trading expedition to the Papuan Gulf. In C.G. Seligman (ed.), *The Melanesians of British New Guinea*, pp. 96–120. Cambridge University Press, Cambridge.

Beale, H. 1974. Moresby, J. (1830–1922), admiral, hydrographer and explorer. *Australian Dictionary of Biography* 5:285–287.

Belshaw, C.S. 1955. *In search of wealth: A study of the emergence of commercial operations in the Melanesian society of southeastern Papua*. American Anthropological Association Memoirs, No. 80. Menasha, Wisconsin.

Bevan, T.F. 1890. *British New Guinea from the protectorate to the sovereignty, 1884–1888: Toil, travel and discovery in British New Guinea*. Kegan Paul, London.

Bickler, S.H. 1998. Eating stone and dying: Archaeological survey on Woodlark Island, Milne Bay Province, Papua New Guinea. Unpublished PhD thesis. University of Virginia, Madison.

Bickler, S.H. and M. Turner 2002. Food to stone: Investigations at the Suloga adze manufacturing sites, Woodlark Island, Papua New Guinea. *The Journal of the Polynesian Society* 5(2):28–91. www.jstor.org/stable/20707040.

Brown, G. 1908. *Pioneer-missionary and explorer: An autobiography*. Charles Kelly, London.

Campbell, S.F. 1983. Attaining rank: A classification of shell valuables. In J.W. Leach and E. Leach (eds), *The Kula: New perspectives on Massim exchange*, pp. 229–248. Cambridge University Press, Cambridge.

Cernohorsky, W.O. 1978. *Tropical Pacific marine shells*. Pacific Publications, Sydney.

Chalmers, J. 1887. Explorations in south-eastern New Guinea: Discussion. *Royal Geographical Society, London, Proceedings*, (new series) 9:71–86. www.jstor.org/stable/1800803.

D'Albertis, L.M. 1877. *Journal of the Expedition for the Exploration of the Fly River*. Frederick, Sydney.

Damon, F. 1980. The Kula and generalised exchange: Considering some unconsidered aspects of the elementary structures of Kinship. *Man* 15(2):267–292. doi.org/10.2307/2801671.

Damon, F. 1983. On the transformation of Muyuw into Woodlark Island: Two minutes in December, 1974. *The Journal of Pacific History* 18(1):35–56. doi.org/10.1080/00223348308572457.

Davies, S. 2012. Andrew Goldie: His ethnological collecting and collections. *Memoirs of the Queensland Museum – Culture* 6: 29–161. search.informit.org/doi/10.3316/INFORMIT.213648204461397.

Douglas, J. and J. Burns 1887. *British New Guinea annual report* for 1886. Memorandum of Agreement. Appendix A:12–3.

Edelfeld, E.G. 1887. Travels in the neighbourhood of Mount Yule. In J.W. Lindt, *Picturesque New Guinea, with an historical introduction and supplementary chapters on the manners and customs of the Papuans*, pp. 126–134. Longman Green and Co, London.

Finsch, O. 1887. Abnorme Eberhauer, Pretiosen im Schmuck der Südsee-Völker. *Mitteilungen der Anthropologischen Gesellschaft in Wein* 17:153–159, Tafel VI.

Finsch, O. 1888. *Samoafahrten. Reisen in Kaiser Wilhelms-Land und Englisch-Neu-Guinea in den Jahren 1884 und 1885 an Bord des Deutschen Dampfers Samoa*. Ferdinand Hirt and Sohn, Leipzig.

Gibbney, H.J. 1974a. Lawes, William George (1839–1907). *Australian Dictionary of Biography*, National Centre of Biography, The Australian National University. adb.anu.edu.au/biography/lawes-william-george-3999/text6329, published first in hardcopy 1974, accessed online 12 June 2020.

Gibbney, H.J. 1974b. Macfarlane, Samuel (1837–1911). *Australian Dictionary of Biography*, National Centre of Biography, The Australian National University. adb.anu.edu.au/biography/macfarlane-samuel-4090/text6535, published first in hardcopy 1974, accessed online 31 May 2020.

Gray, A.C. 1989. From windfall to copra: Trading contacts in the Bismarck Archipelago during the whaling era, 1799–1884. Unpublished BA (Hons) thesis. University of Otago, Dunedin.

Gray, A.C. 1999. Trading contacts in the Bismarck Archipelago during the whaling era, 1799–1884. *The Journal of Pacific History* 34(1):23–43. doi.org/10.1080/00223349908572889.

Howes, H. 2018. A 'perceptive observer' in the Pacific: Life and work of Otto Finsch. In *BEROSE – International Encyclopaedia of the Histories of Anthropology*, IIAC-LAHIC, Paris. www.berose.fr/article1468.html.

Hunter, R.L. 1839. Gower's Harbour New Ireland. *Nautical Magazine and Naval Chronicle* 8:37–39.

Jones, A. 1974. Hula since 1850: A social history of a Papua New Guinea village. Unpublished MA thesis. College of Advanced Education, Salisbury.

Lacey, R.J. 1972. Missions. In *Encyclopaedia of Papua New Guinea*, vol. 2, pp. 773–782. Melbourne University Press, Melbourne.

Langdon, R. 1976. Romilly, Hugh Hasting (1856–1892). *Australian Dictionary of Biography*, National Centre of Biography, The Australian National University, Canberra. adb.anu.edu.au/biography/romilly-hugh-hastings-4502/text7361, published in hardcopy 1976, accessed online 6 July 2014.

Langley, M.C., S. Bedford, M. Spriggs and I. Phillip 2019. Manufacture and use of Lapita *Conus* multi-segment broad rings: Evidence from the Teouma site, Central Vanuatu. *The Journal of Island and Coastal Archaeology* 15(3):364–383. doi.org/10.1080/15564894.2019.1570989.

Laracy, H. 2010. Of missionaries and mariners: Marists, Milanese and the vicariate of Melanesia, 1845–1859. *Forum Novum* Dec 12:132–152.

Lepowsky, M. 1983. Sudest Island the Louisiade archipelago in Massim exchange. In J.W. Leach and E. Leach (eds), *The Kula: New perspectives on Massim exchange*, pp. 467–501. Cambridge University Press, Cambridge.

Liep, J. 2009. *A Papuan plutocracy: Ranked exchange on Rossel Island*. Aarhus University, Aarhus.

Liep, J. and D. Affleck 1983. 'This civilizing influence': The colonial transformation of Rossel Island society. *The Journal of Pacific History* 18(2):113–133. doi.org/10.1080/00223348308572462.

Lindt, J.W. 1887. *Picturesque New Guinea*. Longmans, London.

Lyne, C. 1885. *New Guinea: An account of the establishment of the British Protectorate over the southern shores of New Guinea*. Samson Low, London.

MacFarlane, S. 1877. Voyage of the *Ellangowan* to China Straits, New Guinea. *Proceedings of the Royal Geographical Society of London* 21(4):350–360. doi.org/10.2307/1799963.

Macgillivray, J. 1852. *Voyage of HMS* Rattlesnake, vol. 1. T. and W. Boone, London.

MacGregor, W.M. 1893. Despatch reporting visits to the D'Entrecasteaux and Trobriand Groups. *Annual Report British New Guinea*, July 1891 to June 1892, Appendix A:1–7.

Macintyre, M. 1983a. Changing paths: An historical ethnography of the traders of Tubetube. Unpublished PhD thesis. The Australian National University, Canberra.

Macintyre, M. 1983b. *The Kula: A bibliography*. Cambridge University Press, Cambridge.

Malinowski, B. 1922. *Argonauts of the Western Pacific*. Routledge and Kegan Paul, London.

Malinowski, B. 1988. *Malinowski among the Magi: The natives of Mailu*. Edited by M.W. Young. Routledge, London.

Mira, W.J.D. 1986. *From cowrie to kina: The coinages, currencies, badges, medals, awards and decorations of Papua New Guinea*. Spink and Son, Sydney.

Monckton, C.A.W. 1921. *Some experiences of a New Guinea Resident Magistrate*. John Lane, London.

Moore, C. 1991. The life and death of William Bairstow Ingham: Papua New Guinea in the 1870s. *Journal of the Royal Historical Society of Queensland* 14(10):414–432. doi.org/10.2307/j.ctvsrfkh.

Moore, C. 2003. *New Guinea: Crossing boundaries and history*. University of Hawai'i Press, Honolulu.

Moresby, J. 1875. Recent discoveries in the South-Eastern part of New Guinea. *Proceedings of the Royal Geographical Society of London* 18(1):22–31. doi.org/10.2307/1799800.

Moresby, J. 1876. *Discoveries and surveys in New Guinea and the D'Entrecasteaux Islands*. John Murray, London.

Musgrave, A. 1889. Past and present trade with British New Guinea. In *British New Guinea Annual Report for 1888*:32–37.

Norick, F.A. 1976. An analysis of the material culture of the Trobriand Islands based upon the collection of Bronislaw Malinowski. Unpublished PhD thesis, University of California, Berkeley.

Oram, N. 1982. Pots for sago: The *hiri* trading network. In T. Dutton (ed.), *The* hiri *in history*, pp. 1–33. The Australian National University, Canberra.

Salerio, C., D. Lithgow and D. Affleck 1983. Manuscript XVIII: Information on customs and practices of the people of Woodlark Island. *The Journal of Pacific History* 18(1):57–72. doi.org/10.1080/0022334830 8572458.

Saville, W.J.V. 1926. *In unknown New Guinea*. Seeley Service, London.

Seligman, C.G. 1910. *The Melanesians of British New Guinea*. Cambridge University Press, London.

Shaw, B., S. Coxe, V. Kewibu, J. Haro, E. Hull and S. Hawkins 2020. 2500-year cultural sequence in the Massim region of eastern Papua New Guinea reflects adaptive strategies to small islands and changing climate regimes since Lapita settlement. *The Holocene* 30(7):1075–1090. doi.org/10.1177/095968362 0908641.

Shaw, B., G. Irwin, A. Pengilley and S. Kelloway 2021. Village-specific Kula partnerships revealed by obsidian sourcing on Tubetube Island, Papua New Guinea. *Archaeology in Oceania* 56:32–44. doi.org/10.1002/arco.5224.

Shaw, B. and M.C. Langley 2017. Investigating the development of prehistoric cultural practices in the Massim region of eastern Papua New Guinea: Insights from the manufacture and use of shell objects in the Louisiade Archipelago. *Journal of Anthropological Anthropology* 48:149–165. doi.org/10.1016/j.jaa.2017.07.005.

Stone, O.C. 1879. *A few months in New Guinea*. Franklin Square Library, Number 92. Harper and Brothers, New York.

Swadling, P. and P. Bence 2016. Changes in Kula valuables and related supply linkages between the Massim and the South Papuan Coast between 1855 and 1915. *Archaeology in Oceania* 51, Supplement 1:50–60. doi.org/10.1002/arco.5106.

Swadling, P., R. Torrence, J. Hasell, S. Davies and S. Bickler 2022. *Conus* armshells in British New Guinea: The effects of economic change on cross-cultural engagement. *Memoirs of the Queensland Museum – Culture* 13:309–326.

Turner, W.Y. 1878. The ethnology of the Motu. *The Journal of the Anthropological Institute of Great Britain and Ireland* 7:470–499. doi.org/10.2307/2841436.

Webster, E.M. 1984. *The moon man: A biography of Nikolai Miklouho-Maclay*. Melbourne University Press, Carlton.

Weiner, A. 1988. *The Trobrianders of Papua New Guinea*. Holt, Rinehart and Winston, New York.

Wetherell, D. 1998. First contact mission narratives from Eastern Papua New Guinea. *The Journal of Pacific History* 33(1):111–116. doi.org/10.1080/00223349808572862.

Wisse, D.C.J. 2018. All things Trobriand: A portrait of Dr. G.J.M. (Fred) Gerrits' Trobriand Island collections, 1968 to 1972. Unpublished PhD thesis. University of East Anglia, Norwich.

12

Raided and traded: Sourcing Marind-anim exotic stone objects, south-east Papua (Indonesia)

Ian J. McNiven and Friedrich E. von Gnielinski

Abstract

The Marind-anim of the south-east corner of Papua, Indonesia, live in a stoneless world but venerate stone objects. As expected, stone objects of the Marind, such as axes, club heads and 'spearthrower' attachments, are exotic, with ethnographic information pointing to acquisition through a complex portfolio of trading and raiding (headhunting) relationships with multiple neighbours who had either direct or indirect access to tool stone. Ethnographic and geological information indicates that the two closest sources of tool stone to the Marind are located over 100 km away—the southern flanks of the Central Ranges (especially the Upper Digul River) to the north and Torres Strait to the south-east. These two source options are consistent with our petrographic assessment of a sample of three Marind stone club heads and three 'spearthrower' stones. Beyond ethnographically documented trading and raiding processes of stone implement provisioning, we hypothesise that the Marind may have manufactured their own stone implements by accessing igneous outcrops at Mabaduan on the northern mainland coast of Torres Strait during headhunting expeditions.

Introduction

Chemical fingerprinting and petrographic analysis of raw materials have been fundamental to archaeological understandings of past stone artefact movements and associated exchange networks in New Guinea for half a century (e.g. Gaffney and Summerhayes 2019; Key 1968; McNiven et al. 2004; Mialanes et al. 2016; Rhoads and MacKenzie 1991; Shaw et al. 2021; Summerhayes 2009; Summerhayes et al. 1998; Sutton et al. 2015). For over 30 years, Glenn Summerhayes has had a critical role in innovative methodological and analytical developments in these sourcing studies, particularly in understanding obsidian exchange systems over the past 20,000 years, and especially over the past 3300 years in tandem with sourcing of Lapita and Post-Lapita ceramics (e.g. Summerhayes 2000; Summerhayes and Allen 1993). In marked contrast to the importance of these studies for understanding Papua New Guinea's past, little stone artefact sourcing research has been undertaken across the western half of New Guinea in Indonesian Papua (e.g. Harlow et al. 2012;

Pétrequin and Pétrequin 1993a, 1993b, 2020; Torrence et al. 2009). This chapter provides the first published account of the raw materials and potential geological sources of ground stone implements (club heads and 'spearthrower' attachments) used by the Marind-anim of south-east Papua. These ground stone implements had an exotic origin as the Marind inhabit a stoneless world. Ethnographic records from the early twentieth century invite discussion of the relative roles of headhunting raids and exchange in the provisioning of these exotic objects.

Marind-anim

The Marind-anim are hunter–forager–agriculturalists who inhabit tropical coastal lowlands of the south-east corner of Indonesian Papua (van Baal 1966). Usually, their name is shortened to Marind as *anim* = people/person/human in Marind language (Chao 2021:248; Olsson 2017; Usher and Suter 2015). The territorial domain of the Marind stretches 200 km eastwards along the coast from Selat Muli (Muli Strait, formerly known as Princess Marianne Strait) in the west to 25 km east of Merauke (a town located 100 km along the coast from the Indonesian – Papua New Guinea border). It extends 200 km inland, taking in the drainage basins of the Bian and Kumbe Rivers and the lower reaches of the Merauke (Maro) River (van Baal 1966:10–11; see Figure 12.1). A linguistic division exists between the (inland) Bian Marind (of the upper Bian River) and the Coastal and Central Marind (Olsson 2017:25; Usher and Suter 2015). The stoneless world of the Marind is mostly elevated <40 m above sea level and comprises Quaternary sediments (Reynders 1961; Schroo 1964). Much of this low-lying area was probably inundated following higher sea levels associated with the end of the postglacial sea level rise c. 6000–7000 years ago (Chappell 2005:Fig. 4; see also Dougherty et al. 2019; Woodroffe et al. 2000).

Population estimates of the Marind at the start of the twentieth century and before depopulation (see below) range from c. 15,000 to c. 20,000, divided between the coast (c. 10,000–13,000) and inland (c. 5000–7000) (Kooijman et al. 1958:44–45; see also van Baal 1966:710). In reality, the Marind 'world', especially the region taken in by large-scale headhunting expeditions that could last for months, encompassed a much larger area than the region defined by the extent of the Marind language. As pointed out by Dutch colonial anthropologist Jan van Baal, these 'extra-regional' domains included Yos Sudaro (formerly Frederik Hendrik) Island to the west/south-west, the Digul River to the north/north-west, and the Trans-Fly and northern Torres Strait to the south-east (van Baal 1966:348). These areas had cosmological referents in numerous mythological narratives where the creative activities of *dema* spirit beings extend from the Digul River to the Fly River (van Baal 1966:348).

Sustained colonial occupation and pacification of the Marind commenced in 1902 with the establishment of the Dutch settlement of Merauke on the lower Merauke (Maro) River and the establishment of Okaba in 1908 (Kooijman et al. 1958:103; van Baal 1966:681). Roman Catholic (Sacred Heart) missionaries established major missions at Merauke (1905) and Okaba (1910) (Boelaars 1969; Kooijman et al. 1958:104–105; Steenbrink 2007). Diseases (e.g. donovanosis), influenza epidemics, Dutch government administrative control, and missionisation resulted in radical changes to Marind culture and society (Kooijman et al. 1958:53; Kooijman 1959:19; Richens 2022; van Baal 1966:25–26). In 1962, the peoples of western New Guinea (including the Marind) became part of Indonesia and what are known today as the various provinces of Papua.

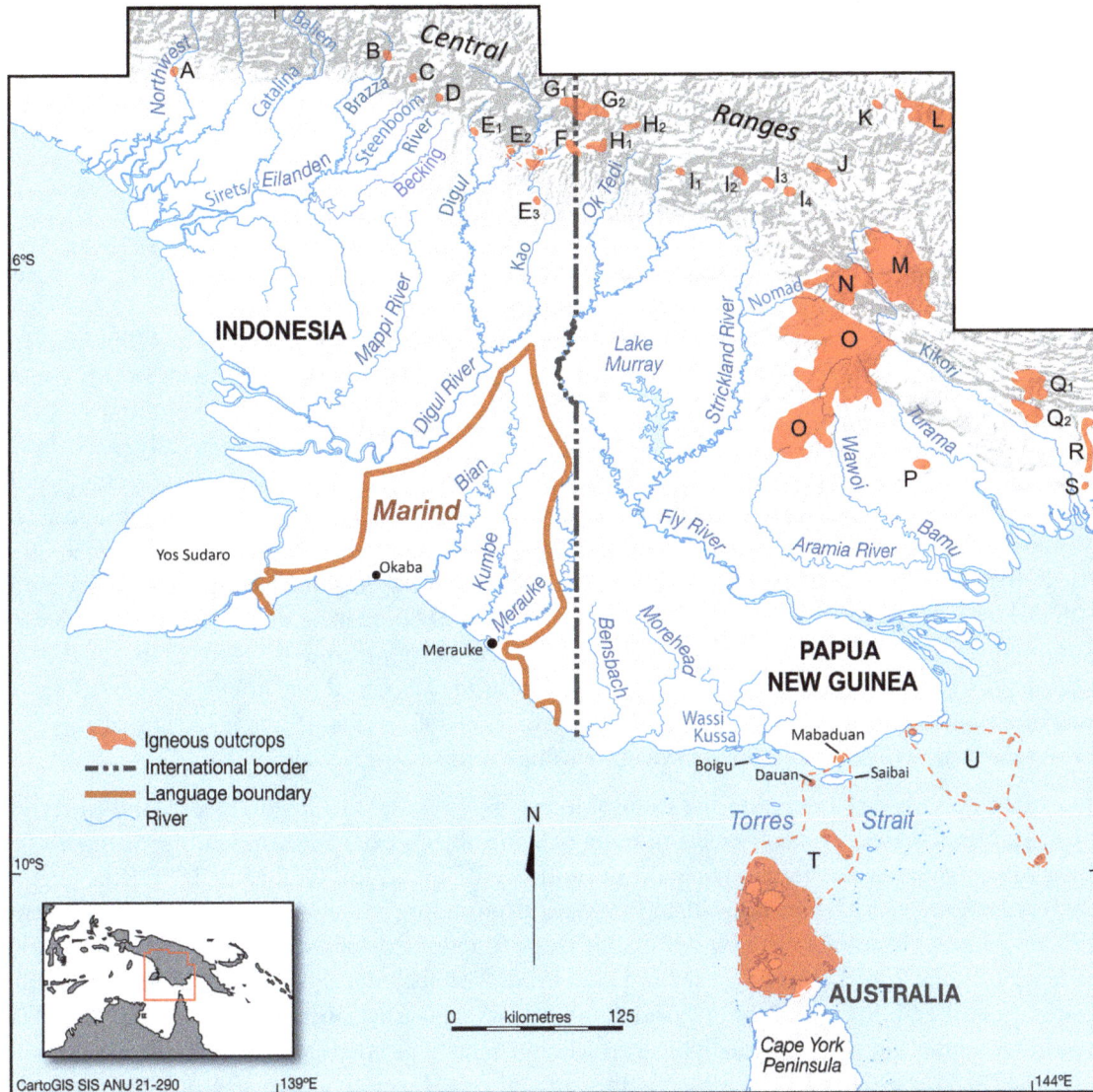

Figure 12.1: Map of central-southern New Guinea showing Marind territory (brown line) and igneous rock outcrops.

Note: For details on igneous rock outcrop locations/zones labelled A to U see Table 12.2.

Sources: After van Baal (1966); Kooijman (1959:12); Voorhoeve (1983); Bain and Haipola (1997); D'Addario et al. (1976); Dow et al. (1986).

Archaeological understandings of the Marind past are essentially non-existent, as they are for most of the southern lowlands of Indonesian Papua (Simanjuntak 1998; Wright et al. 2013). It is likely that archaeological evidence of settlement sites (e.g. villages) is relatively recent and concentrated within fossil beach ridges aligned parallel to the coast (Reynders 1961; see also McNiven 2010). These fossil beach ridges extend up to 100 km inland according to Heldring (1910:Pl. III), and probably track the progressive fall in sea level over the past c. 6000–7000 years (see also Paijmans et al. 1971:67, Fig. 8). Archaeological evidence of older village sites is likely to be found on elevated relict river terraces located further inland (see Visser and Hermes 1962:188). Following Swadling (1983:23–29), the newly formed coastal lowlands of Papua were likely colonised by inland peoples, a hypothesis consistent with genetic evidence for similarities between both regions and an absence of an influx of coastal (Austronesian) peoples (Purnomo et al. 2021; Tommaseo-Ponzetta et al. 2002:59; see also van Baal 1966:944; Djami and Suroto 2023). The Asmat, who occupy lowlands to the north-west, hold a myth recounting how their ancestors migrated southwards from inland mountains (Konrad and Konrad 1996:268).

Stone use by the Marind: Ethnographic picture

The limited number of published references to the use of stone by the Marind is due in large part to the simple fact that Marind territory is 'completely devoid of stony matter except for loose concretions of sand or weathered loam' (van Baal 1966:16; see also Heldring 1910). In 1905, Austrian anthropologist Rudolf Pöch travelled across Marind territory, noting that 'Nowhere in this region did I notice any stone' (1907:614; see also van Baal 1966:8). Living in a stoneless environment, stone had a special meaning for the Marind, as all stone artefacts had to be obtained externally (see below). Despite an absence of locally available stone, the Marind used stone for tools (e.g. axes, club heads, and 'spearthrower' attachments—see below), while references to stone objects and features occur in a number of *dema* mythological narratives (e.g. Kooijman et al. 1958:73; van Baal 1966:279, 299, 461, 880). Ethnographic records say nothing about the use of flaked stone cutting or scraping tools. Such tasks were performed by tools manufactured from bamboo, marine shell, bone and boar's tusk (Kooijman et al. 1958:46; van Baal 1966:313, 907). The rarity of stone is reflected also in the use of pieces of termite nest as heat retainers in Marind ground ovens, and not stones as occurred across most other parts of New Guinea (van Baal 1966:16, 799–800, 847–848). It is likely that clay ball heat retainers were also used, as seen in neighbouring groups (Owen et al. 2008).

The earliest published record of Marind stone objects is by William MacGregor, Lieutenant-Governor of British New Guinea, who collected a number of stone objects from a Marind raiding camp on the Wassi Kussa (river) in the Trans-Fly region of south-west Papua New Guinea in 1896 (MacGregor 1897) (see Figure 12.1). The objects include a Marind 'pounding stone' with 'a fossil shell in one end of it', and a series of stone objects with possible ritual functions (MacGregor 1897:56). Despite the existence of stone implements (e.g. axes and club heads—see below), the majority of the admittedly limited published information on Marind stone objects concerns spiritual/ritual stones. Van Baal noted that stones can have spiritual power in Marind society as 'many' *dema* 'changed into stones' (1966:182–185, 209, 223, 229–230, 233, 237, 267, 392, 461; see also Wirz 1946). More generally, 'déma stones' were a 'preoccupation' of 'medicine-men' (*messav*) (van Baal 1966:883). These stones often took the form of a 'peculiar pebble' that was obtained through ritual interactions by *messav* at locations where *dema* reside. *Dema* stones were associated with rituals to heal sick people, increase the fertility of gardens, including coconuts, assist with hunting of crocodiles and help bring rain (van Baal 1966:803, 873–874, 881–882, 894, 899–900, 926).

Stone axes

Marind stone axes were hafted into a single piece of wood with a slot to accommodate the axe head (van Baal 1966:22, 230) (Figure 12.2A). This distinctive form of socketed hafting has a restricted distribution in New Guinea, centring on the southern lowlands of Indonesian Papua (Le Roux 1950, 3:Map III; Pétrequin and Pétrequin 2020:Figs 32–37). The Marind also possessed a variant of socketed hafting using a section of bamboo with a root node, known as *hong-ti* (van Baal 1966:230; see also Wirz 1946:85) (Figure 12.2B).

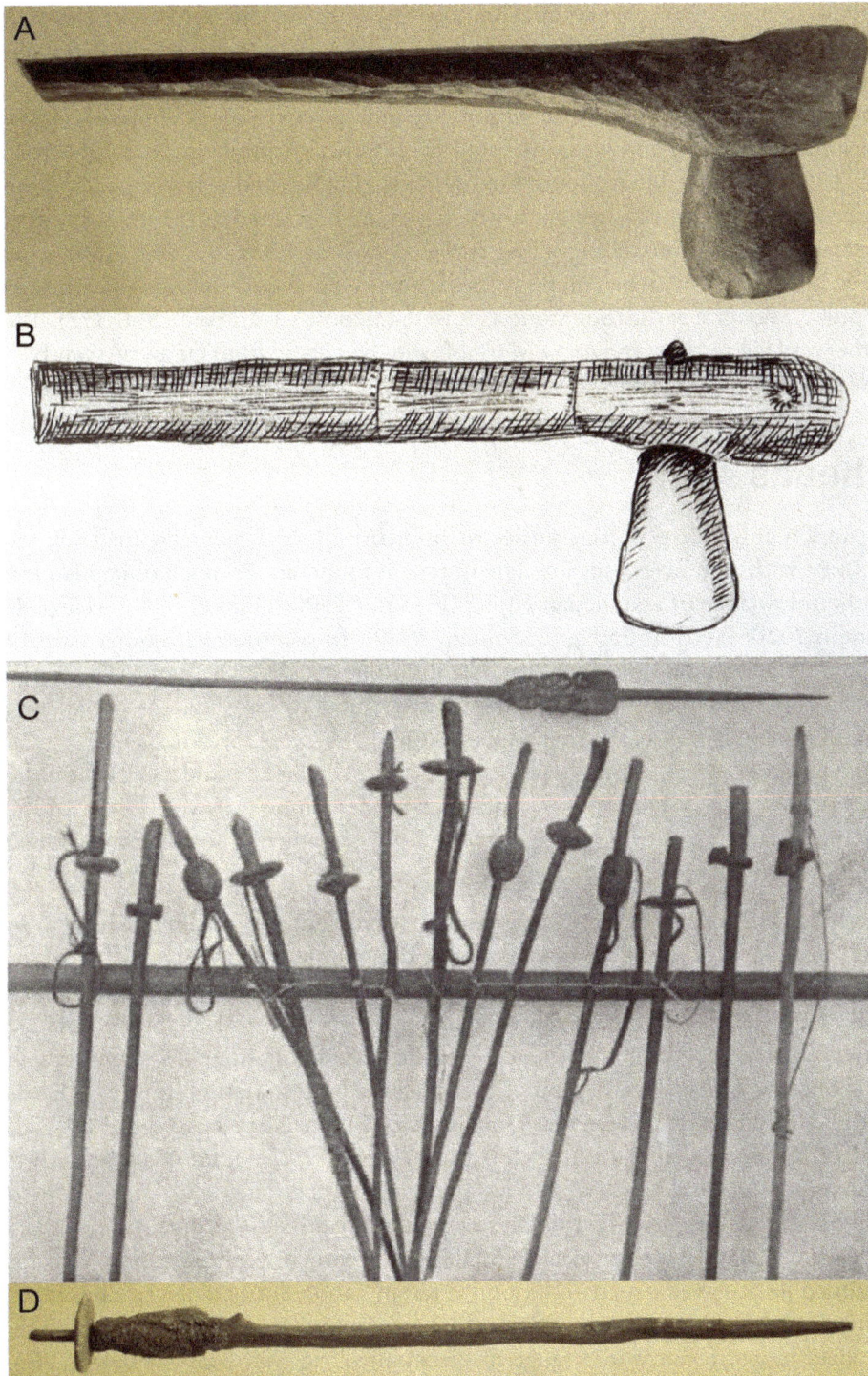

Figure 12.2: Marind stone axes and stone-headed clubs.

Notes: (A) Marind hafted stone axe from Merauke, collected 1904–05; (B) Marind stone axe hafted to the 'root end of a bamboo stalk'. Length of haft = 60 cm; (C) stone-headed clubs (ovoid and disc-shaped), metal-headed clubs, and a spear collected by William MacGregor from a Marind raiding camp on the Wassi Kussa (river), Trans-Fly region, south-west Papua New Guinea, 1896; (D) Marind stone-headed club from Merauke, collected 1904-05. Piece of spiky skin of a stingray wrapped around wooden haft. Weight = 1.5 kg, Length = 1.32 m.

Source: (A) from Expedition (1908:Plate VI, No. 183); (B) from Wirz (1922, I:Plate 37.1, English translation); (C) MacGregor (1898:Plate 6, Fig. 11); (D) from Expedition (1908:Plate VII, No. 179).

Similar bamboo hafts were used by the Asmat and Kamoro (Mimika) to the north-west (Konrad and Sowada 2002:369; Kooijman 1984:117; Le Roux 1950, 3:Map III; Pétrequin and Pétrequin 2020:Figs 34–36) and in the Morehead River area to the south-east (Williams 1936:429). These status/wealth objects had a range of secular uses within Marind society, such as chopping down sago trees, and ceremonial functions, and were inherited from father to son (van Baal 1966:466, 771, 861). Van Baal (1966:841) noted that 'stones axes, birds of paradise and other ornaments' are attached to a platform made of arrows (*tanggé*) upon which pigs are butchered for feasts. Stone axes are mentioned in a range of Marind mythological narratives (van Baal 1966:227, 255, 466). One mythological narrative refers to a time when 'nobody knew how to go about' chopping down sago trees 'to prepare the pith … because at the time stone axes were unknown' (van Baal 1966:337). The first axe was one of the 'very big teeth' of the *dema* Monubi who 'had come from far away' (van Baal 1966:337; see also Wirz 1922, II:153, 1946:85).

Stone club heads

Stone-headed clubs were highly prized objects possessed by many Marind men (Figure 12.3; see also Corbey 2010:37). As with stone axes, this implement type is found across much of Papua New Guinea and the southern lowlands of Indonesian Papua (Haddon 1900; Höltker 1940–41:Fig. 1; Pétrequin and Pétrequin 2020; Pretty 1965:Fig. 2; Soukup 2020). In common with other parts of New Guinea, they were used as raiding weapons (e.g. headhunting raids) and as status/ceremonial objects. They came in two main forms (ovoid or egg-shaped, and disc-shaped), and two rare forms (star-shaped, and knobbed/'pineapple'-shaped) (van Baal 1966:22, 273; Wirz 1922, I:112). The earliest recorded Marind examples are by MacGregor (1897:56) who at a raiders camp on the Wassi Kussa observed no 'stone axes' but a number of stone-headed clubs that were 'either of the thick disc type or shaped nearly like a turkey's egg. One at least is made of a fossiliferous whitish stone' (Figure 12.2C).

Of the 38 stone club heads (13 hafted) depicted in the online catalogue of the Tropen Museum in Amsterdam, most (79 per cent) ($N = 30$) are disc-shaped and eight are ovoid-shaped. The ovoid-shaped club (*waganê*) was a symbol of the male sex and the disc-shaped club (*kupa*) a symbol of the female sex (van Baal 1966:273, 732, 742). Van Baal (1966:730) was emphatic: 'Stone discs are rare'. Such rarity may explain in part the manufacture of wooden 'imitation' stone discs (Grottanelli 1951:106; van Baal 1966:734, 736) and the acceptance of imported brass imitation stone club heads in the early twentieth century (McNiven and von Gnielinski 2004; see also MacGregor 1897:56) (see below). Men obtained their first stone-headed club at the important age-grade ceremony when boys change status to young single men (*ewati*) and are presented with an 'heirloom' stone-headed club (van Baal 1966:151; 1994:135). They continued to be status/wealth objects until at least 1919 (Alder 1922:24; Alder and Bailey 1921; van Baal 1966:861). Adventurist and filmmaker William Alder (1922:110) claimed he observed a man 'fashioning a rattan handle for a stone war-club head' in 1919. They are mentioned in numerous mythological narratives (van Baal 1966:284, 292, 315, 317, 464) and were held by participants in a range of ceremonies (e.g. van Baal 1966:483, 904, 906). A *kupa* club was used to kill a pig for a feast associated with a ceremony (van Baal 1966:567) and Alder (1922:102) observed a stone-headed club used to break open coconuts. In some cases, club heads were hafted loosely such that they could slide down the wooden haft to increase impact (Kooijman 1952:97). In at least one case, spiky stingray hide was attached to the haft under the stone club head to increase the severity of impact (Figure 12.2D).

Figure 12.3: Marind men and stone-headed clubs.

Notes: (A) Marind man holding a stone-headed club, Merauke, c. 1906–1909; (B) Marind man holding a stone-headed club, c. 1902–1920; (C) Marind man holding a stone-headed club; (D) Marind man with a stone club head hanging around his neck.

Source: (A) photography by Father Henricus Nollen and published in Nollen (1909:Fig. H IVc); see also Reichgelt (2016:24) (collection of the University of Leiden library, KITLV D6224); (B) from Alder (1922:opp. p. 161); (C) photograph taken during the 'De Zuidwest Nieuw-Guinea-Expeditie 1904/05' (collection of the Museum Volkenkunde, Leiden, RV-A30-23); (D) photograph by Nicholas at Merauke in 1904 and published in Expedition (1908:Fig. 142) (collection of the Museum Volkenkunde, Leiden, RV-A30-25).

'Spearthrower' stones

The Marind used wooden (bamboo) spearthrowers (e.g. Geurtjens 1949; Wirz 1922, I:Plates 32.3 and 36.3). However, ethnographically collected objects in the form of wooden shafts with hafted stones that were beautifully crafted with a shaped hook feature (known as *imbassum*) are unique to the Marind (Figure 12.4).

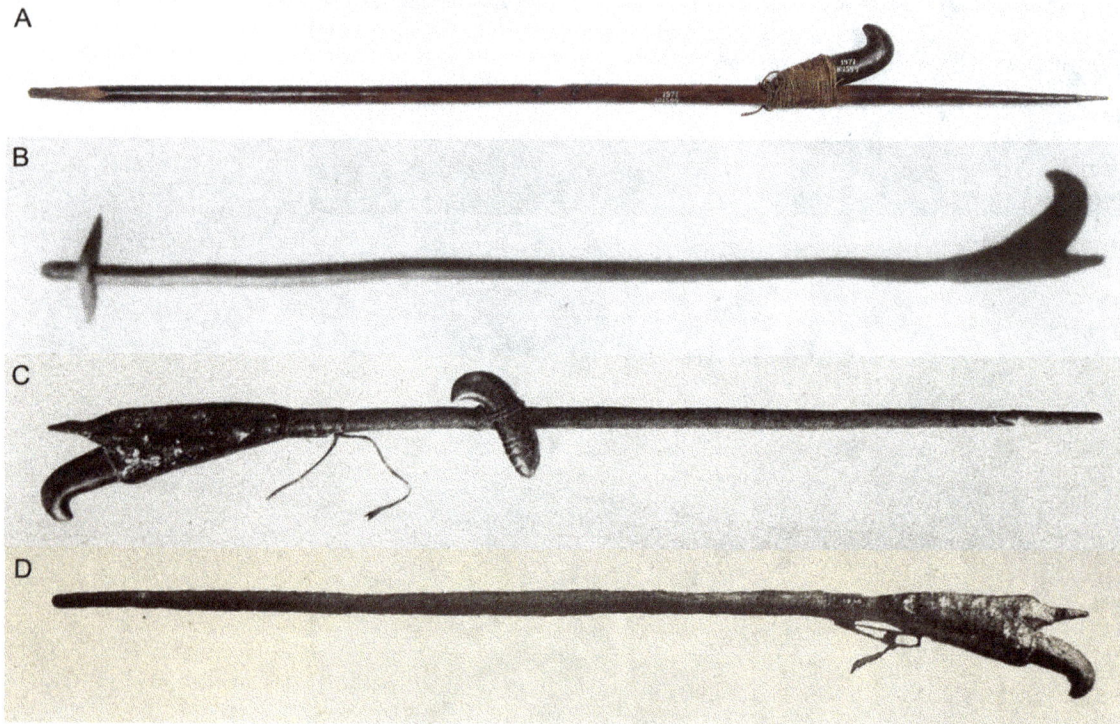

Figure 12.4: Various hafted *imbassum*.

Notes: (A) Marind hafted *imbassum*, Sanggase coastal village, collected c. 1913 by A.J. Gooszen. Length = 116 cm; (B) hafted *imbassum* at one end and 'bone plate' at the other end. Provenanced to the Digul River. Length = 80 cm; (C) Marind hafted *imbassum* (with two shaped stones); (D) 'ornamental weapon or symbol' comprising a hafted *imbassum* and cassowary toenail, Okaba coastal village, collected 1907–1915.

Source: (A) Geurtjens (1949:Figs 1–2) (collection of the Museum Volkenkunde, Leiden, RV-1971-1594); (B) Geurtjens (1949:Fig. 4) (collection of the Nederlandsch Volkenkundig Missiemuseum, Tilburg); (C) Wirz (1922, I:Plate 36.12); (D) Expedition (1920:345–346, Fig. 155, English translation).

According to Swiss ethnologist Paul Wirz (1925 cited in van Baal 1966:413), *imbassum* 'combines the functions of spear-thrower, striking weapon and thrusting weapon'. The spearthrower function of *imbassum* was supported by Geurtjens (1949:221) and van Baal (1966:413–415). Anthropologists agree that *imbassum* also had an important ceremonial/ritual function. Wirz (1925, III:20) noted that *imbassum* were carried by *kapiog* (black cockatoo) performers in *mayo* cult initiation ceremonies, adding that the hooked form of the stone 'has some resemblance to the beak of a cockatoo' (Wirz 1925, IV:138, English translation) or more generally 'the shape of a bird's head' (Wirz 1946:88, English translation). Father Henri Geurtjens (1949) argued that the rarity of *imbassum* is consistent with a restricted, ceremonial use. Van Baal (1966:414) was adamant that 'there is ample reason to accept that the *imbassum* is a ceremonial spear-thrower. It fits in perfectly with the ritual performance' of the *kapiog*. Marind mythological narratives refer to *dema* using *imbassum* to facilitate hunting of wallabies (e.g. van Baal 1966:286, 328, 412). At Senégi village, missionary Father Jan Verschueren (cited in van Baal 1966:415) recorded a large (12-cm-long) *imbassum* (stone) said to be a banana *dema*. The rarity of hafted *imbassum* (see Figure 12.4) and unhafted *imbassum* stones in museum collections is consistent with their apparent rarity among the Marind and their restricted ceremonial use (Smidt 2006:429). The combined online catalogue of the Tropen Museum (Amsterdam), Rijksmuseum voor Volkenkunde (Leiden), and World Museum (Rotterdam) lists seven Marind *imbassum* stones (one with a haft), with a length range of 6.5–14.5 cm. Length measurements made by Wirz (1946:88) of five *imbassum* stones in the Museum für Völkerkunde (Basel) range from 9.5 to 16.2 cm (Figure 12.5).

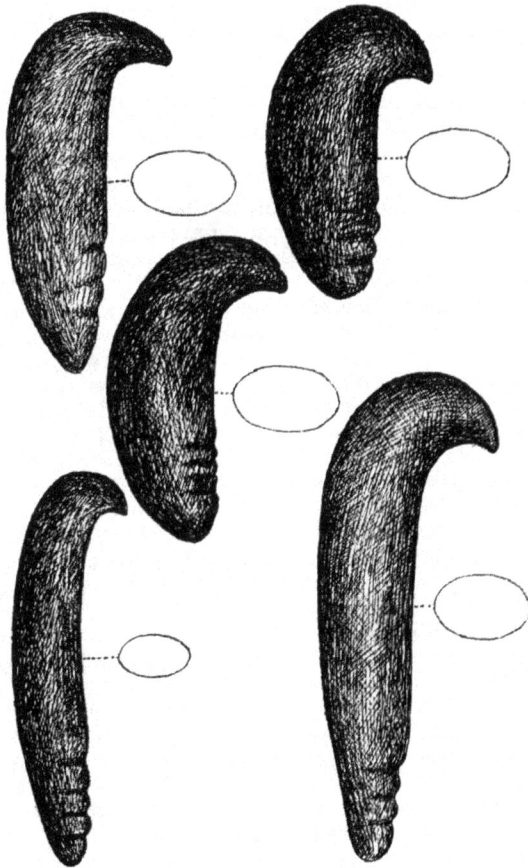

Figure 12.5: Marind *imbassum* stones collected by Paul Wirz between 1915 and 1922 and housed in the Museum für Völkerkunde (now Museum of Cultures), Basel, Switzerland.

Source: After Wirz (1946:Fig. 9–13).

Potential sources of stone implements

All stone implements used by the Marind must originate from beyond their territory, given the absence of local stone. Less consensus exists within anthropological literature on specifically where and how stone implements were obtained by the Marind. Van Baal suggested:

> stone axes as well as the stone clubs had to be obtained through trade or robbery during one of their frequent headhunting expeditions. The fact that there are different types of axes and clubs points to a diversity of origin (van Baal 1966:23; see also Wirz 1946:85)

Three regions external to the Marind have been identified ethnographically (based on interviews with elderly Marind during the first half of the twentieth century) as known and potential sources of stone implements—inland regions to the west and north (Digul River) and to a lesser extent the north-east (Fly River) and south-east (Torres Strait) (see Figure 12.1).

Upper Digul River

Wirz (1922, I:114, English translation) was informed by the Marind that their stone axes originated in the 'upper Digul and the Fly river'. Dutch anthropologist Simon Kooijman and colleagues (1958:46) noted that the Marind obtained stone axes and club heads from 'inland peoples … by barter or otherwise by robbery'. Archaeologist Pam Swadling (1983:85–86, Fig. 35) hypothesised that stone axes manufactured in the Upper Digul River ('Red Digul River quarry') 'were traded southwards as far as the Marind-anim'. Ethnoarchaeologists Pierre Pétrequin and Anne-Marie Pétrequin (2020:18, 143–144, 184–185) argued that most basalt stone axes traded down the Digul River originated from ethnographically documented quarries to the immediate north-west across the headwaters of the Eilanden (Sirets) River system located c. 200 km north-west of the Marind (see also

Hampton 1999:Chap 7). For example, Langda andesite/basalt axes (Eilanden River headwaters) have been documented among stone axes collected from the Digul River (Pétrequin and Pétrequin 2020:172). Axes manufactured from andesite/basalt (possibly from Langda) were also used by the Kombai of the Upper Mappi River (Konrad and Ligabue 1996:58) located immediately west of the Digul River, and the Marind on the Merauke River (Pétrequin and Pétrequin 2020:16, 18).

Wirz (1922, I:112) also recorded that the Marind obtained most ovoid- and disc-shaped stone club heads from the Digul River through trading and raiding. German ethnologist Hans Nevermann (1939:33) was informed that the Marind obtained stone club heads from the Digul River area. Similarly, Verschueren (cited in van Baal 1966:730) was informed in 1936 that disc-shaped stone club heads were 'traded, being passed down from the Star Mountains [Digul River headwaters] to the south'.

The hafted *imbassum* collected from the Marind coastal village of Okaba during the 1907–1915 'Verslag van de Militaire Exploratie van Nederlandsch-Nieuw-Guinee' was said to have come from 'Jamboeike in the interior' (Expedition 1920:345, English translation) (see Figure 12.4D). Jamboeike is located 90 km north-east of Okaba and 25 km south-east of the Digul River. Geurtjens (1949:223) was of the opinion that *imbassum* originated from the Digul River region.

Upper Fly River

Wirz (1922, I:112) recorded that Marind star- and pineapple-shaped stone club heads were obtained through headhunting and were thought by the Marind of the Upper Bian River to come from the Upper Fly River. He also noted that the 'Fly river' was a source of some Marind stone axes (Wirz 1922, I:114). Swadling (1983:79–84) added that Wirz's Fly River source may have been the Boazi people of the Lake Murray area who imported stone axes from the Upper Fly River, including gneiss axes from the Upper Wario River within the Sepik River system.

Torres Strait

Van Baal (1966:699) observed that the 'stone-headed clubs' of the Marind:

> are very much like some of the stone clubs of the Torres Str. islands and it is a fair guess that they obtained them from the Fly River district as well as from the interior.

Wirz (1933:121) was of the opinion that while the Marind visited the granite outcrops at Mabaduan on the Trans-Fly south coast, they only viewed the granite hill of Dauan, the northernmost rocky island of Torres Strait, from a distance. He added: 'Even on the calmest sea the crossing [10 km] in their canoes would have been a foolhardy venture' (Wirz 1932:285). The Marind informed Wirz (1933:120) that Dauan, a close but unreachable hill of stone, 'occupied their imagination more than anything else they had got to know on their journeys'. McNiven (in press) hypothesises that the Marind likely obtained stone objects manufactured by Torres Strait Islanders through trading and raiding after they had passed northwards into the hands of Trans-Fly peoples similarly through raiding and trading. Preliminary sourcing studies of stone club heads from Torres Strait and the Torassi or Bensbach River area of the Trans-Fly indicate manufacture from Torres Strait stone (Hitchcock 2004; McNiven 1998; McNiven and von Gnielinski 2004). Although *imbassum* ('spearthrower' stones) have never been recorded in Torres Strait, Swadling (1983:103) suggested that Torres Strait may have been the source of raw materials.

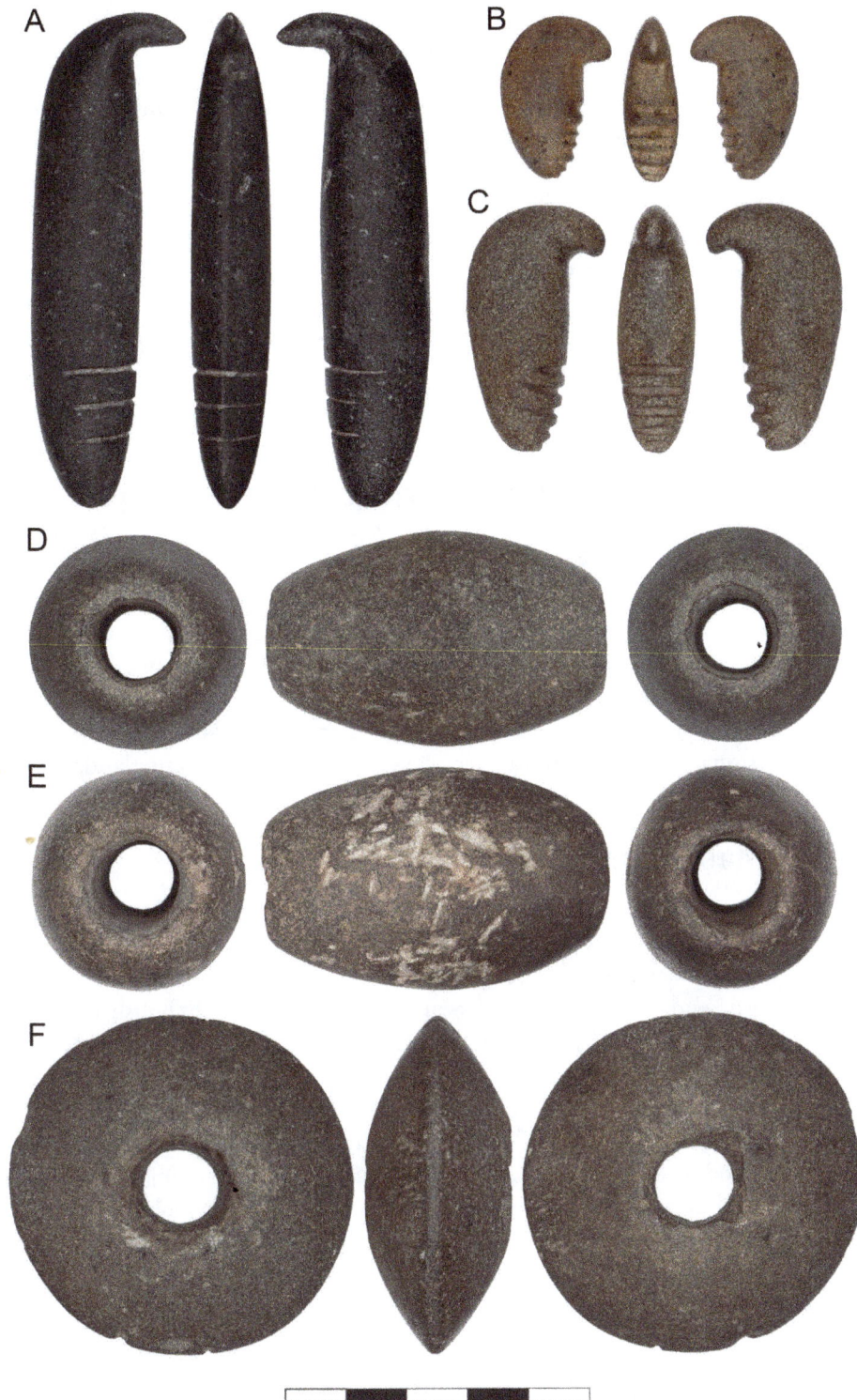

Figure 12.6: Marind *imbassum* and stone club heads, examined by IM and FvG.

Notes: (A) Marind *imbassum*, Okaba area (#498); (B) Marind *imbassum*, Merauke area (#541); (C) Marind *imbassum*, Merauke area (#542); (D) Marind ovoid stone club head (*wagané*), Merauke area (#479); (E) Marind ovoid stone club head (*wagané*), Merauke area (#480); (F) Marind discoid stone club head (*kupa*), Merauke area (#463). Scale in 1 cm units.

Source: All objects in private collection. Photographs by Steve Morton, Monash University.

China

Wirz (1922, I:112) recorded that Chinese traders introduced brass copies of stone club heads to the Marind in the early twentieth century. Similarly, Nevermann (1939:34, English translation) noted that 'recently' (i.e. early twentieth century) 'club discs made of stone or iron' were introduced to the Marind by Chinese traders. He observed that in contrast to the 'hourglass pierced shape' of the hafting shaft in 'old stone knobs', the hafting shaft of the Chinese imports was 'smoothly pierced' (Nevermann 1939:34). However, Swadling (1983:103–104), following Wirz (1922, I;112), rightly pointed out that straight-sided hafting shafts on stone club heads from south-western Papua New Guinea predate the arrival of Chinese traders at Merauke after 1902. Furthermore, ethnographic observations indicate the indigenous production of straight-sided hafting shafts in stone club heads in Papua New Guinea using cylindrical drills of bamboo (Austen 1923:344; McNiven and von Gnielinski 2004:298).

Six Marind stone implements: Manufacture and raw materials

To shed further light on the source(s) of Marind stone objects, one of us (IM) gained access to three 'spearthrower' stones (*imbassum*) and three club heads (ovoid and discoid) (Figure 12.6). Provenance information on the six objects is based on personal communication by IM with three ethnographic artefact 'dealers' in Australia, the Netherlands and Germany. Objects 463, 498, 541, and 542 were obtained by two of the 'dealers' directly from Marind in Okaba and Merauke. Objects 479 and 480 were part of an old missionary collection from Merauke taken back to the Netherlands. All six objects are in the custodianship of IM in Melbourne.

'Spearthrower' stones (*imbassum*)

The three 'spearthrower' stones (*imbassum*) (Objects A to C) vary considerably in weight (42, 112, 238 g), maximum length (55, 81, 164 mm) and maximum thickness (18, 25, 27 mm) (Table 12.1, Figure 12.6A–C). All exhibit the characteristic hook feature at one end and a series of three to six abraded grooves at the opposite end. The three *imbassum* have ground and highly polished surfaces and reveal no evidence of earlier stages of manufacture and shaping such as flaking or pecking. Rock types represented by each implement were described by one of us (FvG) by visual inspection of the surface with the aid of a 10× hand lens. Object B is manufactured from extrusive igneous rock, specifically rhyolite or rhyodacite. Objects A and C are manufactured from intrusive igneous rocks, specifically diorite/microdiorite (Object A) and microdiorite (Object C). Object A, though, has a fresh, very coherent, and crystalline appearance, different from any other objects observed in McNiven (1998) and McNiven et al. (2004). These characteristics may indicate a different provenance for Object A. That Object A may have been obtained from Chinese traders in the early twentieth century is a hypothesis for future testing.

Stone club heads

The three stone club heads represent examples of the two major forms of ethnographically known Marind stone club heads—ovoid (*waganê*) (Objects D and E) and discoid (*kupa*) (Object F) (Table 12.1, Figure 12.6D–F). The range of weights (540, 614, 669 g) and maximum diameter of the hafting shafts (25, 26, 27 mm) is similar for all three club heads, and the two ovoid club heads have near-identical lengths (99, 106 mm) and maximum diameters (66, 71 mm). All three club heads exhibit ground and polished surfaces (with scattered pits indicative of a prior manufacturing phase of shaping by pecking) and reasonably straight-sided hafting shafts. Numerous deep impact marks across the surface of Object E are consistent with secondary use as a hammerstone and/or anvil. All three club heads are manufactured from intrusive igneous rocks, specifically microdiorite (Object D) and microdiorite or micromonzodiorite (Objects E and F).

Table 12.1: Descriptions of Marind stone objects.

Fig. 12.6 ref. (private coll. #) collection location	Size Wt = weight L = length Th = thickness D = diameter HS = hafting shaft	Object type Method of manufacture	Rock type Raw materials
A (498) Okaba area	Wt: 237.5 g Max. L: 164 mm Max. Th: 27 mm	**'Spearthrower' stone (*imbassum*)** The entire surface of the implement has been ground and polished smooth, thus obliterating evidence of prior stages of shaping/manufacture (e.g. flaking, pecking). The three parallel (straight-sided) grooves were created using a thin-bladed saw (probably metal). In contrast to the other objects, the polished surface appears fresh with little or no patination.	**Diorite/microdiorite** Black equigranular (0.01–2.2 mm) microdiorite (intrusive igneous), with fresh biotite flakes (mostly weathered on surface), white plagioclase, translucent fine quartz/silica, dark green to black augite, dark grey pyroxene/hornblende. There also is a dark blue mineral, that is not yet identified.
B (541) Merauke area	Wt: 42.0 g Max. L: 55 mm Max. Th: 18 mm	**'Spearthrower' stone (*imbassum*)** The entire surface of the implement has been ground and polished smooth, thus obliterating evidence of prior stages of shaping/manufacture (e.g. flaking, pecking). The six parallel (U-shaped) grooves were created by abrasion.	**Rhyolite or rhyodacite** Brown-oxidised greenish-grey crystal and lithic-rich rhyolite or rhyodacite. Common euhedral plagioclase laths and less common larger volcanic quartz crystals, which are translucent, but appear dark grey (up to 2 mm). The matrix is aphanitic and quartz-feldspar–dominant—hence an extrusive/volcanic rock, possibly a lava or an ignimbrite.
C (542) Merauke area	Wt: 111.7 g Max. L: 81 mm Max. Th: 25 mm	**'Spearthrower' stone (*imbassum*)** The entire surface of the implement has been ground and polished smooth, thus obliterating evidence of prior stages of shaping/manufacture (e.g. flaking, pecking). The five parallel (U-shaped) grooves were created by abrasion.	**Microdiorite** Altered very fine to fine-grained (0.01–1.2 mm) intrusive rock, even-grained equigranular microdiorite with distinctive euhedral-shaped crystals of plagioclase (white-cream), smaller brownish K-feldspar, less distinct translucent to buff-coloured quartz-silica and dark grey-green hornblende (chloritised).

Fig. 12.6 ref. (private coll. #) collection location	Size Wt = weight L = length Th = thickness D = diameter HS = hafting shaft	Object type Method of manufacture	Rock type Raw materials
D (479) Merauke area	Wt: 539.8 g L HS axis: 99 mm Max. D: 66 mm Max. D HS: 25 mm	**Ovoid club head (*wagané*)** Most of the outer surface is ground smooth with scattered small pits indicative of a prior manufacturing phase of shaping by pecking. Central hafting shaft is largely parallel-sided, suggesting creation by drilling augmented by abrasion. Minor chipping on the inside circular edge of both entrances to the hafting shaft possibly reflects impact from a wooden handle during use. Both hafting shaft entrances have been ground flat.	**Microdiorite** Altered very fine to fine-grained (0.03–1.1 mm) intrusive rock, fairly even-grained equigranular microdiorite with distinctive euhedral-shaped crystals of plagioclase (cream-brown), less distinct translucent to buff-coloured quartz-silica, very fine black flakes of biotite. Some rare aggregates of biotite and other mafic minerals were observed, but this rock has less hornblende compared to #480. Also, some rare K-feldspar laths (up to 3 mm) were observed. The rock appears to be hardened by silica alteration.
E (480) Merauke area	Wt: 669.0 g L HS axis: 106 mm Max. D: 71 mm Max. D HS: 27 mm	**Ovoid club head (*wagané*)** Most of the outer surface is ground smooth with scattered small pits indicative of a prior manufacturing phase of shaping by pecking. Central hafting shaft is largely parallel-sided, suggesting creation by drilling augmented by abrasion. Minor chipping on the inside circular edge of both entrances to the hafting shaft possibly reflects impact from a wooden handle during use. Both hafting shaft entrances have been ground flat. One half of the implement exhibits multiple impact pits, suggesting use as an anvil and/or hammerstone.	**Microdiorite or micromonzodiorite** Altered very fine to fine-grained (0.05–1.2 mm) intrusive rock, fairly even-grained microdiorite with distinctive euhedral-shaped crystals of plagioclase (cream-brown), less distinct translucent to buff-coloured quartz-silica and dark grey-green hornblende (possibly chloritised), also some altered pseudomorphs after pyroxene. The rock appears to be hardened by silica alteration.
F (463) Merauke area	Wt: 614.2 g L HS axis: 45 mm Max. D: 111 mm Max. D HS: 26 mm	**Discoid club head (*kupa*)** Most of the outer surface is ground smooth with scattered small pits indicative of a prior manufacturing phase of shaping by pecking. Central hafting shaft is largely parallel-sided, suggesting creation by drilling augmented by abrasion. Minor chipping on the inside circular edge of both entrances to the hafting shaft possibly reflects impact from a wooden handle during use. Outer edge of implement exhibits a series of flake scars from impact.	**Microdiorite or micromonzodiorite** Fresh very fine to fine-grained (0.05–1.2 mm) intrusive rock, fairly even-grained microdiorite with distinctive euhedral-shaped crystals of plagioclase (cream-brown), less distinct translucent to buff-coloured quartz-silica and dark grey-green hornblende (possibly chloritised), also some altered pseudomorphs after pyroxene. The rock appears to be hardened by silica alteration.

Source: Authors' summary.

Discussion

Characterised implements: Potential sources

All six Marind implements are made from igneous rocks. No outcrops of igneous stone occur within an area of ~100,000 km² across the vast lowlands of Quaternary sediments located south of the Central Ranges between the Digul River (west) and the Fly River (east) and north of the south coast and Torres Strait (D'Addario et al. 1976; Dow et al. 1986; Willmott 1972) (Figure 12.1). On the eastern side of the Fly River, igneous outcrops do not occur across ~40,000 km² of Quaternary lowlands located south of the Central Ranges, taking in the Strickland and Aramia Rivers, and north of the south coast (Dow et al. 1986) (Figure 12.1). As such, the nearest sources of igneous tool stone to the Marind are located to the south-east across northern Torres Strait and to the north and north-east in the Central Ranges and associated southern foothills. As discussed below, some of the identified raw materials for the six Marind implements are known to outcrop in the Central Ranges, while others occur in Torres Strait. That is, microdiorite and microdiorite/micromonzodiorite (intrusive igneous) are available in the Central Ranges and Torres Strait, while rhyolite/rhyodacite (extrusive igneous) are available in Torres Strait. The diorite/microdiorite (intrusive igneous) of Object A is of a form currently unknown in Torres Strait.

Torres Strait

The Torres Strait takes in the northern (Papua New Guinea) and southern (Cape York, Australia) mainland coasts and intervening islands (mostly within Australia). The geology of Torres Strait islands is divided into the Torres Strait Volcanic Group of rhyolites, ignimbrites and andesites (western Torres Strait); the Badu Suite of granites (western Torres Strait) and the Maer Volcanics of basalts and tuffs (eastern Torres Strait) (von Gnielinski 2015; von Gnielinski et al. 1997; Willmott et al. 1973). On the south coast of Papua New Guinea forming the northern boundary of Torres Strait, igneous outcrops are limited to the settlement of Mabaduan and nearby islets (e.g. Marakara Island) which feature boulders of Badu Suite granites and small areas of Torres Strait Volcanics, which, due to their proximity to the 'hot' Badu Suite granites, were hornfelsed and silicified. Across the northern section of Cape York Peninsula (within the area delimited in Figure 12.1), igneous outcrops are restricted to the immediate surrounds of Cape York (Powell and Smart 1977; Willmott and Powell 1977).

Except for the form of diorite/microdiorite of Object A, the other identified raw materials of rhyolite/rhyodacite, microdiorite and microdiorite/micromonzodiorite are known to outcrop in western Torres Strait. Rhyolite/rhyodacite is part of the Torres Strait Volcanic Group, especially the Goods Island Ignimbrite and the Muralug Ignimbrite of south-west Torres Strait. Microdiorite and micromonzodiorite are very fine-grained intrusive rocks that possibly derive from dyke outcrops within the Badu Granite, especially in north-west Torres Strait. Previous research has similarly identified Torres Strait as the likely source of ground stone implements (stone axes and club heads) collected from Torres Strait and the Trans-Fly region (Hitchcock 2004; McNiven 1998; McNiven and von Gnielinski 2004; McNiven et al. 2004).

Central Ranges

In Indonesia, the Central Ranges covering the area taken in by Figure 12.1 are dominated by marine sedimentary rocks, limestones, sandstones and mudstones (Dow et al. 1986). Metamorphic rocks such as mica-schist metadiorite and slate occur across the northern flanks of the ranges. In Papua New Guinea, the Central Ranges covering the area taken in by Figure 12.1 are similarly dominated by marine sedimentary rocks and limestones (Bain et al. 1972). However, a range of locations within the Central Ranges located to the north (within Indonesia) and north-east (within Papua New Guinea) of the Marind exhibit igneous rock outcrops and potential sources of raw materials matching the rock types used to manufacture the characterised Marind implements. That is, localised igneous outcrops with diorite and microdiorite are found across the upper (headwater) catchments of the Digul, Sepik, Fly and Strickland Rivers (Figure 12.1, Table 12.2). None of the characterised Marind implements were made from lavas (e.g. basalts) and ash (tuff) deposits associated with the Dome Peaks, Mt Sisa and Mt Bosavi volcanoes located to the east of the middle Strickland River, or gneiss from quarries of the Upper Wario River of the Sepik River system.

Erosion of igneous outcrops extended the availability and potential source locations of tool stone raw materials to include secondary deposits of boulders, cobbles and pebbles in rivers draining the southern flanks of the Central Ranges (see Swadling 1983:89). Visser and Hermes (1962:177) note that 'Torrential rivers flowing down the range have laid down extensive boulder beds in foothills and adjoining plains'. For example, average annual rainfall exceeds 10 m in the Ok Tedi River area of the Upper Fly River catchment (Pickup and Marshall 2009:5). Most riverine pebbles of the eastern Central Ranges in Indonesian Papua 'can be fitted into the groups of igneous rocks known from outcrops' (Visser and Hermes 1962:122). The size of these eroded rock fragments decreases from boulders to fine sands as they travel down towards the sea. Löffler (1977:133) pointed out that 'gravel banks and bars' occur up to 100 km downstream from where the Strickland River leaves the mountains (i.e. c. 700 km from the Fly River mouth). Cobbles and boulders occur down to 120 km from the source of the Ok Tedi River (i.e. c. 900 km from the Fly River mouth) (Bolton et al. 2009:54–56). Austen (1926:438) noted that the Ok Tedi River contains 'volcanic gravels … in great quantities'.

In Indonesian Papua, Saulnier and Bisiaux (1963:147, 159–160, 163) documented pebble banks along the Steenboom River where it leaves the Central Ranges and enters the lowland plains. In lowlands to the immediate east of the Upper Eilanden River, extensive cobble banks occur along the Upper Becking River (Raffaele 2006:55; van Enk and de Vries 1997:274 n. 16). 'Cobbles' are well documented for the mountainous headwaters of the Digul River in elevations above 400 m above sea level (e.g. Reijnders 1964:27–28, 33, 81–83, 103, 119, 138–139). Schroo (1964:14) noted that 'gravel terraces' begin occurring c. 460 km upstream from the Digul River mouth, along both the main Digul River channel and the Kao (Oewimmerah) River tributary. Whether cobbles occur within these gravels, or are restricted to further upstream (e.g. Schoorl 1993:72), is unknown. Van den Bold (1942) noted that many of Heldring's (1913) samples from 'pebble banks' of the Upper Digul River were diorite.

The downstream extent of cobbles is complicated further by transport within the roots of dislodged and floating trees. For example, people of the stoneless Middle Fly River region would 'pick stones out of the roots of trees that were floating down the river to obtain stones for axe blades' (Busse 1987:50; see also Swadling 1983:89). The Asmat (located > 200 km north-west of the Marind) used stones recovered from roots of floating trees along the lower Sirets (Eilanden) River as 'grinding tools, as they are not ordinarily suitable for processing into ax blades' (Konrad and Ligabue 1996:56; see also Trenkenschuh 1982:83).

Table 12.2: Outcropping igneous rock units across central New Guinea (Indonesia and Papua New Guinea) and Torres Strait (Australia). Rock types in bold match identified raw material types for sampled Marind stone objects (Table 12.1).

Fig. 12.1 reference	Geographical location	Geological unit (Unit map code)	Rock types/Comments	References
A	Upper Mumugo (Northwest) River valley	Unmapped geologically	Schist, greywackes, sandstone. Known mostly from ethnographic descriptions of the Mumugo tool stone quarry sites	Pétrequin and Pétrequin (2020:189–190); Swadling (1983:88)
B	Sela/Phu Valley and headwaters of the Brazza River (Eilanden River catchment)	Unmapped geologically	Metabasalt/andesite; metamorphosed igneous, formerly dolerite; andesite dykes Known mostly from ethnographic descriptions of the Sela tool stone quarry sites	Hampton (1999:85, 276); Pétrequin and Pétrequin (2020:168–169); Terpstra (1939); van der Wegen (1966:258)
C	Langda area Ey/Mumyeme/Heime Rivers, headwaters of the Steenboom River (Eilanden River catchment)	Unmapped geologically	Andesite/basalt, meta-andesite/basalt; biotite-muscovite granite, quartz-biotite-cordierite schist. Known mostly from ethnographic descriptions of the Langda tool stone quarry sites	Hampton (1999:85, 252, 274); Pétrequin and Pétrequin (2020:143–144); Toth et al. (1992:88); van den Bold (1942:850); van der Wegen (1966:259)
D	Suntamon Valley/Yamyhi River and headwaters of the Eilanden River	Unmapped geologically	Metavolcanics, metamorphosed basalts, probably a dyke (possibly dolerites); biotite-muscovite granite, hornblende granodiorite. Known mostly from ethnographic descriptions of the Suntamon tool stone quarry sites	Pétrequin and Pétrequin (2020:15, 175, 182–186); van der Wegen (1966:259)
E_1–E_3	Headwaters of the Digul River and its multiple tributaries—E_1 (Red/West Digul), E_2 (East Digul and Kao) and E_3 (Kao) Rivers	Timepa Monzonite (Tpt)	Tpt: Quartz **diorite**, minor monzonite, porphyry **diorite**, quartz andesite, biotite-muscovite granite E_1 = corresponds to location of Red Digul ('basaltic rock'?) tool stone quarry	Bär et al. (1961:59, Geological map); Soetrisno dan and Amiruddin (1995); Pétrequin and Pétrequin (2020:185); Swadling (1983:85–86, Fig. 35)
F	Headwaters of the Kao River (Digul River catchment) and Ok Mat River (Ok Tedi and Fly River catchment)	Birim Formation	Andesites; **diorite**, augite-hornblende basalt, augite-plagioclase basalt, olivine basalt, basalt-tuff with zeolite or aragonite as cement, chlorite-augite andesite	Bär et al. (1961:59, Geological map); van der Wegen (1966:255, 257)

Fig. 12.1 reference	Geographical location	Geological unit (Unit map code)	Rock types/Comments	References
G_1–G_2	Star Mountains. Headwaters of the Digul River and Kongfale, Fatik and Bun Rivers, Ok Werp Al, Tingeri, Ban, Din and Nong Rivers (Upper Sepik River)	Timepa Monzonite (Tpt) Antares Complex (Tpa) Volcanics (Tpv) Porphyry (Tpp) Ban Quartz **Monzodiorite (Tpb)** Tumfakama **Microdiorite (Tpt)** Stolka Quartz **Diorite (Tpo)**	Tpt: Quartz **diorite**, minor monzonite, porphyry **diorite**, quartz andesite, biotite-muscovite granite (Indonesian side of border) Tpa: Quartz **monzodiorite**, quartz monzonite, **diorite**, **microdiorite**, granodiorite, granite, some porphyry, some volcanics Tpv: Andesitic and dacitic volcanic agglomerate, volcaniclastic sandstone and mudstone, crystal tuff Tpp: Andesitic and dacitic porphyry; phenocrysts are hornblende, plagioclase, minor pyroxene, rare biotite Tpb: Quartz **monzodiorite**, granodiorite, quartz monzonite, equigranular, medium to coarse-grained; characteristically includes pale green clinopyroxene Tpt: **Microdiorite**, some **diorite** and microgranodiorite; medium to fine-grained and equigranular Tpo: Quartz **diorite**, quartz **monzodiorite**, minor porphyry	Bär et al. (1961:53–57, Fig. 4); Davies (1982:28–29); Davies et al. (1983)
H_1–H_2	Headwaters of the Kwirok and Iram Rivers (Upper Sepik River) and Ok Tedi River (Fly River catchment)	Star Mountains Intrusives (Tps)	Tps: Porphyritic micromonzonite, microdiorite, microgranodiorite, minor medium-grained equivalents; magnetite, sulphide and epidotegarnet skarns	Davies et al. (1974); Davies and Norvick (1974:20)
I_1–I_4	Headwaters of the Bol (Upper Fly River) and Strickland Rivers	Intrusives (Tpi) I_1 = Bolivip Stock I_2 = Tabe Stock I_3 = Idawe Stock I_4 = Tumbudu Stock	Tpi: Porphyritic micromonzonite, **microdiorite**	Davies et al. (1974); Davies and Norvick (1974:20)
J	Headwaters of the Strickland River	Kendupwa Volcanics (Tpk)	Tpk: Andesitic agglomerate, tuff and volcanic sandstone, minor marl. Andesite has clinopyroxene and labradorite phenocrysts, and large hornblende xenocrysts, in groundmass of matted plagioclase microlites and much magnetite	Davies and Eno (1983); Davies (1983:51)
K	Headwaters of Nekiei River (Upper April River) (Sepik River catchment)	Nekiei batholith (Tmi)	Tmi: **Diorite**, quartz **diorite**; granodiorite, some porphyry	Davies and Baloiloi (1983); Davies and Hutchison (1982:37)
L	Headwaters of the Karawari River (Sepik River catchment)	Karawari batholith (Tmr)	Tmr: **Diorite**, quartz **diorite**; granodiorite, quartz gabbro, hornblende gabbro, anorthite gabbro, pyroxenite and hornblendite; some **diorite** pegmatite, some **microdiorite** porphyry. Inclusions of hornfelsed and mineralised calcareous sediments	Davies and Baloiloi (1983); Davies and Hutchison (1982:37); Davies and Eno (1983); Davies (1983:53)

Fig. 12.1 reference	Geographical location	Geological unit (Unit map code)	Rock types/Comments	References
M	Headwaters of the Kikori River with three volcanic cones known as the Doma Peaks	Tephra (Qt) Lumu Volcanics (Qiv) Doma Volcanics (Qdn, Qda, Qdb, Qdd, Qde, TQn) Un-named (TQp) Kerewa Volcanics (TQk, Qvk, Qvkl)	Qt: volcanic ash, some coarser pyroclastics: tephra Qiv: Porphyritic olivine tholeiite lava Qdn: Probably trachyandesite lava Qda: Lahar and pyroclastic flow deposits, some coarse volcanogenic sediments: basal volcanics Qdb: Trachyandesite lava, some pyroclastics and volcanogenic sediments: old cone Qdd: Trachyandesite and olivine trachybasalt lava flows Qde: Chaotic deposits of large clasts of lava in finer volcanic debris, clay; pyroclastic flow TQn: andesite lava TQp: Probably pyroclastics TQk: Trachyandesite lava and lava breccia, some agglomerate and tuff Qvk: Fine-grained basaltic lava, lava breccia, andesitic agglomerate, tuff Qvkl: Volcaniclastic andesite and basaltic breccia; reworked agglomerate, tuff minor intercalated volcanically derived conglomerate, sandstone: laharic deposits	Davies and Eno (1983); Davies (1983:41, 48–50); Brown et al. (1983)
N	Headwaters of the Nomad River (Strickland River catchment) with two volcanic cones, one known as Mt Sisa	Sisa Volcanics (TQsl, TQvs)	TQsl: Volcaniclastic andesitic and basaltic breccia, reworked agglomerate, tuff; minor intercalated volcanically derived conglomerate, sandstone; exotic blocks of limestone; laharic deposits TQvs: Andesitic and basaltic agglomerate, tuff lava	Brown et al. (1983)
O	Headwaters of the Rentoul, Tomu and Aiema Rivers (Strickland River catchment); Aramia River; Wawoi and Guavi Rivers (Bamu River catchment); and Turama River. Centres on the Mt Bosavi cone	Sisa Volcanics (TQsl) Bosavi Volcanics (Qvb, Qvbl)	TQsl: Volcaniclastic andesitic and basaltic breccia, reworked agglomerate, tuff; minor intercalated volcanically derived conglomerate, sandstone; exotic blocks of limestone; laharic deposits Qvb: Basaltic (shoshonitic) and andesitic lava, agglomerate, tuff; minor derived volcaniclastic conglomerate, sandstone Qvbl: Volcaniclastic basaltic and minor andesitic breccia; reworked agglomerate, tuff intercalated volcanically derived conglomerate, sandstone: laharic deposits	Brown et al. (1983)
P	Turama River catchment centring on the Biwai Hills cone	Unnamed (Qv2)	Qv2: Basic to intermediate lavas and pyroclastic rocks (shoshonitic and calc-alkaline), lahars, fanglomerate, lacustrine deposits	Bain et al. (1972)

Fig. 12.1 reference	Geographical location	Geological unit (Unit map code)	Rock types/Comments	References
Q₁–Q₂	Lower Kikori River catchment, centring on the Mount Murray cone	Q₁ = Mount Murray Volcanics (Qvm) Q₂ = Mount Murray Volcanics (Qvml)	Qvm: Basaltic (shoshonitic) to andesite lava, agglomerate, tuff, porphyritic **microdiorite** dykes Qvml: Volcaniclastic basaltic and andesitic breccia, reworked agglomerate, tuff, minor intercalated volcanically derived conglomerate, sandstone: laharic deposits	Bain and MacKenzie (1974a:30, 1974b); Brown et al. (1983)
R	Sirebi River (Kikori River catchment)	Duau Volcanics (Qvd)	Qvd: Andesite and basalt agglomerate, tuff, minor lava at central parts of cones; volcanic sandstone, conglomerate and tuff on lower slopes and aprons	Pieters (1980:17–18, 1983)
S	Lower Kikori River (delta)	Aird Hill Volcanics (Qva)	Qva: Aphyric to porphyritic plagioclase-rich, leucocratic andesite or dacite lava and volcanic breccia	Pieters (1980:16, 1983)
T	Western Torres Strait, taking in numerous islands (e.g. Dauan, Gebar, Mabuyag, Mua, Badu and Muralag) and isolated outcrops on the adjacent north coast (Mabaduan, PNG) and south coast (Cape York, Australia)	Badu Suite (Cub) Torres Strait Volcanics (Ct) Muralug Ignimbrite (Cm) Goods Island Ignimbrite (Cg) Endeavour Strait Ignimbrite (Cn) Eborac Ignimbrite (Ce)	Cub: Leucocratic biotite granite, hornblende-biotite granite, porphyritic biotite granite, adamellite, hornblende-biotite adamellite, granodiorite, microdiorite, aplite and numerous quartz veins and dykes of aplite, pegmatite, porphyritic microgranite, dacite (?), hornblende andesite, hornblende-augite andesite and augite andesite. Ct: **Rhyolite** welded tuff, **rhyolite**, hornfels, andesite, siltstone and arenite Cm: Brownish grey **rhyolite** welded tuff; some **rhyolite** volcanic breccia and dacite? welded tuff Cg: Dark grey dellenite to dacite welded tuff; some interbedded siltstone and sandstone Cn: Greenish-grey **rhyolite** welded tuff; some **rhyolite**, andesite, agglomerate and hornfels Ce: Light grey **rhyolite** welded tuff; some **rhyolite** and agglomerate	Maitland (1892:16–17); von Gnielinski (2015); von Gnielinski et al. (1997); Willmott (1972:8); Willmott and Powell (1977:9–12); Willmott et al. (1973:98–106, 113–118),
U	Eastern Torres Strait, taking in the islands of Daru (PNG) and Bramble Cay, Ugar and Erub, and well-preserved cones at Mer, Dauar and Waier (Australia)	Maer Volcanics (Qpm)	Qpm: Basalt lava and tuff	Willmott (1972:9); Willmott et al. (1973:50–53)

Source: See sources listed throughout table. See also Figure 12.1.

Characterised implements: Potential processes of acquisition

Ethnographic information indicates that the Marind obtained stone implements from their immediate neighbours by trading and raiding. These neighbours similarly obtained supplies of stone implements by trading with and/or raiding neighbouring groups who had direct or indirect access to tool stone supplies/quarries. The following discussion of ethnographic information reveals that the Marind were part of trading and raiding networks that linked them directly or indirectly with potential sources of stone implement raw materials (i.e. Upper Digul River, Upper Fly–Strickland Rivers and Torres Strait). Indeed, such links suggest strongly that the Marind strategically positioned themselves with a wide range of stone implement provisioning options involving trading, raiding and perhaps direct stone procurement by quarrying.

Trading

As noted above, elderly Marind informed anthropologists during the first half of the twentieth century that at least some exotic stone implements were obtained from neighbours through exchange (e.g. Kooijman et al. 1958:46; van Baal 1966:23; Wirz 1946:85). The Digul River is the only specific area identified as the source of exchanged stone implements (Wirz 1922, I:112), with the Upper Digul River (Star Mountains) identified as the ultimate source (Verschueren cited in van Baal 1966:730).

A wide range of ethnographic information reveals that stone axes originating from quarry sites scattered along the southern flanks of the Central Ranges in Indonesian Papua were traded southwards along various river systems and across the vast lowlands towards the coast. In each case, and in the broader context of bi-directional movements of a variety of objects, stone axes from the mountainous interior moved downriver and marine shells (used as valuables and body adornments) from the coast moved upriver: Mumugo/Pomatsi–Northwest River system (Eyde 1967:15–16, 25; Pétrequin and Pétrequin 2020:188–190), Eilanden–Catalina–Baliem River system (Hampton 1999:278; Matthiessen 1962:94; Mitton 1972:8; Swadling 1983:87, Fig. 35), Eilanden–Brazza River system (Hampton 1999:278: Pétrequin and Pétrequin 2020:167, 175–176), Eilanden–Steenboom River system (Toth et al. 1992:92), Eilanden River (van Enk and de Vries 1997:11, 48-49) and Digul River (Kooijman 1962:18–19, 31–32, 37; Pétrequin and Pétrequin 2020:167, 172, 186, 253; Schoorl 1993:87, 94; Swadling 1983:86).

For the Fly–Strickland River system in Papua New Guinea, Swadling (1983:82) noted that the Duna of the headwaters of the Strickland River traded (imported) axes (made of glaucophane blueschists, greenschists and metavolcanics—White and Modjeska 1978:279) southwards through various groups to the Middle Strickland River and Lake Murray area (see also Austen cited in McCarthy 1939:185–186). The Boazi of the Middle Fly River (Lake Murray) obtained stone axes from Upper Fly River (Ok Tedi River) people in exchange for marine shells sourced to the Suki and Kiwai (Lower Fly River mouth) and Marind (Busse cited in Craig and Swadling 1983:117). The Samo of the Middle Strickland (Nomad River) obtained stone axes from the Upper Strickland in exchange for marine shells sourced to the Gulf of Papua coast via riverine trade routes (e.g. Bamu and Turama Rivers) (Craig and Swadling 1983:118). People of the Oriomo area at the mouth of the Fly River obtained stone implements 'through the Fly River people, who traded them from up-river' (Pretty 1965:127). Government anthropologist F.E. Williams (1936:416) recorded that the Wiram/Suki of the Lower Fly River obtained stone club heads from 'higher up the Fly River' in exchange for *Melo* shells 'collected on the coast'.

People of Mawata village on the northern mainland coast of Torres Strait apparently obtained stone implements from Torres Strait Islanders, telling Finnish anthropologist Gunnar Landtman (1927:34) that 'Torres Strait islanders obtained the stones out of which axes (or adzes) and club-heads were made principally from the bottom of the sea, by diving'. The upshot of these ethnographically known exchange networks is that the borders of Marind territory abutted supplies of traded stone implements (e.g. axes, club heads) available along the Digul River (western, north-western and northern borders), the Middle Fly River (north-eastern border) and the Trans-Fly/Torres Strait region (south-eastern border). The close linguistic and social relationships between the Boazi and Bian Marind provided considerable potential for Upper Fly River stone implements to enter Marind society (see Busse 1987, 2005; van Baal 1966:110, 706).

Raiding

Elderly Marind also informed anthropologists during the first half of the twentieth century that exotic stone implements were obtained mostly from neighbours during headhunting raids (e.g. Kooijman et al. 1958:46; van Baal 1966:23; Wirz 1946:85). Again, the only area specially mentioned as a source of raided stone implements was the Digul River (Wirz 1922, I:112), with the far northern Marind (Upper Bian River) adding that the Upper Fly River was the ultimate source of stone club heads (Wirz 1922, I:112). Yet Marind headhunting expeditions engaged a wide range of neighbours to the south-west (Yos Sudarso Island), west, north-west and north (Digul River), east (Middle and Upper Merauke River) and south-east (Trans-Fly and northern Torres Strait) (McNiven in press; Schoorl 1993; Swadling 1996:Fig. 39; van Baal 1966). The relationship between headhunting and stone implement procurement was not unique to the Marind, with Busse (1987:50) noting that 'The absence of stone was also one motivation for the head-hunting raids by the tribes of the Middle Fly on the groups to the north of them' (see also Kirsch 1991:22). Marind headhunting expeditions allowed engagement with a wide range of neighbouring groups who had supplies of stone implements sourced either directly (e.g. Torres Strait) or indirectly (e.g. Digul River).

Ethnographic observations from northern Torres Strait during the late nineteenth century reveal extra dimensions to Marind tool stone procurement. Missionary Rev. Samuel McFarlane (1888:106) was informed by people of Boigu that they fought off a Marind attack using spears and stone missiles. Boigu is a stoneless island with the nearest potential stone source being their neighbours and allies on the granite island of Dauan (Figure 12.1). It is likely that retreating Marind kept the stone missiles as a rare and valuable source of tool stone. In another instance, in the 1880s the missionary Rev. Edwin B. Savage observed the Marind trading with Saibai Islanders instead of the usual raiding interaction (Wirz 1933:108; see also McNiven 1998:108).

Quarrying

While not mentioned in the ethnographic literature, it is possible that the Marind directly accessed the Mabaduan stone source located on the northern mainland coast of Torres Strait (opposite the island of Saibai) during south-eastern headhunting expeditions to the Trans-Fly region (Figure 12.1). The process of direct procurement is not without precedent for southern lowland groups of central New Guinea, with some coastal Asmat groups travelling upriver to foothills of the Central Ranges to load up canoes with river cobbles which were ferried back to coastal villages for shaping into axes (Konrad and Ligabue 1996:54). Within the ethnographic context of Marind mobility patterns, Mabaduan provided the only opportunity for the Marind to directly access igneous tool stone and manufacture their own ground stone implements. Whether or not axe-grinding grooves at Mabaduan were used by the Marind is unknown (Landtman 1927:287). Wirz (1933:119) was informed by the Marind that 'occasionally' they established a 'big camp' (including women and children) at Mabaduan during the headhunting season. Marind access to northern Torres Strait (including Mabaduan) tool stone helps explain the apparent restricted distribution of 'spearthrower' stones (*imbassum*) to the Marind.

Conclusion

In 2009, Glenn Summerhayes pointed out that documenting chronological and spatial dimensions of stone tools and their geological sources provide important insights into trade and exchange systems and the social and economic worlds of New Guinea societies in the past. Indeed, Papua New Guinea was at the centre of the most extensive distributional array of obsidian in the ancient world (Summerhayes 2009:115). The analytical foundation of these studies is accurate characterisation of stone artefact raw materials and detailed understanding of the locations of potential geological sources of these raw materials. Although such studies (especially by Summerhayes) are well developed for some areas of Papua New Guinea, the same is not true for Indonesian Papua across the western half of New Guinea. The major exception is the detailed ethnoarchaeological research by Pierre Pétrequin and Anne-Marie Pétrequin (1993a, 1993b, 2020) on ground-edge axes in the stone-rich regions of the Central Ranges. While that research was focused on axe production at quarry sites, insights into axe distributions was limited largely to examination of selected museum collections of axes obtained from locations away from sources. Our examination of Marind ground stone implements (club heads and 'spearthrower' stones) builds on the foundational work of the Pétrequins but in the stoneless region of south-east Indonesian Papua. The social and cultural relationships that developed between the stone-rich and stoneless regions of Indonesian Papua reveal that processes of provisioning extended beyond trading and exchange to include raiding and headhunting. Indeed, the Marind developed one of the most extreme stone tool provisioning systems in the world. Further research is required to extend our pilot study of six Marind stone implements to include comprehensive petrographic characterisation of museum collections of stone axes, club heads and 'spearthrower' stones. Archaeological excavation of old Marind village sites would furnish further examples of stone implements for sourcing, and shed light on the representativeness of museum collections of Marind objects. In addition, archaeological research at Mabaduan on the northern mainland coast of Torres Strait may reveal its critical role in provisioning tool stone across the southern lowlands of central New Guinea.

Acknowledgements

Thanks to Anne Ford, Ben Shaw and Dylan Gaffney for the invitation to contribute to this special volume. For assistance with reproduction of historical photographs and images of museum objects we thank Nicolien Karskens (Leiden University, Libraries Special Collections Services) and Myrthe Duin and Ingeborg Eggink (World Museum, Rotterdam). Thanks to Karina Pelling (CartoGIS Services, The Australian National University) for creating the base map for Figure 12.1, and Steve Morton (Monash University) for photographic images in Figure 12.6. Special thanks to Raymond Corbey, Hugh Davies, Peter Pieters and Pamela Swadling for reading and providing helpful comments on an earlier draft of this chapter. One of us (IM) would like to extend a huge thanks to Glenn Summerhayes for his decades of friendship, built around our mutual passion for New Guinea anthropology and archaeology, Indian cuisine, old books, old red wine and old jokes.

References

Alder, W.F. 1922. *The isle of vanishing men: A narrative of adventure in cannibal-land.* The Century Co., New York.

Alder, W.F. and E. Bailey 1921. Six months among the head-hunters. *Wide World Magazine* 47:205–210.

Austen, L. 1923. The Tedi River district of Papua. *The Geographical Journal* 62(5):335–349. doi.org/10.2307/1780585.

Austen, L. 1926. Recent explorations in the north-west district of Papua. *The Geographical Journal* 67(5): 434–441. doi.org/10.2307/1782209.

Bain, J.H.C., H.L. Davies, P.D. Hohnen, R.J. Ryburn, I.E. Smith, R. Grainger, R.J. Tingey and M.R. Moffat 1972. *Geology Papua New Guinea.* Map. 1:1,000,000 scale. Bureau of Mineral Resources, Geology and Geophysics, Canberra; Department of Lands, Surveys and Mines, Port Moresby.

Bain, J.H.C. and D. Haipola 1997. North Queensland geology map, 1:1,000,000. In J.H.C. Bain and J.J. Draper (eds), *North Queensland geology.* Australian Geological Survey Organisation Bulletin 240, and Queensland Department of Mines and Energy Queensland Geology 9, Brisbane.

Bain, J.H.C. and D.E. MacKenzie 1974a. *Karimui, Papua New Guinea.* 1:250,000 geological series. Sheet SB 55-9. Explanatory notes. Australian Government Publishing Service, Canberra.

Bain, J.H.C. and D.E. MacKenzie 1974b. *Karimui, Papua New Guinea.* 1:250,000 geological series. Sheet SB 55-9. Map. First edition. Bureau of Mineral Resources, Geology and Geophysics, Department of Minerals and Energy, Canberra.

Bär, C.B., H.J. Cortel and A.E. Escher 1961. Geological results of the Star Mountains ('Sterrengebergte') Expedition. *Nova Guinea, Geology* 4:39–99.

Boelaars, J. 1969. South-western Irian missionary activities, 1905-1966. *Euntes Docete* 22:241–264.

Bolton, B.R., J.L. Pile and H. Kundapen 2009. Texture, geochemistry, and mineralogy of sediments of the Fly River system. In B. Bolton (ed.), *The Fly River, Papua New Guinea: Environmental studies in an impacted tropical river system*, pp. 51–112. Developments in Earth & Environmental Sciences 9. Elsevier, Amsterdam. doi.org/10.1016/s1571-9197(08)00402-3.

Brown, C.M., G.P. Robinson and D.L. Gibson 1983. *Kutubu, Papua New Guinea.* 1:250,000 geological series. Sheet SB 54-12. Map. Department of Minerals and Energy, Port Moresby.

Busse, M.W. 1987. Sister exchange among the Wamek of the Middle Fly. Unpublished PhD thesis, University of California, San Diego. www.proquest.com/docview/303549483.

Busse, M. 2005. Wandering hero stories in the southern lowlands of New Guinea: Culture areas, comparison, and history. *Cultural Anthropology* 20(4):443–473. doi.org/10.1525/can.2005.20.4.443.

Chao, S. 2021. Children of the palms: Growing plants and growing people in a Papuan Plantationocene. *Journal of the Royal Anthropological Institute* 27(2):245–264. doi.org/10.1111/1467-9655.13489.

Chappell, J. 2005. Geographic changes of coastal lowlands in the Papuan past. In A. Pawley, R. Attenborough, J. Golson and R. Hide (eds), *Papuan pasts: Cultural, linguistic and biological histories of Papuan-speaking peoples*, pp. 525–539. Pacific Linguistics 572. Research School of Pacific and Asian Studies, The Australian National University, Canberra.

Corbey, R. 2010. *Headhunters from the swamps: The Marind Anim of New Guinea as seen by the missionaries of the Sacred Heart, 1905–1925.* KITLV Press and C. Zwartenkot Art Books, Leiden.

Craig, B. and P. Swadling 1983. Trading spheres in the Ok Tedi impact region. In P. Swadling, *How long have people been in the Ok Tedi region?*, pp. 111–121. PNG National Museum Record 8. Trustees of the PNG National Museum, Port Moresby.

D'Addario, G.W., D.B. Dow and R. Swoboda 1976. *Geology of Papua New Guinea.* Map. 1:2,500,000. Bureau of Mineral Resources, Australia, Canberra.

Davies, H.L. 1982. *Mianmin, Papua New Guinea.* 1:250,000 geological series. Sheet SB/54-3. Explanatory notes. Department of Minerals and Energy, Geological Survey of Papua New Guinea, Port Moresby.

Davies, H.L. 1983. *Wabag, Papua New Guinea.* 1:250,000 geological series. Sheet SB/54-8. Explanatory notes. Department of Minerals and Energy, Geological Survey of Papua New Guinea, Port Moresby.

Davies, H.L. and S.J. Baloiloi 1983. *Ambunti, Papua New Guinea.* 1:250,000 geological series. Sheet SB 54-4. Map. First edition. Geological Survey of Papua New Guinea, Department of Minerals and Energy, Port Moresby.

Davies, H.L. and P. Eno 1983. *Wabag, Papua New Guinea.* 1:250,000 geological series. Sheet SB 54-8. Map. First edition. Geological Survey of Papua New Guinea, Department of Minerals and Energy, Port Moresby.

Davies, H.L. and D.S. Hutchison 1982. *Ambunti, Papua New Guinea.* 1:250,000 geological series – Explanatory notes. Sheet SB/54-4. Department of Minerals and Energy, Geological Survey of Papua New Guinea, Port Moresby.

Davies, H.L., D.S. Hutchison, M. Norvick, J. Rau Aeava, R.J. Ryburn and P.G. White 1983. *Mianmin, Papua New Guinea.* 1:250,000 geological series. Sheet SB 54-3. Map. First edition. Geological Survey of Papua New Guinea, Department of Minerals and Energy, Port Moresby.

Davies, H.L. and M. Norvick 1974. *Blucher Range, Papua New Guinea.* 1:250,000 geological series. Sheet SB/54-7. Explanatory notes. Port Moresby: Department of Lands, Surveys and Mines, Papua New Guinea, Geological Survey of Papua New Guinea, Port Moresby; Australian Government Publishing Service, Canberra.

Davies, H.L., M. Norvick, D.S. Hutchison, R.J. Ryburn and P.G. White 1974. *Blucher Range, Papua New Guinea.* 1:250,000 geological series. Sheet SB/54-7. Map. First edition. Bureau of Mineral Resources, Geology and Geophysics, Department of Minerals and Energy, Canberra; Geological Survey of Papua New Guinea, Port Moresby.

Djami, E.N.I. and H. Suroto, 2023. Distribution of Austronesian languages and archaeology in Western New Guinea, Indonesia. *L'Anthropologie* 127(3), p.103153.

Dougherty, A.J., Z.A. Thomas, C. Fogwill, A. Hogg, J. Palmer, E. Rainsley, A.N. Williams, S. Ulm, K. Rogers, B.G. Jones and C. Turney 2019. Redating the earliest evidence of the mid-Holocene relative sea-level highstand in Australia and implications for global sea-level rise. *PLoS ONE* 14(7):p.e0218430. doi.org/10.1371/journal.pone.0218430.

Dow, D.B., G.P. Robinson, U. Hartono dan and N. Ratman 1986. *Peta Geologi Irian Jaya, Indonesia/Geological map of Irian Jaya, Indonesia.* 1:1,000,000. Sheets 1 & 2. Pusat Penelitian Dan Pengembangan Geologi/Geological Research and Development Centre, Bandung.

Expedition. 1908. *De Zuidwest Nieuw-Guinea-Expeditie 1904/05 van het Koninklijk Aardrijkskundig Genootschap.* E.J. Brill, Leiden.

Expedition. 1920. *Verslag van de Militaire Exploratie van Nederlandsch-Nieuw-Guinee 1907–1915.* Landsdrukkerij, Weltevreden.

Eyde, D. 1967. Cultural correlates of warfare among the Asmat of south west New Guinea. Unpublished PhD thesis, Yale University, Ann Arbor. www.proquest.com/docview/302306163.

Gaffney, D. and G.R. Summerhayes 2019. Coastal mobility and lithic supply lines in northeast New Guinea. *Archaeological and Anthropological Sciences* 11(6):2849–2878. doi.org/10.1007/s12520-018-0713-8.

Geurtjens, R.P.H. 1949. A propos d'un ustensile de l'âge de pierre au Sud de la Nouvelle-Guinée. *Anthropos* 41/44(1/3):219–224. www.jstor.org/stable/40449180.

Grottanelli, V.L. 1951. On the 'mysterious' baratu clubs from Central New Guinea. *Man* 51:105–107. www.jstor.org/stable/2793639.

Haddon, A.C. 1900. A classification of the stone clubs of British New Guinea. *Journal of the Anthropological Institute of Great Britain and Ireland* 30:221–250. doi.org/10.2307/2842629.

Hampton, O.W. 1999. *Culture of stone: Sacred and profane uses of stone among the Dani.* Texas A & M University Press, College Station.

Harlow, G.E., G.R. Summerhayes, H.L. Davies and L. Matisoo-Smith 2012. A jade gouge from Emirau Island, Papua New Guinea (Early Lapita context, 3300 BP): A unique jadeitite. *European Journal of Mineralogy* 24(2):391–399. doi.org/10.1127/0935-1221/2012/0024-2175.

Heldring, O.G. 1910. De quickest van Nieu-Guinea door den mijningenieur. *Jaarboek van het mijnwezen in Nederlandsch Oost-Indie 1909* 38:85–203.

Heldring, O.G. 1913. Verslag over Zuid-Nieuw-Guinea door den mijningenieur. *Jaarboek van het mijnwezen in Nederlandsch Oost-Indie 1911* 40:40–207.

Hitchcock, G. 2004. Torres Strait origin of some stone-headed clubs from the Torassi River, southwest Papua New Guinea. *Memoirs of the Queensland Museum Cultural Heritage Series* 3(1):305–313. search.informit.org/doi/abs/10.3316/ielapa.889850103336082.

Höltker, G. 1940–41. Einiges über steinkeulenköpfe und steinbeile in Neuguinea. Tatsachen und probleme in ausschnitten und perspektiven. *Anthropos* 35/36(4/6):681–736. www.jstor.org/stable/40459836.

Key, C. 1968. Trace element identification of the source of obsidian in an archaeological site in New Guinea. *Nature* 219:360. doi.org/10.1038/219360a0.

Kirsch, S. 1991. The Yonggom of New Guinea: An ethnography of sorcery, magic, and ritual. Unpublished PhD thesis, University of Pennsylvania, Philadelphia.

Konrad, U. and G. Konrad 1996. *Bis Pokumbu*: The ancestor pole feast. In G. Konrad and U. Konrad (eds), *Asmat: Myth and ritual. The inspiration of art*, pp. 264–301. Erizzo Editrice, Venezia.

Konrad, G. and G. Ligabue 1996. Stone tools and ritual stones: Production and trade. In G. Konrad and U. Konrad (eds), *Asmat: Myth and ritual. The inspiration of art*, pp. 44–63. Erizzo Editrice, Venezia.

Konrad, U. and A. Sowada 2002. The collection of the museum of Agats. In U. Konrad, A. Sowada and G. Konrad (eds), *Asmat: Perception of life in art. The collection of the Asmat Museum of Culture and Progress*, pp. 111–381. B. Kühlen, Verlag.

Kooijman, S. 1952. The function and significance of some ceremonial clubs of the Marind-anim, Dutch New Guinea. *Man* 52:97–99. doi.org/10.2307/2793498.

Kooijman, S. 1959. Population research project among the Marind-anim and Jeeo-nan peoples in Netherlands South New Guinea: Summary of a report. *Nieuw-Guinea Studiën* 3:9–34.

Kooijman, S. 1962. Material aspects of the Star Mountains culture. *Nova Guinea, Anthropology* 2:15–44.

Kooijman, S. 1984. *Art, art objects, and ritual in the Mimika culture.* E.J. Brill, Leiden. doi.org/10.1163/9789004545106.

Kooijman, S., M. Dorren, L. Veeger, J. Verschueren and R. Luyken 1958. Report of the Investigation into the Problem of Depopulation among the Marind-anim of Netherlands New Guinea 1953–1954. South Pacific Commission Population Studies S.18 Project. Nouméa, New Caledonia.

Landtman, G. 1927. *The Kiwai Papuans of British New Guinea.* Macmillan & Co, London.

Le Roux, C.C.F.M. 1950. *De Bergpapoea's van Nieuw-Guinea en hun woongebied.* Vol. 3. E.J. Brill, Leiden. doi.org/10.1163/9789004665293.

Löffler, E. 1977. *Geomorphology of Papua New Guinea.* CSIRO with Australian National University Press, Canberra. openresearch-repository.anu.edu.au/bitstream/1885/114888/2/b12297859.pdf.

MacGregor, W.M. 1897. Appendix K: Despatch reporting expedition undertaken to repel Tugeri invaders. In *Annual Report on British New Guinea from 1st July, 1895, to 30th June, 1896, with Appendices,* pp. 52–56. Edmund Gregory, Government Printer, Brisbane.

MacGregor, W.M. 1898. *Annual Report on British New Guinea from 1st July, 1897, to 30th June, 1898; with Appendices.* Edmund Gregory, Government Printer, Brisbane.

Maitland, A.G. 1892. *Geological observations in British New Guinea in 1891.* Queensland Geological Survey Publication No. 85. J.C. Beal, government printer, Brisbane.

Matthiessen, P. 1962. *Under the mountain wall: A chronicle of two seasons in the Stone Age.* Heinemann, London.

McCarthy, F.D. 1939. 'Trade' in Aboriginal Australia, and 'trade' relationships with Torres Strait, New Guinea and Malaya. *Oceania* 9(4):405–439, 10(1):80–104, 10(2):171–195. doi.org/10.1002/j.1834-4461.1939.tb00275.x.

McFarlane, S. 1888. *Among the cannibals of New Guinea.* London Missionary Society, London.

McNiven, I.J. 1998. Enmity and amity: Reconsidering stone-headed club (gabagaba) procurement and trade in Torres Strait. *Oceania* 69:94–115. doi.org/10.1002/j.1834-4461.1998.tb02697.x.

McNiven, I.J. 2010. 'Oh wonderful beach': The Marind-anim of Papua and ethnographic foundations for an archaeology of a littoral sea people. *The Artefact (Journal of the Anthropological & Archaeological Society of Victoria)* 33:91–108. search.informit.org/doi/abs/10.3316/ielapa.005095043358499.

McNiven, I.J. (in press). Agentive seas and animate canoes: Tangible and intangible dimensions of marine voyaging by the Marind-anim of central-southern New Guinea. In D. Gaffney and M. Tolla (eds), *The archaeology and material culture of Western New Guinea.* Terra Australis. ANU Press, Canberra.

McNiven, I.J. and F. von Gnielinski. 2004. Manufacture of stone club heads from Dauan Island, Torres Strait. *Memoirs of the Queensland Museum, Cultural Heritage Series* 3(1):187–200. search.informit.org/doi/abs/10.3316/ielapa.889794204422308.

McNiven, I.J., F. von Gnielinski and M. Quinnell 2004. Torres Strait and the origin of large stone axes from Kiwai Island, Fly River Estuary (Papua New Guinea). *Memoirs of the Queensland Museum, Cultural Heritage Series* 3(1):271–289.

Mialanes, J., B. David, A. Ford, T. Richards, I.J. McNiven, G.R. Summerhayes and M. Leavesley 2016. Imported obsidian at Caution Bay, south coast of Papua New Guinea: Cessation of long distance procurement c. 1,900 cal BP. *Australian Archaeology* 82(3):248–262. doi.org/10.1080/03122417.2016.1252079.

Mitton, R. 1972. Stone as a cultural factor in the central and eastern Highlands. *Irian: Bulletin of West Iran Development* 1(3):4–11.

Nevermann, H. 1939. Die Kanum-irebe und ihre Nachbarn. *Zeitschrift für Ethnologie* 71(1/3):1–70. www.jstor.org/stable/25839800.

Nollen, P.H. 1909. Les différentes classes d'age dans la société kaia-kaia, Merauke, Nouvelle Guinée Néerlandaise. *Anthropos* 4(3):553–573. www.jstor.org/stable/40442582.

Olsson, B. 2017. The coastal Marind language. Unpublished PhD thesis, Nanyang Technological University, Singapore. dr.ntu.edu.sg/bitstream/10356/73235/1/Olsson2017_Coastal_Marind.pdf.

Owen, I.L., L. Muke and H.L. Davies 2008. Trichinellosis: A possible link between human infection and the traditional earth-oven or 'mumu' method of cooking in Morehead District, Western Province, Papua New Guinea. *Anthropology & Medicine* 15(3):189–197. doi.org/10.1080/13648470802355582.

Paijmans, K., D.H. Blake, P. Bleeker and J.R. McAlpine 1971. *Land resources of the Morehead-Kiunga area, Territory of Papua and New Guinea.* Land Research Series 29. Commonwealth Scientific and Industrial Research Organization, Melbourne. doi.org/10.1071/lrs29.

Pétrequin, P. and A.-M. Pétrequin 1993a. *Écologie d'un outil: La hache de pierre en Irian Jaya (Indonésie).* Monographie du CRA 12. CNRS editions, Paris.

Pétrequin, P. and A.-M. Pétrequin 1993b. From polished stone tool to sacred axe: The axes of the Danis of Irian Jaya, Indonesia. In A. Berthelet and J. Chavaillon (eds), *The use of tools by human and non-human primates*, pp. 359–377. Clarendon Press, Oxford. doi.org/10.1093/acprof:oso/9780198522638.003.0021.

Pétrequin, P. and A.-M. Pétrequin 2020. *Ecology of a tool: The ground stone axes of Irian Jaya (Indonesia).* Oxbow, Oxford & Philadelphia. www.jstor.org/stable/j.ctv138wsr5.

Pickup, G. and A.R. Marshall 2009. Geomorphology, hydrology, and climate of the Fly River system. In B. Bolton (ed.), *The Fly River, Papua New Guinea: Environmental studies in an impacted tropical river system*, pp. 3–49. Developments in Earth and Environmental Sciences 9. Elsevier, Amsterdam. doi.org/10.1016/s1571-9197(08)00401-1.

Pieters, P.E. 1980. *The geology of the Kikori.* 1:250,000 sheet area, PNG. Record 1980/79. Bureau of Mineral Resources, Geology and Geophysics, Canberra.

Pieters, P. 1983. *Kikori, Papua New Guinea.* 1:250,000 geological series. Sheet SB/55-13. Explanatory notes. Department of Minerals and Energy, Geological Survey of Papua New Guinea, Port Moresby.

Pöch, R. 1907. Travels in German, British, and Dutch New Guinea. *The Geographical Journal* 30(6):609–616. doi.org/10.2307/1776812.

Powell, B.S. and J. Smart 1977. *Jardine River–Orford Bay, Queensland.* 1:250,000 Geological Series – Explanatory Notes and Map. Australian Government Publishing Service, Canberra.

Pretty, G.L. 1965. Two stone pestles from western Papua and their relationship to prehistoric pestles and mortars from New Guinea. *Records of the South Australian Museum* 15(1):119–130.

Purnomo, G.A., K.J. Mitchell, S. O'Connor, S. Kealy, L. Taufik, S. Schiller, A. Rohrlach, A. Cooper, B. Llamas, H. Sudoyo and J.C. Teixeira 2021. Mitogenomes reveal two major influxes of Papuan ancestry across Wallacea following the last glacial maximum and Austronesian contact. *Genes* 12(7):965. doi.org/10.3390/genes12070965.

Raffaele, P. 2006. Sleeping with cannibals. *Smithsonian* 37(6):48–59.

Reichgelt, M.G.W. 2016. Marind children through the lens of the missionaries of the Sacred Heart: Missionary photography on Netherlands New Guinea, 1906–1935. Unpublished MA thesis, Radboud University, Nijmegen.

Reijnders, J.J. 1964. A pedo-ecological study of soil genesis in the tropics from sea level to eternal snow. Star Mountains, Central New Guinea. Published doctoral thesis, University Utrecht. E.J. Brill, Leiden.

Reynders, J.J. 1961. The landscape in the Maro and Koembe River district (Merauke, southern Netherlands New Guinea). *Boor en Spade* 11:104–119.

Rhoads, J.W. and D.E. MacKenzie 1991. Stone axe trade in prehistoric Papua: The travels of python. *Proceedings of the Prehistoric Society* 57(2):35–49. doi.org/10.1017/S0079497X00004497.

Richens, J. 2022. *Tik Merauke: An epidemic like no other*. Melbourne University Press, Melbourne. doi.org/10.2307/jj.1176760.

Saulnier, T. and M. Bisiaux 1963. *Headhunters of Papua*. Paul Hamlyn, London.

Schoorl, J.W. 1993. *Culture and change among the Muyu*. KITLV Press, Leiden.

Schroo, H. 1964. An inventory of soils and soil suitabilities in West Irian. IIB. *Netherlands Journal of Agricultural Science* 12(1):1–29. doi.org/10.18174/njas.v12i1.17530.

Shaw, B., G. Irwin, A. Pengilley and S. Kelloway 2021. Village-specific Kula partnerships revealed by obsidian sourcing on Tubetube Island, Papua New Guinea. *Archaeology in Oceania* 56(1):32–44. doi.org/10.1002/arco.5224.

Simanjuntak, T. 1998. Review of the prehistory of Irian Jaya. In J. Miedema, C. Odé and R.A.C. Dam (eds), *Perspectives on the Bird's Head of Irian Jaya, Indonesia: Proceedings of the conference Leiden, 13–17 October 1997*, pp. 941–950. Rodopi B.V., Amsterdam; Atlanta, GA. doi.org/10.1163/9789004652644_043.

Smidt, D. 2006. The Marind-anim art. In P. Peltier and F. Morin (eds), *Shadows of New Guinea: Art from the great island of Oceania in the Barbier-Mueller collections*, pp. 248–259, 428–430. Musée Barbier-Mueller, Geneva.

Soetrisno dan and Amiruddin. 1995. *Geological map of the Oksibil quadrangle, Irian Jaya*. Scale 1:250,000. Geological Research and Development Centre, Bandung.

Soukup, M. 2020. Stone clubs of New Guinea. *Annals of the Náprstek Museum* 41(2):55–70. doi.org/10.37520/anpm.2020.007.

Steenbrink, K. 2007. *Catholics in Indonesia, 1808–1942: A documented history. Volume 2: The spectacular growth of a self-confident minority, 1903–1942*. KITLV Press, Leiden. brill.com/display/title/23356.

Summerhayes, G. 2000. *Lapita interaction*. Terra Australis 15. Department of Archaeology and Natural History, The Australian National University, Canberra. openresearch-repository.anu.edu.au/bitstream/1885/127430/1/TA_15.pdf.

Summerhayes, G.R. 2009. Obsidian network patterns in Melanesia—Sources, characterisation and distribution. *Bulletin of the Indo-Pacific Prehistory Association* 29:109–123.

Summerhayes, G.R. and J. Allen 1993. The transport of Mopir obsidian to late Pleistocene New Ireland. *Archaeology in Oceania* 28(3):144–148. doi.org/10.1002/j.1834-4453.1993.tb00305.x.

Summerhayes, G.R., R. Bird, R. Fullagar, C. Gosden, J. Specht and R. Torrence 1998. Application of PIXE-PIGME to archaeological analysis of changing patterns of obsidian use in West New Britain, Papua New Guinea. In M.S. Shackley (ed.), *Archaeological obsidian studies: Method and theory*, pp. 129–158. Plenum Press, New York. doi.org/10.1007/978-1-4757-9276-8_6.

Sutton, N., G. Summerhayes and A. Ford 2015. Regional interaction networks in southern Papua New Guinea during the late Holocene: Evidence from the chemical characterisation of chert artefacts. *Proceedings of the Prehistoric Society* 81:343–359. doi.org/10.1017/ppr.2015.14.

Swadling, P. 1983. *How long have people been in the Ok Tedi region?* PNG National Museum Record 8. Trustees of the PNG National Museum, Port Moresby.

Swadling, P. 1996. *Plumes from paradise*. Papua New Guinea National Museum, Port Moresby.

Terpstra, H. 1939. Resultaten van een goud-exploratie in het stroomgebied van de Lorentz- en de Eilanden-rivier in Nederlandsch Nieuw-Guinea. De Ingenieur in Nederlandsch-Indië IV. *Mijnbouw en Geologie* 1:1–6.

Tommaseo-Ponzetta, M., M. Attimonelli, M. De Robertis, F. Tanzariello and C. Saccone 2002. Mitochondrial DNA variability of west New Guinea populations. *American Journal of Physical Anthropology* 117(1):49–67. doi.org/10.1002/ajpa.10010.

Torrence, R., P. Swadling, N. Kononenko, W. Ambrose, P. Rath and M. Glascock 2009. Mid-Holocene social interaction in Melanesia: New evidence from hammer-dressed obsidian stemmed tools. *Asian Perspectives* 48(1):119–148. doi.org/10.1353/asi.0.0014.

Toth, N., D. Clark and G. Ligabue 1992. The last stone ax makers. *Scientific American* 267(1):88–93. doi.org/10.1038/scientificamerican0792-88.

Trenkenschuh, F. 1982. Border areas of the Asmat: The Dani people. In F.A. Trenkenschuh (ed.), *An Amsat sketch book*, vols 1 and 2, pp. 83–85. Asmat Museum of Culture and Progress, Agats.

Usher, T. and E. Suter 2015. Anim languages of southern New Guinea. *Oceanic Linguistics* 54(1):110–142. doi.org/10.1353/ol.2015.0003.

van Baal, J. 1966. *Dema: Description and analysis of Marind-anim culture (South New Guinea)*. Martinus Nijhoff, The Hague.

van Baal, J. 1994. The dialectics of sex in Marind-anim culture. In G.H. Herdt (ed.), *Ritualized homosexuality in Melanesia*, pp. 128–166. Paperback edition. University of California Press, Berkeley. doi.org/10.1525/9780520341388-004.

van den Bold, W.A. 1942. Some rocks from the course of the Digoel, the Oewi-Merah and the Eilanden River (South New Guinea). *Proceedings of the Koninklijke Nederlandse Akademie van Wetenschappen* 45(8):850–854.

van der Wegen, G. 1966. Contribution of the Bureau of Mines to the geology of the Central Mountains of West New Guinea. *Geologie en Mijnbouw* 45(8):249–261.

van Enk, G.J. and L. de Vries 1997. *The Korowai of Irian Jaya: Their language in its cultural context*. Oxford University Press, New York and Oxford.

Visser, W.A. and J.J. Hermes 1962. *Geological results of the exploration for oil in Netherlands New Guinea carried out by the 'Nederlandsche Nieuw Guinee Petroleum Maatschappij' 1935–1960*. Verhandelingen van het Koninklijk Nederlands Geologisch Mijnbouwkundig Genootschap Geological Series 20. Delft, Netherlands.

von Gnielinski, F. 2015. The geology of the Mabuyag Island Group and its part in the geological evolution of Torres Strait. *Memoirs of the Queensland Museum – Culture* 8(1):55–78. search.informit.org/doi/10.3316/INFORMIT.630649989430634.

von Gnielinski, F.E., T.J. Denaro, P. Wellman and C.F. Pain 1997. Torres Strait region. In J.H.C. Bain and J.J. Draper (eds), *North Queensland geology*, pp. 159–164. AGSO Bulletin 240 / Queensland Geology 9. Australian Geological Survey Organisation, Canberra; Geological Survey of Queensland, Brisbane.

Voorhoeve, C.L. 1983. South-eastern Irian Jaya. In S.A. Wurm and S. Hattori (eds), *Language atlas of the Pacific area. Pt. 1. New Guinea area, Oceania, Australia.* Pacific Linguistic Series C, pp. 66–67. Australian Academy of the Humanities in collaboration with the Japan Academy, Canberra.

White, J.P. and N. Modjeska 1978. Acquirers, users, finders, losers: The use axe blades make of the Duna. In J. Specht and J.P. White (eds), *Trade and exchange in Oceania and Australia*, pp. 276–287. Special issue of *Mankind* 11(3). Sydney University Press, Sydney. doi.org/10.1111/j.1835-9310.1978.tb00658.x.

Williams, F.E. 1936. *Papuans of the Trans-Fly.* Claredon Press, Oxford.

Willmott, W.F. 1972. *Daru-Maer. Papua and Queensland.* 1:250,000 Geological Series. Explanatory Notes and Map. Australian Government Publishing Service, Canberra.

Willmott, W.F. and B.S. Powell 1977. *Torres Strait–Boigu–Daru, Queensland.* 1:250,000 Geological Series. Explanatory Notes and Map. Australian Government Publishing Service, Canberra.

Willmott, W.F., W.G. Whitaker, W.D. Palfreyman and D.S. Trail 1973. *Igneous and metamorphic rocks of Cape York Peninsula and Torres Strait.* Department of Minerals and Energy, Bureau of Mineral Resources, Geology and Geophysics. Bulletin 135. Australian Government Printing Service, Canberra.

Wirz, P. 1922. *Die Marind-anim von Holländisch-Süd-Neu-Guinea. I. Band. Teil I. Die materielle kultur de Marind-anim. Teil II: Die religiösen vorstellungen und die mythen der Marind-anim, sowie die herausbildung der totemistisch-sozialen gruppierungen.* L. Friederichsen & Co, Hamburg. www.degruyter.com/document/doi/10.1515/9783111588902/html.

Wirz, P. 1925. *Die Marind-anim von Holländisch-Süd-Neu-Guinea. II. Band. Teil III. Das soziale leben der Mardin-anim. Teil IV. Die Marind-anim in ihren festen, ihrer kunst und ihren kenntnissen und eigenschaften.* Kommissions-Verlag L. Friederichsen & Co, Hamburg.

Wirz, P. 1932. Legend of the Dauan Islanders (Torres Straits). *Folklore* 43(3):285–294. doi.org/10.1080/0015587x.1932.9718449.

Wirz, P. 1933. Head-hunting expeditions of the Tugeri into the Western Division of British New Guinea. *Tijdschrift voor Indische Taal-, Land- en Volkenkunde* 73:105–122.

Wirz, P. 1946. Einiges ilher die Steinverehrung und den Steinkult in Neuguinea. *Verhandlungen der Naturforschenden Gesellschaft in Basel* 57:75–117.

Woodroffe, C.D., D.M. Kennedy, D. Hopley, C.E. Rasmussen and S.G. Smithers 2000. Holocene reef growth in Torres Strait. *Marine Geology* 170(3-4):331–346. doi.org/10.1016/S0025-3227(00)00094-3.

Wright, D., T. Denham, D. Shine and M. Donohue 2013. An archaeological review of western New Guinea. *Journal of World Prehistory* 26(1):25–73. doi.org/10.1007/s10963-013-9063-8.

Part 4: Cultural landscapes

13

Mid–late Holocene diversification of cultural identities in the Massim islands and the formative development of *Kula*: Excavations at the Mumwa site, Panaeati Island

Ben Shaw, Simon Coxe, Jemina Haro, Vincent Kewibu, Kenneth Miamba and Lachlan Sharp

Abstract

Anthropological, linguistic and genetic research has suggested that the Massim islands of south-east New Guinea have a complex human history. Archaeological research has gone some way to model the long-term trajectories of island settlement in this region. However, the role of inter-island interaction and connections with mainland populations in shaping cultural diversity remains poorly understood, particularly as it relates to the formative development of the ethnographically described *Kula* network within which Panaeati Island (Louisiade Archipelago) was once a central node. Excavations at the Mumwa site on Panaeati Island have revealed a mid-Holocene cultural deposit (4350 cal. BP), with overlying pottery-bearing layers (750–500 cal. BP) spanning a period of profound social change across the Massim and south Papuan coast, during which time *Kula* is thought to have commenced in earnest. Our data suggests that more regular human habitation of the Massim islands from the end of the mid-Holocene coincided with similarly timed population expansions and changes in tool technologies in other parts of New Guinea that influenced subsequent population dispersals, and likely contributed to the diversification of regional cultural identities. Within the last millennium, inter-island connections had been established with population on Woodlark and perhaps along the south Papuan coast, facilitating the spread of shared cultural behaviours that overlaid established local practices. The gradual withdrawal of islands in the Louisiade Archipelago from regular involvement in regional maritime networks over the last 500 years contributed to deepening linguistic, genetic and cultural boundaries, and were thereafter on the periphery of the *Kula* network.

Introduction

The island of New Guinea is well recognised as a global hotspot of linguistic and cultural diversity, having more extant languages than the Eurasian continent, despite having only 0.5 per cent of the world's land area (Eberhard et al. 2022; Hua et al. 2019). In part, such remarkable diversity can be attributed to a long human history spanning more than 50,000 years that involved innovative behavioural adaptations to a wide range of landscapes and ecologies (Allen and O'Connell 2020; Nettle 1998; Summerhayes et al. 2017). Yet it has become increasingly apparent that the last few millennia have been profoundly influential in the diversification of unique but often interconnected cultural identities following the arrival of Lapita-affiliated groups (McNiven et al. 2011; Shaw et al. 2022; Spriggs 1997; Summerhayes and Allen 2007). The Massim region of south-east Papua New Guinea, in particular, has been the focus of ethnographic investigations attempting to understand the idiosyncratic social practices of island populations and the varying institutions that connected them (Haddon 1894; Seligman 1910). The best known is the *Kula* network that still operates and involves cross-cultural negotiations between trade partners from different islands (Kuehling 2021; Malinowski 1922; Uberoi 1962). Although *Kula* in its ethnographically recorded form is a relatively recent cultural institution that (re)intensified following colonial suppression of warfare, antecedent networks on which it developed have far greater time depths and varied both in function and geographic scope (Irwin et al. 2019). Identifying changes to inter-island connections and the underlying social drivers can therefore provide a robust heuristic framework within which to investigate the diversification of cultural identities in past populations (Allen 1985; Earle and Ericson 1977; Irwin and Holdaway 1996).

Here we present results of archaeological investigations at the newly discovered open site of Mumwa (site code: BAPF[1]) on Panaeati Island, located 170 km from the New Guinea mainland at the western end of the Louisiade Archipelago (Figure 13.1). Systematic excavations at Mumwa have demonstrated that cultural material accumulated rapidly between 720 and 490 years ago and included a more diverse range of pottery styles than previously reported in the archipelago. The predominant pottery style has characteristic 'Massim' art motifs still in use today, reflecting the development of regional cultural identities. Underlying sediments tentatively associated with a mid-Holocene radiocarbon date contained the first tanged blade and stone mortar fragment to be recovered from an excavated context in the Massim region. Our results expand on regional models by suggesting that closer social connections between Massim island populations within the last millennium reflects the formative development of the *Kula* network. A human presence from 4350 cal. BP coincides with population expansions and the development of formalised tool technologies in other parts of New Guinea (south Papuan coast, Bismarck Archipelago, Highlands) and on other Massim islands (Brooker) that likely influenced subsequent population dispersals, distributions and densities (Araho et al. 2002; David et al. 2022; Shaw 2021; Shaw, Field et al. 2020; Shaw et al. 2022; Swadling 2016). Although commonly defined as a singular cultural area (cf. Haddon 1894; Young 1983), this was a relatively recent phenomenon with the long-term history of the Massim islands best modelled as 'pulses' of habitation interspersed by periods of sporadic use or abandonment, particularly in the Louisiade Archipelago, that contributed to the development of diverse regional cultural identities.

---

1   National Museum and Art Gallery of Papua New Guinea site code register, with each site having a three or four-digit code. Codes provided in text for Massim sites.

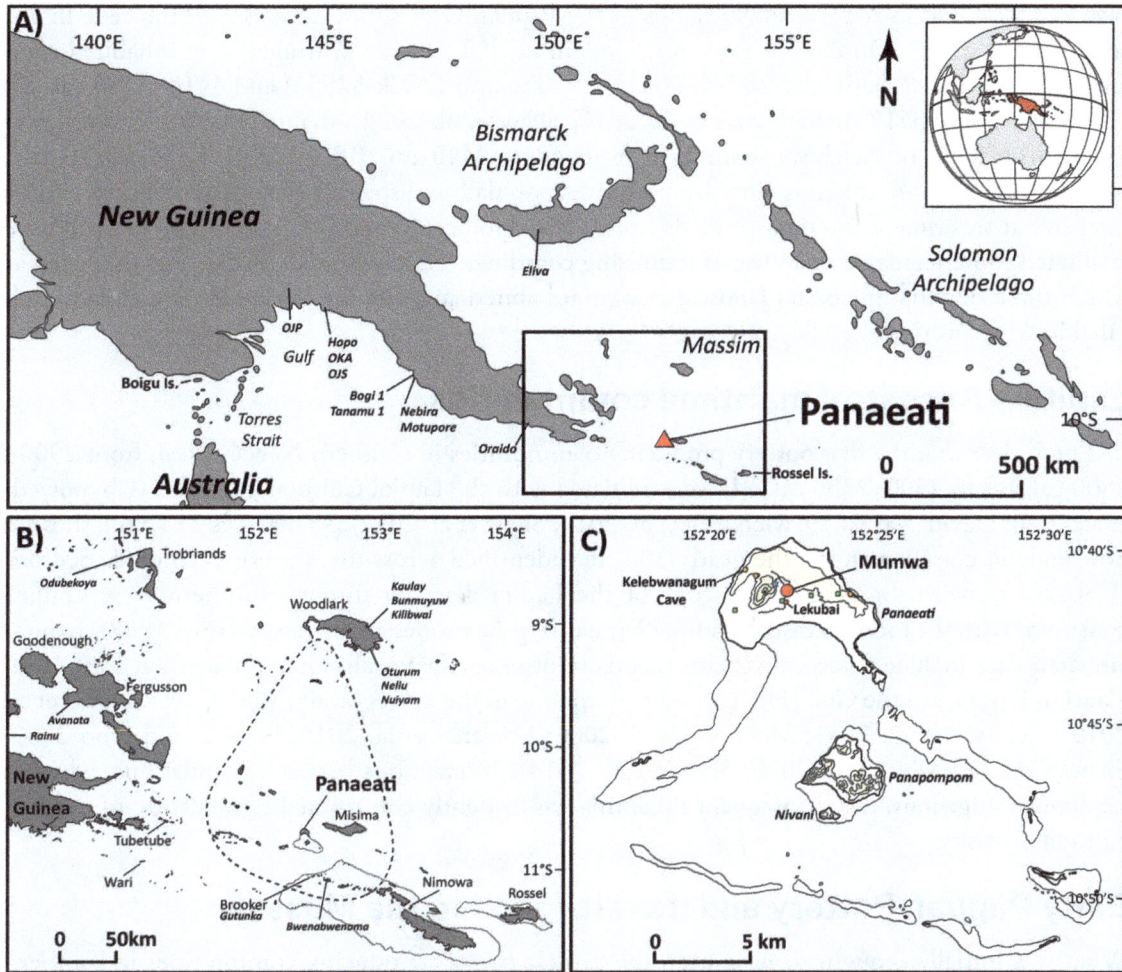

Figure 13.1: (A) Map of Island New Guinea; (B) Massim island region; (C) Panaeati Island.

Notes: (B) The dashed line marks the distribution of people speaking Misima language as their primary language; (C) recorded archaeological sites marked with 40 m contours drawn. Place names mentioned in the text are labelled. Inset: Global location of island New Guinea.

Source: Authors.

The Massim islands in a regional context

Pre-pottery settlement of the southern lowland and island New Guinea

The Massim islands and southern lowlands of Papua New Guinea, spanning 1500 km from Rossel Island in the east to Boigu Island in the west, have a long human history that is currently not well understood (Figure 13.1A). Of ~107 excavated and radiocarbon-dated sites, only eight have cultural chronologies older than 3000 cal. BP[2] (Shaw 2021). The earliest evidence for a human presence has been documented at Kelebwanagum cave (site code: BAPI) on Panaeati Island from 17 cal. ka (cal. kilo annum, thousands of years) (Shaw, Coxe, Haro et al. 2020). Except for OJP

---

2   Kelebwanagum, OJP, Wokoi Amoho, Ruisasi 2, Tanamu 1, Bogi 1, Kukuba and Gutunka. Excludes single dates from Nebira 4 and Popo, considered by the original authors as erroneous.

cave (13.5 cal. ka) in the riverine lowlands of the Papuan Gulf, all other sites are Holocene in age (David et al. 2007). On current evidence, modern coastal and island fringes were inhabited soon after they developed, between 5200–4880 cal. BP (Tanamu 1, Wk-32553) and 4410–4150 cal. BP (Gutunka, Beta-535172) (McNiven et al. 2011; Shaw et al. 2022; Thangavelu 2015; Vanderwal 1973). The reuse of Kelebwanagum cave from 4810–4440 cal. BP (OZX-905, Marine20 ΔR: −135±20) after an ~8 ka hiatus tentatively suggests population dispersals were more frequent and/or intensive at this time. Lowering sea levels from a mid-Holocene peak (+1.5–3 m, 7–4 ka) will have facilitated more regular human use of stabilising coastlines (cf. Lewis et al. 2013). Yet, the speed at which these developing coastal landscapes were inhabited suggests the lowlands were already well inhabited by this time.

Lapita — Ancestral maritime communities

It is now clear that the first pottery producing communities in southern New Guinea, from 2900–2800 cal. BP to 2500–2350 cal. BP, were affiliated with the Lapita Cultural Complex (Chynoweth et al. 2020; David et al. 2019; McNiven et al. 2011; Shaw et al. 2022). As many as 21 Lapita sites are now known, complementing the nearly 300 sites identified across the western Pacific (cf. Bedford et al. 2019), with the geographic scope of the Lapita diaspora through southern New Guinea consistent with the modern distribution of Papuan Tip Austronesian languages (Ross 1988). Lapita-affiliated sites include three on Massim islands (Gutunka, Kasasinabwana, Malakai), at least 16 in Caution Bay, one in the Gulf (Hopo), and perhaps one in the Torres Strait (Mask Cave) (David et al. 2019; McNiven et al. 2011; McNiven et al. 2006; Mialanes et al. 2016; Negishi and Ono 2009; Shaw, Coxe, Kewibu et al. 2020; Skelly et al. 2014). Interactions between populations, whether Lapita or indigenous, over subsequent millennia has evidently contributed significantly to modern cultural diversity.

Early Papuan Pottery and its relevance to the Massim

What was initially thought to have been the earliest pottery producing communities in southern Papua New Guinea are likely cultural descendants of both Lapita-affiliated and indigenous populations (Shaw et al. 2022; Summerhayes and Allen 2007). Defined as 'Early Papuan Pottery' (EPP), the term broadly describes a set of pottery traditions spanning a millennium or so from 2300–2100 cal. BP to 1300–1100 cal. BP documented at several archaeological sites along the south coast. The earliest pottery was predominantly made locally, with some having similar intricate shell-impressed motifs (Allen 2010). Such similarities suggest the populations were culturally related and, like the preceding Lapita diaspora, had migrated rapidly along the south coast (Allen 1972; Bulmer 1978; Irwin 1985; Vanderwal 1973). Although the initial development of EPP represents a second large-scale population migration, evidence now indicates that at least in some areas (Caution Bay) there was continuity in pottery production and use since its introduction with Lapita (David et al. 2012). From 1600–1500 cal. BP, pottery styles along the south Papuan coast had diversified but continued similarities of some styles is evident, namely the Papuan Gulf and Port Moresby areas, indicating pottery trade and use of some decorative motifs was maintained (Allen 2010; Rhoads 1980).

Whether EPP and the social influences that facilitated its widespread production and distribution also occurred in the Massim islands remains uncertain. Pottery dating from 2200–1600 cal. BP has now been recovered at the Kasasinabwana (BALU), Malakai (BYP) and Gutunka (BANA) sites. With the exception of lip incision on one sherd, all pottery has thus far been undecorated

(Shaw et al. 2022). Although there are similarities in vessel forms and the application of red slip, these assemblages bear no apparent resemblance to contemporary south coast EPP (Negishi and Ono 2009; Shaw, Coxe, Kewibu et al. 2020; Shaw et al. 2022). Currently, shell-impressed pottery from the excavated but undated Avanata site (BALZ) on Fergusson Island provides the only potential link between Late Lapita and initial EPP (Ford et al. 2021). Irwin (1991) included the southern Massim islands within the EPP distribution and argued that the Louisiade islands were on the periphery of core maritime dispersals, presumably inferring that the earliest EPP styles were not present in the region. Irwin et al. (2019) have since illustrated excavated pottery from the Bwenabwenama site (BADD/BADL) on Moturina Island associated with two dates that encompass the full EPP range (2330–1830 cal. BP and 1350–940 cal. BP, ANU-5131/5133) (Figure 13.2). The pottery has closest parallels in rim form and motif elements with Bulmer's thick-rimmed Style II (~1200–1000 cal. BP) that was initially thought to have represented pottery imported from the Massim to the Port Moresby area (Bulmer 1971; Swadling 1981). A lack of shell-impressed motifs and the presence of comparative stylistic attributes supports an association with the later of the two dates. As such, closer social connections between the Louisiade Archipelago and the south coast may have only been re-established around the last millennium, with earlier social connections evident, at least initially, during the rapid diaspora of Lapita cultural groups through these regions (Figure 13.2).

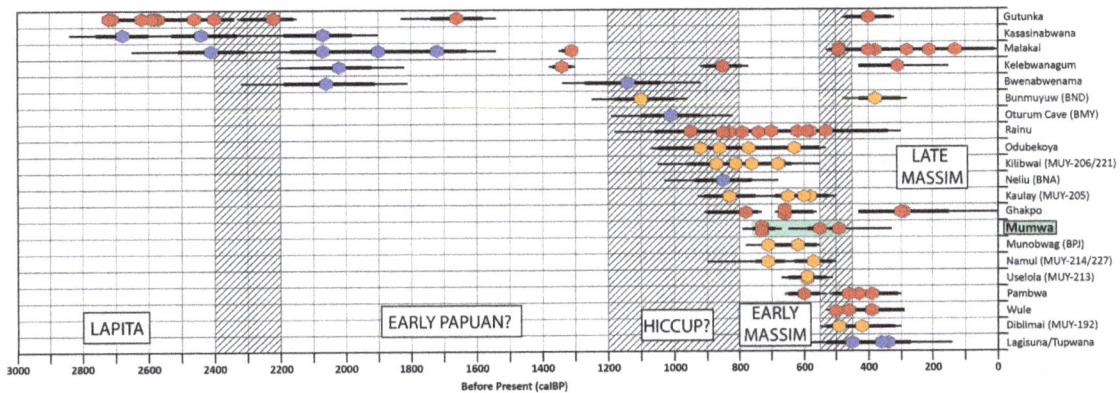

Figure 13.2: Calibrated radiocarbon dates from systematically excavated sites in the Massim region with heuristic chronological divisions based on south coast and Massim datasets.

Notes: Red dots = charcoal, blue dots = marine shell, orange dots = human bone. Site names are listed on the right margin. Note the good chronological coverage across the Hiccup–Early Massim boundary but limited coverage of the preceding Early Papuan (EPP). Hashed areas indicate broadly defined periods of change in archaeological assemblages.

Source: Authors.

Last millennium social change in the Massim

There are now nine Massim sites with median dates between 1200 and 800 cal. BP,[3] contemporary with the so-called 'hiccup'. The hiccup heuristically defines the end of EPP on the south coast when a myriad of localised pottery styles had emerged (Summerhayes and Allen 2007; Vilgalys and Summerhayes 2016) (Figures 13.1 and 13.2). In the Massim during this time, pottery import from the mainland (Rainu) was gradually replaced by inter-island connections, and by 600–500 cal. BP communal burial grounds associated with megalithic arrangements had been superseded by an apparent preference for secondary pot burials (Bickler 1998; Burenhult 2002; Egloff 1979).

---

3   Kelebwanagum, Bwenabwenama, Oturum cave (BMY), Neliu (BNA), Bunmuyuw (BND), Rainu, Odubekoya, Kilibwai (MUY-206) and Kaulay (MUY-205).

Elaborately carved *Conus* shell valuables recovered from Rainu and several northern Massim islands have characteristic spiral motifs still in use today, with four directly dated to between 910–640 cal. BP (Wk-25781) and 650–380 cal. BP (Wk-31234) (Ambrose et al. 2012). It has been convincingly argued that the *Conus* objects reflect the earliest known representation of 'Massim' art, and together with regional evidence demonstrate the expansion of social networks at this time through which the cultural significance of these motifs was shared and reinforced.

Site setting, survey and excavations

Panaeati Island (30 km², 206 m above sea level) is located in the Louisiade Archipelago of the Massim region. It comprises a central metavolcanic hill surrounded by an uplifted coral limestone platform (Smith and Pieters 1973) (Figure 13.1B). Uplift of the plateau has created a basin into which rainwater draining off the mountain accumulates that would have been the only regular water source on the island before the introduction of modern water storage tanks. Archaeological investigations were initiated on Panaeati because it forms a natural 'bottleneck' island through which people would often travel to reach the Louisiade Archipelago. A barrier reef and shallow lagoon encloses the southern side of Panaeati and encompasses two smaller islands—Panapompom and Nivani (Figure 13.1C). Despite the relative isolation of Panaeati from New Guinea, it is near the larger island of Misima and the Calvados Island chain where more regular maritime connections have been documented historically and archaeologically (Berde 1974; Shaw et al. 2016). The Panaeati population speak Misima language, which is also spoken on the small offshore islands near Woodlark, suggesting regular social connections had been maintained with these northern islands in the past (Figure 13.1B). Close ancestral ties are also attested through oral histories with populations on Misima and Brooker in the Louisiade Archipelago, Woodlark in the north, and Tubetube and Wari in the west (Damon 1990; Kinch 2020; Macintyre 1983; Lincoln Wesley, pers. comm, 2021).

A foot survey of Panaeati in 2017–18 resulted in 11 sites being recorded, including four secondary pot burial niches, four caves, two surface artefact scatters and a clay quarry used historically for pot production (Figure 13.1C). One excavated cave—Kelebwanagum—has yielded Late Pleistocene evidence for human use. Two other caves contained secondary burials associated with pots typologically attributed to Southern Massim Pottery (SMP) and antecedent Southern Massim Combed Pottery (SMCP), tentatively suggesting the pots were intermittently deposited over the last 1000–500 years. The two dense surface scatters—Mumwa and Lekubai—are located 600 m apart on the edge of the limestone plateau near the base of the hill where pottery, obsidian and lithics were collected, with Mumwa 1.7 km from the southern coast (Figures 13.1B and 13.3A). Lekubai (BAPC) predominately contained SMP that has been dated in secure excavated contexts elsewhere in the region to within the last 550–500 cal. BP (Irwin et al. 2019; Shaw, Coxe, Kewibu et al. 2020). Mumwa yielded SMCP and several other styles that have not been widely documented in the Louisiade Archipelago, tentatively suggesting it was inhabited earlier than Lekubai. Nine spade test pits were subsequently dug across Mumwa to determine the nature and depth of cultural material relative to surface concentrations (Figure 13.3B). A total of 2731 g (*n* = 624 sherds) of pottery was excavated, one third of which was recovered from SP3 where the deepest sedimentary deposits were also identified.

Figure 13.3: Aerial drone images of Mumwa and the surrounding landscape.

Notes: (A) Looking south across the limestone plateau and Deboyne lagoon from Mumwa, showing the site's location relative to geological and geomorphological boundaries. The Lekubai site is 600 m from Mumwa and mainly contains Southern Massim Pottery (SMP); (B) cleared garden plots at Mumwa close to the edge of the limestone plateau showing the distribution of spade pits and the Square A–C excavations.

Source: Authors.

Table 13.1: Stratigraphic layers identified in Squares A–C at the Mumwa site.

Layer	Approx. depth below surface (cm)	Spits			m³ excavated	% organic	pH	Munsell	Description
		Sq. A	Sq. B	Sq. C					
1	0–14	1–3	1–3	1–2	0.457	19	8–7	5YR 3/3 (Dark reddish brown)	Poorly sorted lightly compacted sediment of silt (60%), clay (23%) and fine sand (17%) sized particles, with friable nodules, dense root matter and moderately dense angular metavolcanic stone inclusions. Few limestone nodules. Ant bioturbation noted.
2	14–46	4–9	4–8	3–5	0.751	17	8–7	5YR 4/4 (Reddish brown)	Poorly sorted, moderately compacted friable sediment predominantly silt (73%) and fine sand (19%) sized particles, with 8% clay. Root matter and natural stone inclusions decreasing with depth, and limestone nodules increasing. Ant bioturbation still evident.
3	46–99	10–18	–	6–7	0.301	16	7–6.5	2.5YR 4/4 (Reddish brown)	Poorly sorted sandy silt sediment with moderate limestone nodule inclusions, increasing with depth. Only few fibrous roots present. Moisture content increases near baserock with sediment increasingly compact. Limited bioturbation present. Pockets of sediment with higher clay content in some basal limestone crevices.

Notes: % organic obtained by loss on ignition analysis, and clay–silt–sand proportions from particle size analysis. Sediment colour obtained using Munsell (2000) colour charts. Source: Authors' summary of site.

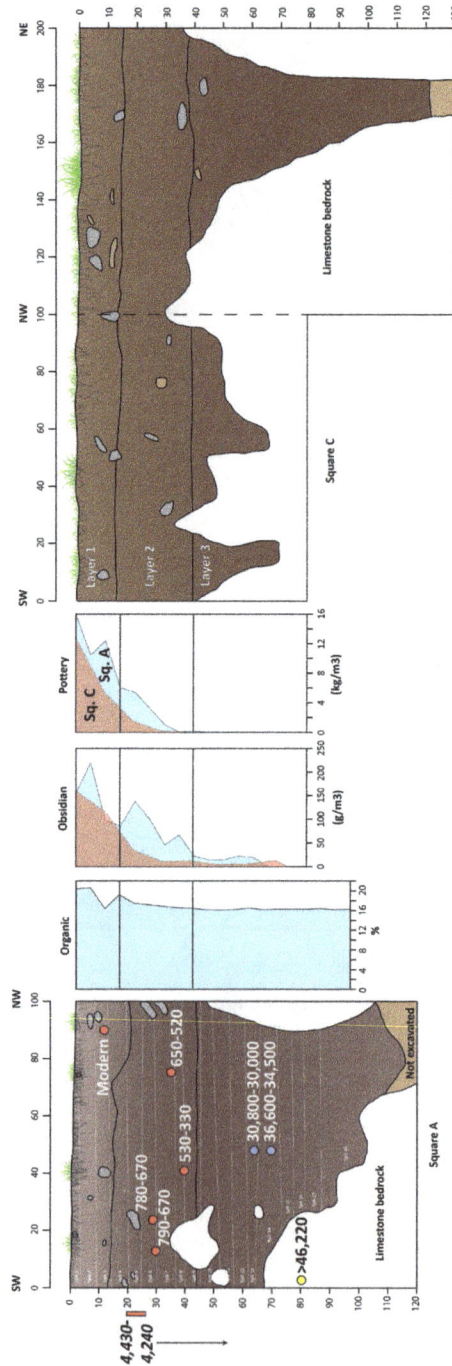

Figure 13.4: Stratigraphic profile of the Mumwa site, Squares A and C.

Notes: The organic component of the sediment is shown, as well as the corrected volume (g/m³) of excavated obsidian and pottery. The 95.4 per cent confidence index range of calibrated radiocarbon dates are indicated. Red circle: charcoal. Blue: *Tridacna* sp. shell. Yellow: coral. Source: Authors.

In 2018–19 three 1 m² squares were systematically excavated near SP3 within apparent stratigraphic layers in 5 cm spits for Squares A–B and 10 cm spits for Square C. All excavated sediment was sieved through 5 mm mesh onsite, with remaining sediment wet sieved through 3 mm mesh. Neutral (pH 8–6.5) sediments provided good conditions for the preservation of organic materials. The notably high organic component (19–16 per cent) suggests sediment formation was primarily a result of in situ decomposition of plants. A lack of reaction of sediments in hydrogen peroxide suggests the underlying limestone did not contribute to soil formation (Figure 13.4). Three stratigraphic layers were identified based on colour and particle size analysis, with two major cultural horizons (Layers 1–2 and Layer 3) defined based on the distribution of cultural material and radiocarbon dating (Table 13.1, Figure 13.4).

The depth of the sediment deposit varied due to undulating basal reef limestone exposed in places 25–30 cm below the surface, with Layer 3 largely defined by infilled sediment within pockets of reef limestone. Squares A and C were excavated to basal limestone, whereas Square B ceased within Layer 2 (~40 cm) due to a landowner dispute temporarily halting work.

Radiocarbon chronology

Nine AMS (accelerator mass spectrometry) radiocarbon determinations established a chronology at Mumwa (Table 13.2). Three additional samples did not survive pretreatment. Seven in situ charcoal samples from Square A indicate that Layer 2 was deposited between 790–670 cal. BP and 530–330 cal. BP (2σ ranges), possibly reflecting two separate pulses of occupation within this timeframe (Figure 13.2). A modern charcoal date (1956 AD) from Layer 1 suggests mid-twentieth-century garden plot preparation had disturbed the topsoil, with some degree of post-depositional disturbance in Layer 2 indicated by inversion of the radiocarbon dates within a 10 cm depth range. However, pottery from both layers was similar, suggesting it was deposited relatively quickly. A charcoal date from SP3 of 4430–4240 cal. BP at a depth (23 cm) equivalent to Layer 2 was clearly out of context. It is considerably earlier than the other determinations and predates the introduction of pottery in Oceania by a millennium (Kirch 2021; Summerhayes 2007). The charcoal was collected from an exposed section and may have been dragged up by the spade, or the enclosing sediment had been disturbed during past land use. In any case, a mid-Holocene age for the aceramic Layer 3 is likely.

Table 13.2: Radiocarbon accelerator mass spectrometer determinations from the Mumwa site.

Lab code	Context	Spit	Depth	Sample	Date	Error	68.3% range	95.4% range	Median
Beta-515727	Sq. A	3	11 cm	Charcoal	Modern	–	–	–	–
Beta-502623		6	29 cm	Charcoal	820	30	740–680	780–670	720
UNSW-1204		6	30 cm	Charcoal	821	36	740–680	790–670	720
UNSW-1205		7	34 cm	Charcoal	586	36	640–540	650–520	600
Beta-515728		8	39 cm	Charcoal	420	30	520–470	530–330	490
UNSW-1202		13	60–64 cm	*Tridacna* shell	27,016	170	30,600–30,100	30,800–30,000	30,400
UNSW-1203		14	64–73 cm	*Tridacna* shell	31,904	480	36,100–35,000	36,600–34,500	35,500
Beta-482842	SP3	–	23 cm	Charcoal	3,920	30	4,420–4,290	4,430–4,240	4,350
Beta-502624			110 cm	Coral	>43,500	–	>46,220		–

Notes: Calibrated ranges rounded to 10 years for Holocene dates and 100 years for Pleistocene dates. Radiocarbon dates are noted as before present (BP), with BP being AD 1950. Error is noted to 1 sigma. Calibrations were undertaken using OxCal 4.4 and the IntCal20 curve for terrestrial samples, and Marine20 with a ΔR of 0 for marine shell samples (Heaton et al, 2020; Reimer et al. 2020). The modern determination was calibrated using CALIbomb and the SHZ3 post-bomb dataset.

Source: Authors' summary.

Pre-Last Glacial Maximum human use or complex uplift history?

Two fragments of *Tridacna* sp. shell from Layer 3 (Spits 13–14) returned pre-Last Glacial Maximum ages of 30,800–30,000 cal. BP and 36,100–34,500 cal. BP. Although it is possible the dates reflect early human landscape use at Mumwa, the shell more likely derived from a relic shellfish bed on the underlying coral limestone. The dates therefore provide a tentative indication of when the Mumwa area was still submerged underwater prior to substantive uplift. If correct, it demonstrates that much of the limestone plateau of Panaeati Island was a lagoon even when sea levels were ~80–60m below modern levels at 36–30 ka. Branch coral from basal reef deposits in SP3 returned an age beyond the limits of detection (<46,220 cal. BP), indicating that the relic shellfish bed had formed on top of a well-established coral reef system.

Relatively recent uplift may explain the relatively dense concentrations of metavolcanic rock fragments on the limestone plateau that would have eroded off the adjacent hillside before uplift subsequently created a basin around its base. Sediment formation on limestone is generally slow, and at Mumwa the uplift history and human use has evidently influenced the sedimentation rate. It is possible that sediment had accumulated very slowly within the last 30 ka when the reef uplifted above sea level, but had probably increased in the mid-Holocene during more regular human landscape use that may have resulted in relict shell being dislodged from the fossil reef or having been used for some purpose.

Excavated material

Pottery, obsidian and lithics were the most abundant excavated cultural material recovered (Tables 13.S1 to 13.S3: see Appendix). A total of 1787 potsherds weighing 5144 g were recorded. Except for two fragments with fresh breaks in Layer 3 (Square C) that had almost certainly fallen from the exposed section, all sherds were attributed to Layer 1 (74 per cent by weight) and Layer 2 (26 per cent). Obsidian was found in all layers with a total of 342 pieces weighing 103.4 g recorded, of which 3.7 g (n = 22) came from Layer 3 in low but consistent quantities in both Squares A and C where Layer 3 was exposed, suggesting its presence in this context was cultural rather than a result of downward post-depositional movement. Considerable quantities of obsidian were present on the surface, with 683 g collected by five people over a 10-minute period, of which the largest piece weighed 10 g. A small amount of pumice (9.3 g), marine shell (7 g) and faunal bone (6.4 g) was identified, including 2.2 g of shell and 0.2 g of fishbone in Layer 3. Pig and fish remains were present in Layers 1–2.

A total of 27 lithic artefacts of hornfels, tuff, limestone, siltstone and schist were also recovered from systematic excavation (Table 13.S4: see Appendix). Of these, 11 were flakes or flaking debris (e.g. Figure 13.5C–D), nine were ground/polished fragments likely broken from an adze-axe blade during use (e.g. Figure 13.5A–B), two were unmodified manuports (e.g. Figure 13.5J) and one was a core (Figure 13.5F). The remaining four were from formally manufactured tools, including a tanged blade and a mortar/stone bowl rim (Figure 13.6A, B), as well as an axe-adze fragment or possibly a grindstone with cut marks, and a retouched axe-adze blade (Figure 13.5G–H). The latter blade had a weathered surface with fresh stone revealed in the retouch scars, indicating the tool had been recycled and may therefore be older than its in situ depositional context. A hornfels axe-adze preform found on the surface of the nearby Lekubai site had also been recycled in the same manner (Figure 13.5I).

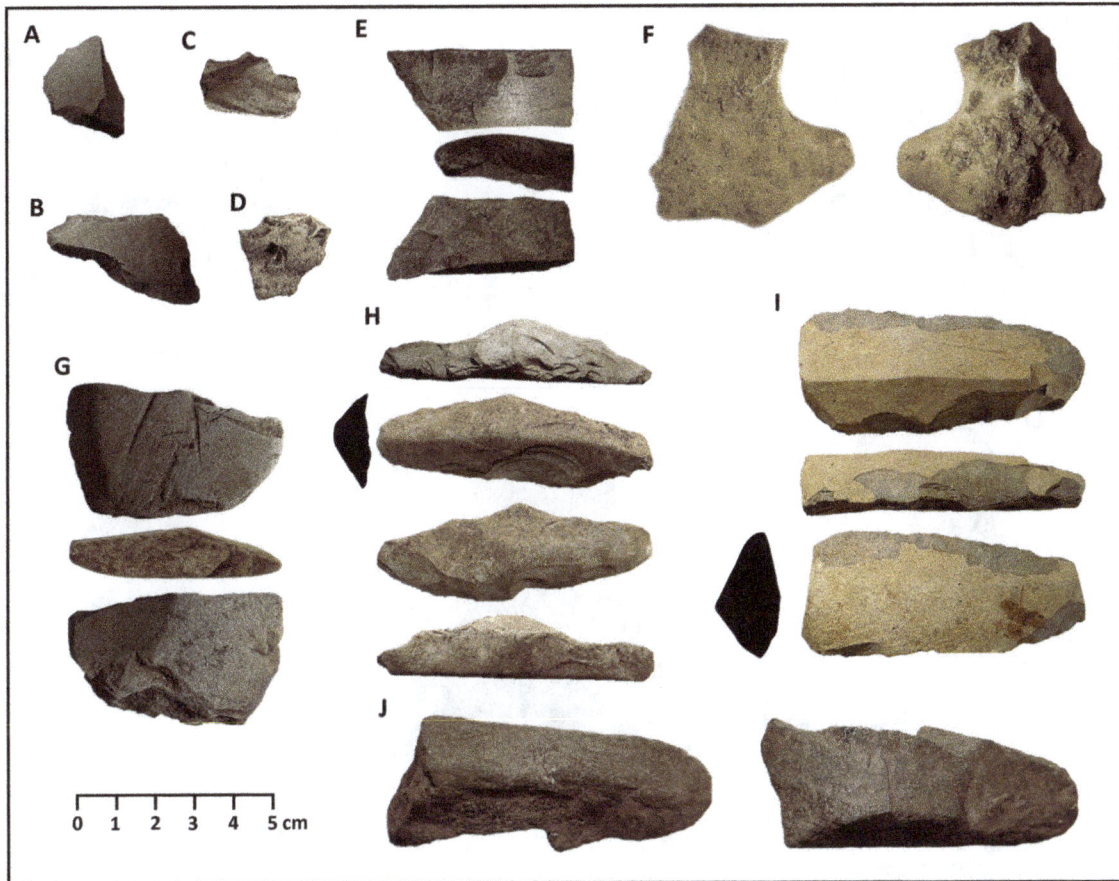

Figure 13.5: Lithic artefacts from Mumwa.

Notes: (A) C.1.1, layer 1, hornfels, ground fragment; (B) C.3.1, layer 1, hornfels, ground fragment; (C) A.4.2, layer 1, limestone, flake; (D) A.14.1, layer 3, limestone, flake; (E) C.4.1, layer 2, hornfels, ground fragment with partial bevel; (F) A.13.1, layer 3, limestone, possible core with flaked edge; (G) A.5.1, layer 2, quartz siltstone, axe-adze preform fragment or grindstone with incisions; (H) B.6.1, layer 2, fine-grained tuff, axe-adze preform with retouch; (I) Lekubai, surface, hornfels, axe-adze preform; (J) C.2.2, metavolcanic, layer 1, manuport.

Source: Authors.

A mid-Holocene human presence at Mumwa

The radiocarbon evidence for burning at 4430–4240 cal. BP cannot on its own be unequivocally associated with human activity, not least because it is out of stratigraphic order. However, the heavily weathered tanged blade and mortar rim are consistent with those recorded in mid-Holocene sites elsewhere in New Guinea, and are the first to be recorded in an excavated Massim context (Figure 13.6A, B) (Bulmer 2005; Swadling 2016; Torrence et al. 2013). Both tool forms are absent from Australasian archaeological contexts spanning the last three millennia and are unknown in Massim ethnographic records and to modern populations.

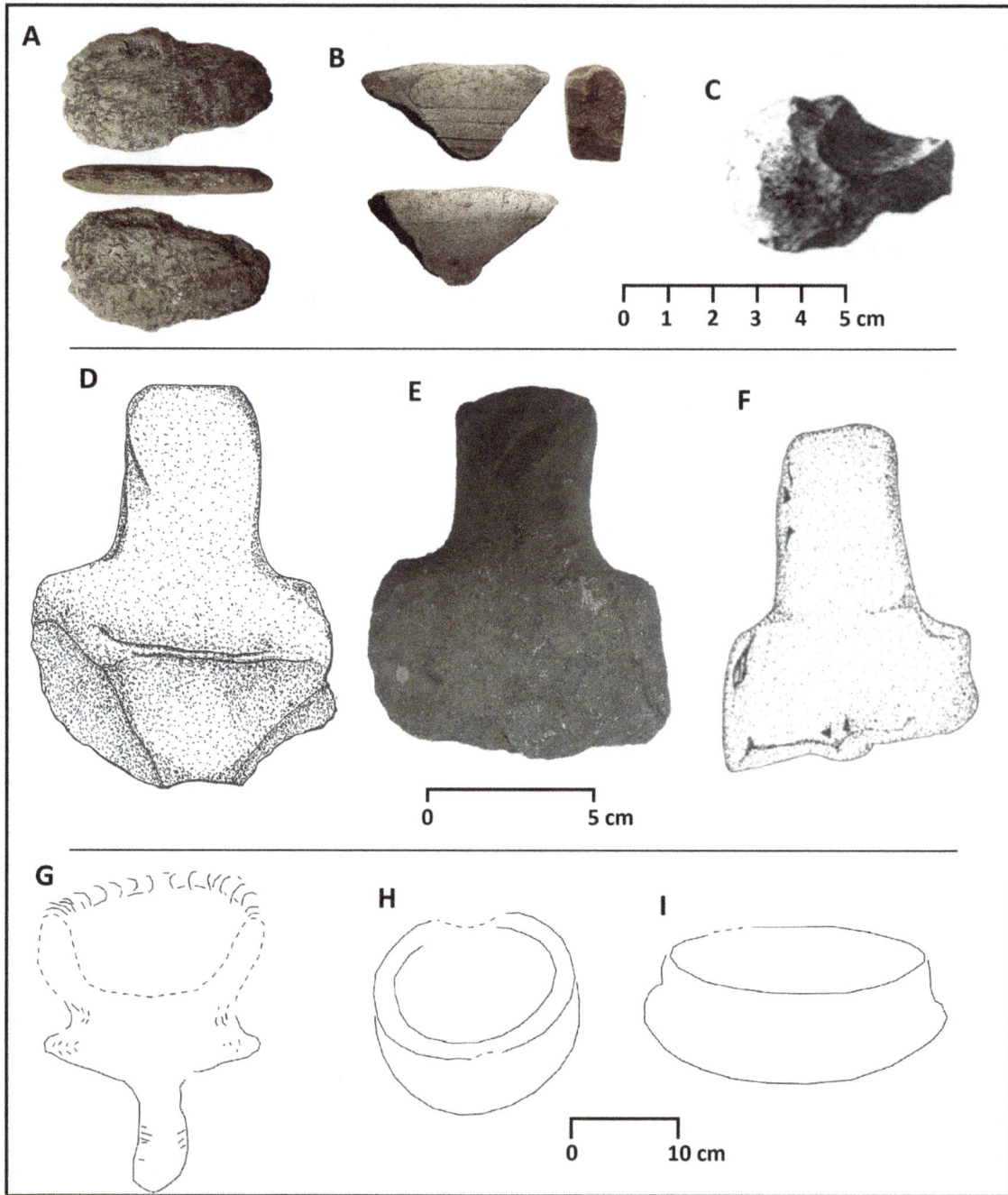

Figure 13.6: Tanged blade (A) and mortar rim (B) from Mumwa compared with other examples from the Massim and island New Guinea.

Notes: (A) Tanged schist blade, Mumwa, Layer 3, spit 14 (64–73 cm below surface, or bs); (B) quartz siltstone mortar rim with four horizontal incised lines, Mumwa, Unit C, Layers 1–2, Spit 2 (92–197 cm bs), possibly out of stratigraphic context; (C) tanged blade from Yombon-Eliva-Asiu, Chronological unit 3 dated to Mid-Holocene; (D) and (F) tanged blades from Okaiboma village, Kiriwina Island recorded by Fernstal et al. (2002); (E) tanged blade (E3054, BOI) from Okabulula, Kitava Island, Trobriand Group collected by G. Gerritz and held by the National Museum and Art Gallery of Papua New Guinea; (G) Pedastalled and bossed mortar, surface, Misima Island; (H) flat rim mortar, surface, Goodenough Island; (I) bowl mortar, surface, South coast.

Source: (A–B, E): Author supplied; (C) from Pavlides 1999; (D, F) from Fernstal et al. (2002); (G–I) adapted from Swadling (2016: Fig. 3).

Tanged blades

The tanged blade from Mumwa was recovered in situ within Layer 3, 689 mm below the ground surface (bs) (Square A, Spit 14). It is made from a grey-green lightly foliated chlorite schist, and could have been obtained locally on the island (Smith and Pieters 1973). A limestone flake and a larger limestone piece with a flaked edge of local origin were also found in Layer 3, the latter recorded in situ 636 mm bs (Square A, Spit 13) (Figure 13.5D, F), suggesting low-intensity utilisation of locally available material for tool production during the mid-Holocene.

Several tanged stone blades have previously been found in undated surface contexts in the Massim, all larger and all recorded on the limestone Trobriand archipelago, about which nothing is known of their use by local residents (Fernstal et al. 2002; Norick 1976). On the northern boundary of the Massim at Eliva in the interior of New Britain, tanged chert tools of a broadly similar size and morphology as the Mumwa tool were found in excavations dated to between 4860–4090 cal. BP and 4410–3900 cal. BP (Pavlides 1999:Unit 3). Obsidian tanged/stemmed blades with similar profiles but larger in size have been found elsewhere in the Bismarck Archipelago, with the few recovered from secure contexts mainly constrained between 6160–5740 and 3480–3160 cal. BP (Araho et al. 2002; Torrence 2016). A stemmed obsidian blade was found under 4 m of sediment on Misima Island, only 14 km from Panaeati, tentatively suggesting the Louisiade Archipelago was within the ambit of mid-Holocene social networks spanning island and mainland New Guinea (Seligman and Joyce 1907; Swadling 2016). Larger tanged and waisted tools on mainland New Guinea date to at least 45 ka, with similar undated examples also known on the Massim island of Rossel (Bulmer 1977; Groube et al. 1986; Shaw 2017).

Mortar rim

Whereas the tanged blade can be tentatively attributed to a mid-Holocene context on both morphological and stratigraphic grounds, the mortar rim was recovered from Layer 2 (92–197 mm bs, Spit 2, Square C) and is either out of stratigraphic context or is a later tool form. Later manufacture of mortars in the Massim can be parsimoniously discounted as they have not been recorded in archaeological sites spanning the last millennium, and are similarly not known in ethnographic collections or to modern communities (Swadling 2013). The quartz rich siltstone from which it was made likely came from the larger island of Misima (Gulewa formation) (de Keyser 1961). Hundreds of mortars and pestles have been recovered in undated surface contexts across highland and lowland New Guinea and adjacent islands, including the Massim (Swadling 2016; Swadling et al. 2008). The most securely dated excavated example has been documented in the Ivane Valley at 4410–4150 cal. BP, with two pestles probably used with mortars dated at the Waim site to 4850–4640 cal. BP and 4300–4080 cal. BP, respectively (Field et al. 2020; Shaw, Field et al. 2020). It is, therefore, probable that the mortar had been displaced from an underlying context and is mid-Holocene in age. Certainly, if the charcoal date of 4430–4240 cal. BP from Mumwa is associated with the tanged blade and mortar it would be chronologically consistent with what is currently known about the age and distribution of these stone technologies in island New Guinea (Shaw 2017). However, a later age for the Mumwa mortar cannot be presently ruled out.

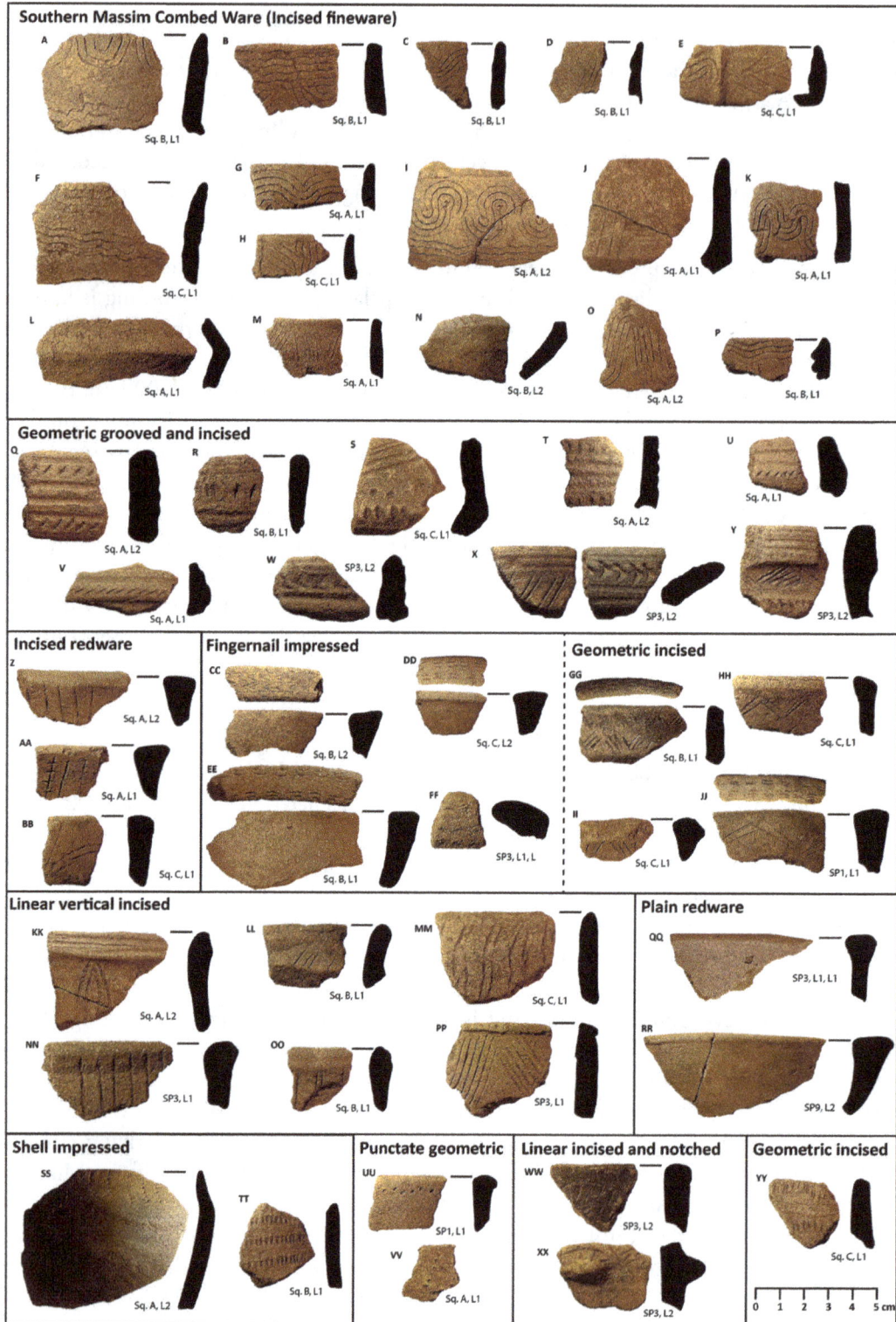

Figure 13.7: Excavated pottery from Squares A–C and spade pits.

Notes: The majority of the pottery was Southern Massim Combed Pottery (SMCP) but contained pottery styles identified by Bickler (1998:98–131) that were likely manufactured on Woodlark Island (Muyuw). Some were likely also manufactured in the D'Entrecasteaux Islands. Except SMCP, names are those defined by Bickler (1998).

Source: Author supplied.

Pottery reveals connections with Woodlark Island and south Papuan coast

The identification of several distinct pottery styles at Mumwa indicates that from 720–490 cal. BP the population had been socially connected with the northern Massim island of Woodlark—still a major *Kula* hub (Damon 1990). Sites elsewhere in the Louisiade Archipelago dating after 500 cal. BP have notably less diversity in pottery styles and are dominated by SMP (Shaw, Coxe, Kewibu et al. 2020). The majority of sherds large enough to determine morphological characteristics and motif elements could be attributed to SMCP (Figure 13.7A–P).

Smaller quantities were attributed to 'Early Period' styles defined by Bickler (1998) on Woodlark Island broadly dated to 1050–500 cal. BP (Figures 13.S1–13.S2: see Appendix). The age range overlaps with the Mumwa chronology and suggests either that (1) pottery deposition at Mumwa may have commenced slightly earlier than the radiocarbon dates currently indicate, (2) production and use of the same pottery styles occurred earlier on Woodlark, or (3) the earliest dates on Woodlark are not securely associated with the pottery. As most radiocarbon dates on Woodlark are on marine shell and human bone that are not associated with a local ΔR marine correction it is possible that the pottery on both islands has a core date range of 720–490 cal. BP, with antecedent forms made earlier.

The complete lack of SMP on the surface or in excavation at Mumwa indicates settlement ceased before its widespread production and trade from 550–450 cal. BP. The presence of SMP at Lekubai only 600 m away implies that the focus of settlement may have shifted further along the plateau towards the coast. As such, stylistic change in pottery at Mumwa and Lekubai may be associated with broader social changes that influenced settlement location as well as pottery production.

Southern Massim Combed Pottery

Mumwa is the only excavated site where SMCP is the predominant style, providing the first chronological constraints for its production and trade. SMCP vessels are made by coiling, often with only the exterior having a smoothed finish. Rim courses are generally straight or have a slight concavity between shoulder and lip, with the lip typically shaped from folded clay to form an interior or exterior swelling (see also Irwin et al. 2019). Elders on Panaeati Island recall that their great-grandparents were told by their own grandparents that pottery was once made with folded clay rims (Aliti Luyana, pers. comm, 16 October 2017). Comb incision motifs are geometric and limited to the upper half of the vessel above a carination or shoulder with notching, appliqué strips or applied nubbins occasionally demarcating the lower motif boundary (see Figure 13.7).

Trace quantities of SMCP have been recovered at the Wule (BAOT), Ghakpo (BAOP) and Pambwa (BAMY) sites on Rossel Island associated with larger amounts of SMP and dated from 540–470 cal. BP (Shaw 2015). Earlier dates at Ghakpo and Pambwa (910–530 cal. BP) overlap with the Mumwa chronology but are not associated with pottery, suggesting SMCP was not imported as far as Rossel at this time and that its production and trade volume had declined by the time pottery was introduced *en masse* to the island (Shaw 2016). SMCP has otherwise been found in surface contexts on several southern Massim islands and in trace qualities on the northern island of Woodlark—defined by Bickler (1998:107–108) as 'incised fineware'. It was not recovered from the contemporary Rainu deposits, indicating that the distribution of SMCP was primarily limited to the southern Massim islands. Chemical sourcing analyses by Irwin et al. (2019) identified Tubetube Island as one probable production centre. The high concentration of SMCP at Mumwa suggests Panaeati was probably another.

Northern Massim pottery

Bickler (1998:98–131) defined pottery styles on Woodlark by combining decorative elements and vessel morphology; those identified at Mumwa included geometric grooved and incised, fingernail impressed, geometric incised, linear vertical incised, incised redware, punctate geometric, linear incised and notched, and geometric incised (Figures 13.7, 13.8 and 13.S1).

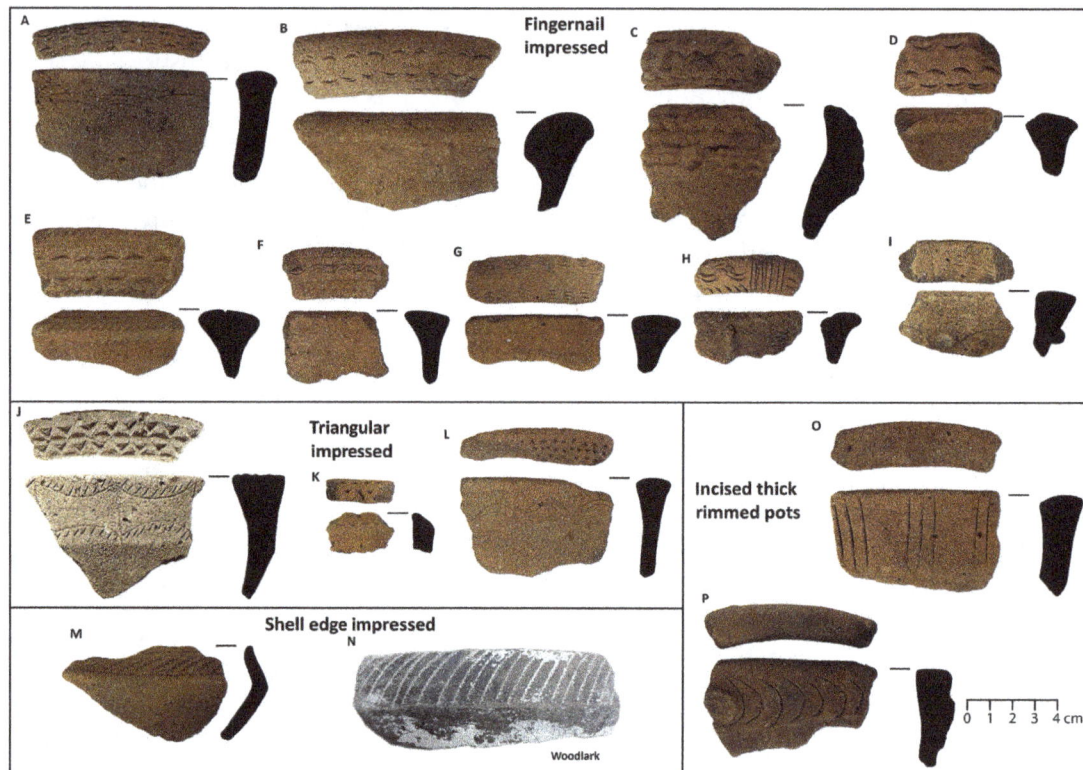

Figure 13.8: Surface pottery from Mumwa not well represented in excavation.

Notes: A range of thick-rimmed fingernail-impressed pottery, suggesting multiple wares with similar decorative conventions. Triangular-impressed sherds were not found in excavation but are known from the Rainu excavations. Shell-impressed pottery has thus far only been reported on Fergusson Island. The right-hand shell-impressed sherd was collected on Woodlark by Ollier and Pain (1978) and photographed in the National Museum and Art Gallery of Papua New Guinea.

Source: Author supplied, except where cited.

Although some of these styles likely belong to the same tradition, their presence together at Mumwa confirms they are broadly contemporary. Allocation of Mumwa pottery to Bickler's Woodlark styles was clear when motifs were preserved, although sherds with eroded surfaces could generally be distinguished from SMCP by rim form and a thicker wall profile (Figure 13.9). Of the Woodlark styles, fingernail-impressed pottery, well represented at Mumwa, was determined by Bickler (1998) through radiocarbon and seriation analyses to have been manufactured from 1050 cal. BP (median age). However, it was more likely produced later as it had also been found more securely associated with secondary pot burials dating to 800–500 cal. BP. Fingernail-impressed pottery has so far not been found to be associated with secondary cave or niche burials on Panaeati. Chemical and petrographic sourcing analyses of the Woodlark 'Early Period' pottery has been interpreted as evidence for local production. However, the geometric grooved and incised pottery is strikingly similar to historically recorded pottery made on Goodenough Island, so a D'Entrecasteaux Archipelago origin remains a possibility (Lauer 1973).

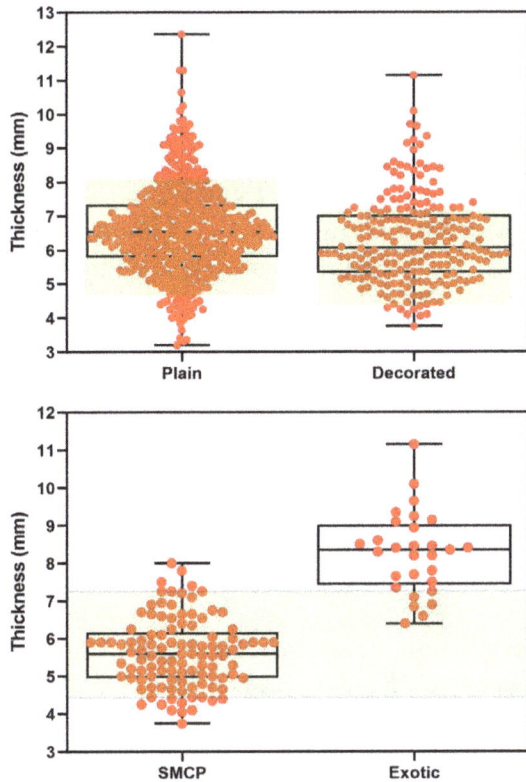

Figure 13.9: Box and whisker plot of decorated sherd thickness recovered from Square A, Mumwa, attributed to SMCP or styles defined by Bickler (1998) for Woodlark Island.

Notes: Although there is overlap, the SMCP is thinner than contemporary pottery manufactured elsewhere in the Massim. The green band marks the 1-standard deviation range of SMP recorded on Rossel Island, showing consistency with antecedent SMCP vessels.

Source: Author supplied.

Shell-impressed pottery

Two shell-impressed sherds were recovered from excavation that do not fit into any known regional Massim style and may belong to an as-yet undefined style, or was imported into the region from elsewhere. Shell-impressed pottery is rare in Massim island archaeological contexts but is common in the Rainu mounds on the adjacent mainland. There is, however, no clear correlation between the Mumwa and Rainu shell-impressed sherds (Egloff 1979). On Woodlark Island, shell impression is combined with incision on a northern variant of SMP dated to within the last ~600 years. On Fergusson, sherds from the Avanata site are probably associated with terminal Lapita or EPP (Ford et al. 2021).

The first excavated shell-impressed Mumwa sherd (Figure 13.7SS) is a rim and carination of a shallow vessel with bivalve edge impression, consistent with an *Anadara* sp. shell. A rim sherd found on the surface at Mumwa and a rim recorded in association with secondary burials in Nuiyam Cave (BMW) on Woodlark recorded by Ollier and Pain (1978) also have similar vessel forms and edge impressions (Figure 13.8M–N). An association with secondary burials is consistent with regional models for changing attitudes to interment. This excavated sherd is also similar to shell-impressed bowls at the contemporary Motupore site on the south coast dated to 800–300 cal. BP (Allen 2017:Fig. 8.12).

The second excavated sherd (Figure 13.7TT) is stamped with individual impressions consistent with the umbo of a bivalve shell. The impressions may have been made by a similarly shaped end of a stick but this is less likely based on comparisons with other shell-impressed sherds. It is broadly similar to EPP pottery dating from ~2200–1600 cal. BP at OKA and OJS in the Gulf, and Nebira 4 and Bogi 1 in the Central Province (Allen 1972; David et al. 2012; Skelly 2014). Two other shell-impressed surface sherds at Mumwa have small triangle umbo impressions on thickened rims (Figure 13.8K–L) and are identical to pottery from Rainu (Mound C, Group P, 1000–600 cal. BP) and the Oraido site (Layer C,1600–1300 cal. BP) in Amazon Bay (Egloff 1979; Irwin 1977). Production of shell-impressed pottery in the Massin islands may therefore have commenced as early as 1600–1300 cal. BP, but given the relatively small number of shell-impressed potsherds at Mumwa, they were likely imported to Panaeati at the later end of its production lifespan as has also been suggested for Rainu. Petrographic and elemental analyses are also underway to confirm regional connections.

Stone tools suggest multiple island connections

The Suloga peninsula on the south coast of Woodlark has the highest quality fine-grained stone in the region for the manufacture of axe/adze blades, with most islands in the Louisiade Archipelago having smaller outcrops or foliated base rock not well suited for tool manufacture (Bickler and Turner 2002). The surface collected axe-adze preform from Lekubai (Figure 13.5I) is consistent with the metamorphosed hornfels (*Kaitalamai*) from Suloga and its triangular cross-section is consistent with the predominant tool form produced on Woodlark. The presence of similar ground fragments of the same lithology at Mumwa suggests Suloga stone may have been imported to Panaeati from at least 790–670 cal. BP (Figure 13.5A–B, C). The tuff blade preform at Mumwa, clearly imported to Panaeati, also had a triangular cross-section and may indicate the use of other lithic materials from Woodlark, where tuff occurs, to manufacture tools using similar conventions (Trail 1967) (Figure 13.5H). Again, elemental and petrographic analyses also underway to confirm the source.

Obsidian implies direction and extent of inter-island trade

Obsidian does not occur naturally in the Louisiade Archipelago and its presence on Panaeati indicates that it was imported to the island through maritime networks. Known obsidian source regions are geochemically distinct from each other and include three in the Bismarck Archipelago (Willaumez Peninsula, Mopir and Admiralties) and one (Fergusson Island) in the Massim. Multiple outcrops occur within each of these regions (Bird et al. 1981; Smith 1974). Portable X-ray fluorescence (pXRF) analysis of 91 Mumwa obsidian pieces demonstrate it was all sourced from western ($n = 87$) and eastern ($n = 4$) Fergusson Island sub-sources, 190–240 km west of Panaeati. Sampled Layer 3 obsidian ($n = 12$) was imported exclusively from western sub-sources. Obsidian volume in Layers 1–2 at Mumwa (Squares A and C) is similar to the lowest pottery-bearing Lapita layer at the Gutunka site on nearby Brooker island (87 g/m^3), with volumes considerably lower in Mumwa, Layer 3 (10.2 g/m^3). The obsidian volume data suggests import to Panaeati occurred regularly from 720–490 cal. BP but less frequently in earlier contexts. The size of obsidian pieces on the surface further suggests obsidian import to Panaeati occurred in relatively large pieces. Flakes comprise 70 per cent ($n = 241$) of the excavated assemblage, angular fragments 20 per cent ($n = 67$) and cores 10 per cent ($n = 32$). The obsidian pieces are relatively small in length (5–28 mm, $\bar{x} = 12$ mm) and weight (0.02–2.65 g, $\bar{x} = 0.30$ g), with cores smaller than the largest flakes. No formal tools were present. The metric data collectively indicates that reduction occurred onsite and was relatively intensive, with all cores exhausted to the smallest practical size prior to discard. More detailed analyses of the Mumwa obsidian will be presented in forthcoming publications by one of the authors (LS).

Maritime pathways to Panaeati

Potential maritime import pathways to Panaeati can be inferred when the Mumwa obsidian data is considered against contemporary sites elsewhere in the region. The obsidian density at Rainu (950–530 cal. BP) on the mainland, 140 km west of Fergusson Island, was considerably higher than at Mumwa (203–282 g/m³) (Egloff 1979). However, at Kasasinabwana on Wari Island, 170 km south of Fergusson, only 63 pieces were recovered from a 2 m² trench spanning the last 2680 cal. years, of which 59 came from layer one that likely dates to the last 500 years or so (Negishi and Ono 2009). In the Trobriand group, 130 km from Fergusson, densities at Odubekoya (BALP) were surprisingly much lower than at Mumwa, as only 787 pieces were recovered from 66 m² of excavated sediment, with most collected on the surface (Fernstal et al. 2002). Finally, on Woodlark, although Bickler (1998) did not provide any site-specific obsidian data, he noted it was plentiful on the surface in association with pottery styles identified at Mumwa. Sites on the island's northern side contained larger flakes than those in the south, with the implication that obsidian may have been imported through northern communities and redistributed across the island and to other islands. In later contexts within the Louisiade Archipelago (<550 cal. BP), obsidian densities decrease significantly (<20–5 g/m^3) indicating that these communities were not as regularly connected to social networks through which obsidian was imported (Shaw, Coxe, Kewibu et al. 2020). Given the low densities of obsidian at the contemporary sites on Wari and Kiriwina, obsidian may have been transported to Panaeati through Woodlark, perhaps via smaller 'stepping stone' islands such as Gawa and Iwa that are connected through *Kula* exchange routes (Munn 1992).

Discussion

Archaeological investigations at Mumwa have filled a conspicuous gap in cultural chronologies of the Louisiade Archipelago and the southern Massim, with analyses indicating the site was occupied during a period of marked social change in the region when inter-island maritime networks were augmenting and cultural identifies diversifying. The results suggest that connections that had been maintained with Woodlark and other islands nearer to the New Guinea mainland were closer between 720 and 490 years ago than in later centuries. Potential links with south coast pottery production centres also suggest the Louisiade Archipelago was integrated into overlapping regional social networks, including those antecedent to *Kula*, and appear to have excluded some contemporary maritime-focused Massim and south coast communities where similar pottery has not been found. Prior to *Kula* and the establishment of other historically recorded networks there was a fluidity of interactions throughout the Massim islands and with the New Guinea mainland that included the production of more diverse pottery than is known within the last 500 years. Such fluidity was likely to have been foundational to the development of the *Kula* network and was driven by intergenerational social linkages.

EPP and the 'hiccup'

The pottery recovered from Mumwa is consistent with the pottery from Moturina Island defined by Irwin et al. (2019) as EPP, and on Woodlark Island defined by Bickler (1998) as 'early style pottery'. Although this pottery, or antecedent forms of it, may have been produced regionally from 1300–1050 cal. BP or slightly earlier, it was evidently more widespread from 720–490 cal. BP, and broadly overlaps with the 'ceramic hiccup' when local styles had proliferated. There is currently no substantive evidence for an EPP sequence in the Massim islands like that of the south Papuan coast beyond the broad similarities in vessel form that probably derived from a shared history of Lapita-affiliated pottery production. Bulmer (1971) and Swadling (1981) considered that pottery from the Eriama and Boera sites (Style II) was reminiscent of historic Massim styles. The pottery from Mumwa confirms contemporary Massim pottery does have close similarities, and the potential presence of south coast pottery at Mumwa implies some maritime connections, albethey irregular.

There is a notable absence of deposition between 1300 and 550 cal. BP on small Massim islands, including Nimowa (3.5 km^2), Brooker (1.4 km^2), Wari (2.2 km^2) and perhaps also Tubetube (2.5 km^2). Reduced annual rainfall and shortages in available fresh water have been suggested as a reason for the abandonment of small islands in favour of larger islands during this time. It may also be a driver of the identified 'ceramic hiccup' on the south coast, where changes in settlement patterns also occurred (Allen 2010; Shaw, Coxe, Kewibu et al. 2020; Sutton et al. 2015). The Mumwa site, near a natural watershed on Panaeati Island, was one such settlement maintained over this time of apparent social disruption. A shift in settlement from Mumwa to locations nearer the coast from or after 550 cal. BP coincided with a large-scale influx of pottery import to Rossel Island (290 km²) and reoccupation of Nimowa and Brooker Islands, all associated with the deposition of SMP. The Mumwa sequence, therefore, demonstrates that SMCP is ancestral to SMP, and stylistic change was associated with changes in settlement location and social organisation that involved cross-cultural maritime networking.

Pulses of population movements since the mid-Holocene

The tentative correlation of a tanged blade and mortar rim with a radiocarbon date of 4420–4320 cal. BP at Mumwa suggests that the overlapping mid-Holocene social networks spanning the Bismarck Archipelago and the New Guinea mainland also included the Massim islands, as suggested by Swadling (2016). A later age for the mortar is possible, but evidence is mounting for the more regular habitation of Massim islands from 5–4 ka, although populations were relatively mobile because as yet there is no evidence for continuous use of any one island since this time (Shaw, Coxe, Haro et al. 2020; Shaw et al. 2022). It is likely that until the last millennium many small islands were mostly used as short-term fishing and bird hunting camps, or refuges during longer sea voyages between larger islands. 'Pulses' of population expansion would likely have been supported by a network of culturally related groups occupying surrounding islands, such as was likely the case during Lapita expansion, that contributed to the maintenance of ancestral connections within archipelagos as inferred by genetic analyses (Shaw et al. 2022; van Oven et al. 2014). Innovations occurring within these interconnected maritime-focused social systems led to the deepening diversification of cultural identities. The greater number and smaller geographic range of languages in the D'Entrecasteaux might suggest that different social processes influenced diversity in this island group. We must now look to increase the resolution of existing sequences and to fill the many blanks in archaeological coverage so more nuanced models can be developed.

Acknowledgements

The authors would like to thank the Panaeati Islands communities for permission and support to undertake the archaeological research. We also thank the National Museum and Art Gallery of Papua New Guinea, the National Research Institute and the Provincial Government of Milne Bay for supporting the research program. Thanks also to Pamela Swadling, Glenn Summerhayes, Rob Skelly and two anonymous reviewers for comments on the manuscript. This paper is dedicated to Glenn Summerhayes, who nurtured Shaw's interest in New Guinea archaeology as an undergraduate student, provided sage advice as a postgraduate student, and has long been a mentor, colleague and friend. There is a generation of archaeologists who owe much to Glenn for his enthusiastic encouragement—Shaw counts himself among them.

References

Allen, J. 1972. Nebira 4: An early Austronesian site in Central Papua. *Archaeology and Physical Anthropology in Oceania* 7:92–124. www.jstor.org/stable/40386170.

Allen, J. 1985. Comments on complexity and trade: A view from Melanesia. *Archaeology in Oceania* 20:41–49. doi.org/10.1002/j.1834-4453.1985.tb00102.x.

Allen, J. 2010. Revisiting Papuan ceramic sequence changes: Another look at old data. *Artefact* 33:4–15. search.informit.org/doi/10.3316/informit.004778282847109.

Allen, J. 2017. *Excavations on Motupore Island, Central District, Papua New Guinea*. 2 Vol. Working Papers in Anthropology, No. 4. University of Otago, Dunedin.

Allen, J. and J. O'Connell. 2020. A different paradigm for the initial colonisation of Sahul. *Archaeology in Oceania* 55:1–14. doi.org/10.1002/arco.5207.

Ambrose, W.R., F. Petchey, P. Swadling, H. Beran, L. Bonshek, K. Szabo, S. Bickler and G. Summerhayes 2012. Engraved prehistoric *Conus* shell valuables from southeastern Papua New Guinea: Their antiquity, motifs and distribution. *Archaeology in Oceania* 47:113–132. doi.org/10.1002/j.1834-4453.2012. tb00124.x.

Araho, N., R. Torrence and J.P. White 2002. Valuable and useful: Mid-Holocene stemmed obsidian artefacts from West New Britain, Papua New Guinea. *Proceedings of the Prehistoric Society* 68:61–81. doi.org/ 10.1017/s0079497x00001444.

Bedford, S., M. Spriggs, D. Burley, C. Sand, P. Sheppard and G. Summerhayes 2019. Debating Lapita: Distribution, chronology, society and subsistence. In S. Bedford and M. Spriggs (eds), *Debating Lapita: Distribution, chronology, society and subsistence*, pp. 5–33. ANU Press, Canberra. doi.org/10.22459/ta52. 2019.01.

Berde, S. 1974. Melanesians as Methodists: Economy and marriage on a Papua and New Guinea island. Unpublished PhD thesis, University of Pennsylvania, Philadelphia.

Bickler, S. 1998. Eating stone and dying: Archaeological survey on Woodlark Island, Milne Bay province, Papua New Guinea. Unpublished PhD thesis, University of Virginia, Charlottesville.

Bickler, S.H. and M. Turner 2002. Food to stone: Investigations at the Suloga adze manufacturing sites, Woodlark Island, Papua New Guinea. *Journal of the Polynesian Society* 111:11–43. www.jstor.org/stable/ 20707040.

Bird, J.R., W.R. Ambrose, L.H. Russell and M.D. Scott 1981. *The characterisation of Melanesian obsidian sources and artefacts using proton induced gamma-ray emission (PIGME) technique*. Australian Atomic Energy Commission, Lucas Heights.

Bulmer, S. 1971. Prehistoric settlement patterns and pottery in the Port Moresby area. *Journal of Papua New Guinea Society* 5:28–91.

Bulmer, S. 1977. Waisted blades and axes: A functional interpretation of some early stone tools from Papua New Guinea. In R.V.S. Wright (ed.), *Stone tools as cultural markers: Change, evolution and complexity*, pp. 40–59. Humanities Press Inc., New Jersey.

Bulmer, S. 1978. Prehistoric culture change in the Port Moresby region. Unpublished PhD thesis, University of Papua New Guinea, Port Moresby.

Bulmer, S. 2005. Reflection in stone: Axes and the beginning of agriculture in the Central Highlands of New Guinea. In A. Pawley, R. Attenborough, J. Golson and R. Hide (eds), *Papuan pasts: Cultural, linguistic and biological histories of Papuan-speaking peoples*, pp. 387–450. Pacific Linguistics, Canberra.

Burenhult, G. 2002. *The archaeology of the Trobriand Islands, Milne Bay Province, Papua New Guinea: Excavation season 1999*. British Archaeological Reports. Archaeopress, Oxford. doi.org/10.30861/97818 41714578.

Chynoweth, M., G.R. Summerhayes, A. Ford and Y. Negishi 2020. Lapita on Wari Island: What's the problem? *Asian Perspectives* 59:100–116. doi.org/10.1353/asi.2020.0009.

Damon, F.H. 1990. *From Muyuw to the Trobriands: Transformations along the northern side of the Kula ring*. The University of Arizona Press, Tucson.

David, B., K. Aplin, H. Peck, R. Skelly, M. Leavesley, J. Mialanes, K. Szabo, B. Koppel, F. Petchey, T. Richards, S. Ulm, I.J. McNiven, C. Rowe, S.J. Aird, P. Faulkner and A. Ford 2019. Moiapu 3: Settlement on Moiapu Hill at the very end of Lapita, Caution Bay hinterland. In S. Bedford and M. Spriggs (eds), *Debating Lapita: Distribution, chronology, society and subsistence*, pp. 61–88. ANU E Press, Canberra. doi.org/10.22459/ta52.2019.03.

David, B., A.S. Fairbairn, K. Aplin, L. Murepe, M. Green, J. Stanisic, M. Weisler, D. Simala, T. Kokents, J. Dop and J. Muke 2007. OJP, a terminal Pleistocene archaeological site from the Gulf Province lowlands, Papua New Guinea. *Archaeology in Oceania* 42:31–33. doi.org/10.1002/j.1834-4453.2007.tb00013.x.

David, B., I.J. McNiven, M. Leavesley, B. Barker, H. Mandui, T. Richards and R. Skelly 2012. A new ceramic assemblage from Caution Bay, South Coast of Mainland PNG: The linear shell edge-impressed tradition from Bogi 1. *Journal of Pacific Archaeology* 3:73–89. pacificarchaeology.org/index.php/journal/article/view/69.

David, B., K. Szabo, M. Leavesley, I.J. McNiven, J. Ash and T. Richards 2022. *The archaeology of Tanamu 1: A pre-Lapita to Post-Lapita site from Caution Bay, south coast of mainland Papua New Guinea*. Archaeopress, Oxford. www.archaeopress.com/Archaeopress/Products/9781803270883.

de Keyser, F. 1961. *Misima Island—Geology and gold mineralization*. Bureau of Mineral Resources, Geology and Geophysics, Canberra.

Earle, T.K., J.E. Ericson 1977. *Exchange systems in prehistory*. Academic Press, Inc, New York.

Eberhard, D.M., G.F. Simons and C.D. Fennig 2022. *Ethnologue: Languages of the world*. 25th edition. SIL International, Dallas. www.ethnologue.com.

Egloff, B.J. 1979. *Recent prehistory in Southeast Papua*. Terra Australis 4. Australia National University, Canberra. openresearch-repository.anu.edu.au/handle/1885/127419.

Fernstal, C., B. Hjulstrom and A. Sterner 2002. The lithic material from Labai and Mwatawa. In G. Burenhult (ed.), *The archaeology of the Trobriand Islands, Milne Bay Province, Papua New Guinea*, pp. 115–125. Archaeopress, Oxford. doi.org/10.30861/9781841714578.

Field, J., G. Summerhayes, S. Luu, A.C.F. Coster, A. Ford, H. Mandui, R. Fullagar, E. Hayes, M. Leavesley, M. Lovave and L. Kealhofer 2020. Functional studies of flaked and ground stone artefacts reveal starchy tree nut and root exploitation in mid-Holocene Highland New Guinea. *The Holocene* 30:1360–1374. doi.org/10.1177/0959683620919983.

Ford, A., V. Kewibu and K. Miamba 2021. Avanata: A possible Late Lapita site on Fergusson Island, Milne Bay Province, Papua New Guinea. In J. Specht, V. Attenbrow and J. Allen (eds), *From field to museum: Studies from Melanesia in honour of Robin Torrence*, pp. 61–70. Australian Museum, Sydney. doi.org/10.3853/j.1835-4211.34.2021.1743.

Groube, L., J. Chappell, J. Muke and D. Price 1986. A 40,000 year-old human occupation site at Huon Peninsula, Papua New Guinea. *Nature* 324:453–455. doi.org/10.1038/324453a0.

Haddon, A.C. 1894. *The decorative art of British New Guinea: A study in Papuan ethnography*. Cunningham Memoirs. Royal Irish Academy, Dublin.

Heaton, T., P. Köhler, M. Butzin, E. Bard, R. Reimer, W. Austin, C. Bronk Ramsey, P. Grootes, K. Hughen, B. Kromer, P. Reimer, J. Adkins, A. Burke, M. Cook, J. Olsen and L. Skinner 2020. Marine20—the marine radiocarbon age calibration curve (0–55,000 cal BP). *Radiocarbon* 62:1–42. doi.org/10.1017/rdc.2020.68.

Hua, X., S.J. Greenhill, M. Cardillo, H. Schneermann and L. Bromham 2019. The ecological drivers of variation in global language diversity. *Nature Communications* 10:2047. doi.org/10.1038/s41467-019-09842-2.

Irwin, G. 1977. The emergence of Mailu as a central place in the prehistory of Coastal Papua. Unpublished PhD. thesis, The Australian National University, Canberra. doi.org/10.25911/5d73949645f52.

Irwin, G. 1985. *The emergence of Mailu: As a central place in Coastal Papuan prehistory.* Terra Australis 10. The Australian National University, Canberra. hdl.handle.net/1885/127425.

Irwin, G. 1991. Themes in the prehistory of Coastal Papua and the Massim. In A. Pawley (ed.), *Man and a half: Essays in Pacific anthropology and ethnobiology in honour of Ralph Bulmer*, pp. 503–510. Polynesian Society, Auckland.

Irwin, G. and S. Holdaway 1996. Colonization, trade and exchange: From Papua to Lapita. In J.M. Davidson, G. Irwin, B.F. Leach, A. Pawley and D. Brown (eds), *Oceanic culture history: Essays in honour of Roger Green*, pp. 225–235. New Zealand Journal of Archaeology Special Publication, Wellington.

Irwin, G., B. Shaw and A. McAlister 2019. The origins of the Kula ring: Archaeological and maritime perspectives from the southern Massim and Mailu areas of Papua New Guinea. *Archaeology in Oceania* 54:1–16. doi.org/10.1002/arco.5167.

Kinch, J.P. 2020. Changing lives and livelihoods: Culture, capitalism and contestation over marine resources in Island Melanesia. Unpublished PhD thesis, The Australian National University, Canberra. openresearch-repository.anu.edu.au/handle/1885/202679.

Kirch, P.V. (ed.) 2021. *Talepakemalai: Lapita and its transformations in the Mussau Islands of Near Oceania.* Cotsen Institute of Archaeology Press, Los Angeles. doi.org/10.2307/j.ctv27tctrd.10.

Kuehling, S. 2021. Winds and seas: Exploring the pulses of place in *kula* exchange and yam gardening. In J.J. Fox (ed.), *Austronesian paths and journeys*, pp. 231–274. ANU Press, Canberra. doi.org/10.2307/j.ctv1prsr48.13.

Lauer, P.K. 1973. *The technology of pottery manufacture on Goodenough Island and in the Amphlett group, S.E. Papua.* Anthropology Museum Occasional Papers no. 2. University of Queensland, Brisbane.

Lewis, S.E., C.R. Sloss, C.V. Murray-Wallace, C.D. Woodroffe and S.G. Smithers 2013. Post-glacial sea-level changes around the Australian margin: A review. *Quaternary Science Reviews* 74:115–138. doi.org/10.1016/j.quascirev.2012.09.006.

Macintyre, M. 1983. Changing paths. An historical ethnology of the traders of Tubetube. Unpublished PhD thesis, The Australian National University, Canberra. openresearch-repository.anu.edu.au/handle/1885/7534.

Malinowski, B. 1922. *Argonauts of the Western Pacific.* Routledge and Kegan Paul, London.

McNiven, I., B. David, T. Richards, K. Aplin, B. Asmussen, J. Mialanes, M. Leavesley, P. Faulkner and S. Ulm 2011. New direction in human colonisation of the Pacific: Lapita settlement of south coast New Guinea. *Australian Archaeology* 72:1–6. doi.org/10.1080/03122417.2011.11690525.

McNiven, I.J., W.R. Dickinson, B. David, M. Weisler, F.V. Gnielinski, M. Carter and U. Zoppi 2006. Mask Cave: Red-slipped pottery and the Australian-Papuan settlement of Zenadh Kes (Torres Strait). *Archaeology in Oceania* 41:49–81. doi.org/10.1002/j.1834-4453.2006.tb00610.x.

Mialanes, J., B. David, A. Ford, T. Richards, I.J. McNiven, G.R. Summerhayes and M. Leavesley 2016. Imported obsidian at Caution Bay, south coast of Papua New Guinea: Cessation of long distance procurement c. 1900 cal BP. *Australian Archaeology* 82:248–262. doi.org/10.1080/03122417.2016. 1252079.

Munn, N.D. 1992. *The fame of Gawa: A symbolic study of value transformation in a Massim society (Papua New Guinea)*. Duke University Press, Durham.

Munsell, C. 2000. *Munsell soil color charts*. Gretagmacbeth, New Windsor.

Negishi, Y. and R. Ono 2009. Kasasinabwana shell midden: The prehistoric ceramic sequence of Wari Island in the Massim, eastern Papua New Guinea. *People and Culture in Oceania* 25:23–52.

Nettle, D. 1998. Explaining global patterns of language diversity. *Journal of Anthropological Archaeology* 17:354–374. doi.org/10.1006/jaar.1998.0328.

Norick, F.A. 1976. An analysis of the material culture of the Trobriand Islands based upon the collection of Bronislaw Malinowski. Unpublished PhD thesis, University of California, Berkeley. ehrafworldcultures. yale.edu/cultures/ol06/documents/031.

Ollier, C.D. and C.F. Pain 1978. Some megalithics and cave burials: Woodlark Island (Murua), Papua New Guinea. *Archaeology and Physical Anthropology in Oceania* 13:10–18.

Pavlides, C. 1999. The Story of Imlo: The organisation of flaked stone technologies from the lowland tropical rainforest of West New Britain, Papua New Guinea. Unpublished PhD thesis, La Trobe University, Melbourne.

Reimer, P., W. Austin, E. Bard, A. Bayliss, P. Blackwell, C. Bronk Ramsey, M. Butzin, H. Cheng, R. Edwards, M. Friedrich, P. Grootes, T. Guilderson, I. Hajdas, T. Heaton, A. Hogg, K. Hughen, B. Kromer, S. Manning, R. Muscheler, J. Palmer, C. Pearson, J. van der Plicht, R. Reimer, D. Richards, E. Scott, J. Southon, C. Turney, L. Wacker, F. Adolphi, U. Büntgen, M. Capano, S. Fahrni, A. Fogtmann-Schulz, R. Friedrich, P. Köhler, S. Kudsk, F. Miyake, J. Olsen, F. Reinig, M. Sakamoto, A. Sookdeo and S. Talamo 2020. The IntCal20 Northern Hemisphere radiocarbon age calibration curve (0–55 cal kBP). *Radiocarbon* 62:1–33. doi.org/10.1017/RDC.2020.41.

Rhoads, J.W. 1980. Through a glass darkly: Present and past land use of Papuan sagopalm users. Unpublished PhD thesis, The Australian National University, Canberra. openresearch-repository.anu.edu.au/handle/ 1885/96947.

Ross, M.D. 1988. *Proto Oceanic and the Austronesian languages of Western Melanesia*. Pacific Linguistics, Canberra.

Seligman, C.G. 1910. *The Melanesians of British New Guinea*. Cambridge University Press, Cambridge.

Seligman, C.G. and T.A. Joyce 1907. On prehistoric objects in British New Guinea. In W.H.R. Rivers (ed.), *Anthropological essays presented to Edward Burnett Tylor, in honour of his 75th birthday*, pp. 325–341. Clarendon, Oxford.

Shaw, B. 2015. The archaeology of Rossel Island, Massim, Papua New Guinea: Towards a prehistory of the Louisiade Archipelago. 2 Vol. Unpublished PhD thesis, The Australian National University, Canberra.

Shaw, B. 2016. The late prehistoric introduction of pottery to Rossel Island, Louisiade Archipelago, Papua New Guinea: Insights into local social organisation and regional exchange in the Massim. *Archaeology in Oceania* 51:61–72. doi.org/10.1002/arco.5104.

Shaw, B. 2017. Late Pleistocene colonisation of the eastern New Guinea islands? The potential implications of robust waisted stone tool finds from Rossel Island on the long term settlement dynamics in the Massim region. *Journal of Pacific Archaeology* 8:1–16. pacificarchaeology.org/index.php/journal/article/view/234.

Shaw, B. 2021. Palaeolandscapes, radiocarbon chronologies, and the human settlement of southern lowland and island Papua New Guinea. In M.T. Carson (ed.), *Palaeolandscapes in archaeology: Lessons for the past and future*, pp. 215–290. Routledge, New York. doi.org/10.4324/9781003139553-9.

Shaw, B., S. Coxe, J. Haro, K. Privat, S.G. Haberle, F. Hopf, E. Hull, S. Hawkins and G. Jacobsen 2020. Smallest Late Pleistocene inhabited island in Australasia reveals the impact of post-glacial sea-level rise on human behaviour from 17,000 years ago. *Quaternary Science Reviews* 245:106522. doi.org/10.1016/j.quascirev.2020.106522.

Shaw, B., S. Coxe, V. Kewibu, J. Haro, E. Hull and S. Hawkins 2020. 2500-year cultural sequence in the Louisiade Archipelago (Massim region) of eastern Papua New Guinea reflects adaptive strategies to remote islands since Lapita settlement. *The Holocene* 30(7):1–16. doi.org/10.1177/0959683620908641.

Shaw, B., J. Field, G. Summerhayes, S. Coxe, A.C.F. Coster, A. Ford, J. Haro, H. Arifeae, E. Hull, G. Jacobsen, R. Fullagar, E. Hayes and L. Kealhofer 2020. Emergence of a Neolithic in Highland New Guinea by 5000–4000 years ago. *Science Advances*:eaay4573. doi.org/10.1126/sciadv.aay4573.

Shaw, B., S. Hawkins, L. Becerra-Valdivia, C. Turney, S. Coxe, V. Kewibu, J. Haro, K. Miamba, M. Leclerc, M. Spriggs, K. Privat, S.G. Haberle, F. Hopf, E. Hull, A. Pengilley, S. Brown, C. Marjo, G. Jacobsen and Brooker and Panaeati communities. 2022. Frontier Lapita interaction with resident Papuan populations set the stage for initial peopling of the Pacific. *Nature Ecology and Evolution* 6:802–812. doi.org/10.1038/s41559-022-01735-w.

Shaw, B., M. Leclerc, W.R. Dickinson, M. Spriggs and G.R. Summerhayes 2016. Identifying prehistoric trade networks in the Massim: Evidence from petrographic and chemical compositional pottery analyses from Rossel and Nimowa Islands in the Louisiade Archipelago, Massim region, Papua New Guinea. *Journal of Archaeological Science: Reports* 6:518–535. doi.org/10.1016/j.jasrep.2016.03.034.

Skelly, R. 2014. From Lapita to the *Hiri*: Archaeology of the Kouri Lowlands, Gulf of Papua, Papua New Guinea. Unpublished PhD thesis, Monash University, Clayton. bridges.monash.edu/articles/thesis/From_Lapita_to_the_Hiri_archaeology_of_the_Kouri_Lowlands_Gulf_of_Papua_Papua_New_Guinea/4697263.

Skelly, R., B. David, F. Petchey and M. Leavesley 2014. Tracking ancient beach-lines inland: 2600-year-old dentate-stamped ceramics at Hopo, Vailala River region, Papua New Guinea. *Antiquity* 88:470–487. doi.org/10.1017/S0003598X00101127.

Smith, I.E. 1974. Obsidian sources in Papua-New Guinea. *Archaeology and Physical Anthropology in Oceania* 9:18–25. www.jstor.org/stable/40386213.

Smith, I.E. and P.E. Pieters 1973. The geology of the Deboyne Island Group, southeastern Papua. *Bureau of Mineral Resources, Geology and Geophysics Australia* 139:71–74.

Spriggs, M. 1997. *The Island Melanesians*. Blackwell Publishers, Oxford.

Summerhayes, G.R. 2007. The rise and transformation of Lapita in the Bismarck Archipelago. In S. Chui and C. Sand (eds), *From Southeast Asia to the Pacific: Archaeological perspectives on the Austronesian expansion and the Lapita Cultural Complex*, pp. 129–172. Academic Sinica, Taipei.

Summerhayes, G.R. and J. Allen 2007. Lapita writ small? Revisiting the Austronesian colonisation of the Papuan South Coast. In S. Bedford, C. Sand and S.P. Connaughton (eds), *Oceanic explorations: Lapita and Western Pacific Settlement*, pp. 97–122. ANU E Press, Canberra. doi.org/10.22459/TA26.2007.05.

Summerhayes, G., J. Field, B. Shaw and D. Gaffney 2017. The archaeology of forest exploitation and change in the tropics during the Pleistocene: The case of Northern Sahul (Pleistocene New Guinea). *Quaternary International* 448:14–30. doi.org/10.1016/j.quaint.2016.04.023.

Sutton, N., G. Summerhayes and A. Ford 2015. Regional interaction networks in southern Papua New Guinea during the Late Holocene: Evidence from the chemical characterisation of chert artefacts. *Proceedings of the Prehistoric Society* 81:343–359. doi.org/10.1017/ppr.2015.14.

Swadling, P. 1981. The settlement history of the Motu and Koita speaking people of the Central Province, Papua New Guinea. In D. Denoon and R. Lacey (eds), *Oral tradition in Melanesia*, pp. 240–251. University of PNG and the Institute of Papua New Guinea Studies, Port Moresby.

Swadling, P. 2013. Prehistoric stone mortars. In L. Bolton, N. Thomas, E. Bonshek, J. Adams and B. Burt (eds), *Melanesia: Art and encounter*, pp. 78–82. British Museum Press, London. doi.org/10.14434/mar. v9i1-2.19614.

Swadling, P. 2016. Mid Holocene social networks in far eastern New Guinea. *Journal of Pacific Archaeology* 7:7–19. pacificarchaeology.org/index.php/journal/article/view/179.

Swadling, P., P. Weissner and A. Tumu 2008. Prehistoric stone artefacts from Enga and the implication of links between the highlands, lowlands and islands for early agriculture in Papua New Guinea. *Journal de la Societe des Oceanistes* 126–127:271–292. doi.org/10.4000/jso.2942.

Thangavelu, A. 2015. 'Unshelling the past'—An archaeological study of shellfish assemblages from Caution Bay, Papua New Guinea. Unpublished PhD thesis, University of Southern Queensland, Toowoomba. research.usq.edu.au/item/q33yz/-unshelling-the-past-an-archaeological-study-of-shellfish-assemblages-from-caution-bay-papua-new-guinea.

Torrence, R. 2016. Social resilience and long-term adaptation to volcanic disasters: The archaeology of continuity and innovation in the Willaumez Peninsula, Papua New Guinea. *Quaternary International* 394:6–16. doi.org/10.1016/j.quaint.2014.04.029.

Torrence, R., S. Kelloway and P. White 2013. Stemmed tools, social interaction, and voyaging in early-mid Holocene Papua New Guinea. *The Journal of Island and Coastal Archaeology* 8:278–310. doi.org/10.1080/15564894.2012.761300.

Trail, D.S. 1967. *Geology of Woodlark Island, Papua*. Bureau of Mineral Resources, Geology and Geophysics, Canberra.

Uberoi, J.P.S. 1962. *Politics of the Kula ring: An analysis of the findings of Bronislaw Malinowski*. Manchester University Press, Manchester.

van Oven, M., S. Brauer, Y. Choi, J. Ensing, W. Schiefenhovel, M. Stoneking and M. Kayser 2014. Human genetics of the Kula Ring: Y-chromosome and mitochondrial DNA variation in the Massim of Papua New Guinea. *European Journal of Human Genetics*:1–11. doi.org/10.1038/ejhg.2014.38.

Vanderwal, R.L. 1973. Prehistoric studies in Central Coastal Papua. Unpublished PhD thesis, The Australian National University, Canberra.

Vilgalys, G. and G. Summerhayes 2016. Do hiccups echo? Late Holocene interaction and ceramic production in southern Papua New Guinea. *Asian Perspectives* 55:62–88. doi.org/10.1353/asi.2016.0011.

Young, M. 1983. The Massim: An introduction. *The Journal of Pacific History* 18:3–10. doi.org/10.1080/00223348308572455.

Appendix: Supplementary tables and figures

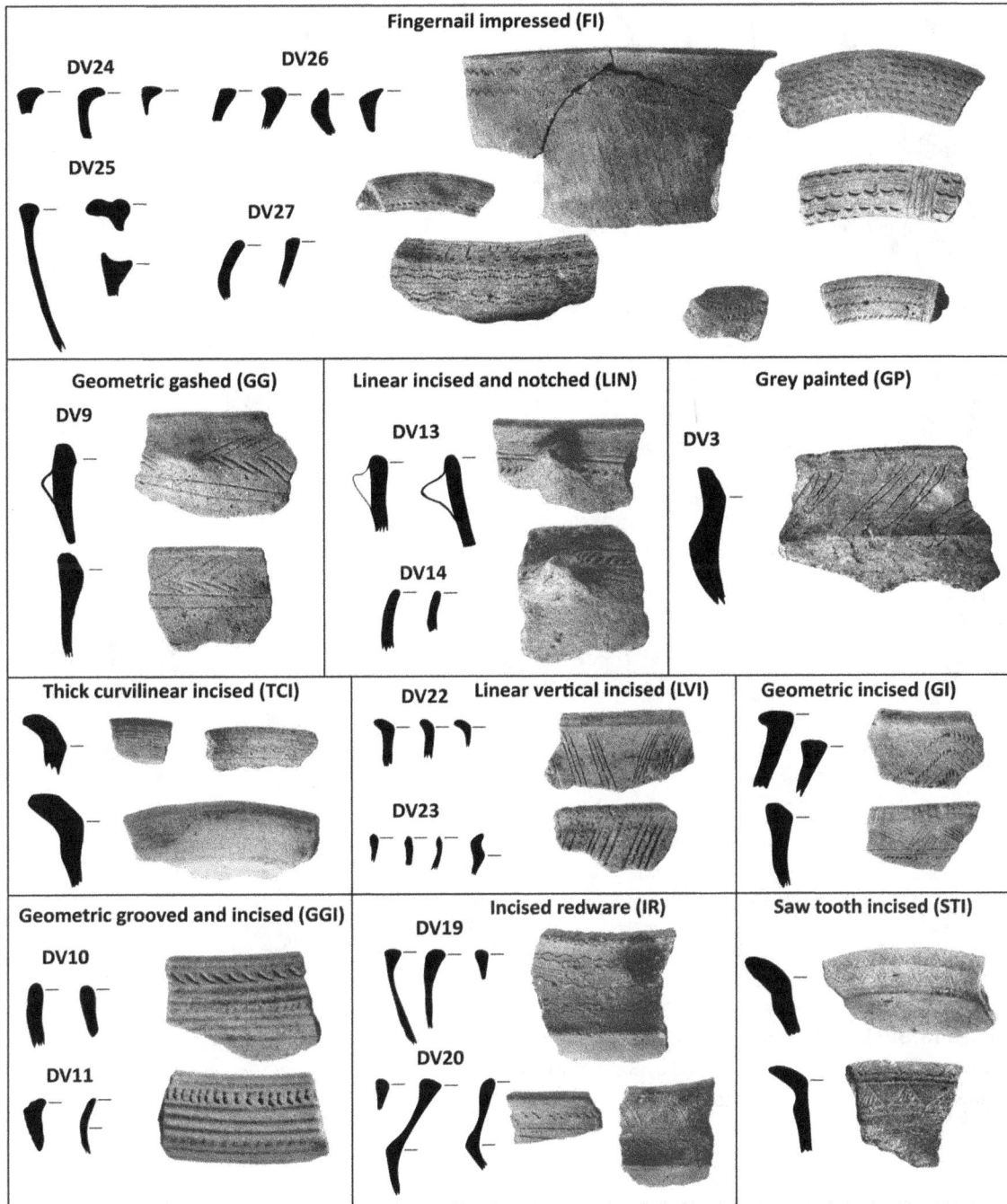

Figure 13.S1: Early Period pottery (~1050–500 cal. BP) recorded on Woodlark Island.

Note: DV = Decorated vessel as defined by Bickler (1998).

Source: Recorded by Simon Bickler (1998).

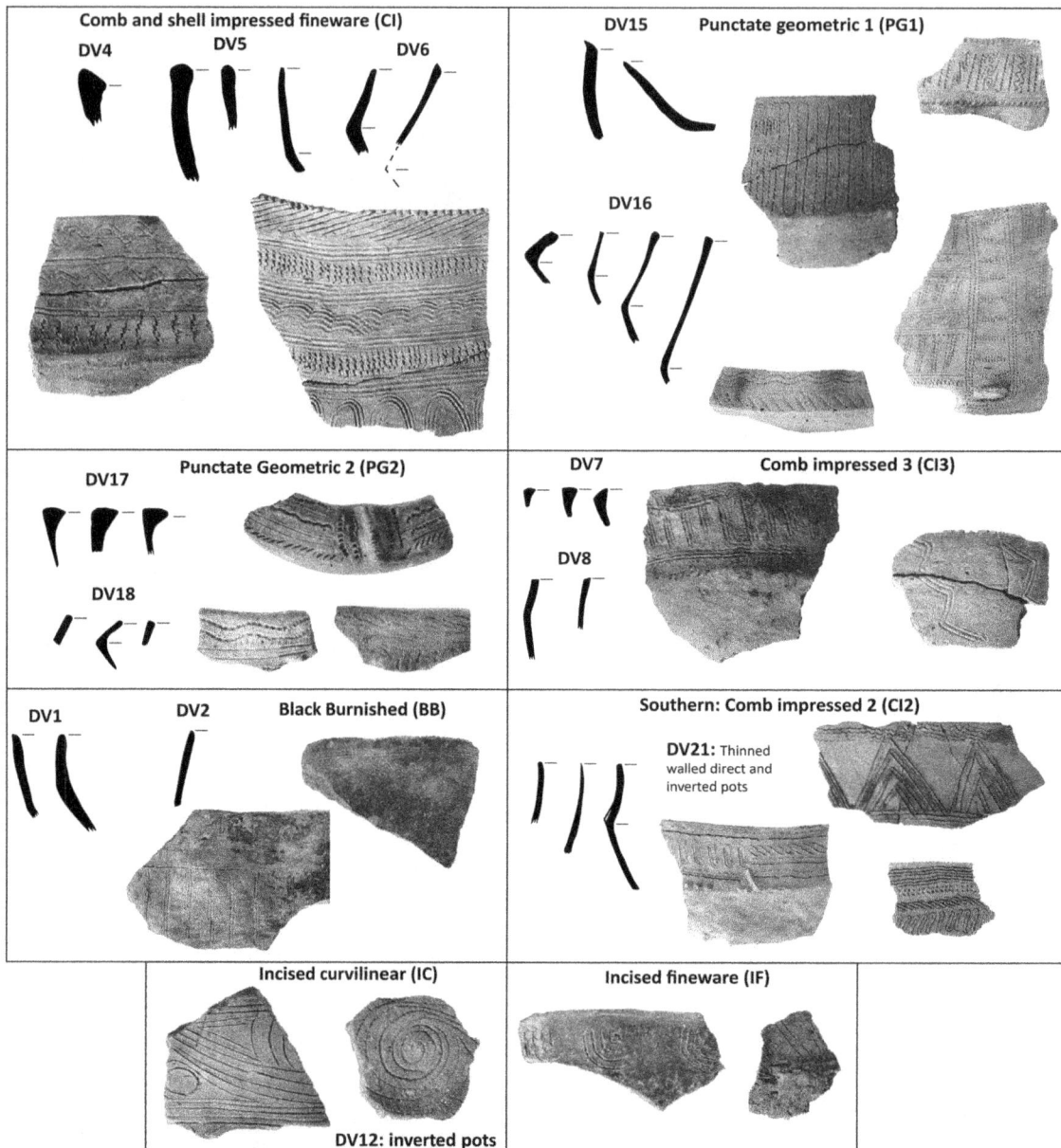

Figure 13.S2: Late Period pottery (<500 cal. BP) recorded on Woodlark Island.

Note: DV = Decorated vessel as defined by Bickler (1998).

Source: Recorded by Simon Bickler (1998).

Table 13.S1: Excavation data from Square A, Mumwa.

Spit	Layer	Area (m²)	Depth range (mm)	Average spit depth (mm)	Spit volume (m³)	Sediment weight (kg)	Sediment volume (L)	Kg/L	Obsidian (no.)	Obsidian (g)	Obsidian (g/m³)	Pottery (no.)	Pottery (g)	Pottery (g/m³)	Lithic (no.)	Lithic (g)	Shell (g)	Bone (g)
1	1	1.0	0–34	34	0.0340	44.8	35.5	1.26	15	5.262	155	219	543.4	15,982	3	1.14	0.86	0.28
2			34–88	54	0.0540	65.4	55.5	1.18	25	11.84	219	216	562.8	10,422	3	2.94	–	2.54
3			88–135	47	0.0470	67	54	1.24	16	4.584	98	202	583.4	12,413	2	0.37	0.12	–
4	2	1.0	135–203	68	0.0680	93.4	81	1.15	22	5.815	86	140	408.9	6013	2	3.14	–	–
5			203–254	51	0.0510	66.4	59.5	1.12	22	7.042	138	69	274.6	5384	1	31.32	–	0.28
6			254–299	45	0.0450	57.8	58	1.00	13	4.490	100	36	140.1	3113	–	–	–	–
7			299–354	55	0.0550	74.4	72	1.03	7	2.568	47	14	60.6	1102	–	–	–	–
8		0.9	354–397	43	0.0387	49	45	1.09	7	2.615	68	1	1.2	31	–	–	–	–
9		0.8	397–458	61	0.0488	75.6	71.5	1.06	4	1.133	23	4	9	184	–	–	0.27	–
10	3	0.7	458–503	45	0.0450	54.8	51.5	1.06	3	0.666	15	–	–	–	–	–	–	–
11		0.6	503–561	58	0.0348	53.6	46	1.17	4	0.516	15	–	–	–	–	–	0.1	0.08
12		0.4	561–606	45	0.0450	61.7	51	1.21	6	1.026	23	–	–	–	–	–	0.15	–
13		0.3	606–643	37	0.0111	68.2	55	1.24	1	0.224	20	–	–	–	1	25.75	1.31	–
14			643–725	82	0.0246	46.8	36.5	1.28	–	–	–	–	–	–	2	10.22	0.68	–
15		0.2	725–771	46	0.0092	7	6	1.17	–	–	–	–	–	–	–	–	–	–
16			771–811	40	0.0080	6.5	6	1.08	–	–	–	–	–	–	–	–	–	–
17			811–868	57	0.0114	7.2	7	1.03	–	–	–	–	–	–	–	–	–	–
18			868–990	122	0.0244	9.2	8	1.15	–	–	–	–	–	–	–	–	–	–
Total					**0.6550**	**908.8**	**799**	**1.14**	**145**	**47.781**	**83**	**901**	**2584**	**5853**	**14**	**74.88**	**3.49**	**3.18**

Source: Author supplied.

Table 13.S2: Excavation data from Square B, Mumwa.

Spit	Layer	Area (m²)	Depth range (mm)	Average spit depth (mm)	Spit volume (m³)	Sediment weight (kg)	Sediment volume (L)	Kg/L	Obsidian (no.)	Obsidian (g)	Obsidian (g/m³)	Pottery (no.)	Pottery (g)	Pottery (g/m³)	Lithic (no.)	Lithic (g)	Shell (g)	Bone (g)
1	1	1	0–46	46	0.046	46.2	38	1.22	0	0	0	37	144.5	3141	–	–	–	0.60
2			46–76	30	0.030	40.6	36	1.13	4	1.516	51	34	82.5	2750	–	–	–	–
3			76–125	49	0.049	67.1	57	1.18	9	3.995	82	48	191.7	3912	–	–	–	–
4	2	1	125–186	61	0.061	71.7	61	1.18	15	6.229	102	36	98.3	1611	–	–	–	–
5		0.9	186–232	46	0.041	54	48	1.13	14	7.592	183	27	96.7	2336	–	–	–	–
6		0.8	232–287	55	0.044	50.7	53	0.96	16	3.257	74	24	68.9	1566	1	26.75	–	0.17
7		0.7	287–338	51	0.036	46.1	44	1.05	3	1.156	32	3	3.0	84	–	–	–	–
8		0.6	338–398	60	0.036	–	–	–	1	0.021	1	1	0.7	19	–	–	–	–
Total					**0.343**	**376.4**	**337.0**	**1.12**	**62**	**23.766**	**69**	**210**	**686.3**	**2000**	**1**	**26.75**	**0**	**0.77**

Source: Author supplied.

Table 13.S3: Excavation data from Square C, Mumwa.

Spit	Layer	Area (m²)	Depth range (mm)	Average spit depth (mm)	Spit volume (m³)	Sediment weight (kg)	Sediment volume (L)	Kg/L	Obsidian (no.)	Obsidian (g)	Obsidian (g/m³)	Pottery (no.)	Pottery (g)	Pottery (g/m³)	Lithic (no.)	Lithic (g)	Shell (g)	Bone (g)	Pumice (g)
1	1	1.0	0–92	92	0.0920	113.2	109	1.04	52	14.519	158	432	1165	12,663	8	8.46	3.15	1.7	6.3
2	1/2	1.0	92–197	105	0.1050	139.2	124	1.12	52	12.07	115	194	549.4	5232	2	92.93	0.28	–	2.98
3	2	1.0	197–295	98	0.0980	118	110	1.07	21	3.35	34	44	145	1480	1	7.73	0.09	0.62	–
4		0.7	295–384	89	0.0630	89.4	89	1.00	2	0.657	10	4	11.7	186	1	25.53	–	–	–
5	2/3	0.7	384–478	94	0.0658	83.6	74	1.13	3	0.78	12	1	1.6	24	–	–	–	–	–
6	3	0.5	478–588	110	0.0550	96.8	79.5	1.22	3	0.214	4	1	0.9	16	–	–	–	0.14	–
7		0.2	588–649	61	0.0122	46.2	47.5	0.97	1	0.064	5	–	–	–	–	–	–	–	–
Feature		0.04	–	–	0.0200	54.2	56	0.97	1	0.247	12	–	–	–	–	–	–	–	–
Total					**0.5110**	**740.6**	**689**	**1.07**	**135**	**31.654**	**62**	**676**	**1873.6**	**3913**	**12**	**134.65**	**3.52**	**2.46**	**9.28**

Source: Author supplied.

Table 13.S4: Excavated lithic artefacts from Mumwa.

Square	Spit	Layer	Depth (mm)	Context	Artefact no.	Mass (g)	Lithic	Artefact	Length (mm)	Width (mm)	Weathering	Notes
A	1	1	0–34	Sieve	A.1.1	0.37	Hornfels	Ground axe-adze fragment	14	13	No	–
					A.1.2	0.6	Hornfels	Flake	17	10	No	–
					A.1.3	0.17	Hornfels	Angular fragment	11	8	No	Fragment
	2		34–88	Sieve	A.2.1	0.73	Hornfels	Flake	19	13	No	–
					A.2.2	0.44	Hornfels	Ground axe-adze fragment	13	11	No	–
					A.2.3	1.77	Tuff	Manuport	19	16	Yes	Possible bowl carination
	3		88–135	Sieve	A.3.1	0.31	Hornfels	Ground axe-adze fragment	11	10	No	–
					A.3.2	0.06	Hornfels	Ground axe-adze fragment	9	8	No	–
	4	2	135–203	Sieve	A.4.1	0.58	Hornfels	Flake	16	13	No	–
					A.4.2	2.56	Limestone	Flake	26	16	Yes	–
	5		232	In situ	A.5.1	31.32	Quartz siltstone	Axe-adze preform or grindstone	53	32	Yes	Bevelled edge with 3 cut marks on body surface and 3 on bevel
	13	3	636	In situ	A.13.1	25.75	Limestone	Possible core	52	51	Yes	flaked edge
	14		643–725	Sieve	A.14.1	2.12	Limestone	Flake	26	22	Yes	–
			689	In situ	A.14.2	8.1	Chlorite schist	Tanged blade	47	29	Yes	–
B	6	2	279	In situ	B.6.1	26.75	Fine-grained tuff	Axe-adze blade	71	25	Yes	Retouched edge
C	1	1	0–92	Sieve	C.1.1	2.42	Hornfels	Ground axe-adze fragment	26	17	No	–
					C.1.2	1.83	Hornfels	Flake	21	16	No	Distal notch
					C.1.3	1.75	Hornfels	Flake	23	17	No	–
					C.1.4	1.01	Hornfels	Flake	21	16	No	–
					C.1.5	0.68	Hornfels	Ground axe-adze fragment	18	13	No	–
					C.1.6	0.28	Hornfels	Flake	14	13	No	Fragment
					C.1.7	0.37	Hornfels	Ground axe-adze fragment	13	11	No	–
					C.1.8	0.12	Hornfels	Flake	10	8	No	–
	2		92–197	Sieve	C.2.1	12.17	Quartz siltstone	stone bowl fragment	40	21	Yes	4 x incised lines
			209	In situ	C.2.2	80.76	Metavolcanic	Manuport	82	31	Yes	–
	3	2	197–295	Sieve	C.3.1	7.73	Hornfels	Ground axe-adze fragment	39	20	No	Retouched edge, reused as core.
	4		335	In situ	C.4.1	25.53	Hornfels	Ground axe-adze fragment	45	22	No	Partial bevel

Source: Author supplied.

14

Echoes of distant pasts? New Britain, Vanuatu and Felix Speiser

Jim Specht

Abstract

Recent papers on the genetics of the First Remote Oceanians raised questions about the nature of two population movements into the islands of Vanuatu, particularly the dominance of 'Papuan' lineages in the second phase. The papers identified potential ancestral lineages in New Britain, Papua New Guinea and cited Vanuatu linguistic features and cultural practices as additional evidence for the origin of the second phase in that region. This paper reviews these claims through an examination of ethnographic and archaeological records, focusing on the head binding of babies (artificial cranial modification), the raising of full-circle tusker pigs and their tusks, aspects of pottery forms, and stone arrangements. While noting some differences, the review broadly supports the claims of Speiser, the geneticists and the archaeologists, and proposes likely contacts between Vanuatu and the New Guinea – New Britain – north Solomons areas during the last 1000 years or so. There is currently no cultural evidence for the postulated earlier secondary movement that introduced 'Papuan' genetic ancestry to Vanuatu.

Introduction

Recent papers on the genetic history of Vanuatu identified settlement by three population movements into these islands, with the second pointing to the Bismarck Archipelago, and specifically to New Britain, as its likely source (Skoglund et al. 2016; Lipson et al. 2018, 2020; Posth et al. 2018) (Figure 14.1).

From an archaeological perspective the primacy of the Bismarck Archipelago in the settlement of Remote Oceania has long been accepted (Golson 1961) and confirmed by the identification of Bismarck Archipelago obsidian at Lapita sites in Remote Oceania (Ambrose and Green 1972; Galipaud et al. 2014; Reepmeyer et al. 2011), and stylistic analyses of Lapita pottery (e.g. Green 1979:Fig. 2.10). The purpose of the present paper is to assess this claim from archaeological and recent material culture aspects, some of which have previously been canvassed by archaeologists and linguists but not explicated in relation to the genetics' studies. The paper addresses four questions:

1. Can we confirm New Britain as a specific source area for the 'second wave' into Vanuatu?

2. If the answer is 'yes', when did this occur?

3. Can we define other potential source areas?

4. What do the results of points (1) to (3) tell us about relationships (if any) between genetics/ biology, language and material culture?

The paper summarises the main points of the genetics and related studies in relation to these questions and reviews the non-genetic and non-linguistic evidence for two cultural practices—head binding and boars' tusks—cited by the genetics' papers, and on the late-sequence pottery comparisons of Bedford and Spriggs (2008:99, 107). To these I add the treatment of the dead and aspects of stone arrangements. I conclude that the northern Solomon Islands, the New Guinea mainland and possibly even the south-east islands of New Guinea should be added to New Britain as likely source areas for so-called Papuan cultural components of Vanuatu, consistent with the preferred phylogenetic model of 'Papuan' ancestry in Vanuatu (Lipson et al. 2018:1162).[1] The paper ends with some observations on the relationship between genetics, languages and culture.

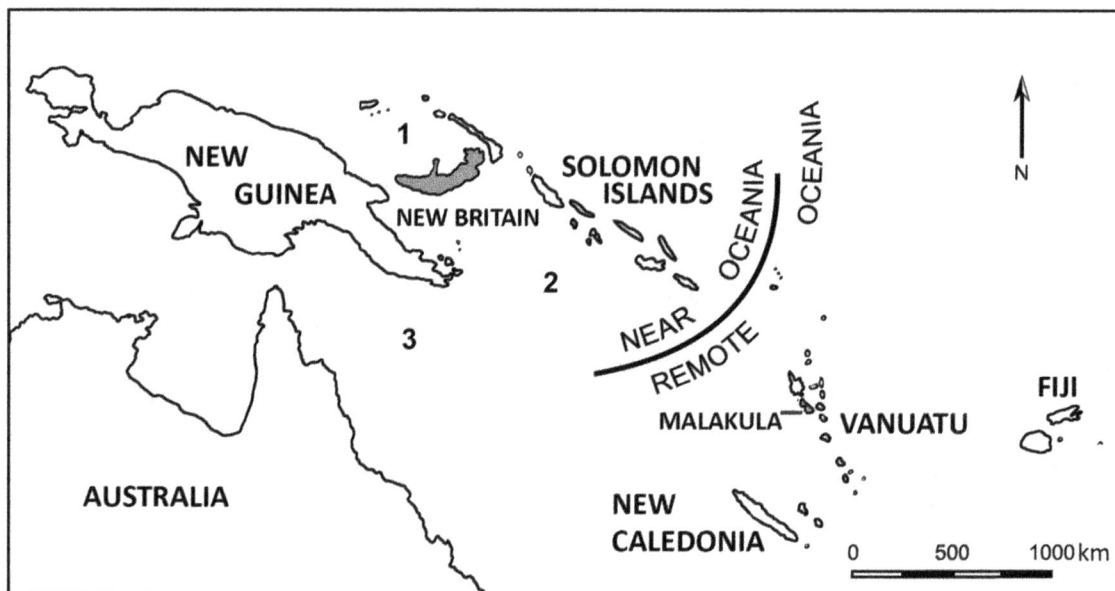

Figure 14.1: The western Pacific islands, showing the Near and Remote Oceania boundary, the major island groups and the Bismarck (1), Solomon (2) and Coral (3) Seas.
Source: Original map by Fiona Roberts, modified by Jim Specht.

---

1   The term Papuan is variously used to denote unrelated languages that are not Austronesian, people of a range of phenotypes, kinds of material culture and as a geographical term for people of the former colony of Papua in Papua New Guinea. Here 'Papuan' in quotation marks refers to 'the deep ancestral lineage that contributes the majority of the ancestry found in present-day populations from Near Oceania' (Lipson et al. 2020:4847). This avoids confusing genomic populations with geographical, cultural, archaeological or linguistic ones (Skoglund et al. 2016:512; Spriggs and Reich 2019:5). Papuan without quotation marks represents the cited author's usage.

Genetics and Vanuatu

Based on genome analyses of burials from Teouma and other Vanuatu archaeological sites, together with modern samples from Vanuatu and elsewhere, the genetics' papers demonstrated initial settlement of Vanuatu at ca 3000–3100 BP by people with almost unadmixed East Asian and Southeast Asian genomes, whereas people with predominantly 'Papuan' genomes were present by 2800–2400 cal. BP, suggesting a secondary settlement phase (Spriggs and Reich 2019:625–626). Archaeological individual TAN002 from Tanna Island, dated to 2630–2350 cal. BP (Posth et al. 2018:Table 1), was genetically close to modern-day Baining people of New Britain, who were therefore considered living proxies for the ancient 'Papuan' genetic lineage of the secondary movement (Posth et al. 2018:734). Lipson et al. (2020:4849–4850) later generalised this to 'a subset of populations from New Britain', having previously noted that 'three Papuan source lineages' from New Guinea, New Britain and Bougainville were needed for their preferred phylogenetic model of 'Papuan' ancestry in Vanuatu (Lipson et al. 2018:1162).

Independently of the genomic data, Bedford and Spriggs (2008, 2018:174–175) and Bedford (2018), citing Speiser (1996 [1923]), supported likely contacts between Vanuatu and New Britain marked by the common practices of head binding of babies and the raising of full-circle tusker pigs, adding similarities between the late-sequence pottery of Buka and Malakula. These contacts were placed around 600–1000 years ago (Bedford 2018:137; Posth et al. 2019:58). Initially Blust (2005:554, fn. 3, 2008:453–454) and Posth et al. (2018:736) proposed that these cultural elements and non-Austronesian (NAn) linguistic features were shared 'almost exclusively' between Vanuatu and NAn-speakers in the northern regions, but Lipson et al. (2020:4854) later dropped the reference to NAn languages.

The genetics studies sparked debate between geneticists, linguists and archaeologists (Bedford et al. 2018; Posth et al. 2019; Spriggs and Reich 2019; Spriggs et al. 2019). The claims about cultural practices, however, escaped scrutiny, perhaps because the archaeological evidence was convincing, and it was obvious that migrants would have taken their cultural practices with them. Furthermore, claims for links between Vanuatu and New Britain based on head binding and boars' tusks were not new. Ethnologist Felix Speiser devoted his career to the history of cultural connections across the islands of Southeast Asia (ISEA) and the western Pacific (e.g. Speiser 1996 [1923], 1932, 1934a, 1934b, 1938; Adam 1950; Kaufmann 1996). He conducted archaeological excavations on several islands in Vanuatu with little success and turned to comparisons of contemporary cultural practices that he observed in the island groups from New Caledonia to New Guinea, including a five months' visit to New Britain's south coast (Gosden and Knowles 2001:101–128; Kocher Schmid 2001; Speiser 1996 [1923]:83–86). He claimed four practices were shared exclusively between the 'Arue' (Arawe) area of New Britain and Malakula: head binding, the raising of tusker pigs, the production of full-circle tusk ornaments, and tusker pig sacrifices (Speiser 1934a:131, 155–156).

New Britain, languages and the Baining

At ca 36,500 km² New Britain is the largest tropical island in the Pacific east of New Guinea. Similar in size to Taiwan and three times the land area of Vanuatu, it comprises a main landmass and several dozen offshore islands (Figure 14.2). About 51 Austronesian (AN) and NAn languages are spoken on New Britain and adjacent islands (SIL 2015). These languages present 'one of the most complex linguistic geographies of the region', and 'probably display greater genetic [i.e. linguistic] diversity than those of any similarly sized area in Oceania' (Ross 1996:v, 2). This complexity reflects

New Britain's deep human history (ca 40,000 years) and its geographical position between New Guinea to the west and New Ireland to the east. This position has facilitated exchange networks involving frequent short-distance movements of people in each direction that contributed to the present linguistic complexity (Ross 2014).

The AN languages belong to the Meso-Melanesian and North New Guinea Clusters in the Western branch of the Oceanic group (Ross 1988). Proto-Oceanic probably developed in the New Britain area from interaction between immigrant speakers of AN languages and the NAn residents, with today's Western Oceanic languages emerging after the dispersal of Proto-Oceanic–speakers into Island Melanesia (Ross 1996:2; Lynch et al. 2002:96–97). Today only 12 NAn languages are known in New Britain, but formerly there were probably many more (Stebbins et al. 2018:Map 7.1). Five languages form the Baining family on the Gazelle Peninsula in eastern New Britain (Stebbins 2009:224; Stebbins et al. 2018:775, Map 7.2). The Baining individuals with 'Papuan' genetic lineages came from inland villages speaking the Kaket and Mali languages. The other NAn languages are isolates. Kol, Makolkol, Sulka, Taulil and Butam are also on or close to the Gazelle Peninsula, though Butam is no longer spoken and Makolkol is possibly extinct (Rohatynskyj 2001:28; Stebbins et al. 2018:797). Ata is in the interior to the west of the Peninsula, and Anêm is located near the western end of the island (Ross 1996:ix).

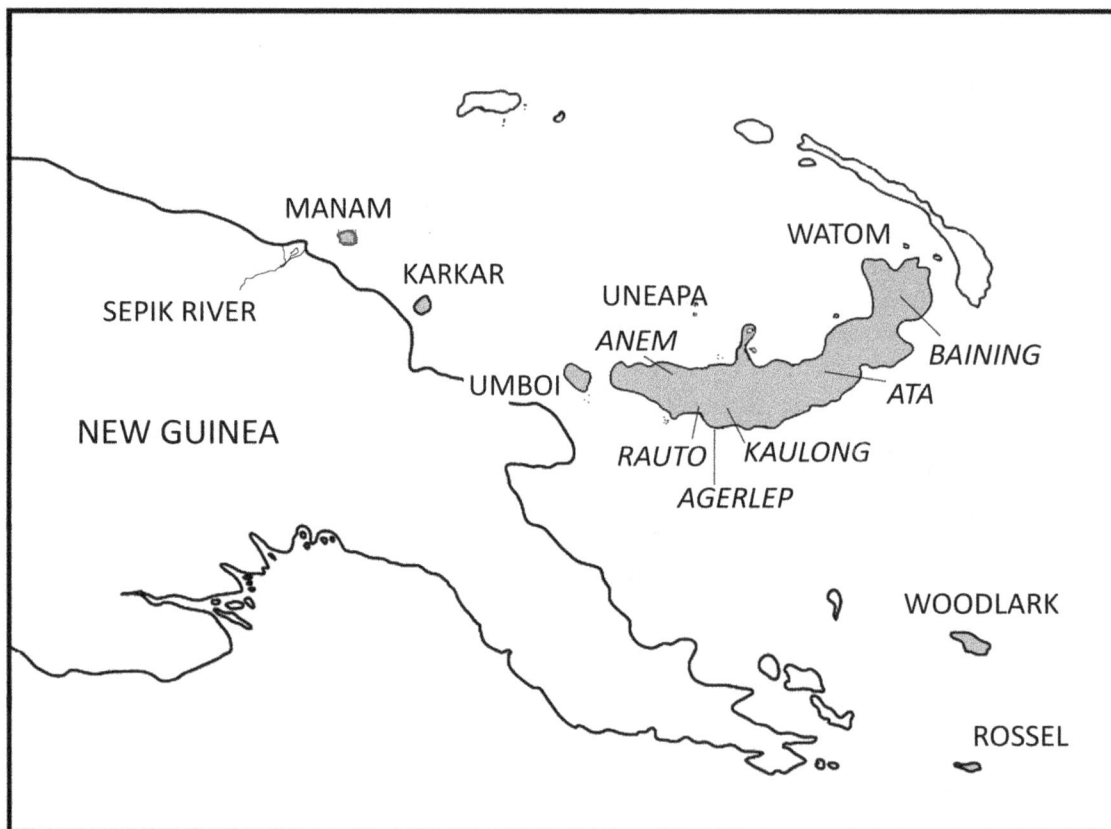

Figure 14.2: New Guinea and the Bismarck Archipelago, showing the main places and language areas cited in the text.

Source: Map prepared by Jim Specht.

The Baining claim to be the original indigenous people on the Gazelle Peninsula and describe themselves as conquered by the Oceanic-speaking Tolai, who came from New Ireland several hundred years ago (Neumann 1992:117; Rohatynskyj 2001:26; Salisbury 1972). The Taulil, Butam and Sulka speakers also came from New Ireland; when is not known, though recently enough for people on New Ireland to remember the Butam, and for the Butam and Sulka to believe that the spirits of their dead return there (Stebbins 2009:229–230). All three groups presumably arrived after the cataclysmic Rabaul eruption of AD 667–699 (1283–1251 cal. BP: McKee et al. 2015). The Mali language of the Baining family was influenced by an Oceanic language before the Tolai arrival (Stebbins et al. 2018:806), and a similar influence on Sulka has also been identified (Reesink 2005; Reesink and Dunn 2018:97), though in neither case has the Oceanic source language been identified. These interactions probably contributed to the 4 per cent East Asian/Southeast Asian ancestry of the Baining (Lipson et al. 2020:Fig. 5; Posth et al. 2018:734).

Previous genetic studies on New Britain showed only a 'modest association between language and genetic affiliation' in New Britain (Friedlaender et al. 2008:10). Hunley et al. (2008:10–11) noted that 'Oceanic-speaking groups without the "Austronesian" signature are often genetically indistinguishable from their immediate Papuan-speaking neighbors', and that NAn-speakers contributed more genetically to Oceanic-speakers than vice versa. The AN Meramera, Mamusi and Nakanai (Loso), for example, have become genetically 'predominantly Papuan' like their NAn neighbours, the Ata (Friedlaender et al. 2008:8, 10).

Artificial cranial modification (head binding)

Artificial cranial modification (ACM) involves various methods of applying pressure to the head of a newborn child to modify permanently the shape of the cranium, creating an elongated or flattened shape depending on the technique applied (Tubbs et al. 2006). ACM has a long history in Australia and Asia, from the late Pleistocene at Zhoukoudian, China (Brothwell 1975; Li et al. 2018) to terminal Pleistocene – early Holocene in Australian contexts (Anton and Weinstein 1999; Brown 1981, 2010; Durband 2008). The oldest record in ISEA is dated to the sixteenth or seventeenth century in the Philippines (Clark 2013; Meyer 1881:133–134), and by the nineteenth century various practices including binding and hand massaging the child's skull were widespread in Sulawesi (Meyer 1885:85), Timor (Garson 1884:387), Sumatra, Borneo, and Java (Meyer 1881, 1885).[2]

Records of ACM practices are discontinuous across the Pacific Ocean. In the Mariana Islands during the Latte Period (950–1521 AD) several archaeological skulls had posterior flattening, a practice probably introduced by Spanish colonists (Ikehara-Quebral et al. 2018). In nineteenth-century Fiji (Fison 1885:20, fn. 1) and Samoa (Speiser 1934a:156), manual pressure was applied to the baby's head, whereas a skull from Niue was posteriorly flattened (Virchow 1884:153). In Hawai'i, Stokes (1920) recorded various techniques employed in historic times and cases of ACM occur among the undated Mokapu skulls (Schendel et al. 1980). The best historical evidence comes from the Arawe area of New Britain (Blackwood and Danby 1955; Parkinson 1999 [1907]:26, 88–89) and southern Malakula in Vanuatu (Layard 1928:218, 220; Speiser 1934a:156–157, 1996 [1923]:162–163).[3]

---

2   Meyer (1881:Fig. 2) illustrated a device from Sarawak allegedly used to flatten a child's head, but its weight and size (the wooden part was 325 mm long) would make it inappropriate for attaching to a baby's head; it is more likely to have been an adult's carrying device.

3   Reche (2015 [1913]:103, plate LXXIII.1) acquired three crania with posterior flattening at the Sepik River mouth which he believed were not of local origin as he saw no village people with deformed heads. Speiser (1934a:156) suggested that they were Arawe skulls that had been traded, though the skull in Reche's plate does not resemble those illustrated by Blackwood and Danby (1955).

The Arawe area extends along the south coast of New Britain from Gasmata westwards to beyond the Arawe Islands and into the hinterland (Figure 14.2). Today it contains about a dozen languages within the North New Guinea Cluster of Western Oceanic (Ross 1996:map, p. ix), some displaying what Blust (2009:685) called 'undeniable lexical deviance'. Of these, Kaulong has the lowest retention rate (5.2 per cent) among Oceanic languages of Proto-Malayo-Polynesian lexical reconstructions (Pawley 2006:234), which is as low or lower than NAn adoption rates from the AN lexicon (Blust 2009:686–687). On this basis Kaulong and its lexically aberrant neighbours could be mistaken as NAn languages, but grammatically they are Oceanic (Chowning 1985, 1996:23; Ross 2002:387; Reesink and Dunn 2018:946–948). ACM was practised within the distribution of these languages.[4]

On Malakula and in the Arawe area, the heads of newborn children were coated with black pigment made from charred nuts or wood. On Malakula, the baby's head was then wrapped with a banana leaf and covered with a tight, woven cap (Layard 1928:220, Fig. 5; Speiser 1934a:140). On New Britain the Kaulong, Rauto and Agerlep speakers wound barkcloth around the baby's head and secured it with a vine 'string' (Blackwood and Danby 1955:173–174; Goodale 1995:plate opp. 81; Gosden and Knowles 2001:Fig. 1.1; Maschio 1994:182; Todd 1934:202). The binding was removed each day and the baby's head was washed, massaged, painted again and re-bound (Blackwood and Danby 1955:174; Maschio 1994:224). This process was repeated for about a year. The procedures in New Britain and on Malakula essentially differ only in the use of a woven cap instead of bark cloth on Malakula.

There is little archaeological evidence for ACM practices in New Britain and none for Malakula. The New Britain evidence is an adult male burial (W15) in the late-to-post Lapita cemetery on Watom Island dated to 2750–2050 cal. BP (human bone, 95.4 per cent probability), though there are issues about its stratigraphic integrity (Petchey et al. 2016:27, Fig. 21). This date range embraces that for TAN002, the oldest dated individual with a 'Papuan' lineage in Vanuatu (2630–2350 cal. BP, 95.4 per cent probability: Posth et al. 2018:Table 1). The genetic lineage of W15 is unknown, but Pietrusewsky et al. (2014:16) concluded from a morphometric study that the Watom crania and mandibles are most like those of inhabitants of Near Oceania and western Remote Oceania and least like those of Polynesians. In a separate study, Valentin et al. (2016:294) explicitly linked the Watom craniofacial forms with the secondary movement into Remote Oceania. There are, however, no cases of ACM among the Lapita-age burials of Teouma or the later burials of Uripiv and Vao that were contemporary with Watom W15 (Valentin et al. 2010, 2016; Bedford et al. 2011:Table 1). There may be several reasons for this lack of archaeological evidence for ACM among these early Vanuatu people, the most obvious being that the practice was not taken to Vanuatu until after the Lapita and immediate Post-Lapita periods, although other issues like sample sizes, status associations and taphonomic issues also merit consideration.

Treatment of the dead

The post-mortem manipulation of human remains was formerly widespread in the western Pacific Islands in various forms of memorialising and paying of respect to ancestors, particularly in the form of skull cults (Layard 1928; Speiser 1934a). This section discusses an unusual form of manipulation identified in the Teouma cemetery (Valentin et al. 2010) that seems to be echoed among the Kaulong people of New Britain in the recent past.

---

4   Head binding was still practiced inland from Kandrian in 1979–1981, but I did not see evidence for the raising of tusker pigs either on the coast or inland. As I do not have up-to-date information whether these practices are still followed, I use the past tense here.

According to Goodale (1985:239–240) the Kaulong followed a complex process involving exhumation and washing of the skull, mandible and sometimes clavicles, scapulae, arms and sternum (Goodale 1985:239–240). The skull and mandible were painted red, a perforated stone was placed in each eye socket, and the bones were then displayed with the deceased's valuables. A ceremony was held at which a tusker pig was sacrificed, and the dead man's skull and other bones were presented with the sacrificial pig skull to one of the deceased man's exchange partners to restore the link broken by his death. Over time, the bones passed through the network and eventually returned 'home' for secondary burial.[5] The Rauto people to the west of the Kaulong also exhumed the skull, mandible, ulna and hand bones and conducted various rituals, but did not circulate them through the exchange network (Maschio 1994:92–93, 187–189).

Similar bone removals were apparently practised 3000 years earlier at the Teouma cemetery where 25 adult burials lacked skulls and incomplete sets of clavicles, scapulae and arm bones (Valentin et al. 2010:217, Fig. 3). The skeletal remains in three jar burials were similarly incomplete (Valentin et al. 2016:83, Table 1). Some removed bones were given secondary burial (Bedford et al. 2010:155, Fig. 12; Valentin 2010:167, Fig. 3).

There is no evidence for similar patterns of bone removals in the later burials on Vao and Uripiv Islands (Bedford et al. 2011:34) or among the Watom burials (Pietrusewsky et al. 2014), though on Watom there are instances of the removal of skulls and other bones (Valentin et al. 2010). There is little skeletal evidence elsewhere in the Bismarck Archipelago, with only fragmentary skeletal elements and no identifiable burials in the Mussau Islands (Kirch 2021:511, Table 6.1). The similarity of practices across 3000 years and thousands of kilometres, however, invites speculation whether this is coincidence or persistence of cultural performances. While this question currently cannot be resolved, the possibility of some degree of relationship or continuity should be kept in mind.

Pigs, tusks and ornaments

Beran (2014) and Bedford (2018) reviewed the production and distribution of full-circle boars' tusks in the New Guinea – Bismarck Archipelago region and Vanuatu respectively, with Bedford also exploring the archaeological evidence for their use and their scarcity in excavations apart from certain burials.[6] In Vanuatu, the raising of tusker pigs and their full-circle tusks is limited to the northern and central islands. It takes many years to produce the circle tusks, during which the boars receive special attention, being treated with great respect and regarded as sacred. Production of these tusks is intimately linked to grade-taking ceremonies through which men gain increasing status and receive armbands of full-circle tusks appropriate to their grade (Bonnemaison 1996; Huffman 2005; Layard 1942:241–246; Speiser 1996 [1923]:143–144). Bedford (2018:128) notes that old photos show relatively few people wearing full-circle tusks, which were often left embedded in the mandible and displayed on racks, presumably to show the wealth and success of individuals and the social group.

Full-circle boars' tusks occur throughout Papua New Guinea and Torres Strait, including the Fly River delta and the Massim (Davies 2011:87; Lawrence with Varjola 2010:151; Swadling and Bence 2016), though their actual production seems very restricted. Beran (2014:10–11) identified

---

5   Goodale (1985:232) recounts a myth about a child-eating monster Yumihin who 'looked like the butchered head of a pig, with his cloak detached from the body but left attached to the fore-legs and skull'. This echoes the human remains circulated among the deceased's exchange partners.

6   Vanuatu pigs come in three genders - male, female and intersex (Baker 1929:115–130; Layard 1942:240ff; Huffman 2005; Lum et al. 2006). The intersex variety does not occur on New Britain (Hide 2003).

production on New Britain in the Arawe area, probably in the Bariai area, and possibly on Umboi, the north New Guinea coast and adjacent islands, and in the Massim. Most information, however, is about obtaining tusks by exchange or their role in performances (e.g. Gaffney and Summerhayes 2017:1, 15; Hogbin 1978:39; Lipset 1990; Lutkehaus 1990:300, 2013; Swadling and Bence 2016), and there is no information about the raising of the boars. McSwain (1977:7) recorded that each village on Karkar had a specialist to remove the tusks from the mandible, but there is no indication that these were locally raised full-circle tuskers. In fact, photos of boars' tusks incorporated into body ornaments throughout the islands and New Guinea mainland rarely show full-circle tusks.[7]

Goodale (1985:234–235) described the process of producing full-circle tusks among the Kaulong as taking about 10 years. After the boar is sacrificed, the tusks are removed from the mandible and bound together, sometimes decorated with gastropods (Beran 2014:Fig. 2; Goodale 1966:24; Kaufmann 1975:Fig 62; Parkinson 1999 [1907]:Fig. 27). These paired tusks are insignia worn by senior men on the back of their necks. Formerly, during warfare, they were clenched in the wearer's teeth to signal aggression and power (Goodale 1985:234), but today they are worn in ceremonial and celebratory performances on New Britain and Manam Island and along the north coast of New Guinea (Beran 2014:Fig. 5; Lutkehaus 2013:8, Fig. 5).

In Vanuatu the most valuable tusks have double or triple circles (Huffman 2005:41–43), but these forms are not mentioned in the anthropological literature of New Britain and do not appear in photographs of people wearing boars' tusks in New Britain or the broader New Guinea region. Paired circle tusks are not the prerogative of men in southern New Britain, as both Chinnery (n.d.:19, plate 4, plate 6) and Todd (1934:plate IIB) photographed coastal women wearing paired tusks round their necks. In Todd's case the tusks belonged to one of the woman's male relatives, and among the Rauto, women could receive them during puberty rites to mark their new status as 'big women' (Maschio 1994:134, 1995:136, 156–160). In northern Vanuatu wives of high-ranking men can wear a tusk if they have completed the requisite rites, but not at puberty, which is regarded as far too early in life (Speiser 1996 [1923]:plate 8 Fig. 8; Kirk Huffman, pers. comm. 17 November 2021).

A change in the use of tusks might have occurred in New Britain over the last 180 years, for Jacobs (1844:252, 260) commented that people assembled for a ceremony on the south coast wore 'boars' tusks bangles' on their arms. As this is the only record of circle tusks being worn this way in New Britain, it is likely that Jacobs saw *Trochus* shell armbands.

In Vanuatu full-circle tusks only appear about 400–600 years ago, though an earlier date ca 1050 BP in the Banks Islands is possible (Bedford 2018:130–131). The earliest evidence comes from burials on Tongoa Island that postdated the Kuwae eruption of ca AD 1452 (Robin et al. 1994), and from Roi Mata's cemetery on Eretok (Retoka) Island dated to the early seventeenth century AD (Bedford 2018:130), where 22 individuals had over 50 full-circle tusks as arm/wrist bands (Garanger 1972:Table 11, Figs 192–196). The absence of full-circle tusks in other contexts may reflect gaps in the archaeological record (Bedford 2018:138, endnote 5), or the practice of smashing of a man's boar's tusk and replacing it with a new one when he progresses to a higher grade on Malakula and Vao (Layard 1928:149, 154). No whole tusks have been reported from archaeological sites in the Bismarck Archipelago. On Watom Island, canine fragments were found in Late and Post-Lapita contexts at the SAC site but appear to be from normal tusks (Smith 2000 [1998]:141; Specht, unpublished data). There were no pig canines in the Lapita levels of the Anir Islands (Summerhayes et al. 2019:382, Tables 18.1, 18.2); and none among the pig remains from

---

7   Neither Bedford nor I have been able to access Speiser's (1932) paper on the production and use of full-circle tusks on New Britain cited by the late Harry Beran.

the Tanga Islands' excavations (Cath-Garling 2017:Table 3.8). Pig remains were common in sites on the Siassi Islands near Umboi and on mainland New Guinea, but no breakdown of body parts is available (Lilley 1986:Table 10.1). Consequently, the antiquity of producing full-circle tusks in the Bismarck Archipelago is unknown but this does not eliminate the possibility of a time depth like that of Vanuatu.

Pottery of Malakula and Buka/Bougainville

It is unclear whether pottery production on Malakula continued between 1200 and 600 cal. BP (Bedford 2006:168, Fig. 8.16), but from ca 600 BP bullet-shaped vessels with vertical sides termed Chachara ware appeared and continued in elongated form as *Naamboi* ware during the last 200 years (Bedford 2006:143, 151–155, Figs 7.14, 7.19–7.23). These bullet-shaped pots are unique in the archipelago and there is no predecessor in the Vanuatu industry from which they might have developed. Layard's Malakulan informants were uncertain about the origin of these vessels and attributed them to the *Ambat*, a light-skinned people of the past whose origin is unclear (Layard 1928:210–214). They certainly did not originate in New Britain, where there is no evidence for pottery production during the last 2000 years.

Bedford (2006:151; Bedford and Spriggs 2008:107) proposed possible connections between Chachara ware and the modern/recent bullet-shaped *tabeli* vessels of Buka Island in the northern Solomon Islands (May and Tuckson 2000:Fig. 11.2; Specht 1972:130). Related tall, cylindrical- to bullet-shaped vessels with everted rims also occur in the Bougainville industries of Siwai (Oliver 1967:Fig. 34) and Buin, where Terrell excavated one at the Loiai stone arrangement site dated to the last 1000 years (Terrell 1976:300–329, Figs 4.19c, 5.4a, 5.5). Terrell (1976:360, Fig. 6.1) grouped the pottery industries of Buka, Bougainville (Nasioi, Buin, Siwai), Shortland Islands and Choiseul into the North Solomons Tradition with two sub-traditions, Buka and the rest. Chachara ware is similar to the Buka sub-tradition in form, decoration and chronology and is highly likely to have been introduced from the Buka region (Bedford and Spriggs 2018). This would rule out the light-skinned *Ambat* as the carriers of the pottery tradition since the people of Buka–Bougainville have 'extremely dark' skins.

The large size and poor quality of *Naamboi* vessels led Bedford (2006:155) to propose a shift in their function from domestic to ritual use. *Naamboi* were used in ceremonies for fertility and resource increase, burials and control of weather, and were kept in sacred places (Deacon 1934:597; Layard 1928:210). In contrast, the Buka *tabeli* was a domestic cooking vessel (Blackwood 1935:399–400; Specht 1972:130), though Blackwood recorded (but did not see) a large form known as *abonon* that was used for feasts. The *Naamboi* vessels are more tubular than *tabeli* (Buka: Blackwood 1935:plate 61; Specht 1972:Figs 2, 3; Malakula: Bedford 2006:143–156, Figs 7.14, 7.19–7.23; Galipaud 1996:122, Fig. 102; Layard 1928:plate XVIII.3), though they are similar in size: the mean height of 10 *Naamboi* vessels is 344 mm and maximum 458 mm (Bedford 2006:Figs 7.19–7.23), and the mean height of 11 Buka *tabeli* is 324 mm and a maximum of 465 mm (Specht 1972:131). An unusual *Naamboi* form is a simple cylinder open at each end that was associated with burials (Layard 1928:plate XVIII.3, plate XIX, Fig. 1). Such cylinders are unknown on Buka and Bougainville.

Stone arrangements

Malakula and the Small Islands have one of the densest concentrations of stone arrangements in the western Pacific Islands, and these are prominent in grade-taking cycles and other rites (Geismar and Herle 2009:45–46; Layard 1928:153–154, 1943:12–20). Riesenfeld (1950) surveyed these features in his study of the 'megalithic cultures' of the western Pacific, and since then further information has been published (e.g. Bedford 2019; Bickler 2006; Riebe 1967; Terrell 1978). The arrangements come in many forms, often with rich oral histories and mythologies. Along with Speiser (1934a), Riesenfeld saw parallels between Vanuatu and the New Guinea – Bismarck Archipelago region, with both citing the stone 'seat' on Uneapa Island in the Vitu group (Parkinson 1999 [1907]:plate 14). This kind of feature comprises a tabular slab supported on two or more 'legs' and is a common sight on Oceanic-speaking Uneapa Island off northern New Britain, where some are identified as sacrificial tables (Ambrose and Johnson 1986; Byrne 2008:Figs 5.3, 5.4, 2013:Table 1; Torrence et al. 2002). The form is also present on Umboi Island between New Britain and New Guinea (Byrne 2008:Fig. 9.2). Similar structures, called 'dolmens' by Layard, are common on Malakula and the Small Islands around dancing grounds where they form parts of skull shrines (Geismar and Herle 2009:48–49; Layard 1928:frontispiece). Structurally related features occur in NAn-speaking areas of the middle Sepik River (Schindlbeck 2018), in south Bougainville and on Choiseul Island in the Solomon Islands (Leavesley and Mandui 2004; Terrell 1976:267–329, 1978:226, Fig. 79; Thomas et al. 2001:Fig. 4; Thurnwald 1934). These features are grouped here under the single term 'capstone features' that includes those called 'seats' and 'tables' on Uneapa (Byrne 2013).

The variety of capstone features and the range of reported functions complicate simple comparisons between Vanuatu and the New Guinea – Bismarck Archipelago – Solomons region, but in both areas they are associated with ritual spaces and 'dancing grounds' (Layard 1942:293, 365–368) and 'meeting places' (Byrne 2008:175–176, 2013:70–71). Monoliths, some of massive size, are associated with dancing grounds (e.g. Geismar and Herle 2009:50, 54; Layard 1928:Figs V.1, XVI.3, 4, XVII.1, 2). On Vao, some are made from coral or beach rock slabs that are roughly dressed, but others are dressed pillars engraved with male anthropomorphic figures, and these stand inside a circle of smaller stones (Bedford 2019; Layard 1928:154, 186).

Both plain and engraved monoliths are found widely in the western Pacific Islands and have a diversity of functions (Bedford 2019; Byrne 2013:Fig. 9; Riesenfeld 1950; Schindlbeck 2018:photos 1, 5; Specht et al. 2021:Fig. 15). Some memorialise ancestors, provide backrests for seats, mark graves, form avenues and delineate sacred spaces. They are associated with special plants such *Cycas* and *Cordyline* species (e.g. Layard 1928:184, Plate XV.4; Schindlbeck 2018:214–215). In south-east Papua New Guinea and on Bougainville they form rectangular or circular enclosures or components of stone platforms or pavements (Bickler 2006; Bickler and Ivuyo 2002; Egloff 1970; Kahn 1990; Ollier et al. 1970; Terrell 1978), but elsewhere they stand alone or within a circle of smaller stones (e.g. Blackwood 1935; Byrne 2008; McPherson 2007:Fig 7). As with capstone features, pillars engraved with anthropomorphic figures occur in both Oceanic and NAn language areas.

In the Bismarck Archipelago, none of the monoliths, capstone features or other stone arrangements have been directly dated. In south-east New Guinea, Bickler and Ivuyo (2002:Table 3) suggested that stone arrangements at the Bunmuyuw site on Woodlark (Muyuw) Island date to around 1300–400 cal. BP based on ^{14}C dates for burials. On Rossel Island, Shaw (2015:163–166) obtained a charcoal date of 500–300 cal. BP (ANU 32531) from 40 cm below a stone feature associated with a small monolith, placing the construction of the stone arrangement within the last 500 years. Similar dates have been obtained for capstone features on Bougainville (Terrell 1978:34–36) and Nusa Roviana, Solomon Islands (Sheppard et al. 2000:32, Table 2).

Layard (1928:200) referred to historical records for the late introduction of monoliths to Malakula but did not cite the evidence. On Tongoa Island monoliths postdate the Kuwae eruption of ca 1452 AD (ca 500 BP: Garanger 1972:92–94, Figs 246–260; Robin et al. 1994), and at Roi Mata's cemetery on Eretoka Island they date to the early seventeenth century (ca 400 BP: Garanger 1972:Figs 149, 152–153). Assuming that these were not an independent local invention, the dates place their introduction around the same time as the appearance of boars' tusks, and well within the timeframe for the Woodlark, Rossel and Solomon Islands' stone features.

Discussion

The review of head binding (ACM) and boars' tusks on Malakula and its adjacent Small Islands and the Arawe area of New Britain has followed well-worn paths of evidence but yielded new information and new questions. Whereas ACM was present in the late Pleistocene to early Holocene in Australia, it is known in ISEA only from much later times, arguably reflecting the paucity of skeletal remains of this early period. Its presence among the Watom burials in the Late to Post-Lapita period (ca 2750–2050 cal. BP) invites consideration whether this was a local development or an introduced practice. If the latter, there is currently no likely source area; Malakula is highly unlikely in view of the absence of ACM among the Teouma Lapita burials and later ones on Vao and Uripiv Islands. At this stage it is reasonable to accept a plausible connection between the practice on New Britain and Malakula, while not assigning a date for its initiation in either area.

The pattern of the Kaulong and Rauto bone removals from inhumations are reminiscent of those in the Teouma cemetery. In Vanuatu it appears restricted to the earliest Lapita period, implying the practice was current at initial colonisation of the archipelago. Its absence from the later Watom burials, where more restricted bone removals were practised, and the lack of skeletal evidence on New Britain in general limit discussion. The great length of time separating the practices on New Britain and at Teouma makes a link between them seem improbable, though further research might resolve the matter.

The review of full-circle boars' tusks in the New Guinea – Bismarck Archipelago region supports previous views that their production was probably restricted to New Britain, though their production in other areas remains a possibility. Nevertheless, the similarities of practices on New Britain and Malakula are sufficient to support transmission between them, but the direction of transmission is not known. There is no evidence yet for their production on New Britain before historical times, but in Vanuatu they appeared ca 550–600 years ago. In the New Guinea – Bismarck Archipelago region it appears that only single circle tusks have been produced, whereas double- and triple-circle tusks are produced in Vanuatu, perhaps to accommodate increasing complexity of grade-taking and the addition of extra higher grades as recorded by Layard (1928:143, 202; 1942:290). In recent times the practices associated with the tusks in Vanuatu and New Britain differed: Rauto girls could receive full-circle tusks at puberty, but in Vanuatu only adult women of high status could possess and wear them.

The late-sequence pottery opens possibilities for contacts between Vanuatu and the north Solomons and islands in southeast Papua New Guinea. The bullet-shaped forms of Chachara and *Naamboi* wares of 600–200 cal. BP (Bedford 2006:Table 6.1) are likely to have been introduced from Buka in the northern Solomons, though their functions and context of use changed on Malakula.

The final comparisons concerned stone arrangements. As Riesenfeld's (1950) survey showed, this is a complex field as there are obvious structural similarities between stone features throughout the western Pacific Islands and beyond. They could have been introduced to Vanuatu from the Buka – Bougainville – western Solomon Islands region, or from Woodlark Island in south-east New Guinea (via the western Solomons?). If from Woodlark, this followed connections in Late Lapita and Post-Lapita times (Tochilin et al. 2012) and could have been through the later short-lived interaction sphere across the Solomon Sea proposed by Sheppard et al. (2015). The dates for some stone features place them within the time range for the introduction of bullet-shaped pottery and full-circle boars' tusks in the later stages of Vanuatu's history. It remains to be seen whether there was any connection between these events.

Conclusions

There is no disagreement that the first settlement of Remote Oceania (as opposed to possible 'scouting' visits) came from the New Guinea – Bismarck Archipelago region around 3000–3100 BP. The two-phase process previously discussed by linguists and speculations about the movement of people and specific cultural practices into Vanuatu recall the diffusionism of Speiser, Riesenfeld and others who sought answers in multiple migration events between ISEA, New Guinea and the Melanesian islands. Speiser (1934a) even proposed a nonstop migration direct to New Britain from the island of Nias on the western side of Sumatra. While such a proposal exceeds the bounds of credulity, the genetic studies discussed here and one relating to the Solomon Islands (Pugach et al. 2018) generally support the archaeological model for a 'leapfrog' initial movement of people from the Bismarck Archipelago into Remote Oceania (Sheppard 2011, 2019; cf. Felgate 2007). The discussions on ACM and full-circle boars' tusks indicate the possibility of one or more later 'leapfrog' movements (Spriggs and Reich 2019:632).

Lipson et al. (2018:1162) inferred three source populations to explain the 'Papuan' genetic input to Vanuatu in the secondary population movement, citing New Britain, Bougainville and the New Guinea Highlands, the latter presumably a portmanteau term for potential ancestral populations across New Guinea. Spriggs and Reich (2019:632) view the secondary movement as 'a continuing migration stream but in changed circumstances' from the initial colonising event. The discussion presented here does not conflict with this stream of people with 'Papuan' lineages but opens possibilities for movements, accidental or planned, from several directions consistent with the Lipson et al. conclusion. The Late Lapita transport of pottery or temper from Woodlark Island across the Solomon Sea to the western Solomon Islands (Tochilin et al. 2012) suggests forms of contact other than migration, though there is no evidence at this stage that this involved Vanuatu.

This review has covered many communities with diverse languages and cultural practices that are the products of millennia of change and modification, reflecting what Spriggs (1997:186) termed '2000 years of contingent history and cultural drift'. Increasingly, the evidence for people moving within and across the Bismarck, Solomon and Coral Seas (e.g. Lilley 2019; McNiven 2021; Sheppard et al. 2015; Tochilin et al. 2012; Torrence et al. 2013) supports this view and challenges the unidirectional and bounded thinking about the region's past that has often tended to become embedded in discourses about interaction spheres and networks. It is a warning not to expect straightforward relationships between language, genes and cultural practices. Previous studies have revealed complex patterns of association in modern populations of the western Pacific; even a small island can yield levels of complexity across all three fields (Cox and Lahr 2006; Friedlaender et al. 2008; Hunley et al. 2008; Ricaut et al. 2008). There is no reason to assume that the past was different.

Acknowledgments

My thanks to the National Museum and Art Gallery, National Research Institute of Papua New Guinea, and the University of Papua New Guinea for granting permits and affiliations for research and other assistance over many years. I also thank successive West New Britain governments, various businesses and people for permission to work in the province and for numerous forms of assistance. Funding was primarily through the Australian Research Council and its predecessors, and the Australian Museum, Sydney. I thank Kirk Huffman and Michael Pietrusewsky for advice on various points; Chris Gosden and Robin Torrence and an anonymous reviewer for their constructive comments; and the editors of this volume for the invitation to contribute a paper. My warmest thanks, however, go to Glenn Summerhayes for decades of friendship, collegiality and good humour, and I look forward to many more years of the same with Glenn and his family.

References

Adam, L. 1950. In memoriam Felix Speiser. *Oceania* 21(1):66–72. www.jstor.org/stable/40328271.

Ambrose, W.R. and R.C. Green 1972. First millennium B.C. transport of obsidian from New Britain to the Solomon Islands. *Nature* 237:31. doi.org/10.1038/237031a0.

Ambrose, W.R. and R.W. Johnson 1986. Unea: An obsidian non-source in Papua New Guinea. *Journal of the Polynesian Society* 95(4):491–497. www.jstor.org/stable/20706035.

Anton, S.C. and K.R. Weinstein 1999. Artificial cranial deformation and fossil Australians revisited. *Journal of Human Evolution* 36(2):195–209. doi.org/10.1006/jhev.1998.0266.

Baker, J.R. 1929. *Man and animals in the New Hebrides*. Routledge, London.

Bedford, S. 2006. *Pieces of the Vanuatu puzzle: Archaeology of the North, South and Centre*. Terra Australis 23. Pandanus Books, Research School of Pacific and Asian Studies, The Australian National University, Canberra. doi.org/10.22459/pvp.02.2007.

Bedford, S. 2018. Modified canines: Circular pig's tusks in Vanuatu and the wider Pacific. In M.C. Langley, M. Litster, D. Wright, and S.M. May (eds), *The archaeology of portable art: Southeast Asian, Pacific and Australian perspectives*, pp. 125–141. Routledge, London and New York. doi.org/10.4324/9781315299112-9.

Bedford, S. 2019. The complexity of monumentality in Melanesia: Mixed messages from Vanuatu. In M. Leclerc and J. Flexner (eds), *Archaeologies of Island Melanesia: Current approaches to landscapes, exchange and practice*, pp. 67–79. Terra Australis 51. ANU Press, Canberra. doi.org/10.22459/TA51.2019.05.

Bedford, S., R. Blust, D. Burley, M. Cox, P. Kirch, E. Matisoo-Smith, A. Naess, A. Pawley, C. Sand and P. Sheppard 2018. Ancient DNA and its contribution to understanding the human history of the Pacific Islands. *Archaeology in Oceania* 53(3):205–219. doi.org/10.1002/arco.5165.

Bedford, S., H.R. Buckley, F. Valentin, N. Tayles and N.F. Longga 2011. Lapita burials: A new Lapita cemetery and Post-Lapita burials from Malakula, northern Vanuatu, Southwest Pacific. *Journal of Pacific Archaeology* 2(2):26–48. pacificarchaeology.org/index.php/journal/article/view/62.

Bedford, S. and M. Spriggs 2008. Northern Vanuatu as a Pacific crossroads: The archaeology of discovery, interaction, and the emergence of the 'ethnographic present'. *Asian Perspectives* 47(1):95–106. doi.org/10.1353/asi.2008.0003.

Bedford, S. and M. Spriggs 2018. The archaeology of Vanuatu: 3,000 years of history across islands of ash and coral. In E.E. Cochrane and T.L. Hunt (eds), *The Oxford handbook of prehistoric Oceania*, pp. 162–184. Oxford University Press, New York. doi.org/10.1093/oxfordhb/9780199925070.013.015.

Bedford, S., M. Spriggs, H. Buckley, F. Valentin, R. Regenvanu and M. Abong 2010. Un cimetière de premier Peuplement: le site de Teouma, au sud d'Efaté, au Vanuatu/A cemetery of first settlement: The site of Teouma, South Efate, Vanuatu. In C. Sand and S. Bedford (eds), *Lapita: Ancêtres océaniens/Oceanic ancestors*, pp. 146–161. Musée du quai Branly, and Somogy Éditions d'Art, Paris.

Beran, H. 2014. Where do mainland New Guineans get their circular boars' tusks from? *Pacific Arts* 15(2): 5–20. www.jstor.org/stable/44737321.

Bickler, S.H. 2006. Prehistoric stone monuments in the northern region of the Kula Ring. *Antiquity* 80(307): 38–51. doi.org/10.1017/S0003598X00093248.

Bickler, S.H. and B. Ivuyo 2002. Megaliths of Muyuw (Woodlark Island), Milne Bay Province, PNG. *Archaeology in Oceania* 37(1):22–36. doi.org/10.1002/j.1834-4453.2002.tb00498.x.

Blackwood, B. 1935. *Both sides of Buka Passage*. Clarendon Press, Oxford.

Blackwood, B.M. and P.M. Danby 1955. A study of artificial cranial deformation in New Guinea. *Journal of the Royal Anthropological Institute* 85:173–192. doi.org/10.2307/2844190.

Blust, R. 2005. Review of Lynch, Ross and Crowley, *The Oceanic Languages*. *Oceanic Linguistics* 44:544–558. doi.org/10.1353/ol.2005.0030.

Blust, R. 2008. Remote Melanesia: One history or two? An addendum to Donohue and Denham. *Oceanic Linguistics* 47:445–459. www.jstor.org/stable/20542824.

Blust, R. 2009. *The Austronesian languages*. Pacific Linguistics, Canberra.

Bonnemaison, J. 1996. Graded societies and societies based on title: Forms and rites of transitional power in Vanuatu. In J. Bonnemaison, C. Kaufmann, K. Huffman and D. Tryon (eds), *Arts of Vanuatu*, pp. 200–203, 208–216. Crawford House Publishing, Bathurst.

Brothwell, D. 1975. Possible evidence of a cultural practice affecting head growth in some late Pleistocene East Asian and Australasian populations. *Journal of Archaeological Science* 2(1):75–77. doi.org/10.1016/0305-4403(75)90048-5.

Brown, P. 1981. Artificial cranial deformation: A component of the variation in Pleistocene Australian Aboriginal crania. *Archaeology in Oceania* 16(3):156–167. doi.org/10.1002/j.1834-4453.1981.tb00026.x.

Brown, P. 2010. Nacurrie 1: Mark of ancient Java, or a caring mother's hands, in terminal Pleistocene Australia? *Journal of Human Evolution* 59:168–187. doi.org/10.1016/j.jhevol.2010.05.007.

Byrne, S.E. 2008. A practice-centred approach to Uneapa Island's archaeology in a long-term context. Unpublished PhD thesis, 2 vols. University College, London.

Byrne, S. 2013. Rock art as material culture—A case study on Uneapa Island, West New Britain, Papua New Guinea. *Archaeology in Oceania* 48(2):63–77. doi.org/10.1002/arco.5004.

Cath-Garling, S. 2017. *Evolutions or revolutions? Interaction and transformation at the 'transition' in Island Melanesia*. University of Otago Studies in Archaeology 27. University of Otago, Dunedin.

Chinnery, E.W.P. n.d. *Certain natives in South New Britain and Dampier Straits*. Territory of New Guinea, Anthropological Report 3. Government Printer, Melbourne.

Chowning, A. 1985. Rapid lexical change and aberrant Melanesian languages. In A. Pawley and L. Carrington (eds), *Austronesian linguistics at the 15th Pacific Science Congress*, pp. 169–198. Pacific Linguistics C-88. Australian National University, Canberra.

Chowning, A. 1996. Relations among languages of West New Britain: An assessment of recent theories and evidence. In M.D. Ross (ed.), *Studies in languages of New Britain and New Ireland. 1: Austronesian languages of the North New Guinea Cluster in Northwest New Britain*, pp. 7–62. Pacific Linguistics Series C-135. The Australian National University, Canberra.

Clark, J.L. 2013. The distribution and cultural context of artificial cranial modification in the Central and Southern Philippines. *Asian Perspectives* 52(1):28–42. www.jstor.org/stable/24569880.

Cox, M.P. and M.M. Lahr 2006. Y-chromosome diversity is inversely associated with language affiliation in paired Austronesian- and Papuan-speaking communities from Solomon Islands. *American Journal of Human Biology* 18:35–50. doi.org/10.1002/ajhb.20459.

Davies, S.M. 2011. Plumes, pipes and valuables: The Papuan artefact-trade in southwest New Guinea, 1848–1888. In S. Byrne, R. Harrison, A. Clarke and R. Torrence (eds), *Unpacking the collection: Networks of material and social agency in the museum*, pp. 83–115. Springer, New York. doi.org/10.1007/978-1-4419-8222-3_4.

Deacon, A.B. 1934. *Malekula: A vanishing people in the New Hebrides.* Edited by C.H. Wedgwood. Routledge, London.

Durband, A.C. 2008. Artificial cranial deformation in Pleistocene Australians: The Coobool Creek sample. *Journal of Human Evolution* 54:795–813. doi.org/10.1016/j.jhevol.2007.10.013.

Egloff, B.J. 1970. The rock carvings and stone groups of Goodenough Bay, Papua. *Archaeology and Physical Anthropology in Oceania*, 5(2):148–156. www.jstor.org/stable/40386115.

Felgate, M.W. 2007. Leap-frogging or limping? Recent evidence from the Lapita littoral fringe, New Georgia, Solomon Islands. In S. Bedford, C. Sand and S. Connaughton (eds), *Oceanic explorations: Lapita and Western Pacific Settlement*, pp. 123–140. Terra Australis 26. ANU E Press, Canberra. doi.org/10.22459/ta26.2007.06.

Fison, L. 1885. The Nanga, or sacred stone enclosure, of Wainimala. *Journal of the Anthropological Institute of Great Britain and Ireland* 14:14–30. doi.org/10.2307/2841476.

Friedlaender, J.S., F.R. Friedlaender, F.A. Reed, K.K. Kidd, J.R. Kidd, G.K. Chambers, R.A. Lea, J.H. Loo, G. Koki, J.A. Hodgson, D.A. Merriwether and J.L. Weber 2008. The genetic structure of Pacific Islanders. *PLoS Genetics* 4(1):e19. doi.org/10.1371/journal.pgen.0040019.

Gaffney, D. and G.R. Summerhayes 2017. *An archaeology of Madang, Papua New Guinea.* Working Papers in Archaeology 5. University of Otago, Dunedin.

Galipaud, J.-C. 1996. Le Rouge et le Noir: la poterie Mangaasi et le peuplement des îles de Mélanésie. In M. Julien, M. Orliac, C. Orliac, B. Gérard, A. Lavondès, H. Lavondès and C. Robineau (eds), *Mémoire de Pierre, Mémoire d'Homme. Tradition et archéologie en Océanie: Hommage à José Garanger*, pp. 115–130. Collection Homme et Société 23. Université de Paris 1, Panthéon-Sorbonne, Paris.

Galipaud, J.-C., C. Reepmeyer, R. Torrence, S. Kelloway and P. White 2014. Long-distance connections in Vanuatu: New obsidian characterisations for the Makué site, Aore Island. *Archaeology in Oceania* 49(2): 110–116. doi.org/10.1002/arco.5030.

Garanger, J. 1972. *Archéologie des Nouvelles Hébrides.* Publications de la Société des Océanistes 30. ORSTOM, Paris. doi.org/10.4000/books.sdo.859.

Garson, J.G. 1884. On the cranial characters of the natives of Timor-Laut. *Journal of the Anthropological Institute of Great Britain and Ireland* 13:386–394. doi.org/10.2307/2841555.

Geismar, H. and Herle, A. 2009. *Moving images: John Layard, fieldwork and photography on Malakula since 1914.* Crawford House Publishing Australia, Belair (South Australia).

Golson, J. 1961. Report on New Zealand, Western Polynesia, New Caledonia and Fiji. *Asian Perspectives* 5(2):166–180.

Goodale, J.C. 1966. Imlohe and the mysteries of the Passismanua, Southwest New Britain. *Expedition* 8(3): 20–31. www.penn.museum/sites/expedition/?p=1571.

Goodale, J.C. 1985. Pig's teeth and skull cycles: Both sides of the face of humanity. *American Ethnologist* 12(2):228–244. www.jstor.org/stable/644218.

Goodale, J.C. 1995. *To sing with pigs is human.* University of Washington Press, Seattle.

Gosden, C. and C. Knowles 2001. *Collecting colonialism: Material culture and colonial change.* Berg, Oxford. doi.org/10.4324/9781003084952.

Green, R.C. 1979. Lapita. In J.D. Jennings (ed.), *The prehistory of Polynesia*, pp. 27–60. Harvard University Press, Cambridge, Massachusetts. doi.org/10.4159/harvard.9780674181267.c3.

Hide, R. 2003. *Pig husbandry in New Guinea. A literature review and bibliography.* Australian Centre for International Agricultural Research, Canberra. www.aciar.gov.au/publication/books-and-manuals/pig-husbandry-new-guinea-literature-review-and-bibliography.

Hogbin, I. 1978. *The leaders and the led: Social control in Wogeo, New Guinea.* Melbourne University Press, Melbourne.

Huffman, K. 2005. *Traditional money banks in Vanuatu. Project survey report.* Vanuatu National Cultural Council, Port Vila. ich.unesco.org/doc/src/00418-EN.pdf.

Hunley, K., M. Dunn, E. Lindstrom, G. Reesink, A. Terrill, M.E. Healy, G. Koki, F.R. Friedlaender and J.S. Friedlaender 2008. Genetic and linguistic coevolution in Northern Island Melanesia. *PLoS Genetics* 4(10):e1000239. doi.org/10.1371/journal.pgen.1000239.

Ikehara-Quebral, R., M. Pietrusewsky and M. Toomay Douglas 2018. Cranial vault modification in the Mariana Islands. Paper presented at the 82nd Annual Meeting of the Society for American Archaeology, Washington, DC. 2018. core.tdar.org/document/443527/cranial-vault-modification-in-the-mariana-islands.

Jacobs, T.J. 1844. *Scenes, incidents, and adventures in the Pacific Ocean, Or, the islands of the Australasian Seas, during the cruise of the clipper Margaret Oakley under Capt. Benjamin Morrell.* Harper Brothers, New York.

Kahn, M. 1990. Stone-faced ancestors: The spatial anchoring of myth in Wamira, Papua New Guinea. *Ethnology* 29(1):51–66. doi.org/10.2307/3773481.

Kaufmann, C. 1975. *Papua Niugini: Ein Inselstaat im Werden.* Museum für Völkerkunde, Basel.

Kaufmann, C. 1996. Felix Speiser, ethnologist. In F. Speiser, *Ethnology of Vanuatu: An early twentieth century study.* Translation by D.Q. Stephenson of *Ethnographische Materialen aus den Neuen Hebriden und den Banks Inseln*, pp. 411–415. Crawford House Publishing, Bathurst.

Kirch, P.V. (ed.) 2021. *Talepakemalai: Lapita and its transformations in the Mussau Islands of Near Oceania.* Monumenta Archaeologica 47. Cotsen Institute of Archaeology Press, Los Angeles. doi.org/10.2307/j.ctv27tctrd.

Kocher Schmid, C. 2001. Felix Speiser's ethnography of Southwest New Britain: Annotated edition of Felix Speiser's fieldnotes and complementing documents from Arawe, Kandrian, and Gasmata (1930). Unpublished typescript held by the Museum der Kulturen, Switzerland.

Lawrence, D. with P. Varjola 2010. *Gunnar Landtman in Papua 1910–1912*. ANU Press, Canberra. doi.org/10.22459/GLP.02.2010.

Layard, J.W. 1928. Degree-taking rites in South West Bay, Malekula. *Journal of the Royal Anthropological Institute* 58:139–223. www.jstor.org/stable/4619530.

Layard, J. 1942. *Stone men of Malekula. Vao*. Chatto and Windus, London.

Leavesley, M.G. and H. Mandui 2004. *Report of the Pioneers of Island Melanesia Project archaeological fieldwork in Bougainville Province, Papua New Guinea*. Leverhulme Centre for Human Evolutionary Studies, Cambridge.

Li, F., C.J. Bae, C.B. Ramsey, F. Chen and X. Gao 2018. Re-dating Zhoukoudian Upper Cave, northern China and its regional significance. *Journal of Human Evolution* 121:170–177. doi.org/10.1016/j.jhevol.2018.02.011.

Lilley, I. 1986. Prehistoric exchange in the Vitiaz Strait, Papua New Guinea. Unpublished PhD thesis, The Australian National University, Canberra.

Lilley, I. 2019. Lapita: The Australian connection. In S. Bedford and M. Spriggs (eds), *Debating Lapita: Distribution, chronology, society and subsistence*, pp. 105–114. Terra Australis 52. ANU Press, Canberra. doi.org/10.22459/ta52.2019.05.

Lipset, D. 1990. Boars' tusks and flying foxes: Symbolism and ritual of office in the Murik Lakes. In N. Lutkehaus, C. Kaufmann, W.E. Mitchell, D. Newton, L. Osmundsen and M. Schuster (eds), *Sepik heritage: Tradition and change in Papua New Guinea*, pp. 286–297. Crawford House Press, Bathurst.

Lipson, M., P. Skoglund, M. Spriggs, F. Valentin, S. Bedford, R. Shing, H. Buckley, I. Phillip, G.K. Ward, S. Malick, N. Rohland, N. Broomandkhoshbacht, O. Cheronet, M. Ferry, T.K. Harper, M. Michel, J. Oppenheimer, K. Sirak, K. Stewardson, K. Auckland, A.V.S. Hill, K. Maitland, S.J. Oppenheimer, T. Parks, K. Robson, T.N. Williams, D.J. Kennett, A.J. Mentzer, R. Pinhasi and D. Reich 2018. Population turnover in Remote Oceania shortly after initial settlement. *Current Biology* 28:1–9. doi.org/10.1016/j.cub.2018.02.051.

Lipson, M., M. Spriggs, F. Valentin, S. Bedford, R. Shing, W. Zinger, H. Buckley, F. Petchey, R. Matanik, O. Cheronet, N. Rohland, R. Pinhasi and D. Reich 2020. Three phases of ancient migration shaped the ancestry of human populations in Vanuatu. *Current Biology* 30(24):4846–4856. doi.org/10.1016/j.cub.2020.09.035.

Lum, J.K., J.K. McIntyre, D.L. Gregers, K.W. Huffman and M.G. Vilar 2006. Recent Southeast Asian domestication and Lapita dispersal of sacred male pseudohermaphroditic 'tuskers' and hairless pigs of Vanuatu. *Proceedings of the National Academy of Sciences of the United States of America* 103(46):17190–17195. doi.org/10.1073/pnas.0608220103.

Lutkehaus, N. 1990. The *tambaran* of the *tanepoa*: Traditional and modern forms of leadership on Manam Island. In N. Lutkehaus, C. Kaufmann, W.E. Mitchell, D. Newton, L. Osmundsen and M. Schuster (eds), *Sepik heritage: Tradition and change in Papua New Guinea*, pp. 298–308. Crawford House Press, Bathurst.

Lutkehaus, N.C. 2013. Bodily transformations: The politics and art of men as pigs and pigs as men on Manam Island, Papua New Guinea. *Pacific Arts* 13(1):5–13. www.jstor.org/stable/44737246.

Lynch, J., M. Ross and T. Crowley 2002. *The Oceanic languages*. Curzon Press, Richmond, Surrey.

Maschio, T. 1994. *To remember the faces of the dead: The plenitude of memory in southwestern New Britain.* The University of Wisconsin Press, Madison.

Maschio, T. 1995. Mythic images and objects of myth in Rauto female puberty ritual. In N.C. Lutkehaus and P.B. Roscoe (eds), *Gender rituals: Female initiation in Melanesia*, pp. 131–161. Routledge, New York and London. doi.org/10.4324/9781315021836.

May, P. and M. Tuckson 2000. *The traditional pottery of Papua New Guinea.* Revised edition. Crawford House Publishing, Hindmarsh (South Australia).

McKee, C.O., M.G. Baillie and P.J. Reimer 2015. A revised age of AD 667–699 for the latest major eruption at Rabaul. *Bulletin of Volcanology* 77:article 65. doi.org/10.1007/s00445-015-0954-7.

McNiven, I.J. 2021. Coral Sea Cultural Interaction Sphere. In I.J. McNiven and B. David (eds), *The Oxford handbook of the archaeology of Indigenous Australia and New Guinea online*, pp. 1–29. Oxford University Press, Oxford. doi.org/10.1093/oxfordhb/9780190095611.013.28.

McPherson, N. 2007. Tracing tradition: Twenty-five years of vernacular architecture in Bariai, West New Britain, Papua New Guinea. *Pacific Arts* 6:31–40. www.jstor.org/stable/23412145.

McSwain, R. 1977. *The past and future people: Tradition and change on a New Guinea island.* Oxford University Press, Melbourne.

Meyer, A.B. 1881. On artificial deformation of the human skull in the Malay Archipelago. *Nature* 25(632): 132–135. doi.org/10.1038/025132b0.

Meyer, A.B. 1885. On artificial deformation of the head in Sumatra, Celebes, and the Philippine Islands. *Journal of the Anthropological Institute of Great Britain and Ireland* 14:85–87. archive.org/details/journalofroyalan14royauoft/page/84/mode/2up.

Neumann, K. 1992. *Not the way it really was: Constructing the Tolai past.* Pacific Islands Monograph series 10. University of Hawai'i, Honolulu. doi.org/10.1515/9780824847098.

Oliver, D.L. 1967. *A Solomon Island society: Kinship and leadership among the Siuai of Bougainville.* Beacon Press, Boston. doi.org/10.4159/harvard.9780674183117.

Ollier, C.D., D.K. Holdsworth and G. Heers 1970. Megaliths of Kitava, Trobriand islands. *Records of the Papua New Guinea Public Museum and Art Gallery* 1(1):5–15.

Parkinson, R.R.H. 1999 [1907]. *Thirty years in the South Seas: Land and people, customs and traditions in the Bismarck Archipelago and on the German Solomon Islands.* Translated by J. Dennison, edited by J.P. White. Crawford House Publishing with Oceania Publications, University of Sydney, Bathurst.

Pawley, A. 2006. Explaining the aberrant languages of Southeast Melanesia: 150 years of debate. *Journal of the Polynesian Society* 115(3):215–258. www.jstor.org/stable/20707348.

Petchey, P., H. Buckley, R. Walter, D. Anson and R. Kinaston 2016. The 2008–2009 excavations at the SAC locality, Reber-Rakival Lapita site, Watom Island, Papua New Guinea. *Journal of Indo-Pacific Archaeology* 40:12–31. doi.org/10.7152/jipa.v40i0.14928.

Pietrusewsky, M., H. Buckley, D. Anson and M. Toomay Douglas 2014. Polynesian origins: A biodistance study of mandibles from the Late Lapita site of Reber-Rakival (SAC), Watom Island, Bismarck Archipelago. *Journal of Pacific Archaeology* 5(1):1–20. pacificarchaeology.org/index.php/journal/article/view/121.

Posth, C., K. Nägele, H. Colleran, F. Valentin, S. Bedford, K.W. Kami, R. Shing, H. Buckley, R. Kinaston, M. Walworth, G.R. Clark, C. Reepmeyer, J. Flexner, T. Maric, J. Moser, J. Gresky, L. Kiko, K.J. Robson, K. Auckland, S.J. Oppenheimer, A.V.S. Hill, A.J. Mentzer, J. Zech, F. Petchey, P. Roberts, C. Jeong, R.D. Gray, J. Krause and A. Powell 2018. Language continuity despite population replacement in Remote Oceania. *Nature Ecology and Evolution* 2:731–740. doi.org/10.1038/s41559-018-0498-2.

Posth, C., K. Nägele, H. Colleran, F. Valentin, S. Bedford, R. Gray, J. Krause and A. Powell 2019. Response to 'Ancient DNA and its contribution to understanding the human history of the Pacific Islands'. *Archaeology in Oceania* 54(1):57–61. doi.org/10.1002/arco.5181.

Pugach, I., A.T. Duggan, D.A. Merriwether, F.R. Friedlaender, J.S. Friedlaender and M. Stoneking 2018. The gateway from Near into Remote Oceania: New insights from genome-wide data. *Molecular Biology and Evolution* 35(4):871–886. doi.org/10.1093/molbev/msx333.

Reche, O. 2015 [1913]. *The empress Augusta/Sepik River by Dr Otto Reche.* Translated by J. Dennison and edited by J. Dennison and G.R. Summerhayes from *Der Kaiserin-Augusta Flüss* by Otto Reche, 1913. University of Otago Working Papers in Anthropology 3. University of Otago, Dunedin.

Reepmeyer, C., M. Spriggs, S. Bedford and W.R. Ambrose 2011. Provenance and technology of lithic artefacts from the Teouma Lapita site, Vanuatu. *Asian Perspectives* 49(1):205–225. doi.org/10.1353/asi.2010.0004.

Reesink, G. 2005. Sulka of East New Britain: A mixture of Oceanic and Papuan traits. *Oceanic Linguistics* 44(1):145–193. doi.org/10.1353/ol.2005.0026.

Reesink, G. and M. Dunn 2018. Contact phenomena in Austronesian and Papuan languages. In B. Palmer (ed.), *The languages and linguistics of the New Guinea Area. A comprehensive guide*, pp. 939–985. De Gruyter Mouton, Berlin. doi.org/10.1515/9783110295252-009.

Ricaut, F.X., T. Thomas, C. Arganini, J. Staughton, M. Leavesley, M. Bellatti, R. Foley and M. Mirazon Lahr 2008. Mitochondrial DNA variation in Karkar Islanders. *Annals of Human Genetics* 72:349–367. doi.org/10.1111/j.1469-1809.2008.00430.x.

Riebe, I. 1967. Anthropomorphic stone carvings on Unea Island. *Journal of the Polynesian Society* 76(3):374–378. www.jstor.org/stable/20704487.

Riesenfeld, A. 1950. *The megalithic cultures of Melanesia.* E.J. Brill, Leiden.

Robin, C., M. Monzier and J.-P. Eissen 1994. Formation of the mid-fifteenth century Kuwae caldera (Vanuatu) by an initial hydroclastic and subsequent ignimbritic eruption. *Bulletin of Volcanology* 56(3):170–183. doi.org/10.1007/BF00279602.

Rohatynskyj, M.A. 2001. On knowing the Baining and other minor ethnic groups of East New Britain. *Social Analysis* 45(2):23–40. www.jstor.org/stable/23170109.

Ross, M.D. 1988. *Proto Oceanic and the Austronesian languages of Western Melanesia.* Pacific Linguistics Series C-98. The Australian National University, Canberra.

Ross, M.D. (ed.) 1996. *Studies in languages of New Britain and New Ireland. 1: Austronesian languages of the North New Guinea Cluster in Northwest New Britain.* Pacific Linguistics Series C-135. The Australian National University, Canberra.

Ross, M. 2002. Kaulong. In J. Lynch, M. Ross and T. Crowley, *The Oceanic languages*, pp. 387–409. Curzon Press, Richmond, Surrey.

Ross, M. 2014. Reconstructing the history of languages in northwest New Britain. *Journal of Historical Linguistics* 4(1):84–132. doi.org/10.1075/jhl.4.1.03ros.

Salisbury, R.F. 1972. The origins of the Tolai people. *Journal of the Papua and New Guinea Society* 6(2):79–84.

Schendel, S.A., G. Walker and A. Kamisugi 1980. Hawaiian craniofacial morphometrics: Average Mokapuan skull, artificial cranial deformation, and the 'rocker' mandible. *American Journal of Physical Anthropology* 52(4):491–500. doi.org/10.1002/ajpa.1330520406.

Schindlbeck, M. 2018. Stones in swamps: remains of a mythical past in the Sepik area. *Journal de la Société des Océanistes* 146:213–225. doi.org/10.4000/jso.8123.

Shaw, B. 2015. The archaeology of Rossel Island, Massim, Papua New Guinea: Towards a prehistory of the Louisiade Archipelago. 2 volumes. Unpublished PhD thesis. The Australian National University, Canberra.

Sheppard, P.J. 2011. Lapita colonization across the Near/Remote Oceania Boundary. *Current Anthropology* 52(6):799–840. doi.org/10.1086/662201.

Sheppard, P. 2019. Early Lapita colonisation of Remote Oceania: An update on the leapfrog hypothesis. In S. Bedford and M. Spriggs (eds), *Debating Lapita: Distribution, chronology, society and subsistence*, pp. 135–153. Terra Australis 52. ANU Press, Canberra. doi.org/10.22459/ta52.2019.07.

Sheppard, P.J., R. Walter and T. Nagaoka 2000. The archaeology of headhunting in Roviana Lagoon. *Journal of the Polynesian Society* 109(1):9–37. www.jstor.org/stable/20706906.

Sheppard, P., R. Walter, W. Dickinson, M. Felgate, C. Ross-Sheppard and C. Azémard 2015. A Solomon Sea interaction sphere? In C. Sand, S. Chiu and N. Hogg (eds), *The Lapita Cultural Complex in time and space: Expansion routes, chronologies and typologies*, pp. 63–80. Institut d'archéologie de la Nouvelle-Calédonie et du Pacifique, Nouméa.

SIL (Summer Institute of Linguistics) 2015. Language maps for East and West New Britain Provinces, PNG. pnglanguages.sil.org/resources/language_maps.

Skoglund, P., C. Posth, K. Sirak, M. Spriggs, F. Valentin, S. Bedford, G.R. Clark, C. Reepmeyer, F. Petchey, D. Fernandez, Q. Fu, E. Harney, M. Lipson, S. Mallick, M. Novak, N. Rohland, K. Stewardson, S. Abdullah, M.P. Cox, F.R. Friedlaender, J.S. Friedlaender, T. Kivisild, G. Koki, P. Kusuma, D.A. Merriwether, F.X. Ricaut, J.T.S. Wee, N. Patterson, J. Krause, R. Pinhasi and D. Reich 2016.Genomic insights into the peopling of the Southwest Pacific. *Nature* 538:510–513. doi.org/10.1038/nature19844.

Smith, I.W.G. 2000 [1998]. Terrestrial fauna from excavations at the Kainapirina (SAC) locality, Watom Island, Papua New Guinea. *New Zealand Journal of Archaeology* 20:137–147.

Specht, J. 1972. The pottery industry of Buka Island, T.P.N.G. *Archaeology and Physical Anthropology in Oceania* 7(2):125–144. www.jstor.org/stable/40386171.

Specht, J., R. Torrence and K. Mulvaney 2021. Petroglyphs and place: Complex histories at four sites in New Britain. *Archaeology in Oceania* 56(3):196–228. doi.org/10.1002/arco.5243.

Speiser, F. 1932. Note à propos des dents de cochon déformées dans les mers du Sud et en Indonésie. *Revista del Instituto de Etnologia de la Universidad Nacional de Tucuman* 2:441–444.

Speiser, F. 1934a. Versuch einer Kulturanalyse der zentralen Neuen Hebriden. *Zeitschrift für Ethnologie* 66(1/3):128–186. www.jstor.org/stable/25839472.

Speiser, F. 1934b. Observations on the cultural history of New Caledonia and the New Hebrides. *Man* 34(May):74. doi.org/10.2307/2790656.

Speiser, F. 1938. Melanesien und Indonesien. *Zeitschrift für Ethnologie* 70(6):463–481. www.jstor.org/stable/25839767.

Speiser, F. 1996 [1923]. *Ethnology of Vanuatu: An early twentieth century study*. Translation by D.Q. Stephenson of *Ethnographische Materialen aus den Neuen Hebriden und den Banks Inseln*. Crawford House Publishing, Bathurst.

Spriggs, M. 1997. *The Island Melanesians*. Blackwell, Oxford.

Spriggs, M. and D. Reich 2019. An ancient DNA Pacific journey: A case study of collaboration between archaeologists and geneticists. *World Archaeology* 51(4):620–639. doi.org/10.1080/00438243.2019.173 3069.

Spriggs, M., F. Valentin, S. Bedford, R. Pinhasi, P. Skoglund, D. Reich and M. Lipson 2019. Revisiting ancient DNA insights into the human history of the Pacific Islands. *Archaeology in Oceania* 54(1):53–56. doi.org/ 10.1002/arco.5180.

Stebbins, T.N. 2009. The Papuan languages of the Eastern Bismarcks: Migration, origins and connections. In B. Evans (ed.), *Discovering history through language: papers in honour of Malcolm Ross*, pp. 223–243. Pacific Linguistics 605. Pacific Linguistics, Canberra.

Stebbins, T., Evans, B., Terrill, A. 2018. The Papuan languages of Island Melanesia. In B. Palmer (ed.), *The languages and linguistics of the New Guinea area: A comprehensive guide*, pp. 775–894. The World of Linguistics 4. De Gruyter Mouton, Berlin. doi.org/10.1515/9783110295252-007.

Stokes, J.G. 1920. Artificial deformations in Hawaii. *American Journal of Physical Anthropology* 3(4):489–491. doi.org/10.1002/ajpa.1330030406.

Summerhayes, G.R., K. Szabó, A. Fairbairn, M. Horrocks, S. McPherson and A. Crowther 2019. Early Lapita subsistence: The evidence from Kamgot, Anir Islands, New Ireland Province, Papua New Guinea. In S. Bedford and M. Spriggs (eds), *Debating Lapita: Distribution, chronology, society and subsistence*, pp. 379–402. Terra Australis 52. ANU Press, Canberra. doi.org/10.22459/ta52.2019.18.

Swadling, P. and P. Bence 2016. Changes in kula valuables and related supply linkages between the Massim and the south Papuan coast between 1885 and 1915. *Archaeology in Oceania* 51, Supplement 1:50–60. doi.org/10.1002/arco.5106.

Terrell, J.E. 1976. Perspectives on the prehistory of Bougainville Island, Papua New Guinea. Unpublished PhD thesis, 2 vols. Harvard University, Cambridge, Massachusetts.

Terrell, J.E. 1978. Archaeology and the origins of social stratification in southern Bougainville. In J. Guiart (ed.), *Rank and status in Polynesia and Melanesia: Essays in honour of Professor Douglas Oliver*, pp. 23–43. Publications de la Société des Océanistes 39. Musée de l'Homme, Paris. doi.org/10.4000/books.sdo.949.

Thomas, T., P. Sheppard and R. Walter 2001. Landscape, violence and social bodies: Ritualized architecture in a Solomon Islands society. *Journal of the Royal Anthropological Institute* 7(3):545–572. doi.org/10.1111/ 1467-9655.00077.

Thurnwald, R. 1934. Stone monuments in Buin (Bougainville, Solomon Islands). *Oceania* 5(2):214–217. doi.org/10.1002/j.1834-4461.1934.tb00141.x.

Tochilin, C., W.R. Dickinson, M.W. Felgate, M. Pecha, P. Sheppard, F.H. Damon, S. Bickler and G.E. Gehrels 2012. Sourcing temper sands in ancient ceramics with U-Pb ages of detrital zircons: A southwest Pacific test case. *Journal of Archaeological Science* 39:2583–2591. doi.org/10.1016/j.jas.2012.04002.

Todd, J.A. 1934. Report on research work in South-west New Britain, Territory of New Guinea. *Oceania* 5(1):80–101. doi.org/10.1002/j.1834-4461.1934.tb00132.x and *Oceania* 5(2):193–213. doi.org/10.1002/ j.1834-4461.1934.tb00140.x.

Torrence, R., S. Kelloway and P. White 2013. Stemmed tools, social interaction, and voyaging in early-mid Holocene Papua New Guinea. *Journal of Island and Coastal Archaeology* 8(2):287–310. doi.org/10.1080/15564894.2012.761300.

Torrence, R., J. Specht and B. Vatete 2002. *Report of an archaeological survey of the Bali-Witu Islands, West New Britain Province, PNG*. Report prepared for the West New Britain Provincial Government, Papua New Guinea.

Tubbs, R.S., E.G. Salter and J. Oakes 2006. Artificial deformation of the human skull: A review. *Clinical Anatomy* 19(4):372–377. doi.org/10.1002/ca.20177.

Valentin, F. 2010. Sépultures et pratiques funéraires du Ier millénaire avant J.-C. de Mélanésie et de Polynésie occidentale/Burials and funerary practices of the 1st millennium BC in Melanesia and western Polynesia. In C. Sand and S. Bedford (eds), *Lapita, Ancêtres océaniens/Oceanic ancestors*, pp. 162–175. Somogy Éditions d'Art, and Musée du quai Branly, Paris.

Valentin, F., S. Bedford, H.R. Buckley and M. Spriggs 2010. Lapita burial practices: Evidence for complex body and bone treatment at the Teouma cemetery, Vanuatu, Southwest Pacific. *Journal of Island and Coastal Archaeology* 5(2):212–235. doi.org/10.1080/15564891003648092.

Valentin, F., F. Détroit, M.J.T. Spriggs and S. Bedford 2016. Early Lapita skeletons from Vanuatu show Polynesian craniofacial shape: Implications for Remote Oceanic settlement and Lapita origins. *Proceedings of the National Academy of Sciences of the United States of America* 113(2):292–297. www.pnas.org/cgi/doi/10.1073/pnas.1516186113.

Virchow, R. 1884. Zwei künstlich deformirte Schädel von Niue und den Neu-Hebriden, letzerer mit temporaler Theriomorphie. *Zeitschrift für Ethnologie* 16:153–158.

15

New 'mysterious mounds' in Southern Melanesia: An archaeological study of the Tivoli plateau (Lifou, Loyalty Islands, New Caledonia) and regional comparisons

Christophe Sand, Jacques Bolé and David Baret

Abstract

The identification of numerous earthen mounds on the central plateau of the Isle of Pines in the south of New Caledonia has led, over the past 70 years, to a number of hypotheses about their origin and possible uses. As an appreciation to the long-lasting work of Glenn Summerhayes on the Melanesian past, we report here on the first discovery of a large group of tumuli in the Loyalty Archipelago, on Lifou Island, unknown to the local inhabitants. The mapping of the site and subsequent excavation of some structures allows us to characterise these remains and propose a first set of hypotheses about their uses, by confronting our results with the larger corpus of interpretations proposed for New Caledonia's 'mysterious mounds'.

Introduction

Early studies of the past of the Pacific have in some archipelagos made abundant use of the idea of 'population replacements' to build temporal frames, each 'archaeological culture' being supposedly associated to a different 'race'. This approach was especially popular in the colonial context of New Caledonia, where during most of the twentieth century, amateur archaeologists repeatedly published supposed proofs of the existence of 'pre-Papuan' inhabitants, eradicated by later arrivals from Northern Melanesia (see Archambault 1901; Avias 1949; summary in Sand 2020:274–276). Aside from the long-held claim of a Polynesian ancestry of the producers of the Lapita tradition in New Caledonia, culturally and ethnically distinct from the Melanesian ancestry of the producers of Manga'asi-affiliated pottery traditions (Brou 1977), one of the central archaeological site-types used to demonstrate the presence of a pre-Kanak 'white population', has been 'mysterious mounds'.

Hundreds of rounded tumuli of various sizes, the largest reaching nearly 4 m high and over 30 m in diameter, have especially been surveyed on the central sterile ferralitic plateau and along the calcareous seashores of the Isle of Pines, at the southern extremity of the archipelago (Frimigacci 1986). Some large tumuli are also recorded in different plains on the west coast of nearby Grande Terre (Chevalier 1959–62). Salvage excavations identified the presence of a central column of lime in some of these mounds, but aside from human remains discovered in seashore tumuli, these structures appear to be devoid of archaeological items.

Until recently, tumuli had only been recorded in the western half of the archipelago. Here we report on the discovery of a large site of mounds on the calcareous plateau of Lifou Island in the Loyalties, east of Grande Terre. The mapping of the numerous mounds and excavation of some of the structures allow for the comparison of Lifou's tumuli to the corpus of data known for the Isle of Pines and Grande Terre, and to reconsider the chronological timeframes and the possible uses of New Caledonia's tumuli.

Location of the Tivoli site (LWT085), description of the tumuli and excavations

Lifou Island (1200 km^2), in the centre of the Loyalty chain, is formed from a series of uplifted karstic plateaux reaching 100 m high, resting on a deep volcanic cone (Figure 15.1). As part of an archaeological mapping program centred on the north-western region of the Island (Wetr chiefdom), in November 2012 we surveyed along a new path reaching the seashore west of the tribe of Mucaweng. This led us to cross an area in the forest, halfway between Mucaweng and the abandoned seashore of Nonime, characterised by an environment of numerous karst outcrops, resulting in a chaotic landscape with very little arable soil. Where soil can be identified, it appears of limited thickness, although a set of abandoned fields can be identified in the surrounding areas, where karst outcrops are all but absent. Along this section of the trail we identified mounds in a land-plot called Tivoli (Kofias land, archaeological code LWT085). Although the human origin of these tumuli appeared unquestionable at the time of the discovery, no knowledge of them appeared present in the local community.

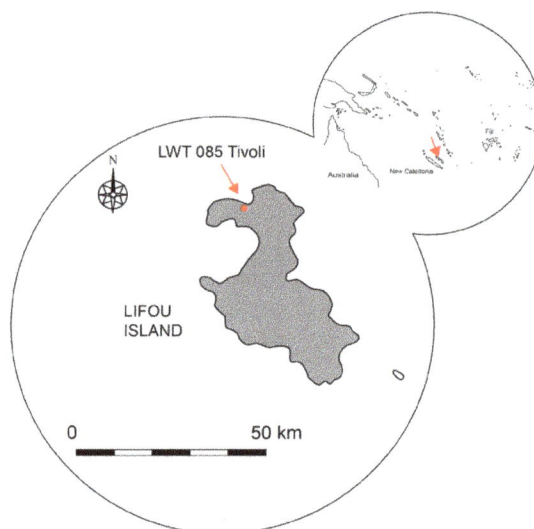

Figure 15.1: Location of Lifou Island in the western Pacific and positioning of site LWT085 of Tivoli.

Source: Figure prepared by D. Baret.

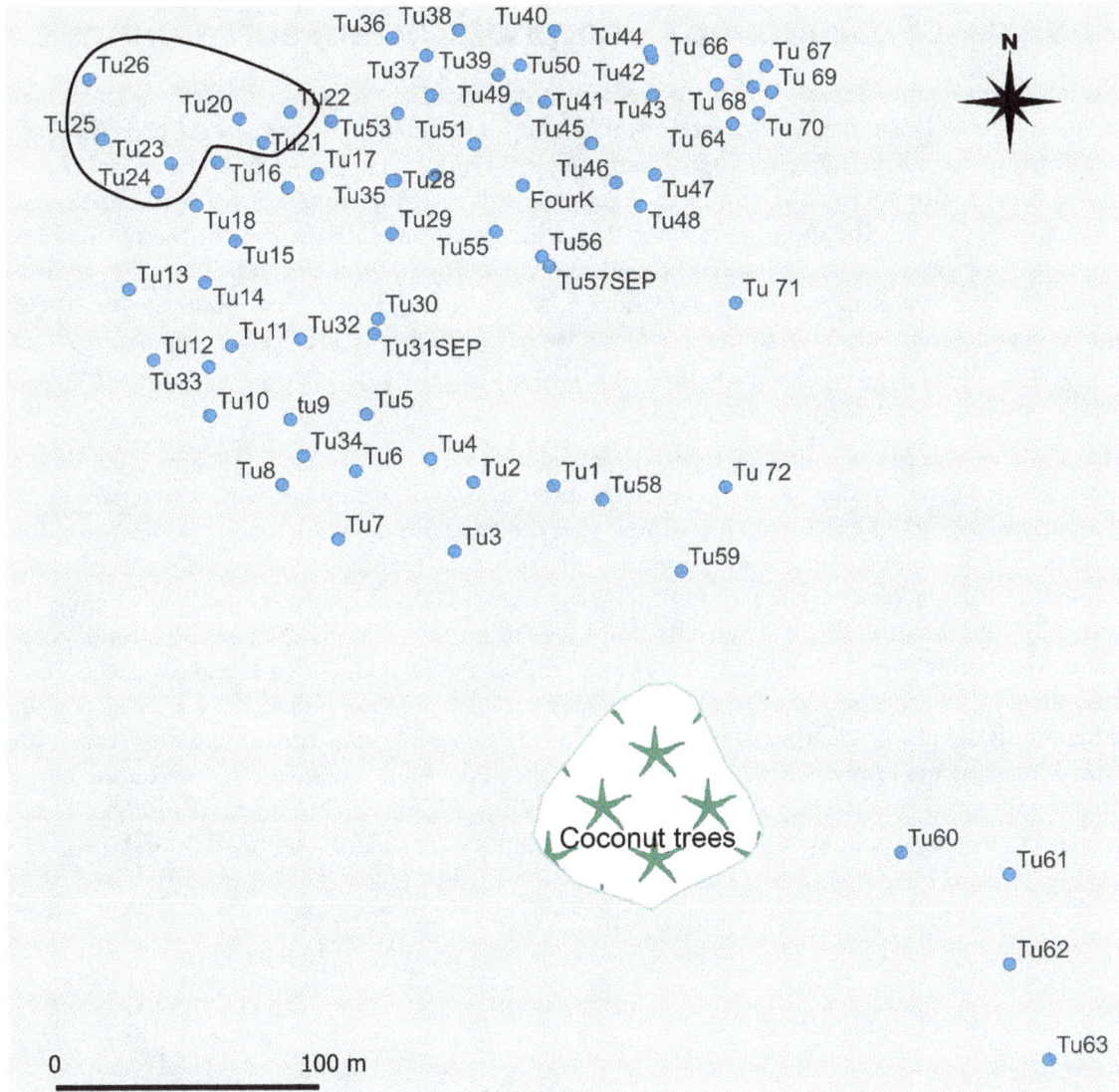

Figure 15.2: GPS map of the location of the tumuli recorded in Tivoli. The group of low flat mounds is highlighted.

Source: Figure prepared by D. Baret.

A general map of the site, displaying every individual mound, was fulfilled by recording their location with GPS and their size and height. A total of 67 structures (recorded as Tu.+number), mainly constituted of fossil coral gravels and karst blocks of different sizes mixed with soil, have been recorded to date for site LWT085, along with three burial areas and two large stone-oven mounds (Figure 15.2). This count does not represent the total number of raised structures present on this site, as other mounds remain to be recorded in the vicinity of the mapped area. A grouping of most of the recorded structures in an area of about 5 ha can be identified; a second group of four large tumuli are located about 200 m to the south-east of this central core, near a cultivable plot free of karstic outcrops. No clear organisation pattern can be identified for the main grouping at this stage, aside from an empty zone in the eastern area. The partial clearing of the dense fern cover has, however, allowed for the identification of what appear to be a set of rough low raised paths, some connecting various tumuli. Future studies should highlight the presence of a more structured pattern.

Analysis of the mounds' morphology and surroundings

The fern cover on the site was such that we refrained from clearing each mound before measurement, as we considered that the natural erosion of the top and sides of the structures prevented any possibility to record their precise original morphology (Table 15.1). The study of the recorded sizes shows that the diameter of the tumuli varies significantly, ranging from 4.5 m for the smallest to 15 m for the largest. The mean diameter is 9 m when amalgamating the data of the 60 mounds. The height of the mounds varies between 40 cm and 240 cm, with the indication of a positive correlation between diameter and height (Figure 15.3). A set of seven low mounds (Tu.20–26) appear typologically unrelated to the rest of the corpus, with a height not exceeding about 20 cm and a large flat top formed of small to medium-sized gravel. These mounds group in the north-west corner of the site, on less rocky soil.

The study of the tumuli's morphology has shown that, aside from the seven low mounds just mentioned, a great number of the higher structures also have a flattened top. The repetition of this pattern appears to exclude the hypothesis that the flat summits result from a natural erosional process. The partial erosion of some mound sides has also highlighted repeatedly the existence of a circle of large karst blocks forming the partly buried basis of the structures, invalidating the possibility that the tumuli are simple cleaning heaps of horticultural fields or refuse piles of coral-stone ovens. Only two of the mounds, Tu.42 and Tu.72, have been identified as cooking areas. These mounds were built from the accumulation of burnt coral blocks and ashes, the last oven used on the mounds being still identifiable in the centre of the two structures. A natural cavity containing human remains was located near Tu.19 and Tu.36. The only visible modification observed on one of the mounds was a small depression, 100 cm deep, arranged in the wall of the large tumulus Tu.62, inside which were seen human remains. No bone samples were collected for analysis or dating.

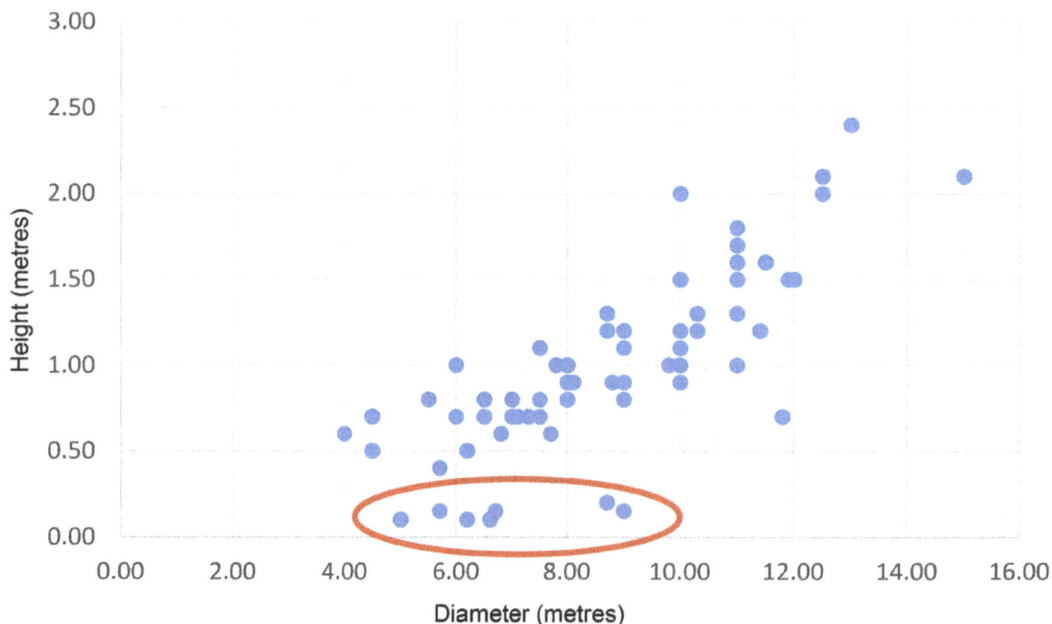

Figure 15.3: Graph of the diameter/height of the tumuli recorded at Tivoli, differentiating the group of low flat mounds.

Source: Figure prepared by D. Baret.

Table 15.1: Morphological data of the tumuli recorded at Tivoli.

Number/Location	Base diameter	Top diameter	Height
Tu.1-723007/7705646	7.50 m	2.50 m	1.10 m
Tu.2-722977/7705647	9 m	4.50 m	1.20 m
Tu.3-722970/7705621	5.50 m	2 m	80 cm
Tu.5-722936/7705673	11 m	4.80 m	1.50 m
Tu.6-722933/7705652	12 m	4.70 m	1.50 m
Tu.7-722926/7705626	12.50 m	4.90 m	2.10 m
Tu.8-722905/7705646	11.90 m	4.40 m	1.50 m
Tu.9-722908/7705671	8.70 m	2.60 m	1.30 m
Tu.10-722878/7705673	10 m	3 m	2 m
Tu.11-722885/7705699	11.40 m	5 m	1.20 m
Tu.12-722857/7705694	7.80 m	2.70 m	1 m
Tu.13-722847/7705721	8.10 m	2.70 m	90 cm
Tu.14-722876/7705724	10.30 m	1.90 m	1.30 m
Tu.15-722887/7705739	10.30 m	4.30 m	1.20 m
Tu.16-722908/7705759	8 m	3.30 m	1 m
Tu.17-722919/7705765	8.80 m	5 m	90 cm
Tu.18-722873/7705753	7.70 m	2.10 m	60 cm
Tu.19-722881/7705769	7.30 m	2.70 m	70 cm
Tu.20-722889/7705786	6.70 m	–	15 cm
Tu.21-722898/7705777	5.70 m	–	15 cm
Tu.22-722908/7705788	6.60 m	–	10 cm
Tu.23-722864/7705769	5 m	–	10 cm
Tu.24-722858/7705758	6.20 m	–	10 cm
Tu.25-722838/7705778	8.70 m	–	20 cm
Tu.26-722833/7705801	9 m	–	15 cm
Tu.27-722924/7705785	9.80 m	7.30 m	1 m
Tu.28-722947/7705762	9 m	3 m	1.10 m
Tu.29-722947/7705742	11.50 m	5 m	1.60 m
Tu.30-722941/7705710	11 m	3.70 m	1.80 m
Tu.31-722940/7705704	Burial cavity		
Tu.32-722913/7705702	11 m	3.60 m	1.70 m
Tu.33-722877/7705691	11.80 m	5.50 m	70 cm
Tu.34-722913/7705658	8.70 m	2.50 m	1.20 m
Tu.35-722947/7705762	10 m	4.30 m	1.20 m
Tu.36-722947/7705816	6.50 m	3 m	70 cm
Tu.37-722959/7705810	6 m	3.60 m	70 cm
Tu.38-722972/7705819	7.10 m	3.20 m	70 cm
Tu.39-722986/7705802	8 m	4 m	80 cm
Tu.40-723008/7705819	8 m	2.50 m	1 m
Tu.41-723005/7705792	8 m	2.70 m	1 m
Tu.42-723045/7705808	'Hna sa zi' oven mound		

Number/Location	Base diameter	Top diameter	Height
Tu.43-723045/7705794	4.50 m	2 m	70 cm
Tu.44-723043/7705811	7 m	3 m	70 cm
Tu.45-723022/7705776	7.50 m	3.30 m	70 cm
Tu.46-723031/7705761	8 m	3.90 m	90 cm
Tu.47-723046/7705764	7 m	2.50 m	80 cm
Tu.48-726304/7705752	8 m	3 m	90 cm
Tu.49-722993/7705789	8 m	2.20 m	80 cm
Tu.50-722995/7705806	10 m	4.70 m	1.10 m
Tu.51-722978/7705776	11 m	4.70 m	1.30 m
Tu.52-722962/7705794	10 m	3.90 m	1 m
Tu.53-722949/7705787	10 m	4.50 m	90 cm
Tu.54-722963/7705764	9 m	4.50 m	90 cm
Tu.55-722986/7705742	11 m	6 m	1.60 m
Tu.56-723003/7705733	10 m	4 m	1.50 m
Tu.57-723005/7705729	Burial cavity		
Tu.58-723026/7705640	7.50 m	4.50 m	80 cm
Tu.59-723055/7705613	9 m	6.70 m	80 cm
Tu.60-723139/7705506	11 m	6.50 m	1 m
Tu.61-723180/7705497	13 m	4.50 m	2.40 m
Tu.62-723180/7705463	12.50 m (with burial)	4.90 m	2 m
Tu.63-723195/7705427	15 m	2.70	2.10 m
Tu.64-723076/7705783	6.50 m	4.60 m	80 cm
Tu.65-723069/7757798	6.80 m	3.90 m	60 cm
Tu.66-723076/7705807	4 m	2.40 m	60 cm
Tu.67-723088/7705805	5.70 m	2.80 m	40 cm
Tu.68-723083/7705797	4.50 m	2.50 m	50 cm
Tu.69-723090/7705795	6.20 m	4.30 m	50 cm
Tu.70-723086/7705787	4.50 m	3 m	50 cm
Tu.71-723076/7705715	6 m	3.50 m	1 m
Tu.72-723073/7705645	'Hna sa zi' oven mound		

Source: Authors' summary.

Excavations

In order to understand more precisely the stratigraphic context of these mounds, four tumuli were selected for test pit excavations. The main scopes were to identify possible construction phases, to record the presence of archaeological items and to collect samples for dating.

Tumulus Tu.17

This structure is located in an area with numerous karstic outcrops and where the trees are not tall. The mound has an overall rounded structure about 10 m in diameter, with a height of about 90 cm. Its oval-shaped flat top is 6.5 m wide and 5.5 m long, covered with small coral pebbles, with the top of the karstic bedrock emerging in some places. The remains of an arrangement of large coral boulders half-buried at the base of the mound has been identified on the eroded slopes. A 5.5-m-long and 1-m-wide trench was excavated from the edge towards the centre of the tumulus, up to the bedrock. The stratigraphy can be divided into four levels (Figure 15.4):

- Level 1, 40–45 cm thick, is formed of a dark brown sediment incorporating numerous pebbles of coral, about 3–5 cm in diameter, along with a few larger blocks. The lower part of the level has more sediment, due to natural percolation.

- Level 2 is present irregularly at the interface between the upper fill and the karstic bedrock, and is formed of the decomposition of the fossil coral into an oxidised orange or white soft sediment.

- Level 3 is only present on the outer margin of the mound and is formed of a loose brown sediment rich in roots and enclosing small pebbles resulting from the mound's erosion.

- Level 4 is the in situ coral bedrock, of irregular morphology, on which the mound has been built.

No human-made items were recovered in the mound. A fragment of a *Cypraea* sp. and numerous shells of the local *Placostylus* sp. terrestrial gastropod were the only non-coral remains present in the fill. Considering the distance from the ocean and the height of the site above the sea, the *Cypraea* shell can only have been brought by human agency. It was dated to 2454+/−25 BP (Wk-38472), calibrated at two sigma to 2240–1990 cal. BP.

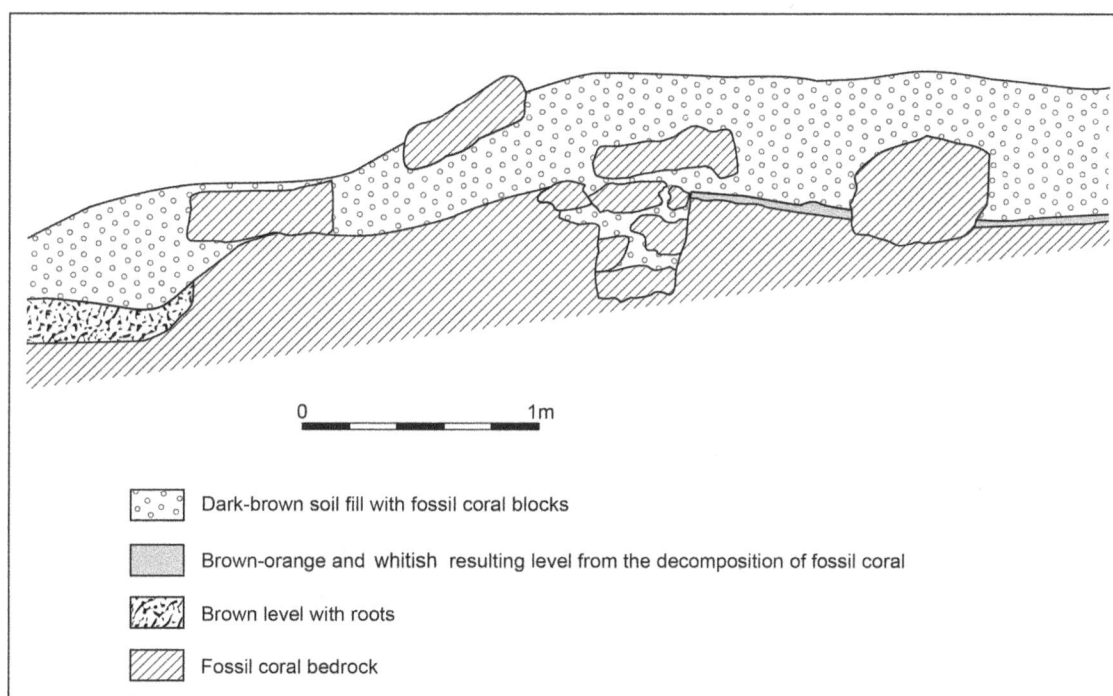

0 _____ 1m

▫ Dark-brown soil fill with fossil coral blocks

▪ Brown-orange and whitish resulting level from the decomposition of fossil coral

▨ Brown level with roots

▨ Fossil coral bedrock

Figure 15.4: Stratigraphic profile of the trench excavated in mound Tu.17.

Source: Figure prepared by D. Baret.

Tumulus Tu.53

This structure, located close to the path leading to the seashore, has an overall rounded shape with a diameter of 10 m and a height of over 90 cm. The flat top, about 6 m wide, is mainly covered with medium-sized coral blocks about 20–30 cm wide, a pattern clearly different from Tu.17. The excavation of a one-square-metre test pit positioned in the centre of the mound identified a fill divided into four levels:

- Level 1, reaching over 110 cm depth, is formed of fossilised coral boulders, becoming larger in the lower half of the fill, with blocks reaching 40–50 cm width and weighing over 30 kg.
- Level 2 (110–135 cm) is irregular in shape and thickness due to the presence of outcrops of the karstic bedrock (Level 4). It is composed of infilled soil mixed with pebbles.
- At the interface between this level and the bedrock (Level 4), oxidation and decomposition of the fossil coral has created thin orange-coloured lenses (Level 3).

The excavation has shown that the build-up of tumulus Tu.53 was achieved in one chronological episode, with a pattern of accumulating the largest blocks in the basal rows and smaller blocks in the top rows. A charcoal sample was collected at 115 cm deep, and was dated to 373+/–20 BP (Wk-38473), calibrated at two sigma to 470–320 cal. BP. This recent result confirms the hypothesis reached during the excavation, that this isolated sample is an outlier infiltrated into the soil matrix, as from experience with Loyalty Islands excavations, recent layers are rich in charcoal remains due to poorly acidic soil characteristics.

Low mound Tu.20

This structure, about 7 m in diameter, is located 30 m to the west of Tu.17, in an area mainly composed of low mounds. The surrounding landscape is characterised by a floor of coral pebbles about 3–5 cm in diameter, in an area of small trees. The excavation of a one-square-metre test pit in the centre of the mound allowed for the differentiation of four stratigraphic levels (Figure 15.5):

- Level 1 is only about 10–15 cm thick and is formed entirely of a layer of fossil coral pebbles of different sizes, wrapped in a humiferous dark brown sediment.
- Level 2 (10–40 cm) is composed of a light brown loose soil, full of tree roots and pebbles as well as some larger coral blocks.
- Level 3 (40–45 cm) is the oxidised interface between the soil fill and the bedrock, with lenses of loose orange sediment.
- Level 4 is the natural coral bedrock.

A *Tridacna* sp. bivalve fragment was collected from the mound's surface, and dated to 2229+/–24 BP (Wk-38471), calibrated at two sigma to 1920–1740 cal. BP. An operculum from a *Trochus* sp. gastropod was recovered at 20–35 cm, underneath the mound's base, and dated to 2249+/–29 BP (Wk-38470), calibrated at two sigma to 1950–1760 cal. BP. The bivalve and the operculum cannot have reached Tivoli by a natural process like crab activity, and must have been deposited by human agency.

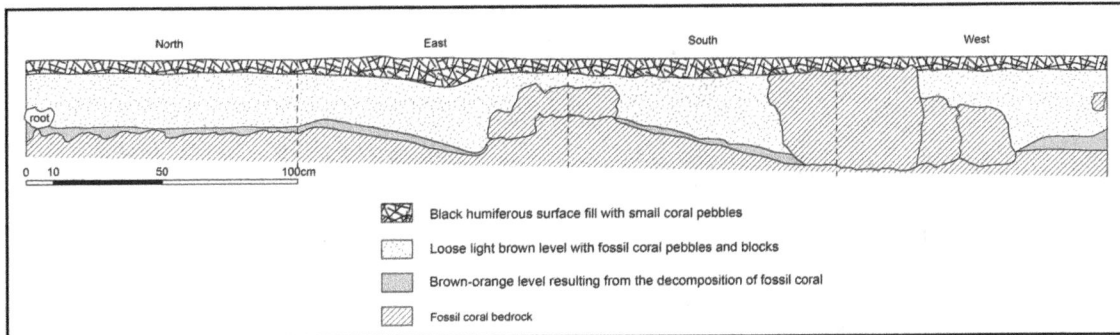

Figure 15.5: Stratigraphic profile of Test pit 1 in mound Tu.20.

Source: Figure prepared by D. Baret.

Oven mound Tu.42

This mound is located at the north-eastern limit of the tumuli area, in an environment of rugged karstic outcrops. Surveys further east did not discover other tumuli. Tu.42 has a unique typology only identified on one other structure of the Tivoli site (Tu.72, diameter 7.5 m, height 0.7 m). The centre of the 6.5-m-wide and 1-m-high rounded mound has a 2.6-m-wide pit containing the remains of a stone oven. The basis of the mound is surrounded by a ring of burnt coral fragments about 1.5–3 m wide, with two higher heaps in the north-west and south-west corners, indicating an original larger size of the cooking mound and successive cleaning episodes of the coral stones. A one-square-metre test pit was positioned in the southern part of the oven pit, and encompassed part of the remaining stone-oven structure as well as the flat summit of the mound. The main objective was to recover dating material and see if any chronological phasing of the build-up of the mound was identifiable. A total of four different levels were identified (Figure 15.6):

- After a thin topsoil, Level 1 is a loose soil fill about 35 cm thick, with numerous roots, mainly formed of the oven's ashes and soil. It encloses the infill of stones from the remaining oven in the northern profile. The lower half of the level, after 20 cm depth, is harder, probably due to the progressive compaction of the sediment.

- Level 2 (35–45 cm) is a loose reddish fill of burnt coral enclosing large charcoal fragments.

- Level 3 (45–70 cm) is a succession of ash lenses, mixed in some cases with charcoal fragments.

- Level 4 is the fossil coral bedrock, which has a smooth surface, possibly related to the severe heating process that led to partial decomposition of the bedrock's upper surface. It can be concluded that the first burning was probably made directly on the coral outcrop surface.

Two charcoal fragments were sent for dating. The first, from Level 2 (35 cm), returned a date of 155+/–21 BP (Wk-38474), calibrated to the last two centuries. The second sample, from Level 3 (60 cm), returned a date of 174+/–21 BP (Wk-38475), also calibrated to the last two centuries.

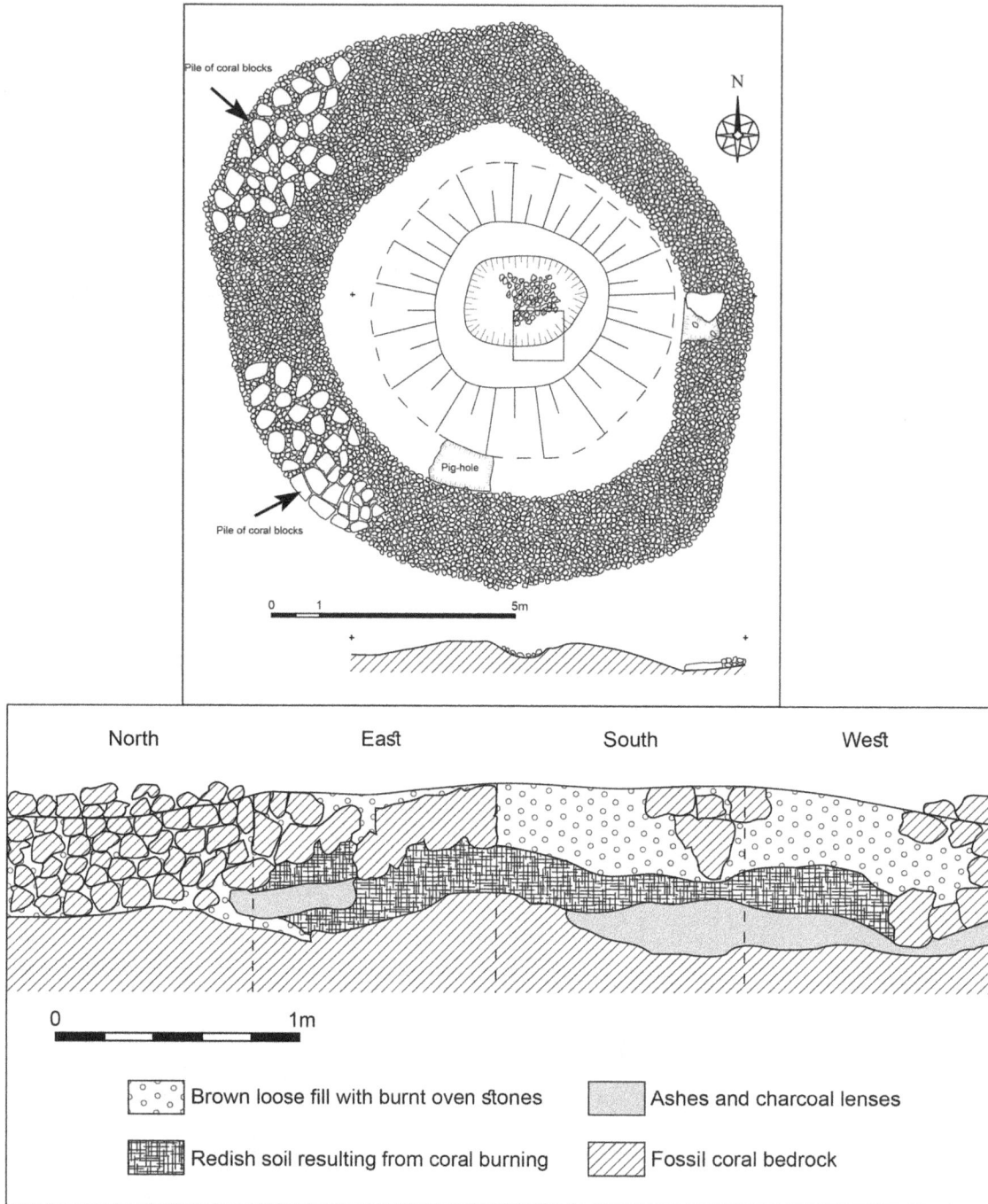

Figure 15.6: Map of mound Tu.42 and stratigraphic profile of Test Pit 1.
Source: Figure prepared by D. Baret.

Summary on the tumuli of the Tivoli site

The mapping of about 70 tumuli on the site of Tivoli, and the partial excavation of four structures, has added new information about New Caledonia's unique mounds. All the mounds were man-made through the piling-up of karstic material retrieved from the immediate surroundings; the site appears to have been chosen because of its rugged environment. Although we concentrated our study on only one location, the diversity of sizes and forms has nonetheless differentiated three types of tumuli:

- Type A, the most represented in our sample (61/70), is characterised by a large diversity of sizes and heights, with an estimated total volume infill ranging from five to over 70 cubic metres above ground. The excavations fulfilled in two of these structures appear to indicate only one main building episode, with a fill of diverse sizes of karst blocks and pebbles on top of the bedrock substratum, often placed inside a circular layout of large coral blocks (Figure 15.7). Most of the tumuli less than 10 m in diameter have a flattened top, while the largest and highest mounds, located closer to productive planting grounds, have a more rounded summit (Figure 15.8). The absence of archaeological items and pit structures prevents at this stage any definitive conclusion about their use(s). It can only be said that they are not waste stone piles of horticultural gardening.

- Type B mounds, characterised by a total of seven low rounded flat structures of an overall smaller diameter than Type A, have tentatively been interpreted as the floors of simple house-structures or as the remains of deconstructed mounds.[1]

- Type C has only two occurrences, with the oven mounds Tu.42 and Tu.72. The elders of Mucaweng tribe identified these structures as a cooking area (*Hna sa zi*) for *Cordyline fruticosa* or *terminalis* (*zi* in Drehu language), a root supposed to have been used by the inhabitants of Lifou well before the arrival of yams on the Island, and eaten especially during times of food shortage.[2] The contact-period dating of *Hna sa zi* Tu.42 was anticipated, as the preserved remains of the stone oven on the surface of the mound indicated a recent use of the structure. While the oral tradition specifies that this type of mound was used only once, the two dates from Tu.42 do not allow us to confirm this, although the stratigraphy appears to point to a single use of the oven.

Significantly, the three C14 dates of Tivoli completed on shell all pool in a chronological bracket just before (two samples, Type B mound) or around (one sample, Type A mound) 2000 cal. BP. That the two samples of mound Tu.20 returned near-identical dates strengthens the conclusion that these results indicate the use of Tivoli and the building of at least some of the tumuli about 2000 years ago.

---

1   It must be acknowledged that these two hypotheses are at this stage a first tentative explanation. Elevated house-mounds are uncommon in the Loyalty Islands, as the draining karstic subsoil of the Islands does not necessitate the raising of the house floors above ground. Clear cases of 'deconstruction' of mounds, allowing for the reuse of the raw material to build other mounds, has been identified in sites on Grande Terre.

2   Several days of cooking are needed to ensure the preparation of the mature *Cordyline fruticosa* or *terminalis* and especially to melt the toxic fibres and oxalic crystals contained in the root (Carson 2002; Guillaumin et al. 1946). In Lifou, a set of rituals had to be followed before consumption, the first *zi* eaten being collected from the outer side of the oven. Once cooked, the roots of *Cordyline* could be kept over a month inside the cooking mound.

Figure 15.7: Profile of the fill of large coral blocks forming mound Tu.53.

Source: Figure prepared by D. Baret.

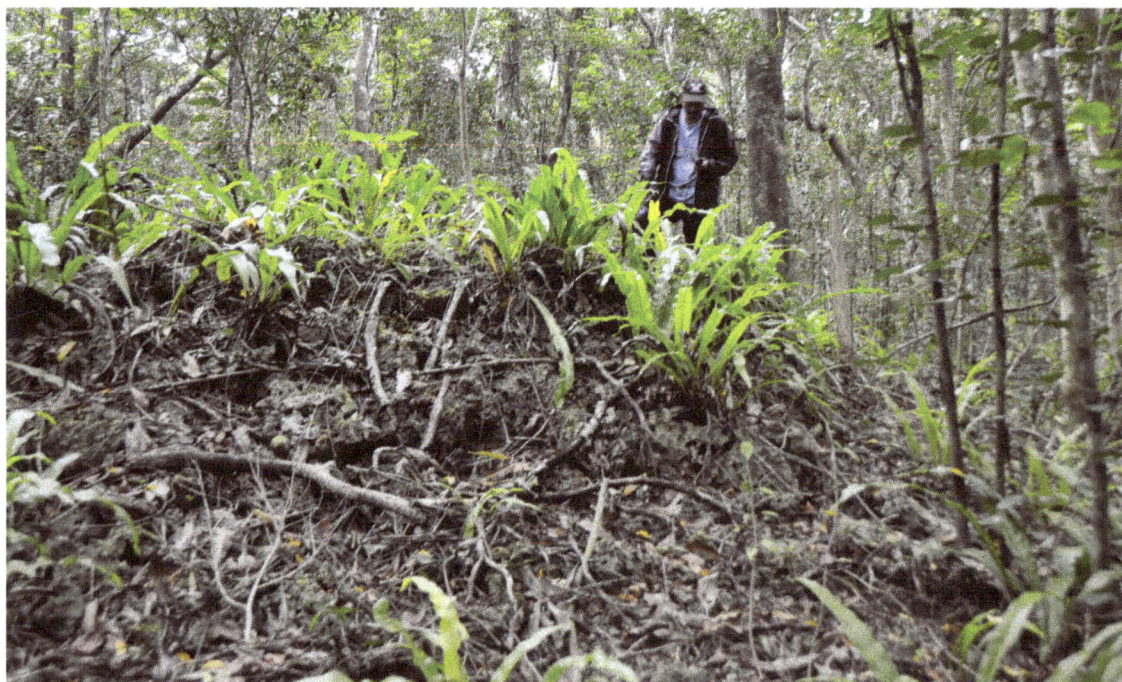

Figure 15.8: Example of mound Tu.61, a large tumulus at the south-east edge of the site of Tivoli.

Source: Figure prepared by D. Baret.

Moving forward on New Caledonia's 'mysterious mounds': Unsustainable hypotheses and possible interpretations

The presence of tumuli in New Caledonia has led to a rich array of interpretations over the last century. A geological origin for these structures was proposed by some authors (Brou 1977:102; Golson 1996:314), although the concentration of mounds in some unique locations like the central ferralitic plateau of the Isle of Pines, and their total absence in similar geological settings on Grande Terre, invalidates this explanation for the vast majority of them. After the discovery of the remains of extinct flightless birds of megapode affiliation (Poplin et al. 1985), R.C. Green proposed to interpret these raised structures as megapode nests, comparable to what is still observable in Northern Melanesia and Western Micronesia with living megapodes (Green 1988). But this non-human interpretation is today weakened by the new classification of the large flightless bird *Sylviornis neocaledoniae* in the galliform family (Worthy et al. 2016). Remains of a true megapode, *Megapodius molistructor*, have been discovered on the Isle of Pines (Balouet and Olson 1989:9–11), but also in the Pindai region on the north-west coast of Grande Terre (cf. Anderson et al. 2010:Table 3-4), where not a single tumulus has been recorded during archaeological surveys so far. It can therefore be concluded that most of the tumuli in New Caledonia do not have a natural origin and are thus anthropogenic.

To disentangle the histories behind this specific type of structure, it is necessary to challenge previous assumptions, which all searched for a single explanation. We need to change our analytical paradigm by taking into account that there appears to have been different periods of construction and different uses of the mounds around the archipelago over time. The hypothesis that the tumuli were built by Palaeolithic or early pre-ceramic occupants appeared, in the 1970s and 1980s, to be sustained by the dating of *Placostylus* sp. terrestrial shells or fragments of 'mortar' collected in the central column of a number of excavated or partly destroyed mounds. Dates ranking from nearly 13000 BP to the fourth millennium BP were obtained by several researchers (Table 15.2). Unfortunately, the exact nature of the 'mortar/concrete' column remains unresolved (see Golson 1996:311–313; Green and Mitchell 1983:22–31). Likewise, the dating of land snails is made hazardous by carbonate contamination and has been shown to be useless for archaeology (see Golson 1996:312). Finally, the last 30 years of research in Central and Southern Melanesia have definitely confirmed that first settlement of this region was linked to the arrival of Lapita sailors, and it appears today that all these early results, although they potentially inform on geological and pedological processes, cannot be used as proof of any remote settlement of New Caledonia.

Table 15.2: Radiocarbon dates obtained from samples collected in tumuli from the plateau of the Isle of Pines (IoP) and from Païta (south-west Grande Terre).

Location	Sample type	Uncalibrated date	Reference number
Païta (date I)	*Placostylus*	12900+/–450 BP	Gif 298
Païta (date III)	Mortar	9600+/–400 BP	Gif 300
Tumulus 5 (IoP)	Land snail shells	8180+/–75 BP	NZ3347
Tumulus 5 (IoP)	Coral aggregate	7710+/–70 BP	NZ3348
Tumulus 5 (IoP)	Land snail shells	7590+/–180 BP	NZ3589
Tumulus 5 (IoP)	Land snail shells	7540+/–160 BP	NZ3587
Tumulus 5 (IoP)	Land snail shells	7090+/–110 BP	NZ3588
Païta (date II)	Mortar/*Placostylus*	7070+/–350 BP	Gif 299
Tumulus 5 (IoP)	Old concrete	5090+/–130 BP	NZ3585

Location	Sample type	Uncalibrated date	Reference number
Tumulus 5 (IoP)	New concrete	4120+/–90 BP	NZ3584
Païta (WPT102)	Mortar	3450+/–70 BP	Beta-66643
Tumulus 121 (IoP)	Concrete	3380+/–80 BP	NZ3593
Tumulus (IoP)	Mortar	3380+/–70 BP	Beta-67061
Tumulus 121 (IoP)	Concrete	3370+/–80 BP	NZ3590
Tumulus 121 (IoP)	*Placostylus*	3150+/–80 BP	NZ3591
Tumulus 121 (IoP)	*Placostylus*	3070+/–80 BP	NZ3592

Source: Authors' summary.

At the other end of the chronological spectrum, the antiquity of some of the tumuli recorded on the south-west coast of Grande Terre need also to be questioned. Indeed, artificial mounds continue to be created today when cleaning large wooded plains with heavy machinery, as the compacting of burnt *Melaleuca* tree (*Myrtaceae* family) remains and soil in piles creates in a few years 'perfect tumuli'. Another set of distinctive tumuli has been recorded in some peridotite regions of Grande Terre, dotting some high-altitude plateaux of tens or hundreds of large and high mounds made by accumulating chrome and iron blocks (Avias 1949:18–21). Recent studies have shown that these mounds were mainly raised during the second millennium AD (Sand et al. 2012:33–38; Sand in preparation). On the Bogota peninsula near Canala (south-east coast of Grande Terre), oral traditions describe these mounds as memorials of exchange ceremonies between seashore and inland communities (Gony 2014). On Maré Island south of Lifou, oral traditions relate to a number of massive tumuli built possibly during the last few centuries as boundary markers between chiefdoms or as a memorial to old alliances (Dubois 1981:32; Sarasin 2009 [1929]:Fig. 3(1)). The case of the *Cordyline* oven mounds of Tivoli, probably built by refugees during the wars of the middle of the nineteenth century, parallel larger mounds used for the same purpose discovered on the Isle of Pines.

While a diversity of mound uses must be highlighted for the archipelago, it would be a mistake to conclude that there are no identifiable patterns that may connect a significant set of these tumuli. This appears to be especially the case between the Isle of Pines and the new discovery on Lifou presented in this paper. Since the first publication of the Tivoli report in 2013, a number of other sites around Lifou containing mounds have been reported to archaeologists, indicating that this type of structure has a wider incidence than just one isolated site. On the Isle of Pines, following pioneering work by J. Golson, archaeologist D. Frimigacci recorded over 300 tumuli (*Pure* in Kwenyi language), in two distinct geological settings. About 160 tumuli are located on the flat central ferralitic plateau of the Island (Frimigacci 1986:Fig. 3; Lagarde 2020:Fig. 2). Two main types of mounds were distinguished by J. Golson:

> (d)imensions of the bowl-shaped category (including the conical) are diameter 12.3 to 28.3 m, height 0.9 to 3.8 m; of the saucer-shaped, diameter 13 to 37 m, height 0.6 to 1.7 m. (Golson 1996:311)

Detailed mapping of some of them has revealed the presence of simple path constructions or stone alignments at the base of the mounds (Figure 15.9) (Lagarde 2020:Figs. 6, 8).

Figure 15.9: Tumulus KTU049 on the central plateau of the Isle of Pines, showing the double alignment of pebbles of the path leading to the top of the mound.

Source: Figure prepared by D. Baret.

No intelligible pattern has however been identified in the spatial layout of these tumuli. Studies on a number of partly destroyed mounds, and three proper archaeological excavations, have shown that the fill is mainly composed of chromite gravel. An important number of mounds appear to have a central cylinder of carbonaceous material whose origin is still debated. Remains of basin/post-hole depressions were observed during excavations, but their exact origin and use is unclear (Golson 1959–62:20-22, 1961:171). No archaeological remains have to date been discovered inside these plateau mounds, although some potsherds have been collected in the immediate vicinity.

A minimum number of 185 tumuli have also been recorded in different parts of the karstic seashore edge that completely encircles the Isle of Pines' central plateau (Frimigacci 1986:Fig. 3; Lagarde 2020:Fig. 2). In the coastal areas, the mounds are mainly made of sand, coral gravel and coral blocks, and appear to be overall of lower height than those recorded on the plateau. Local inhabitants have repeatedly reported that human bones are systematically uncovered during the quarrying of these seashore tumuli (Frimigacci 1986:31; Golson 1959–62:22; Lagarde 2020:215). Archaeological excavation of one of these partly destroyed mounds by D. Frimigacci at Tü'ü (Wi Mwa, KVO005), on the south-west coast of the Isle of Pines, confirmed the presence of human burials incorporated in the fill. The original mound would have been about 30 m in diameter and 2 m high, with a buried 'concrete' column in its centre. In a basal layer a complete skeleton, broken up in three parts (sample 5, level III), was dated to 1845+/–35 BP (Seattle 766), calibrated at two sigma to 1860–1630 cal. BP. In a layer above (level II), the disturbed remains of a number of skeletons were retrieved, among which was one apparently still positioned in its original elongated layout. One of the human bones was dated to 1845+/–65 BP (Seattle 765), calibrated at two sigma to 1925–1590 cal. BP. A charcoal collected about 40 cm under the surface, in the upper part of level II, was dated to 1930+/–70 BP (Seattle 655), calibrated at two sigma to 2040–1645 cal. BP (Frimigacci 1986:29–31). Recently, L. Lagarde has dated a human bone retrieved from a seashore tumulus (KGJ003) at Gadji on the north coast of the Isle of Pines, to 2208+/–39 BP (Wk 20880), calibrated at two sigma to 2309–2003 cal. BP (Lagarde 2020:214).

The main question that confronts archaeologists is the link between the coastal tumuli of the Isle of Pines, evidently built up over time as burial mounds, and the plateau tumuli. The set of three dates on human bones point to a period around 2000–1500 BP for the main construction of the burial mounds. Considering the old age of these remains and the severe decomposition of the bones excavated at Tü'ü, although they were buried in alkaline sandy/coral fill, different researchers envision a similar burial finality for the plateau tumuli (Frimigacci 1986:32; Lagarde 2020; Sand 1995:50). The absence of bones in these upland structures is explained by the rapid decomposition of the bodies and skeletons in the acidic chromite and iron gravel used as cover, which has a pH over 4.5 (L'Huillier et al. 2010:39). Expanding our focus, we suggest a similar explanation for the majority of the mounds of Tivoli in Lifou presented in the first part of the paper, interpreted as a grouping of burials forming a cemetery. The absence of any remains (aside from the recently added bones of Tu.62) results in this case from the fossil coral blocks' acidity and permanent water drainage through the rain, which have since long decomposed any bone that would have been buried in the tumuli. But contrary to the coastal mounds of the Isle of Pines, most of Lifou's mounds might have only contained a single or a few bodies. To explain the flat top observed on numerous structures during the survey at Tivoli, it might be hypothesised that the raised burial ground was protected for some time by a vegetal roof cover.

The proposal of a similar use of the mounds on the Isle of Pines and Tivoli, mainly as burial repositories during what appears to be the same overall chronological period, questions the cultural processes that might have led to this specific burial ritual about 2000–1500 years ago. Interestingly, the chronological period which appears associated with the building of at least some of the tumuli studied on site LWT085 of Tivoli is known through other archaeological studies in the Loyalty Islands as a time of major cultural transformations in the region. Excavations have shown the rapid demise, after about 2000 BP, of regular contacts between the Loyalties and nearby Grande Terre. At about the same time period, a number of enclosures of megalithic size, incorporating massive karst boulders in the wall's constructions, started to be built on Maré, Lifou and Tiga Islands (Sand 1996). One of these enclosures (site LWT092) has been discovered on the coastal flat of Nonime, at the end of the trail crossing the site of Tivoli (Sand et al. 2013:12–15). This significant cultural change appears to have been concomitant with the emergence of stronger chiefdoms. The progressive hierarchical centralisation might be explained by a process of demographic growth during the last centuries of the first millennium BC in the Loyalty Islands, intensification of the landscape's occupation forcing settlements to expand towards marginal ecological areas, before a progressive reduction of relations between the Islands for centuries, due to inner tensions. Interestingly, archaeological data from the Isle of Pines has highlighted the similarity of cultural changes between this Island and the Loyalties at the end of the first millennium BC (Lagarde and Ouetcho 2015:Fig. 14), strengthening the suggestion of a connection between the tumuli of the two regions.

Conclusion

This paper has proposed to bring new archaeological data pertaining to the 'mysterious mounds' of New Caledonia, one of the long-held debates about Melanesia's past, as a tribute to the decades of work of Glenn Summerhayes on the Islands of the Southwestern Pacific. The topic remains to this day far from simply a scientific question. In Southern Melanesia, some people still claim that these mounds were built by 'pre-indigenous' (possibly 'white') inhabitants. Others want to see them as natural features, considering that they are 'too numerous and too large' to be human constructions. A number of the tumuli located in south-western Grande Terre might have been built only during the last century as part of mechanised dryland forest clearing. Although partial at best, the restricted archaeological data at hand nonetheless point to a clear concentration around 2000 BP of the few valid C14 dates retrieved from the excavated structures. Our interpretation of the results gained from Tivoli, analysed in a broader context, led us to hypothesise that on Lifou Island, after about one millennium of human settlement, constraints imposed on some communities led them to sanctuarise some of the less cultivable zones, characterised by karstic outcrops, by transforming them into cemeteries. A similar process appears to have been at play at the same time period on the Isle of Pines, as has been suggested by different researchers over the last decades.[3]

This conclusion raises intriguing questions on the dynamics and reasons fostering the social, cultural and political changes at play at that time throughout a number of archipelagos of the south-western Pacific (see Sand 2018:192–194 for New Caledonia). Explanations ranging from inner changes (Bedford and Clark 2001) to the arrival of new populations (Burley 2013) and impacts of natural phenomena (Spriggs 1997:178) have been proposed. Although little acknowledged for Island Melanesia, the role of demographic pressure appears to us to be a central node to consider in our analysis of the changes witnessed throughout the region during the first millennium AD. Evidently the tradition of burying family members in a dedicated mound, generation after generation, was not sustained for long in New Caledonia. But archaeological studies on Grande Terre have shown that, up to the nineteenth century, some Kanak communities had the tradition of burying their relatives under a pile of stones, in marginal areas like rock shelters (Sand and Ouetcho 2010). This example demonstrates that there is no need to invoke a 'pre-Kanak' population to account for an old tradition of burial mounds in some regions of Southern Melanesia. Evidently, the way forward to definitively retrieve the 'mystery' out of New Caledonia's mounds, should be to dedicate a pluri-disciplinary research program on this specific topic. This sounds like a good collaborative project to envision with retired Emeritus Professor Glenn Summerhayes.

Acknowledgements

This research was fulfilled between 2012 and 2014 by the Institute of Archaeology of New Caledonia and the Pacific (IANCP) as part of the research program for the Loyalty Islands Province. The customary authorisation for the archaeological study at Tivoli and the permission to excavate were given by the Chiefdom of Wetr and Mucaweng tribe. The text has been written by the senior author (CS) as research fellow at the French National Research Institute for Sustainable Development (IRD) in Nouméa, as part of his publication program for the government of New Caledonia. The figures have been prepared by D. Baret.

---

3   Large artificial mounds are not unique to New Caledonia. They have also been uncovered on Erromango Island in Southern Vanuatu (Bedford 2006:36) and burial mounds are present in the Sigatoka dunes cemeteries dated to the first centuries of the first millennium AD (Best 1987; Marshall et al. 2000:Plate 10). Further east, Tongatapu saw, during the first millennium AD, the first repeated use of mounds to bury the dead, a tradition that led over the succeeding millennium to the building of thousands of tumuli (Freeland et al. 2016).

References

Anderson, A., C. Sand, F. Petchey and T.H. Worthy 2010. Faunal extinction and human habitation in New Caledonia: Initial results and implications on new research at the Pindai Caves. *Journal of Pacific Archaeology* 1(1):89–109. pacificarchaeology.org/index.php/journal/article/view/12/0.

Archambault, M. 1901. Les mégalithes néo-calédoniens. *L'Anthropologie* 12:257–268.

Avias, J. 1949. Contribution à la préhistoire de l'Océanie: Les tumulis des plateaux de fer en Nouvelle-Calédonie. *Journal de la Société des Océanistes* 5:15–50. doi.org/10.3406/jso.1949.1625.

Balouet, J.C. and S. Olson 1989. *Fossil birds from late Quaternary deposits in New Caledonia.* Smithsonian Contributions to Zoology 469. Smithsonian Institution Press, Washington D.C. doi.org/10.5479/si.00810282.469.

Bedford, S. 2006. *Pieces of the Vanuatu puzzle: Archaeology of the North, South and Central.* Terra Australis 23. ANU Press, Canberra. doi.org/10.22459/pvp.02.2007.

Bedford, S. and G. Clark 2001. The rise and rise of the incised and applied relief tradition: A review and reassessment. In G.R. Clark, A.J. Anderson and T. Vunidilo (eds), *The archaeology of Lapita dispersal in Oceania: Papers from the Fourth Lapita Conference, June 2000, Canberra, Australia*, pp. 61–74. Terra Australis 17, Pandanus Books, Canberra.

Best, S. 1987. A preliminary report on the Sigatoka Dune burials. *Domodomo* 3:2–15.

Brou, B. 1977. *Préhistoire et société traditionnelle de la Nouvelle-Calédonie.* Société d'Etudes Historiques de la Nouvelle-Calédonie 16, Nouméa.

Burley D. 2013. Fijian polygenesis and the Melanesian/Polynesian divide. *Current Anthropology* 54:436–462. doi.org/10.1086/671195.

Carson M. 2002. Ti ovens in Polynesia: Ethnological and archaeological perspectives. *Journal of the Polynesian Society* 111(4):339–370.

Chevalier, L. 1959–62. Le problème des tumuli en Nouvelle-Calédonie. *Etudes Mélanésiennes* 14–17:24–42.

Dubois, Joseph-Marie. 1981. *Histoire résumée de Maré.* Publications de la Société d'Etudes Historiques de la Nouvelle-Calédonie 27, Nouméa.

Freeland T., B. Heung, D.V. Burley, G. Clark and A. Knudby 2016. Automated feature extraction for prospection and analysis of monumental earthworks from aerial LIDAR in the Kingdom of Tonga. *Journal of Archaeological Science* 69:64–74. doi.org/10.1016/j.jas.2016.04.011.

Frimigacci, D. 1986. Archéologie. *Notice explicative sur la feuille 'Ile des Pins'. Carte géologique à l'échelle du 1/50000*, pp. 27–37. BRGM, Paris.

Golson, J. 1959–62. Rapport sur les fouilles effectuées à l'île des Pins (Nouvelle-Calédonie) de décembre 1959 à février 1960. *Etudes Mélanésiennes* 14–17:11–23.

Golson, J. 1961. D. Report on New Zealand, Western Polynesia, New Caledonia, and Fiji. *Asian Perspectives* V(2):166–180.

Golson, J. 1996. Roger Green: Early and late encounters. In J. Davidson, G. Irwin, F. Leach, A. Pawley and D. Brown (eds), *Oceanic culture history. Essays in honour of Roger Green*, pp. 307–317. New Zealand Journal of Archaeology Special Publication, Dunedin.

Gony, Y-B. 2014. *Recueil de traditions orales. Site archéologique de Bogota, Nakety (Commune de Canala)*. Rapport de l'Institut d'Archéologie de la Nouvelle-Calédonie et du Pacifique, Nouméa.

Green, R.C. 1988. Those mysterious mounds are for the birds. *Archaeology in New Zealand* 31(3):153–158.

Green, R.C. and J.S. Mitchell 1983. New Caledonian culture history: A review of the archaeological sequence. *New Zealand Journal of Archaeology* 5:19–67.

Guillaumin A., R.-H. Leenhardt and P. Pétard 1946. Le ti. *Journal de la Société des Océanistes* 2:191–208. doi.org/10.3406/jso.1946.1526.

Lagarde, L. 2020. 'Were those mysterious mounds really for the birds?' Reappraising the Isle of Pines' puzzling Tumuli (New Caledonia). In I.E. Dotte-Sarout, A. Di Piazza, F. Valentin and M. Spriggs (eds), *Towards a history of Pacific prehistory: Historiographical approaches to Francophone archaeology in Oceania*, pp. 211–232. Publication de la Maison des Sciences de l'Homme du Pacifique, Papeete. doi.org/10.4000/books.pacific. 1292.

Lagarde, L. and A.-J. Ouetcho 2015. Rocks, bird bones and pottery: New evidence in local and regional exchanges from site KTT006 (Isle of Pines). In C. Sand, S. Chiu and N. Hogg (eds), *The Lapita Cultural Complex in time and space: Expansion routes, chronologies and typologies*, pp. 103–123. Archeologia Pasifika 4, IANCP-Academia Sinica, Nouméa.

L'Huillier, L.T. Jaffré and A. Wulff (eds), 2010. *Mines et environnement en Nouvelle-Calédonie: Les milieux sur substrats ultramafiques et leur restauration*. Institut Agronomique Néo-Calédonien, Nouméa.

Marshall, Y., A. Crosby, S. Matararaba and S. Wood 2000. *Sigatoka: The shifting sands of Fijian prehistory*. Oxbow Books, Oxford.

Poplin, F. and C. Mourer-Chauviré 1985. *Sylviornis neocaledoniae* (Aves, Galliformes, Megapodiidae), oiseau géant éteint de l'Ile des Pins (Nouvelle-Calédonie). *Geobios* 18(1):73–97. doi.org/10.1016/s0016-6995 (85)80182-0.

Sand C. 1995. *'Le temps d'avant': La préhistoire de la Nouvelle-Calédonie*. L'Harmattan, Paris.

Sand, C. 1996. Structural remains as markers of complex societies in southern Melanesia during prehistory: the case of the monumental forts of Maré Island, New Caledonia. In I.C. Glover and P. Bellwood (eds), *Indo-Pacific prehistory: The Chiang Mai papers*, pp. 37–44. Bulletin of the Indo-Pacific Prehistory Association 15, Canberra.

Sand, C. 2018. Archaeology of a piece of Gondwanaland: The past of New Caledonia. In E. Cochrane and T.L. Hunt (eds), *The Oxford handbook of prehistoric Oceania*, pp. 185–205. Oxford University Press, Oxford. doi.org/10.1093/oxfordhb/9780199925070.013.014.

Sand, C. 2020. The question of the 'First Inhabitants' of New Caledonia (Southern Melanesia): Archaeological writings in a colonial context and one of decolonisation. In I.E. Dotte-Sarout, A. Di Piazza, F. Valentin and M. Spriggs (eds), *Towards a history of Pacific prehistory: Historiographical approaches to Francophone archaeology in Oceania*, pp. 279–306. Publication de la Maison des Sciences de l'Homme du Pacifique, Papeete. doi.org/10.4000/books.pacific.1103.

Sand C. (ed.), in preparation. *Archéologie d'un plateau minier calédonien: La presqu'île de Bogota (Canala)*. Archeologia Pasifika, Nouméa.

Sand C., J. Bolé, A-J. Ouetcho, Y. Gony and D. Baret 2012. Occupations anciennes des plateaux miniers calédoniens et datations. *Journal de la Société des Océanistes* 134:31–44. doi.org/10.4000/jso.6582.

Sand C., D. Baret and J. Bolé 2013. *Tumuli de Lifou: Abris de bord de mer, enclos monumental et amas de* Xaca *du chemin de Nonime (Mucaweng, district du Wetr)*. Rapport de l'Institut d'archéologie de la Nouvelle-Calédonie et du Pacifique, Nouméa.

Sand C. and A.-J. Ouetcho 2010. Étude d'une grotte sépulcrale préservée de Nouvelle-Calédonie. *Journal de la Société des Océanistes* 130–131:221–228. doi.org/10.4000/jso.6172.

Sarasin, F. 2009 [1929]. *Ethnologie des Kanak de Nouvelle-Calédonie et des Iles Loyauté*. Ibis Press, Paris.

Spriggs, M. 1997. *The Island Melanesians*. Blackwell, Oxford.

Worthy, T.H., M. Mitri, W.D. Handley, M.S.Y. Lee, A. Anderson and C. Sand 2016. Osteology supports a stem-galliform affinity for the giant extinct flightless bird *Sylviornis neocaledoniae* (Sylviornithidae, Galloanseres). *PLoS ONE* 11(3):1–62. doi.org/10.1371/journal.pone.0150871.

16

The commons in prehistory: The case of Japan

Chris Gosden

Abstract

The notion of the commons derives originally from material things, such as grazing land, held and used in common by a group. I have broadened the idea of a commons to include a range of important skills, practices and resources that people share. I would also see commoning as a process that helps maintain access to vital aspects of life, operating best when groups are relatively egalitarian. I have used the case of the Jomon of Japan to explore how such egalitarian groups might work, holding in common knowledge about vital resources, such as plants or fish, but also aesthetic products such as fine pottery or stone circles created through cosmological engagements. Human history has often been written as a story of progress and such progress is often seen as a small group of people gaining power over the majority, eroding the commons in the process. The Jomon show that commoning can exist over many millennia, maintaining the egalitarian ethos of the group and this occurs even when Japanese groups were in close contact with people in mainland East Asia organised in a more hierarchical manner. The Jomon show that many human histories are possible and that we need to broaden the scope of the narratives told about the past.

Introduction

In this chapter, I want to explore the idea of the commons and its utility in thinking about past cultural forms. My use of the term commons differs somewhat from its most usual usage, so that it is necessary to explore what I mean. In English usage and in law, most often the word 'commons' refers to shared physical resources, such as grazing land, which exist in distinction to privately owned resources. People had rights to use things like shared grazing land and a duty not to overuse them. Over-exploitation results in the so-called 'tragedy of the commons' and can arise from pressure on a common resource through overpopulation, but equally can come about when personal advantage is placed before the general good, as when, for example, someone puts more cows than they are allowed on public grazing land, leading to the decline of the grassland (Hardin 1968). Hardin's famous 'tragedy of the commons' is based on the premise that selfishness and the pursuit of individual advantage are natural human traits, so that compromising the commons is inevitable. Important counterarguments to Hardin's are found in the work of Elinor Ostrom (Ostrom 1990; Ostrom and Chang 2012), who cites numerous examples of the careful joint management of common resources existing over the long term. Others have pointed out that increased use of a commons can in fact benefit everyone: greater usage of Wikipedia helps enrich its content and scope. In all such usages and debates the commons are open not enclosed, public rather than private, shared not individually owned. Within a Japanese context, it has been pointed out that a number of ecosystems have been created and maintained by long-term and cooperative human management. For instance, the ecotone known as satoyama exists as a mosaic of habitats encompassing paddy fields, grasslands and woodlands. People have worked between these habitats, for instance taking fallen leaves from the forests to act as fertiliser in the paddy fields, over long periods of time. Recently a combination of rural depopulation, the move to chemical fertilisers and loss of skills needed to integrate these habitats has meant that areas designated as satoyama have decreased markedly, a case of a commons declining due to underuse (Miyama and Shimada 2018).

The idea of the commons links physical resources with the politics and constitution of the group. For me, one of the benefits of the idea of the commons is its political dimension, exploring the balance between group provision and responsibility as against private benefit.

I wish to use the idea of the commons more broadly and to include not just physical resources, but also the technologies, techniques, practices and knowledges needed to use them. Indeed, I would make little distinction between a physical resource, such as grazing land, and knowledgeable engagement with it: understanding when to graze animals, the size of the herd and for how long are all things that develop as people husband both the animals and the land that nourishes them. Such knowledge develops over the long term, is distributed across the group, is handed down to be used strategically. A herder today can vary their herd size depending on whether this is a dry, hot year or a cool, wet one, whether an important feast is coming up or if there is a suspicion that the spirits of the land are disturbed in some way. Common knowledge is flexible, strategic and experimental, not a set of techniques to be applied by rote. The land, the animals and knowledgeable human engagement are all part of the commons, all part of developing cultural projects and desires. If the commons is defined by combined material elements, skills and knowledges, it is not to be defined mainly in terms of scarcity, as Hardin attempted when emphasising the tragedy of the commons, nor is it easily quantified.

In such a broad view, the commons becomes a process, not a physical thing, as much a verb as a noun. The commons has spatial extent, as determined by its physical properties, but also temporal shape, as relevant skills, knowledges and their material referents unfold over time.

The commons is an important element of the material engagements of human life, with, for instance, clay, wood, metal, cows, wheat or rice. The commons is not purely shaped by human desires and needs, but rather though all its participants, so that the needs and habits of cows are important, as are the properties of clay or metal when worked and heated. The commons is a complex field with multiple actors and is always unstable, changing and potentially creative. There is a spontaneity about the commons as process, so that novelty is always arising: it is an engine of creativity and alteration, for better or worse from the point of view of humans. People are also altered by the commons—all our senses, skills and desires are educated by the cultural world in which we live. We create the commons and it in turn creates us. Some expansion or sequestering of the commons shifts our powers to think, to feel, to see, to relate to one another, to love. The commons starts and ends with the group: it is always political. The commons is also always a process, a verb not a noun, the means through which life unfolds.

Following this line of thought, the commons is not just about pragmatics, not purely about how many head of cattle we can graze on an area of land; it also concerns models of the universe, of cause and effect, of how people can place themselves within a universe made up of spiritual forces in addition to what we might see as physical ones. The commons is enacted not just through the *chaîne opératoire* of stone tool making, but through ritual forms and observances. Ritual helps us understand how the world works, and generates understanding, immersion, alienation or transcendence. Making a living is pragmatic, requiring us to think what is possible or necessary, what is the relationship between people and other entities, or the balance between the group and the individual. But for some time there has been a reaction against the standard Childean model of human history being powered by three revolutions (Neolithic, the urban and the industrial), where history is powered by technology and technological change, which in turn shifts society from an early state of equality to rank or class-based societies. But of course ritual forms are central elements of technology, guiding human action in the everyday and at significant moments of the calendar.

In consequence, each commons is based on a model of reality, which specifies in very broad terms whether the world is animistic or mechanistic, how far people are a separate creation from everything else or whether everything can be seen as sentient in some manner. Such models of reality always contains a morality and an ethics: how should we act towards other people, what duty of care or of exploitation do we owe to the world? The answer to these questions will be very different if we think we live in a mechanistic, uncaring universe without gods and spirits or in an animate world where spirits of things and of the human dead are spread throughout the material aspects of the universe. A mechanistic universe is ripe for exploitation, a spirit-infused one requires care and respect.

The process of the commons creates social value: things that are necessary to live, in a physical and emotional sense. It is only relatively recently that value has come to be viewed in transactional terms, as money or some form of currency that exists as an objective and agreed-upon measure of value. Most forms of social value are best thought about in terms of quality, primarily the quality of life as understood by people and all their significant others. A healthy commons will maximise value for the greatest number.

No commons is ever totally held in common; there are always distinctions made in who has access to what sorts of knowledge, skills and resources, whether these distinctions are made through gender, class or ethnicity. Or, to put the same point another way, no one in society holds all the skills and capabilities that exist within that society: there is women's knowledge and work, as there are tasks and skills restricted to men. On the other hand, the commons is impossible to extinguish, so that even in societies in which private rights are strong, such as our own, there is the spontaneous generation of activities and effects, beyond the power of any elite to control. No commons are entirely positive or negative, they can lead to exploitation or to care.

The advantage of the commons for archaeologists is that ideas of control, desire and power can be given material form, through looking at landscapes, material culture and the remains of people, plants and animals, and thinking about the sets of skills and processes which shaped all of them and the politics surrounding such processes.

Let us now think about the case of the commons through a particular example, one of the most intriguing in global prehistory: that of Jomon Japan. In the brief account that follows, I am aware of the dangers of essentialising and simplifying the Jomon, making it appear a single entity or approach to the world. Much recent Japanese work has shown how much variability there is over both time and space. It is very hard to give a true sense of this in the account that follows.

The Jomon as commons

The most conventional view of prehistory, one which many are now reacting against (e.g. Graeber and Wengrow 2021), is that derived from Gordon Childe and others, as mentioned above. For Childe, human history was revolutionary, with three revolutions powering progress: the Neolithic, the urban and the industrial. Of these three, the farming revolution was primary and fundamental, leading to sedentism, surplus, superior craft production and ultimately private property and the state. In the terms I am developing, Childe's view of the Neolithic was that it brought about the severe compromise of the commons (not that he uses the term), as, over time, people started to own land, develop a stress on surplus and means of exchange that came to emphasise wealth. Of recent years, the Neolithic revolution has been much critiqued, often making the point that few places see a sudden change to farming, that the process of domestication was frequently long and drawn out, or that changes previously associated with farming, such as sedentism and pottery, developed either before or long after farming did (e.g. Denham et al. 2007). The so-called origins of agriculture have been freighted with enormous historical significance, moving humans away from an original state of equality and eventually giving us all the aspects of modern life (Mizoguchi 2019).

We can question what farming was—the classic definition centred on the controlled husbandry of domesticated species—partly because many early modes of food-getting combined wild and domesticated forms, or cultivated wild forms of grasses especially, which only later became domesticated. Nowhere we know of does farming develop rapidly or with immediate consequences, so that it is very rarely revolutionary. China is a classic case of a slow move towards rice cultivation in the south and millet in the north, both happening so slowly that the point at which a group became agricultural is impossible to pinpoint. Systems of getting food are unfolding processes, only rarely subject to revolutionary change, often occasioned by a new crop or, more often, outsiders coming into an area. Nor can we say that the advantages of farming were so self-evident that whenever people knew of agriculture they would adopt it: here Japan is the classic case.

The Japanese islands were never isolated from the mainland to the west and north, so that Kyushu had regular contact with the Korean Peninsula and Hokkaido enjoyed links with Sakhalin in the north (Figure 16.1). From the Palaeolithic onwards, common tool types are found in the Japanese archipelago and the mainland, with obsidian from Hokkaido found in Sakhalin and that from southern sources occurring in the Tongsamdong shell midden in south-eastern Korea (Imamura 1996:213). Shell middens are found along the coast of China and up to Japan and north into Sakhalin and east Russia. The most discussed ancient artefacts linking what are now China, Russia and Japan are the world's oldest pots, being some 20,000 years old in China and currently some 4000 years younger in Japan—although a single find can change this chronology, being found also in eastern Russia. Such sharing indicates regular early seafaring connecting a huge area at an early date (Gaffney 2021:290–293). Shared pottery technology does not exist in cultural isolation, but indicates similarities in boiling and steaming technologies in both places, as well as what is now eastern Russia. It is likely that vessels of fired clay diffused through a network of relationships throughout the region, by people able to travel by sea even at the height of the last glaciation. Connections across the Japan Sea are ancient and longstanding, with no reason to believe these ended in the Holocene. When agriculture gradually crystallised out of earlier broad-spectrum practices in China some 6000 BC, a fact most likely known to contemporary inhabitants of Japan given the long contacts across the Sea of Japan, the Jomon groups chose to go their own way, refusing agriculture for many thousands of years while receiving a range of material culture from Korea and China (Hudson et al. 2021). There was eventually something of a farming revolution in Japan, but this did not occur until around 800 BC (the Yayoi period), many millennia after paddy field rice occurred in China and Korea.

Figure 16.1: The major regions of Japan.
Source: Author supplied.

For much of the Holocene, Japanese groups lived on wild plants, animals, fish and shellfish, resisting cultivation practices, as a result of a set of deliberate choices. From the point of view I am developing here, they were preserving the commons.

Let us look in a little more detail at Jomon culture. First of all, the Jomon period lasted for an immensely long time, some 13,000 years in all, so it is obvious much changed over those millennia; it also had considerable geographical variation from Kyushu in the south to Hokkaido in the north. For long periods in the final glacial and early Holocene, settlements were ephemeral and stone tool types suited for hunting indicate small populations that were very mobile (Imamura 1996:56–57, 88–91; Mizoguchi 2020:8) (Table 16.1).

Table 16.1: Chronology Jomon to Kofun.

Initial and Incipient Jomon	13500–5000 BC
Early Jomon	5000–3500 BC
Middle Jomon	3500–2470 BC
Late and Final Jomon	2470–800 BC
Yayoi	800 BC–250 AD
Kofun	250–538 AD

Source: Author's summary.

By the end of the Initial phase and into the Middle Jomon people settled, with some larger settlements, probably lived in all year round, with a series of smaller, special-purpose sites, these differentiated from one another by specialist tool kits. It is possible to recognise a repeated pattern of a central large settlement, surrounded by smaller ones, with each of these combinations forming a territorial and social unit (Mizoguchi 2020:8). There is evidence of burning the landscape in a controlled manner. Jomon landscapes were ones without domesticated plants and animals, or indeed agriculture, but they were highly managed and regulated by people with very deep pools of knowledge.

The larger permanently occupied settlements often have a circular structure. The Nishida site (Figure 16.2) in its Middle Jomon phase is typical: at the centre of the circle are burials around which are pillared structures which might either be for the exposure of the dead or food storage. In a last outer ring are storage facilities and pit dwellings. Many settlements seem to have their circular structures divided into radial segments, indicating perhaps that a lineage of the living and the dead occupied each segment (Mizoguchi 2020:9). On occasions, radial segments are marked by stones and these can be aligned with significant points on the horizon, such as the setting sun at a solstice or a prominent local mountain. A settlement combines several lineages with no indication of differences in status between them within a strong cosmological orientation.

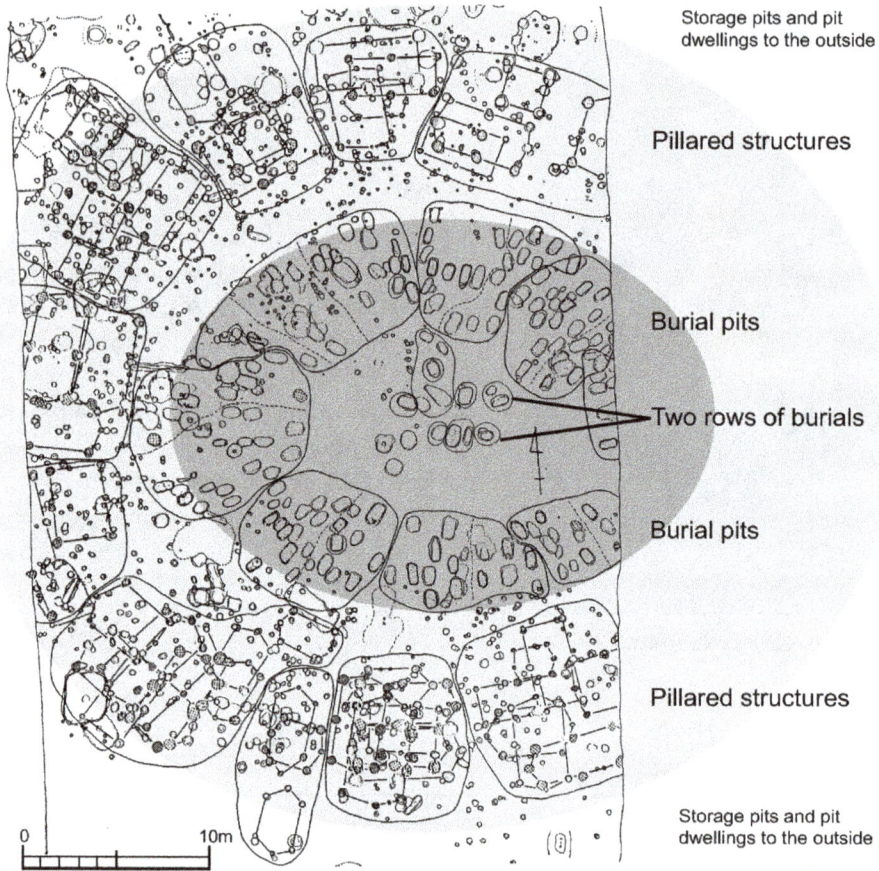

Figure 16.2: The Nishida site, Middle Jomon phase (Iwate prefecture).
Source: After Mizoguchi (2020:Fig. 2).

Figure 16.3: Jomon pots excavated at the Komakino site.
Source: Author supplied.

The strong spatial structure of the settlement gave structure and pattern to the activities of the living whose repeated actions would have helped shape the group in which they lived, with mundane daily activities of food processing, eating, sleeping or raising children on the outside and recognition of the ancestors towards the middle, perhaps with the exposed bodies of the recently dead in between. Children brought up in a circular settlement internalised a series of rules of correct action—perhaps including how to move through the parts of the site belonging to their lineage, what you were allowed to do in each circle and the manner in which the settlement as a whole was oriented on features of the landscape or the sky. A series of both pragmatic and more cosmological strictures were written into arms, legs and bodies as children moved and acted, becoming not something people knew, but something they were. And, of course, there would also have been movement across the landscape and between the large sites and smaller ones. It might have been that the big and small settlements had different social compositions, with a good proportion of a lineage living together in a radial segment of a larger site, with their different mixtures of age, gender and kinship affiliation in the smaller ones. Some sites might have been camps for hunting, especially those at the base of wooded mountains home to deer and other animals, and others for plant gathering. Without slipping into clichéd notions that men hunted and women gathered, there might have been differences in gender and age groups coming together for the various activities. Such regular shuffling of people would have led to a range of affiliations and affective networks.

If the activities necessary for making a living created forms of mobility which mixed and complicated groups, then the vibrant ritual lives of middle and later Jomon communities held them together. The extraordinary pots of the Middle Jomon had applied clay motifs added to their surfaces which combined the abstract with human and animal figures, as well as occasional phallic designs (Figure 16.3). A great variety of pottery style zones have been seen across Japan, distinguished by stylistic variations in pots. The heads and bodies of quasi-human creatures on pots may have been seen as emerging out of another dimension beyond the wall of the pot. Some figures are probably engaged in ritual activities such as dancing. Further links with lifeworlds may have been embodied in the undulating rims of the pots that some have compared with salmon tails—the salmon being a crucial food on the west of the islands especially (Steinhaus et al. 2020). Pots were used for storage and cooking, transforming raw into cooked states in containers constructed from important figures of this world or some other. Not only was food transformed, but also the figures on the pots do not fit into simple categories of species, so that transformation occurred in human and animal bodies, or it might be better to say that the strict division we tend to make between human bodies and those of other species did not exist for Jomon people, perhaps indicating a rather more animistic world, a point I will come back to.

A further feature of note in our whistle-stop tour of the Jomon, and again focusing on the Middle Jomon after 3500 BC, are the so-called *dogū* figures. Fired clay figures have been made, used, broken and deposited since the start of the Jomon period, but their numbers gradually increase so that many of the roughly 18,000 figures known date from the Middle and Late Jomon periods (Kaner 2009:16). The greatest concentrations are found in central and northern Honshu, with a number also from southern Hokkaido. A good percentage of the figures appear human, many with female attributes, commonly with ornate designs such as coiled snakes. A lot of attention was paid to the face with prominent eyes, sometimes round mouths and occasionally well-modelled noses. Many figures wear clothing and some have lines which might indicate tattoos. In the Late Jomon, clay masks were made and indeed some of the figurines of all periods may have been wearing masks. There is greater abstraction through time and in the Late Jomon some very large figures were made. Numbers wax and wane: the end of the Middle Jomon sees a decline, but from the middle of the Late Jomon large numbers were made and deposited. *Dogū* overlap in date with the advent of rice agriculture and their large numbers in some areas have been seen as a form of resistance to the new ways (Kaner 2009:18, 24–39). Not only were *dogū* made in recognisable forms, but they were broken in standard ways, with some having head and arms removed and others various parts of the torso and legs (Harada 2009:Fig. 43).

Quite what the role or meaning of *dogū* for various Jomon people might have been has been much discussed, with common interpretations circling around the idea of an Earth Mother or Mother Goddess, due in part to the prevalence of the female form. It is worth noting that the two Chinese characters for *dogū* represent earth and spirit. The fact that these figurines, like Jomon pots, were made from the earth and potentially embodied with spirit again hints at an animistic world, wherein aspects of the landscape we might take to be inanimate, such as clay, were seen by Jomon groups as living in some way, to be given extra energies through forming into the human body or a pot, hardened by fire and then sometimes broken with the pieces distributed across Jomon sites. The lively world of the Jomon did not respect boundaries between people and other aspects of that world, so that people put a lot of effort into recreating parts of the world to use, break and distribute in graves, pits and other contexts. It has been argued that *dogū* emphasised the female form and may have been involved in rites emphasising reproduction, an emphasis reinforced by stone rods which may have been phalluses, as well as stone tools shaped as genitalia (Mizoguchi 2013:Chapter 5). Reproduction encourages a cyclical view of reality, an emphasis on replacement and generation, contained perhaps also within an ethics of care, points we will return to below. The seasonal nature of site use in the Jomon, with gatherings at large permanent sites at some times, alternating with movement to smaller, special purpose camps at others, might have encouraged notions of repetition and cycles.

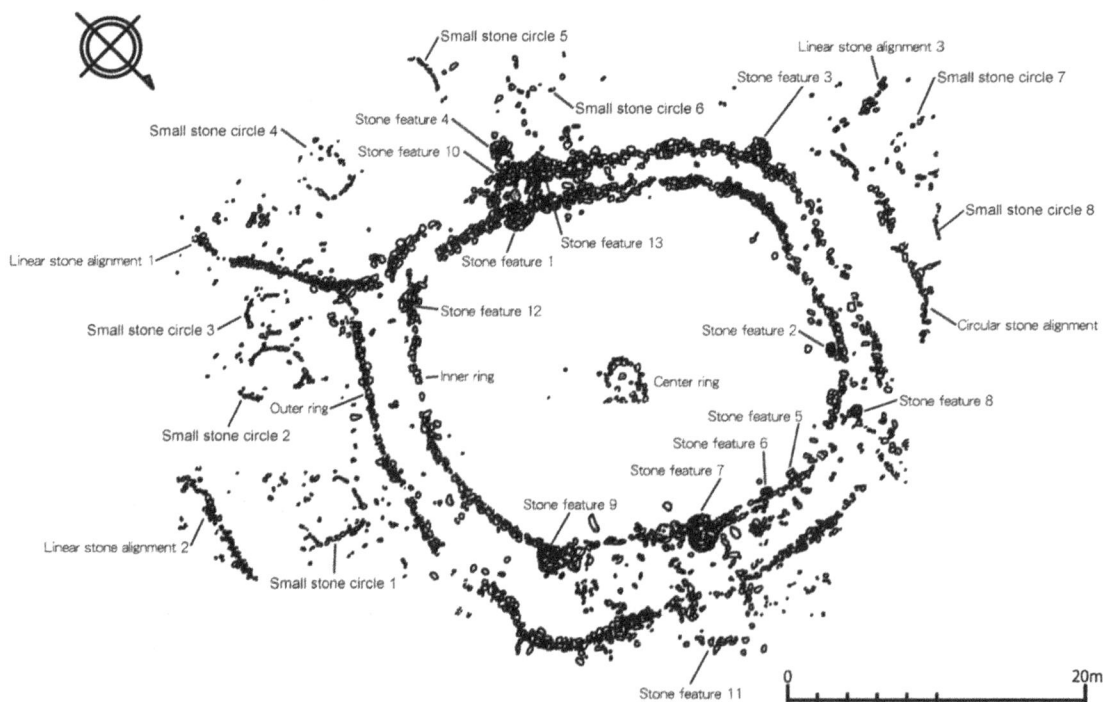

Figure 16.4: The Komakino stone circles with a small central ring, two larger concentric circles with hints of a fourth ring outside of those and a series of stone alignments oriented on the movement of the sun or prominent features of the landscape.

Source: After Kodama (2003:Fig. 13.7).

Clay was obviously crucial to the Jomon world, with changing uses over time, and so too was stone. Many circles and some rectangles of stone are found across the Jomon area. There are so-called 'sundial' circles with a vertical stone in the centre and stones laid flat radiating out from it.

Much more complicated stone circles are also known, such as those from the broader site complex at Komakino within Aomori city (Figure 16.4). On a slope overlooking the sea an artificial terrace was cut into the hillside some 1500 BC. On this terrace were constructed a series of stone circles and other stone features, indicating a series of activities perhaps stretching over hundreds of years. The stone circles were constructed from around 2,400 boulders from the Arakawa riverbed which was some 70 m below the artificial terrace. The cutting of the terrace and the movement of the stones would have necessitated a considerable amount of labour. The site was much more complicated than that, made up of more than 100 burials (both barrows and graves) containing pottery coffins and miniature pottery vessels. In addition, animal and human figures in clay have been found on the gentle slope to the east of the circles. These include more than 400 triangular-shaped stones, also found at other neighbouring sites. There is also a rich midden area and a nearby spring (Kodama 2003).

In the worsening climate of the Late Jomon after around 1500 BC large permanent settlements disappear and it is assumed that people became more mobile, distributing their lives and activities across a range of camps. The coming into being of small mobile groups would have had implications for broader group cohesion, so that large ritual sites such as Komakino were created as crucial gathering points where the ancestral dead were buried and then honoured and observances carried out at important times of the solar or lunar calendar. Labour needed to construct the stone circles would also have helped construct the group, as would smaller-scale activities, such as burials, the deposition of triangular stones or clay figurines. The group worked with a variety of substances, minimally clay and stones, but more likely also a range of organics now hard to detect.

If we compare the Nishida and Komakino sites we can see that in both the Middle and Late Jomon the spatial arrangement of sites was complex and meant that human activities were structured, as bodies were educated to move and act in appropriate ways on each of the sites. Such sites derive from, and help strengthen, a commons: a mode of distributed intelligence that guided group action across the landscape. But we can also see that forms of group intelligence were never static and always changing, with the reorientation of the landscape in the Late Jomon there was a major set of changes, which took place not just at one site, but across the landscape as a whole. The Middle to Late Jomon saw the shift from one commons to another, with no evidence of hierarchy in houses or burials, indicating that everyone had general access to the physical and psychological skills and resources they needed for life.

The Yayoi, agriculture and the compromise of the commons

Agriculture appeared relatively suddenly in Japan perhaps around 800 BC (although rice and millet had been known for some time). The question to be posed here is: did agriculture destroy the commons and, if so, how? In historic periods, Japan is well known for growing rice in paddy fields and still today Japan grows enough rice to feed its own population of 126 million people, a remarkable feat given the relatively paucity of lowland areas suitable for intensive agriculture. Paddy field cultivation starts in the Yayoi period, some 800 BC.

Farming of rice and millet without irrigation started in Korea around 3000 BC, broadly contemporary with the Middle Jomon. There is no evidence of such a phase of dry-field farming in Japan as yet, although claims have been made on the basis of possible cereal inclusions in pottery back into the Middle Jomon; these are undermined by the lack of evidence for widespread occurrence of domesticated grains on archaeological sites (Endo and Leipe 2022; Mizoguchi 2013:54). If farming on the Korean Peninsula was known, but not adopted, this indicates that it held no attraction for Jomon people for perhaps two millennia, probably because it did not fit in with people's deeply held values concerning the nature of social relations and the place of humans within an active cosmos. As the final Jomon unfolded, however, from around 1000 to 500 BC, the cultivation of rice began, so that by the later date it is likely that rice was grown in paddy fields, which required considerable labour and also brought high returns.

The process by which paddy field agriculture enters Japan is complicated and debated. There was undoubtedly some movement of people from southern Korea into northern Kyushu, the point of the Japanese archipelago closest to Korea. Conversely there are Japanese assemblages of the Yayoi period found in Korea, so that movement was two-way at least since the Early Jomon period, when pottery changes in similar ways in Korea and Kyushu, with Japanese obsidian also being found in the Tongsamdong shell midden in south-eastern Korea (Imamura 1996:213). In many ways the modern nation-state distinction between Korea and Japan may be historically unhelpful here with the sea being a bridge as much as a barrier to competent seafarers, with shared elements but considerable distinctions on both sides of the strait.

A recent wide-ranging study of impressions of grains in pottery shows some of the complexity of the introduction of both rice and millet, together with their subsequent spread from Kyushu into Honshu (Endo and Leipe 2022). During the five phases of use of Tottaimon pottery assemblages, spanning the final Jomon through to Early Yayoi, rice and two sorts of millet are found in small amounts, quickly increasing to a dominant crop in the case of rice.

The grain impression study (Endo and Leipe 2022) provides evidence to argue that the three newcomer crops (rice, foxtail millet and broomcorn millet) arrived together most probably from the Korean Peninsula. Choices of crops were selective however, as barley and wheat were part of the crop repertoire of Mumun period farmers on the Korean Peninsula by the time arable agriculture spread to Japan, but no evidence of them exists either from impressions or charred remains in Kyushu or Honshu until the end of the Kofun period.

Once established in northern Kyushu, the rice and millets spread eastwards with Tottaimon pottery as far as the central Tokai region by the end of the Initial Yayoi period, around 500 BC (Figure 16.5). The Initial Yayoi period in the Central Highlands shows complications and only millet was grown here, partly because creating paddy fields was more difficult in the Highlands and maybe also because these were indigenous Jomon populations rather than incomers. Rice-based farming then spread across the western part of the archipelago as far as central Tokai, accompanied by Ongagawa-type pottery during the Early Yayoi period, arriving in southern Kanto by the Middle Yayoi period after 300 BC. The rice-centred agriculture in Hokuriku is also suggested to have appeared during the Middle Yayoi period. Influenced by the millet-centred agriculture in the Central Highlands, a mixed rice–millet cultivation system spread to northern Kanto during the Middle Yayoi period. There are clear indications that agricultural practices focused on rice appeared in northern Tohoku during the Early Yayoi period. People who made pottery similar to Ongagawa pottery might have helped establish rice cultivation (Endo and Leipe 2022).

Age (BCE)	Periodi-sation (this study)	Cultural phase	Phase	Northern Kyushu	Chugoku/Shikoku	Kinki	Tokai	Hoku-riku	Central Highlands		Kanto	Southern Tohoku	Northern Tohoku
2000	Late–Final Jomon	Late Jomon	Pre-Tottai-mon	Tottaimon			Jokonmon		Phase	Fusenmon			
?	Final Jomon	Final Jomon	1	Kurokawa (M) / (Osayuki) / (Etsuji SX-1)	Tanijiri / Maeike	Shinohara / Shigasato IV							
800/700	End of Final Jomon/ Initial Yayoi	End of Final Jomon/ Initial Yayoi	2	Yusu I	(Agata)	Kuchisakai							
			3	Yusu IIa / Yusu IIb	Tsushima-okadai	Funabashi	Gokanmori		1	Metobagawa			
500/400	Early Yayoi	Early Yayoi	4	Yusu IIb/ Itazuke I	Sawada	Nagahara	Mamizuka		2	Hanareyama/ Kori I (O)			
			5	Itazuke I	(Kawatsushi-motoi)				3	Kori I (M)/(L)			
					Ongagawa		Kashio		4	Kori II			
300							Suijinbira				Jokonmon		Sunazawa
											Oki II		Yubune-zawa
	Middle Yayoi	Middle Yayoi					Komatsu				Ajima		
							Uto			Kuribayashi	Ikegami / Kitajima	Nakazato / Miyanodai	Minami oyama 2 / Kawahara machiguchi	Inakadate
1													

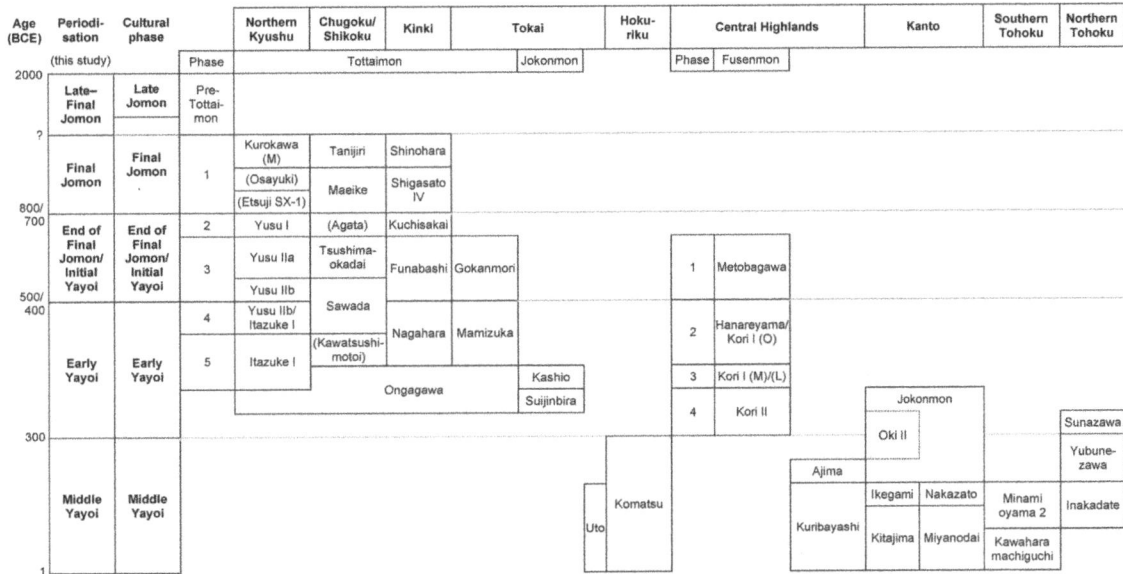

Figure 16.5: The detailed chronology from the Late Jomon to Middle Yayoi showing the main pottery types and some important sites across Japan.

Source: From Endo and Leipe (2022:Fig. 3).

In sum, we can see cereal cultivation spread across Kyushu, Shikoku and Honshu islands during the Yayoi period and continuing subsequently, with the spread possibly faster in western Japan than eastern regions, where the Jomon relationship with the landscape resisted change. Much later, in the period of state formation from the seventh century AD rice had become the food of the elite, extracted from commoners through taxes, so that those who farmed themselves eating mainly millets, wheat and barley, supplemented by wild foods. We will look briefly at these later periods below.

Returning to the Yayoi period, we can see that there was a complicated story concerning the spread of rice and millet, with the former becoming the dominant crop in many areas by the Middle Yayoi, but millet also important at higher altitudes. The adoption of these new crops was only possible through wholesale changes to people's lives, with the dispersed Jomon pattern of a large permanent site and smaller camps for specific functions collapsing down into permanent settlements near paddy fields, some of which were not far from earlier Jomon sites (Mizoguchi 2019). Movements across the landscape changed, but so too did the seasonal round, with much of life now focused on rice production between spring and autumn. Paddy field rice is famously labour intensive, but is equally known to be productive. The basic sequence of a rice cultivator's year can be summarised as follows. In the spring, seedlings are planted in nurseries, while the main paddy fields are ploughed and weeded. Transplanting then occurs from the nurseries to the paddy field in late spring, followed by regular weeding and tending. Harvest occurs in the autumn, with large-scale drying, processing and storage of rice either in pits or granaries raised from the ground. The rice can be eaten from harvest onwards and through the winter. It is possible that wild foods were added to the diet from at least spring onwards. Mizoguchi (2019) has argued that rice was initially readily adopted because the main work on this crop fell into periods of the year where the workload was somewhat lighter for Jomon people. However, the needs of rice soon came to predominate, pushing out other activities, changing relations between men and women, allowing for a steep rise in population, perhaps because a larger labour force was needed in the paddy fields, and fairly soon the breakdown of the long period of equality and commitment to the commons found over the millennia of the Jomon period.

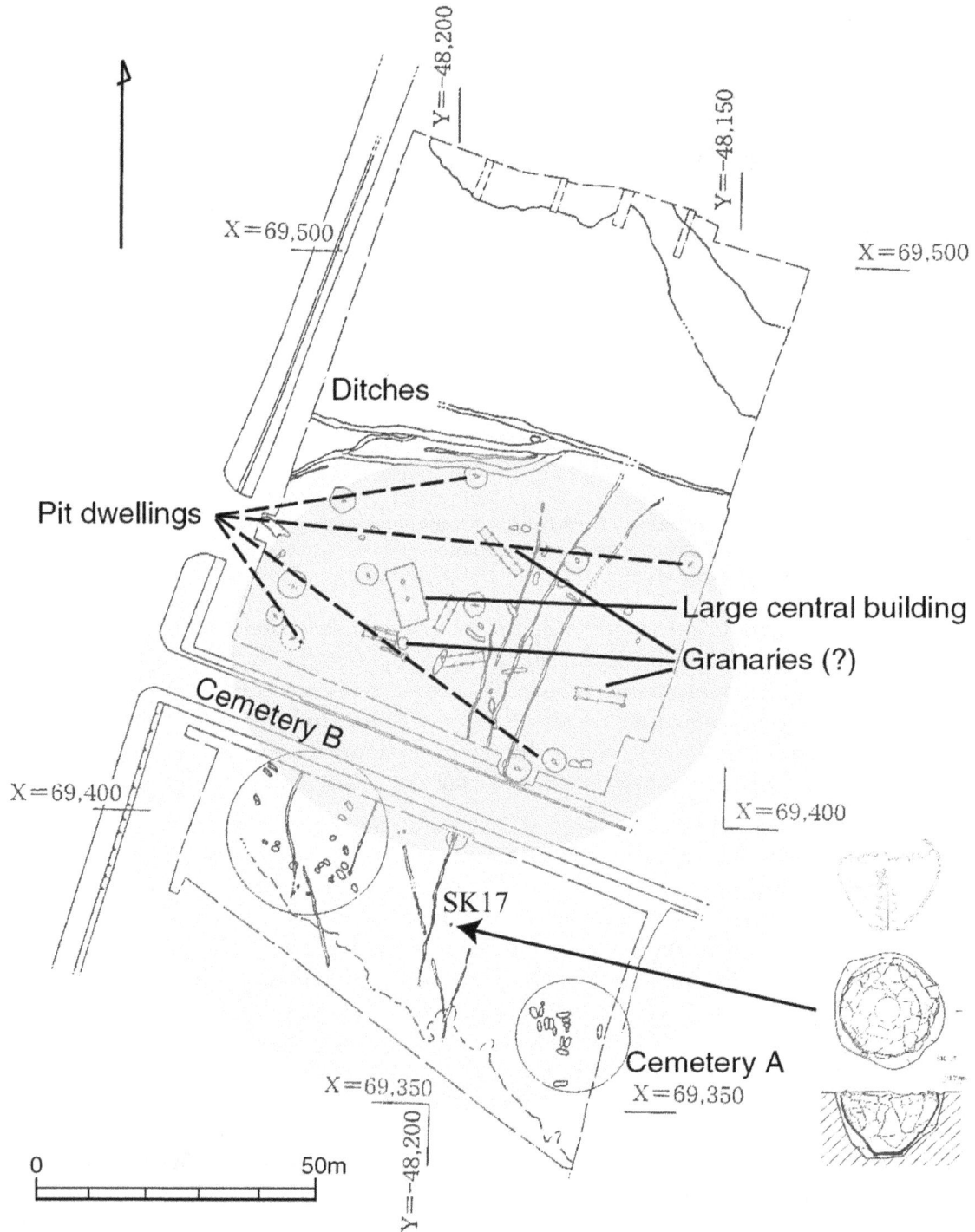

Figure 16.6: The Yayoi settlement at Etsuji village, Fukuoka prefecture, with a large rectangular building and granaries surrounded by a circle of round pit houses and two cemeteries to the south.
Source: After Mizoguchi (2013:Fig. 5.1).

The balance between change and continuity is made more interesting by the fact that some of the earliest Yayoi settlements were laid out on a circular plan in the same way that preceding Jomon ones had been, showing some initial attempt to preserve known ways in the face of novelty. A prime example is the site of Etsuji near present-day Kasuya township, in the Fukuoka prefecture in northern Kyushu, established in the Initial Yayoi period. Etsuji is a hamlet on slightly raised ground within a floodplain where several rivers met, creating a naturally swampy landscape which was an ideal habitat for early rice cultivation. Reaping knives have been found, indicating rice harvesting took place, but no paddy fields contemporary with the settlement are known. Obsidian arrowheads indicate hunting took place, quite possibly in the nearby hills. This had been an area of dense Jomon inhabitation, with a Late Jomon pit dwelling only 300 m to the north of the Yayoi site and a scattering of Jomon artefacts 500 m east and a series of pit dwellings occupied between the Late and Final Jomon phases some 600 m south-east. Such habitations had probably been sustained by combinations of hunting and the cultivation or gathering of wild plants in the wetter lowlands (Mizoguchi 2013:56).

Initial Yayoi Etsuji had a circular plan defined by round pit dwellings arranged in a circle with a large central rectangular building and a number of granaries in the middle (Figure 16.6)—although its full plan has not definitely been revealed by the excavation. The settlement was occupied for some length of time as there is evidence of rebuilding of new structures adjacent to older ones. While the smaller rectangular buildings probably had floors raised off the ground and were granaries, the largest building (5.5 m wide and 10.3 m long) may have been communally used. From the Middle Yayoi onwards, such buildings have been connected to elite burial grounds, being perhaps used for activities honouring the ancestors (Mizoguchi 2013:57–58). Mizoguchi (2013:58) wonders whether the activities honouring the ancestors were restricted to only part of the group, perhaps indicating that some lineages or moieties within the community were now able to control the ritual life of the group to some extent. The fact that the largest building was surrounded by granaries storing rice might have helped associate the dead ancestors with the new basis of life, which was rice. Furthermore, the structure of the various buildings at Etsuji—the circular pit dwellings, the rectangular granaries and the large rectangular buildings—directly recalled types of construction for these buildings known from the Middle Mumun period on the Korean Peninsula.

A further feature is intriguing. Jomon settlements, especially in eastern Japan, seem to have had a segmentary structure, with indications that the community who lived in them was divided into two parts. The division of burials at Etsuji into two groups (Cemetery A and B in Figure 16.6) further echo such a social distinction. Mizoguchi describes the two sets of burials as follows:

> Cluster A, the eastern cluster, consisted of thirteen composite wooden coffin burials, one pit burial (also possibly a wooden coffin burial) and two jar burials (in one, a large globular jar was used as a coffin, while the other's shape-type could not be determined). The graves were generally laid out to form several linear alignments. Burial cluster B, the western cluster, consisted of nine composite wooden coffin burials and fifteen pit burials. The latter might have included some composite wooden coffin burials, but it is impossible to identify them exactly due to the severe disturbance of the upper layers. The graves appear to have been situated in a circular layout. (Mizoguchi 2013:62).

The circular arrangement in Cluster B appears to be following a Jomon tradition, whereas the linear arrangement in A links to Korean traditions. Are we dealing here with an immigrant and local group, within a community that as a whole is embracing novelty, living in a settlement in which the structures echoed Korean architecture, while the circular structure of the site continued Jomon ways of doing things? People were both breaking with the Jomon past and also sticking with it. Overall, novelty is considerable, containing within it the germ of a new society in which the old ethics of equality broke down, leading to more hierarchical modes of action by the later Yayoi and certainly into the Kofun period. Mizoguchi (2013:Chapter 12) has argued that the flexibility of Jomon relations, where groups moved to various sites in parts of the landscape with particular plants, animals and fish, which they exploited before returning to the major settlement with food they had procured, made hierarchy an undesirable option. Jomon landscapes were not just or mainly pragmatic ones, but were endowed with spirits of the land, living things and humans, or, most likely a combination of all three of these. Jomon landscapes were ritualised, with a series of shrines and features, large and small, constructed across it, as we have seen briefly. This very spatially varied landscape would have been used following a complicated calendar, with observances happening in the high hills, on the plains and by the coast at times of the year significant to each locale. These complications over time and space would have been hard to control by any one part of the group, even if they had conceived a desire to do.

With the concentration of group activities into the rice paddy field (and indeed through the cultivation of millet), following the spring to autumn calendar of planting to harvesting, the time and space of Yayoi communities was simplified and regularised, giving all aspects of the group an interest in a good rice harvest. Spatial and temporal concentration of pragmatic activity and, perhaps especially ritual actions, was either easier to control by one clan or lineage, or at least allowed the group to think that such a ritual specialisation would have been desirable. By the late Yayoi and into the Kofun periods, a bit before 250 CE, particular lineages may have been deemed efficacious, so that at least some ritual activity focused on the burial mounds of such a lineage. This focus resulted in the construction of ever larger and more formalised burial mounds, best known through the famous keyhole shape of the *kofun*, but also developed into continued activity indicated by deposited stones, shells or the clay *haniwa* figures in a variety of human forms. The power of some ancestors were needed to guarantee and maintain the fertility of the world, both for humans and for rice, whose life cycles seem to have become entangled in the Yayoi period, so that jars for storing rice were also used to bury the human dead (Mizoguchi 2013).

The long equality of the Jomon came to an end, seeing the decline of a commons that persisted for more than 10 millennia. The death of the commons and the redistribution of power and resources into fewer hands (it might have only been the Kofun period elite that ate rice) might not have resulted from the fact that agriculture could generate storable surpluses to be controlled and used by a section of the community, but rather because the responsibility for maintaining the order and fertility of the world was taken into a few hands. Internal differentiation within a group was mirrored by a fragmented social landscape in which clan fought clan, with one group occasionally and rather temporarily aspiring to imperial status, where the overall ruler had the status of a god, in the ultimate indication of the death of the commons. Those who were guarantors of fertility also regulated the flows of the increasing numbers and ranges of prestigious items both produced in Japan and overseas, especially China. The world of the commons derived from the quality of relations between people and also between people and transcendent forces. Quality existed through the respect and honour shown in relations with all significant others, a state of extended reciprocity. As the first millennium CE unfolded, relations of quality gave way to those of quantity, where exchanges were designed to be unequal, to extract for the few the labour of the many. Without reciprocity the commons cannot exist, so that profit is the negation of the commons.

Final thoughts

We should not romanticise the commons and no perfect state of equality, deriving from shared skills and resources, has ever existed. The Jomon were violent on occasion, although less so than many groups, and where violence did occur it was probably due to fighting between groups: power relations always existed, often between women and men, or the old who use access to systems of esoteric knowledge to control the young. Furthermore, the commons is not one thing but many, existing in countless forms. Each commons is based upon a model of reality, notions of how various biological kinds are interrelated or divided, or the manner in which transcendental, spiritual powers are manifest across the world. It might be that the rims of Jomon pots evoked the tails of salmon (Steinhaus et al. 2020), perhaps hinting in turn that these fish might not have been separate from humans, deriving from an entangled worldview contrasting with a Linnean view of the separate nature of species. Each model of the world contains within it an ethics, specifying not just how the world works but also the correct sorts of action within that world, not just between human and human, but among and between all the things that are distinguished in that world. An equality of action and outcome is only possible if people believe that that is how the world is constituted, as flat and open fields of cultural interaction, in which power of one thing over another is a temporary state, calmed by respect, reciprocity and care. The commons is not a thing but a style of action, an active and ongoing process not a singular outcome. We are better thinking of commoning than of a commons. A stress on commoning is in many ways the negation of a more Darwinian idea of the survival of the fittest, where nature is always red in tooth and claw and the strong not only do triumph, but should, because this is the way nature works. Acting against the inherent striving and competitive nature of the world is quite literally unnatural. Not only can Darwinian theory be seen as an encoding of the spirit of capitalism, but it also provided a naturalisation of the desire to thrive at the expense of others. The Jomon established a commons and maintained it in changing forms over 13 millennia, indicating that it is not human nature to subvert the commons for individual gain, as people like Hardin argued. The Jomon encoded an immensely long ethic of care and reciprocity, carefully maintained and curated.

But also, in these days when the deleterious consequences of competitive capitalism are obvious so that many doubt that the spirit of capitalism is natural and certainly worry about the results of all our striving for material advantage, it is not surprising that many are turning to the idea of the commons as the basis for a more sustainable and equitable life (e.g. Bollier and Hilfreich 2012; Hyde 2010; Ostrom 1990). The standard model of Childe and others assumed that equality was an original state of society and that the surplus-generating capacity of farming supported the specialist production of prestige items then used to control spheres of exchange. The Jomon shows that this is not necessarily so. People can know about, ignore and resist farming, preferring more equal states of society. Jomon is just one of the more striking counter cases that are accumulating against the standard model, indicating that a considerable range of historical trajectories were possible.

I am very happy to write this piece for Glenn who has always been a political and egalitarian person, who I feel will be in sympathy with the idea of the commons, although we have never had a chance to discuss it. I hope that the Japanese case study will chime with the Japanese dimension of his life. For my part, it has been a great privilege and pleasure to know Glenn these almost 40 years and rather too occasionally working with him. We have a lot in common.

Acknowledgements

I am very grateful to Anne Ford for all her care and attention during the editorial process. I would also like to thank Koji Mizoguchi, who managed to find time in his busy schedule to give me some extremely insightful comments on Jomon and later developments. An anonymous referee was also most helpful in pointing out relevant references and correcting a number of errors—any remaining mistakes are my own.

References

Bollier, D. and S. Helfrich (eds). 2012. *The life of the commons: A world beyond market and state.* Levellers Press, Amherst, MA.

Denham, T., J. Iriarte and L. Vrydaghs 2007. *Rethinking agriculture: Archaeological and ethnoarchaeological perspectives.* Taylor and Francis, Abingdon.

Endo, E. and C. Leipe 2022. The onset, dispersal and crop preferences of early agriculture in the Japanese archipelago as derived from seed impressions in pottery. *Quaternary International* 623:35–49. doi.org/10.1016/j.quaint.2021.11.027.

Gaffney, D. 2021. Pleistocene water crossings and adaptive flexibility within the *Homo* genus. *Journal of Archaeological Research* 29:255–326. doi.org/10.1007/s10814-020-09149-7.

Graeber, D. and D. Wengrow 2021. *The origins of everything: A new history of humanity.* Allen Lane, London.

Harada, M. 2009. Dogū broken and enshrined: Traces of a Jomon world view. In S. Kaner (ed.), *The power of dogū: Ceramic figures from ancient Japan,* pp. 50–59. British Museum Press, London.

Hardin, G. 1968. The tragedy of the commons: The population problem has no technical solution; it requires a fundamental extension in morality. *Science* 162:1243–1248. doi.org/10.1126/science.162.3859.1243.

Hudson, M., I. Bausch, M. Robeets, T. Li, A. White and L. Gilaizeau 2021. Bronze age globalisation and Eurasian impacts on Later Jomon social change. *Journal of World Prehistory* 34:121–158. doi.org/10.1007/s10963-021-09156-6.

Hyde, L. 2010. *Common as air: Revolution, art and ownership.* Farrar, Straus and Giroux, New York.

Imamura, K. 1996. *Prehistoric Japan: New perspectives on insular East Asia.* Routledge, London.

Kaner, S. (ed.) 2009. *The power of dogū: Ceramic figures from ancient Japan.* British Museum Press, London.

Kodama, D. 2003. Komakino stone circle and its significance for the study of Jomon social structure. *Senri Ethnological Studies* 63:235–226.

Miyanaga, K. and D. Shimada 2018. 'The tragedy of the commons' by underuse: Toward a conceptual framework based on ecosystem services and satoyama perspective. *International Journal of the Commons* 12(1):332–351. doi.org/10.18352/ijc.817.

Mizoguchi, K. 2013. *The archaeology of Japan: From the earliest rice farming villages to the rise of the state.* Cambridge University Press, Cambridge. doi.org/10.1017/CBO9781139034265.

Mizoguchi, K. 2019. Re-thinking the origin of agriculture through the 'beginnings' in the Japanese archipelago. *Japanese Journal of Archaeology* 6:95–107.

Mizoguchi, K. 2020. Making sense of material culture transformation: A critical long-term perspective from Jomon- and Yayoi-Period Japan. *Journal of World Prehistory* 33:1–23. doi.org/10.1007/s10963-020-09138-0.

Ostrom, E. 1990. *Governing the commons: The evolution of institutions for collective action.* Cambridge University Press, New York. doi.org/10.1017/CBO9780511807763.

Ostrom, E. and C. Chang 2012. *The future of the commons: Beyond market failure and government regulation.* Institute of Economic Affairs Occasional Paper 148, London. doi.org/10.2139/ssrn.2267381.

Steinhaus, W., S. Kaner, S. Shoda and M. Jinno (eds) 2020. *An illustrated companion to Japanese archaeology.* Archaeopress, Oxford.

Part 5:
Cultural objects

17

Late Holocene potting traditions in the far western Pacific: Evidence from the Raja Ampat Islands, 3500–1000 BP

Dylan Gaffney and Daud Tanudirjo

Abstract

The question of where Lapita groups derived from, immediately prior to their appearance in the Bismarck Archipelago, is a perennial one; it is a question that remains largely unaddressed owing to a dearth of research in West Papua. This chapter describes two pottery sequences from Waigeo Island in the Raja Ampat group, off the Bird's Head of New Guinea. Mololo Cave preserves pottery from 3100–2700 years ago and possibly 3800–3500 years ago. Some of the sherds are red-slipped and incised, with similarities to Island Southeast Asian Neolithic ceramics, while other sherds share morphological similarities with Lapita plainware. However, intricate decorations like dentate stamping and lime infilling, characteristic of the earliest Island Southeast Asian and Lapita ceramics, are absent. Manwen Bokor Cave preserves pottery from 1300–1000 years ago, with fewer instances of red slip, but more intricate decorations including circle stamping, impression and incision. These later ceramics share affinities with pottery from eastern Wallacea and northern New Guinea, showing a more restricted sphere of influence later in time; that is, there was a process of network contraction and regionalisation between c. 3500 and 1000 BP.

Introduction

The challenge that Glenn Summerhayes set archaeologists at the beginning of this century was to model the nature of maritime colonisation and interaction that could account for the rapid and widespread appearance of Lapita pottery in the western Pacific from about 3350 years ago (Summerhayes 2000:1). Not content to sit about and let the challenge linger, Glenn's ongoing field projects in the Bismarck Archipelago and on the New Guinea mainland, undertaken alongside numerous students, Papua New Guinean archaeologists and local stakeholders, have dramatically refined our understanding of these processes (e.g. Summerhayes 2007b, 2010, 2022). It is now apparent that Early Lapita pottery was produced primarily by Austronesian speakers that established enclaves on the offshore islands of the Bismarcks and maintained high levels of interconnectivity during initial periods of colonisation (Summerhayes 2001), introducing to the region distinctive settlement patterns (Summerhayes, Szabó, Leavesley et al. 2019), domesticated animals (Summerhayes, Szabó, Fairbairn et al. 2019) and visual communication systems (Summerhayes 2007a).

The clarity of this research legacy in the east, in large part generated by Glenn's unparalleled drive to piece together the Lapita puzzle, starkly contrasts the archaeological record to the west. The islands off the Bird's Head Peninsula of West Papua may have formed a staging post immediately prior to Lapita movements into the Bismarck Archipelago (Bellwood 1998); this is supported by linguistic, bioarchaeological and genetic evidence that indicates ancient people from nearby north-east Wallacea were closely related with Lapita groups in Remote Oceania (Bulbeck 2019; Oliveira et al. 2022; Pawley and Ross 1993). However, owing to an almost total lack of archaeological research in the area, several outstanding questions remain. Did a cohesive 'Far, Far Western Lapita' or 'Proto Lapita' province exist in the islands of West Papua prior to movements into the Bismarck Archipelago? Alternatively, did early Lapita cultures in the Bismarck Archipelago emerge from disparate influences in eastern Indonesia (Ono et al. 2019), New Guinea (Summerhayes 2019) and perhaps even Micronesia (Carson et al. 2013), prior to becoming interlinked with indigenous Island Melanesian practices? Moreover, did interconnectivity between West Papua and the Bismarck Archipelago persevere, and how was this reflected in changes to pottery-making traditions?

To take up these questions, this chapter presents crucial pottery data from the Raja Ampat Islands, off the Bird's Head of West Papua. One of the goals of our archaeological project in these islands was to empirically bridge the well-established traditions of research in Papua New Guinea and the wider Pacific with that in Indonesia. As such, the chapter begins by summarising the characteristics of ceramics from Wallacea, New Guinea, the Bismarck Archipelago and the Marianas. It then presents a summary of the Raja Ampat area including 2018–2019 excavations at Mololo Cave and Manwen Bokor Cave on Waigeo Island. The ceramic finds from each site are then laid out in detail, with especial focus on which vessel forms, decorations and fabrics were discarded in different chronostratigraphic contexts. These results are discussed in a regional context with the aim of describing similarities and discontinuities with other circum-New Guinea ceramic traditions.

Early ceramics in Island Southeast Asia and the western Pacific

The Island Southeast Asian Neolithic

The pottery trail that leads from Southeast Asia to Near Oceania is so far a discontinuous one (Figure 17.1). The early ceramics of the Batanes and Philippines are primarily red-slipped plainware, reflecting their connections with Taiwan from about 4000 years ago (Hung 2005); later dentate, lime-infilled, circle-stamped and incised sherds date to sometime between 3800 and 3300 years ago (Bellwood et al. 2013; Hung 2008). Strong similarities exist between the ceramics of the northern and central Philippines and those excavated at Unai Bapot on Saipan, in the Mariana Islands (Carson and Hung 2017:104; Hung et al. 2011). Although the dating of the Unai Bapot pottery remains debated (Carson 2014, 2020; Petchey et al. 2018; Petchey and Clark 2021), it is likely that pottery makers of the Philippines, the Marianas, Wallacea and the Bismarck Archipelago were interconnected, whether directly or indirectly, by voyaging networks between 3500 and 3000 years ago. This is evident by the similar dentate, circle-stamped and lime-infilled pottery recovered from open sites like Kalumpang in the Karama Valley and at Mansiri, Sulawesi, dating to about 3500–3400 years old (Anggraeni et al. 2014; Azis et al. 2018) and at Bukit Tengkorak on Borneo, where initial pottery dates sometime between 3300 and 3000 years old (Bellwood and Koon 1989; Chia 2016).

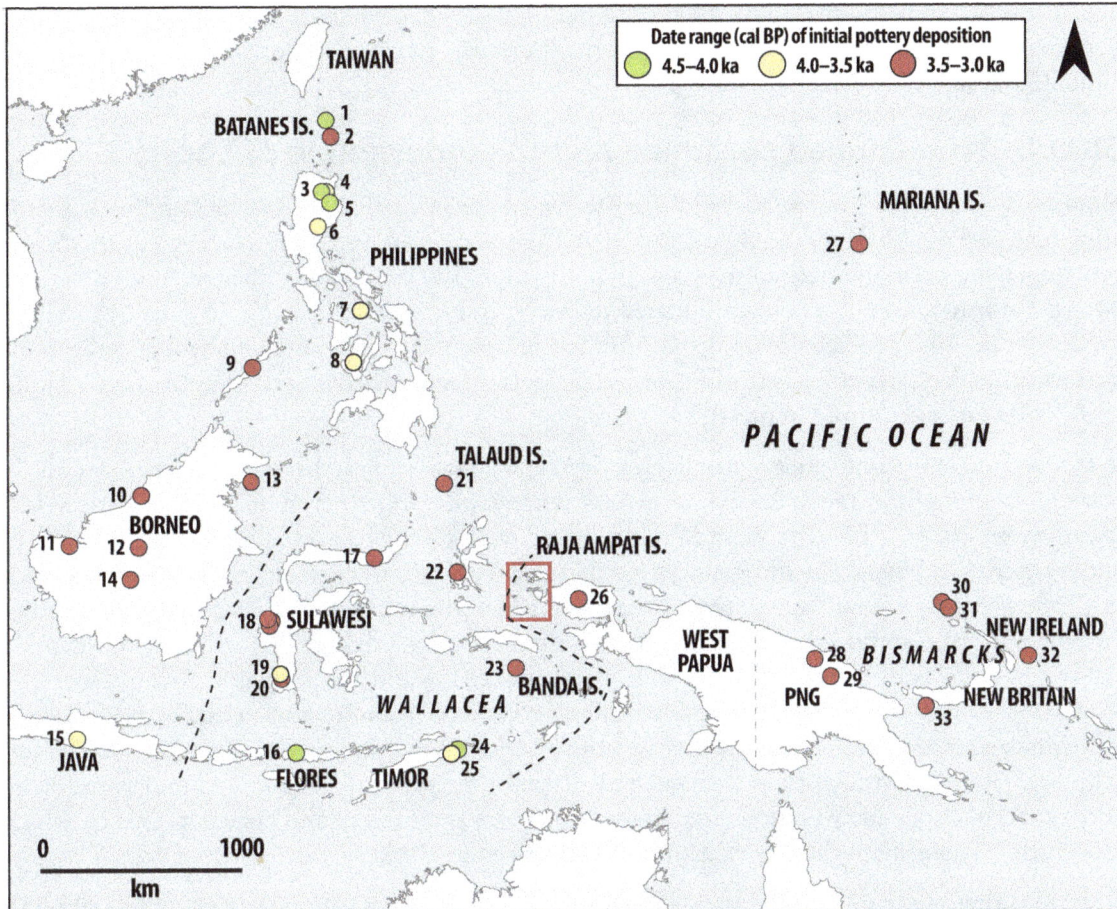

Figure 17.1: Map of circum-New Guinea islands showing key early pottery sites.

Notes: (1) Torongan; (2) Sunget; (3) Rabel; (4) Andarayan; (5) Dimolit; (6) Pintu; (7) Batungan; (8) Edjek; (9) Manunggul; (10) Niah; (11) Gua Sireh; (12) Liang Kaung; (13) Bukit Tengkorat; (14) Nangabalang; (15) Song Keplek; (16) Liang Bua; (17) Mansiri; (18) Kalumpang; (19) Ulu Leang 1; (20) Leang Burung; (21) Leang Tuwo Mane'e; (22) Uattamdi 1; (23) PA1; (24) Lene Hara; (25) Uai Bobo 2; (26) Toé; (27) Unai Bapot; (28) Kowekau; (29) Wañelek; (30) Talepakemalai; (31) Tamuarawai; (32) Kamgot; (33) Apalo.

Source: Authors' illustration.

The earliest known ceramics in eastern Wallacea are predominantly characterised by red-slipped globular vessels, and are similar to plainware sherds from Sulawesi and Borneo. In the Talaud Islands, red-slipped sherds from Leang Tuwo Mane'e date by association with a marine shell to 3690±70 BP (Bellwood 1976; Tanudirjo 2001). When calibrated using a new ΔR of −129±47 from the nearby Raja Ampat Islands (Gaffney 2021:168), this date suggests the sherds were deposited anytime between 3850 and 3350 years ago (cal. BP), with 95.4 per cent probability. The Talaud vessels are very similar to those at Uattamdi 1 on Kayoa Island, where red-slipped sherds date to no earlier than about 3500–3050 years ago, although more convincingly begin around 3350 years ago (Bellwood 2019). However, it should be noted that Leang Tuwo Mane'e and Uattamdi 1 are cave sites and so their pottery may be functionally and decoratively different from those used at open sites. PA1 in the Banda Islands provides the only open site with early ceramics in eastern Wallacea; the pottery dates by association with charcoal to sometime before 3350 years ago and possibly up to 3550 (Lape et al. 2018; Peterson 2015). In each of these sites, 'Neolithic Age' pottery came to be replaced by 'Metal

Age' ceramics dating to after 2300–2200 years old, and which were less frequently red-slipped, but were characterised by more elaborate decorations including incision, circle stamping and appliqué (Ono, Oktaviana et al. 2018).

Circum-New Guinea ceramics and the emergence of Lapita

Almost no pottery has been published from the West Papuan mainland. A small handful of sherds from Toé Cave on the Bird's Head Peninsula date to sometime around 3000 years ago or thereafter, perhaps having been produced in the Raja Ampat Islands (Pasveer 2004). Other ceramics described from the north coast either remain undated or were produced more recently in time (e.g. Miller 1950; Schmitt 1947; Solheim 1958, 1998). Around Jayapura and Lake Sentani, ongoing excavations by Balai Arkeologi Papua (Centre of Papuan Archaeology) are recovering red-slipped sherds dating after 2000 years old (Suroto in press).

In the eastern New Guinea region, in what is today Papua New Guinea, the only published pre-3000-year-old ceramics from the mainland occur inland at Wañelek (Gaffney et al. 2015) and Kowekau (Northwood 2015). Although most of these sherds were probably made around the foothills of the Sepik–Ramu Inland Sea (providing a similar geographical arrangement to Cenderawasih Bay and Lake Sentani in West Papua), some are red-slipped and tempered with beach sands indicating their manufacture around the northeast coast. These ceramics, although few in number, resemble plainwares from both eastern Wallacea (e.g. Bellwood 2019) and the Bismarck Archipelago (e.g. Kirch 1997:146). Additionally, two undated sherds recovered from the north coast of New Guinea are dentate stamped, and one was demonstrated to be locally produced (Golitko 2011; Terrell and Schechter 2007). A much more frequent red-slipped pottery manufacture occurred around the north coast of Papua New Guinea after about 2000 years ago (Terrell and Schechter 2011), which continued to intensify in the last millennium (Gaffney et al. 2018).

Notably earlier are 'Early Lapita' sherds from sites like Talapakemalai, Tamuarawai, Kamgot and Apalo in the Bismarck Archipelago, which were the result of local pottery manufacture commencing around 3350–3100 years ago (Kirch 2021; Kirch et al. 2015; Summerhayes et al. 2010; Summerhayes, Szabó, Leavesley et al. 2019; Summerhayes 2000). These sherds were usually red-slipped plainware, sometimes with minor decoration around vessel lips, although a small component were dentate-stamped, lime-infilled, circle-stamped and incised (Chiu and Sand 2005). Similarities in decoration and vessel form during this period suggest these pots were produced by people who were tightly interconnected (Summerhayes 2001); assuming that these pottery makers were female and matrilocal (Jordan et al. 2009), but sometimes moving long distances during voyaging (Bentley et al. 2007), it implies that they had learned potting traditions from parent communities. However, the extent to which Early Lapita groups (or the Far Western Lapita province) interacted with home communities in Island Southeast Asia is limited to a few known instances of exchange (Harlow et al. 2012; Summerhayes 2017). Where these parent communities to the west were located, and how they were connected with communities in the east, will now be examined with new data from the Raja Ampat Islands, West Papua.

The Raja Ampat excavations

The Raja Ampat Islands

The Raja Ampat archipelago lies just off the north-western coast of New Guinea (Figure 17.2). In the last few centuries, the islands were a key location mediating the transfer of goods and people between Island Southeast Asia and the Pacific (Sollewijn Gelpke 1994; Warnk 2010). Today, Raja Ampat is home to speakers of several Austronesian languages belonging to the South Halmahera – West New Guinea branch of East Malayo-Polynesian (Arnold 2020; Kamholz 2014).

Earthenware pottery is made by Ambel speakers in Waigeo's Mayalibit Bay, and by Biak speakers around the north coast of Batanta; both groups produce rectilinear sago flour ovens, but globular pots for cooking or water storage are not commonly used or known about (Gaffney and Tanudirjo 2019). In 2018, the Raja Ampat Archaeological Project surveyed the northern islands—Waigeo, Gam, Batanta and offshore satellites—locating several promising cave sites and open locations with surface pottery. This was subsequently followed by systematic excavations in 2018–2019, targeting cave sites (Gaffney 2021).

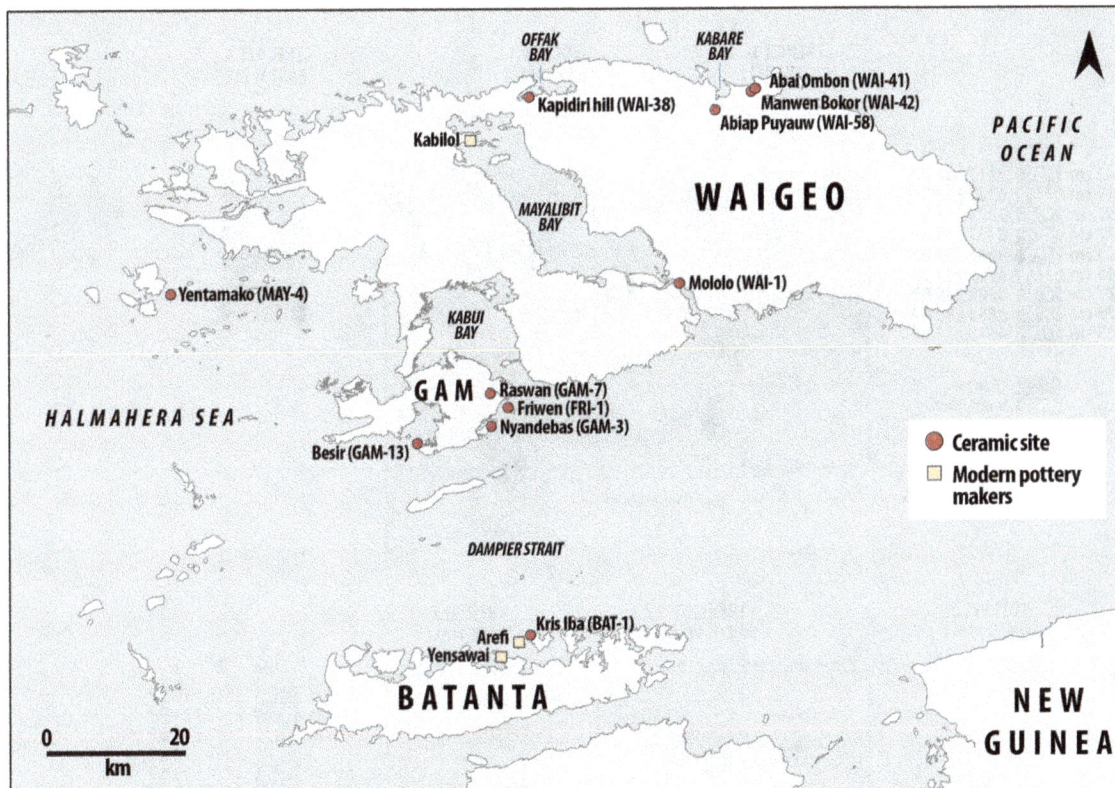

Figure 17.2: The northern Raja Ampat Islands.

Note: This map shows location of ceramic sites, including key excavated sites, Mololo at the entrance to Mayalibit Bay, and Manwen Bokor on the north coast of Waigeo.

Source: Authors' illustration.

Excavations at Mololo Cave

Mololo Cave (WAI-1 in the Raja Ampat Archaeological Project database) is located at the entrance to Mayalibit Bay, the large water body that almost bisects Waigeo (Figure 17.3). It is a limestone system comprised of a light outer chamber, exposed to sunlight but sheltered from rain, and a dark inner chamber that is home to several bat colonies. The 2018 excavations focused on two parts of the outer chamber (Area 1 and Area 2), where 0.5 × 0.5 m test pits were followed by 2 × 1 m trenches. Trench excavations followed stratigraphic boundaries, constrained by 50 mm spits. A 0.5 × 1 m test pit was also excavated in Area 3, at the edge of the dark inner chamber, but this recovered sparse archaeological evidence.

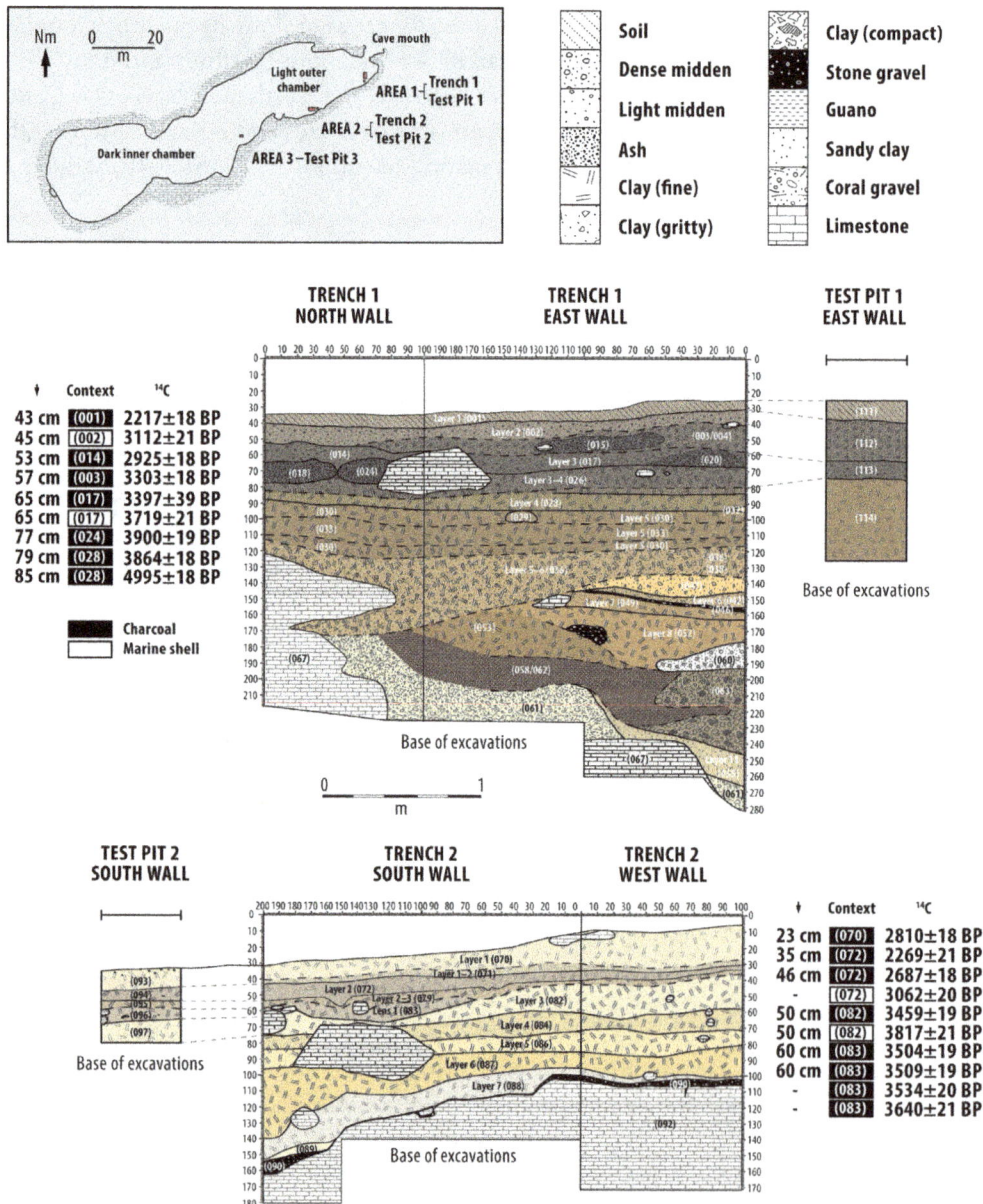

Figure 17.3: Mololo Cave (WAI-1) site plan and excavation sequence showing Late Holocene radiocarbon determinations.

Source: Authors' illustration.

Table 17.1: Late Holocene radiocarbon dates from Mololo (TR1 and TR2) and Manwen Bokor (Unit 1 and TP2).

Lab code	Area	Quad	Spit	Layer	Context #	Material	X	Y	Z	Determination	d13C	Calibrated 2 sig	Cal curve
Mololo – TR1													
Wk-53106	B	SE	2	1	1	Charcoal	90	143	43	2217±18 BP	–	2320–2291 cal. BP (14.6%) 2271–2149 cal. BP (80.8%)	IntCal2020
OxA-39721	A	NW	3	2	2	Marine shell	23	66	45	3112±21 BP	0.35	3077–2721 cal. BP (95.4%)	Marine20
Wk-53110	B	NE	4	F10	14	Charcoal	82	185	53	2925±18 BP	–	3160–2998 cal. BP (95.4%)	IntCal2020
Wk-53108	A	NE	5	2	3	Charcoal	91	51	57	3303±18 BP	–	3565–3466 cal. BP (95.4%)	IntCal2020
OxA-40144	B	SW	7	3	17	Wood charcoal	100	109	65	3397±39 BP	-28.46	3821–3795 cal. BP (4.1%) 3762–3755 cal. BP (0.5%) 3724–3552 cal. BP (86.5%) 3533–3493 cal. BP (4.3%)	IntCal2020
OxA-39722	B	SW	7	3	17	Marine shell	100	109	65	3719±21 BP	1.14	3828–3444 cal. BP (95.4%)	Marine20
Wk-53107	B	SE	9	F17	24	Charcoal	100	115	77	3900±19 BP	–	4414–4286 cal. BP (87.1%) 4275–4249 cal. BP (8.4%)	IntCal2020
Wk-53109	A	SE	11	4	28	Charcoal	70	10	79	3864±18 BP	–	4406–4233 cal. BP (91.2%) 4198–4184 cal. BP (3.7%) 4166–4162 cal. BP (0.6%)	IntCal2020
Wk-53105	A	SE	12	4	28	Charcoal	51	2	85	4995±18 BP	–	5856–5827 cal. BP (8.9%) 5752–5654 cal. BP (83.5%) 5620–5607 cal. BP (3.1%)	IntCal2020
Mololo – TR2													
Wk-53103	A	NE	1	1	70	Charcoal	68	61	23	2810±18 BP	–	2960–2857 cal. BP (95.4%)	IntCal2020
Wk-53102	B	SE	4	2	72	Charcoal	183	15	35	2269±21 BP	–	2345–2301 cal. BP (50.8%) 2239–2158 cal. BP (44.6%)	IntCal2020
Wk-53101	B	SE	5	2	72	Charcoal	185	42	46	2687±18 BP	–	2848–2810 cal. BP (28.0%) 2792–2753 cal. BP (67.5%)	IntCal2020
OxA-X-3054-10	B	NE	5	2	72	Marine shell	–	–	–	3062±20 BP	2.01	3023–2681 cal. BP (95.4%)	Marine20
OxA-39444	B	NE	6	3	82	Wood charcoal	168	70	50	3459±19 BP	-27.2	3828–3789 cal. BP (28.6%) 3775–3740 cal. BP (15.4%) 3733–3684 cal. BP (38.5%) 3667–3642 cal. BP (12.9%)	IntCal2020
OxA-39723	B	NE	6	3	82	Marine shell	168	70	50	3817±21 BP	1.24	3960–3560 cal. BP (95.4%)	Marine20

Lab code	Area	Quad	Spit	Layer	Context #	Material	X	Y	Z	Determination	d13C	Calibrated 2 sig	Cal curve
OxA-39445	B	SW	8	Lens 1	83	Wood charcoal	107	51	60	3504±19 BP	-28.87	3838–3699 cal. BP (95.4%)	IntCal2020
OxA-39446	B	SW	8	Lens 1	83	Wood charcoal	107	51	60	3509±19 BP	-28.77	3842–3699 cal. BP (95.4%)	IntCal2020
Wk-53034	A	SE	10	Lens 1	83	Wood charcoal (Gymnosperm)	–	–	–	3640±21 BP	–	4079–4038 cal. BP (13.1%) 3995–3886 cal. BP (82.4%)	IntCal2020
Wk-53036	B	SW	10	Lens 1	83	Wood charcoal	–	–	–	3534±20 BP	–	3888–3818 cal. BP (45.6%) 3799–3721 cal. BP (49.9%)	IntCal2020
Manwen Bokor Unit 1													
OZZ-315	–	SW	–	1	1	Marine shell	42	26	62	1630±25 BP	0.8	1299–977 BP (95.4%)	Marine20
Manwen Bokor TP2													
OZZ-314	–	E	7	3	5	Wood charcoal	–	–	66	1290±35 BP	-27.3	1293–1173 BP (91.1%) 1159–1130 BP (4.4%)	IntCal2020

Source: Authors' data.

Late Holocene discard was focused in Area 1, near the entrance to the cave. This is indicated by large midden and ash contexts near the top of Trench 1 and Test Pit 1. These contexts, particularly Layer 2 and 3 and associated features, represent several discrete cooking and discard events between c. 4400–4250 and c. 2300–2150 years ago (Table 17.1). Contemporaneous layers were excavated in Area 2, although material was more sparse. In Trench 2 and Test Pit 2, Layer 2 and Lens 1 represent smaller-scale cooking events, dating from c. 4100–3900 to c. 2350–2150 years ago. At both Area 1 and 2, the middens predominantly contained mammal and fish bone, and marine and brackish water shell. Along with pottery that was found in small numbers (see below for further detail), shell ornaments, chert flake tools and bone point artefacts were extremely rare in these upper deposits.

Excavations at Manwen Bokor Cave

Manwen Bokor (WAI-42) sits near the end of the Rainkan River, which outflows into the Pacific along the north coast of Waigeo. The site itself is a cave and rock shelter at the base of a c. 100-m-high limestone escarpment (Figure 17.4). A small tidal creek runs through the western part of the cave and has created mudflats around most of the site. A dry sandy area with surface pottery is located in the east, near an ossuary of secondary burials. Similar ossuaries are present on a limestone boulder to the west of the creek, with bones having been placed inside small wooden coffins carved in the shape of marine animals, characteristic of Biak graves in Cenderawasih Bay (Corbey 2019).

The 2019 excavations included a 1 × 1 m pit (Unit 1) in the dry sandy part of the cave, excavated with 50 mm spits, along with two test pits (Test Pit 1 = 0.5 × 0.5 m, Test Pit 2 = 1 × 0.5 m) on the mud flats, excavated in 100 mm spits. Given the proximity of the excavations to human remains, custom leaders oversaw our research in the cave and made the area safe for our work.

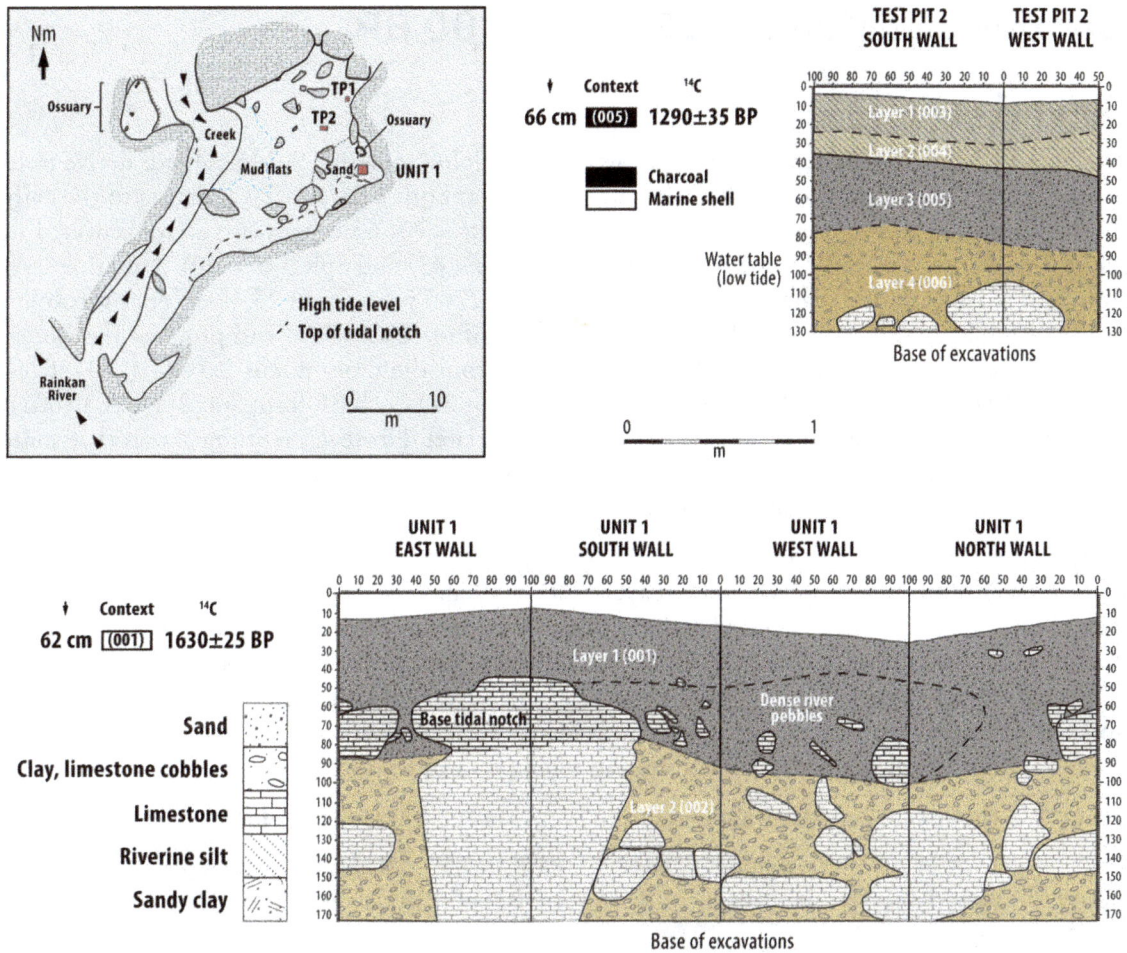

Figure 17.4: Manwen Bokor Cave (WAI-42) site plan and excavation sequence showing radiocarbon determinations.

Source: Authors' illustration.

Based on the excavated stratigraphy, the black sand in the east of the site had been covered by the mud flats, suggesting that the tidal creek is a recent incursion into the site. These changes likely occurred within the past millennium, because charcoal and marine shell in the black sand layer dates to c. 1300–1000 years old (see Table 17.1). The black sand is associated with shell and fish bone, along with pottery. Below the sand layer is a clay, densely packed with coral limestone cobbles toward the cave wall. In Unit 1, excavations captured the base of a tidal notch, which may have been carved out during Mid to Late Holocene high stands (Dickinson 2003), when the Pacific abutted the edge of the limestone escarpment. No archaeological material in primary deposition was recovered from the basal clay layer, although loose overlying sediment and periodic flooding likely accounts for occasional vertical displacement of material from above.

Ceramics at Mololo, c. 3500–2300 BP

Chronology

One hundred and fifty-six ceramics were recovered at Mololo (Table 17.2). Most sherds derive from contemporary habitation and midden deposits (Layer 2) at both TR1 and TR2, dating to the early third millennium before present. At TR1, most sherds (n = 73, 65.8 per cent) were recovered in Layer 2 (002), with many of those coming from Spit 2 (n = 43) and Spit 3 (n = 20). A marine shell from Spit 3, Layer 2 (002) dates to 3112±21 BP, c. 3100–2700 years ago at 95.4 per cent probability using a Mololo-specific ΔR of –129±47 (reported in Gaffney 2021:172), and provides the closest age estimate for these sherds. Thirty-four sherds come from the more recent Layer 1 (001), from both Spit 1 (n = 14) and Spit 2 (n = 20). A charcoal date of 2217±18 BP from Spit 2, Layer 1 (001), suggests these sherds date to c. 2300–2150 years ago or later. However, refitting shows that some sherds from Layer 1 (001) and 2 (002) derive from the same vessel and the Layer 1 (001) sherds may alternatively have been deposited earlier than 2300 years ago.

Only four plain body sherds from TR1 derive from pre-3000-year-old contexts, in Spit 5, midden context (003/004), and in Spits 5 and 7, Layer 3 (017). A charcoal date of 3303±18 BP, or c. 3550–3450 years ago, from Spit 5, midden (003/004), provides an estimate for one of these sherds. The deepest sherds from Layer 3 (017) are most closely associated with a wood charcoal date of 3397±39 BP from Spit 7, Layer 3 (017), or c. 3800–3500 years old. Each sherd weighs less than 2 g and was collected from the sieves; there is no evidence for downward displacement from overlying contexts, although owing to their small size this remains a real possibility.

Table 17.2: Number of ceramic fragments from excavated contexts at Mololo Cave.

Layer	Cont.	Date ka	Rim n	Rim %	Neck n	Neck %	Carination n	Carination %	Body n	Body %	Appliqué n	Appliqué %	Total n	Total %
Area 1														
TR1														
Layer 1	(001)	2.2	4	11.8	4	11.8	–	–	26	76.5	–	–	34	100.0
Layer 2	(002)	2.9	8	11.0	7	9.6	2	2.7	56	76.7	–	–	73	100.0
Midden	(003)	3.5	–		–		–		1	100.0	–	–	1	100.0
Layer 3	(017)	3.6	–		–		–		3	100.0	–	–	3	100.0
Subtotal			**12**	**10.8**	**11**	**9.9**	**2**	**1.8**	**86**	**77.5**	**–**	**–**	**111**	**100.0**
TP1														
Layer 1	(111)	–	–	–	–	–	–	–	2	66.7	1	33.3	3	100.0
Layer 2	(112)	–	–	–	–	–	–	–	2	100.0	–	–	2	100.0
Subtotal			**–**	**–**	**–**	**–**	**–**	**–**	**4**	**80.0**	**1**	**20.0**	**5**	**100.0**
Area 2														
TR2														
Layer 2	(072)	2.8	–	–	–	–	–	–	31	100.0	–		31	100.0
Lay. 2-3	(079)	–	–	–	–	–	–	–	6	100.0	–		6	100.0
Subtotal			**–**	**–**	**–**	**–**	**–**	**–**	**37**	**100.0**	**–**		**37**	**100.0**
TP2														
Layer 2	(094)	–	–	–	–	–	–	–	2	100.0	–	–	2	100.0
Lay. 2-3	(095)	–	–	–	–	–	–	–	1	100.0	–	–	1	100.0
Subtotal			**–**	**–**	**–**	**–**	**–**	**–**	**3**	**100.0**	**–**	**–**	**3**	**100.0**
TOTAL			**12**	**7.7**	**11**	**7.1**	**2**	**1.3**	**130**	**83.3**	**1**	**0.6**	**156**	**100.0**

Note: ka = thousand years ago; n = number of fragments; % = percentage by stratigraphic context.
Source: Authors' data.

At TR2, the majority of sherds (n = 29; 78.4 per cent) were excavated in Spit 5, Layer 2 (072), most closely associated with a date of 2687±18 BP, c. 2850–2750 years ago, from the same spit and context, making them contemporary with sherds from TR1, Layer 2 (002). Two sherds recorded in Spit 4, Layer 2 (072), associated with a date of 2269±21 BP, c. 2350–2150 years old, are contemporary with those from TR1, Layer 1 (001). The deepest sherds at TR2 derive from Spit 6, Layer 2–3 (079), which are related to mixing and vertical displacement from Layer 2 (072). These sherds were recorded in situ at 46 cm below the datum line, about 31 cm below the ground surface.

Ceramic technology

The minimum number of vessels at Mololo is four, and each vessel is a distinct technical class of globular pot with restricted neck (Table 17.3). Class 1 rims belong to a thick-walled globular pot with red slip applied to the interior and exterior of the rim (Figure 17.5).

The pot was discarded sometime in the third millennium before the present, but it is not possible to be more precise about its age because Class 1 sherds were found in both Layer 1 (001) and Layer 2 (002). The vessel was tempered with a mixed sand (Fabric A; Figure 17.6) and is incised with gashes around the neck. Linear incisions were also inscribed around the vessel shoulders forming zones for combining decorative configurations into motifs involving diagonal incisions, wavy lines, and ovoids (see 'incision and fingernail incision' in Figure 17.7).

Class 2 rims belong to a thin-walled globular pot with everted rim that lacks red slip surface treatment. The shoulder has a slight corner point, suggestive of paddle and anvil construction, but it was not deliberately carinated during the forming stages. The vessel was produced with Fabric B and was probably discarded earlier than the Class 1 vessel, about c. 3100–2700 years ago.

Table 17.3: Formal and decorative description of pottery technical classes at Mololo Cave.

Class	Lay.	Cont.	Spit	Form	Rim direction	Rim profile	Rim course	Lip profile	Lip feature	External finish	Internal finish	Rim thickness (mm)	Neck thickness (mm)	Ø (mm)	Decoration
1	1	(001)	1–2		Everted	Parallel	Straight	Flat sharp edge	Absent	Red slip	Red slip	A: 6.8–8.3	?	180	Fingernail impression around exterior of neck
	2	(002)	2												
2	2	(002)	2–3		Everted	Parallel	Straight	Flat round edge	Asym. thick interior	Absent	Absent	A: 4.8–6.2 B: 3.6–5.8	3.5–4.5	210	?
3	2	(002)	2–3		Everted	Conver. gradual	Straight	Flat sharp edge	Absent	Absent	Absent	A: 2.4 B: 4.4	?	?	Diagonal groove incisions around exterior rim and below neck
4	2	(002)	2		Outcurving	Parallel	Convex	Flat sharp edge	Impressed	Absent	Absent	A: 6.6–6.8 B: 5.9–5.9	?	c. 200	Circular impressions around exterior lip

Note: Silhouettes show hypothetical reconstructions of complete vessels based on available data.
Source: Authors' data.

Class 1   **WAI-1-1476**

Class 2   **WAI-1-1437**

Class 3   **WAI-1-1251**

0   5

cm

Class 4   **WAI-1-1438-A/B**

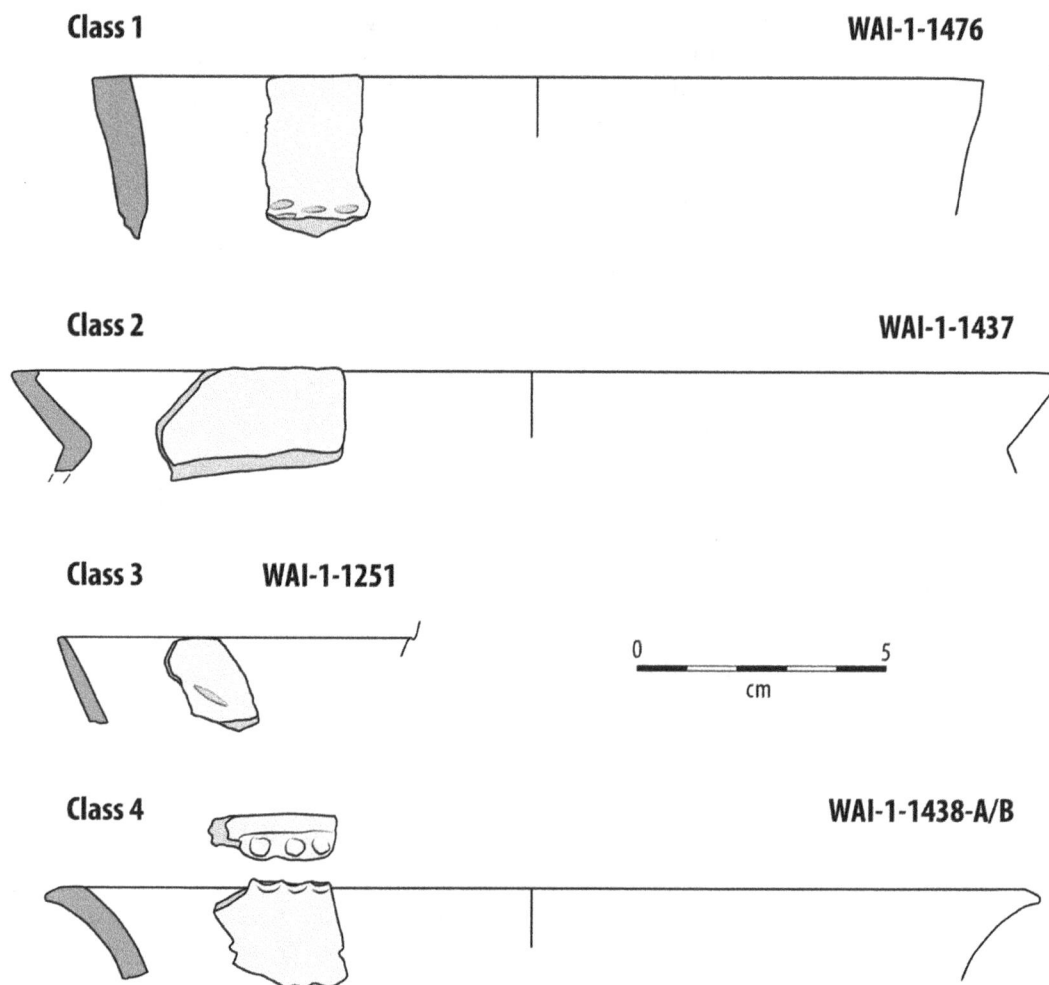

Figure 17.5: Rims from Mololo Cave, Trench 1.

Notes: Class 1 rim (WAI-1-1469) with gash incision from Spit 1, Layer 1 (001); Class 2 rim (WAI-1-1437) from Spit 2, Layer 2 (002); Class 3 rim (WAI-1-1251) with diagonal groove incision on exterior rim from Spit 2, Layer 2 (002); Class 4 rim (WAI-1-1438-A refitted with WAI-1-1438-B) with lip impressions and shoulder carination from Spit 2, Layer 2 (002).

Source: Authors' illustration.

The Class 3 vessel was deposited at a similar time and is represented by four sherds from Layer 2 (002). It may be technologically related to the Class 2 vessel, in that it is a thin-bodied, globular pot with an everted rim. Surface treatment is absent, and it was formed from Fabric C. However, it lacks the asymmetrical thickening at the lip and has a carinated shoulder. The vessel was incised with diagonal grooves around the exterior rim and below the neck. Specimen WAI-1-1687 (Figure 17.6) is made from the same paste (Fabric C) and appears to be a broken coil with parallel grooves produced with a blunt point or a comb, possibly suggesting that Class 3 vessels involved initial coil formation followed by paddling.

The Class 4 vessel is represented by three sherds from Layer 2 (002) and likely dates to about c. 3100–2700 years ago (Figure 17.5). The pot had an outcurving rim with circular impressions around a flat lip made with a blunt point rather than a hollow stamp. The shoulder was carinated and it was formed from Fabric I. One non-slipped appliqué piece was also recovered in Spit 1, Layer 1 (001), produced from Fabric E, but an association with vessel form cannot be determined (see 'appliqué' in Figure 17.7).

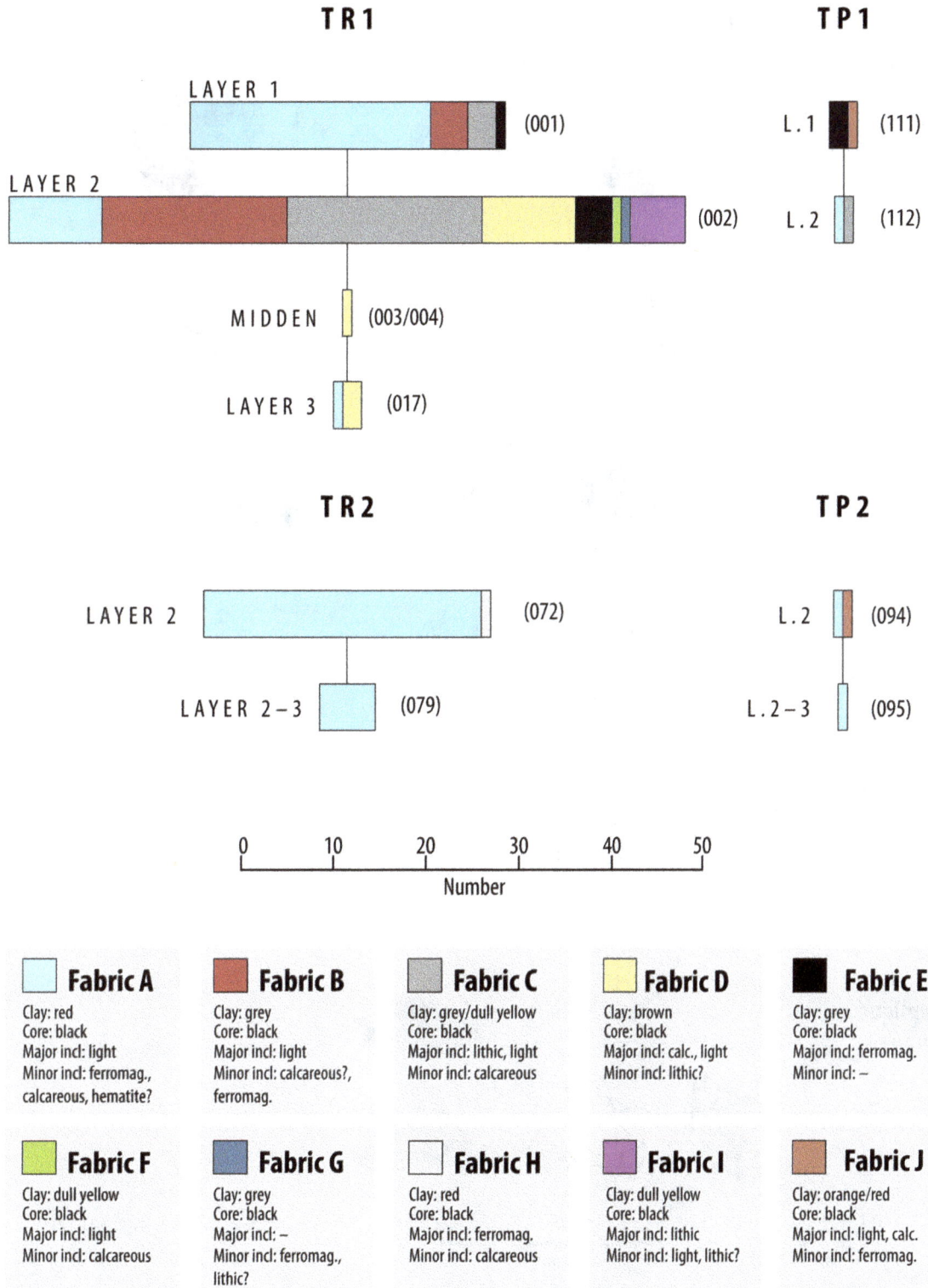

Figure 17.6: Harris matrix showing number of sherds per fabric group in each stratigraphic context at Mololo Cave.

Source: Authors' illustration.

Incision and fingernail incision

WAI-1-1470

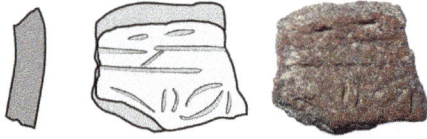

WAI-1-1472

WAI-1-1467

WAI-1-1471

WAI-1-1468-A

WAI-1-1691/1689

WAI-1-1389

Groove incisions

WAI-1-1687

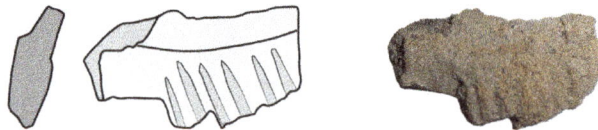

Appliqué
WAI-1-4-B

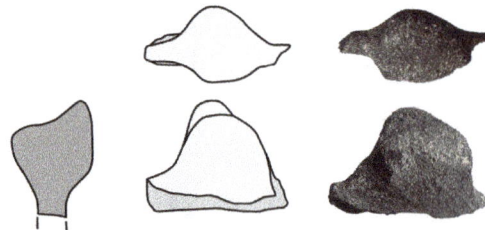

0   5

cm

Figure 17.7: Decorated sherds from Mololo Cave.

Notes: Incised and fingernail-incised body sherds, WAI-1-1470, WAI-1-1472, WAI-1-1467, WAI-1-1471 and WAI-1-1468-A from TR1, Spit 2, Layer 1 (001); WAI-1-1691 refitted with WAI-1-1689 from TR1, Spit 2, Layer 2 (002); WAI-1-1389 from TR1, Spit 1 Layer 1 (001). Groove-incised (comb marked) coil, WAI-1-1687 from TR1, Spit 2, Layer 2 (002). Appliqué fragment from TP1, Spit 1, Layer 1 (111).

Source: Authors' illustration.

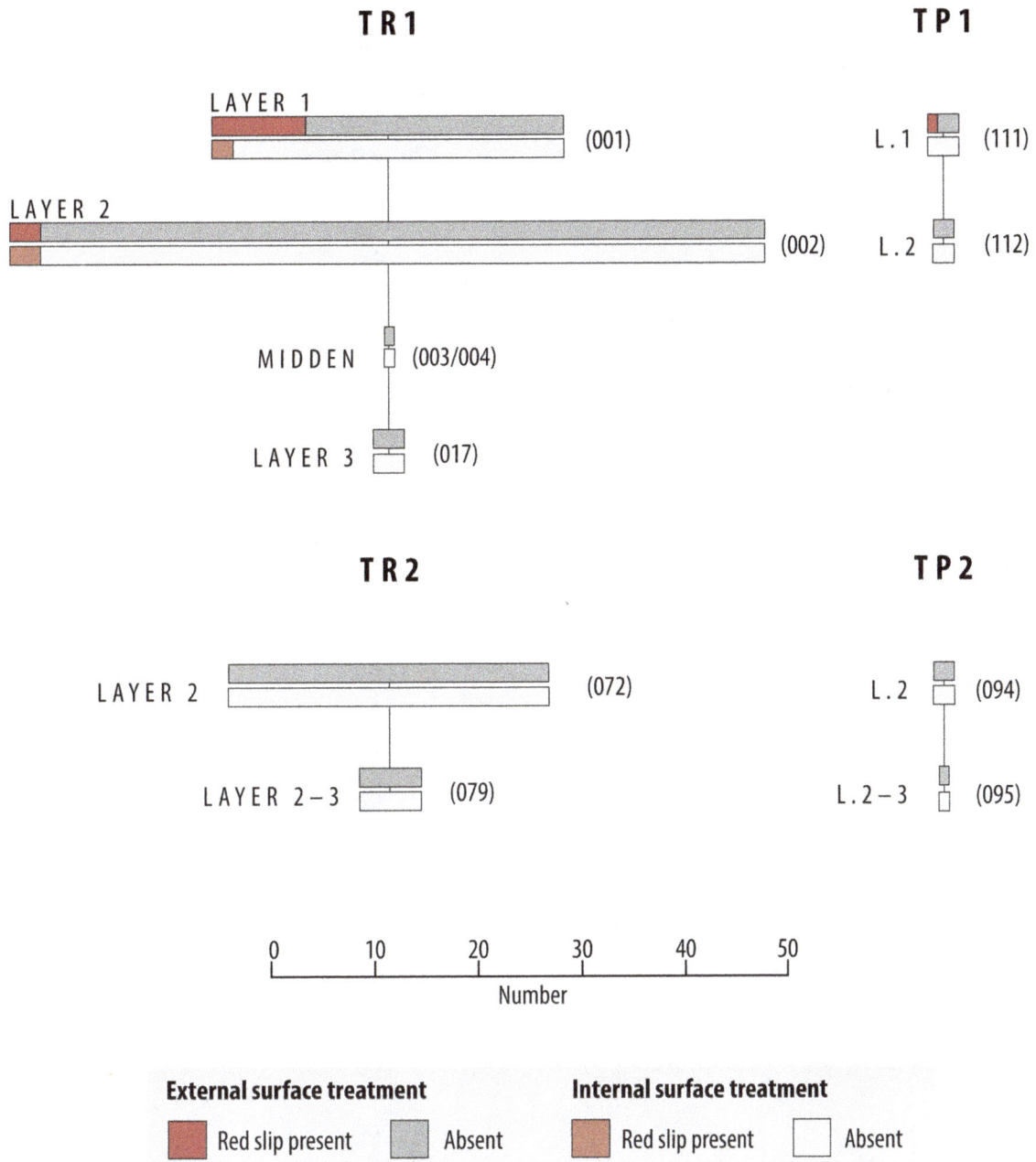

Figure 17.8: Harris matrix showing number of sherds with surface treatment in each stratigraphic context at Mololo Cave.

Source: Authors' illustration.

A small number of sherds retain surface treatment applied following the decorating stage. Red slip is rare, but more common in the most recent contexts at TR1 and TP1 (Figure 17.8), particularly in Layer 1 (001) associated with Class 1 rims and incised body sherds. No plain sherds from the earliest contexts at TR1—midden (003) and Layer 3 (017)—are slipped, and no sherds display slip at TR2 or TP2.

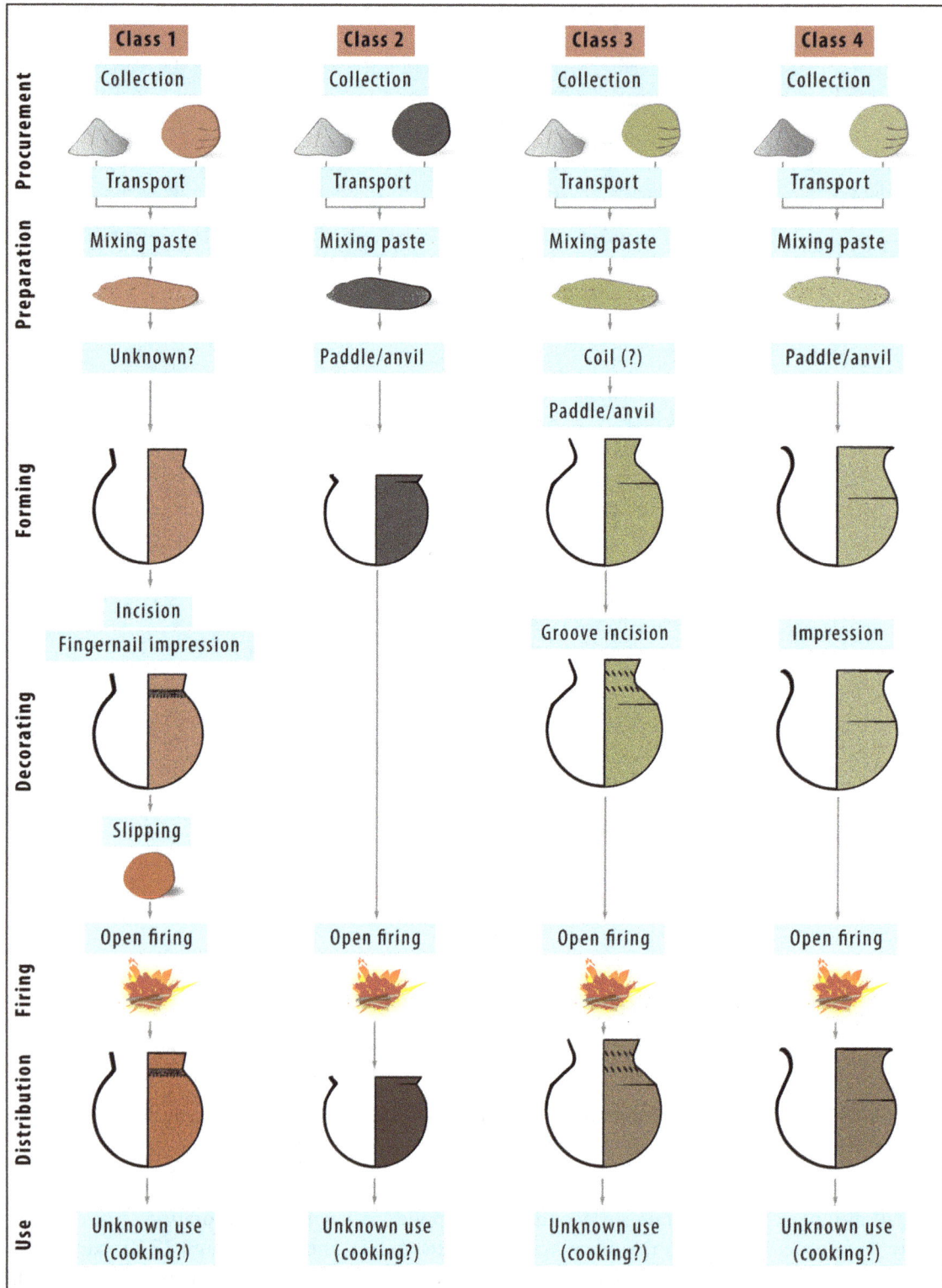

Figure 17.9: Provisional *chaînes opératoires* for four ceramic technical classes at Mololo Cave.

Notes: Several techno-fabric groups and technical variants based on decorating could not be reconstructed owing to small sample sizes. The lack of technological variation within each class almost certainly reflects small sample sizes.

Source: Authors' illustration.

Based on technological analysis, Figure 17.9 presents very provisional *chaînes opératoires* to illustrate how the Mololo pots were produced. It should be noted that owing to very limited sample sizes, representing a small number of vessels, these remain hypotheses that will be revised.

Ceramics at Manwen Bokor, c. 1300–1000 BP

Chronology

In total, 50 pottery sherds were recovered from the Manwen Bokor excavations (Table 17.4). At Unit 1, all ceramics were recovered in Layer 1 (001), in which there is a relatively low density distribution of sherds across Spits 1–14 (each spit contains between one and four sherds). A marine shell date of 1630±25 BP from Spit 11 provides an approximation of c. 1300–1000 years old for these sherds (calibrated with Mololo ΔR). At TP1, only three sherds were recovered, both from the sandy Layer 2 (008) that connects with Unit 1, Layer 1 (001), as well as in Layer 1 (007), which represents more recent sedimentation forming the mud flats. At TP2, pottery was recovered in low numbers in each layer; half of all sherds were excavated in Layer 3 (005), which again links with Unit 1, Layer 1 (001), and dates by association with wood charcoal to 1290±35 BP, c. 1300–1150 years old. At each excavation unit, it remains unclear whether all sherds represent a single depositional event with subsequent redeposition in secondary contexts; the absence of sherds that could be refitted suggests that there has been substantial horizontal displacement. Alternately (or additionally), the sherds might represent an aggregation of ceramic traditions spanning several centuries.

Table 17.4: Number of ceramic fragments from excavated contexts at Manwen Bokor Cave.

Layer	Cont.	Date ka	Rim		Body		Total	
			n	%	*n*	%	*n*	%
Unit 1								
Layer 1	(001)	1.2	10	27.0	27	73.0	37	100.0
Subtotal			**10**	**27.0**	**27**	**73.0**	**37**	**100.0**
TP1								
Layer 1	(007)	–	–	–	2	100.0	2	100.0
Layer 2	(008)	–	–	–	1	100.0	1	100.0
Subtotal			**–**	**–**	**3**	**100.0**	**3**	**100.0**
TP2								
Layer 1	(003)	–	1	50.0	1	50.0	2	100.0
Layer 2	(004)	–	–	–	2	100.0	2	100.0
Layer 3	(005)	1.2	3	60.0	2	40.0	5	100.0
Layer 4	(006)	–	1	100.0	–	–	1	100.0
Subtotal			**5**	**50.0**	**5**	**50.0**	**10**	**100.0**
TOTAL			**15**	**30.0**	**35**	**70.0**	**50**	**100.0**

Note: ka = thousand years ago; *n* = number of fragments; % = percentage of stratigraphic context.

Source: Authors' data.

Ceramic technology

The earthenware rims at Manwen Bokor were classified into five technical classes (Table 17.5; Figure 17.10). Unlike at Mololo Cave, no attempt is made to illustrate reconstructions of vessel form because of a dearth of formal sherds belonging to the same vessel. Long-distance import porcelain and white glazed ceramics (*n* = 5, 10 per cent of total assemblage) were not assigned a classification.

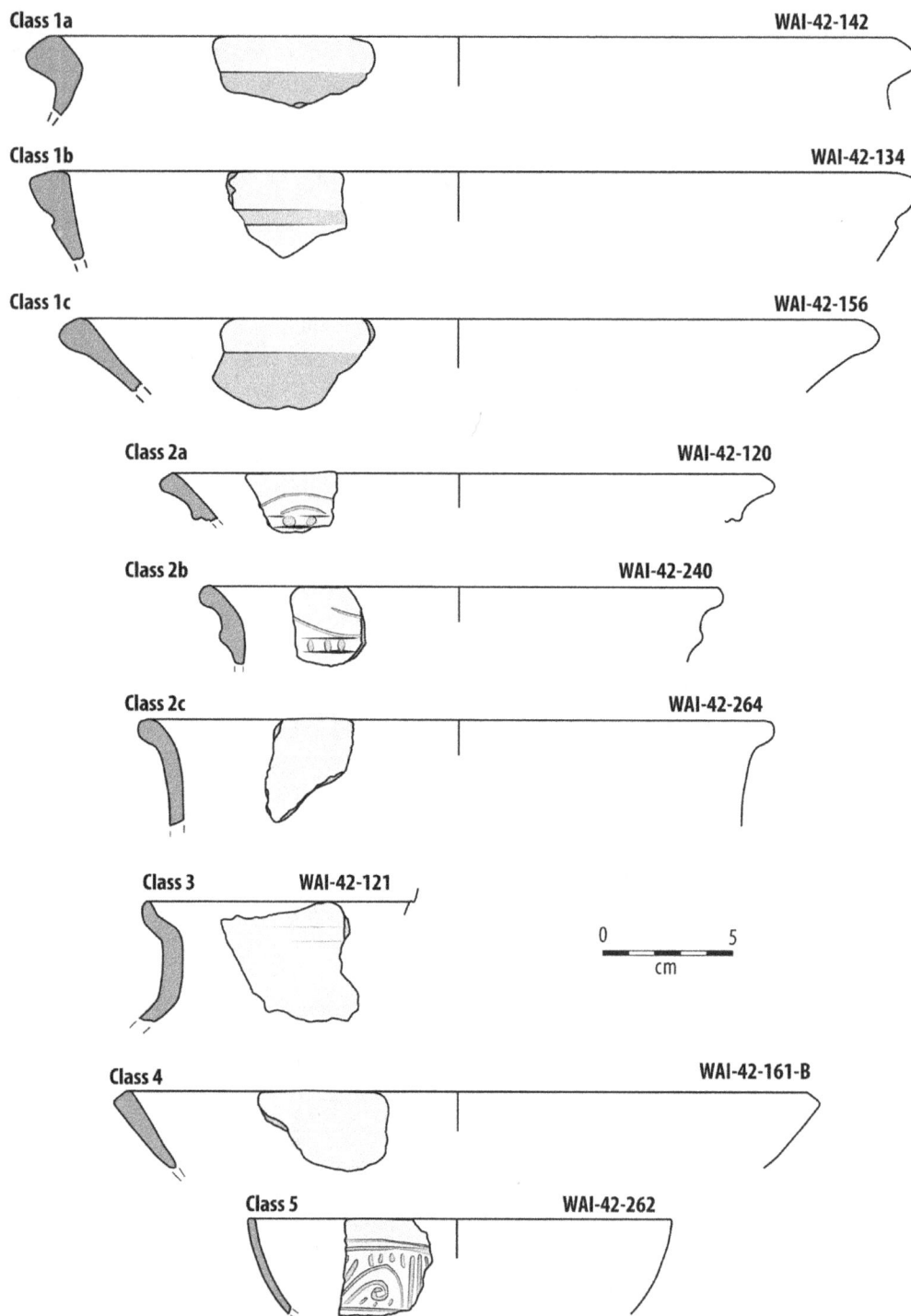

Figure 17.10: Rims from Manwen Bokor.

Notes: Class 1a rim (WAI-42-142) from globular pot, Unit 1, Layer 1 (001), Spit 9; Class 1b rim (WAI-42-134) from bowl or globular pot, Unit 1, Layer 1 (001), Spit 8; Class 1c rim (WAI-42-156) from bowl, globular pot or pedestal in Unit 1, Layer 1 (001), Spit 10; Class 2a rim (WAI-42-120) from Unit 1, Layer 1 (001), Spit 7; Class 2b rim (WAI-42-240) from Unit 1, Layer 1 (001); Class 2c rim (WAI-42-264) from TP2, Layer 3 (005), Spit 5; Class 3 rim (WAI-42-121) from Unit 1, Layer 1 (001), Spit 7; Class 4 rim (WAI-42-161-B) from Unit 1, Layer 1 (001); Class 5 incised rim (WAI-42-262) from TP2, Layer 3 (005), Spit 5.

Source: Authors' illustration.

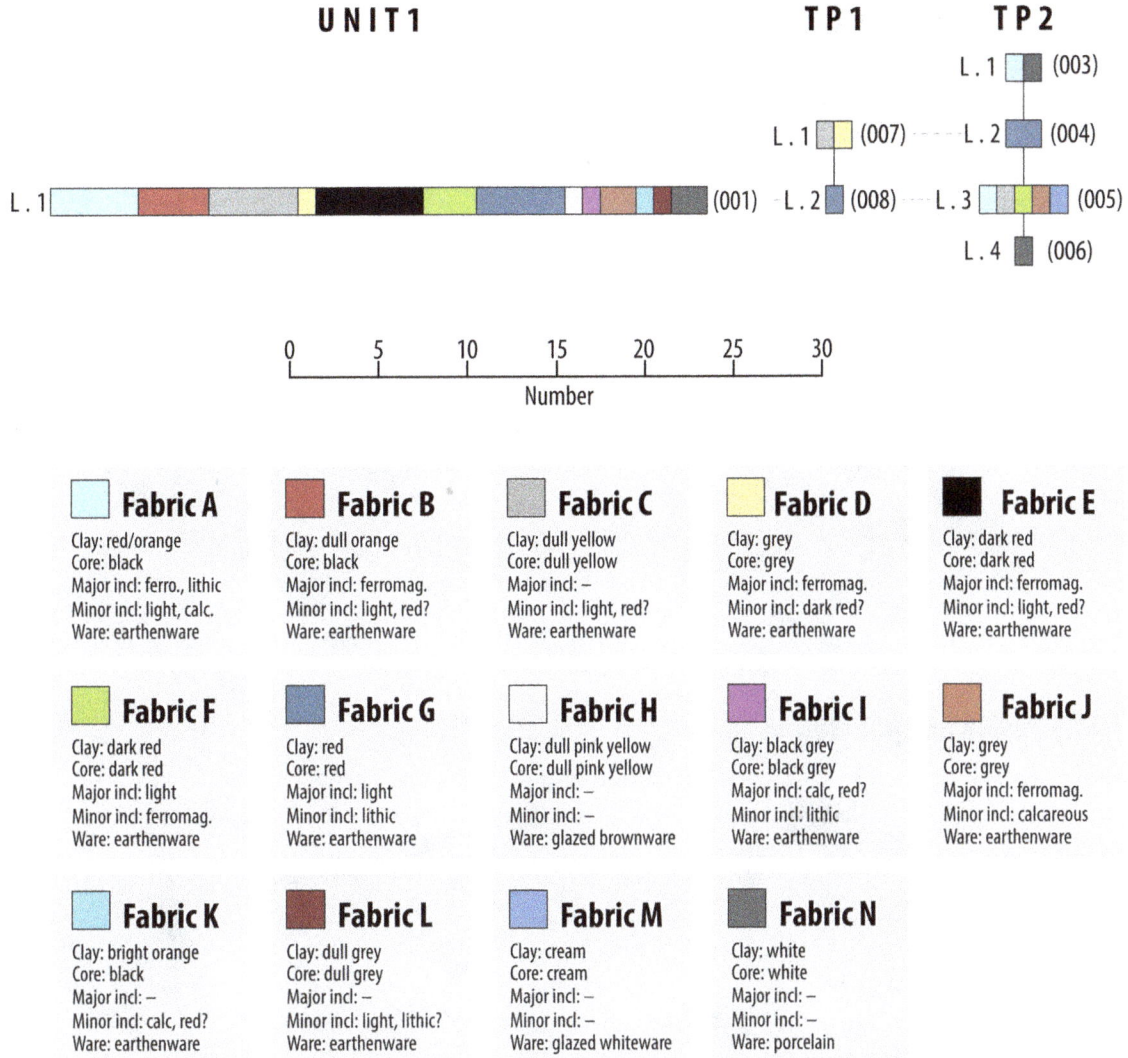

Figure 17.11: Number of sherds per techno-fabric group in each stratigraphic context at Manwen Bokor Cave.

Source: Authors' illustration.

Class 1 rims are thick-rimmed, red-slipped/burnished globular pots with a wide orifice and asymmetrically thickened exterior lips (Figure 17.10). Within Class 1, variant 1a is plain with an everted rim, variant 1b is a collared everted rim with a sub-lip bevel, and variant 1c is a plain direct rim. All Class 1 variants were formed from Fabric G (Figure 17.11). Class 2 rims are thin-walled pots with asymmetrically thickened exterior lips and sub-rim grooves. Within Class 2 rims, variant 2a is a plain direct rim, variant 2b is a curved everted rim with external and internal red slip and 2c is a collared everted rim. On Class 2a–b vessels from Unit 1, Layer 1 (001), a wave was inscribed around the sub-rim groove, coupled with circular impressions around the sub-rim ridge (see Figure 17.12). These variants were produced from Fabric B, while variant 2c was made from a similar paste, Fabric A.

Incision and fingernail incision

WAI-42-166

WAI-42-158

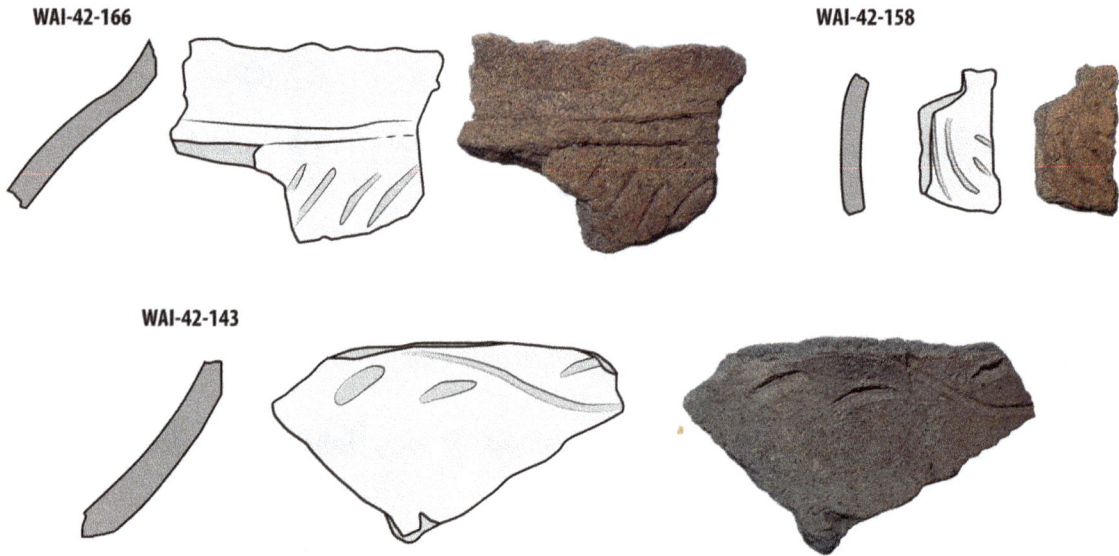

WAI-42-143

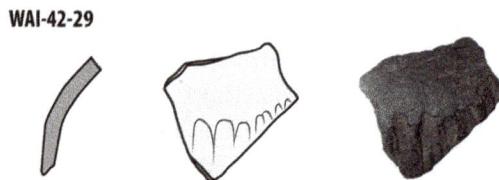

Impression and punctation

WAI-42-102

Incised

Punctation

Impression

WAI-42-155

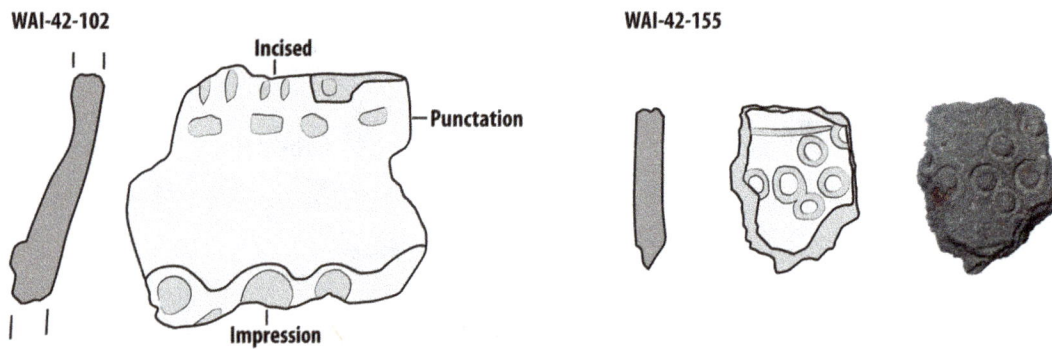

Groove incision

WAI-42-29

0 ————————————— 5
cm

Figure 17.12: Decorated potsherds from Manwen Bokor Cave, Unit 1, Layer 1 (001).

Notes: Incision: WAI-42-166, Spit 11; WAI-42-158, Spit 10; WAI-42-143, Spit 9; impression: WAI-42-102, Spit 6; WAI-42-155, Spit 10; groove incision: WAI-42-29, Spit 8.

Source: Authors' illustration.

Table 17.5: Formal and decorative description of pottery technical classes at Manwen Bokor.

Class	Unit	Lay.	Cont.	Spit	Form	Rim direction	Rim profile	Rim course	Lip profile	Lip feature	External finish	Internal finish	Rim thickness (mm)	Neck thickness (mm)	Ø (mm)	Decoration
1a	1	1	(001)	9	Globular pot	Everted	Divergent gradual	Convex	Flat rounded	Asymmetrically thickened exterior	Red slip, burnish	Red slip, burnish	A: 16.1 B: 10.6	4.9	320	–
1b	1	1	(001)	8	Globular pot or bowl	Direct (or everted)	Divergent abrupt	Straight	Flat rounded	Asymmetrically thickened exterior	Red slip, burnish	Red slip, burnish	A: 15.4 B 10.3	6.3	320	–
1c	1	1	(001)	10	Bowl, pot or pedestal	Direct (or everted)	Divergent gradual	Straight	Flat rounded	Asymmetrically thickened exterior	Red slip, burnish	Red slip, burnish	A: 13.3 B: 9.6	?	300	Impression around exterior lip
2a	1	1	(001)	7	Globular pot or bowl	Direct	Divergent gradual	Straight	Flat rounded	Asymmetrically thickened exterior	Absent	Absent	A: 8.6 B: 6.0	3.4	230	Incision on sub-rim groove and impression on sub-rim ridge
2b	1	1	(001)	–	Globular pot(?)	Outcurving (or everted)	Parallel	Convex	Rounded	Asymmetrically thickened exterior	Red slip	Red slip	A: 7.7 B: 6.6	5.5	200	Incision on sub-rim groove and impression on sub-rim ridge
2c	TP2	3	(005)	5	Globular pot	Outcurving (or everted)	Parallel	Convex	Rounded	Asymmetrically thickened exterior	Red slip	Red slip	A: 8.8 B: 8.1	?	240	–
3	1	1	(001)	7	Globular pot	Everted	Convergent gradual	Concave	Rounded	Absent	Absent	Absent	A: 4.3 B: 6.9	8.4	?	–
4	1	1	(001)	–	Bowl	Direct	Divergent gradual	Concave	Flat sharp edge	Absent	Absent	Absent	A: 8.5 B: 6.1	?	260	–
5	TP2	3	(005)	5	Bowl or pedestal	Incurving	Parallel	Concave	Flat sharp edge	Absent	Absent	Absent	A: 3.7 B: 3.0	?	160	Incision on body

Note: All rims derive from the black sand layer at the site: Unit 1, Layer 1 (001) and Test Pit 2, Layer 3 (005).
Source: Authors' data.

The Class 3 sherd has a long, collared neck and internally concave rim, and was formed from Fabric K. The Class 4 rim is direct and gradually divergent with a flat lip that may derive from a bowl or everted rim. This rim was assigned to Fabric L. The Class 5 rim has parallel sides and an internally concave rim course, indicating it derives from a small bowl. An intricate motif was incised with spirals and horizontal lines within the borders of linear incisions on the body (see Figure 17.10). This vessel was produced from Fabric J, which is also associated with a body sherd decorated with wavy linear incisions flanked by possible fingernail incisions (see WAI-42-143 in Figure 17.12).

Incised body sherds from Unit 1, Layer 1 (001), included one specimen with rows of diagonal incisions flanking linear incisions (see WAI-42-166 in Figure 17.12). The sherd was made from Fabric A and these decorations may therefore be associated with Class 2c vessels. Another sherd (WAI-42-29), possibly slipped or burnished on the interior and exterior, was marked with groove incisions in a similar manner to those at Mololo, possibly using a comb or blunt wooden tool. Finally, a single small body sherd (WAI-42-155) was marked with groups of circle stamps, probably made with bamboo or truncated long bone. This sherd was excavated in Unit 1, Layer 1 (001), Spit 10, one spit above the marine shell date of c. 1300–1000 years ago.

Discussion

Early ceramics: Connections with the Island Southeast Asian Neolithic and Lapita

The presence of ceramics at Mololo Cave from, perhaps, 3800–3500 years ago and, more abundantly, 3100–2700 years ago represents the earliest known movement of pottery makers into the West Papua area. Although it remains unclear whether these ceramics were made locally around the Raja Ampat archipelago, the technological analysis gleaned meaningful insights about the production of the Mololo pots. For instance, the presence of calcareous tempers in the earliest Mololo sherds may suggest that pottery produced before 3000 years ago was made around limestone zones or on offshore coral islands, whereas later ceramics with light (feldspathic and quartz) and ferromagnesian grains could derive from sedimentary and volcanic zones on mainland Waigeo or other large islands. Similarly, most early sherds at Uattamdi 1 and Leang Tuwo Mane'e were coral tempered (Bellwood 2019; Tanudirjo 2001:207). Geochemical and petrographic analyses, now underway, will provide further detail.

In terms of morphological comparisons, the plainware from Mololo overlaps with rim forms recorded at Island Southeast Asian and Lapita sites (Figure 17.13). In particular, the Class 4 vessel discarded at Mololo c. 3100–2700 years ago is very similar to Bellwood's (2019) 'inflected rim v' from Uattamdi on Koyoa Island; globular pots with an outcurving or flaring rim that have a generally 'Lapitoid' appearance (e.g. Gaffney et al. 2019; Kirch 2021:341; Summerhayes 2000:117). This vessel form is also similar to sherds from a surface collection made at Kapidiri hill (WAI-38) on the north coast of Waigeo, suggesting that the use of pottery by coastal groups was not restricted to Mayalibit Bay.

Molol - Class 4

Kapidiri Hill - Surface finds

Uattamdi 1 - Inflected Rim V

Talepakemalai - Class IIA

Apalo - Vessel Form V

0 _____ 5
cm

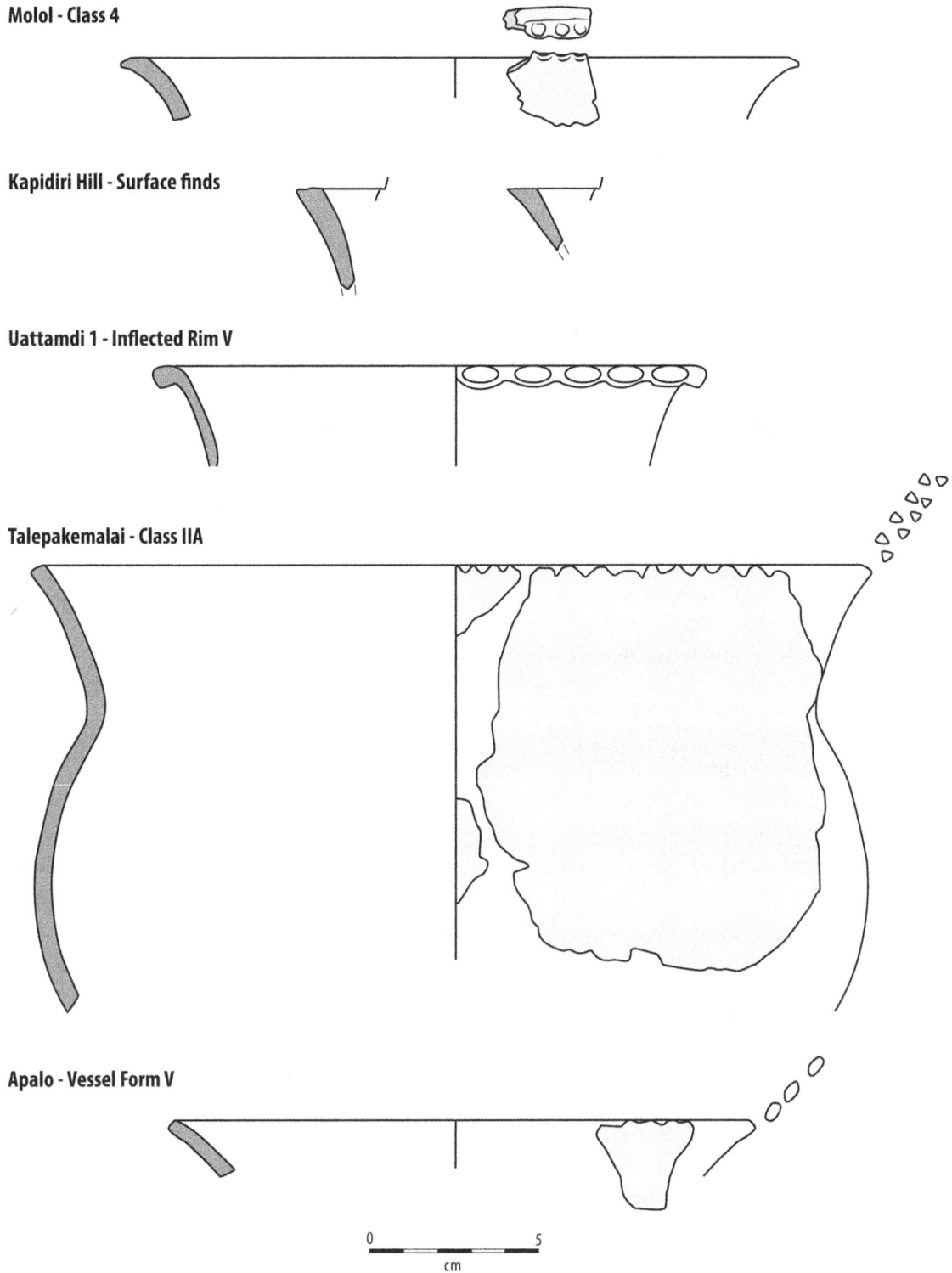

Figure 17.13: Rim form comparisons.

Notes: Class 4 rims at Mololo Cave, dating c. 3100–2700 years ago, in comparison with surface finds at Kapidiri hill, north Waigeo, and inflected rims from Uattamdi (Northern Maluku Is.), Talepakemalai (St Matthias Is.), and Apalo (Arawe Is.).

Sources: Redrawn from Bellwood (2019); Gaffney (2021); Kirch (2021:335); Summerhayes (2000:117).

When these Raja Ampat ceramics are considered alongside similar evidence from northern Maluku (Bellwood 2019), it seems likely that Lapita emerged from various influences in eastern Wallacea, New Guinea and possibly Micronesia, before becoming intertwined with extant communities in the Bismarck Archipelago. However, the sherds recovered from cave sites like Mololo may not represent large-scale settlements or ceramic production centres, and could have been occupied by non-pottery makers who obtained plain ceramics via trade (the same may not be true for Uattamdi, where larger numbers of ceramics have been recorded, see Ono 2022; Ono et al. 2021). Moreover, the earliest ceramics from these sites are contemporary with, but not earlier than, Early Lapita ceramics. As such, it is possible that open sites in the Raja Ampat Islands will provide more substantive evidence for a 'Far, Far Western Lapita' enclave occupied prior to 3350 years ago by people speaking Proto East Malayo-Polynesian (EMP) or dialects of Malayo-Polynesian that later evolved into the EMP languages upon contact with Papuan languages in the area. Future field excavations in the Raja Ampat and Cenderawasih Bay area will resolve this.

Changes to pottery making: Network contraction and regionalisation

Class 1 rims at Mololo are identical to Bellwood's (2019) red-slipped 'long rims' from Uattamdi Layer C. There is a large error range in the associated date (ANU-7775) that places the Uattamdi rims sometime between c. 3150 and 2300 years old, which corresponds with the date from Mololo. However, incised decorations associated with Class 1 rims are identical to 'inverted comma' designs described on pedestal bowls, lids and asymmetrically thick-rimmed pots at Aru Manara and Tanjong Pinang on Morotai Island dating to c. 2100–1900 years ago (Bellwood 2019; Ono, Aziz et al. 2018; Ono, Oktaviana et al. 2018), and carinated pots at Buwawansi 3 and 5 on Gebe Island (Bellwood 2019). If the incised motifs at Mololo are associated with the early Metal Age decorative complex in Maluku, then it implies the same decorations and associated Class 1 rims at Mololo are in situ in Layer 1 (001) and therefore date to c. 2300–2150 years ago. The appliqué piece recovered in Layer 1 (001) is also similar to moulded decorations on Metal Age ceramics from Maluku (Bellwood 2019; Ono, Oktaviana et al. 2018), and from Yenbekaki hill fort on Batanta (Galis and Kamma 1958).

The third millennium BP ceramics from Mololo are distinct from sherds recovered at Manwen Bokor, which date to 1300–1000 years ago and possibly thereafter. The Manwen Bokor ceramics show few similarities with contemporaneous potting traditions in the Bismarck Archipelago (e.g. Cath-Garling 2017; Spriggs 1991) and central Indonesia (e.g. Hasanuddin 2018; Plutniak et al. 2016). However, they do show similarities, of a more restricted range, with pottery to the east and the west. Class 1c and Class 4 rims are similar, but not identical, to bowls from Mare Island in North Maluku (Mahirta 2000). Class 3 rims resemble water pots from Ambon in Central Maluku (see Pétrequin and Pétrequin 2006:370). Many of the incised linear decorations on the Manwen Bokor sherds are common motifs around the north coast of New Guinea (e.g. Terrell and Schechter 2011), and Class 1a–b rims with sub-rim ridges and impressions are similarly characteristic of forming techniques found along the north coast of New Guinea (Gaffney 2020:214; Terrell and Schechter 2011), and resemble sherds recorded at Kaibatu near Jayapura (see Pétrequin and Pétrequin 2006:416). Notably, there is no evidence for the import of painted pots of the Banda, Kei and Aru Islands (e.g. Ellen 2019; Veth et al. 2005).

This process of regionalisation, or glocalisation, has been previously proposed by Tanudirjo (2006) for Island Southeast Asia and Allen (1985) for New Guinea. The presence of porcelain and glazed whiteware alongside earthenware at Manwen Bokor indicates that trade links (probably indirect) between mainland East Asia and the Pacific had been established about 1300–1000 years ago or slightly later. Therefore, although technological connections in earthenware pottery making were compressed during the Metal Age, trade connections with new exotic pottery centres expanded. The exception to this trend is circle stamping, like on sherd WAI-42-155. This decorative method is widespread in the late Neolithic and early Metal Age of Island Southeast Asia. For instance, stamping occurs on ceramics from nearby Morotai Island dating to c. 2100–1900 years ago (Ono, Aziz et al. 2018) and the Banda Islands dating to c. 2700–2350 years ago (Lape et al. 2018), and further afield in the Batanes (Bellwood et al. 2013), Sulawesi (Mulvaney and Soejono 1972) and on Taiwan (Tsang 2000) particularly common around 2500 years ago. Stamping is present but less common in Late Lapita and Post-Lapita traditions (Cath-Garling 2017; Wu 2016). We suggest that these similarities result from a diffusion of design elements across a sphere of culture inherited from earlier pottery makers, rather than the mobility of potters themselves.

Conclusion

There is yet to be evidence for a cohesive Lapita occupation in the Raja Ampat Islands prior to its emergence in the Bismarck Archipelago. It is plausible that such evidence remains to be excavated at open sites around Raja Ampat and Cenderawasih Bay, or, alternatively, that Lapita developed in the Bismarck Archipelago from different strands of influence, some of which came from Raja Ampat. The Mololo Cave ceramics that date to 3100–2700 years ago (possibly even 3800–3500 years ago) show that the earliest known Raja Ampat ceramics are technologically related with contemporaneous pottery in Island Southeast Asia and the Bismarck Archipelago. However, the nature of these relationships needs to be clarified. Were the Early Lapita potters of the Bismarck Archipelago in direct contact with those around West Papua? Does Early Lapita pottery represent a daughter tradition, or offshoot, from parts of West Papua? Conversely, did Early Lapita potters emerge in the Bismarcks to become important ceramic producers that then influenced potters in West Papua?

Figure 17.14: Circle stamp traditions from Island Southeast Asian late Neolithic and early Metal Age ceramics, alongside Lapita pottery.

Notes: (A) Ying Pu, Taiwan, c. 2500 BP; (B) Sunget, Batanes, c. 2500 BP; (C) Malawa, South Sulawesi; (D) Pulau Ay, Banda Islands; (E) Manwen Bokor, Waigeo, c. 1200 BP; (F) Lapita pottery.

Source: Authors' photographs.

The Manwen Bokor ceramics date to about 1300–1000 years ago and are distinct from those at Mololo. Decorative similarities with pottery from North Maluku and north New Guinea suggest a geographical contraction of the networks that potters operated within. Some instances of widespread decorations like circle stamping are suggestive of descent from common Neolithic and Lapita potters (Figure 17.14).

This process of regionalisation went hand-in-hand with a process of globalisation as Raja Ampat became connected, indirectly, with ceramic exporters in mainland East Asia. Lingering questions remain, however, about exactly when Southeast Asia – Bismarck connections began to fragment and how the mobility patterns of pottery makers changed accordingly. Asking these questions is just the first step; as Glenn Summerhayes' career has shown, it is only through years of survey, excavation, laboratory studies—and a bit of hard yakka—that we will come closer to resolving them.

Acknowledgements

We hope this article pays homage to Glenn Summerhayes' long career studying the ceramics of the Indo-Pacific; from his cutting-edge master's research on Javanese pottery to his later work pushing the boundaries of ceramic analysis in Papua New Guinea. Dylan Gaffney wishes to thank Glenn for 10 years of supervision, guidance and friendship. He is fortunate to have been taught ceramic analysis by Glenn during his MA at Otago, and remembers their fieldwork in Madang, Simbai and Karkar fondly. Daud Tanudirjo thanks Glenn for introducing to him a former student, Dylan, which led to the collaborative research project in Raja Ampat being set up. At The Australian National University, Daud often sought Glenn's advice about analysing and interpreting pottery collections from eastern Indonesia, and is grateful for their discussions about his PhD thesis. Glenn also provided his early writing on Javanese pottery which became a key resource, and his Lapita articles have become important touchstones for studying the archaeology of Indonesia.

We thank the people of Warsambin and Asokweri for their support during excavations. In particular, we thank the Mambrasar family at Warsambin and the Rumbarak family at Asokweri for their hospitality. Excavators on the Raja Ampat Archaeological Project included Erlin Novita Idje Djami, Abdul Razak Matcap, Tristan Russell and Yulio Ray. We also thank Moses Dailom Melkion Amberbaken, Olos, Nathanial, Otniel, Otto, Robert, Isak, Demianus, Demersis, Septinus, Peter, Yan, Fernandes and Paul for their assistance at Mololo and Moses, Yansen, Alex and Daud for their assistance at Manwen Bokor. We thank Simson Wanma and Ababnar, custom leaders at Asokweri, for making the Manwen Bokor area safe during our research.

The field research was carried out as part of the Raja Ampat Archaeological Project, funded collectively by a National Geographic Explorer Grant, an Evans Fund Fellowship, the Royal Anthropological Institute Horniman and Sutasoma Awards, the University of Cambridge School of the Humanities and Social Sciences Research Grant, the Magdalene College Anthropology and Archaeology Fund, and the Leakey Foundation Research Grant. The project was carried out under Indonesian research permit 359/SIP/FRP/E5/Dit.KI/X/2018. Dylan Gaffney was supported by Gates Cambridge. Radiocarbon dating was supported by Natural Environment Research Council Radiocarbon Facility (NRCF) and Australian Nuclear Science and Technology Organisation (ANSTO) grants.

References

Allen, J. 1985. Comments on complexity and trade: A view from Melanesia. *Archaeology in Oceania* 20(2): 49–56. doi.org/10.1002/j.1834-4453.1985.tb00102.x.

Anggraeni, T. Simanjuntak, P. Bellwood and P. Piper 2014. Neolithic foundations in the Karama valley, West Sulawesi, Indonesia. *Antiquity* 88(341):740–756. doi.org/10.1017/s0003598x00050663.

Arnold, L. 2020. Four undocumented languages of Raja Ampat, West Papua, Indonesia. *Language Documentation and Description* 17:25–43. doi.org/10.25894/ldd95.

Azis, N., C. Reepmeyer, G. Clark and D.A. Tanudirjo 2018. Mansiri in North Sulawesi: A new dentate-stamped pottery site in Island Southeast Asia. In S. O'Connor, D. Bulbeck and J. Meyer (eds), *The archaeology of Sulawesi: Current research on the Pleistocene to the Historic period*, pp. 191–205. ANU Press, Canberra. doi.org/10.22459/ta48.11.2018.12.

Bellwood, P. 1976. Archaeological research in Minahasa and the Talaud Islands, northeastern Indonesia. *Asian Perspectives* 19(2):240–288. www.jstor.org/stable/42927924.

Bellwood, P. 1998. From Bird's Head to bird's eye view: Long term structure and trends in Indo-Pacific prehistory. In J. Miedema, C. Odé and R.A.C. Dam (eds), *Perspectives on the Bird's Head of Irian Jaya, Indonesia: Proceedings of the Conference*, pp. 951–975. Rodopi, Leiden. doi.org/10.1163/9789004652644 _044.

Bellwood, P. 2019. The earthenware pottery from the North Moluccan excavations. In P. Bellwood (ed.), *The Spice Islands in prehistory: Archaeology in the Northern Moluccas, Indonesia*, pp. 81–106. ANU Press, Canberra. doi.org/10.22459/ta50.2019.07.

Bellwood, P. and P. Koon 1989. 'Lapita colonists leave boats unburned!' The question of Lapita links with Island Southeast Asia. *Antiquity* 63(240):613–622. doi.org/10.1017/s0003598x00076572.

Bellwood, P., E. Dizon and A. De Leon 2013. The Batanes pottery sequence, 2500 BC to recent. In P. Bellwood and E. Dizon (eds), *The 4000 years of migration and cultural exchange: The archaeology of the Batanes Islands, Northern Philippines*, pp. 77–113. ANU Press, Canberra. doi.org/10.22459/ta40.12. 2013.06.

Bentley, R.A., H.R. Buckley, M. Spriggs, S. Bedford, C.J. Ottley, G.M. Nowell, C.G. Macpherson and D.G. Pearson 2007. Lapita migrants in the Pacific's oldest cemetery: Isotopic analysis at Teouma, Vanuatu. *American Antiquity* 72(4):645–656. doi.org/10.2307/25470438.

Bulbeck, D. 2019. Bioarchaeological analysis of the Northern Moluccan excavated human remains. In P. Bellwood (ed.), *The Spice Islands in prehistory: Archaeology in the Northern Moluccas, Indonesia*, pp. 167–200. ANU Press, Canberra. doi.org/10.22459/ta50.2019.11.

Carson, M.T. 2014. *First settlement of Remote Oceania: Earliest sites in the Mariana Islands*. Springer, New York. doi.org/10.1007/978-3-319-01047-2.

Carson, M.T. 2020. Peopling of Oceania: Clarifying an initial settlement horizon in the Mariana Islands at 1500 BC. *Radiocarbon* 62(6):1733–1754. doi.org/10.1017/rdc.2020.89.

Carson, M.T. and H.C. Hung 2017. *Substantive evidence of initial habitation in the remote Pacific: Archaeological discoveries at Unai Bapot in Saipan, Mariana Islands*. Archaeopress, Oxford. www.jstor.org/stable/j.ctv1 zcm0fj.

Carson, M.T., H.-C. Hung, G. Summerhayes and P. Bellwood 2013. The pottery trail from Southeast Asia to Remote Oceania. *Journal of Island and Coastal Archaeology* 8(1):17–36. doi.org/10.1080/15564894.2012. 726941.

Cath-Garling, S. 2017. *Evolutions or revolutions? Interaction and transformation at the 'Transition' in Island Melanesia.* Department of Anthropology and Archaeology, University of Otago, Dunedin.

Chia, S. 2016. *Arkeologi Bukit Tengkorak.* Penerbit Universiti Sains Malaysia, Penang.

Chiu, S. and C. Sand 2005. Recording of the Lapita motifs: Proposal for a complete recording method. *Archaeology in New Zealand* 48(2):133–150.

Corbey, R. 2019. *Korwar: Northwest New Guinea ritual art according to missionary sources.* C. Zwartenkot Art Books, Leiden.

Dickinson, W.R. 2003. Impact of mid-Holocene hydro-isostatic highstand in regional sea level on habitability of islands in Pacific Oceania. *Journal of Coastal Research* 19(3):489–502. www.jstor.org/stable/4299192.

Ellen, R. 2019. Pottery production and trade in the Banda zone, Indonesia. *Indonesia and the Malay World* 47(138):133–159. doi.org/10.1080/13639811.2019.1582862.

Gaffney, D. 2020. *Materialising ancestral Madang: Pottery production and subsistence trading on the Northeast Coast of New Guinea.* University of Otago, Dunedin.

Gaffney, D. 2021. Human behavioural dynamics in Island rainforests: Evidence from the Raja Ampat Islands, West Papua. Unpublished PhD thesis, University of Cambridge, Cambridge.

Gaffney, D. and D. Tanudirjo 2019. Sago oven pottery production in the Raja Ampat Islands of the far western Pacific. *Journal of Pacific Archaeology* 10(2):63–72.

Gaffney, D., G.R. Summerhayes, A. Ford, J.M. Scott, T. Denham, J. Field and W.R. Dickinson 2015. Earliest pottery on New Guinea mainland reveals Austronesian influences in highland environments 3000 years ago. *PLoS ONE* 10(9):e0134497. doi.org/10.1371/journal.pone.0134497.

Gaffney, D., G.R. Summerhayes, M. Mennis, T. Beni, A. Cook, J. Field, G. Jacobsen, F. Allen, H. Buckley and H. Mandui 2018. Archaeological investigations into the origins of Bel trading groups around the Madang Coast, Northeast New Guinea. *Journal of Island and Coastal Archaeology* 13(4):501–530. doi.org/10.1080/ 15564894.2017.1315349.

Gaffney, D., G.R. Summerhayes and M. Mennis 2019. A Lapita presence on Arop/Long Island, Vitiaz Strait, Papua New Guinea? In S. Bedford and M. Spriggs (eds), *Debating Lapita: Distribution, chronology, society and subsistence*, pp. 115–133. ANU Press, Canberra. doi.org/10.22459/ta52.2019.06.

Galis, K.W. and F.C. Kamma 1958. Het fort te Jémbakaki. *Nieuw-Guinea Studien* 2:206–222.

Golitko, M. 2011. Provenience investigations of ceramic and obsidian samples using laser ablation inductively coupled plasma mass spectrometry and portable X-ray fluorescence. *Fieldiana Anthropology* 42:251–287. doi.org/10.3158/0071-4739-42.1.251.

Harlow, G.E., G.R. Summerhayes, H.L. Davies and L. Matisoo-Smith 2012. Jade gouge from Emirau Island, Papua New Guinea (Early Lapita context, 3300 BP): A unique jadeitite. *European Journal of Mineralogy* 24(2):391–399. doi.org/10.1127/0935-1221/2012/0024-2175.

Hasanuddin. 2018. Prehistoric sites in Kabupaten Enrekang, South Sulawesi. In S. O'Connor, D. Bulbeck and J. Meyer (eds), *The archaeology of Sulawesi: Current research on the Pleistocene to the Historic period*, pp. 171–189. ANU Press, Canberra. doi.org/10.22459/ta48.11.2018.11.

Hung, H. 2005. Neolithic interaction between Taiwan and northern Luzon: The pottery and Jade evidences from the Cagayan Valley. *Journal of Austronesian Studies* 1(1):109–133.

Hung, H.C. 2008. Migration and cultural interaction in Southern Coastal China, Taiwan and the Northern Philippines, 3000 BC to AD 1. Unpublished PhD thesis, The Australian National University, Canberra.

Hung, H., M.T. Carson, P. Bellwood, F.Z. Campos, P.J. Piper, E. Dizon, M.J.L.A. Bolunia, M. Oxenham and Z. Chi 2011. The first settlement of Remote Oceania: The Philippines to the Marianas. *Antiquity* 85(329): 909–926. doi.org/10.1017/s0003598x00068393.

Jordan, F.M., R.D. Gray, S.J. Greenhill and R. Mace 2009. Matrilocal residence is ancestral in Austronesian societies. *Proceedings of the Royal Society B: Biological Sciences* 276(1664):1957–1964. doi.org/10.1098/rspb.2009.0088.

Kamholz, D.C. 2014. Austronesians in Papua: Diversification and change in South Halmahera–West New Guinea. Unpublished PhD thesis, University of California, Berkeley.

Kirch, P.V. 1997. *The Lapita peoples.* Blackwell, Oxford.

Kirch, P.V. (ed.) 2021. *Talepakemalai: Lapita and its transformations in the Mussau Islands of Near Oceania.* Cotsen Institute of Archaeology Press, Los Angeles. doi.org/10.2307/j.ctv27tctrd.

Kirch, P.V, S. Chiu and Y. Su 2015. Lapita ceramic vessel forms of the Talepakemalai site, Mussau Islands, Papua New Guinea. In C. Sand, S. Chiu and N. Hogg (eds), *The Lapita Cultural Context in time and space: Expansion routes, chronologies, and typologies,* pp. 49–61. Archeologia Pacifika 4, Instiut d'archeologie de la Nouvelle-Calédonie et du Pacifique, Nouméa.

Lape, P., E. Peterson, D. Tanudirjo, C.C. Shiung, G.A. Lee, J. Field and A. Coster 2018. New data from an open Neolithic site in Eastern Indonesia. *Asian Perspectives* 57(2):222–243. doi.org/10.1353/asi.2018.0015.

Mahirta. 2000. The development of the Mare pottery tradition in the northern Moluccas. *Bulletin of the Indo-Pacific Prehistory Association* 20:124–132.

Miller, C.F. 1950. Pottery types from kitchen middens of Dutch New Guinea. In E.K. Reed and D.S. King (eds), *For the dean: Essays in anthropology in honor of Byron Cummings on his eighty-ninth birthday,* pp. 277–289. Hohokam Museums Association, Tucson AZ.

Mulvaney, D. and R. Soejono 1972. The Australian–Indonesian archaeological expedition to Sulawesi. *Asian Perspectives* 13:163–177. www.jstor.org/stable/42929097.

Northwood, L. 2015. Pots on the inland shore: Investigating the nature of Austronesian interaction in the Sepik-Ramu Basin, Papua New Guinea. Unpublished BA Hons thesis, University of Otago, Dunedin.

Oliveira, S., K. Nägele, S. Carlhoff, I. Pugach, T. Koesbardiati, A. Hübner, M. Meyer, A.A. Oktaviana, M. Takenaka, C. Katagiri, D.B. Murti, R.S. Putri, Mahirta, T. Higham, C. Higham, S. O'Connor, S. Hawkins, R. Kinaston, P. Bellwood, R. Ono, A. Powell, J. Krause, C. Posth and M. Stoneking 2022. Ancient genomes from the last three millennia support multiple human dispersals into Wallacea. *Nature: Ecology and Evolution* 6:1024–1034. doi.org/10.1038/s41559-022-01775-2.

Ono R. 2022. Early Austronesian migration and pottery culture during the Neolithic times in northern Maluku: a view from Uattamdi assemblages. In T. Simanjuntak, R. Handini and M. Ririmasse (eds), *Membumikan Arkeologi: Tribute untuk Kepala Pusat Penelitian Arkeologi Nasional Dr. I Made Geria,* pp. 89-107. Pusat Penelitian Arkeologi Nasional and Yayasan Pustaka Obor Indonesia, Jakarta.

Ono, R., F. Aziz, A.A. Oktaviana, D. Prastiningtyas, M. Ririmasse, N. Iriyanto, I. Zesse, Y. Hisa and M. Yoneda 2018. Development of regional maritime networks during the Early Metal Age in Northern Maluku Islands: A view from excavated glass ornaments and pottery variation. *Journal of Island and Coastal Archaeology* 13(1):90–108. doi.org/10.1080/15564894.2017.1395374.

Ono, R., H. Octavianus Sofian, N. Aziz, Sriwigati, A.A. Oktaviana, N. Alamsyah and M. Yoneda 2019. Traces of early Austronesian expansion to east Indonesia? New discovery of dentate-stamped and lime-infilled pottery from Central Sulawesi. *The Journal of Island and Coastal Archaeology* 14(1):123–129. doi.org/10.1080/15564894.2018.1481897.

Ono, R., A.A. Oktaviana, M. Ririmasse, M. Takenaka, C. Katagiri and M. Yoneda 2018. Early Metal Age interactions in Island Southeast Asia and Oceania: Jar burials from Aru Manara, northern Moluccas. *Antiquity* 92(364):1023–1039. doi.org/10.15184/aqy.2018.113.

Ono, R., H.O. Sofian, A.A. Oktaviana, S. Wigati and N. Aziz 2021. Human migration and maritime networks in Northern Wallacea during Neolithic to Early Metal ages. In M.F. Napolitano, J.H. Stone and R.J. DiNapoli (eds), *The archaeology of island colonization*, pp. 293–326. University Press of Florida, Gainesville. doi.org/10.2307/j.ctv1m9x2s3.16.

Pasveer, J.M. 2004. *The Djief hunters: 26,000 years of rainforest exploitation on the Bird's Head of Papua, Indonesia*. A.A. Balkema, Leiden. doi.org/10.1201/b17006.

Pawley, A. and M. Ross 1993. Austronesian historical linguistics and culture history. *Annual Review of Anthropology* 22:425–549. doi.org/10.1146/annurev.an.22.100193.002233.

Petchey, F. and G. Clark 2021. Clarifying the age of initial settlement horizon in the Mariana Islands and the impact of hard water: A response to Carson (2020). *Radiocarbon* 63(3):905–913. doi.org/10.1017/rdc.2021.27.

Petchey, F., G. Clark, I. Lindeman, P. O'Day, J. Southon, K. Dabell and O. Winter 2018. Forgotten news: Shellfish isotopic insight into changing sea-level and associated impact on the first settlers of the Mariana Archipelago. *Quaternary Geochronology* 48:180–194. doi.org/10.1016/j.quageo.2018.10.002.

Peterson, E.J. 2015. Insularity and adaptation: Investigating the role of exchange and inter-island interaction in the Banda Islands. Unpublished PhD thesis, University of Washington, Washington.

Pétrequin, A. and P. Pétrequin 2006. *Objets de Pouvoir En Nouvelle-Guinée: Catalogue de La Donation Anne-Maire et Pierre Pétrequin*. Musée d'Archéologie nationale de Saint-Germain-en-Laye, Paris.

Plutniak, S., A. Araujo, S. Puaud, J.G. Ferrié, A.A. Oktaviana, B. Sugiyanto, J.M. Chazine and F.X. Ricaut 2016. Borneo as a half empty pot: Pottery assemblage from Liang Abu, East Kalimantan. *Quaternary International*: 416:228–242. doi.org/10.1016/j.quaint.2015.11.080.

Schmitt, K. 1947. Notes on some recent archaeological sites in the Netherlands East Indies. *American Anthropologist* 49(2):331–334. doi.org/10.1525/aa.1947.49.2.02a00260.

Solheim, W. 1958. Some potsherds from New Guinea. *The Journal of the Polynesian Society* 67(2):155–157. www.jstor.org/stable/20703660.

Solheim, W.G. 1998. Preliminary report on Makbon archaeology, the Bird's Head, Irian Jaya. In G.-J. Bartstra (ed.), *Bird's Head approaches: Irian Jaya studies, a programme for interdisciplinary research*, pp. 29–40. A.A. Balkema, Rotterdam.

Sollewijn Gelpke, J.H.F. 1994. The report of Miguel Roxo de Brito of his voyage in 1581–1582 to the Raja Ampat, the MacCluer Gulf and Seram. *Bijdragen tot de Taal-, Land- en Volkenkunde van Nederlandsch-Indië* 150(1):123–145. doi.org/10.1163/22134379-90003096.

Spriggs, M. 1991. Nissan, the island in the middle: Summary report on excavations at the north end of the Solomons and the south end of the Bismarcks. In J. Allen and C. Gosden (eds), *Report of the Lapita Homeland Project*, pp. 222–243. Department of Prehistory, Research School of Pacific Studies, The Australian National University, Canberra.

Summerhayes, G.R. 2000. *Lapita interaction*. Terra Australis 15. Department of Archaeology and Natural History and Centre for Archaeological Research, The Australian National University, Canberra. hdl.handle.net/1885/127430.

Summerhayes, G.R. 2001. Lapita in the far west: Recent developments. *Archaeology in Oceania* 36(2):53–63. doi.org/10.1002/j.1834-4453.2001.tb00478.x.

Summerhayes, G.R. 2007a. The rise and transformations of Lapita in the Bismarck Archipelago. In S. Chiu and C. Sand (eds), *From Southeast Asia to the Pacific: Archaeological perspectives on the Austronesian expansion and the Lapita Cultural Complex,* pp. 141–184. Center for Archaeological Studies, Academia Sinica, Taipei.

Summerhayes, G.R. 2007b. Island Melanesian pasts: A view from archeology. In J.S. Friedlaender (ed.), *Population genetics, linguistics, and culture history in the Southwest Pacific*, pp. 10–35. Oxford University Press, Oxford. doi.org/10.1093/acprof:oso/9780195300307.003.0002.

Summerhayes, G.R. 2010. Lapita interaction: An update. In L. Xiuman (ed.), *2009 International Symposium on Austronesian Studies,* pp. 11–40. National Museum of Prehistory, Taidong.

Summerhayes, G.R. 2017. Island Southeast Asia and Oceania interactions. In J. Habu, P. Lape and J. Olsen (eds), *Handbook of East and Southeast Asian archaeology*, pp. 659–771. Springer, New York. doi.org/10.1007/978-1-4939-6521-2_38.

Summerhayes, G.R. 2019. Austronesian expansions and the role of mainland New Guinea: A new perspective. *Asian Perspectives* 58(2):250–260. doi.org/10.1353/asi.2019.0015.

Summerhayes, G.R. 2022. Kisim save long graun: Understanding the nature of landscape change in modelling Lapita in Papua New Guinea. In M.T. Carson (ed.), *Palaeolandscapes in archaeology: Lessons for the past and future*, pp. 291–312. Routledge, Abingdon. doi.org/10.4324/9781003139553-10.

Summerhayes, G., E. Matisoo-Smith, H. Mandui, J. Allen, J. Specht, N. Hogg and S. McPherson 2010. Tamuarawai (EQS): An Early Lapita site on Emirau, New Ireland, PNG. *Journal of Pacific Archaeology* 1(1):62–75. pacificarchaeology.org/index.php/journal/article/view/10.

Summerhayes, G.R., K. Szabó, A. Fairbairn, M. Horrocks, S. Mcpherson and A. Crowther 2019. Early Lapita subsistence: The evidence from Kamgot, Anir Islands, New Ireland Province, Papua New Guinea. In S. Bedford and M. Spriggs (eds), *Debating Lapita: Distribution, chronology, society and subsistence*, pp. 379–402. ANU Press, Canberra. doi.org/10.22459/ta52.2019.18.

Summerhayes, G.R., K. Szabó, M. Leavesley and D. Gaffney 2019. Kamgot at the lagoon's edge: Site position and resource use of an Early Lapita site in Near Oceania. In S. Bedford and M. Spriggs (eds), *Debating Lapita: Distribution, chronology, society and subsistence*, pp. 89–103. ANU Press, Canberra. doi.org/10.22459/ta52.2019.04.

Suroto, H. in press. Prehistorical sites in the western Lake Sentani area, Papua. In D. Gaffney and M. Tolla (eds), *West New Guinea: Social, biological, and material histories*. ANU Press, Canberra.

Tanudirjo, D.A. 2001. Islands in between: Prehistory of the Northeastern Indonesian archipelago. Unpublished PhD thesis, The Australian National University, Canberra.

Tanudirjo, D.A. 2006. The dispersal of Austronesian-speaking people and the ethnogenesis of Indonesian people. In T. Simunjuntak, I.H. Pojoh and M. Hisyam (eds), *Austronesian diaspora and the ethnogeneses of people in Indonesian archipelago*, pp. 83–98. Indonesian Institute of Sciences, Jakarta.

Terrell, J.E. and E.M. Schechter 2007. Deciphering the Lapita code: The Aitape ceramic sequence and late survival of the 'Lapita face'. *Cambridge Archaeological Journal* 17(1):59–85. doi.org/10.1017/s0959774307000066.

Terrell, J.E. and E.M. Schechter 2011. Prehistoric pottery wares in the Aitape area. *Fieldiana Anthropology* 42(42):87–157. doi.org/10.3158/0071-4739-42.1.87.

Tsang, C. 2000. Recent advances in the Iron Age archaeology of Taiwan. *Bulletin of the Indo-Pacific Prehistory Association* 20:153–158.

Veth, P., M. Spriggs, S. O'Connor and A.D. Saleh 2005. Wangil midden: A late prehistoric site, with remarks on ethnographic pottery making. In S. O'Connor, M. Spriggs and P. Veth (eds), *The archaeology of the Aru Islands, Eastern Indonesia*, pp. 95–124. ANU Press, Canberra. doi.org/10.22459/ta22.2007.06.

Warnk, H. 2010. The coming of Islam and Moluccan-Malay culture to New Guinea c.1500–1920. *Indonesia and the Malay World* 38(110):109–134. doi.org/10.1080/13639811003665454.

Wu, P. 2016. What happened at the end of Lapita: Lapita to Post-Lapita pottery transition in West New Britian, Papua New Guinea. Unpublished PhD thesis, University of Otago, Dunedin. ourarchive.otago.ac.nz/handle/10523/6817.

18

Ancient starch and usewear analyses of an excavated pestle fragment from the Upper Kaironk Valley, Madang Province, Papua New Guinea

Judith H. Field, Adelle C. Coster, Ben Shaw, Elspeth Hayes, Richard Fullagar, Michael Lovave, Jemina Haro and Glenn R. Summerhayes

Abstract

During archaeological survey and excavation along the Kaironk and Simbai Valleys of the New Guinea Highlands in 2016, a ground and pecked tool fragment was recovered from a subsurface context immediately adjacent to the Imbiben (JRQ) open area excavations where a well-preserved cultural deposit including hearth stones and a flaking floor has been dated to the mid-Holocene (4.4–4.3 cal. ka (ka: thousands of years ago). Technological and usewear analyses of the fragment identified a formally manufactured surface shaped by pecking, with minimal traces of use but consistent with the side of a pestle, on which starch residues were preserved. Ancient starch analysis identified *Castanopsis acuminatissima* as the primary contributing species in the residue sample. *C. acuminatissima* is an upper canopy tree found in primary forest across the highlands. It belongs to the acorn family (Fagaceae) and produces an edible starchy nut that can be eaten raw or roasted. The Imbiben pestle fragment is the fourth formally manufactured artefact with pecked and/or ground surfaces recovered from subsurface sediments during the current project, all of which date to the mid-Holocene. The other artefacts include two pestle fragments and a fragment of a carved face excavated at the Waim site. Pestles, mortars and carved stones are widely known from unprovenanced contexts across the Kaironk/Simbai Valleys, New Guinea and the Bismarck Archipelago. The functional study of the Imbiben pestle fragment described here aids in our understanding of the range, antiquity and use of these formally manufactured stone tools to process starchy plant foods.

Introduction

The enigmatic mortar and pestle complex of formally manufactured ground, pecked and sometimes exquisitely carved stone objects from New Guinea and neighbouring islands has a remarkable range of form and decoration, providing a unique opportunity to investigate the role of these objects in traditional societies across different landscapes and language groups (see Swadling 1986, 2013, 2021; Swadling et al. 2008). The vast majority of stone mortars and pestles currently known are from poorly provenanced contexts with no associated chronological information (Swadling 2021). Local communities have no knowledge about their manufacture or intended use. Despite much speculation among researchers for over 100 years, the primary function of these implements is only now becoming clearer (Barton 1908; Bulmer 1964; Field et al. 2020; Seligman and Joyce 1907; Shaw et al. 2020; Swadling and Hide 2005; Watson 1968). The recent discoveries of mortar and pestle fragments from securely excavated and dated contexts in widely separated geographic locations, and the significant advances in ancient starch studies over the past two decades, and in combination with usewear analyses, have yielded much-needed new information on the associated uses of these tools (e.g. Coster and Field 2015, 2018; Field et al. 2016, 2020; Hayes et al. 2021). As mortars, pestles and carved objects are found across New Guinea and the Bismarck Archipelago (see Swadling 2021:Fig. 1), it is highly likely that the function and use of these implements also varied according to resource availability and subsistence patterns, as well as locale and context of their manufacture (e.g. Ambrose 1964; Berndt 1954; Chappell 1964). The study presented here adds to the growing corpus of archaeological knowledge about the past uses of these remarkable tools, especially the range of plants that were being processed.

Functional studies of pestles and mortars in New Guinea

Usewear residue studies have previously been undertaken on one excavated mortar fragment from the Joe's Garden site in the Ivane Valley (Central Province), and on two excavated pestle fragments from the Waim site in the Schrader Range (Madang Province) (Field et al. 2020; Shaw et al. 2020). The starch grains identified on all three artefacts were attributed to *Castanopsis acuminatissima*, a forest tree species that is ubiquitous across the highlands, occurring between 570–2440 m asl (above sea level) and documented in the vegetation histories of the region (e.g. Haberle 2007). *C. acuminatissima* produces small hazelnut-size starchy kernels which are abundant between November to April. The starchy nuts can be eaten either raw or roasted and are likely to have been processed by pounding. *C. acuminatissima* starch grains were identified along with starch grains from the geophytes of *Dioscorea alata* and *Pueraria lobata*, these latter species considered to have considerable antiquity as important plant foods prior to the arrival of the sweet potato (*Ipomoea batatas*) (Roullier et al. 2013; Watson 1964, 1968). Bulmer (1964:149) has argued that *C. acuminatissima* may have been considered important across the New Guinea Highlands because of its edibility, abundance and size. While it has been documented from mid-Holocene contexts, it is likely to have been exploited over a longer period (Bourke 1996; Field et al. 2020; Shaw et al. 2020).

C. acuminatissima (*sawey*—pronounced 'sar-way', Gardner 2010:36) is just one of 13 plants identified by Ralph Bulmer (1964) when he canvassed the range of edible tree nuts likely to be processed in the mortars and pestles in the Kaironk Valley (Table 18.1). *C. acuminatissima* trees were observed in village gardens in the Ivane Valley, while in the Kaironk Valley a grove of *C. acuminatissima* has been set aside as a reserve in recognition of the importance attributed to the annual availability of these edible tree nuts during the wet season. The *C. acuminatissima* reserve is on the northern side of the Kaironk River on the Schrader Range, though Bulmer (1964) described almost pure stands of *Castanopsis* on exposed ridge crests on the southern side of the valley on the Bismarck Range at around 2100 m asl (c. 7000 feet) (see also Paijmans 1976). There has been, and continues to be, considerable clearing of forests across the Kaironk/Simbai system leading to a severe contraction of their availability. Local population increases have resulted in considerable pressure for more land clearing to develop new gardens.

Table 18.1: A summary of the 13 tree taxa identified by Bulmer (1964) and updated by Gardner (2010), including local names and judged by Bulmer to likely be processed in mortars and pestles in the Kaironk Valley.

No.	Family	Species	Kalam name(s)	Ethnographic notes
1–3	Pandanaceae	*Pandanus* sp.	*algaw, gdi/gdl, kmi*	3 categories, roasted, cooked in ground oven
		P. brosimos (cf. *julianettii*)	*alngaw*	>2250 m,[a] oily nuts roasted and eaten; 1800–3300 m asl[b]
		P. cf. *julianetti*	*kumi, snay*	to c. 2400 m,[a] nuts eaten roasted or raw; 1450–2800 m asl[b]
4–6	Elaeocarpaceae	*Elaeocarpus* sp.	*ymges*	3 species, eaten raw or roasted, tedious to extract
		E. leucanthus	*kodjop*	Grows to higher altitude than *kodlap*, single edible kernel
		E. womersleyi	*kodlap*	to c. 2100 m,[a] eaten raw or roasted
		E. schlechterianus	*ttaman*	tree of mid-altitude forest, kernels eaten
7	Elaeocarpaceae	*Sloanea archboldiana* (syn. *tieghemii*)[a]	*tlum, tlm*	to c. 2400 m,[a] not recorded as eaten by Kalam, though Maring people do; 1100–2300 m asl[c]
8	Fagaceae	*Castanopsis acuminatissima*	*sawey, kabj, wusij, kabi nqem*	eaten raw or roasted; 570–2440 m asl[b]
9	Moraceae	*Artocarpus* sp. 1	no known Kalam name	not in Kalam area but adjacent groups. Seeds eaten roasted; 0–1450 m asl[b] (*A. altilis*)
10		*A. lacucha*	*abok*	Shrader Range at 1800–2100 m,[a] nuts eaten
11	Proteaceae	*Finschia chloroxantha*	*sog*	roasted and then pounded with a rock; 0–2000 m asl[b]
12	Malvaceae	*Sterculia* sp. cf. *monticola*	*dkpn, dkbn*	tree to c. 1800 m,[a] seeds from bean-like pod, roasted and eaten: up to 2150 m asl[d]
13	Pittosporaceae	*Pittosporum pullifolium*	*slknuw**	Shrub, pod roasted, seeds extracted and eaten, bitter taste

Notes: * not documented by Gardner (2010); powo.science.kew.org/taxon/324460-1; [a] Bulmer (1964); [b] Bourke (2010), extreme altitudinal range in PNG; [c] Coode (1983); [d] uses.plantnet-project.org/en/Sterculia_monticola (PROSEA). asl = above sea level. Further Kalam names for the various species can be found in Pawley and Bulmer (2011). (Also note *E. schlechterianus* has been added following Gardner (2010).)

Source: See sources listed throughout notes.

Other important tree nuts include *Elaeocarpus womersleyi*, the nuts known locally as *kodlap*, while *Elaeocarpus leucanthus*, which grows to a higher altitude, is known as *kodjop* (Gardner 2010:28). It is not clear whether these nuts are starchy, and although we encountered carbonised remains of both types of seeds in excavated sequences (identified by local collaborators), we have not yet been able to acquire any fresh reference samples for study. *Finschia chloroxantha* (*sog*, Gardner 2010:39) is also widely eaten and numerous trees were observed in the Kaironk and Simbai Valleys. Unfortunately, prepared slide samples from field collections did not contain any starch. *Pandanus* species (*alngaw/kumi* Gardner 2010:12) are common in the Kaironk Valley, as they are across the highlands. *Pandanus* sp. seeds are high in protein and oil (Hyndman 1984) but yield low quantities of starch. While *Pandanus* drupes are pounded in some contexts, the number of starch grains may consequently be under-represented in archaeological contexts. Although *Pandanus* drupes were recovered from the Kosipe Mission excavations (in the Ivane Valley) and dated to around 35 ka (Fairbairn et al. 2006), no *Pandanus* sp. starch was identified in tool residues. *Pandanus* kernels (endosperm) and the pulp (mesocarp) (Hyndman 1984:295) may be cooked and consumed away from the villages, as observed elsewhere in the Ivane Valley (Summerhayes et al. 2010).

Functional analyses of mortars and pestles likely to be associated with food processing have provided important insights into the range of foods exploited over time in domestic contexts, and into the types of plant materials that are pounded and/or ground. The residues recovered from these artefacts contribute important functional and contextual information that supplements other microfossil records, such as those preserved in sediment cores. The study discussed here is no exception, as the aim of this paper is to present a functional study of an excavated formally manufactured stone artefact recovered from subsurface sediments of probable mid-Holocene age from the Kaironk Valley in the Papua New Guinea.

Study area

The Upper Kaironk Valley, in the Madang Province, is part of the Kalam-speaking territory of the Papua New Guinea Highlands (Field et al. 2021). Anthropological, linguistic and botanical research in the Kaironk Valley has been undertaken since the 1960s (Gardner 2010; Majnep and Bulmer 1997, 2007; Pawley and Bulmer 2011). The initial archaeological investigations were pursued by Sue Bulmer at the Wañelek site (JAO) and elsewhere in the Kaironk Valley in the 1970s (see Bulmer 1975).

The archaeological survey and excavation described in this paper are part of an Australian Research Council – funded project titled 'Pathway to the Highlands Project' (see Field et al. 2021; Shaw et al. 2020), aimed at investigating whether the highland fringe valleys were conduits for the movement of people, plants and technology, between the coastal lowlands and highland valleys, and ultimately to develop a more nuanced model for the peopling of Sahul and New Guinea. Previous research by Pawel Gorecki had explored the human record in the adjacent, but lower-lying, Jimi Valley (<500 m asl). Notably, these valleys are less than 100 km from the Wahgi Valley and the Kuk Swamp records (Golson et al. 2017; Gorecki and Gillieson 1989). In 2015, a survey of the Upper Simbai and Kaironk Valley was undertaken to identify past settlements and whether areas of cultural activity in the form of subsurface cultural materials were present and in concentrations justifying excavation (Field et al. 2021).

Imbiben (JRQ), Upper Kaironk Valley, Madang Province

During a survey of the Alvan Spur in the Upper Kaironk Valley (Figure 18.1), a range of surface finds were recovered at Imbiben, while some were observed in the Alvan village museum (Figure 18.2). Similar artefacts are often revealed during garden construction, emerging as the soil is turned over for planting. The small museum at Alvan was only recently constructed to house a range of artefacts collected by locals.

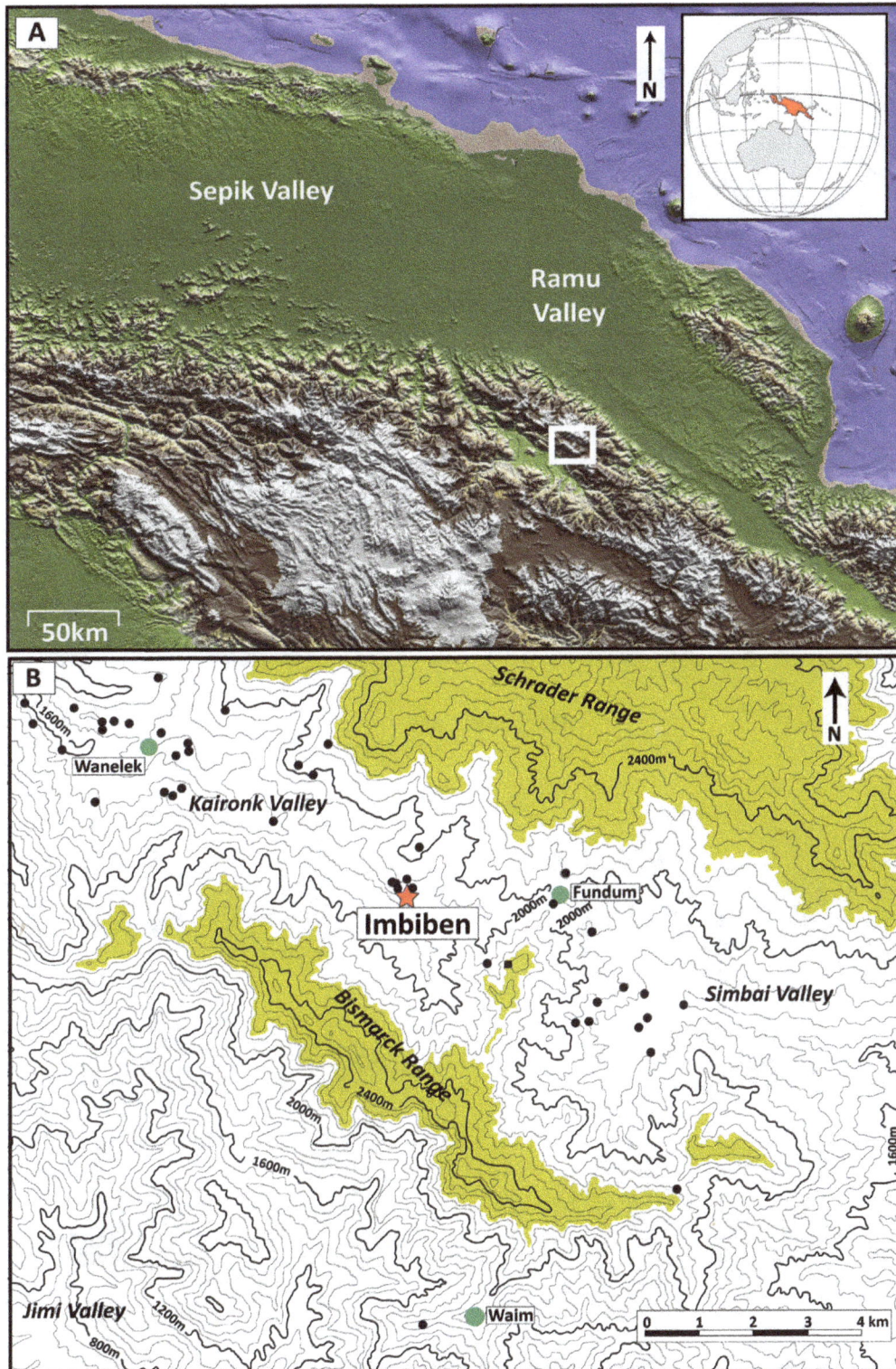

Figure 18.1: The location of the Simbai–Kaironk Valleys.

Notes: B. KAI-25 (JRQ,* red star) is associated with a cluster of other recorded sites below the Alwan village on a prominent spur system. The map shows 80 m contours. Fundum (JQQ,* green dot) lies on the saddle between the Kaironk and Simbai River valleys. * National Museum and Art Gallery site codes.

Source: Illustration by Ben Shaw.

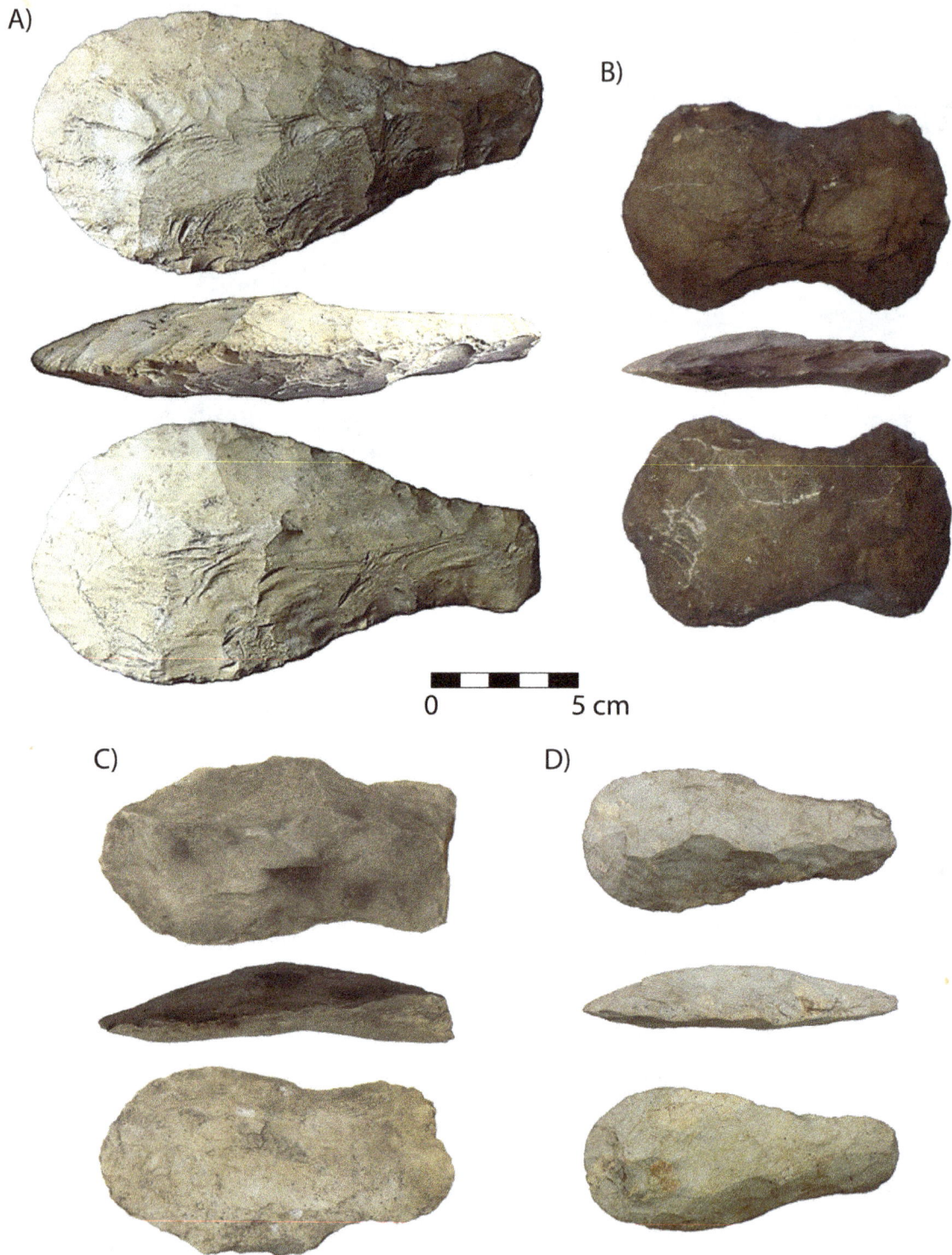

Figure 18.2: Waisted chert artefacts as surface finds from the Upper Kaironk Valley.

Notes: (A) From the local Alvan collection; (B) Skow (KAI-6); (C) near Alvan (KAI-22) above Imbiben. All three artefacts had a weathered cortex overlying a green chert interior; (D) Fundum (SIM-11).

Source: Illustrations by Ben Shaw.

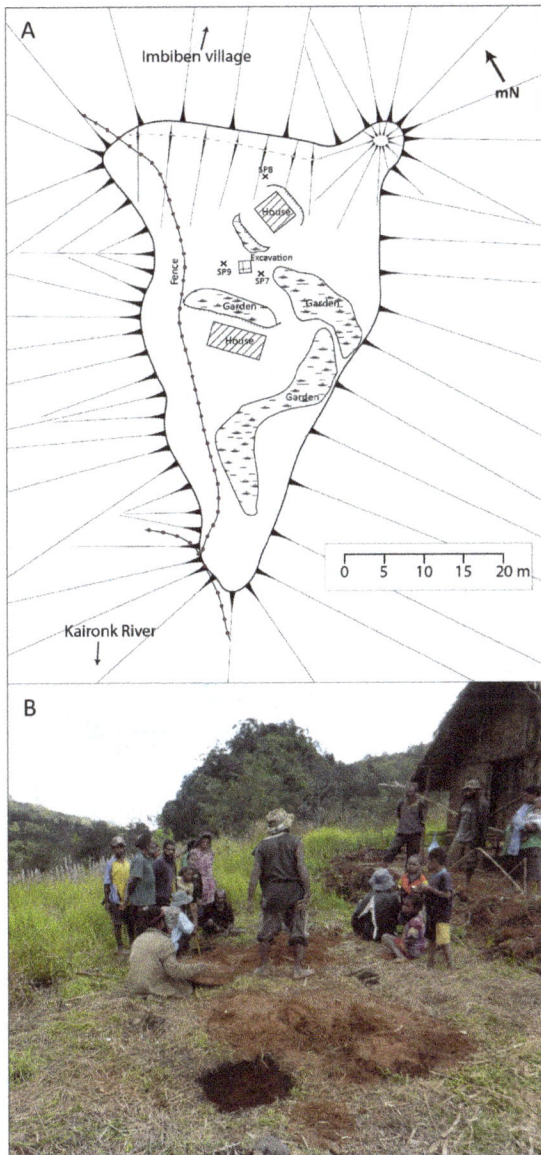

Figure 18.3: Alvan spur excavation.

Notes: (A) Survey plan of the flattened part of the Alvan spur where systematic archaeological investigations were undertaken; (B) test pit excavations in progress (SP9), with spade pit 7 (SP7) open in the foreground. The artefact KAI25-SP7-20cm-bs was recovered from SP7 and is immediately adjacent to the later systematic excavation (Field et al. 2021). The Kolkop limestone outcrop covered in dense vegetation can be seen in the background to the southwest.

Source: Illustrations and photo Ben Shaw.

Prior to systematic and targeted subsurface investigations at Imbiben (JRQ) in 2016, a series of nine spade pits were excavated down the Alvan spur, with three (SP7–SP9) dug across a 1300 m² triangular area of relatively flat ground (JRQ: Imbiben site, 1860 m asl), ~ 40 m above and 100 m north of the Kaironk River, to ascertain the nature and extent of any cultural remains and their correlation to sediments and stratigraphy (Figure 18.3). The highest concentration of flaked lithic artefacts was in SPs 7–9, including a fragment from SP7 (Layer 2, 20 cm below the surface (bs)) with a smooth, rounded surface that appeared to be similar to those found at Waim (WAA), where they were recovered from excavation, in addition to several samples held by the local community (see Shaw et al. 2020). To better understand details of its manufacture, use and breakage, a technological and functional analysis was undertaken.

The three stratigraphic layers identified in SPs 7–9, and confirmed in later systematic excavation, include an organic topsoil (Layer 1, 0–15 cm), a dense cultural horizon (Layer 2, 15–40 cm) and an underlying compact, culturally sterile basal clay (Layer 3). Bedrock was not reached. Two radiocarbon determinations from the systematic excavation situated between the two spade pits, and adjacent to SP7, bracket Layer 2 between 5460–5070 cal. BP (OSV218, 4595±30 BP, 50–60 cm) and 4510–4240 cal. BP (OZV217, 3930±30 BP, 20–30 cm). The latter date was associated with a well-defined stone cooking area (*mumu*) and a dense scatter of flaked and ground stone artefacts, revealing the remarkable preservation of a mid-Holocene cooking place and associated knapping floor (Field et al. 2021). A radiocarbon determination from SP9 of 1690–1410 cal. BP (OZU286, 1645±25 BP) from 37 cm bs is inconsistent with the established age of Layer 2, and is likely to have been deposited within an intrusive pit feature from Layer 1, as identified in the section of the spade pit. The date is therefore not considered further here.

Methods

Technological and usewear analysis

A 3D scan of the artefact was generated using a Polyga Compact C210 3D scanner with FlexScan3D software (Version 3.3). The 3D image and snapshots of the artefact were viewed and obtained in MeshLab (Version 1.3.4BETA).

Wear traces were documented under low and high magnification. Low magnification examination (up to ×45) was undertaken using an Olympus SZ61 stereo-zoom microscope with an external fibre optic, 150-watt halogen light source (Olympus LG-PS2). High magnification examination was undertaken using an Olympus metallographic microscope (model BX53M) with vertical incident light (brightfield and darkfield) with objective lenses of ×5, ×10, ×20 and ×50 and various polarising filters. Microscopic images were captured with an Olympus Infinity 2 camera attachment (TIF files). Multifocal images of the artefact surface were taken with both microscopes and stacked to create a focused image using Helicon Focus software Version 7.6.3.

A reference library of experimental usewear patterns from grinding/pounding a variety of materials is available (e.g. Hayes et al. 2018), the results of which contributed to our functional interpretations.

Residue analysis

Residue extraction and documentation

The pecked dorsal surface was immersed in an ultrasonic bath of deionised water for two minutes to remove adhering residues. The solution, including residues, was then reduced in volume by centrifugation. Starch and phytoliths were isolated using heavy liquid separation (sodium polytungstate, S.G.2.35) by centrifugation at 1000 RPM for 15 minutes. The sample was then rinsed with water by centrifugation, dried in acetone and mounted in water. A negative control sample was processed in parallel with the archaeological sample and subsequently checked for modern starch contamination.

Modern comparative reference collections

The principal aid in identifying from which plant taxa the unknown starch gains originate is a modern comparative collection of starchy plants parts known to be exploited and possibly pounded or ground, from the region of interest (see Field et al. 2016, 2020; Hayes et al. 2021). Plant parts were sampled, visualised, documented and digitised (Coster and Field 2015, 2018) (Table 18.2).

Table 18.2: Comparative reference starch and archaeological sample.

Sample name	Common name	Altitudinal range	n	Plant part	Processed	Size range (μ)	Median (μ)
KAI25-SP7-20cm-bs pestle frag	–	(1860 m)	121	–	–	6.62-43.21	15.65
Castanopsis. acuminatissima	Castanopsis	570–2440 m	233	Fruit	Raw/roasted	5.07–49.6	20.52
Colocasia esculenta	Taro	0–2760 m	458	Tuber	Roasted/baked	2.53–9.9	5.15
Dioscorea alata	Greater yam	0–2100 m	199	Tuber	Roasted/baked	10.53–68.18	29.44
D. bulbifera	Bitter/Hairy yam	0–2110 m	207	Tuber	Cooked/leached	8.29–51.00	28.33
D. esculenta	Lesser yam	0–1620 m	284	Tuber	Roasted/baked	2.27–9.3	5.56

Sample name	Common name	Altitudinal range	n	Plant part	Processed	Size range (μ)	Median (μ)
D. nummularia	Common yam	0–2050 m	114	Tuber	Roasted/baked	19.20–53.37	32.45
D. pentaphylla	Five leaflet yam	0–1620 m	146	Tuber	Roasted/baked	14.60–110.78	65.07
Gnetum gnemon	Tulip nuts	0–1330 m	125	Nuts	–	3.51–21.32	12.58
Homalomena sp.	–	2000 m	103	Root	–	6.49–43.79	16.29
Hydriastele sp.	Palm	2000 m	102	Root	–	2.24–23.02	5.93
Musa acuminata	Banana	0–2350 m	94	Fruit	Raw	1.53–19.52	3.46
M. ingens	Banana	0–<2000 m	160	Fruit	Raw	4.66–18.11	9.65
M. peekelii	Banana	0–<2000 m	121	Fruit	Raw	2.49–22.22	5.25
Psophocarpus tetragonolobus	Winged bean	0–2070 m	151	Tuber	Baked/roasted	5.15–35.95	11.42
Pueraria lobata	Kudzu bean	0–2740 m	278	Tuber	Baked/roasted	2.93–25.07	10.05
Saccharum officinarum	Sugar cane	0–2760 m	105	Root	Raw	4.83–19.45	9.50
Zingiberaceae	Ginger	0–2200 m	144	Root	–	2.18–20.14	7.21

Notes: 'n' indicates the number of digitised grains in the analysis. *Musa acuminata* has numbers less than 100. Many of these plant taxa are often roasted and baked while others are eaten raw. It is well known that some foodstuffs are pounded when feeding the elderly and the young, though there may be other reasons why they are processed, perhaps to improve palatability or combining less abundant resources.

Source: Table prepared by Judith Field, Michael Lovave and other sources cited in text (e.g. Bourke 2010).

Microscopy and documentation

The residue sample and modern reference samples were viewed using a Zeiss Axioskop II transmitted brightfield microscope with Nomarksi optics. Total slide scans were undertaken for the archaeological sample. For the reference set, a minimum of 100 starch grains were documented. Starch grains were photographed using a Zeiss HRc camera as .ZVI files with Zeiss Axiovision software.

The outline and hilum position of individual starch grains from the archaeological sample and the reference starch assemblages were digitised (from the micrographs) using custom Matlab (Mathworks R2018b) code and a Wacom Intuos Pen Tablet (CTH-480). Damaged starch grains were not included.

Analysis of starch assemblages

A range of quantitative macroscopic geometric features were determined for each starch grain from the digitised grain outlines. In this analysis, area, perimeter, maximum length through the hilum (MaxD) and hilum offset measurements were used. The individual grain shapes were assessed at their original (actual) size and as 'normalised' grain shapes.

Normalised shapes are determined by scaling the size of individual grains whereby the average radius about the hilum of each grain is one. The shapes can then be rotationally aligned and compared. The use of normalised shapes controls for growth stage or inherent variations in size across each assemblage. The aligned normalised shapes of each reference species and the archaeological assemblage were hierarchically clustered into self-similar groups, using a common cut-off to ensure the same levels of self-similarity between the different subsets.

The grain shapes (original and normalised) were analysed for similarity by rotationally aligning pairs about their hilum positions and minimising the area between the two shapes. The area between shapes provided a distance measure for pairs of shapes. The distribution of the distances between the normalised shapes and the distributions of the macro-scale geometric features within each reference subset were then analysed for overlaps with those of the assemblage. If any of the comparative reference subset distributions did not overlap with the distributions of the unknown (archaeological) assemblage, then those reference subsets were removed from subsequent analyses.

Independent expert visual verification

Once the geometric analyses have removed non-contributing reference species, then the closest grains from the reference set are established for the unknown grains. More than one species from the reference set may be identified for one unknown grain. As the quantitative geometric measures used in the first stage of the analysis derive from the (2D) digitised outline of the grain and the position of the hilum, other morphological features may need to be considered to identify the reference species. Thus, the second stage of the analysis is the expert visual verification: comparing the digitised outlines and the categorical features of the grains in the micrographs. The categorical starch grain features considered in the verification process were presence/absence of fissures, presence/absence of lamellae, presence/absence of facets, open/closed hilum and compound/single starch grains.

Results

Technology and usewear traces

The Imbiben artefact (KAI25-SP7-20cm-bs) appears to be a broken flake made from coarse-grained gabbro. It has a pecked/ground dorsal surface, which has two partial flake scars, and a slightly weathered ventral surface, which has a hackly fracture and lacks a clear bulb of percussion or striking platform (Figure 18.4A). The morphology suggests an abrupt lateral break at the (possible) proximal margin, although we cannot be certain of its orientation since there is no remnant of the platform or any clear indication of an impact zone. Consequently, it is uncertain whether the flake is the result of deliberate or accidental breakage. On the pecked/ground dorsal surface, there is a group of shallow grooves or scratch marks which are not typical of grinding/pounding; and it is uncertain whether these are cultural (e.g. damage caused by past tool handling), or the result of post-depositional alterations (taphonomic) (Figure 18.4B).

Microscopic examination of the dorsal surface indicates that the original surface was shaped by pecking. Under low magnification, individual grains on the dorsal surface are angular and don't appear to be smoothed or levelled, with the exception of a few isolated areas (Figure 18.4C, D). Under high magnification, many grains on the dorsal surface appear to have relatively fresh fracture surfaces (Figure 18.4E–I). These fracture surfaces are considered to be wear resulting from pecking during manufacture to shape the artefact. Pecking and minimal abrasive smoothing are the only techniques documented. The abrasive smoothing could have formed during manufacture and diagnostic traces of use are absent.

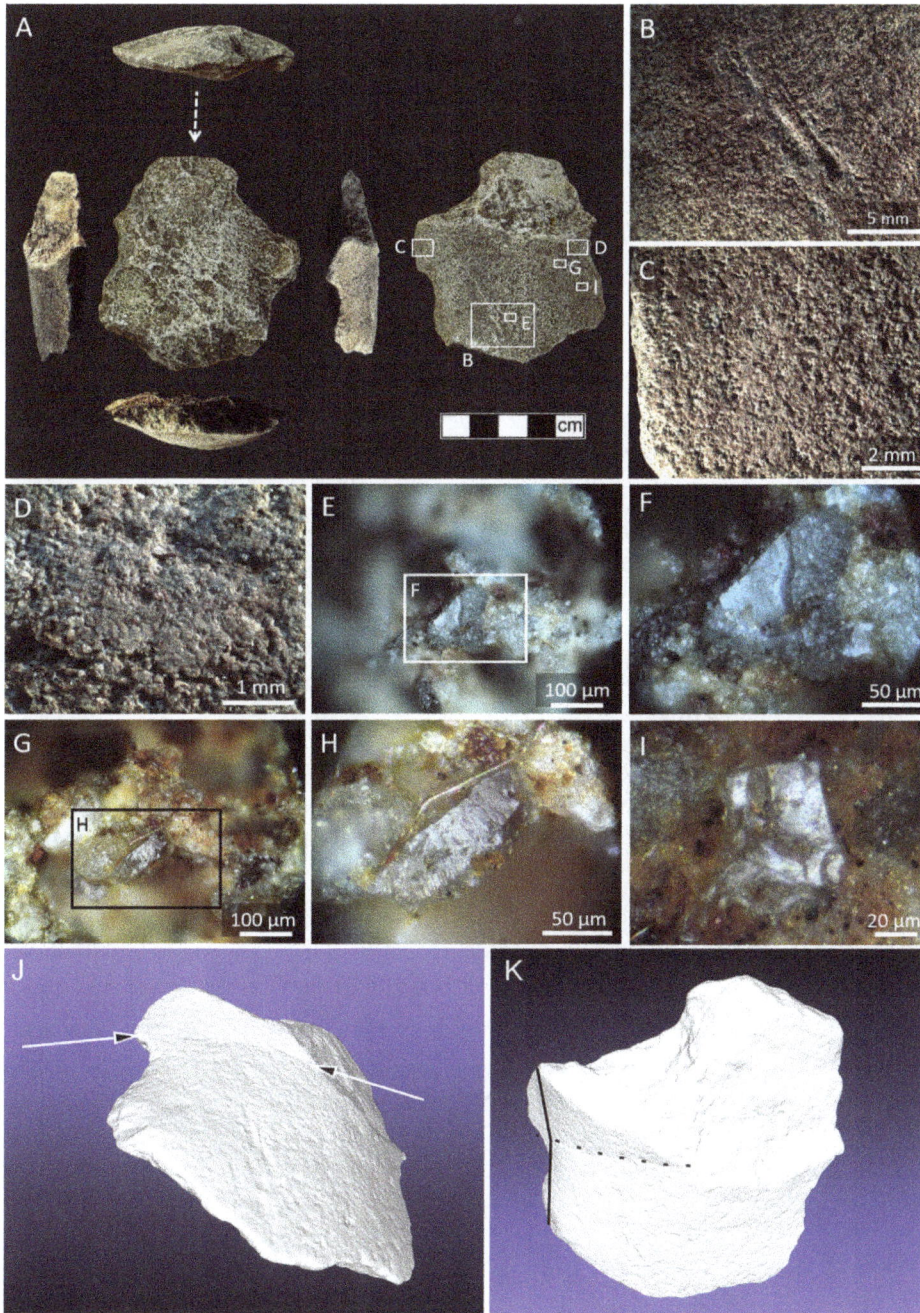

Figure 18.4: Microscopic wear documented on artefact KAI25-SP7-20cm-bs.

Notes: (A) KAI25-SP7-20cm-bs views: ventral (left) and dorsal (right), orientated with the proximal end up. The dashed arrow indicates the likely direction of force that detached the flake. White squares show locations of the microscope images D–I; (B) macroscopically visible scratch marks on the dorsal surface (stereo-zoom stereomicroscope); (C–D) isolated zones of levelled grains, indicating grinding and smoothing (stereo-zoom stereomicroscope); (E–I) individual crystal grains in the stone matrix lack scratch marks or striations and mostly have natural fracture features that are likely the result of hard impact, probably from hard hammer percussion — pecking to shape the pestle (metallographic microscope); (J–K) 3D model snapshots of the dorsal surface of KAI25-SP7-20cm-bs (proximal end up), showing possible inflexion or waist; (J) a possible waist on the artefact indicated by arrows; (K) alternate view of the artefact with inflexion indicated by solid lines and waist indicated by dotted lines. Note that curvature at the proximal end appears to get wider in diameter more steeply than at the distal end, possibly indicating that the missing proximal end would be pestle base.

Source: Illustration by Richard Fullagar and Elspeth Hayes.

It is difficult to reconstruct the diameter or general shape of the complete artefact prior to breakage but a partial 'waist' is discernible in a rotated 3D image (Figure 18.4F, G). The waist may indicate deliberate widening at the working end or base, as seen on the base of some formally manufactured pestles (e.g. Shaw et al. 2020:Fig. 4e). But we cannot determine whether the working end or base of the artefact is 'above' or 'below' the apparent waist. If the working end or base of the artefact is 'above' the waist—that is, beyond what we identify as the possible proximal end—then only a small portion of the working end has survived. Either way, the flake is from near the junction of a handle and the base, and the wear is mostly from manufacture (stone on stone). It is possible that the force of pounding, when using the artefact as a pestle, caused the flake to be detached from the side. The lack of impact percussion marks perhaps makes it less likely that the artefact was deliberately broken as part of some ritual (e.g. Adams 2008).

Only minimal abrasive smoothing was noted, and the general lack of usewear is intriguing. Is the flake from near the working end of an implement or part of a carved stone object that was not a utilitarian tool? A change in surface morphology was noted on the carved head fragment from Waim, though it was not considered to be part of a pestle (see Shaw et al. 2020:Fig. S14a–b). Many other formally manufactured implements also bear elaborately carved surfaces, but in this case, the artefact is most likely a combination of both: a pestle with a carved handle (see Swadling 2021).

The original function/use of the artefact could not be determined from the microscopic usewear analysis alone, reinforcing the advantage of a multidisciplinary approach. A lack of distinctive usewear could be related to several factors:

1. We have concluded that the flake represents part of a pestle and is likely to derive from near the junction of the handle and not directly from the working end of the implement. As such, usewear is expected to be minimal, while residues from use are present. If the flake is from a stone carving, then we would expect no usewear or residues.

2. The pestle is made from coarse-grained gabbro (see also Shaw et al. 2020). The hardness of the raw material means that usewear may be slow to develop and hard to recognise. Moreover, the artefact studied here may have been detached very early on in the life-history of the object.

3. It is possible that weathering of the stone surface may have removed or obscured wear traces. The presence of slight but uniform edge-rounding on the flake margins and fracture ridges on dorsal and ventral surfaces indicates partial weathering. However, the microscopic fresh fracture features on the dorsal surface are typical of the deliberate stone-on-stone pecking technique with minimal abrasive smoothing. Chemical alterations were not observed on those surfaces.

Ancient starch

A total of 134 starch grains were analysed from the artefact's pecked surface, of which 121 starch grains were digitised for analysis (Table 18.2, Figure 18.5). Those starch grains which were not digitised (*n* = 13) and therefore excluded from the analysis were damaged, did not have complete margins or were partially obscured by other tissues/detritus in the slide preparation.

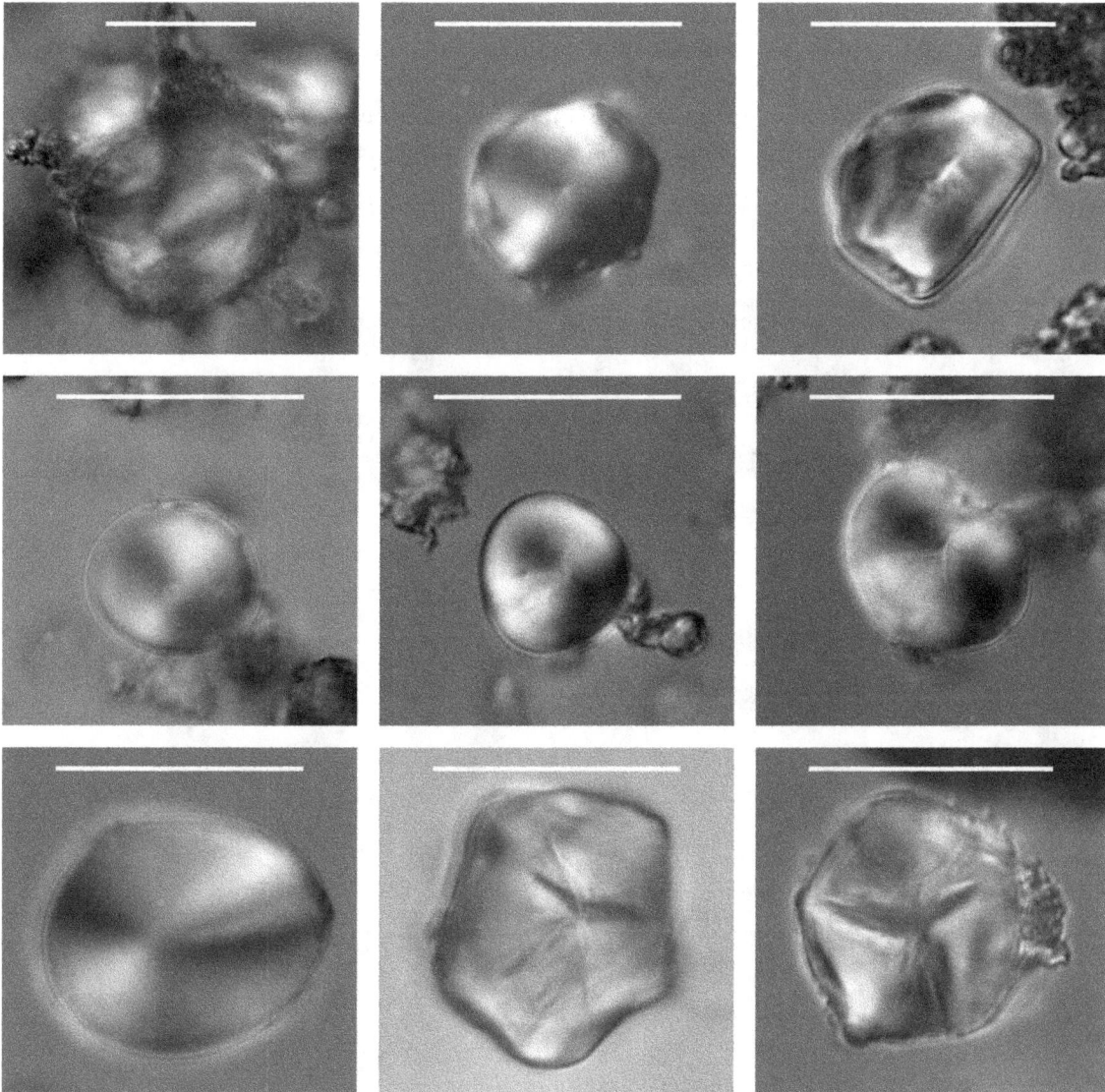

Figure 18.5: A sample of the starch grains recovered from the surface of KAI25-SP7-20cm-bs.

Notes: There is notable dominance in the assemblage of faceted grains with either fissures or pits/vacuoles/open hila. Scale Bar = 20 microns.

Source: Images J. Field.

Modern comparative reference set

A modern comparative reference collection is essential to canvas the size, shape and variability of starches from plants known to be culturally and economically important in the Kaironk Valley and surrounding highland landscapes, which can then be compared with the starch assemblage recovered from the pestle (cf. Field et al. 2020; Shaw et al. 2020) (Table 18.1). The reference collection included plants that are known to be exploited and possibly pounded or ground (see Field et al. 2016, 2020; Hayes et al. 2021). Various sources were used to construct the plant list, and importantly, plants known to have been used in the past, as well as those important in the present day, were included (Coster and Field 2015, 2018). Many plant species that have been exploited by people in the past are still commonly used across the highlands (Bulmer 1964; Gardner 2010; Watson and Cole 1977). The sweet potato (*Ipomoea batatas*), which was introduced c. 300 years ago, is now ubiquitous in the highland landscape (Roullier et al. 2013). Over the last decade, a database of starch isolated from field collected specimens or from herbaria from Australia, New Guinea and North America has been created at the University of New South Wales Ancient Starch laboratory. Over 32,000 starch grains from a range of plant taxa and archaeological samples have now been added to the starch database, of which c. 23,000 are from 432 samples of modern comparative reference species.

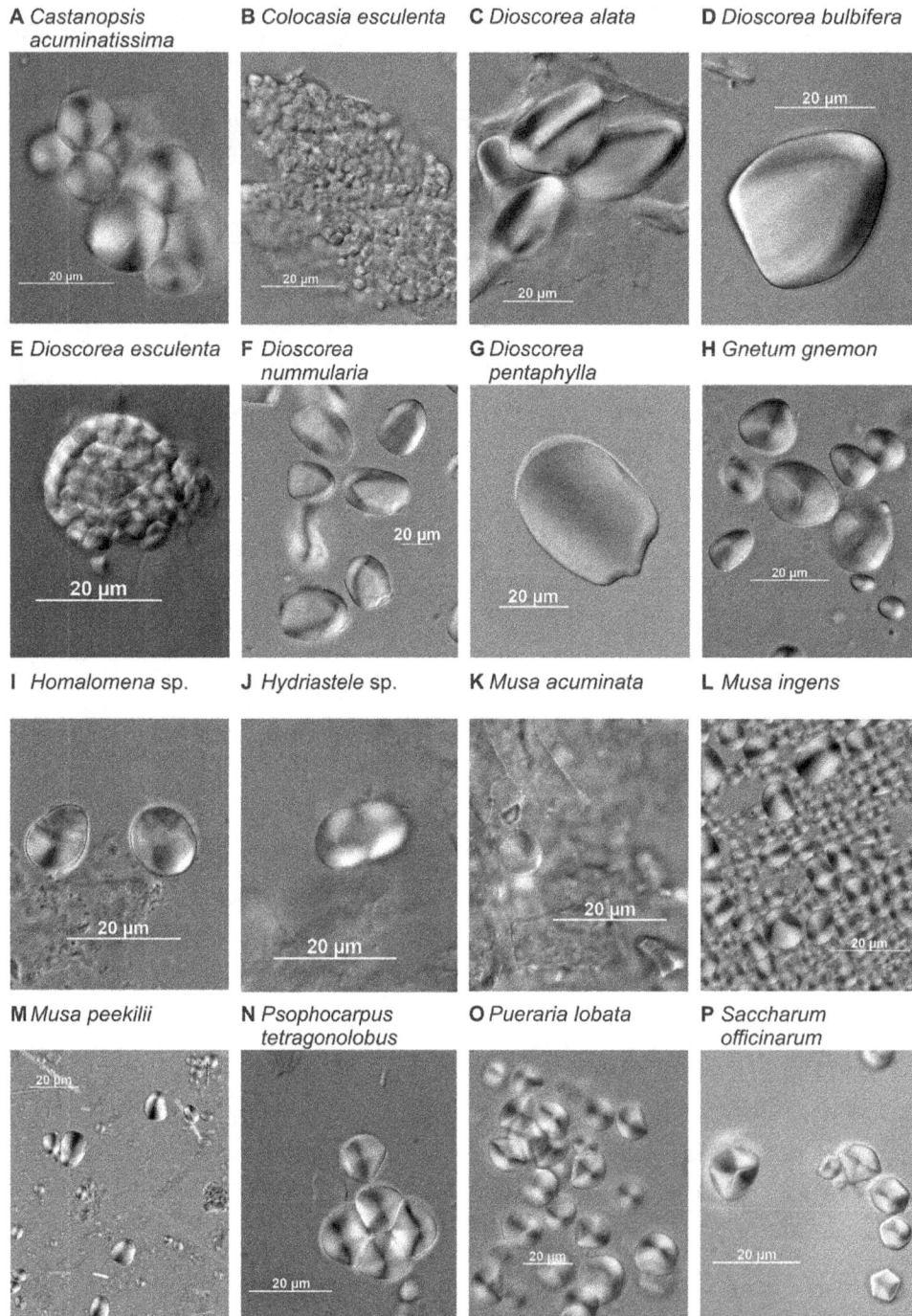

Figure 18.6: Representative examples of starch grains from the comparative reference set used in the analysis of the pestle fragment (KAI25-SP7-20cm-bs), Kaironk Valley, Madang Province, PNG.

Source: Images J. Field.

The inclusion of 17 plant species in this study is based on our general knowledge of starchy plant use in the highlands, and more specifically the flora in the Kaironk/Simbai Valleys (Gardner 2010) (Table 18.1; Figure 18.6). The comparative reference set is conservative, in the sense that the plant list reflects the most likely candidates for the region of interest. As the Simbai–Kaironk are highland fringe valleys, some flexibility was required to account for the potential movement of plants and people between the coastal lowlands and the highland fringe. *Gnetum gnemon* was included as it is a tree species that produces a starchy nut and has an altitudinal range close to the elevations documented in the Simbai–Kaironk Valleys (see also *Dioscorea esculenta* and *D. pentaphylla)*. Sago (*Metroxylon sagu*) was not included, despite the proximity of coastal lowlands where it is used, primarily because it has very distinctive and diagnostic morphologies and that were not observed in the starch residues recovered from the pestle fragment.

Refining the comparative reference set

The range of metrics plotted for all the starch grains in the study are presented in Figures 18.7 and 18.8. Of these metrics, the maximum diameter through the hilum (MaxD) (Figure 18.7) assessed in the first pass through the data, often facilitates the elimination of non-contributing reference species (see Coster and Field 2015). For this study, the range of starch grain attributes identified in the KAI25 sample meant that further refining of the comparative reference sample was required.

To further reduce the number of potential contributing plant species to the unknown sample, the analysis of normalised grain shapes was undertaken. It allowed us to explore overall grain shape variability independent of size in both the reference set and for the unknown archaeological sample. The normalisation of grains shapes effectively reduces anomalous within-species variations due to small differences in growth stage and size and was determined by scaling each grain so that the average radius about the hilum was one. The normalised grain shapes were then rotationally aligned about the grain hila, minimising the radial distance between the grains within each of the species and unknown archaeological sample.

Variability in normalised starch grain shapes was further explored by the identification of within-sample subgroups across the archaeological and comparative reference set (see Hayes et al. 2021). Normalised grain shapes were compared within-species using hierarchical clustering (average distance between radii about the shapes) to determine whether there were distinct subgroups of grain shapes within the sample. Subgroups of the sets were determined using a cut-off equal to 0.25 of the maximum separation across all grains (from all reference species and archaeological samples). All starch grains (reference species and archaeological samples) were subgrouped using this cut-off to ensure uniform within-subgroup similarity. Subgroups were denoted by adding the subgroup number to the end of the sample name, such as KAI25-SP7-20cm-bs pestle frag-1, KAI25-SP7-20cm-bs pestle frag-2 and KAI25-SP7-20cm-bs pestle frag-3. The same suffix labelling was used for the reference species.

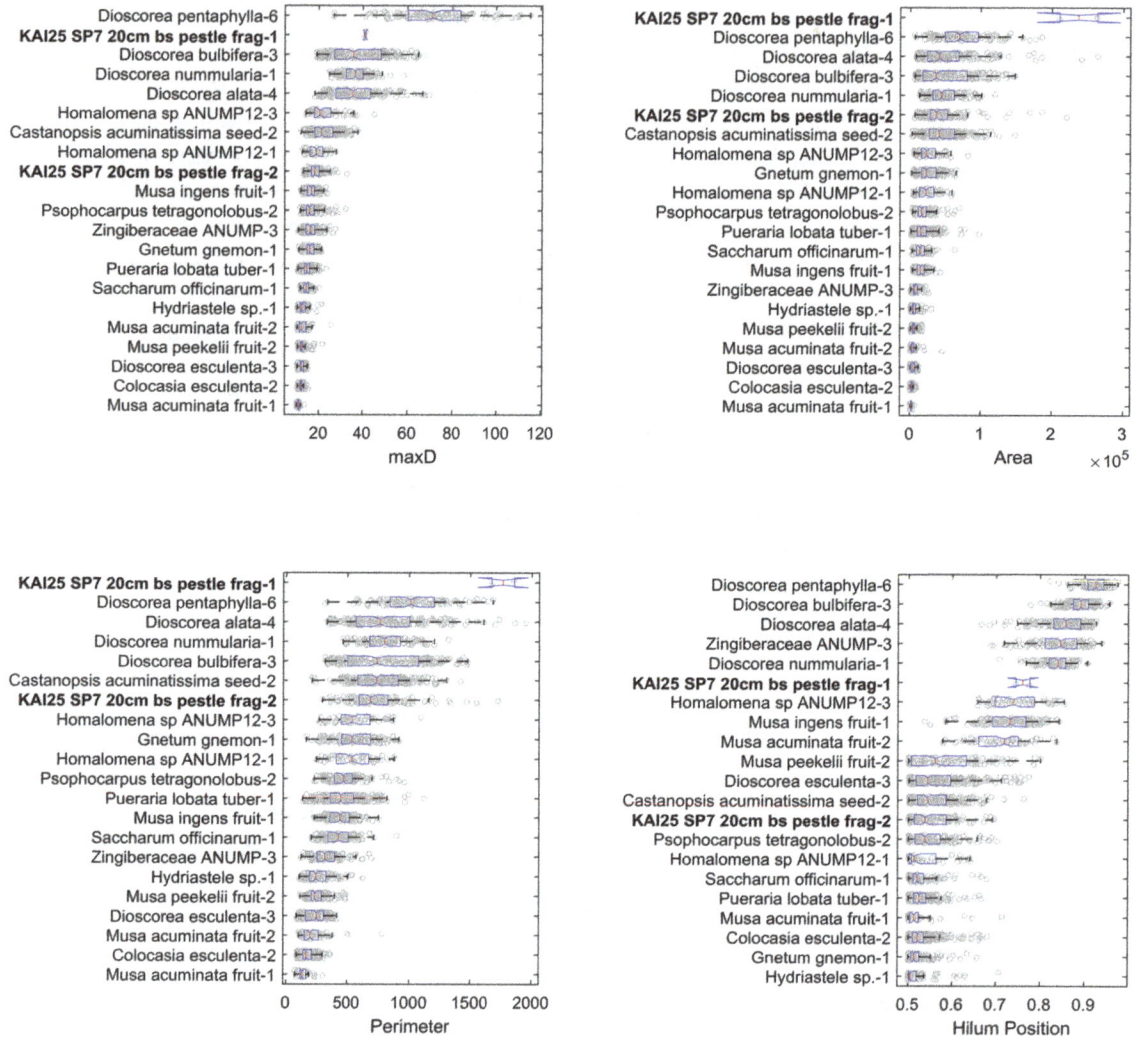

Figure 18.7: Box plots of maximum diameter through the hilum, MaxD, starch grain area, starch grain perimeter and starch grain hilum position for the comparative reference set and the archaeological samples KAI25-SP7-20cm-bs (indicated in bold).

Notes: The subgroup KAI25-SP7-20cm-bs pestle frag-1 contained only two starch grains and was not further analysed. All the data points are shown. The boxes indicate the values of the data quartiles q_1, q_2 and q_3. The whiskers indicate the re-transformed range of less than $q_3 + 1.5(q_3 - q_1)$ and greater than $q_3 - 1.5(q_3 - q_1)$.

Source: Illustration by Adelle Coster.

The distributions of the macro-scale metrics (maximum diameter through the hilum, area, perimeter and hilum position—a measure of the offset of the hilum from the grain centre) for each of the reference subgroups with greater than 25 grains were compared to the archaeological samples (cf. Hayes et al. 2021) (Figure 18.7). Note the subgroup KAI25-SP7-20cm-bs pestle frag-1 contained only two starch grains and was not further analysed. The subgroup KAI25-SP7-20cm-bs pestle frag-2 however, contained 118 grains, the macro-scale metrics of which also indicate a large degree of similarity within this subgroup across these measures—and that it may be largely composed of a single species.

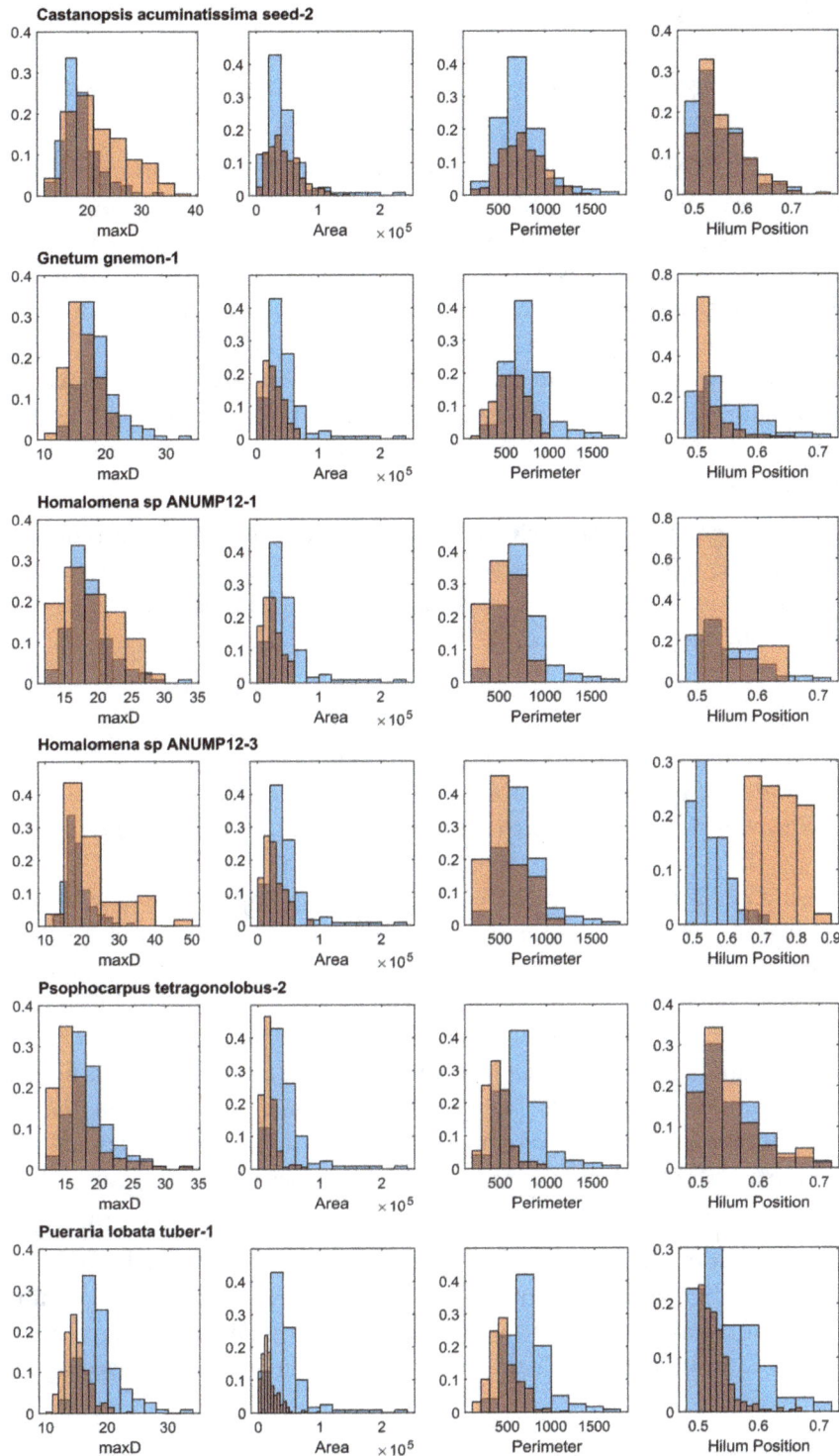

Figure 18.8: Histogram plots of size metrics.

Notes: The plots show maximum diameter through the hilum, area, perimeter and hilum position for the populations of grains comparing the archaeological sample with the five species that have the best overlap with the unknown sample: *Castanopsis acuminatissima* seed-2; *Gnetum gnemon*-1; *Psophocarpus tetragonolobus*-2; *Homalomena* sp. ANUMP12-1; Homalomena sp. ANUMP12-3; *Pueraria lobata* tuber-1. KAI25-SP7-20cm-bs is in blue, reference species in orange.

Source: Illustration by Adelle Coster.

Six subgroups were identified as having significant overlaps across all the macro-scale metrics with the larger unknown subgroup (KAI25-SP7-20cm-bs-2, 118 grains): *Castanopsis acuminatissima* seed-2, *Gnetum gnemon*-1, *Psophocarpus tetragonolobus*-2, *Homalomena* sp. ANUMP12-1, *Homalomena* sp. ANUMP12-3 and *Pueraria lobata* tuber-1.

The proximity of the archaeological (KAI25-SP7-20cm-bs) assemblage and *C. acuminatissima* across the four metrics indicate their close association and overlap. *Homalomena* sp. is also in close proximity to the KAI25 sample for MaxD. *D. pentaphylla* overlaps in the outlier grains for this metric but is unlikely to be a contributing species. There was also good correspondence in area between the archaeological sample and *C. acuminatissima*. The intervening *Dioscorea* samples do not match when compared using other attributes. The hilum position of *C. acuminatissima* and KAI25 assemblages completely overlap, whereas the large *Dioscorea* groups are clearly differentiated on this measure. *Homalomena* does overlap in hilum position as do the two *Musa* species and *D. esculenta*, however *D. esculenta* and *M. acuminata* can be excluded as dominant contributors to the archaeological assemblage due to the size of the grains.

Histogram plots of the unknown grains overlaid with the six identified subgroups illustrate the overlaps in the distributions of the macro-scale metrics (Figure 18.8). The remaining reference subgroups had distinctly different metric distributions over one or more of the attributes and were excluded from further comparison.

The six reference subgroups were then analysed to determine the similarity of characteristics with the archaeological grains. For each unknown archaeological starch grain, and each reference subgroup, the five closest matching grains, based on the normalised grain shape, were then independently verified (by JF) in which the correspondence was evaluated of the non-quantitative grain characteristics in the micrographs to those of the reference species (Note that categorical features were not used in the identification of the matching references.). The analysis focused on the removal of non-attributable species based on a population analysis of the samples (recalling that the samples were determined with uniform within-group similarity of their normalised shapes). Thus, for each reference subgroup, the proportion of unknown grains that could not be attributed to that species was determined, with some archaeological grains being attributed to more than one reference subgroup. The attributions of the KAI25-SP7-20cm-bs-2 archaeological subgroup is shown in a Venn diagram (Figure 18.9). Note that the two *Homalomena* subgroups (although distinct in shape) have been combined in this figure. Of the 118 unknown grains, 68 unknown grains (57 per cent) were attributed to *C. acuminatissima* (42 of which were to only *C. acuminatissima*), 28 were not attributed to any of the species (24 per cent), and 22 were attributed to species other than *C. acuminatissima* (19 per cent) (see Figure 18.9).

When all the metric distributions of the grains were examined (Figures 18.7–8), along with visual verification and population attribution (Figure 18.9), the best correlation of the archaeological assemblage is to *C. acuminatissima*. The species attribution does not necessarily hold for all the grains in the archaeological sample, but certainly accounts for the majority of the features documented, reinforcing the conclusion that *C. acuminatissima* is the primary contributor to the archaeological assemblage.

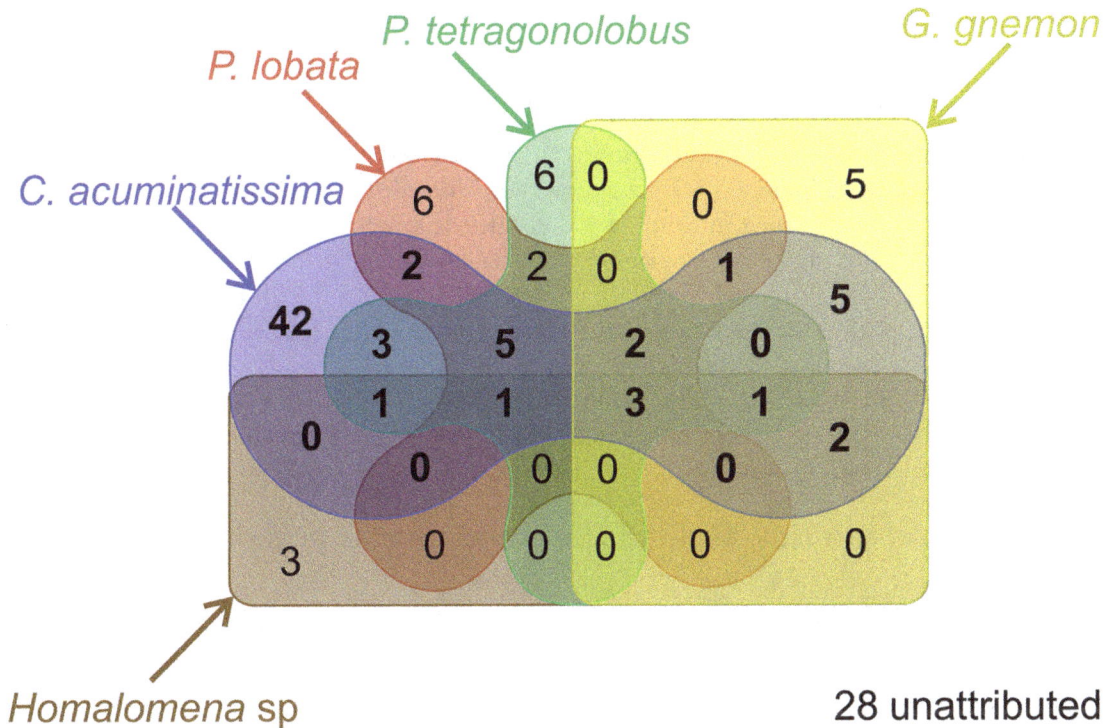

Figure 18.9: Venn diagram indicating the number of grains of the KAI25-SP7-20cm-bs-2 artefact sample attributed to species in the reference set.

Notes: *C. acuminatissima* attributions are shown in bold. The colours of the species names shown on the diagram correlate to the colours in the Venn diagram. In several cases, the starch grain features (size, hilum position, shape and surface morphologies) are shared between some species making it difficult to differentiate between them. Where a starch grain cannot be differentiated from another species, then these are shown as an overlap with that species. For example, 42 of the starch grains have been solely attributed to *C. acuminatissima*. The remaining numbers shown in the purple 'dumbbell shape' represent starch grains that are indistinguishable from *C. acuminatissima* and one or more of the other species in the reference set. For instance, two grains of *P. lobata* share common features with *C. acuminatissima* (upper left), while five grains share similarities with *P. tetragonolobus*, *P. lobata* and *C. acuminatissima* (centre left). It was found that 28 of the 118 grains analysed could not be attributed to any species in the reference set.

Source: The base intersections for the figure were adapted from output of the Venn diagram tool at and prepared by Adelle Coster.

Discussion and conclusion

Starchy tree nut use and human diet

Functional studies of stone artefacts, particularly ancient starch analyses, have opened an important window on understanding the long-term exploitation and use of starchy plant resources in a broad range of archaeological contexts (e.g. Fullagar et al. 2008; Liu et al. 2010; Nadel et al. 2012; Piperno 2004). Starchy tree nuts were widely used globally in the Holocene, some requiring either simple or complex processing to render them edible and/or palatable, and have been recognised as an important component of human diets (e.g. Basgall 1987; Liu et al. 2010; Pedley 1993; Rosenberg 2008).

The complex processing of toxic starchy tree nuts has been employed since the early–mid-Holocene in the North Queensland rainforests (Cosgrove et al. 2007). Other plant foods requiring comparable preparation methods (e.g. *Cycas* seeds) have a similar or even a greater antiquity of use in Australia (Asmussen 2011; Beck 1992; Smith 1982). Archaeological sequences in rainforest sites contain abundant carbonised shell remains (Cosgrove et al. 2007; Horsfall 1996), as the hard outer shells (endocarp) of tree nuts (primarily family Lauraceae) were discarded after baking in ground ovens and prior to pounding then leaching in running water. Ancient starch studies have demonstrated that these nuts were pounded on the formal manufactured slate pounding/grinding stones called 'morahs' (Field et al. 2009, 2016). Similarly, in North America, China and the Near East, archaeological studies have documented the use of starchy tree nuts (acorns) from oaks in the family Fagaceae, which also required complex processing to render them edible (e.g. Basgall 1987; Liu et al. 2010; Rosenberg 2008). The tradition of exploiting starchy tree nuts that contain chemicals acting as toxins or irritants appears to be common across a range of environmental contexts and continents, and New Guinea is no exception.

Tree nuts and the New Guinea Highland mortar and pestle complex

The New Guinea member of the Fagaceae (oak) family, *Castanopsis acuminatissima,* produces starchy nuts that are generally recorded as being roasted before consumption. They have been reported as eaten raw or cooked (Bulmer 1964), but Swadling has noted from other reports that if eaten raw, 'doing so can cause anaemia, emaciation and mouth ulcers' (Swadling 2021 and references therein). In New Guinea, *C. acuminatissima* nuts are widely available during the wet season and may have been exploited opportunistically and continue to have a place in modern diets. *C. acuminatissima* endocarps are thin, easily removed and discarded, and evidence of their long-term use has come from the identification of use-related residues (starch grains) on stone artefact surfaces (e.g. Field et al. 2020). The discovery of *C. acuminatissima* residues in the current and recent studies has effectively focused our attention on the importance of starchy tree nuts in highland diets from at least the mid-Holocene. When *C. acuminatissima* starch grains have been identified on tool surfaces, the indications are that they were routinely pounded, along with other starchy plants. In the study presented here, the evidence unequivocally confirms the association of *C. acuminatissima* tree nuts with the mid-Holocene Highland mortar and pestle complex.

The decline in the use of stone mortars and pestles in the Late Holocene has been argued to be a response to the decline in *C. acuminatissima* availability due to forest clearance and decreasing connectivity with the coast, the latter associated with the contraction of the Sepik inland sea (Bulmer 1964; Swadling 2021; Swadling and Hide 2005). Nonetheless, *C. acuminatissima* is still widely exploited in highland communities as a traditional food, with the potential to supplement diets in times of drought or other environmental disruptions, as observed for *Pueraria lobata* (Allen and Bourke 2009). The question remains as to whether the decline of mortars and pestles is linked to the arrival of Lapita cultural groups around 3300 years ago. The appearance of pottery and associated technologies in the region may have had a significant impact on methods of food use and preparation and appears to be broadly coincident with decline and subsequent disappearance of the stone mortar and pestle complex (see Gaffney et al. 2015).

The Upper Kaironk pestle fragment

Despite its fragmentary nature, the usewear and technology analyses of the Imbiben artefact have suggested it is part of a formally manufactured pestle, other carved stone object, or a pestle with a carved handle. However, the 'multidisciplinary' approach used here (see Fullagar et al. 1996), which considers a number of lines of evidence—stone raw material, technology, usewear, the tool's life-history and the starch residues—leads us to conclude that the artefact is indeed a fragment from a pestle.

The pestle fragment may be the result of an early break soon after manufacture, in which case usewear associated with plant processing would not have been well developed as it was not subject to high contact with a mortar or working surface. The lack of distinctive usewear is likely a consequence of the fragment origin, namely from the junction of the handle and the working end, where the dominant wear would be from manufacturing rather than use and where abundant residues might be expected with the immersion of the pestle in soft plant tissue. *Castanopsis acuminatissima* starchy nuts were processed along with other starchy plant species as seen in the Waim and Joe's Garden studies.

There are now functional studies of four examples of excavated finds of the mortar and pestle complex from the New Guinea Highlands. Three examples were recovered during the current project, supporting the proposition by Bulmer (1964) that mortars and pestles were used for pounding tree nuts, in this case *C. acuminatissima*. More recently, it was proposed that *Colocasia esculenta* (taro) may have been processed with these implements, mainly because of their co-occurrence with gardened areas (Swadling and Hide 2005). Residue studies have identified *Colocasia esculenta* on at least one flaked stone artefact (K76 S29B) recovered from the Kuk Swamp sediments (Fullagar et al. 2006), but to date there has been no empirical evidence that taro was pounded with mortars and pestles in the highlands. Functional analyses of pestles and mortars from lowland contexts will undoubtedly expand our understanding of the range of uses and associated tasks.

When Ralph Bulmer (Bulmer 1964) first published his paper speculating on the range of tree nuts that may have been processed with mortars and pestles, the notion that techniques and methodologies would be available to accomplish these identifications was beyond consideration. While these methodologies are now developing, the ancient starch analyses undertaken here are complex, time consuming and under continual development as we pursue a quantitative and transparent approach to identifying plant taxa from unknown starch grains. It is a robust and replicable method for identifying the remains of starchy plant processing on these tools. Essential to identifying the pestle fragment described here was the multidisciplinary approach. Usewear, technology and residue analysis combined can provide a high level of confidence that each method on its own may not provide.

In conclusion, the confirmed use of *C. acuminatissima* at Imbiben adds to our understanding of the role of tree nuts in the diet of highlanders from at least the Mid Holocene. Even after the changes wrought following the arrival of Lapita cultural groups just over three millennia ago, the introduction of sweet potato in the 1700s, and despite the well-documented land clearing, traditional foods such as *C. acuminatissima*, *Pandanus* sp., taro and other starchy plants have continued to be a constant in the diets and traditions of highlanders to the present day. As new research investigates the nature of plant foods and technological changes over time, a clearer picture of highland settlement and resource use will also emerge, challenging both current discourse and approaches to archaeobotanical studies in these unique environments.

Acknowledgements

We wish to dedicate this paper to the late Mr Henry Arifeae, a wonderful friend, colleague and mentor, whom we will dearly miss. We are grateful to the Kalam communities of the Kaironk and Simbai Valleys, Madang Province, PNG for their welcome, support and friendships, including Esron Dotch, Makindon Ynemb, Henry Yei, Joel Engini, Sucklyn Gi, Allanson Auseng. We are especially grateful to the staff of the Kalam Guesthouse in Simbai, particularly Ronald Ynemb, John Yama and Dickson Kangi. At Alvan, Councillor Benson Balik, and at Imbiben we wish to thank Nathaniel Imbugu and family and the Imbiben community for their assistance and hospitality. We also thank the National Research Institute, particularly Georgia Kaipu, the Provincial Government of Madang, the sitting Governor at the time the Hon. Jim Kas, and the late Sir Peter Barter for supporting the research program. We thank the National Museum and Art Gallery of Papua New Guinea, namely, the late Henry Arifeae, Alois Kuaso and Dr Andrew Motu. Dr Carol Lentfer kindly supplied the reference samples of all *Musa* species examined here. Funding was provided by Australian Research Council Discovery Grant (ARC DP140103796) awarded to Field and Summerhayes for the period 2015–2017 and the University of New South Wales. 3D scans of the KAI25 artefact were generated with the assistance of Dr Sam Lin (University of Wollongong).

References

Adams, J.L. 2008. Beyond the broken. In J.R. Ebeling and Y.M. Rowan (eds), *New approaches to old stones: Recent studies of ground stone artifacts,* pp. 213–229. Equinox Archaeology Books, London.

Allen, B.J. and R.M. Bourke 2009. People, land and environment. In R.M. Bourke and T. Harwood (eds), *Food and agriculture in Papua New Guinea*, pp. 27–127. ANU E Press, Canberra. doi.org/10.22459/FAPNG.08.2009.01.

Ambrose, W. 1964. Manus, mortars and the Kava concoction. In A. Pawley (ed.), *Man and a half: Essays in Pacific anthropology and ethnobiology in honour of Ralph Bulmer*, pp. 461–469. Memoirs of the Polynesian Society 48. The Polynesian Society, Auckland.

Asmussen, B. 2011. 'There is likewise a nut …' a comparative ethnobotany of Aboriginal processing methods and consumption of Australian *Bowenia, Cycas, Lepidozamia* and *Macrozamia* species. In J. Specht and R. Torrence (eds), *Changing perspectives in Australian archaeology: Papers in Honour of Val Attenbrow*, pp. 147–163. Technical Reports of the Australian Museum Online 23. Australian Museum, Sydney. doi.org/10.3853/j.1835-4211.23.2011.1575.

Barton, F.R. 1908. Note on stone pestles from British New Guinea. *Man* 8:1–2. doi.org/10.2307/2839897.

Basgall, M.E. 1987. Resource intensification among hunter-gatherers: Acorn economics in prehistoric California. *Research in Economic Anthropology* 9:21–52.

Beck, W. 1992. Aboriginal preparation of *Cycas* seeds in Australia. *Economic Botany* 46(2):133–147. doi.org/10.1007/BF02930628.

Berndt, R.M. 1954. Contemporary significance of prehistoric stone objects in the eastern central highlands of New Guinea. *Anthropos* 49:553–587.

Bourke, M. 2010. Altitudinal limits of 230 economic crop species in Papua New Guinea. In S.G. Haberle, J. Stevenson and M. Prebble (eds), *Altered ecologies: Fire, climate and human influence on terrestrial landscapes,* pp. 473–512. Terra Australis 32. ANU E Press, Canberra. doi.org/10.22459/TA32.11.2010.27.

Bourke, R.M. 1996. Edible indigenous nuts in Papua New Guinea. In M.L. Stevens, R.M. Bourke and B.R. Evans (eds), *South Pacific indigenous nuts*, pp. 45–55. ACIAR Proceedings. Australian Centre for International Agricultural Research, Canberra.

Bulmer, R.N.H. 1964. Edible seeds and prehistoric stone mortars in the highlands of east New Guinea. *Man* 64:147–150. doi.org/10.2307/2797699.

Bulmer, S. 1975. Settlement and economy in prehistoric Papua New Guinea: a review of the archaeological evidence. *Journal de la Société des Océanistes* 31:7–75. doi.org/10.3406/jso.1975.2688.

Chappell, J.M.A. 1964. Stone mortars in the New Guinea Highlands: A note on their manufacture and use. *Man* 64:146–147. doi.org/10.2307/2797698.

Coode, M. 1983. A conspectus of *Sloanea* (Elaeocarpaceae). *Old World Kew Bulletin* 38(3):347–427 (+1–27). doi.org/10.2307/4107835.

Cosgrove, R., J. Field and A. Ferrier 2007. The archaeology of Australia's tropical rainforests. *Palaeogeography, Palaeoclimatology, Palaeoecology* 251:150–173. doi.org/10.1016/j.palaeo.2007.02.023.

Coster, A.C.F. and J.H. Field 2015. What starch grain is that? A geometric morphometric approach to determining plant species origin. *Journal of Archaeological Science: Reports* 58:9–25. doi.org/10.1016/j.jas.2015.03.014.

Coster. A.C.F. and J.H. Field 2018. The shape of things to come—Using geometric and morphometric analyses to identify archaeological starch grains. In R.S. Anderssen, P. Broadbridge and Y. Fukumoto (eds), *Agriculture as a metaphor for creativity in all human endeavors*, pp. 1–6. Mathematics for Industry 28. Springer, Singapore. doi.org/10.1007/978-981-10-7811-8_1.

Fairbairn, A.S., G.S. Hope and G.R. Summerhayes 2006. Pleistocene occupation of New Guinea's highland and subalpine environments. *World Archaeology* 38:371–386. doi.org/10.1080/00438240600813293.

Field, J., R. Cosgrove, R. Fullagar and B. Lance 2009. Starch residues on grinding stones in private collections: A study of morahs from the tropical rainforests of NE Queensland. In M. Haslam and G. Robertson (eds), *Archaeological science under a microscope: Papers in honour of Tom Loy*, pp. 218–228. Terra Australis 30. Canberra, ANU Press. doi.org/10.22459/TA30.07.2009.17.

Field, J., L. Kealhofer, R. Cosgrove and A.C.F. Coster 2016. Human–environment dynamics during the Holocene in the Australian Wet Tropics of NE Queensland: A starch and phytolith study. *Journal of Anthropological Archaeology* 44:216–234. doi.org/10.1016/j.jaa.2016.07.007.

Field, J.H., B. Shaw and G.R. Summerhayes 2021. Pathways to the interior: Human settlement in the Simbai-Kaironk Valleys of the Madang Province, Papua New Guinea. *Australian Archaeology* 88:2–17. doi.org/10.1080/03122417.2021.2007600.

Field, J.H., G.R. Summerhayes, S. Luu, A.C.F. Coster, A. Ford, H. Mandui, R. Fullagar, E. Hayes, M. Leavesley, M. Lovave and L. Kealhofer 2020. Functional studies of flaked and ground stone artefacts reveal starchy tree nut and root exploitation in mid-Holocene Highland New Guinea. *The Holocene* 30(9):1360–1374. doi.org/10.1177/0959683620919983.

Fullagar, R., J. Field, T. Denham and C. Lentfer 2006. Early and mid-Holocene tool-use and processing of taro (*Colocasia esculenta*) and yam (*Dioscorea* sp.) and other plants at Kuk Swamp in the highlands of Papua New Guinea. *Journal of Archaeological Science* 33:595–614. doi.org/10.1016/j.jas.2005.07.020.

Fullagar, R., J. Field and L. Kealhofer 2008. Grinding stones and seeds of change: Starch and phytoliths as evidence of plant food processing. In Y.M. Rowan and J.R. Ebeling (eds), *New approaches to old stones: Recent studies of ground stone artefacts*, pp. 159–172. Equinox, London.

Fullagar, R., J. Furby and B. Hardy 1996. Residues on stone artefacts: State of a scientific art. *Antiquity* 70: 270–275. doi.org/10.1017/s0003598x00084027.

Gaffney, D., G.R. Summerhayes, A. Ford, J.M. Scott, T. Denham, J. Field and W.R. Dickinson 2015. Earliest pottery on New Guinea mainland reveals Austronesian influences in Highland environments 3000 years ago. *PLoS ONE* 10(9):e0134497. doi.org/10.1371/journal.pone.0134497.

Gardner, R.O. 2010. Plant names of the Kalam (Upper Kaironk Valley, Schrader Range, Papua New Guinea). *Records of the Auckland Museum* 47:5–50.

Golson, J., T. Denham, P. Hughes, P. Swadling and J. Muke (eds) 2017. *Ten thousand years of cultivation at Kuk Swamp in the Highlands of Papua New Guinea.* Terra Australis 46. ANU Press, Canberra. doi.org/10.22459/TA46.07.2017.

Gorecki, P.P. and D.S. Gillieson (eds) 1989. *A crack in the spine: Prehistory and ecology of the Jimi-Yuat Valley, Papua New Guinea.* Division of Anthropology and Archaeology, School of Behavioural Sciences, James Cook University of North Queensland, Townsville.

Haberle, S.G. 2007. Prehistoric human impact on rainforest biodiversity in highland New Guinea. *Philosophical Transactions of the Royal Society B* 362:219–228. doi.org/10.1098/rstb.2006.1981.

Hayes, E.H., J.H. Field, A.C.F. Coster, R. Fullagar, C. Matheson, S.A. Florin, M. Nango, D. Djandjomerr, B. Marwick, L.A. Wallis and M.A. Smith 2021. Holocene grinding stones at Madjedbebe reveal the processing of starchy plant taxa and animal tissue. *Journal of Archaeological Science: Reports* 35:102754. doi.org/10.1016/j.jasrep.2020.102754.

Hayes, E., C. Pardoe and R. Fullagar 2018. Sandstone grinding/pounding tools: Use-trace reference libraries and Australian archaeological applications. *Journal of Archaeological Science: Reports* 20:97–114. doi.org/10.1016/j.jasrep.2018.04.021.

Horsfall, N. 1996. Holocene occupation of the tropical rainforests of North Queensland. In P. Veth and P. Hiscock (eds), *Archaeology of Northern Australia: Regional perspectives*, pp. 175–190. The Anthropology Museum, University of Queensland, Brisbane.

Hyndman, D.C. 1984. Ethnobotany of Wopkaimin *Pandanus*: A significant Papua New Guinea plant resource. *Economic Botany* 38(3):287–303. doi.org/10.1007/BF02859007.

Liu, L., J. Field, R. Fullagar, S. Bestel, X. Chen and X. Ma 2010. What did grinding stones grind? New light on Early Neolithic subsistence economy in the Middle Yellow River Valley, China. *Antiquity* 84(325): 816–833. doi.org/10.1017/S0003598X00100249.

Majnep, I.S. and R. Bulmer 1977. *Birds of my Kalam country.* Auckland University Press, Auckland.

Majnep, I.S. and R. Bulmer 2007. *Animals the ancestors hunted: An account of the wild mammals of the Kalam area, Papua New Guinea.* Crawford House Publishing, Adelaide.

Nadel, D., D.R. Piperno, I. Holst, A. Snir and E. Weiss 2012. New evidence for the processing of wild cereal grains at Ohalo II, a 23,000-year-old campsite on the shore of the Sea of Galilee, Israel. *Antiquity* 86:990–2013. doi.org/10.1017/S0003598X00048201.

Paijmans, K. (ed.). 1976. *New Guinea vegetation.* ANU Press, Canberra.

Pawley, A. and R. Bulmer 2011. *A dictionary of Kalam with ethnographic notes.* Pacific Linguistics, The Australian National University, Canberra.

Pedley, H. 1993. Plant detoxification in the rainforest: The processing of poisonous plant foods by the Jirrbal-Girramay people. Unpublished MA thesis. James Cook University, Townsville.

Piperno, D.R., E. Weiss, I. Holst and D. Nadel 2004. Processing of wild cereal grains in the Upper Palaeolithic revealed by starch grain analysis. *Nature* 430:670–673. doi.org/10.1038/nature02734.

Rosenberg, D. 2008. The possible use of acorns in past economies of the Southern Levant: A staple food or a negligible food source? *Levant* 40(2):167–175. doi.org/10.1179/175638008X348025.

Roullier, C., J. Benoit, D.B. McKey and V. Lebot 2013. Historical collections reveal patterns of diffusion of sweet potato in Oceania obscured by modern plant movements and recombination. *Proceedings of the National Academy of Sciences USA* 110(6):2205–2210. doi.org/10.1073/pnas.1211049110.

Seligman, C.G. and T.A. Joyce 1907. On prehistoric objects in British New Guinea. In W.H.R. Rivers, R.R. Marett, N.W. Thomas (eds), *Anthropological essays presented to Edward Burnett Tylor, in honour of his 75th birthday*, pp. 325–341. Clarendon Press, Oxford.

Shaw, B., J. Field, G.R. Summerhayes, S. Coxe, A.C.F. Coster, A. Ford, J. Haro, H. Arifeae, E. Hull, G. Jacobsen, R. Fullagar, E. Hayes and L. Kealhofer 2020. Emergence of a Neolithic in Highland New Guinea by 5000 to 4000 years ago. *Science Advances* 6(13):eaay4573. doi.org/10.1126/sciadv.aay4573.

Smith, M. 1982. Late Pleistocene Zamia exploitation in southern Australia. *Archaeology in Oceania* 17(3): 117–121. doi.org/10.1002/j.1834-4453.1982.tb00054.x.

Summerhayes, G.R., M. Leavesley, A. Fairbairn, H. Mandui, J. Field, A. Ford and R. Fullagar 2010. Human adaptation and plant use in highland New Guinea 49,000 to 44,000 years ago. *Science* 330:78–81. doi.org/10.1126/science.1193130.

Swadling, P. 1986. *Papua New Guinea's prehistory*. The National Museum and Art Gallery of Papua New Guinea, Port Moresby.

Swadling, P. 2013. Prehistoric stone mortars. In L. Bolton, N. Thomas, E. Bonshek, J. Adams and B. Burt (eds), *Melanesia: Art and encounter*, pp. 78–82. British Museum Press, London.

Swadling, P. 2021. Mortars and pestles make the mid-Holocene occupation of New Guinea and the Bismarck Archipelago visible. In I.J. McNiven and B. David (eds), *The Oxford handbook of the archaeology of Indigenous Australia and New Guinea*. Online edition. Oxford Academic. doi.org/10.1093/oxfordhb/9780190095611.013.26.

Swadling, P. and R. Hide 2005. Changing landscape and social interaction: Looking at agricultural history from a Sepik-Ramu perspective. In A. Pawley, R. Attenborough, J. Golson and R. Hide (eds), *Papuan pasts: Cultural, linguistic and biological histories of Papuan-speaking peoples*, pp. 289–327. Pacific Linguistics, The Australian National University, Canberra.

Swadling, P., P. Wiessner and A. Tumu 2008. Prehistoric stone artefacts from Enga and the implication of links between the highlands, lowlands and islands for early agriculture in Papua New Guinea. *Le Journal de la Societe des Oceanistes* 126–127:271–292. doi.org/10.4000/jso.2942.

Watson, J.B. 1964. A previously unreported root crop from the New Guinea highlands. *Ethnology* 3(1):1–5. doi.org/10.2307/4617552.

Watson, J.B. 1968. Pueraria: Names and traditions of a lesser crop of the central highlands, New Guinea. *Ethnology* 7(3):268–279. doi.org/10.2307/3772892.

Watson, V.D. and J.D. Cole 1977. *Prehistory of the Eastern Highlands of New Guinea*. University of Washington Press, Seattle.

19

Heirlooming and shell money beads in the Solomon Islands

Katherine Szabó and Fiona Petchey

Abstract

Strings of shell money made up of hundreds, if not thousands, of intensively worked shell beads have featured in the accounts of anthropologists of Melanesia for over a century, and large collections of these strings are to be found in major museum collections around the world. In the Solomon Islands, the tradition of their production continues to this day. Despite new strings still entering circulation, within villages in and around Malaita there are also older strings, either held communally or under tabu. Local wisdom states that some of these are around two hundred years old. The historical and anthropological literature also makes mention of heirloom shell money strings, although how long such strings may be curated and remain active in cultural life has never been quantified. Here, we investigate two large, complex shell money strings from the Solomon Islands, held in the collections of the Museum of Archaeology and Anthropology, University of Cambridge: one from Makira and the other from Nggela. Through direct accelerator mass spectrometry (AMS) radiocarbon dating of individual beads, we establish the restringing and combining of strings of different ages into new strings, as well as the maintenance in use of individual beads for up to two to three hundred years. This demonstrable case of the heirlooming of shell beads has repercussions for archaeology, and the potential cultural longevity of shell valuables such as these should be a consideration in interpretations.

Shell money in museums and on the landscape

Western Island Melanesian shell money and shell valuables are mainstays of both the anthropological literature and ethnographic museum collections. Studies of their production, use and circulation have been used as a window to explore diverse but core facets of anthropological enquiry such as exchange and obligation relationships, alliance formation, peacemaking and prestige acquisition (e.g. Dalton 1965; Graeber 1996; Malinowski 1922; Munn 1986). Their centrality to social affairs was well noted by early European travellers, collectors and residents, with lengthy discussions of the variety of types of shell money produced and circulated and their relative rankings against both each other and different sorts of commodities (e.g. Danks 1888; Petri 1936; Schneider 1905). This almost taxonomic approach to the collection, cataloguing and description of shell money types lent itself well to a museum context, and thus it is no surprise that museums holding early colonial collections from Papua New Guinea and the Solomon Islands have large collections of shell money (e.g. Burt 2009; Lewis 1929; Szabó 2019).

The very structured approach to the European collection and discussion of shell money seems to have given rise to the 'didactic collection' (Szabó 2018): instructive capsule collections of the different stages of production of a variety of shell money types established in the literature, and held in various large museum collections. So focused was the literature on key, formal types of shell money that strands which looked like shell money, and utilised the same types of beads without conforming comfortably to known types, caused consternation. Alison Hingston-Quiggin, author of *A survey of primitive money: The beginnings of currency* (1949:158) protested that:

> The difficulties of identifying shell-money in New Ireland are increased by the custom of stringing several different kinds together, and mixed strings are a special characteristic, the meaning of which is unexplained.

The very sorts of strings to which Hingston-Quiggin was referring are within the collections of the Museum of Archaeology and Anthropology, University of Cambridge, where she volunteered and worked over a number of years in the early twentieth century. Rather than fitting into the rigid formulations of herself and earlier authors, these align much more closely to what would now be recognised as heirloom strings.

Heirlooming and shell money

Heirloom shell money strings have received less attention in the literature than circulating types but Wagner's (2014) discussion of circulating (new) and non-circulating (heirloom) types of shell money (*mangin*) within Barok society in central New Ireland provides a useful starting point. He describes the *mangin* used in transactions in customary contexts, such as the purchase of pigs for *kastom* feasts, as 'circulating *mangin*'. These he contrasts with 'heirloom *mangin*', which are old, polished and often strung in antiquated forms. Although sometimes displayed, these are described as being priceless and without exchange value (Wagner 2014). A similar distinction was made by the Siuai of Bougainville between *pure* shell money, which could be utilised as currency and *tomui* shell money, which could never be used as such and was considered a clan heirloom (Oliver 1955 in Connell 1977:85). Eves (2000) also contrasts circulating and heirloom, clan-held money for the Lelet of central New Ireland. It should be noted that despite titling his well-known article 'Changes in heirloom jewellery in the Central Solomons', the prestige trade valuables Belshaw (1950) discusses do not necessarily fit into either the category of 'jewellery' or 'heirloom'.

Although the findings of Wagner, Oliver and Eves cannot be simply extended to surrounding cultural contexts, the principal findings were mirrored in KS's fieldwork in Malaita, Solomon Islands. The contemporary and historical production of shell money in Malaita is widely known and still supports entire communities (Goto 1996; Ivens 1927; Woodford 1908). However, not as visible in daily life are heirloom shell money strings. These strings were admired for their smoothness and fineness, communally held and displayed at special events (see Figure 19.1). Alternatively, such as in Langalanga Lagoon, they were considered *tambu* ('taboo') by senior men and only accompanied males could look upon them (see Figure 19.2 for key locations mentioned in the text). Although orally recounted histories suggested a time depth for heirloom strands of generations, it was difficult to quantify in calendar years. Local elders consistently suggested around two hundred years, but reinforced that this was a calculated suggestion rather than an assertion. Thus, how long such artefacts can remain in active cultural use is largely unknown.

Figure 19.1: Community-held heirloom shell money being displayed by the priest of Outau Village, south of Lau Lagoon, eastern Malaita, May 2016.

Source: Photograph by K. Szabó.

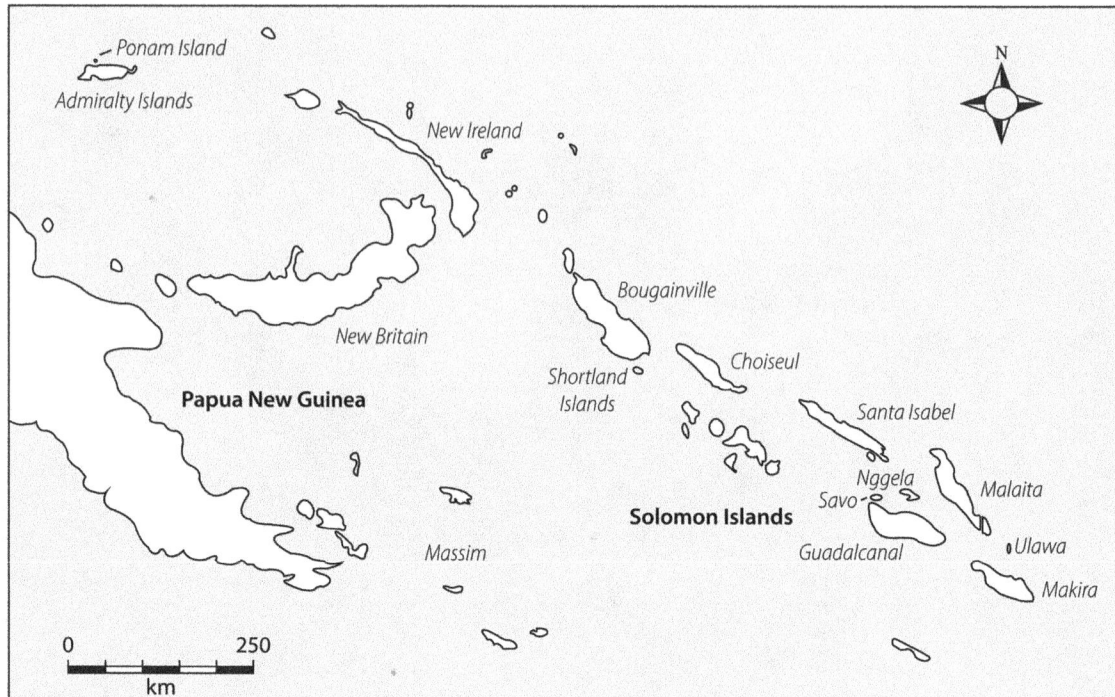

Figure 19.2: Map of the Solomon Islands, showing key locations mentioned in the text.

Source: Original drawing by K. Szabó.

A number of large and often complex shell money strings from the Solomon Islands held in the collections of the Museum of Archaeology and Anthropology (MAA), University of Cambridge, were studied in 2017 by KS. Such strings did not comfortably fit the descriptions of standardised forms of shell money described by those such as Lewis (1929) and were each unique in their construction and use of different bead types. The beads were generally well worn and accorded individually with types typically used in the strings of circulating money. Given commentary on heirloom shell money by Malaitan informants to KS as well as sources such as Wagner (2014), it was hypothesised that these were heirloom shell money strands. The secure places and dates of collection provided a robust starting point from which to investigate: (1) how long individual beads had been in circulation; and (2) whether beads from the same string were contemporaneous. This chapter presents these results.

Two complex shell money strands from the Solomon Islands

Over research visits from 2016 to 2018, 156 western Melanesian shell valuables in the MAA collections were studied in detail by KS. In all instances analysis involved the identification of raw materials, working and use traces, and any curation episodes including refashioning, restringing and recombining components. This analysis was done with the aid of a Dinolite AM4815 Edge series digital microscope. The identification of raw materials utilised two lines of enquiry: (1) the assessment of surface features including colouration, patterning, texture and features indicative of the original shell morphology such as remnant gastropod whorls; and (2) assessment of the microstructural composition and layering in cross-section. The latter drew on a tailor-made reference and image library, collating images and information on the cross-sections of a wide range of molluscan raw materials. This facilitated the identification of numerous ground beads, where surface details had been abraded away. The identification and recording of evidence for manufacture, use and modification followed prior studies undertaken by KS (e.g. Szabó 2018, 2019; Szabó and Koppel 2015; Weston et al. 2017).

The two shell money strings from the Solomon Islands reported on here were both large and complex and had beads which were noted to have come adrift during routine conservation. As there was no way of knowing how these beads had originally been strung, they had been bagged and labelled alongside each string, thereby opening up the possibility of radiocarbon dating with the permission of the MAA Museum Committee.

It should be noted that although the strings studied were termed 'shell money' for museum cataloguing purposes, there seems to be no *a priori* reason to assume they were circulating currency at their time of collection, or indeed that the strings were understood in that manner locally. There may be further information in the MAA archives, but Covid-19 closures means this could not be checked and the archives are as yet undigitised.

String Z10604/E1902.190

MAA Z10604/E1902.190 was collected in the central Solomon Islands chain by the Anglican Melanesian Mission minister David Ruddock. When not at the Melanesian Mission base in Norfolk Island, Ruddock was primarily stationed in Savo, off the north-west coast of Guadalcanal in the central Solomons, from 1880 to 1884, so we can assume the string was collected during this period. The collection location is noted as the 'Florida Islands' (now Nggela), which are just to the east of Savo, and the various mentions of Ruddock as a traveller on Mission journeys around the central Solomon Islands provide plenty of opportunity for an Nggela collection point (see Armstrong 1900; Hilliard 1978). The MAA accession number indicates an accession date into the museum's collections of 1902.

MAA Z10604/E1902.190 is a large, delicate and complex multi-stranded bead string composed of 18 individual strands (Figure 19.3). Given the fragility of the artefact it was not lifted from its packaging for analysis but was studied in situ. Particular attention was paid to raw material identification, condition and usewear assessment of individual beads, and patterns of stringing.

Figure 19.3: Shell money string MAA Z10604/ E1902.190 from the collections of the Museum of Archaeology and Anthropology, University of Cambridge.

Source: Photograph by Josh Murfitt.

Figure 19.4: Detail of *Chama* sp. red beads and white beads mainly manufactured from *Anadara antiquata* and *Tegillarca granosa* from Z10604/E1902.190 at 35× magnification.

Source: Photograph by K. Szabó.

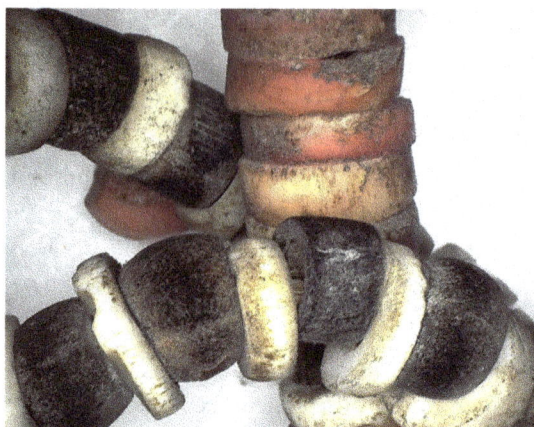

Figure 19.5: Alternating white Arcidae and darker palm endocarp and plant stem beads from Z10604/E1902.190 at 35× magnification.

Source: Photograph by K. Szabó.

The dominant bead type was a disc bead of a reddish hue, manufactured from a species of *Chama* jewel box oyster (Chamidae) (Figure 19.4). These are analogous to the red *Chama* beads still manufactured today in Malaita for shell money (e.g. Woodford 1908; KS pers. obs.). Intermixed either singly or in groups are beads of other types and materials, most notably white beads mostly produced from *Anadara* and *Tegillarca* (Arcidae) valves (Figures 19.4 and 19.5), small, pierced palm endocarps of a dark brown colour and dark tubular beads manufactured from a plant stem (Figure 19.5). Groups of strands are fastened together at different points by large, hewn discs of *Nautilus* shell. Most strands are comprised of disc beads threaded face to face, but there are occasional long stretches where very worn white *Anadara* and *Tegillarca* beads are threaded at angles in a herringbone pattern (see Paravicini 1942–45:168 for a schematic of this type of stringing). Beads in these stretches, as well as elsewhere on other strands, are of variable diameter and the degree of wear in adjacent beads is sometimes highly dissimilar. There are two free ends which dangle separately from the rest of the string, and these terminate in nut shells and red fabric. These two free ends have a greater variety of bead types, including some not seen elsewhere on the main strands (e.g. *Conus* spire beads). There is also less regularity in the pattern of stringing than the strands which form the main body of the artefact.

A number of beads of different types had come adrift from their original strands over the course of time. As there was no way of determining from which strand and location they originated, the Museum Committee of the MAA gave permission for six to be destructively sampled to provide accelerator mass spectrometry (AMS) radiocarbon determinations.

The six beads selected for AMS radiocarbon dating attempted to cover a range of both raw materials and degrees of wear. In all, two red *Chama* sp. beads, two white *Tegillarca granosa* beads and two pierced palm endocarps were selected.

String Z10855

String Z10855 was also collected by a minister of the Melanesian Mission: Reverend Frederick Drew. Described by Hilliard (1978:144) as 'a bank clerk son of an Eton science master', Drew was stationed on Makira (then San Cristobal) off the southern tip of Malaita for two terms (1904–1909 and 1913–1915[†]). No date of collection is recorded in the MAA catalogue but it is assumed to have been during one of these two residencies. He died on Makira in 1915, so if the string is from the second residency it would have had to have been taken to England and MAA via another person; and Stanley (1994:33) suggests this may have been the prolific collector and dealer Beasley.

Again, this is a multi-stranded bead string, comprising four individual strands secured together (see Figure 19.6). The beads are dominantly white discs manufactured from *Tegillarca granosa* and *Anadara antiquata*, although occasional gastropod spires (especially *Imbricariopsis punctata*) are mixed in irregularly (Figure 19.7). At the centre of each strand is a zone of red disc beads made from *Chama* sp. jewel box oyster shells, and occasional *Chama* sp. beads are interspersed among white beads elsewhere on the strands. There is a long zone on one strand comprised of fawn-coloured beads, and these are most likely made from *Beguina semiorbiculata* shells, which are still used in the production of this colour bead today in Malaita. Mead (1973:36) itemised various items of 'costume' noted for Makira, and among these he described *sau* shell money which was both worn and used as an exchange item. It is described as having 'four strings of white shell-money with a short strip of red shell-money at the bottom centre' which, in terms of stringing and configuration, broadly matches Z10855. Indeed, another two strings of south-eastern Solomon Islands shell money held in the MAA collections, acquired by the Templeton Crocker Expedition from either Santa Ana or Santa Catalina islands in 1933, are labelled as *sau* on their accession tags (accession numbers 1934.279 and 1934.280). Both match Mead's description of *sau* and their accession tags further state that the area of production for *sau* was 'Makira Harbour' (see Szabó 2019:123–124).

Figure 19.6: Shell money string Z10855 from the collection of the Museum of Archaeology and Anthropology, University of Cambridge.

Source: Photograph by Lucie Carreau.

Figure 19.7: White beads of various diameters and degrees of wear manufactured from a mix of *Anadara antiquata*, *Tegillarca granosa* and *Imbricariopsis punctata* from Z10855 at 30× magnification.

Notes: The arrow indicates an *I. punctata* bead where the traces of the body whorl, with characteristic fine, punctate concentric grooves, can be seen. When the faces of the other beads are visible, the distinctive radial patterning of the microstructure of *Anadara/Tegillarca* indicating the surface ribbing can be seen.

Source: Photograph by K. Szabó.

Diameters and wear patterns of the individual beads vary widely, indicating that beads from a variety of other sources and strings have been mixed during at least one episode of restringing. As with string MAA Z10604/E1902.190, several beads had come loose, and the MAA Museum Committee gave permission for radiocarbon dating four of these. The four beads selected for AMS radiocarbon dating attempted to cover a range of degrees of wear. Three white *Tegillarca granosa* beads and one *Imbricariopsis punctata* spire bead were chosen.

Radiocarbon dating results

The results of radiocarbon dating are shown in Table 19.1.

Table 19.1: Radiocarbon determinations from bead samples from Z10604/E1902.190 and Z10855.

^{14}C lab number	Acc. no.	Identifier	Material	^{14}C age BP[b]	Modelled Cal. AD 68% prob. range[a]	Modelled Cal. AD 95% prob. range[a]
Wk-47249	Z10604/E1902.190	Bead a	*Tegillarca granosa*	564±18	1690–1850	1650–1920
Wk-47250	Z10604/E1902.190	Bead b	*Tegillarca granosa*	562±17	1690–1850	1650–1920
Wk-47251	Z10604/E1902.190	Bead c	*Chama* sp.	560±19	1700–1850	1660–1920
Wk-47252	Z10604/E1902.190	Bead d	*Chama* sp.	532±17	1730–1890	1680–1920
Wk-48253	Z10604/E1902.190	Bead e	Palm endocarp	Sample abandoned – insufficient carbon		
Wk-47254	Z10604/E1902.190	Bead f	Palm endocarp	115±22	1690–1920	1680–1920
Wk-47255	Z10855	Bead a	*Tegillarca granosa* or *Anadara antiquata*	688±17	1550–1720	1500–1820
Wk-47256	Z10855	Bead b	*Tegillarca granosa* or *Anadara antiquata*	484±17	1800–1920	1710–1920
Wk-47257	Z10855	Bead c	*Imbricariopsis punctata*	702±33	1530–1700	1480–1810
Wk-47258	Z10855	Bead d	*Tegillarca granosa* or *Anadara antiquata*	483±18	1800–1920	1710–1920

[a] All results were calibrated using OxCal v. 4.4 (Bronk Ramsey 2020) and the IntCal20 (Reimer et al. 2020) for terrestrial samples and Marine20 (Heaton et al. 2020) for marine shell. A ΔR value of –116±39 ^{14}C years was applied to account for the regional reservoir offset.

[b] Corrected for isotopic fractionation. δ^{13}C value not reported.

Source: See sources in notes.

To refine the dating of samples, we used Bayesian Sequence Analysis in OxCal v. 4.4 and the *terminus ante quem* ('before') constraint in OxCal, which sets a date before which the calibrated age range must occur, in this case before AD 1915 for Z10855 and AD 1884 for Z10604/E1902.190 (see Figure 19.8). This *prior* historical information is incorporated in a Bayesian statistical model, resulting in more precise calendar results (Bronk Ramsey 2009). All radiocarbon dates were calibrated using the IntCal20 (Reimer et al. 2020) and Marine20 (Heaton et al. 2020) calibration curves. To adjust for regional oceanic variation in ^{14}C, we have applied a location-specific reservoir correction (ΔR) of -116 ± 39 ^{14}C years for non-deposit-feeding shellfish and corals. This value of -116 ± 39 ^{14}C years was derived from modern, pre-AD 1950 shells collected from the Solomon Islands (Guilderson et al. 2004; Petchey et al. 2004) combined using the online tool found at calib.org/marine/ (Reimer and Reimer 2001). This reservoir offset is in keeping with the temporal variation identified across the South Pacific for the last 200 years (Allen et al. 2021; Petchey 2020; Petchey and Schmid 2020).

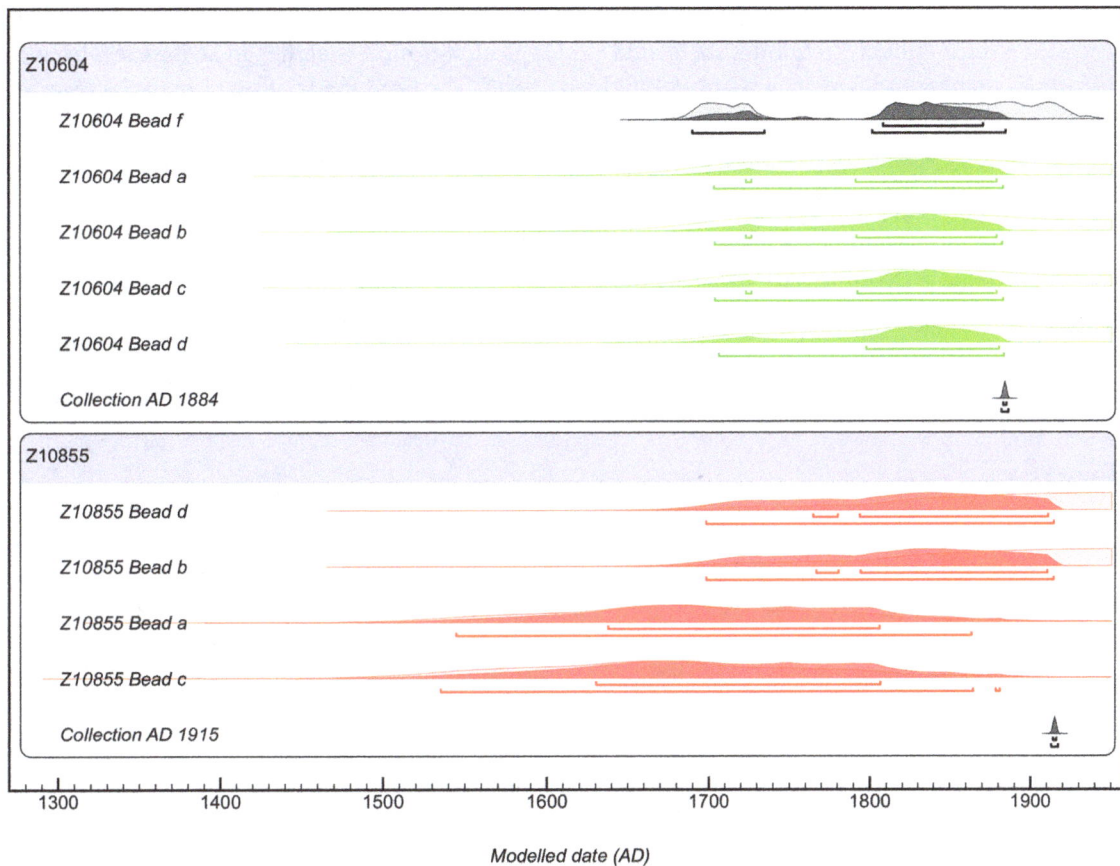

Figure 19.8: Bayesian modelling of calibrated radiocarbon determinations from beads from Z10604/E1902.190 and Z10855.

Source: Figure generated with OxCal v4.4.4 (Bronk Ramsey 2021:r5).

Discussion—Heirlooming qualified and quantified

The AMS radiocarbon dating of individual beads has provided a new window onto the extent and nature of heirlooming in the two shell money strings, although the two strings offer different insights. Given that, they will initially be discussed individually.

MAA Z10604/E1902.190

Of the six beads sampled, five returned determinations, with one of the palm endocarp beads having insufficient carbon. All five dates are in accordance with each other, indicating a broadly contemporaneous period of raw material collection and bead manufacture. The Bayesian modelling (Figure 19.8) suggests that the shell beads were manufactured in the eighteenth, or first half of the nineteenth, century. A later date more synchronous with the date of the string's collection (1880–1884) is possible, but the high degree of variability observed in the shell bead wear patterns and diameters shows that the beads have been restrung from earlier strands making a very late production date unlikely. Regional shell beads are typically ground together in strings resulting in uniform diameters and wear (e.g. Goto 1996; Liep 1981). The bead made of plant material revealed two possible periods of collection: either the early 1700s or the mid-nineteenth century. The later of the two dates is considered most likely here given the nature of the material and the likelihood of degradation under normal tropical conditions.

Together, the dates suggest that the shell beads could have been in circulation for over a century prior to their collection as part of MAA Z10604/E1902.190. If a later production date for the endocarp bead is accepted this would also reinforce that the string, as collected, was not in its original formation. The *Tegillarca granosa* white beads do not seem to be of a radically different date of manufacture to the *Chama* sp. beads, indicating the consistency of both red and white bead production through the early colonial period.

Z10855

The four radiocarbon determinations from Z10855 are intriguing and surprising, with two clear and distinct groupings of dates. Two of the white beads, manufactured from either *Tegillarca granosa* or *Anadara antiquata*, most probably date to sometime in the 1800s (see Figure 19.8). The other two white beads, one of either *Tegillarca granosa* or *Anadara antiquata* and the other made from the small gastropod *Imbricariopsis punctata*, date from substantially earlier. They are likely to have been produced in the 1700s, if not the 1600s (see Figure 19.8). While elsewhere in the Solomon Islands shell valuables are known to be regularly produced from subfossil shell (e.g. see Bogesi 1948), this is restricted to *Tridacna* artefacts. There is no analogue for this tradition relating to either Arcidae bivalves or diminutive species of Mitridae such as *I. punctata*, and the surfaces bear no diagnostic traces of post-mortem raw material collection and working. In short, there appears to be no reason to believe that the radiocarbon dates do not accurately date the production of the beads.

As with MAA Z10604/E1902.190, the irregular dimensions and wear traces on the beads denotes restringing, and the incongruity between the various radiocarbon dates for Z10855 also clearly demonstrate that the beads derive from different original strings. Moreover, the individual original strings are separated in time by up to three, or more likely two, centuries and stretch back beyond the ethnohistoric period of collection into the pre-colonial era.

The presence of beads in *Imbricariopsis punctata* provides evidence of further complexity, as there is seemingly no recorded tradition of bead manufacture in this species in the Malaita/Makira region. *I. punctata*, also mentioned in the literature under its synonyms *Pterygia punctata*, *Conohelix punctata* and *Imbricaria punctata*, is not a standard raw material for bead manufacture across the western Island Melanesian region, but it *is* the dominant raw material during the main period of ethnographic collecting (c. 1880–1935) in some discrete locales. Although confused with small species of *Conus* by some authors (e.g. Schneider 1905:58, 67), it is correctly identified by Ribbe (1903:135–137) for the Shortland Islands, where locally made and used strings of *I. punctata* are termed *perasali* and contrast with another local type (*mauwai*) produced from small *Conus* shells[1] and traded with Bougainville for pigs. It is also identified as the primary material for shell money production on Ponam, north of Manus in the Admiralty Islands (Carrier and Carrier 1989:33, 66, 102–103, again incorrectly identified as small *Conus* for Ponam by Eichhorn 1916). That the species used extensively on the Admiralties for shell money and decorating dance aprons and other items of adornment is indeed *I. punctata* is confirmed by KS's cross-checking of the extensive physical holdings of Admiralties material in the Ethnological Museum, Dresden, Germany.

Although the two known and confirmed centres of production for *I. punctata* beads are the northern Admiralty Islands and the Shortland Islands, shell money strands in museum collections with a recorded provenance of Choiseul also dominantly use this species as a raw material. This was consistently the case across major museum collections in Köln, Dresden, Berlin and Cambridge (Szabó 2019 *passim*). Whether there is local production is unclear, but museum collection evidence suggests that Choiseul—at least at the period of ethnographic collection—consumes and circulates shell money comprised largely of *I. punctata* beads. Short stretches of longer strands and odd, interspersed *I. punctata* beads were also observed in a range of ethnographic shell money strands collected from across New Ireland (Szabó 2019 *passim*).

There are certainly traditions of using small gastropods to produce white shell money in the Malaita/south-eastern Solomon Islands area, and where identifications are given the usual term is 'coneshell' (e.g. Burt 2009 *passim*). This includes the *kofu* money of the Kwaio of Malaita (e.g. Akin 1999), and further north, 'belts of highly-polished cone-shell beads' from Isabel (Burt 2009:54). The white bead manufacturing reported by Ivens (1927:390) for Ulawa and Sa'a, lying in between Makira and Malaita, is stated to use 'an arca' (i.e. Arcidae) termed *huresoso*. Other white shells are referred to as being less frequently used but there is no indication of what these shells might be in terms of Linnean nomenclature. Likewise, Fox (1919:164–165) mentions two types of white shell beads produced in Makira: a fine type (*ngisi*) and a coarse type (termed *h'a machui* in Arosi and *hura toto* in Bauro). There is no further description that would allow us to get a grasp on raw materials, although perhaps we could assume that *hura toto* of Fox in Makira is the *huresoso* of Ivens, produced in ark shell in Ulawa and Sa'a. This would mean *ngisi* remains unidentified.

It would appear that *I. punctata* bead production and circulation forms a tradition which has largely been invisible in (at least the English-language) literature, and although it was possibly used in the south-eastern Solomon Islands, after studying many thousands of shell beads from these islands in museum collections, a vanishingly small number were identified by KS as being made from *I. punctata*. The overwhelming majority of white beads (and indeed beads of all colours) are produced from bivalve shell. It is also worth pointing out that *I. punctata* has not been identified

---

1   Original German text: 'Die Herstellung des Perasali is die gleiche, doch wird viel grössere Sorgfalt auf seine Anfertigung verwendet, auch werden nicht Conusscheiben, sondern solche aus einer Imbricaria verwendet. Perasali ist hauptsächlich auf den Shortlands-Inseln im Verkehr, wohingegen Mauwai [*Conus* money] von den Leuten nach Bougainville zum Einkauf der Schweine mitgenommen wird.' Ribbe 1903:136–137, translated in text KS.

from archaeological deposits as a raw material for bead production anywhere in the Island Melanesia region. On current evidence it seems unlikely that the *I. punctata* bead radiocarbon dated from MAA Z10855 was produced in or around Makira, and it probably entered the region from a location to the north/north-west via the movement of goods and/or people. At what time this movement took place is not possible to discern.

Across the colonial/pre-colonial divide

The impact of European presence in the Solomon Islands on patterns of trade, access to and distribution of wealth, and the production and circulation of goods is well documented. Impacts were felt directly via traders (Belshaw 1950; Burt 2009:39), whalers (Bennett 1987), ethnographic collectors and dealers (Stanley 1994) and missionaries (Kwa'ioloa 2014), but also more broadly through the effects of colonial policies centred on pacification (Bennett 1987:Chapter 5) and currency systems (Connell 1977). All of these intertwining factors, and the complexity in relations between Europeans and indigenous Solomon Islanders, are considered in nuanced detail by Aswani and Sheppard (2003) for the Western Province of the Solomon Islands. That there was expanded traffic in shell valuables and shell money in colonial times in the Solomon Islands is also well attested. For example, Bennett (1987:84) describes European traders procuring red shell money from Langalanga to trade in Vanatinai (also known as Tagula or Sudest Island) in Milne Bay, New Guinea, while gold-lipped pearl oysters (*Pinctada maxima*) were supplied back into the south-eastern Solomons, where they were increasingly in demand for producing *tema* pendants. Aswani and Sheppard (2003:S62) map the shifting centrality of shell rings produced in Roviana, New Georgia, to local exchange systems, through their adoption and redistribution by European traders, to their fall in status in the late nineteenth century. During the course of the twentieth century, a growing curio market supplying foreign visitors spurred local production of shell arts and crafts at the same time as local consumption and use was falling—due at least partially to Christianisation (Burt 2009:50–52, see also Sheppard and Walter 2014 for an analogous rise of arts and crafts production in the Western Province of the Solomon Islands). These transformations doubtless impacted upon the character of museum collections as well as the production and trade of Solomons shell money recorded by anthropologists and observers.

Although it is difficult to know what the prevalence, spread and role of shell money may have been at contact and in the centuries before based on current evidence, the two earlier beads from MAA Z10855 tell us two things: (1) that small shell beads consistent with those produced for shell money strings were produced from very early or pre-colonial times over a period of two to three hundred years; and (2) they remained in circulation in various forms, and thus held their relevance, over this span. This affirms the suspicions of Langalanga elders that shell money can be heirloomed over some hundreds of years, and indeed exceeds their estimates. The fact that such small individual components could survive and pass through many hands for centuries is testimony to their value and the care invested in their maintenance and curation.

These findings also offer insights of a more theoretical nature for archaeologists. Heirlooming, as a general human practice, has the potential to confound archaeological chronologies if undetected: the date of the production of an artefact may not match the chronostratigraphic context in which it is found resulting either in an overestimate of the age of that context or, alternatively, a dismissal of an heirloomed artefact as simply out of context as its date does not match those of surrounding artefacts. If MAA Z10855 had been recovered archaeologically, and its beads dated as here, interpretation would doubtless have been fraught and contested.

Although different areas have distinct shell money traditions and zones of circulation, the geographic spread of these across Papua New Guinea, the Solomon Islands and beyond would in itself imply a degree of time depth. A robust case has been made for specialised shell bead production at Motupore Island on New Guinea's south coast around eight hundred years ago (Allen 2017), however the raw materials being transformed remain unclear, thus limiting our ability to connect beads from elsewhere or contrast traditions (see discussion in Szabó in press). There is surely much to learn about the shifting patterns of connectedness linking specialised shell bead producers and consumers through time, but in order to access these histories, rigour in shell provenance, taxonomic identification and analysis will be required by both archaeologists and anthropologists.

Acknowledgements

KS: It was during fieldwork with Glenn Summerhayes in Anir, Papua New Guinea, that I first came across traditional shell money in anything beyond a museum display or glossy book context. To this day I look back upon that fieldwork as the most enriching and eye-opening fieldwork of my career. For that, alongside the decades of support, tenkyu tumas Glenn. The research presented here was supported by an Australian Research Council Future Fellowship (FT140100504) and a Deutsche Forschungsgemeinschaft (DFG) Mercator Fellowship held at Goethe University, Frankfurt. For access to museum collections, thank you to Anita Herle (MAA, Cambridge), Dorothea Deterts (Ethnological Museum, Berlin), Philipp Schorch (then Grassi Museum, Leipzig) and Oliver Lueb (Rautenstrauch-Joest Museum, Köln). Additional thanks are due to Anita Herle of MAA for supporting and guiding the application for the AMS radiocarbon dating of the MAA beads. Research in the Solomon Islands was undertaken under a research permit in collaboration with the Solomon Islands National Museum, and special thanks are due to Tony Heorake and Edna Belo. Research in Langalanga Lagoon was supported by Serah Kei, while the visit to Outau Village south of Lau Lagoon was organised by Florence Kabi.

References

Akin, D. 1999. Cash and shell money in Kwaio, Solomon Islands. In D. Akin and J. Robbins (eds), *Money and modernity—State and local currencies in Melanesia*, pp. 103–130. University of Pittsburgh Press, Pittsburgh.

Allen, J. 2017. *Excavations on Motupore Island, Central District, Papua New Guinea.* Two volumes. University of Otago Working Papers in Anthropology 4. University of Otago, Dunedin.

Allen, M.S., A. McAlister, F. Petchey, J.M. Huebert, M. Maeva and B. Jones 2021. Marquesan ceramics, Palaeotsunami, and Megalithic architecture: The Ho'oumi Beach site (NHo-3) in regional perspective. *Archaeology in Oceania* 56(2):73–59. doi.org/10.1002/arco.5233.

Armstrong, E.S. 1900. *The history of the Melanesian mission.* Isbister and Company, London.

Aswani, S. and P. Sheppard 2003. The archaeology and ethnohistory of exchange in precolonial and colonial Roviana: Gifts, commodities, and inalienable possessions. *Current Anthropology* 44(S5):S51–S78. doi.org/10.1086/377667.

Belshaw, C.S. 1950. Changes in heirloom jewellery in the Central Solomons. *Oceania* 20:169–184. doi.org/10.1002/j.1834-4461.1950.tb00526.x.

Bennett, J. 1987. *The wealth of the Solomons—A history of a Pacific archipelago, 1800–1978.* University of Hawai'i Press, Honolulu. doi.org/10.1515/9780824850722.

Bogesi, G. 1948. Santa Isabel, Solomon Islands. *Oceania* 18:208–232, 327–357. doi.org/10.1002/j.1834-4461.1948.tb00488.x.

Bronk Ramsey, C. 2009. Bayesian analysis of radiocarbon dates. *Radiocarbon* 51:337–360. doi.org/10.1017/S0033822200033865.

Bronk Ramsey, C. 2021. OxCal program v. 4.4.4. (Radiocarbon Accelerator Unit, Univ. Oxford). Accessed 9 Mar 2022.

Burt, B. 2009. *Body ornaments of Malaita, Solomon Islands.* Trustees of the British Museum, London. doi.org/10.2752/BEWDF/EDch7077.

Carrier J.G., and A.H. Carrier 1989. *Wage, trade, and exchange in Melanesia: A Manus society in the modern state.* University of California Press, Berkeley, Los Angeles, Oxford.

Connell, J. 1977. The Bougainville connection: Changes in the economic context of shell money production in Malaita. *Oceania* 48:88–101. doi.org/10.1002/j.1834-4461.1977.tb01326.x.

Dalton, F.H. 1965. Primitive money. *American Anthropologist* 67:44–65. doi.org/10.1525/aa.1965.67.1.02a00040.

Danks, B. 1888. On the shell-money of New Britain. *The Journal of the Anthropological Institute of Great Britain and Ireland* 17:305–317. doi.org/10.2307/2842168.

Eichhorn, A. 1916. Die Herstellung von 'Muschelperlen' aus Conus auf der Insel Poman und ihre Verwendung im Kunsthendwerk der Admiralitätsinsulaner. *Baessler-Archiv* 6:256–283.

Eves, R. 2000. Sorcery's the curse: Modernity, envy and the flow of sociality in a Melanesian society. *Journal of the Royal Anthropological Institute* (New Series) 6:453–468. doi.org/10.1111/1467-9655.00026.

Fox, C.E. 1919. Social organisation in San Cristoval, Solomon Islands. *Journal of the Royal Anthropological Institute of Great Britain and Ireland* 49:94–179. doi.org/10.2307/2843437.

Goto, A. 1996. Lagoon life among the Langalanga, Malaita Island, Solomon Islands. *Senri Ethnological Studies* 42:11–53.

Graeber, D. 1996. Beads and money: Notes toward a theory of wealth and power. *American Ethnologist* 23:4–24. doi.org/10.1525/ae.1996.23.1.02a00010.

Guilderson, T.P., D.P. Schrag and M.A. Cane 2004. Surface water mixing in the Solomon Sea as documented by a high-resolution coral ^{14}C record. *Journal of Climate* 17:1147–1156. doi.org/10.1175/1520-0442(2004)017<1147:SWMITS>2.0.CO;2.

Heaton, T.J., P. Köhler, M. Butzin, E. Bard, R.W. Reimer, W.E.N. Austin, C. Bronk Ramsey, P.M. Grootes, K.A. Hughen, B. Kromer, P.J. Reimer, J. Adkins, A. Burke, M.S. Cook, J. Olsen and L.C. Skinner 2020. Marine20—The marine radiocarbon age calibration curve (0–55,000 cal BP). *Radiocarbon* 62:779–820. doi.org/10.1017/RDC.2020.68.

Hilliard, D. 1978. *God's gentlemen—A history of the Melanesian Mission 1849–1942.* University of Queensland Press, St Lucia.

Hingston-Quiggin, A. 1949. *A survey of primitive money: The beginnings of currency.* Methuen and Co, London.

Ivens, W. 1927. *Melanesians of the South-East Solomon Islands.* Kegan, Paul, Trench and Trubner, London.

Kwa'ioloa, M. 2014. Traditional money and artefacts in Malaita. In B. Burt and L. Bolton (eds), *The things we value: Culture and history in Solomon Islands*, pp. 47–53. Sean Kingston Publishing, Canon Pyon.

Lewis, A.B. 1929. Melanesian shell money in field museum collections. *Field Museum of Natural History Anthropological Series* 19:1. Field Museum, Chicago. doi.org/10.5962/bhl.title.14027.

Liep, J. 1981. The Workshop of the Kula: Production and trade of shell necklaces in the Louisiade Archipelago, Papua New Guinea. *Folk* 23:279–309.

Malinowski, B. 1922. *Argonauts of the Western Pacific*. Routledge and Kegan Paul, London.

Mead, S. 1973. *Material culture and art in the Star Harbour region, Eastern Solomon Islands*. Ethnography Monograph 1. Royal Ontario Museum, Toronto.

Munn, N. 1986. *The fame of Gawa: A symbolic study of value transformation in a Massim (Papua New Guinea) society*. Cambridge University Press, New York.

Oliver, D.L. 1955. *A Solomon Island society: Kinship and leadership among the Siuai of Bougainville*. Harvard University Press, Cambridge. doi.org/10.4159/harvard.9780674183117.

Paravicini, E. 1942–45. Über das Muschelgeld der südöstlichen Salomonen. *Anthropos* 37–40:158–174.

Petchey, F. 2020. New evidence for a mid- to late-Holocene change in the marine reservoir effect across the South Pacific Gyre. *Radiocarbon* 62(1):127–139. doi.org/10.1017/RDC.2019.103.

Petchey, F., and M. Schmid 2020. Vital evidence: Change in the marine ^{14}C reservoir around New Zealand (Aotearoa). Implications for the timing of Polynesian settlement. *Scientific Reports* 10: 4266. doi.org/10.1038/s41598-020-70227-3.

Petchey, F., M. Phelan and J.P. White 2004. New ΔR values for the southwest Pacific Ocean. *Radiocarbon* 46(2):1005–1014. doi.org/10.1017/S0033822200036079.

Petri, H. 1936. Die Geldformen der Sudsee. *Anthropos* 31:187–212, 509–554.

Reimer, P.J. and R.W. Reimer 2001. A marine reservoir correction database and on-line interface. *Radiocarbon* 43(2A):461–463. doi.org/10.1017/S0033822200038339.

Reimer P.J., W.E.N. Austin, E. Bard, A. Bayliss, P.G. Blackwell, C. Bronk Ramsey, M. Butzin, H. Cheng, R.L. Edwards, M. Friedrich, P.M. Grootes, T.P. Guilderson, I. Hajdas, T.J. Heaton, A.G. Hogg, K.A. Hughen, B. Kromer, S.W. Manning, R. Muscheler, J.G. Palmer, C. Pearson, J. van der Plicht, R.W. Reimer, D.A. Richards, E.M. Scott, J.R. Southon, C.S.M. Turney, L. Wacker, F. Adolphi, U. Büntgen, M. Capano, S.M. Fahrni, A. Fogtmann-Schulz, R. Friedrich, P. Köhler, S. Kudsk, F. Miyake, J. Olsen, F. Reinig, M. Sakamoto, A. Sookdeo and S. Talamo 2020. The INTCAL20 northern hemisphere radiocarbon age calibration curve (0–55 cal kBP). *Radiocarbon* 62(4):725–757. doi.org/10.1017/RDC.2020.41.

Ribbe, C. 1903. *Zwei Jahre unter den Kannibalen der Solomo-Inseln*. Elbgau-Buchdruckerei Hermann Beyer, Dresden-Blasewitz.

Schneider, O. 1905. *Muschelgeld-Studien*. Ernst Engelmann, Dresden.

Sheppard, P. and R. Walter 2014. Shell valuables and history in Roviana and Vella Lavella. In B. Burt and L. Bolton (eds), *The things we value: Culture and history in Solomon Islands*, pp. 33–45. Sean Kingston Publishing, Canon Pyon.

Stanley, N. 1994. Recording Island Melanesia: The significance of the Melanesian Mission in museum records. *Pacific Arts* July 1994, No. 9/10: 25–41.

Szabó, K. 2018. Shell money and context in western Island Melanesia. In L. Carreau, A. Clark, A. Jelinek, E. Lilje and N. Thomas (eds), *Pacific presences. Volume 2: Oceanic art and European museums*, pp. 25–38. Sidestone Press, Leiden.

Szabó, K. 2019. *Shell valuables from the Bismarck Archipelago and Solomon Islands*. Monash University Printery, Clayton.

Szabó, K. In press. Shell valuables and exchange systems in New Guinea. To appear in I. McNiven and B. David (eds), *Oxford handbook of the archaeology of Indigenous Australia and New Guinea*. Oxford University Press, Oxford.

Szabó, K. and B. Koppel 2015. Limpet shells as unmodified tools in Pleistocene Southeast Asia: An experimental approach to assessing fracture and modification. *Journal of Archaeological Science* 54: 65–76. doi.org/10.1016/j.jas.2014.11.022.

Wagner, R. 2014. *Asiwinarong: Ethos, image, and social power among the Usen Barok of New Ireland*. Princeton University Press, Princeton.

Weston, E., K. Szabó and N. Stern 2017. Pleistocene shell tools from Lake Mungo lunette, Australia: Identification and interpretation drawing on experimental archaeology. *Quaternary International* 427: 229–242. doi.org/10.1016/j.quaint.2015.11.048.

Woodford, C.M. 1908. Notes on the manufacture of Malaita shell bead money. *Man* 43:81–4. doi.org/10.2307/2839489.

List of contributors

Jim Allen
School of Archaeology and History,
La Trobe University, Melbourne,
Victoria, Australia.

Wallace Ambrose
School of Culture, History and Language,
The Australian National University, Canberra,
Australian Capital Territory, Australia.

Henry Arifeae
National Museum and Art Gallery of Papua
New Guinea,
Port Moresby, National Capital District,
Papua New Guinea.

David Baret
Institute of Archaeology of New Caledonia
and the Pacific (IANCP),
BP: 11423, 98802, Nouméa,
New Caledonia.

Stuart Bedford
School of Culture, History and Language,
The Australian National University, Canberra,
Australian Capital Territory, Australia.

Department of Linguistic and Cultural
Evolution,
Max Planck Institute for Evolutionary
Anthropology, Leipzig,
Deutscher Platz 6, Germany.

Jacques Bolé
Institute of Archaeology of New Caledonia
and the Pacific (IANCP),
BP: 11423, 98802, Nouméa,
New Caledonia.

Gustavo F. Bonnat
Laboratorio de Arqueología Regional
Bonaerense,
Universidad Nacional de Mar del Plata,
Mar del Plata,
Buenos Aires Province, Argentina.

Elaine Chen
Archaeology program, School of Social Sciences,
University of Otago, Dunedin,
New Zealand.

Scarlett Chiu
Institute of History and Philology,
Academia Sinica, Taipei,
Taiwan, Republic of China.

Adelle C. Coster
School of Mathematics and Statistics,
University of New South Wales, Sydney,
New South Wales, Australia.

Simon Coxe
Monash Indigenous Studies Centre,
Monash University, Melbourne,
Victoria, Australia.

Judith H. Field
School of Biological, Earth and Environmental
Sciences,
University of New South Wales, Sydney,
New South Wales, Australia.

Anne Ford
Archaeology program, School of Social Sciences,
University of Otago, Dunedin,
New Zealand.

Richard Fullagar
School of Earth, Atmospheric and Life Sciences,
University of Wollongong, Wollongong,
New South Wales, Australia.

Dylan Gaffney
School of Archaeology,
University of Oxford, Oxford,
England, United Kingdom

Archaeology Program, School of Social Sciences,
University of Otago, Dunedin,
New Zealand.

Chris Gosden
School of Archaeology,
University of Oxford, Oxford,
England, United Kingdom.

Jemina Haro
National Museum and Art Gallery of Papua
New Guinea,
Port Moresby, National Capital District,
Papua New Guinea.

Jill Hasell
Department of Africa, Oceania, and the
Americas,
The British Museum, London,
England, United Kingdom.

Loretta Hasu
National Museum and Art Gallery of Papua
New Guinea,
Port Moresby, National Capital District,
Papua New Guinea.

Elspeth Hayes
School of Earth, Atmospheric and Life Sciences,
University of Wollongong, Wollongong,
New South Wales, Australia.

Nicholas W.S. Hogg
Archaeology program, School of Social Sciences,
University of Otago, Dunedin,
New Zealand.

Dickson Kangi
Simbai Valley, Madang Province,
Papua New Guinea.

Jason Kariwiga
School of Humanities and Social Sciences,
The University of Papua New Guinea,
Port Moresby,
National Capital District, Papua New Guinea.

School of Social Science,
University of Queensland, Brisbane,
Queensland, Australia.

Vincent Kewibu
School of Humanities and Social Sciences,
The University of Papua New Guinea,
Port Moresby,
National Capital District, Papua New Guinea.

David Killick
School of Anthropology,
University of Arizona, Tucson,
Arizona, United States of America.

Patrick Kirch
Department of Anthropology,
University of Hawaii at Mānoa, Honolulu,
Hawaii, United States of America.

Michael Lovave
Forest Biology Program,
Papua New Guinea Forest Research Institute,
Lae,
Morobe Province, Papua New Guinea.

Elizabeth Matisoo-Smith
Department of Anatomy, School of
Biomedical Sciences,
University of Otago, Dunedin,
New Zealand.

Ian J. McNiven
Australian Research Council Centre
of Excellence for Australian Biodiversity
and Heritage,
Monash Indigenous Studies Centre,
Monash University, Melbourne,
Victoria, Australia.

Kenneth Miamba
National Museum and Art Gallery of Papua
New Guinea,
Port Moresby, National Capital District,
Papua New Guinea.

Betty Neanda
National Museum and Art Gallery of Papua
New Guinea,
Port Moresby, National Capital District,
Papua New Guinea.

Fiona Petchey
Radiocarbon Dating Laboratory,
Te Aka Mātuatua – School of Science,
University of Waikato, Hamilton,
New Zealand.

Christophe Sand
French National Research Institute for
Sustainable Development (IRD),
BP: A5, 98848, Nouméa,
New Caledonia.

Lachlan Sharp
School of Culture, History and Language,
The Australian National University, Canberra,
Australian Capital Territory, Australia.

Ben Shaw
School of Culture, History and Language,
The Australian National University, Canberra,
Australian Capital Territory, Australia.

Jim Specht
Archaeology & Geosciences,
Australian Museum, Sydney,
New South Wales, Australia.
School of Humanities,
The University of Sydney, Sydney,
New South Wales, Australia.

Matthew Spriggs
Vanuatu Cultural Centre, Port Vila,
Vanuatu.
School of Archaeology and Anthropology,
The Australian National University, Canberra,
Australian Capital Territory, Australia.

Yuyin Su
Institute of History and Philology,
Academia Sinica, Taipei,
Taiwan, Republic of China.

Glenn R. Summerhayes
Archaeology program, School of Social Sciences,
University of Otago, Dunedin,
New Zealand.
School of Social Science,
University of Queensland, Brisbane,
Queensland. Australia.

Pamela Swadling
School of Culture, History and Language,
The Australian National University, Canberra,
Australian Capital Territory, Australia.

Katherine Szabó
Pre-construct Archaeology, Cambridge,
England, United Kingdom.

Joyce Taian
National Museum and Art Gallery of Papua
New Guinea,
Port Moresby, National Capital District,
Papua New Guinea.

Daud Tanudirjo
Departemen Arkeologi,
Universitas Gadjah Mada, Yogyakarta,
Special Region of Yogyakarta, Indonesia.

Robin Torrence
Archaeology and Geosciences,
Australian Museum, Sydney,
New South Wales, Australia.
School of Humanities,
The University of Sydney, Sydney,
New South Wales, Australia.

Roxanne Tsang
School of Humanities and Social Sciences,
The University of Papua New Guinea,
Port Moresby,
National Capital District, Papua New Guinea.
School of Humanities, Languages and
Social Science,
Griffith University, Gold Coast,
Queensland, Australia.

Friedrich E. von Gnielinski
Geological Survey of Queensland,
Department of Resources, Brisbane,
Queensland, Australia.

Peter White
School of Humanities,
The University of Sydney, Sydney,
New South Wales, Australia.